The **Rough Guide** to

Corsica

written and researched by

David Abram

NEW YORK · LONDON · DELHI

www.roughguides.com

Contents

Traditional Corsica
colour section following
p.208

Wild Corsica colour
section following p.304

◄◄ GR20 hiking sign ◄ Bonifacio

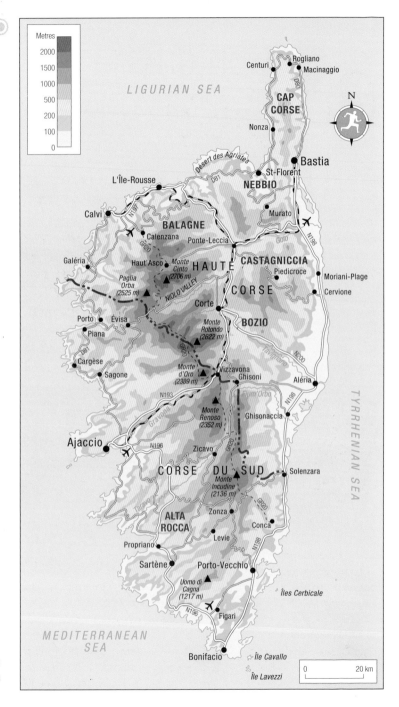

Metres
2000
1500
1000
500
200
100
0

LIGURIAN SEA

N

Centuri   Rogliano
         Macinaggio

CAP
CORSE

Nonza

Bastia

Désert des Agriates

L'Île-Rousse   St-Florent

NEBBIO

Calvi   Murato

BALAGNE
       Calenzana   Ponte-Leccia   CASTAGNICCIA

Galéria   Haut'Asco   Monte   Piedicroce   Moriani-Plage
                           Cinto
               Paglia   (2706 m) HAUTE   Cervione
               Orba   CORSE
               (2525 m)   NIOLO VALLEY

Porto   Évisa   Corte   BOZIO
    Piana   Monte
                      Rotondo
   Cargèse   (2622 m)
       Sagone   Monte   Vizzavona
                          d'Oro   Ghisoni   Aléria
                          (2389 m)
                    N193   Monte
                                  Renoso   Ghisonaccia
                                  (2352 m)

Ajaccio   N196   Zicavo

                  CORSE   DU   SUD   Solenzara
                          Monte
                          Incudine
                          (2136 m)
                     Zonza
            ALTA   Conca
            ROCCA
                     Levie
    Propriano
       Sartène   Porto-Vecchio

              Uomo di
              Cagna   Îles Cerbicale
              (1217 m)

                       Figari

MEDITERRANEAN
    SEA

            Bonifacio   Île Cavallo
                         Île Lavezzi

TYRRHENIAN SEA

0   20 km

Introduction to
Corsica

Kallisté – "the most beautiful" – was what the ancient Greeks called Corsica, and the compliment holds as true today as ever. In few corners of the Mediterranean will you find water as translucent, sand as soft and white, and weather as dependably warm and sunny; and nowhere else has seascapes as dramatic as the red porphyry Calanches of the west coast and the striated white cliffs in the far south. Crowning it all, a mass of forested valleys flow out from the island's granite spine, which rises to a mighty 2706m at Monte Cinto, snow-encrusted even at the height of summer.

Nearly two-and-a-half million visitors descend on the island annually (two-thirds of them in July and Aug), yet purpose-built resorts are few and far between, while high-rise blocks remain outnumbered by extravagant Baroque churches and old fortified houses built to protect families formerly embroiled in vendettas. Overlooked by Corsica's trademark seventeenth-century watchtowers, long stretches of the shore remain backed by unbroken maquis. Forests of holm oak, chestnut trees and magnificent Laricio pines carpet the interior valleys, dotted with pretty stone villages. "Provence without the Brits" is how rural Corsica is often described in holiday brochures, but the gloss fails to convey the island's distinctive grandeur: the wildness of its uplands, the vivid atmosphere of its remote settlements, and arresting emptiness of its valleys and woodlands.

Corsica's pristine state is largely the legacy of economic neglect, compounded by the impact of two world wars and mass out-migration in the twentieth century. Successive invaders – from the Greeks, Carthaginians and Romans to the Aragonese, Italians, British and French – all came and conquered, but none was able to establish lasting prosperity. Nor were they ever able

5

▲ Rodinara beach

to subjugate fully the rebellious spirit of the islanders themselves, who at various times in their history have mounted fierce resistance to colonial occupation. In the eighteenth century, an armed uprising established a fully independent government led by one of the most charismatic political figures of the Enlightenment, Pascal Paoli.

Violent opposition to French rule flared up again in the mid-1970s, since when nationalist paramilitary groups have been waging a bloody campaign against the state and its representatives, both on the island and on the Continent. Among ordinary islanders, support for the armed struggle – whose bombings and shootings have claimed hundreds of lives but seldom, if ever, affect tourists – has dwindled to virtually nil over the past decade. Yet the desire for greater autonomy remains as fervent as ever, in spite of the fact that the island imports virtually everything it needs and receives huge financial support from Paris and the EU.

Having struggled for centuries to preserve their language and customs, Corsicans have gained a reputation for being suspicious of outsiders. You

Forgotten frescoes

During the twelfth and thirteenth centuries, the Pisans constructed dozens of churches across Corsica. Their exteriors were originally embellished with naive sculptures, but the interiors remained plain until the arrival in the fifteenth century of Genoese "**dry-fresco**" (*fresco secco*) artists. Entirely forgotten until their rediscovery in the late 1960s, the murals they created are now regarded as one of the most important hoards of *in situ* medieval art in the western Mediterranean.

For more on the frescoes of Corsica, see the accounts of Santa Maria di e Nevi (see p.76); the Couvent d'Alesani and chapel of Santa Cristina (see p.279); and San Nicholao church at Sermano (see p.313).

will, for example, get a very frosty response if you attempt to broach the subject of nationalist violence. But express admiration for those facets of island life which the islanders are overtly proud of – such as their cuisine, fine wines and polyphony singing – and you'll soon feel the warmth of traditional hospitality.

Save for the ubiquitous nationalist graffiti, sprayed-out road signs and odd fire-bombed villa or beach restaurant, Corsica's dark underbelly is barely discernible these days, as its population is drawn ever closer to the European mainstream. Lasting impressions tend instead to be dominated by the things which have beguiled travellers since Boswell first raved about the island in the mid-eighteenth century: the breathtakingly unspoilt scenery and a distinctive Mediterranean way of life which, although bearing strong resemblances to the cultures of neighbouring Tuscany and Sardinia, the French Riviera and Sicily – somehow manages to remain quite different from any of them.

Fact file

- Corsica's **population** hovers around 260,000, just over eight percent of which is made up of immigrant workers from North Africa. An estimated 800,000 islanders live in mainland France, mostly in Marseille, Paris and the Bouches du Rhône region.

- The island is 183km from north to south and 85km wide at its broadest point, with a **surface area** of 8682 square kilometres – roughly the same as that of Crete, or half of Wales. Its nearest neighbour, Sardinia, is three times larger.

- Corsica has its own regional assembly, answerable to the **national parliament** in Paris.

- Polls show that nearly three-quarters of Corsicans oppose full **independence**, with only fifteen percent in favour of a separate state (the majority of them youngsters). By contrast, nearly half of people questioned in mainland France said they supported independence for Corsica.

- Eighty percent of islanders regard **Corsican** as their mother tongue, but only a tiny number still use it as their first language; **French** is now the lingua franca.

Where to go

C apital of the north, **Bastia** was the principal Genoese stronghold, and its fifteenth-century old town has survived almost intact. Of the island's two large towns, this is the more purely Corsican, and commerce rather than tourism is its main concern. Also relatively undisturbed, the northern **Cap Corse** harbours inviting sandy coves and coastal villages such as Erbalunga and Centuri-Port. Within a short distance of Bastia, the fertile region of the **Nebbio** has a scattering of churches

built by Pisan stone-workers, the prime example being the cathedral of Santa Maria Assunta at the appealingly chic little port of **St-Florent**. To the west of here, **L'Île Rousse** and **Calvi**, the latter graced with an impressive citadelle and a fabulous sandy beach, are the island's major resort towns – and their undulating hinterland, the **Haute-Balagne**, offers plenty of hilltop villages to explore, as well as access to the northern reaches of the vast **Parc Naturel Régional**, an astounding area of forested valleys, gorges and peaks. The spectacular **Scandola** nature reserve, a part of the northwest coast that lies within the boundaries of the park, can be visited by boat from the tiny resort of **Porto**, from where walkers strike into the magnificently wild **Spelunca Gorge** and **Forêt d'Aïtone**.

Sandy beaches and rocky coves punctuate the **west coast** all the way down to **Ajaccio**, Napoleon's birthplace and Bastia's traditional rival. Its pavement cafés and palm-lined boulevards are packed with tourists in summer, but comparatively few of them make it to nearby **Filitosa**, greatest of the many prehistoric sites scattered across this, the most heavily visited, half of the island. The resort of **Propriano** lies close to Filitosa and to stern **Sartène**, seat of the wild feudal lords who once ruled this region and still the quintessential Corsican town.

Le maquis

Napoleon Bonaparte, Corsica's most illustrious son, famously claimed he could smell his homeland while exiled on Elba – it was probably the **maquis** he was talking about. From the minute you set foot on the island, the pervasive fragrance of Corsica's aromatic scrub subtly assails the senses with its peppery blend of rosemary, lavender, cistus, sage, juniper, mastic and myrtle. In spring, the dark green belt, which thrives around the coastal zone below 800m, erupts into a blaze of pink and yellow flowers. Many of the plants are still gathered for their

medicinal or cosmetic properties: the ladanum gum exuded by cistus, for example, is picked from the beards of goats to make myrrh.

Although the bane of walkers, the spiny maquis was a boon for Corsican *bandits d'honneurs*, who traditionally used it for cover when they were forced to flee after committing a vendetta murder. During World War II, the local Resistance also exploited its hidden trails to evade detection by the Italian Gestapo. The partisan movement in time became known as Le Maquis, while its activists were dubbed *maquisards* – monikers that would later be applied to the whole anti-German Resistance network on the Continent.

More megalithic sites are to be found south of Sartène on the way to **Bonifacio**, a comb of ancient buildings perched atop furrowed white cliffs at the southern tip of the island. Equally popular **Porto Vecchio**, the spot that has perhaps suffered most from the tourist boom, provides a springboard for excursions to the dazzling beaches of the south, or alternatively to the pine forest of **Ospédale**, or even to the windswept **Col de Bavella**, whose flattened pines and gigantic cliffs so inspired Edward Lear. The **eastern plain** has less going for it, but the Roman site at **Aléria** is worth a visit for its excellent museum, while to the north of Aléria lies the **Castagniccia**, a swath of chestnut trees and alluring villages.

Corte, standing at the heart of Corsica, is the best base for exploring the stupendous mountains and gorges of the interior, with the remote valleys of the **Niolo** and **Asco** a stone's throw away. Dominating these, **Monte Cinto** marks the northern edge of the island's spine of high peaks, closely tracked by the epic **GR20**, regarded as Europe's toughest and most spectacular hike.

◄ Genoese watchtower, Erbalunga

When to go

Whatever kind of holiday you intend to take, the **best times of year** to visit Corsica are late spring and late summer or early autumn, when you're guaranteed sunshine without the stifling heat or crowds of July and August. The wild flowers carpeting the island in April and May make these delightful months to come, and autumn is just as good for scenic colour – the Castagniccia in particular is a riot of russet tones at this time of year. Beachgoers will be ensured a tan as late as October, and even if you plan a visit in the depths of winter you're unlikely to encounter much rain, though snow on the high mountains can restrict driving through the passes in January, February and March, and visibility is often obscured by mists. **Crowds** are likely to be a problem only in the major resorts such as Porto Vecchio and L'Île Rousse, especially in the summer school holidays – *les grandes vacances* – when the whole of Italy and France take their annual holiday. In the more remote areas you should book **accommodation** in advance, for the simple reason that there is rarely more than a single hotel in any village.

Average daily temperatures (°C) and monthly rainfall (mm)

	Jan	Feb	Mar	Apr	May	Jun	Jul	Aug	Sept	Oct	Nov	Dec
Average daily temperatures												
max (°C)	13	14	16	18	21	25	27	28	26	22	17	14
Monthly rainfall												
mm	76	65	53	48	50	21	10	16	50	88	97	98

20
things not to miss

It's not possible to see everything that Corsica has to offer in one trip – and we don't suggest you try. What follows is a selective and subjective taste of the island's highlights, from wonderful food and drink and superb beaches to dramatic mountains and atmospheric towns. They're arranged in five colour-coded categories to help you find the very best things to see, do and experience. All entries have a page reference to take you straight into the Guide, where you can find out more.

01 **The micheline train** Page **27** • Connecting the three main towns via the high mountains and some gorgeous coast – worth taking for the rattling ride alone.

02 **Bastia Vieux Port** Page **64** • Atmospheric fishing harbour, surrounded by crumbling Genoese tenements.

03 **Apéritif at L'Hôtel Les Roches Rouges** Page **156** • Sublime sea views extend across the Golfe de Porto from the veranda of Corsica's most elegant period hotel. Come for a sundowner of muscat or Cap Corse liqueur.

04 **Calvi** Page **109** • Corsica's hallmark resort, framed by snow peaks and a spectacular blue gulf.

05 Plage de Roccapina Page **239** • Exquisite turquoise cove in the far south, overlooked by a lion-shaped rock.

06 The GR20 Page **337** • France's ultimate Grande Randonnée: ten to fourteen days of punishing gradients and magnificent landscape.

07 Col de Bavella Page **228** • One of the island's defining landscapes: a vertical world of stretched pines and soaring granite escarpments.

08 Boat trips from Bonifacio Page **251** • Catch a navette from the harbour for the most imposing views of Bonifacio's chalk cliffs and *haute ville*.

09 Corsican cheese Page **33** •
In ancient stone *bergeries* high in the mountains, Corsican shepherds produce the island's famously pungent ewe's cheese – the perfect partner for local charcuterie and wine.

10 Plage de Palombaggia
Page **258** • Some of the softest, whitest sand and bluest water in the whole Mediterranean, backed by ranks of umbrella pines.

11 Les Calanches de Piana
Page **154** • A vast mass of red porphyry, eroded into dogs' heads, witches and devils: best viewed at sunset.

12 Spelunca Gorge Page **159** •
Porto to Évisa: Corsica's most dramatic road journey.

13 Corsican wines Page **34** •
Robust, earthy and tinged with distinctive maquis aromas, Corsica's fine wines are all the more wonderful for being little known outside the island.

15 Îles de Lavezzi Page **251** •
Corsica's best snorkelling, in crystal-clear waters around an archipelago of low islets off Bonifacio.

14 Filitosa menhirs Page **206** •
Among the western Mediterranean's greatest archeological treasures, unique for their carved faces.

16 St-Florent Page **88** • An ideal base for explorations of the northeast, with classy eating, spectacular scenery and a pervasively salty atmosphere.

17 **Corte** Page **303** • The former seat of Paoli's independent government and still a nationalist stronghold, with loads of period charm and a high mountain setting.

19 **Scandola Nature Reserve** Page **153** • Remote red granite peninsula in the Golfe de Porto, surrounded by astonishingly clear waters, but accessible only by boat.

18 **Diving** Page **41** • The entire island is ringed by world-class dive sites, from wrecked B-52 bombers to vast underwater escarpments encrusted with red gorgonian coral.

20 **Girolata** Page **152** • The only fishing village on the island still inaccessible by road, set against an extraordinary backdrop of red cliffs and dense maquis.

Basics

Basics

Getting there

Flying is the fastest and most convenient – if not the most romantic – way to reach Corsica, whatever your point of departure. From the UK or mainland France, a direct flight to any of the island's four civil airports – Bastia (in the north), Ajaccio (in the west), Calvi (northwest) or Figari (far south) – takes between one-and-a-half and two-and-a-half hours, or just forty minutes for the short hop from Nice or Marseille on the French Riviera.

The cost of flights varies according to the **season**, peaking in the summer school holidays – the "Grandes Vacances" between early July and the first week in September – and falling off in shoulder season (roughly Easter to late June and early Sept to the end of Oct). From November to Easter, when charter and low-cost flights no longer operate, you'll have to rely on scheduled services from the Continent, the cost of which rises considerably on weekends and during national holidays, such as Christmas, Easter and New Year.

Flights from the UK and Ireland

Flying direct from the UK you've a choice between expensive scheduled tickets with Air France or British Airways (purchased through a travel agent or direct via the companies' websites); the low-cost airline **EasyJet** from London Gatwick; or a charter flight from London or nearly a dozen regional airports, including Manchester, Birmingham, Bristol, East Midlands, Teesside and Edinburgh. With charters, the air ticket may be included in the price of an off-the-peg package holiday, or purchased separately through an agent.

EasyJet operate to and from Corsica from late May until early October, flying four times weekly (twice on Thurs and twice on Sun) from London Gatwick to Bastia and Ajaccio. As with other low-cost carriers, fares fluctuate according to the date of travel, demand and how far in advance you book, but are generally comparable with (and often much cheaper than) charter flights, costing anywhere between £80 and £250 return. Thursday departures are much cheaper than

Sundays. The simplest way to check fares and availability is through the Easyjet website (@www.easyjet.com).

Charter flights to Corsica from the UK start in mid-April and run until mid-October. They're nearly all operated by a firm called **Holiday Options**, who charter planes from airlines such as British Midland, British Airways and FlyBe, and sell the seats on to holiday companies; they (the tour companies) then combine them with accommodation and offer them to the public as packages (see p.23). Any seats left over are sold off – both by the package operators and by Holiday Options – as discounted **flight-only** deals. For this reason, the later you can leave buying a ticket, the more likely you are to come up with a cheap fare, although holding out for a last-minute bargain inevitably entails a degree of risk, particularly if you are travelling in high season.

The best place to start hunting for a flight-only charter ticket is Holiday Options' website (you can also phone them; see p.23), where you'll find published return fares (to Bastia, Calvi, Ajaccio and Figari) from around £175 low or shoulder season to £280–300 in mid-August. In addition, they sometimes advertise "short-notice" or "late-availability" flights for as little as £100 (often with bargain fly-drive or accommodation options thrown in). If Holiday Options is sold out, or has only standard fares on offer, the next step is to check out the websites of tour operators such as Simpson Travel, Corsican Places, Simply Corsica, or others listed on p.23 and p.24 (you can also phone them).

Nearly all charter flights to Corsica from the UK leave and return on Sundays; the ticket price should include airport taxes and an

Fly less – stay longer! Travel and climate change

Climate change is perhaps the single biggest issue facing our planet. It is caused by a build-up in the atmosphere of carbon dioxide and other greenhouse gases, which are emitted by many sources – including planes. Already, **flights** account for three to four percent of human-induced global warming: that figure may sound small, but it is rising year on year and threatens to counteract the progress made by reducing greenhouse emissions in other areas.

Rough Guides regard travel as a **global benefit** and feel strongly that the advantages to developing economies are important, as are the opportunities for greater contact and awareness among peoples. But we also believe in travelling responsibly, which includes giving thought to how often we fly and what we can do to redress any harm that our trips may create.

We can travel less or simply reduce the amount we travel by air (taking fewer trips and staying longer, or taking the train if there is one); we can avoid night flights (which are more damaging); and we can make the trips we do take "climate neutral" via a carbon offset scheme. **Offset schemes** run by climatecare.org, carbonneutral .com and others allow you to "neutralize" the greenhouse gases that you are responsible for releasing. Their websites have simple calculators that let you work out the impact of any flight – as does our own. Once that's done, you can pay to fund projects that will reduce future emissions by an equivalent amount. Please take the time to visit our website and make your trip climate neutral, or get a copy of the *Rough Guide to Climate Change* for more detail on the subject.

www.roughguides.com/climatechange

in-flight meal. When booking, bear in mind which part of the island you intend to travel to first, and where any accommodation you may have pre-arranged is, or you could be faced with a long journey on arrival.

Indirect flights from the UK

Outside the tourist season, from November until Easter, and at those rare times when the charters and EasyJet are sold out, your only option will be to take an **indirect flight** via the French Riviera or northern Italy. The more expensive Air France and British Airways can get you there, while cheaper airlines include **EasyJet**, who fly to Nice from half a dozen UK airports, and to Marseille and Olbia (on the north coast of neighbouring Sardinia, near Bonifacio) from London Gatwick; **Ryanair** fly from London Stansted to Toulon, Alghero (Sardinia) and Genoa (in Italy, but closer to Corsica than any French city); and **BMI Baby** go from East Midlands and Teesside airports to Nice and Pisa.

An indirect flight to Corsica is obviously a longer and more expensive journey. It's also worth bearing in mind that the airline carrying you on your first leg is not contractually obliged to get you to your final destination and will offer no compensation if a delay caused by them means you miss your connecting flight.

Travellers with more time than money might also consider the rock-bottom option of catching a no-frills flight to the French or Italian rivieras, or to Sardinia, and **picking up a ferry** (or hydrofoil) from there (for more on ferry routes to and from Corsica, see opposite). Travelling this way it's sometimes possible to reach the island for £150–200 return, but to do so you'll have to be sure of a prompt connection, otherwise the money saved will disappear in hotel bills.

Flights from Ireland

No airline offers direct flights **from the Republic of Ireland** to Corsica, but you can usually pick up a cheap ticket with Ryanair or EasyJet to London which arrives in time to connect with a direct onward flight on a charter or with EasyJet. Alternatively, you could fly from Dublin to Pisa with Ryanair, and travel overland from there to nearby Savona, from where there are regular ferries to Corsican ports during the summer (see opposite).

From Northern Ireland, British Airways fly directly from Belfast City to Paris-Charles De Gaulle, but you'll have to get from there to Orly on the other side of the city to catch the onward flight with CCM to Corsica. Otherwise, a routing through London to pick up a charter or EasyJet flight is the best option. EasyJet also flies from Belfast International to Nice, arriving early enough (at around 10.30am) for you to jump on an NGV hydrofoil (see below) – if not from Nice, then Toulon or Marseille the same evening.

Flights from the USA and Canada

From North America, Corsica is one of the more obscure European destinations. Discount travel agents – normally the mainstay of budget travellers – concentrate on high-volume routes and are unlikely to be able to ticket you beyond Paris, Marseille or Nice, so you'll probably end up paying a published fare to Corsica.

Whichever company you travel with, flying to Corsica from North America will involve at least one change of plane. Served by flights from over thirty North American cities, Paris is the most convenient gateway. For the onward leg to Corsica, you'll have to purchase a second ticket to Ajaccio, Bastia, Calvi or Figari with CCM, Air France's subsidiary. This can be done before you leave, or – more cheaply – on arrival in France, although bear in mind that flights to Corsica from the mainland are heavily subscribed during the holiday season and should be booked months ahead of departure. Alternatively, pick up a cheap flight to London and then an onward flight with EasyJet or a charter company to Corsica (for more, see p.23).

Fares fluctuate according to the season and are highest from around early June to the end of August; they drop during the shoulder seasons (Sept–Oct & April–May); and you'll get the best deals during the low season (Nov–March, excluding Christmas). Published fares with Air France start at around $1800 from New York; $1675 from Washington DC; or $2000 from LA/San Francisco – though you'll be quoted rates of fifty percent lower than that by consolidators and web-based agents.

From Canada

The strong links between France and Québec's Francophone community ensure regular air services from Canada to Paris, from where you have to change onto the domestic carrier CCM for the onward flight to Corsica.

Air France, Air Canada and Canadian offer nonstop services to Paris from the major Canadian cities. Return fares start at around $1500 from Toronto and Montreal, or $1600 from Vancouver.

Flights from Australia and New Zealand

There are no direct flights from Australia or New Zealand to Corsica, but it's easy enough to fly direct to Paris and change planes there for Ajaccio, Calvi, Bastia or Figari on CCM. Fares tend to be cheaper in low season (mid-Jan to Feb & Oct–Nov), increasing during high season (June–Aug & Dec to early Jan). Travelling in May or late September (shoulder season), count on Aus$1850–2300 from Sydney, around Aus$2100 from Perth, NZ$3100–4000 from Auckland and Wellington.

Most travel agents can book a through-ticket to Corsica before you leave, which can add as little as Aus$100 to the cost of your international flight. Your best chance of finding which airline is currently offering the most competitive fares is to check the websites of the agents listed on p.23 – or try the websites listed on p.22.

Ferries to Corsica from France and Italy

Corsica has six ferry **ports** (Bastia, L'Île Rousse, Calvi, Ajaccio, Propriano and Porto Vecchio), served by three ports on the French Riviera (Marseille, Toulon and Nice) and seven in Italy (Naples, Savona, Genoa, La Spezia, Livorno, Piombo and Santa Teresa di Gallura in Sardinia). From France, crossings take between 6hr (Nice–Bastia) and 13hr 30min (Marseille–Porto Vecchio overnight) on **regular ferries**, and from 2hr 45min (Nice–Calvi) to 4hr (Nice–Ajaccio) on the superfast **NGV** hydrofoils (*Navire à Grande Vitesse*), which travel at a brisk 37 to 43 knots. Coming from the UK, Marseille is the obvious port to head for, but if you want to catch an NGV, you'll have to press on further up the coast to Nice.

Bear in mind that during peak periods demand for ferry tickets to Corsica from both mainland France and Italy may far exceed supply, so book as far in advance as possible. **Reservations** can be made either through your local travel agent or directly with the ferry companies, over the telephone or internet. Some of the ferry companies also have agents in the UK whom you can contact for timetable information and bookings. Tickets for all ferry crossings between the Continent and Corsica may also be booked online through ☻www.aferry.co.uk.

From France, regular and NGV services are run by two companies: SNCM Ferrytér-ranée and Corsica Ferries (see below). **Fares** on their NGVs are around the same as on regular ferries, with both varying according to whether you travel in a blue (off-peak), green (mid-season), white (high-season) or red (peak-season) period. One-way foot passenger tickets to all ports in Corsica, for example, on services from Marseille, Toulon and Nice, cost €30–80 (including port taxes); return fares cost exactly double; and there are reductions for students and OAPs. Note, too, that in order to compete with low-cost airlines, ferry companies nowadays also offer occasional **super deals**, with fares slashed to €3 or less. These are available only through the websites.

Comparatively few British travellers approach Corsica **from Italy**, but ferry services from the seven Italian ports are frequent throughout the summer and often less expensive (their red and white periods tend to be much shorter). Taking around 2hr 30min by NGV, the shortest and least expensive crossing is from Livorno to Bastia; tickets for foot passengers cost €20–30 one way. Again, super deals are sporadically available through the ferry firms' websites.

Ferry contacts

For contact details of ferry company offices in their Corsican ports, see the relevant accounts in the Guide section of this book.
Corsica Ferries ☎00-33/4 92 00 43 76, ☻www.corsicaferries.com (UK agents Via Mare ☎0208/206 3420, ☻www.viamare.com). Toulon to

Bastia, L'Île Rousse and Ajaccio; Nice to Ajaccio, Bastia and Calvi; L'Île Rouse to Calvi; Livorno to Bastia; Santa Teresa di Gallura (Sardinia) to Bonifacio.
Med Mar ☎0815/513352, ☻www.medmargroup .it. Naples to Porto Vecchio via Palau (Sardinia).
Moby Lines ☎49-611/14020, ☻www.mobylines .com (UK agents Via Mare ☎0208/206 3420, ☻www.viamare.com). Genoa and Livorno to Bastia; Santa Teresa di Gallura (Sardinia) to Bonifacio.
Saremar ☎199/30 30 40, ☻www.saremar.it. Santa Teresa di Gallura (Sardinia) to Bonifacio.
SNCM Ferrytérranée ☎00-33/8 25 88 80 88, ☻www.sncm.fr (UK agents Southern Ferries ☎0870/499 1305, ☻www.southernferries.co.uk). From Marseille, Toulon and Nice to Bastia, Ajaccio, L'Île Rousse, Porto Vecchio and Propriano.

Airlines, agents and operators

Online booking agents

☻ **www.expedia.com**
☻ **www.lastminute.com**
☻ **www.opodo.com**
☻ **www.orbitz.com**
☻ **www.travelocity.com**
☻ **www.zuji.com**

Airlines

Aer Lingus Ireland ☎0818/365 000, ☻www .aerlingus.ie.
Air Canada US & Canada ☎1-888/247-2262, ☻www.aircanada.ca.
Air France UK ☎0870/142 4343, US ☎1-800/237-2747, Canada ☎1-800/667-2747, Australia ☎1300/390 190; ☻www.airfrance.com.
Air New Zealand Australia ☎0800/132 476, New Zealand ☎0800/737000; ☻www.airnewzealand .com.
Alitalia US ☎1-800/223-5730, Canada ☎1-800/361-8336; ☻www.alitalia.com.
BMI Baby UK ☎0871/224 0224, ☻www.bmibaby .com.
British Airways UK ☎0844/493 0787, Ireland ☎1890/626 747, US & Canada ☎1-800/AIRWAYS, Australia ☎1300/767 177, New Zealand ☎09/966 9777; ☻www.ba.com.
CCM UK ☎0870/142 4343, US ☎1-800/237-2747, Canada ☎1-800/667-2747; ☻www .ccm-airlines.com.
Delta Air Lines US & Canada ☎1-800/221-1212, ☻www.delta.com.
EasyJet UK ☎0905/821 0905, ☻www .easyjet.com.

Lufthansa US ☎1-800/3995-838, Canada
☎1-800/563-5954; ⓦwww.lufthansa-usa.com.
Ryanair UK ☎0871/246 0000, Ireland
☎0818/303 030; ⓦwww.ryanair.com.
Singapore Airlines Australia ☎131 011, New
Zealand ☎0800/808 909; ⓦwww.singaporeair
.com.
Swiss US & Canada ☎1-877/3597-947, Australia
☎1300/724 666, New Zealand ☎09/977 2238;
ⓦwww.swiss.com.
Thai Airways Australia ☎1300/651 960, New
Zealand ☎09/377 3886; ⓦwww.thaiair.com.
United Airlines ☎1-800/864-8331, ⓦwww
.ual.com.

Agents

Air Brokers International US & Canada
☎1-800/883-3273, ⓦwww.airbrokers.com.
Airtreks.com US & Canada ☎1-877.AIRTREKS,
ⓦwww.airtreks.com.
Charter Flight Centre UK ☎0845/045 0153,
ⓦwww.charterflights.co.uk.
CIE Tours International Ireland ☎01/703 1888,
ⓦwww.cietours.ie.
Flight Centre Australia ☎133 133, New Zealand
☎0800/243 544; ⓦwww.flightcentre.com.
Holiday Options UK ☎0844/477 0451, ⓦwww
.holidayoptions.co.uk.
Holiday Shoppe New Zealand ☎0800/866654,
ⓦwww.holidayshoppe.co.nz.
Joe Walsh Tours Ireland ☎01/241 8000,
ⓦwww.joewalshtours.ie.
Lee Travel Ireland ☎021/427 7111, ⓦwww
.leetravel.ie.
North South Travel UK ☎01245/608291,
ⓦwww.northsouthtravel.co.uk.
STA Travel UK ☎0871/2300 040, US
☎1-800/781-4040, Canada 1-888/427-5639,
Australia ☎133.STA, New Zealand
☎0800/474400; ⓦwww.statravel.com.
Student Flights US & Canada ☎1-800/255-8000
or 480/951-1177, ⓦwww.isecard.com.
Trailfinders Ireland ☎01/677 7888, Australia
☎1300/780212; ⓦwww.trailfinders.com.

Package tours

The cost of package holidays varies
enormously from company to company and
depending on the kind of property you book
and time of year you travel. The list below
summarizes the **tour companies** that
currently offer packages to the island from
the UK, but smaller ones come and go.
Before booking with any travel company,

ensure they are fully bonded – look out for
the IATA or ATOL number given on the
company's brochure.

Corsica is way off the beaten track for
most **North American and Australasian
tour operators**. Your choices basically
come down to a company arranging
upscale tours and a couple of adventure-
travel outfits that do hiking and biking trips
in the mountains. If you're set on going with
a package tour, you might want to consider
contacting an operator in Britain (see
below), where Corsica is a much more
popular destination.

In the UK

For specialist walking holiday firms, see p.336.
BabyGoes2.Com ☎01273 230669, ⓦwww
.babygoes2.com. Web-based holiday-planning
service for parents. You fill in the form and their
consultant (not a search engine) dreams up your ideal
break in Corsica, among many destinations.
Club Med ☎0871/424 4044, ⓦwww.clubmed
.co.uk. Child-friendly holidays in purpose-built
complex on Chiuni Bay, near Cargèse, with excellent
watersports and tennis facilities. See also p.45.
Corsican Affair ☎020/7385 8438, ⓦwww
.corsicanaffair.co.uk. Fly-drive, hotel packages and
self-catering in a wide range of attractive properties
across the island.
Corsican Places ☎0845/330 2059, ⓦwww
.corsica.co.uk. Experienced and knowledgeable
Corsica specialists, offering tailor-made stays, as well
as packages, in period properties and new villas at
very reasonable prices.
Cresta Holidays ⓦwww.crestaholidays.co.uk.
Various hotel-and-flight deals.
Direct Corsica ⓦwww.directcorsica.com. Agency
for rented villas and apartments, as well as rooms in
exclusive hotels and *auberges*, plus a full range of
travel services.
Eurocamp ☎0844/406 042, ⓦwww.eurocamp
.co.uk. Camping holidays at the big Marina d'Erba
Rossa site on the east coast, near Ghisonaccia.
A good all-in budget option, especially for families.
Holiday Options ☎0844/477 0451, ⓦwww
.holidayoptions.co.uk. As well as operating as a flight
agent, Holiday Options offers discounted package
holidays, bundling together accommodation and car
hire, often at rock-bottom rates. See their website for
last-minute deals.
Mark Warner ☎0871 703 3887, ⓦwww
.markwarner.co.uk. Watersports specialists, with
accommodation in beach-club-style hotels and apartments, with special provision for kids.

Nature Trek ☎01962/733051, ⓦwww
.naturetrek.co.uk. Eight-day birdwatching, botanical
and natural history holidays.
Simply Corsica ☎0871/231 4050, ⓦwww
.simplytravel.co.uk. Currently the UK's largest operator on the island. Their portfolio includes a diverse
range of hand-picked properties, from classy hotels to
villas with pools, country cottages and seaside apartments, and they offer unrivalled child-care facilities
(including a crèche and English-speaking nannies).
Check their brochure for special-interest options:
group walking, painting and wild flowers.
Simpson Travel ☎0208/392 5851, ⓦwww
.simpson-travel.co.uk. Expertly tailored holidays in
boutique hotels, rural retreats, character apartments
and villas with private pools. Both their property portfolio and on-island service have set new standards.
VillaFinders.Com ☎0208/607 9988, ⓦwww
.villafinders.com. Internet-based villa specialist
providing package holidays in over 250 properties
around the island from as little as £350 per week per
person, including flights and car hire.
VFB Holidays ☎01452/716841, ⓦwww
.vfbholidays.co.uk. Flexible fly-drive holidays with
accommodation in various standard hotels, small
resort complexes and self-catering properties (some
with pools) all over the island, including nine charming
apartments in the remote mountain village of Lama.
Voyages Ilena ☎0845/330 2048, ⓦwww
.voyagesilena.co.uk. Star hotels and a wide range of
attractive self-catering accommodation all over Corsica.

In the USA and Canada

Kalliste Tours ⓦwww.kallistetours.com. Small,
friendly Corsica specialist whose aim is to provide
"cultural immersion and real-life experiences in
Corsica". Corsican-born guide France-Marie Louvet
escorts the imaginatively devised, themed tours
("Chestnut Week", "Christmas", "Villages and
Artisanat", and so on).
Infohub ⓦwww.infohub.com. Web-based agency
offering various options, from supported cycling and
GR20 trips to scuba diving and cruises – several
combine Corsica with Italian island tours.
World Expeditions US ☎1-800-567-2216,
ⓦwww.worldexpeditions.net; Canada
☎1-800-567-2216 ⓦwww.worldexpeditions.ca.
Fully supported trekking and cycling holidays.

In Australia and New Zealand

Abercrombie and Kent Australia ☎1300/851
800, New Zealand ☎0800/441 638; ⓦwww
.abercrombiekent.com.au. Tailor-made upmarket
tours, with accommodation in select hotels.
Adventure World New Zealand ☎0800/238368,
ⓦwww.adventureworld.co.nz. NZ agent for
Peregrine (see below).
Peregrine Adventures Australia
☎03/8601 4444, ⓦwww.peregrine.net.au.
Guided trekking holidays of various lengths and levels
of comfort.

Getting around

Given the manifest inadequacies of public transport in Corsica – at least outside
peak season, when services to most areas are drastically scaled down – it isn't
surprising that most travellers get around by car. But with a little flexibility and
forward planning you can still reach all but the most remote corners of the island
on buses and trains. Quite apart from reducing the overall cost of your trip, by
travelling on public transport you'll be doing your bit to minimize pollution on an
island that strains to cope with the extra tourists in summer.

Journey times and frequencies for buses,
trains and ferries are given in the Travel details
at the end of each chapter, but bear in mind
that timetables tend to change annually; you
can always check schedules at a tourist
office, or online at ⓦwww.corsicabus.org.

By car

For visitors used to the comparatively
restrained roads and traffic manners of
northern Europe, **driving in Corsica** can
come as a rude shock. Once you're off
the smooth national highways (*routes*

nationales, prefixed with an N), the constantly twisting *routes départementales* (prefixed with a D) present their fair share of hazards, not least of all **Corsican drivers** themselves, who race rally-style around the bends and habitually overtake in perilous situations. For this reason, expect to meet vehicles approaching at speed in the middle of the road, even on blind corners and brows of hills. If you find yourself with a local car breathing down your neck, pull over and let it pass at the first opportunity. Note, also, that the mountain and corniche roads are pitted with great potholes; pigs and goats present further dangers.

EU and US **driving licences** are valid in France. If the vehicle is rented, its registration document (*carte grise*) and the insurance papers must be carried (they are usually stored in the glove compartment of rental cars).

The French law of *priorité à droite* – giving way to traffic coming from your right, even when it is coming from a minor road – is gradually being phased out. It is sometimes respected in built-up areas of Bastia and Ajaccio, however, so you still have to be vigilant in towns, keeping a lookout for signs showing a yellow diamond on a white background that gives you right of way, or for the same sign with an oblique slash, which indicates that vehicles emerging from the right have right of way. At roundabouts the cars on the roundabout have priority. *CÉDEZ LE PASSAGE* means "Give way"; a *STOP* sign means come to a complete halt.

Speed limits are 110kph (68mph) on dual-carriageways, 90kph (56mph) on other roads in non-urban areas, and 60kph (37mph) in towns. Radars are being installed along the main roads (where they're routinely sabotaged by the Corsicans) and there are stiff fines of up to €9000 and suspended licence. The standard fine for exceeding the speed limit by 20kph (12mph), for example, is €90; above 40kph (25mph) you will not only be fined but will also have to go to court. The **alcohol** limit is 0.05 percent (50mg per litre of blood) and random breath tests are increasingly common.

As for **fuel**, note that in remote country areas – such as Cap Corse and the interior – petrol stations are especially scarce, so

See p.436 for useful driving vocabulary.

remember to fill up in the towns. Unleaded fuel (*sans plomb*) is available everywhere.

Car rental

Car rental in Corsica costs upwards of €75 per day and €275 per week, but can be cheaper if arranged before you leave home or online.

To rent a car in Corsica you have to be over 21 (and in some cases over 25) and have been in possession of a clean licence (ie with no more than nine points) for at least one year. All the international rental companies are represented on the island, with branches at the airports and in major towns. You can sometimes save money by booking a **fly-drive deal** with a tour operator (see pp.22–23).

If you **break down** in a rented vehicle, contact the rental company via the emergency number you'll have been given when you collected the car. As in your home country, if you have an **accident**, exchange registration numbers (*numéros d'immatriculation*) with any other drivers involved. **Break-ins** should be reported to the local police in order to make an insurance claim, while in the event of an accident you are also obliged to complete a *constat à l'aimable* (jointly agreed statement), which your car insurers or rental company should give you.

Car rental agencies

Avis US ☎1-800-331-1212, Canada ☎1-800/879-2847, UK ☎0844/581 8181, Republic of Ireland ☎021/428 1111, Australia ☎13 63 33 or 02/9353 9000, New Zealand ☎09/526 2847 or 0800/655 111, South Africa ☎11/923 3660; ⓦwww.avis.com.

Budget US ☎1-800-527-0700, Canada ☎1-800/268-8900, UK ☎0870/156 5656, Australia ☎1300/362 848, New Zealand ☎0800/283 438; ⓦwww.budget.com.

Europcar US & Canada ☎1-877/940 6900, UK ☎0845/758 5375, Republic of Ireland ☎01/614 2800, Australia ☎1300/131 390; ⓦwww.europcar.com.

Hertz US & Canada ☎1-800/654-3131, UK ☎0870/040 9000, Republic of Ireland

☎01/870 5777, Australia ☎13 30 39, New Zealand ☎0800/654 321, South Africa ☎21/935 4800; 🌐www.hertz.com.
Holiday Autos US & Canada ☎0866/392 9288, UK ☎0870/400 4482, Republic of Ireland ☎01/872 9366, Australia ☎1300/554 432, New Zealand ☎0800/144 040, South Africa ☎11/234 0597; 🌐www.holidayautos.co.uk. Part of the lastminute .com group.
National US ☎1-800/227-7368, UK ☎0870/400 4588, Australia ☎0870/600 6666, New Zealand ☎03/366 5574; 🌐www.nationalcar.com.

By bicycle

Corsica is no soft option for **cyclists**, but if you're in good shape you'll enjoy the challenge of the island's convoluted routes and long climbs. The main disadvantage is the traffic, combined with the narrowness of the roads. In summer, you'll also have the fumes to contend with, as well as the ferocious heat. All in all, it's a better idea to come in mid-season – May to June and September to October – and aim to avoid the traffic as much as possible.

A handful of companies around the island **rent cycles**, usually mountain bikes – *vélos tous terrains* (*VTT*) in French. Rates are fairly standard, at €13–17 per day, or €70–80 per week, with discounts of fifteen to twenty percent out of season. You're also usually required to leave a credit card docket or around €300–400 in cash as a deposit (*caution*). See p.436 for useful cycling vocabulary.

Mountain bike rental companies in Corsica

Ajaccio Corse Évasion, Montée St-Jean ☎04 95 20 52 05, 🌐www.corsicamoto.com.
Bastia Objectif Nature, rue Notre-Dame-de Lourdes ☎04 95 32 54 34, 🌐www.objectif -nature-corse.com.
Calvi Garage d'Angeli, rue Villa-Antoine ☎04 95 65 02 13, 🌐www.garagedangeli.com.
Porto Porto Location, opposite Spar supermarket ☎04 95 26 10 13.
Propriano TCC, 25 rue Général-de-Gaulle ☎04 95 76 15 32, 🌐www.ttcmoto.fr.

For more on mountain biking in Corsica, see p.40.

By motorcycle

Corsica is perfect **motorcycle** terrain, and during the summer its roads teem with tourers (most of them from Germany). If you've come without your own vehicle or can't afford to rent a car, you might consider renting a bike – though high insurance premiums have forced prices up to often prohibitive levels.

Bikes can be rented at various towns and resorts around the island, and the **choice of vehicles** on offer is pretty standard; only the prices vary. Cheapest of all, at around €35–40 per day, is a 50cc moped. While these are fine for nipping to and from the beach, they tend to struggle on the hills, which effectively writes off most of the island except the eastern plain. Nor do they tend to have any luggage-carrying facilities. For a trip into the interior or around the coast, you'll need at least a Vespa-style 125cc scooter. Costing around €45–60 per day (or €250–300 per week), these can comfortably carry a rider and pillion passenger on level ground, and will make it over even the highest mountain passes if you're riding solo. Trials-style 125cc bikes are also widely available, though they cost upwards of €50–65 per day (€300–350 per week); anything larger than that – such as a Honda 650cc Transalp – will set you back €100–120 (or €560–660 per week).

In addition to the daily rental rate, you'll need to leave a hefty **deposit** (*caution*) of around €800–1000. Rather than accept a cheque or cash, most companies these days prefer to swipe a credit card through their machine and keep the docket as security, tearing it up if you return the bike in a satisfactory condition.

The cost of rental generally includes a helmet and covers third-party insurance, but not damage incurred to the vehicle in any accident – another reason to ride defensively. Crash your bike, and you'll almost certainly have to foot the bill.

Theft can be problem, especially in car parks above beaches. Owners should issue you with a strong D-lock (*anti-vol*) or chain, which you fasten around the front wheel. This, however, will at best only act as a deterrent, so be sure to use the steering lock as well, each time you park up. If the bike does get stolen, notify the rental company and local police immediately. In theory, the company should be covered by their insurance for theft, but check this before you leave their office; some insist on retaining most or all of your deposit if a bike disappears.

Motorcycle rental companies in Corsica

Ajaccio Cyrnos Location, Hôtel Kallisté, 51 cours Napoléon ☎04 95 51 61 81 or 04 95 23 56 36, ⓦwww.cyrnos.net; Moto Corse Évasion, Montée St-Jean ☎04 95 20 52 05, ⓦwww.corsicamoto.com.
Propriano TCC, 25 rue Général-de-Gaulle ☎04 95 76 15 32, ⓦwww.ttcmoto.fr.

By bus

Buses are Corsica's principal form of public transport, but as most Corsicans own at least one car, demand outside the tourist season is minimal. Even in summer, services on many routes are infrequent, to say the least, and if you rely purely on buses to get around, your travels will be limited to a handful of arterial routes.

In rural areas, **timetables** tend to be constructed to suit working and school hours, which means there's often just one bus a day in any direction, departing at a dauntingly early hour.

To confuse matters, virtually each route is covered by a different **company**. In theory, tourist offices should have up-to-date schedules (*horaires*), but you can't guarantee it. The easiest way to work out which company serves which towns is to consult the Travel details section at the end of each chapter; these include a brief outline of the region's main routes and contact numbers for the relevant bus operators. You can also access up-to-date timetable information on the web at ⓦ**www.corsicabus.org.**

Fares are high, though the buses themselves are comfortable enough and

kept in good condition. Trunk routes are served by large coaches, while the mountain villages of the interior and the northwest coast are connected by modern minibuses.

By train

Corsica's diminutive, bone-shaking train, the *micheline* (or *trinighellu* – little train), crosses the mountains from Ajaccio to Bastia via Corte, with a subsidiary line running from Ponte Leccia, north of Corte, to Calvi. Constructed at the end of the nineteenth century, the 230km line, which boasts 32 tunnels, follows a rattling and precarious route across the mountains, transporting around 800,000 passengers each year. The track had a major re-fit in 2006–08, and state-of-the-art rolling stock is gradually being phased in that will make the ride over the mountains a much smoother one. And what a ride it is: the scenery is wonderful from start to finish, and there are plenty of tempting spots to get off and walk along the route. The line's most impressive feat of engineering is the famous Pont du Vecchio at Vivario, designed by Gustave Eiffel (of Eiffel Tower fame). Crossing it, you get a matchless view across to the dizzying new Pont du Vecchio road bridge, completed in 1999, with a span of 222m and a height of 137.5m. A short way further south, at Vizzavona, the line plunges into the watershed, which it crosses by means of a 3916-metre-long tunnel.

Tickets cost about the same as the buses (€21 for Ajaccio–Bastia and €25 for Ajaccio–Calvi). ISIC card-carrying students are entitled to discounts; bicycles go free.

Timetables can be checked at the stations, at local tourist offices, over the phone using the numbers listed throughout the Guide or, most easily, online at ⓦwww.corsicabus.org.

Accommodation

Protection of the natural environment and traditional architecture has always been a cornerstone of the Corsican nationalist agenda, and as a consequence the island holds few unsightly modern developments. Even around the popular resort beaches of Porto Vecchio, building styles are for the most part low-rise and restrained, with few large and intrusive hotels and a correspondingly high number of private rental properties. Those visitors unable to afford such comforts have little alternative but to pitch a tent in the many campsites that spring up in June.

Wherever you choose to stay, it's advisable to **book ahead**, especially during the "Grandes Vacances" (mid-July to the start of Sept), when the French and Italians take their holidays en masse. The Language section on p.427 should help you make your reservation, as few hoteliers or campsite managers speak any English.

In the event that all the places reviewed by us for the area you're in are full (*complet*), visit the local tourist office, or its website, and consult their accommodation brochure (*guide des hébergements*). These list virtually everywhere within reach and worthy of note, complete with a little photo, contact details, current prices and a rundown of facilities. Once you've settled on a place, you can usually check out its own website and email the owner; alternatively, the tourist office should also be willing to help make the reservation if your French isn't up to it.

Hotels

By comparison with the UK, hotel accommodation in Corsica represents extremely good value for money – at least outside the mid-July through August peak season. Establishments are **graded** on a scale that rises from nought to four stars. Room rates reflect the number of stars, but it's worth remembering that most places offer a spread of differently priced options with varying degrees of comforts, outlined in a list which you'll be presented with at reception.

It's unusual to find rooms costing **less than** €40, and those that are tend to be basic; they'll probably have a washbasin (*lavabo*), and sometimes a bidet, but little else. The shower (*douche*) and toilets (WC) will be outside on the corridor (*à l'étage*).

At the **one-star** level you can expect to pay €40–55 for a double, perhaps with a shower and toilet but probably not a bathtub. **Two-star** places, with fully en-suite facilities and often a small balcony, charge around €55–70. **Three-star** hotels usually cost €70–125, for which you should enjoy a spacious double room with bathroom, television, large terrace or balcony (*loggia*), and access to a pool. **Four-star** establishments, typically costing €125–150 per night, offer international-standard luxury, with big rooms, lots of

---

Accommodation price codes

All accommodation reviewed in this book has been graded according to the following price codes, which indicate the cost of the **cheapest double room available in June and September**. Allow for increases of at least fifty percent during high season (July & Aug), and decreases of around ten to fifteen percent in October and May. Out of season, the few hotels that stay open may offer much-reduced rates.

- ❶ €30 and Under
- ❷ €31–40
- ❸ €41–55
- ❹ €56–70
- ❺ €71–85
- ❻ €86–100
- ❼ €101–125
- ❽ €126–150
- ❾ €151 and over

mod-cons, modern pools and gourmet restaurants. **Single rooms** are typically one-third cheaper than doubles. Some hotels will provide extra beds (*lits supplémentaires*) for three or more, charging around 25 percent per bed.

Breakfast can add €7.50–10 per person to a bill (if it's included you'll be told at check-in time), though you'll be under no obligation to have it and will invariably do better buying your own pâtisserie at a bakery and taking it to a café. The cost of **dinner** in a hotel's restaurant can be a more important factor to bear in mind when picking a place to stay. Despite the introduction of laws banning the practice, some hotels insist you opt for half board (*demi-pension*), particularly in peak season. This may or may not be a good deal, depending on the quality of the restaurant and how much access to the main menu your half board entitles you to.

Note that many hotels **open only in summer**, usually from May to September – we've indicated in the Guide those establishments that close for the winter. The ones that do stay open in winter often offer discounts to off-season visitors.

Chambres d'hôtes and ferme-auberges

Some of the most congenial private accommodation in Corsica is offered in small, rural bed-and-breakfast establishments, or **chambres d'hôtes**. There are dozens of places dotted around the island where you can stay as a paying guest in someone's home, usually in a newly converted wing or modern annexe of a farmhouse. As you'd expect, the experience is more personal, especially in those places where evening meals are offered, giving you a chance to get to know your hosts. Room tariffs are not cheap, averaging from around €55–80 for two, including breakfast, but for many visitors, particularly those keen to practise their French, the off-the-beaten-track locations and warm Corsican hospitality give *chambres d'hôtes* the edge over most hotels.

Ferme-auberges, literally "farm-inns", are similar to *chambres d'hôtes*, but with the emphasis being essentially on the food: classy Corsican speciality dishes, made from locally produced ingredients. The hosts may,

or may not, offer rooms, but if they do you'll be able to stay in one only if you have dinner. For this reason, prices are given as half board (*demi-pension*), which covers the room, breakfast and evening meal.

Rented accommodation

If you're planning to stay a week or more in any one place, it might be worth considering **renting a house, apartment or villa**. The easiest and most reliable way to do this is through a package company before you leave home (see p.23), as holiday firms tend to acquire the pick of the properties in any given area. Alternatively, contact **Gîtes de France Corse** (77 cours Napoléon, BP 10, 20000 Ajaccio ☎04 95 10 54 30, ⓦwww .gites-corsica.com; Mon–Sat 10am–6.30pm) for a brochure, or check their website.

Alternatively, you can wait until you arrive in Corsica and ask any local tourist office for a list of properties to rent (*locations de particulier*) in their region. For somewhere large enough to accommodate a family of four to five, expect to pay €400–650 per week off season, or €750–1500 or more in the school holidays. The rates may be less expensive than renting a villa through an agency, but there's obviously the risk that nothing will be available when you need it.

Gîtes d'étape and refuges

Corsica has dozens of *gîtes d'étape* and refuges situated at stages along the main hiking trails. Although designed primarily for walkers, anyone can stay at them, and in several remote villages of the interior and northwest coast they often constitute the only budget accommodation.

Gîtes d'étape offer basic accommodation, usually in four- to six-bunk-bed dormitories with communal hot showers and toilets; some also have fully en-suite doubles, at far cheaper rates than comparable hotels. When demand is high, you'll be obliged to share the dorm with others, but during off-peak periods the wardens (*gardiens*) try to put clients in separate rooms for the price of a single bed (around €14). Half board is generally offered for around €32–35 per person, and may even be obligatory. It's rare to find a *gîte* that's not kept in immaculate

Rental properties online

Following the introduction of low-cost flights to Corsica from the UK (see p.19), a number of specialist agencies have sprung up in recent years to help visitors find their own villas, holiday cottages and other self-catering properties on the island via the internet. Those listed below are the best established.

Calvi Locations ⓦ uk.calvi-locations.com. Corsican agent for summer and winter lets in the Balagne.

Clévacances ⓦ www.clevacances-haute-corse.com. Government-run agency promoting holiday flats and houses in northern Corsica.

Corse Villa ⓦ www.corsevilla.com. Villa-finding service for the south of the island.

Direct Corsica ⓦ www.directcorsica.com. Agency for rented villas and apartments, as well as rooms in exclusive hotels and *auberges*.

Kalliste Holidays ⓦ www.kallisteholidays.com. Rental properties from apartments and villas to luxury houses, all in the Balagne.

The Villa Company ⓦ www.villa-holiday-company.co.uk. Small UK company that acts as an agent for hand-picked, Corsican-owned properties around the island.

VillaFinders.Com ⓦ www.villafinders.com. UK-based villa specialist with over 250 properties on their books. They also arrange flights and car hire.

Villa Holiday Company ⓦ www.villa-holiday-company.co.uk. "Un-packaged" holidays in villas from another UK company.

Villas du Sud ⓦ www.villas-du-sud.com. A large selection of holiday properties in the south, around Porto Vecchio.

---

condition, and many have attractive terraces or gardens. Self-catering facilities are always provided and included in the cost of the bed, but most walkers opt for half board, which can work out good value. You can also sometimes camp in the garden for around the same price as a cheap campsite. Unlike hotels, the peak periods for *gîtes* are the walking seasons, from late May until early July and through September, when you should reserve a bed as far in advance as possible.

Situated in remote mountain locations, well away from roads, **refuges** are hikers' huts, converted from shepherds' crofts or ancient stone dwellings. While some provide little more than a roof, others have fully equipped kitchens, dining rooms, common dormitory and toilets. Most also have a bivouac area nearby where you can bed down outdoors or pitch a tent. Along the GR20, refuges are manned from late May until mid-September by *gardiens* who also collect the daily fee (€10–12 per bed, or roughly half that for campers and bivouackers). Places in refuges are allocated on a first-come, first-served basis, and cannot be reserved in advance.

All refuges and *gîtes d'étape* are marked on the large-scale IGN maps; you'll also find listings for the *gîtes d'étape*, complete with full contact details, in our coverage of the island's long-distance walks in Chapter 8.

Camping

Practically every locality has at least one **campsite** to cater for the thousands of French, Germans and Italians who spend their holiday under canvas or in recreation vehicles. The cheapest – costing around €15–20 per night for a couple, tent and car – are small, family-run farm campsites (known as *campings à la ferme*), which offer basic amenities in attractive settings. They tend to be a much more pleasant experience, and better value, than the superior categories of campsite dotted around the coast, where you'll pay prices similar to those of a one-star hotel for facilities such as bars, restaurants, tennis courts and swimming pools. People spend their whole holiday in these places – if you plan to do the same, and particularly if you have a caravan or a big tent, it's wise to book ahead.

Lastly, a word of caution: never **camp rough** (*camping sauvage*) on anyone's land without first asking their permission: it's illegal. Camping on beaches is also technically against the law, though a lot of people do it in remote areas such as the Désert des Agriates and Littoral Sartenais. Wherever you camp, be careful with fires, as the maquis burns quickly.

Food and drink

In common with their Continental compatriots, Corsicans take their food and drink very seriously indeed. At 12.30pm sharp, a mini rush hour in towns across the island heralds the return of workers home, or to a local restaurant, for a leisurely three-course meal, whose dishes may well be the subject of avid discussions throughout the afternoon. The quality and authenticity of Corsican cuisine, in particular, can provoke passionate feelings: a former president of the Chamber of Agriculture was murdered for his stand against battery pig farming, while a wine adulteration scandal at Aléria in 1975 led to a bloody armed siege (see p.272).

For some visitors, the islanders' attitude to food can seem obsessive at times, but it does ensure that standards in restaurants are generally high, and prices low. Even travellers on tight budgets should be able to afford to eat in pizzerias, and you'll be missing out on one of the region's undisputed highlights if you don't sample a full-scale Corsican speciality meal at some point. For a **glossary** of food and drink terms see p.437.

Breakfast and snacks

A typical café **breakfast** in Corsica consists of a croissant or pain au chocolat (the barman will usually leave a basket of pastries on your table and bill you according to how many you eat), served with hot chocolate or coffee. In coastal resorts, you'll find many places offering petit déjeuner complet, with half a baguette, butter and jam, fruit juice and a croissant for around €5–9 per person. Hotels invariably do set breakfasts for guests, too, but charge more, while their dining rooms are often less appealing than a sunny café terrace.

For inexpensive **snacks**, head for a café or patisserie where you can fill up on panini (filled and toasted French sticks), bastilles (traditional Corsican pasties stuffed with spinach/onions, or brocciu), or a mixture of all three), slices of pizza, bruscetta, and all kinds of fresh sandwiches. Auberges, refuges and most hotels in the mountains will make you up a casse-croûte, a huge sandwich often filled with a generous slice of lonzu (cured ham) or local saucisse, and fromage corse (local cheese).

Crêpes, thin pancakes with fillings, served up at ubiquitous crêperies, are a popular meal or snack – at least among tourists. The savoury buckwheat variety (often called galettes) provides the main course; the

On the whole, **vegetarians** can expect an easier time than they might in mainland France. Several Corsican standards – including omelette à la menthe and cannelloni al brocciu – are vegetarian and can be found on menus everywhere; and there are always plenty of meat-free options on offer in pizzerias. Remember the phrase "Je suis végétarien(ne). Est-ce qu'il y a quelques plats sans viande?" ("I'm a vegetarian. Are there any non-meat dishes?"). **Vegans**, however, should probably forget about eating in Corsican restaurants and stick to self-catering.

sweet white-flour ones, dessert. **Pizzerias**, serving pizzas usually *au feu de bois* (wood-fired), are also common. Pizzas generally cost around €8–12 but quality varies greatly – look before you leap into the nearest empty seats.

Pastries

Pâtisseries offer a selection of wonderful cakes and local sweet delicacies such as chestnut cake, *fiadone* and *canistrelli* (Corsican speciality-style biscuits), as well as melt-in-the-mouth French standards such as *tarte aux fraises* and *tarte aux pommes*. **Salons de thé**, though few and far between, serve cakes, *glace* (ice cream) and a wide selection of teas. They tend to be a good deal pricier than cafés, as you pay for the swish decor, and they generally have a more female clientele and ambience.

Restaurants and ferme-auberges

During the tourist season, when the island seems to sport as many **restaurants** as it does pleasure boats, there's no reason why you shouldn't eat consistently well for a fraction of what you'd pay at home. The only problem is knowing where to find value for money. The resorts, in particular, are littered with places churning out indifferent microwave meals for large groups of undiscerning tourists.

It's always worth asking locals or French people you meet for restaurant recommendations. Above all, don't be afraid to take a chance on somewhere off the beaten track if it's been recommended. Many of the island's most acclaimed restaurants are lost deep in the maquis, without signs to show you the way. Dependent on word of mouth for their predominantly local custom, they are often classed as **ferme-auberges** (farm-inns), where top Corsican cuisine, made entirely from fresh, locally grown ingredients, is served in appropriately rustic surroundings.

With all *ferme-auberges*, and in touristy areas in high season, it's wise to make **reservations** – easily done on the same day. In small towns and villages, and during the winter, it may be difficult to find something

open after 10pm, though in the larger resorts there's always at least a pizzeria open until midnight through the summer. Don't forget that hotel restaurants are usually open to non-residents.

Menus

Prices, and what you get for them, are posted outside restaurants. Normally there's a choice between one, or more, *menus fixes*, and choosing individually from the à la carte menu. The least expensive option is usually the **menu fixe** – where the number of courses is predetermined and choice is limited. At the bottom of the range, these revolve around standard dishes such as *cannelloni al brocciu*, lasagne, or fried fish of some kind (*friture du golfe*, made with whitebait, is common), and average around €20–22. Further up the scale, there's usually a **menu Corse**; these can often be by far the best-value way of sampling regional cuisine, running to five or more courses that usually include delicious local charcuterie and *fromage*.

The *plat du jour*, often a regional dish, might well be featured on the *menu fixe*, but for unlimited access to the chef's specialities you'll have to go **à la carte**, where you can expect to pay upwards of €20 for a main course. A perfectly legitimate tactic is to order just one course instead of the three or four. You can share dishes or go for several starters – a useful strategy for vegetarians. In Corsica, as in the rest of France, any salad (sometimes vegetables, too) comes separate from the main dish, and you will be offered coffee, which is also charged extra, to finish off the meal. Your Corsican hosts may also offer you a small *digestif* glass of liqueur or *eau de vie* (local firewater) on the house to round off your meal. Fish, incidentally, is sold by weight; the price quoted represents the cost per 100g, so check how much it will come to before the waiter disappears with it into the kitchen, or you could get a nasty shock when your bill arrives. *Service compris* (or *s.c.*) means the service charge is included. *Service non compris* (*s.n.c.*) means that it isn't and you need to allow for an additional fifteen percent. Wine (*vin*) or a drink (*boisson*) is unlikely to be included, though occasionally it is thrown in with cheaper menus (*menus fixes*). When ordering wine, ask for *un quart* (0.25 litre), *un demi-litre* (0.5 litre), *une carafe* (a litre) or *un pichet* (a jug). You'll normally be given the house wine unless you specify otherwise.

Corsican specialities

Whereas French cuisine traditionally relies upon complicated recipes and a large number of often unlikely ingredients for flavour, in Corsica freshness and simplicity are considered the essence of good cooking, with the emphasis more on quality than process.

For any important family meal, meat will invariably form the main course. **Wild boar** (*sanglier*) is probably the dish most closely associated with Corsica, whose forests remain well populated, despite the seasonal onslaught from camouflaged *chasseurs*. These days, however, if you see *sanglier* on a menu it's more likely to be free-range pork than real boar. Pigs, who feed on the chestnuts that were once the staple food in many regions such as Castagniccia, are reared in huge numbers to make **charcuterie**, which in Corsica has been elevated to an art form. Wherever you go you'll find a bewildering selection of cured meats on offer: *prisutu* (smoked ham), *figatellu* and *fitonu* (long liver sausages eaten chilled or grilled), *coppa* (shoulder), *lonzu* (smoked fillet), *salamu* (spicy salami-style sausage), *valetta* (cheek), *boudin* (hard sausage) and *fromage de tête* ("head cheese", made from seasoned pigs' brains).

Other typically Corsican meat dishes include *cabri de lait* (suckling kid), veal (served with local olives) and, in the winter hunting season, slow-cooked game stew (*tianu*). At this time, many *auberges* will also feature locally shot **game** on their menus: roast woodcock (*bécasse*), partridge (*pédrix*) and blackbird (*merle*) pâté. To accompany a meat dish, you might be offered some kind of fresh pasta (tagliatelle is a favourite), or *pulenta* (polenta), a stodgy mash made from chestnut or maize flour, which can be fried or sweetened with caster sugar, and *eau de vie* or liqueur.

As you'd expect, **seafood** predominates on the coast. Reduced fish stocks in the

waters around Corsica (the result of overfishing) mean that supplies are notoriously irregular and prices high. But you can bank on finding farmed red mullet (*rouget*) and sea bass (*loup de mer*) during the summer, as well as a great variety of shellfish – the best crayfish (*langouste*) comes from around the Golfe de St-Florent, whereas oysters (*huîtres*) are a speciality of the eastern plain. **Trout** (*truite*) is a popular alternative to meat dishes in inland areas – sometimes fished from the unpolluted rivers, but more often than not bought from fish farms.

Mountain cooking is dominated by dairy produce, particularly the soft ewe's cheese known as **brocciu** (pronounced "broodge"), produced only in the winter. You'll come across it stuffed into aubergines, cannelloni and omelettes with mint, or deep-fried in dainty little fritters (*beignets*). During the summer months, supplies of ewe's milk dry up and cow's milk is used instead: the result is an inferior product known as *brousse*, which doesn't taste nearly as good. In the high sheep-rearing Niolo and Asco regions, hard cheeses are also widely produced, and can be excellent.

Unlike most Mediterranean countries, Corsica has a fair selection of traditional **desserts**, the majority of them milk-and-egg-based concoctions such as *fiadone* (tart made with soft cheese), which locals love to soak in spirit and flambée. In more serious Corsican restaurants and quality pâtisseries, you'll also come across *beignets*, little fritters made from chestnut flour and often stuffed with ewe's cheese (*brocciu*). Run-of-the-mill French desserts – crème caramel, chocolate mousse or a piece of fruit – are also widely available, although rarely as good. Look out also for Corsica's wonderfully tangy **jams** (*confitures*), made from fig and walnut, fig and almond, lemon, clementine or chestnut. The island also boasts six varieties of AOC (*appellation d'origine contrôlée*) **honey**; those derived from the maquis flowers tend to be more subtly scented than the more full-on chestnut-flower honey.

Drinks

Cafés and bars line the streets and squares of Corsica's towns and tourist resorts, and

Corsican wine

The reputation of Corsican wine has been dogged by scandal over the years. In spite of optimum soils and growing conditions, the output at the top end of the market has lagged well behind the prodigious quantities of wine pouring from the *vin de table* vineyards on the eastern plain around Aléria. Of 100 square kilometres under cultivation, only around ten enjoy *appellation d'origine contrôlée* (AOC) status, the international mark of quality. Nevertheless, several *domaines* have gained a deservedly strong reputation over the past decade or so, combining modern vinification methods with traditional vinestock and know-how.

Well adapted to the maritime climate and granitic soils, the three main Corsican *cépages*, or grape varieties, account for the vast bulk of its quality output. **Vermentino** (sometimes known as "*la malvoisie*") is grown throughout the Mediterranean with varying results, but here produces fine, dry, zesty white wines which offer the perfect accompaniment for seafoods. First introduced by the Genoese, the **nielluccio** (pronounced "ni-*el*-oo-choo") grape yields a deep, earthy red similar to the best Tuscan chiantis. It's sometimes used on its own, but local *vigernons* more often blend it with the indigenous **sciaccarello** (pronounced "shak-a-*rel*-o"), which lends a ruby tint and aromas of maquis herbs to the final wine.

In addition to whites and reds, Corsican vineyards turn out prodigious quantities of excellent **rosé**, mainly for the summer visitor market. Produced by allowing the grape skins to soak in the freshly squeezed juice overnight after harvesting, it's much paler in colour and more subtle than the fruit-driven, bubble-gum-coloured rosés of New World wineries.

Equally popular with foreign visitors (although often undeservingly maligned by some French wine critics) are the delicious **muscats** of Cap Corse and Patrimonio. A rich, sweet, amber-coloured dessert wine, these are produced by spreading the grapes to dry after harvesting to concentrate the sugars, and then arresting the subsequent fermentation with a dose of five-percent pure alcohol. Corsicans love to offer *un p'tit Muscat* as an *apéritif* (some also sing its praises as an accompaniment to strong ewe's cheese). Although it's grown in a relatively small area, with more or less exactly the same mix of *cépages*, the variation in soils ensures that no two muscats are exactly the same, and one of the great pleasures of touring the Cape and Patrimonio regions is tasting your way through them.

these are where you'll likely do most of your drinking, whether as a prelude to food (*apéritif*) or as a sequel (*digestif*).

Wine (*vin*) is the regular drink, with rosé being the type produced in the greatest volume in Corsica. For more on the island's wines, see the box above.

Belgian and German brands account for most of the **beer** you'll find. Draught beer (*bière à la pression*) is the cheapest alcoholic drink after wine – ask for *un demi*

(25cl) – while bottled beer is exceptionally cheap in supermarkets. A brand to look out for, both as *pression* and bottled in the shops, is Pietra, a delicious, purely Corsican beer based on chestnut flour. The same company has also launched a fantastic, if pricey, wheat beer called Colomba, and an amber brew, Torre, flavoured with local maquis herbs.

Strong alcohol is drunk right through the day, the most popular drink being strong

Corsica has nine **AOC regions**, the most famous being Sartène, Figari, Patrimonio, Cap Corse, Calvi and Ajaccio. Enthusiasts can pick up *Route des Vins* leaflets at any local tourist office, which list the top *domaines* in each area. Most welcome visitors and offer **tastings** (*dégustations*), when you can sample their range (*gamme*), beginning with white and rosé, and working through the reds to end on a muscat (if they produce one). As Corsican wines are bottled following a short fermentation period in the barrels, the vast majority do not improve over time and are best drunk after a year or two. If you do taste a *vin de garde* ("wine for keeping"), you'll be advised of it at the time.

Prices are on the high side by French standards, ranging from €8 to €15 for single bottles of quality wines (and two or three times that if you order one in a restaurant). The reason advanced by committed growers for this is that only by tending their vines and harvesting by hand, and minimizing (if not avoiding altogether) the use of pesticides and herbicides – in short, producing small yields from small parcels of land – can vintages of real distinction be obtained from Corsica's granitic soil. However, the tourist market is probably a more influential factor: French and Italian visitors, in particular, are prepared to pay for top quality, and the best Corsican *vigerons* know they could sell what they make two or three times over.

In recent years, the more innovative among them have begun to offer premium **cuvées** – made from the vineyard's best grapes and matured in young oak barrels (*fûts de chêne*). The wood imparts a vanilla flavour that fans of Australian wines and Spanish Riojas will be familiar with, but which is often spurned by devotees of "*le terroir*".

Many wineries only sell direct to restaurants or from their home *caves*, but browsing the shelves of larger supermarkets and Corsican speciality shops you'll come across several *domaines* worth investigating. Stick to the following and you shouldn't go far wrong:

AOC Ajaccio Domaine Abbatucci.

AOC Calvi: Clos d'Alzeto; Clos Culombu.

AOC Figari: Domaine Torraccia; Clos Canarelli; Clos Sarcone.

AOC Patrimonio & Cap Corse: Domaine Antoine Arena; Domaine Leccia; Clos Gentille; Clos Nicrosi; Domaine Venturi-Pieretti.

AOC Sartène: Domaine Fiumiccicoli; Domaine Saparale.

---

aniseed-based *pastis*, especially the local brand, Casanis. **Brandies** and **eaux de vie** are always available – the latter comes in a variety of flavours, such as *prune* (plum) and *cerise* (cherry), and is usually distilled locally in the villages. In many small restaurants and bars you'll be offered these free. You may also be offered Cedratine and Myrthe, locally made sweet liqueurs.

Coffee is invariably espresso and very strong. *Un café* or *un expresso* is black,

un crème is white, *un café au lait* (served at breakfast) is espresso in a large cup or bowl filled up with hot milk. Ordinary **tea** (*thé*) is a Liptons' tea bag nine times out of ten; to have milk with it, ask for "*un peu de lait frais*". **Herb teas** (*infusions*) are served in every café and can be a refreshing alternative. The more common ones are *vervaine* (verbena), *tilleul* (lime blossom) and *tisane* (camomile). *Chocolat chaud* (hot chocolate), unlike tea, is available in any café.

The media

With the island so often in the national spotlight, local media is closely scrutinized in Corsica, especially the ubiquitous daily newspaper, Corse-Matin. Interest in foreign affairs, however, even those of Continental France, tends to lag well behind preoccupation with insular events, which partly explains the widespread indifference to French national news coverage, whether in the Paris-based papers or on television.

Newspapers and magazines

The Corsican **newspaper** with the widest circulation is the local daily, *Corse-Matin*, printed by Nice-Matin. The occasional headlining nationalist atrocity aside, it's a typical regional paper, with far more coverage of local events than national or international news, and is really only useful for listings. Of the **national dailies** *Le Monde* (daily except Mon) is the most intellectual and respected, with no concessions to entertainment (such as pictures), but written in an orthodox French that is probably the easiest to understand. *Libération* (daily except Mon) is moderately left-wing and colloquial, though phrased in a more sophisticated style than *Le Monde* or *Corse-Matin*. All the other nationals are firmly on the right. British newspapers and the *International Herald Tribune* are intermittently available in the larger resorts, and in Ajaccio and Bastia.

Weeklies, on the *Newsweek/Time* model, include the wide-ranging, left-leaning *Le Nouvel-Observateur* and its rightist counterweight, *L'Express*. The best and funniest investigative journalism is in *Le Canard Enchaîné*, but it's almost incomprehensible to non-natives. For a detailed look at the island's political and economic life, hunt out a copy of *Corsica*, a weekly glossy that tackles the issues of the day head-on – the first popular publication in Corsica's modern history to do so.

Radio

There are a few local **radio stations** in Corsica, many of them broadcasting within a tiny area. The best of these is Bastia's RCFM (Radio Corse Frequenza Mora; 103FM), broadcasting in French and Corsican and playing a good variety of music, including traditional folk music and modern Corsican bands.

The **BBC World Service** broadcasts around the clock, but for best reception in Corsica tune in on short wave from 7pm on 6195kHz or 9410kHz. Atmospheric conditions permitting, you can also pick up the World Service on FM, via Radio Riviera in Monaco, on 106 and 106.5.

Television

You get both **French and Italian television** in Corsica. French is slightly better quality, although marred by an unbearable amount of advertising. The third channel – **FR3** – features Corsican regional programmes, with a local news bulletin every lunchtime and evening and a sporadic schedule of documentaries. Italian television is less widely available; the RAI channels are the best, featuring documentaries and good news coverage. Many hotels also have **satellite** channels, featuring a choice of English-speaking stations.

Festivals

Aside from the nationally celebrated religious festivals, such as the Assumption of the Virgin Mary, local saints' days are celebrated in Corsican towns throughout the year, and often include fireworks and processions. Many events are music- and arts-based affairs, with outdoor concerts and film festivals boosting the local tourist industry. There are also a few local country fairs, where you can hear traditional Corsican singing and purchase regional specialities.

Easter celebrations are the most fervent, and interesting to watch or take part in. They often feature a *granitola*, an ancient rite whereby a line of penitents forms a spiral as it moves through the town. The most intense of all Corsican religious ceremonies is the **Catenacciu** in Sartène, an Easter procession led by a penitent who drags a cross through the streets in imitation of Christ's walk to Golgotha.

Of the island's plethora of folk festivals, one that is definitely worth attending is the September **Santa di u Niolu** in Casamaccioli, a riotous event involving much drinking, singing and gambling. Its place as the island's top choral festival, however, has been lost to Calvi's excellent **Rencontres de Chants Polyphoniques**, featuring a cappella groups from all over the world. World, rock, Latin and guitar **music festivals** take place at various locations throughout the summer, and there's a jazz festival at Calvi every June.

Festivals and events

Just about every sizeable village and town in Corsica these days hosts its own festival, whether tagged onto some kind of local produce (olives, almonds, chestnuts) or a musical theme. In addition to cultural events, the calendar below features the island's major religious occasions: saints' day celebrations and the processions at Easter time by Corsica's masked brotherhoods (*confraternités*). These, of course, are free, but for anything involving staged performances, expect to have to pay upwards of €17 for tickets, which should be booked well in advance through local tourist offices.

January–March

A Tumbera: La fête du Porc Courant Renno, late Jan/early Feb. Celebration of the pig-slaughtering season. See *Traditional Corsica* colour section.
Rencontres du Cinéma Italien Bastia, first week of Feb. Pre-release gala screenings, classic Italian films and appearances by stars from across the water.
Rencontres du Cinéma Espagnol Bastia. Spanish cinema comes to town for the whole of March.
Notre-Dame-de-la-Miséricorde Ajaccio, March 18. Religious procession led by the city's patron saint and protectoress. See p.180.

April–June

Fête de la Bande Dessinée Bastia, first week of April. Exhibition of international cartoon art, dominated by Belgian and French styles. For a taster, visit ⓦ www.una-volta.org.
La Cerca Erbalunga (see p.75), **U Catenacciu** Sartène (see p.231), **La Granitola** Calvi, Good Friday. Corsica's sombre Easter rituals involve archaic candlelit processions by masked and robed brotherhoods.
La Passion du Christ Calvi, Easter. Contemporary theatrical re-enactment of the Crucifixion, accompanied by sublime polyphony from the group A Filetta – a spine-tingling event even if you're not a Christian.
Fête du Christ Noir Bastia, May 3. The "Black Christ", found floating in the waves and the patron saint of local fishermen, is carried around Terra Nova.
Fiera di u Mare Solenzara, first week of June. Fishing, sailing, jet-ski races and seafood cooking competitions centred on the marina.
St-Érasme Bastia, Ajaccio and Calvi, June 2. Fishermen's festival celebrated with a Mass, boat jousting and harbour firework displays.
Notre-Dame-des-Neiges Col de Bavella, June 5. Mass pilgrimage to the miracle-working Madonna on one of Corsica's highest mountain passes.

Festival du Jazz Calvi, third week of June ⓦwww
.calvi-jazz-festival.com. A week of top-drawer
jazz performances by internationally renowned
musicians on a stage below the citadelle, with night-
long jam sessions in the bars lining quai Landry.
Festimusica L'Île Rousse, third weekend of June.
Corsican, Sardinian and Tuscan folk music performed
on an open-air stage in the centre of town.
Les Voix du Lazaret Ajaccio, third weekend of
June, just before the Solstice. World music festival
held in the old leper colony on the outskirts of town.

July

Relève des Gouverneurs Bastia, every Thurs in
July and Aug. Historical re-enactment of the French
Governor's arrival in the citadelle, involving lots of
flag waving and military drumming.
Festivoce Pigna, first fortnight in July ⓦfestivoce
.casa-musicale.org. Celebration of Corsican
polyphony revolving around the Casa Musicale.
See p.133.
Fiera di u Vinu Luri, first weekend of July. Wine
and artisanal food festival at the heart of the Cap
Corse muscat region, with glasses of all the island's
finest wines for only €1.
Foire de l'Olivier Montegrosso, July 15–16.
Hugely popular event celebrating the olive tree and
all things made from it.
Interlacs Corte, July 15–16. One of the world's
greatest fell races, with contestants running from
Lac de Nino over the Brêche de Capitello and
around the head of the Restonica Valley.
Calvi on the Rocks Calvi, third week of July
ⓦwww.calviontherocks.com. Rock, hip hop
and contemporary Corsican music live, with the
citadelle as backdrop.
Fête du Livre Corse L'Île Rousse, third and fourth
weeks of July. Corsica's only literary festival.
Fête de la Guitare Patrimonio, last week of
July ⓦwww.festival-guitare-patrimonio.com.
International guitar festival showcasing a range
of styles, from classical to Gypsy jazz and blues.
See p.96.
Au Son Des Mandolines Ajaccio, last week of
July. The world's biggest mandolin festival, staged
on the place du Diamant.
Rencontres Théâtrales Olmi-Capella, last week of
July and first week of Aug ⓦwww.aria-corse.com.
A fortnight of theatre by amateur and professional
actors in the remote Giunssani region, with nature-
based scenery. See p.138.

August

Festival de Musique Erbalunga, first week of Aug.
Jazz, flamenco, classical and Corsican polyphony
around this picturesque port on Cap Corse.

Film festival Lama, first week of Aug. Wonderful
open-air film festival held in the most unlikely
setting of an idyllic Balagne village. The theme is
always "*Le cinéma à la campagne, et la campagne
au cinéma*", with all the films set in rural societies.
See p.128.
Country fair Col de Prato, Castagniccia, first week
of Aug. Traditional rural fair with animal showing,
local handicraft and fresh produce competitions and
polyphony singing (including the rarely performed
Chiama e Rispondi duels).
Foire de l'Amandier Aregno, end of first week of
Aug. Music, food stalls and general revelry loosely
associated with almonds.
Porto Latino St-Florent, mid-Aug ⓦwww
.porto-latino.com. The Nebbio lets its hair down
South American style, with gigs by Cuban and
other Latin bands in the square.
Fêtes Napoléoniennes Ajaccio, mid-Aug.
Processions and parades in period garb, followed
by son et lumière and fireworks in the Jardin du
Casone to celebrate Napoléon's birthday.
L'Assomption Bastia, Ajaccio and Calvi, Aug 15.
Son et lumière in the citadelles.
Festival Pascal Paoli Bastia, third week of Aug.
Dynamic Corsican music festival showcasing the
cream of rising talent on the island.
Violin and Traditional Instrument Festival
Sermano, near Corte, third weekend of Aug. Shows
by fiddlers and folk musicians from across Europe
(notably Ireland), along with workshops in the
village square. A warm-hearted event that's run on
a non-profit basis, so the gigs are free.
Settembrinu di Tavagna In the villages of
Casinca, 30km south of Bastia, end Aug ⓦwww
.tavagna.com. Lively Corsican music festival, under
the direction of one of the island's most prominent
nationalist polyphony groups, A Tavagna.

September–December

Santa di u Niolu Casamaccioli, Sept 8–10.
Arguably Corsica's oldest and best-known festival,
featuring duels of Chiama e Respondi singing in the
village bar. See p.302.
Rencontres de Chants Polyphoniques Calvi,
around Sept 14–18. Hosted by top polyphony
group, A Filetta, this four-day music festival of a
cappella music from around the world is the one
not to miss.
British film festival Bastia, first week of Oct. The
last of the capital's annual film festivals showcases
the best of British cinema, old and modern.
Musicales de Bastia Bastia, first fortnight of
Oct. Eclectic mix of live music at venues around
the town, principally the municipal theatre and
bandstand on the place St-Nicolas.

Les Journées Montagnes Ajaccio and Corte, second week of Oct. Films, talks and exhibitions on the subject of mountaineering.

Festiventu Calvi, last week of Oct and first week of Nov ⓦ www.lefestivalduvent.com/sommaire.html. Hundreds of kites and twenty thousand visitors attend Calvi's fastest-growing festival, held on the beach.

Fête du Marron Évisa, mid-Nov. The largest of several chestnut bashes, providing a chance to gather nuts in the woods with locals and sample some of the wonderful specialities made in the village.

Rencontres du Cinéma Méditerranéan Bastia, second fortnight of Nov. Movies old and new from around the Mediterranean.

Sports and outdoor activities

Corsica's varied landscapes and exceptionally mild climate make it ideal for outdoor pursuits of all kinds. Over the years the Parc Naturel Régional and numerous private activity centres have developed an impressive infrastructure for exploiting the island's potential as an adventure sports destination. Marked footpaths form an extensive network of long-distance trails, and there are plenty of equestrian centres from where you can explore the countryside on horseback. For the more adventurous, mountain biking, climbing and canyoning are also well established, with marked routes and guides on hand at several key locations. In addition, a string of diving schools around the coast offer the chance to sample the island's superb underwater life, which ranks among the most varied in Europe. The one catch with the Corsican adventure sport scene is cost. The seasonal nature of most outdoor pursuits on the island means that instructors and equipment providers tend to charge highly for their services; wherever possible, bring your own gear with you.

Hiking

Hiking (*la randonnée pédestre*, or *la rando* for short) is without doubt the best way to explore Corsica's amazing interior and remote stretches of coast, and there are nearly 1000km of marked trails to help you do just that. For a full rundown of the routes, as well as tips on planning, equipment and safety, see Chapter 8.

Climbing

While not possessing the same allure as the Alps, Pyrénées or Gorges de Verdon in Provence, Corsica offers an impressive range of commendable climbing routes, from short cliff pitches to a number of classic *grandes voies*. Moreover, the rock – with a few exceptions – is solid.

For short climbs, the island's cream-tinted **chalk cliffs** are arguably the most rewarding.

Dotted along a seam running from L'Île Rousse (on the northwest coast) to Solenzara (on the east coast), these are grouped in three main areas: the Nebbio, Ponte Leccia and Solenzara. Pick of the crop are the chalk escarpments at **Caporalino**, Pietralba (in the Ostriconi Valley near Ponte Leccia), but there are also some wonderful pitches around **Patrimonio** and in the **Désert des Agriates**. In the southeast, the **Falaise de Monte Santu**, just north of Solenzara near the hamlet of Penna, offers around fifty routes of varying degrees of difficulty, all of them with superb sea views.

The best known of the island's most demanding climbing sites, the *grandes voies*, are at **Bavella**, in south Corsica. However, you'll find less-frequented routes at several other sites around the island: **Bonifatu**, above the Carozzu refuge; around the lakes

39

at the head of the **Restonica Valley**, near Corte; the famous north cliffs of **Capo d'Ortu**, rising sheer behind Porto on the west coast; and over the red flanks of **Paglia Orba**, the island's shark-finned peak.

In Corsica itself, you can pick up numerous **climbing guides** in French, though to date only one dependable climbing guide to the island has been published in English: *Corsica Mountains* by Robin G. Collomb (West Co, UK).

Less confident climbers may wish to employ the services of a **qualified high-mountain guide** (*guide de haute montagne diplômé*). The following are all qualified to exacting French Alpine standards: Jean-Paul Quilici, who lives at Quenza and is an expert on the Bavella area (☎04 95 78 64 33, ⓦwww .jpquilicimontagne.com); Pierre Griscelli, *gardien* of the Carozzu refuge, Bonifatu, on the GR20 (☎04 95 30 82 51 or 04 95 44 01 95); Pierre Pietri, expert on the Cinto massif and its environs (☎04 95 32 62 76); Joël Guidiceli, who leads treks in and around the Fiumorbo region of the southeast (☎04 95 20 73 51, ⓦperso.wanadoo.fr/rando.corse); and In Terra Corsa, based next to Ponte Leccia station (☎04 95 47 69 48, ⓦwww .interracorsa.fr; see p.294).

A less risky alternative to rock climbing, but one which gives you access to similarly extreme, vertical terrain, is **Via Ferrata**, literally "Iron Way". Originally devised by the Italian army in the 1914–18 war with Austria as a means of penetrating the least accessible cliffs and mountain summits lining the Dolomite frontier, it employs stanchion cables, ramps, fixed ladders and cemented rungs to ease movement over vertical surfaces, with climbers clipped onto steel ropes to ensure they won't fall. The result is that anyone with a head for heights can experience the kind of thrilling exposure normally the preserve of confirmed climbers.

Several Via Ferrata sites have sprung up in Corsica over the past three or four years, the best of them near **Ponte Leccia** in the lower Asco Valley (see p.294), and at **Chisà**, in southeastern Corsica (see p.269). Less demanding routes, featuring adventure playground-style extensions which will appeal to younger kids, have been installed in the Massif de l'Ospédale (see p.261), near Porto Vecchio; the Col de Bavella (see p.228); and just outside Solenzara (see p.269).

Canyoning

An adventure sport that's been catching on fast in Corsica over the past three or four years is **canyoning**, which involves following the course of a river or stream (usually downhill) on foot. Where the water descends steeply, the route may require ropes and abseiling skills (and occasionally even toboggans). For anyone into climbing and swimming (at the same time), this offers the ultimate buzz.

Basic **equipment** for canyoning comprises a wet suit (*combinaison*), canoeing helmet (*casque*), wet sacks and trainers (*tennis*); for more challenging routes, you'll also need quality ropes, harnesses and karabiners. Given the potential dangers involved, it's better to hook up with a **guide company**, who can also rent out the necessary equipment. For trips into the Asco Valley and Bavella hot spots, try the recommended In Terra Corsa (☎04 95 47 69 48, ⓦwww .interracorsa.fr).

See the *Wild Corsica* colour section for the best canyoning areas; more on canyoning in the Bavella area is featured on p.229.

The greatest **danger** faced by canyoneers in Corsica is sudden and dramatic increases in water level caused by heavy rainfall. The non-porous granite rock drains water very quickly, and streams, particularly those in narrow defiles, can fill up at astonishing speeds. It is therefore not advisable to attempt severe routes in wet or unsettled weather.

Mountain biking

Given the terrain and state of most of the roads in Corsica, **mountain bikes**, which the French call **VTTs** (*vélos tous terrains*), have the edge on standard touring cycles as the tool of choice, allowing you to sidestep the congestion and follow forest tracks and old mule paths into the interior. In recent years the island has become popular for VTT enthusiasts of all abilities, and along the marked footpaths you'll encounter fewer of the disapproving looks that can accompany off-road cyclists in Britain.

The most promising **routes**, which we've highlighted in the Guide, are mostly in the south – around the Forêt de l'Ospédale, Bavella and the Coscione Plateau. The jeep tracks of coastal Sartenais, between Campomorro and Tizzano, also offer stunning rides, as do sections of the Tra Mare e Monti Sud long-distance hiking path between Porticcio and Propriano (see p.371). In the north, the Désert des Agriates, between St-Florent and L'Île Rousse, has a rugged coastal path and network of tracks winding through some of the island's most memorable scenery. Serious mountain bikers should seek out Didier Richard's two VTT route guides (for north and south Corsica), which describe fifty of the island's best off-road possibilities, illustrated with reliable contour maps.

In view of the toughness of the trails (and the relative scarcity of shops supplying spares), you might prefer to rent a bike from one of the main towns and tourist resorts. A list of established **rental firms** appears on p.26.

Horseriding

The experience of riding Corsica's hidden bridleways and galloping across immense windswept beaches is one that few horse lovers should pass up. Standards of horsemanship are consistently high, and you won't find an animal that's not in top condition. In fact, few horses are ever sold; Corsicans pride themselves on keeping their horses at home until they die. For a full day's guided excursion, count on €75–90, or €950–1100 for a week. See the *Wild Corsica* colour section.

Diving

Thanks to a virtual absence of pollution and factory fishing, not to mention some enlightened marine-life management, Corsica's coastal waters rank among the cleanest and clearest in the Mediterranean, supporting a profusion of underwater life that's matched by few other regions in Europe. Whether you're an experienced diver or a novice, you'll be spoilt for choice, both in terms of dive sites and schools. The island currently boasts nearly thirty accredited diving centres, where you can rent state-of-the-art equipment and boats, and gain expert advice on local sites and conditions.

Surface **water temperatures** fluctuate hugely throughout the year, from around 14°C in February to a balmy 25°C in August. September and early October are also good months for diving, with the water temperature rarely dipping below 20°C. **Visibility** varies according to the weather, but 25m is about average, rising to nearly double that in perfect conditions. **Winds** can prove problematic, however, whipping up choppy seas and swells at any time of the year around exposed headlands, particularly around the island's two most spectacular diving areas, the Réserve Naturelle de Scandola (on the northwest coast) and the Îles Lavezzi (near Bonifacio).

The island's **underwater landscape** mirrors that of its mountainous interior, with sheer drops plunging to depths of around 700m along stretches of the wild west coast. Coating the contorted granite rock formations underwater is an exciting array of **sea life**: colourful anemones, vibrant gorgonian corals and an amazing wealth of fish. Among the many species unique to the Mediterranean is the brown grouper (*mérou*), whose characteristic fat lips and massive speckled body (which can grow up to more than 1m in length) are a common sight in the crystalline waters around the Îles Lavezzi. Other kinds of fish routinely spotted off Corsica include moray eels, John Dory, forkbeards, damselfish, scorpion fish and the exquisite turquoise-and-red rainbow wrasse.

Several **wrecks** lurk off the coast; among them an American B-17 bomber which crashed in Calvi bay after being shot down by a German fighter in 1944, and a Luftwaffe Heinkel-111, which lies just beyond the breakwater at Bastia harbour. The best source of information on dive sites is the staff at local **diving centres**, who can advise you on the most rewarding places to dive given the prevailing weather conditions and your level of experience. They can also rent you all the equipment you'll need, arrange transport and instruction, usually for an all-in package rate, and will refill your bottles for a fee if you've brought your own.

Typical **costs** for a single dive range from €35 to €450 (plus €7–10 for gear rental); most centres also offer discount cards for three or more outings. After an initial, slightly more expensive, introductory dive – or *plongée baptême* – beginners can also undertake training courses for the compulsory certificates required to dive, including the internationally recognized PADI qualification. Fees for the PADI Open-Water course, after which you're entitled to dive accompanied by an instructor to a depth of 20m, range from €600–650 for level I or €500 for level II.

Whoever you dive with, be sure to respect the **marine environment**. Don't feed the fish (not even grouper, which divers around Bonifacio have traditionally attracted with boiled eggs), as it can upset their metabolisms. Try to keep your feet away from underwater plants while wearing fins: the sudden sweep of water caused by a flipper kick can be enough to destroy coral. And control the speed of your descent, because enormous damage can be caused to marine life by divers landing hard.

Contact details for diving centres are listed throughout the Guide section of this book.

Culture and etiquette

Corsicans have a reputation for being cool with outsiders, and compared with the Continent, service does tend to seem unsmiling, with pleasantries kept to a minimum. That said, once away from the tourist resorts on the coast, particularly up in the hills of the interior where old traditions of hospitality endure, you'll find people generally more responsive to visitors, especially members of the older generation, most of whom will, unlike their younger descendants, have experienced life off the island.

Social life and etiquette

In common with most Mediterranean people, Corsicans socialize more in public places – over a coffee or *pastis*, playing *pétanque*, or taking an evening *passeghiata* on the square – than in each others' homes. If you are invited to someone's house for a **meal**, however, expect it to be conducted with a greater degree of formality than you might be used to. And bear in mind how seriously Corsicans take their food. Expressions of pleasure and interest in local produce – particularly cheese and charcuterie – will always be met with a warm response.

Smoking is now forbidden in all public places, including public transport, cinemas, museums, cafés, restaurants and nightclubs. The ban, however, does not extend to the café terrace or beaches, where non-smokers may well find themselves in the minority.

Complaining about insensitive smoking, or indeed about anything at all in Corsica, should be undertaken with extreme caution. Insular pride is very easily ruffled, and all too often gestures that might be deemed quite innocuous back home – such as asking for unsatisfactory food to be changed in a restaurant, or expressions of frustration on the road – may be perceived as an insult worthy of an aggressive response. So resist the temptation to flash a finger or *bras d'honneur* at Corsican drivers, no matter what the provocation. Road rage on the island can have serious consequences.

If you're a French speaker, avoid getting drawn into **political discussions**. Never express an opinion about local nationalism or, above all, paramilitary activities – even in jest. These are subjects most Corsicans consider off-limits to non-islanders, and which they only discuss among themselves in hushed tones behind closed doors.

When it comes to **clothes**, what you wear will vary little from what you would wear at home. Do bear in mind though that Corsicans like their bling, and in the swankier restaurants, people will dress to impress; scruffiness is generally regarded as showing a lack of respect to yourself and those around you. On the beaches, especially on the Riviera, women young and old tend to go topless.

Bear in mind local attitudes to money. Living on a rock-bottom budget – camping rough, eating nothing but bread and cheese, and avoiding bars and cafés altogether – is unlikely to endear you to the locals, who love to joke about *les mangeurs des tomates* – those die-hard backpackers and camper-van tourists who are so eager to save money that they miss out on one of the things Corsicans are deservedly most proud of: their wonderful cuisine.

Greetings

Although Corsicans are extremely proud of their language, they regard it as something to be shared *entre Corses* – exclusively between themselves. So when greeting people, stick to French conventions.

When **meeting** someone for the first time, it's customary to shake hands. This often (usually only among women and between women and men) progresses quickly to kisses (*la bise*) on the cheek – a custom which can be quite complicated, and embarrassing, if you're not sure how many kisses to expect: as a rule of thumb, go for one on each side and no more. Three or four kisses tend to be reserved for classmates, family members and close friends. Unlike in the rest of France, Corsicans also use *la bise* as a form of greeting between male relatives, such as cousins and uncles. Bear in mind, however, that whatever its context, the kiss isn't exactly a kiss, but more a touching of cheeks whilst kissing into the air. It's usually enough to follow the Corsican person's lead, and accept that from time to time you're bound to make a mistake, though be aware that a single kiss on the cheek is deemed somewhat flirtatious.

Women and gender

Corsican attitudes to gender are fairly typical of the European Mediterranean. In most aspects of life, men and women outwardly conform more closely to Italian norms than to those of the mother country. When in public, women are expected to look feminine and glamorous; men tend to be under less pressure to look good, but where cars and motorbikes are concerned, size definitely matters.

Sex before marriage, while fast becoming the rule, is still regarded as a source of shame when it comes to daughters, whom most families will pressure to be at least engaged before they sleep with a boyfriend. No such opprobrium surrounds the sexual behaviour of men, who are encouraged to "play the field" once over the age of consent (18). This doesn't mean, however, that **sexual harassment** is common: on the contrary. Unlike across the Ligurian Sea, men are invariably polite, with staring regarded as rude. If you feel you've been insulted in the street, don't be afraid to make your feelings known. **Rape** is no more of a risk in Corsica than anywhere else, but as ever when travelling you should be on your guard when walking around at night, especially on unlit beaches and along dark lanes.

Contraception

Condoms (*préservatifs*) are widely available in pharmacies, supermarkets and coin-operated street dispensers. The pill (*la pilule*), and the morning-after pill (*la pilule du lendemain*) are available only on prescription.

Travelling with children

Corsica is an easy place to travel with children of any age: the flight from the UK or Ireland is short, transfers from the airport quick and easy, and the climate – especially in June and September – perfect for little ones. Kids will be well received everywhere, and babies and toddlers, in particular, will be made a fuss of. The traditional pleasures of bucket, spade, sand and sea are never far away, which is just as well as the island has few purpose-made attractions. That said, throughout the Balagne region of the northwest you'll regularly come across signs advertising donkey rides, and if you're anywhere near Ajaccio a visit to the tortoise sanctuary, A Capulatta, is guaranteed to be a big hit. Elsewhere, keep an eye out for aquariums (in Porto and Bonifacio) and boat rides (from resorts across the west coast).

Package operators go out of their way to attract families, and all offer reductions for kids, typically of ten percent for under-12s in low and mid-season. Infants under 2 years go for roughly the cost of the airport tax. Rates are far from standard, however, and parents would do well to compare the small print in the brochures before booking. Some firms – notably the ones listed below – also offer dedicated **child-care facilities**, such as crèches, English-speaking nannies or special watersports instruction, albeit at a price. One final word of advice for parents considering a package holiday: pick properties within easy reach of the airport to keep the transfer times down, which can spare a lot of hassle at the start and end of your stay.

Accommodation shouldn't be a problem. Hotels generally welcome accompanied children and most have rooms with three or four beds (also charged extra). Self-catering villas, apartments and cottages also tend to be well geared up for kids, with highchairs and travel cots as standard – though it's always worth checking in advance. Pool alarms are obligatory by law these days: make sure yours is working and that you know how to switch it off if it sounds.

On the whole, Corsican **beaches** are extremely safe, with gently shelving sand and very little swell, surf or undertow. One hazard parents should always look out for, however, are **anemones** – the little brown spiky balls that lurk on underwater rocks, and whose spines can lodge themselves under the skin and cause painful wounds.

Train and bus **travel** is free for the under-4s, or half-fare for 4- to 12-year-olds. Excursion boats also offer reductions for kids, as do museums and most other places charging admission. Travelling by rented car, a child seat is obligatory these days, just as in the UK. Rental and holiday companies can arrange to have one ready on arrival (for an extra charge) – a less stressful option than bringing your own as you know it will fit and, when pressed, the firm will have someone install it for you.

As in other Mediterranean regions of Europe, children **stay up late** in Corsica, especially in the summer. It's very common for them to be running around pavement cafés or restaurants, and your kids will no doubt enjoy joining in.

Corsicans are, on the whole, very well disposed towards children in **restaurants**, not simply by offering reduced-priced children's menus but in creating an atmosphere that positively welcomes kids. That said, you'll find locals intolerant of undisciplined behaviour; screaming children invariably provoke disapproving looks and gruff comments in Corsican if left unchecked.

For those travelling with **babies**, international brands of formula milk and jars of the usual mush are available everywhere, as are disposable nappies (*couches-culottes*, or *couches à jeter* in French) and wipes. Pampers and Huggies are the most common brands, but you won't find more environmentally friendly equivalents, even in the big hypermarkets.

Other bits of kit parents of babies should consider bringing are a lightweight MacClaren-style stroller, and some kind of front- or backpack if you use one. Sun hats are on sale everywhere, but it won't do any harm to bring a couple of spares.

Useful contacts

UK and Ireland

BabyGoes2.Com ⓦ www.babygoes2.com. Internet-based holiday-planning service for parents. Fill in their form and they'll dream up your ideal break in Corsica. Their site features an enlightening first-hand location report on the island by a woman who travelled there with her 18-month-old child. (ⓦ www.babygoes2 .com/editorial_location_corsica.asp).
Club Med ☎ 0700/007 007 007, ⓦ www.clubmed .co.uk. Specializes in purpose-built holiday resorts, with kids' club, entertainment and sports facilities on site.
Mark Warner Holidays ☎ 0870/770 4222, ⓦ www.markwarner.co.uk. Watersports-oriented holiday vacation campus on the west coast of Corsica, with children's entertainment and childcare included.

US

Rascals in Paradise 2107 Van Ness Ave, Suite 403, San Francisco CA 94109 ☎ 415/921-7000 or 1-800/872-7225, ⓦ www.rascalsinparadise.com. Can arrange scheduled and customized itineraries built around activities for kids.
Travel With Your Children 40 Fifth Ave, New York NY 10011 ☎ 212/477 5524 or 1-888/822-4388. Publishes a regular newsletter, *Family Travel Times* (ⓦ www.familytraveltimes.com), as well as a series of books on travel with children including *Great Adventure Vacations With Your Kids*.

Travel essentials

Costs

It can be disconcertingly easy to spend more money while on holiday in Corsica than you might have intended. Aside from the obvious fact that most commodities have to be imported by sea or air, the main reason for this is the island's economic dependence on tourism, which ensures that from June until September prices of almost everything needed by visitors – principally accommodation – rocket, allowing the locals to make enough cash during the short summer season to see them through the winter. Corsicans themselves lay much of the blame for this seasonal inflation on the supermarkets, who cynically hike prices each May just ahead of the tourist influx – which of course increases the cost of everything else.

Unless you've prearranged somewhere to stay as part of a package holiday (see p.23), **accommodation** will probably be your main expense, particularly if you come in July and August. The majority of hotels charge €60–90 for a double room, though rates typically double in peak season. As a rule of thumb, places on the coast tend to be more expensive, with the best-value deals in the mountains of the interior, where there's far less seasonal price variation. Cheap *pensions* are rare. Staying in **campsites** can be a money-saver as long as you stick to the basic sites found in rural areas (around €15–20 per day for two people, one tent and a car) and avoid the flashy three-star complexes along the coast, which can cost almost as much as a hotel.

As for **food**, in any town you'll find restaurants with three- or four-course menus for €20–25, and the island is full of pizzerias where you can eat for even less than that. Picnic fare tends to be surprisingly expensive, especially if you buy cheese, charcuterie and other treats from Corsican speciality food outlets. Also worth bearing in mind is the expense of drinks in bars and cafés, particularly those situated on beaches, and the cost of wine in restaurants, which can easily double your bill.

Public transport costs around €20–25 for 100km, whether you're travelling by bus or

45

by the *micheline* train (the Bastia–Ajaccio trip currently costs around €21). **Car rental** will set you back anything upwards of €250 per week, depending on the season (see p.25 for more details). Mountain bikes (VTTs) cost about €17–20 per day, while motorbikes start at around €50–60 per day for a 125cc.

Museums and monuments won't prove too much of a drain on your resources, for the simple reason that there are relatively few on the island. Most charge €3–5 and give discounts for holders of ISIC cards or to under-26s on presentation of a passport.

Thus, a **minimum daily requirement** (for food and accommodation only) would be around €60–90 per person, if camping and doing your own catering; a couple staying in budget hotels and eating in cheap restaurants could live comfortably on about €100–120 per person. Move around much, however, and you could easily find yourself spending considerably more than that.

Crime and personal safety

Despite Corsica's reputation for violence and extremist politics, you are unlikely to encounter any trouble during your stay on the island. Petty crime is minimal, though it makes sense to keep a close eye on your valuables in the crowded tourist resorts. If you should get robbed, don't resist. Cars are rarely stolen, but cassette players and luggage left inside are vulnerable to thieves – especially at beach car parks. Try not to leave any valuables in sight, and make sure you have insurance (see p.48).

There are two main types of **French police** (popularly known as *les flics*): the Police Nationale and the Gendarmerie Nationale. For all practical purposes, they are indistinguishable; if you need to report a theft, or other incident, you can go to either. A noticeable presence in Corsica is the CRS (Compagnies Républicaines de Sécurité), a mobile force of heavies posted here to handle demonstrations and the terrorist threat, with whom you should have no contact unless you inadvertently get caught up in a riot.

The police have the right to demand **identification** from any citizen, so if you want to avoid all possible hassle, make sure you're able to produce your passport, or something equally incontrovertible, on the spot. For

---

Emergency numbers

Ambulance ☎15
Fire service ☎18
Police ☎17
Mountain rescue ☎04 95 61 13 95
From a mobile phone ☎112 will connect to emergency services (see p.51).

---

driving violations such as speeding, the police can impose on-the-spot fines (see p.25). Should you be **arrested** on any charge, you have the right to contact your nearest consulate, which is likely to be in Marseille (see below). People caught smuggling or possessing drugs, even a few grams of marijuana, are liable to find themselves in jail, and the consulate will not be sympathetic.

Consulates in Marseille

Britain ☎04 91 15 72 10
Canada ☎04 91 37 19 37
US ☎04 91 54 92 00

Electricity

Electricity is 220v, using plugs with two round pins.

Entry requirements

Citizens of **EU countries** can enter France freely, while those from many **non-EU countries**, including Australia, Canada, New Zealand and the United States, among other countries, do not need a visa for a stay of **up to ninety days**. South African citizens require a short-stay visa for up to ninety days, which should be applied for in advance, and costs €60.

All non-EU citizens who wish to remain **longer than ninety days** must apply for a long-stay visa, for which you'll have to show proof of – among other things – a regular income or sufficient funds to support yourself and medical insurance. Be aware, however, that the situation can change and it's advisable to check with your nearest French embassy or consulate before departure. For further information about visa regulations consult the Ministry of Foreign Affairs website: ⊛www.diplomatie.gouv.fr.

French embassies and consulates

Australia Canberra ☎02/6216 0100, Sydney ☎02/9268 2400; ⊛www.ambafrance-au.org.
Britain London ☎020/7073 1000, ⊛www.ambafrance-uk.org; Edinburgh ☎0131/225 7954, ⊛www.consulfrance-edimbourg.org.
Canada Ottawa ☎613/789 1795, ⊛www.ambafrance-ca.org; Montréal ☎514/878 4385, ⊛www.consulfrance-montreal.org; Québec ☎418/694 2294, ⊛www.consulfrance-quebec.org; Toronto ☎416/847 1900, ⊛www.consulfrance-toronto.org; Vancouver ☎604/681 4345, ⊛www.consulfrance-vancouver.org.
Ireland Dublin ☎01/277 5000, ⊛www.ambafrance-ie.org.
New Zealand Wellington ☎04/384 2555, ⊛www.ambafrance-nz.org.
South Africa Pretoria ☎012/429 7030, ⊛www.ambafrance-rsa.org; Johannesburg ☎011/778 5600, ⊛www.consulfrance-jhb.org; Cape Town ☎021/423 1575, ⊛www.consulfrance-lecap.org.
US Washington ☎202/944 6000, ⊛www.ambafrance-us.org; Atlanta ☎404/495 1660, ⊛www.consulfrance-atlanta.org; Boston ☎617/832 4400, ⊛www.consulfrance-boston.org; Chicago ☎312/327 5200, ⊛www.consulfrance-chicago.org; Houston ☎713/572 2799, ⊛www.consulfrance-houston.org; Los Angeles ☎310/235 3200, ⊛www.consulfrance-losangeles.org; Miami ☎305/403 4150, ⊛www.consulfrance-miami.org; New Orleans ☎504/569 2870, ⊛www.consulfrance-nouvelleorleans.org; New York ☎212/606 3600, ⊛www.consulfrance-newyork.org; San Francisco ☎415/397 4330, ⊛www.consulfrance-sanfrancisco.org.

Gay and lesbian travellers

Corsicans remain much more conservative in their attitude to homosexuality than do their compatriots on the Continent. Gay and lesbian islanders eschew the "we're here, we're queer!" stance of northern Europe and North America in favour of a low profile – which means lots of lavender marriages and creeping off under cover of night to the maquis and deserted beaches. With the exception of Ricanto beach, near Ajaccio airport (where you'll find the island's only out gay bar), you won't often encounter overt cruising, and when you do chances are it'll be someone from outside the island. At the same time, Corsica has long been a popular destination for discreet gay couples and no one is likely to raise much more than an eyebrow if you ask for a double bed when checking into a hotel.

The same doesn't apply to expressing affection in the street. Women can get away with holding hands and walking with arms around each other, but gay men can expect hostile comments if they do the same.

Health

Visitors to Corsica have little to worry about as far as health is concerned. No vaccinations are required, there are no nasty diseases and tap water is safe to drink. The worst that's likely to happen to you is a case of sunburn or an upset stomach from eating too much rich food. If you do need treatment, however, you should be in good hands: the French healthcare system is rated one of the best in the world.

Under the French health system, all services, including doctors' consultations, prescribed medicines, hospital stays and ambulance call-outs, incur a charge which you have to pay upfront. **EU citizens** are entitled to a refund (usually between 70 and 100 percent) of medical and dental expenses, providing the doctor is government-registered (*un médecin conventionné*) and provided you have a European Health Insurance Card (EHIC; *Carte Européenne d'Assurance Maladie*). Note that everyone in the family, including children, must have their own card, which are free. In the UK, you can apply for them through the Department of Health website (⊛www.dh.gov.uk), by phone (☎0845/606 2030) or by post – forms are available at post offices. Even with the EHIC card, however, you might want to take out some additional insurance to cover the shortfall. All **non-EU visitors** should ensure they have adequate medical insurance cover.

For minor complaints go to a **pharmacie**, signalled by an illuminated green cross. You'll find at least one in every small town and even some villages. They keep normal shop hours (roughly 9am–noon & 3–6pm), though some stay open late and in larger towns at least one (known as the *pharmacie de garde*) is open 24hr according to a rota; details are displayed in all pharmacy windows, or the local police will have information.

For anything more serious you can get the name of a **doctor** from a pharmacy, local police station, tourist office or your hotel. Alternatively, look under "Médecins" in the Yellow Pages of the phone directory. The consultation fee is in the region of €21 to €25, and you'll be given a *Feuille de Soins* (Statement of Treatment) for later insurance claims. Any prescriptions will be fulfilled by the pharmacy and must be paid for; little price stickers (*vignettes*) from each medicine will be stuck on the *Feuille de Soins*.

In serious **emergencies** you will always be admitted to the nearest general hospital (*centre hospitalier*). Phone numbers and addresses of hospitals in all the main cities are given in the Guide. The national number for calling an ambulance is ☏15.

Insurance

Even though EU citizens are entitled to health-care privileges in France, you should always have **travel insurance** that covers you against theft, illness and injury. Most policies exclude so-called **dangerous sports** unless an extra premium is paid; in France this can mean skiing, whitewater rafting, rock climbing and potholing.

If you need to **make a claim**, you should keep receipts for medicines and medical treatment, and in the event you have anything stolen, you must obtain an official statement from the police (called a *constat de vol*).

Internet

Virtually every business in Corsica – including hotels and campsites – has a website and is contactable via email. Ownership of personal computers is very low on the island, but

internet cafés can be found in all the major towns, typically charging €4–6.50 per hour; in the resorts, you'll more often than not have to rely on your hotel's connection, usually made available for free to guests.

Laundry

Self-service laundries in Corsica are thin on the ground; details are given in the Listings sections of the relevant accounts. You could discreetly do your own in your hotel room, though technically it's forbidden to wash clothes in hotels.

Living in Corsica

Opportunities for working in Corsica are very limited, even for travellers from EU countries. Casual work in the service sector – in campsites, hotels, bars and on beaches – is plentiful, but it tends to go to French students over for the summer. Cleaning and labouring is the preserve of Moroccan and Algerian guest workers or immigrants from eastern European countries such as Poland or Romania. That said, if your French is fluent and you speak another European language, especially German, you should be able to pick up some kind of temporary job in early June (campsite reception is always worth a try), though don't expect it to pay well.

Mail

Post offices – *postes* or PTTs – are found in the centre of all towns and most sizeable villages. They're generally open Monday to Friday 9am to noon and 2 or 2.30pm to 5pm, plus 9am to noon on Saturday. However, don't depend on these hours: in the major towns you might find the main office open throughout the day, whilst times

---

Rough Guides travel insurance

Rough Guides has teamed up with Columbus Direct to offer you tailor-made **travel insurance**. Products include a low-cost **backpacker** option for long stays; a **short break** option for city getaways; a typical **holiday package** option; and others. There are also annual **multi-trip** policies for those who travel regularly. Different sports and activities (trekking, skiing, etc) can usually be included.

See our website (☺www.roughguides.com/website/shop) for eligibility and purchasing options. Alternatively, UK residents can call ☏0870/033 9988, Australians ☏1300/669 999 and New Zealanders ☏0800/559 911. All other nationalities should call ☏+44 870/890 2843.

vary enormously in the villages. Letters and postcards usually reach the UK in three or four days, and the US in a week or so, depending on where you post them.

Maps

Roads in Corsica are impeccably signposted (even if the signs are frequently defaced by graffiti), and with the maps in this book you should be able to find your way around the places covered in the Guide. All the same, for motorists and cyclists, some kind of additional route map is a good idea.

Michelin's distinctive yellow 1:200,000 (1cm = 2km) map #90 has for years been the benchmark publication, featuring every motorable road on the island with hand-shading to emphasize the topography. It's also tough, unbelievably cheap and readily available at newsagents and bookstores across the island, as well as through the outlets listed below.

Rough Guides also publish an excellent Corsica map at a scale of 1:135,000. Bang up to date and road-tested by the author of this book, it's clearly drawn in a more modern style than the Michelin, and printed on rip-proof, water-resistent plastic paper.

For a more comprehensive topographical picture of individual regions, IGN's beautifully produced **TOP Séries Bleues** maps are second to none. Drawn to a scale of 1:25,000 (1cm = 250m), they cover Corsica in 21 separate sheets. The only catch is that they cost €9 each in France (or £8–9 if you buy them in the UK). All the map suppliers listed below stock the IGN TOP series, but they don't necessarily charge the same prices (especially when you take into account postage surcharges), so shop around.

For more specific advice on maps for walkers, see p.329.

Money

France's **currency** is the euro, which is divided into 100 cents (often still referred to as *centimes*). There are seven notes – in denominations of 5, 10, 20, 50, 100, 200 and 500 euros – and eight different coins – 1, 2, 5, 10, 20 and 50 cents, and 1 and 2 euros. At the time of writing, the **exchange rate** for the euro was around €1.27 to the pound sterling (or £0.79 to €1) and €0.67 to

the dollar (or $1.47 to €1). See ⓦ www.xe.com for current rates.

Currency exchange

You can change cash at most **banks** and main **post offices**, though only the latter will change traveller's cheques. In either case, you'll typically be charged a flat rate of around €5, but rates and commission vary, so it's worth shopping around.

There are **money-exchange counters** (*bureaux de change*) at all Corsican airports, and usually one or two in city centres as well. These services are handy when the banks are closed, though don't always offer the best exchange rates.

ATMs

By far the easiest way to access money in Corsica is to use your credit or debit card to withdraw cash from an **ATM** (known as a *distributeur* or *point argent*). Note that there is often a transaction fee.

Credit and debit cards

Credit and debit cards are widely accepted in shops, hotels and restaurants, although some smaller establishments don't accept cards, or only for sums above a certain threshold. Visa – called Carte Bleue in France – is almost universally recognized, followed by MasterCard (also known as EuroCard). American Express ranks a bit lower. Be aware that French cards are equipped with a chip and require the user to provide a PIN when making a purchase. If your card has a magnetic strip rather than a chip, you may need to explain that that yours is a *carte à piste* and not a *carte à puce*.

Opening hours and public holidays

Basic hours of business are 8am till noon and 2pm till 6pm; almost everything in Corsica – shops, museums, tourist offices, most banks – closes for a couple of hours at midday. In remote parts of the island, lunch breaks tend to be lengthier and opening times less reliable. Food shops all over the island often don't open until midway through the afternoon, closing around 7.30pm or 8pm, just before the evening meal.

Public holidays

There are twelve national holidays (*jours fériés*), when most shops and businesses, though not museums and restaurants, are closed.

January 1 New Year's Day
Easter Sunday
Easter Monday
Ascension Day Forty days after Easter
Pentecost Seventh Sunday after Easter, plus the Monday
May 1 May Day/Labour Day
May 8 Victory in Europe Day
July 14 Bastille Day
August 15 Assumption of the Virgin Mary
November 1 All Saints' Day
November 11 Armistice Day
December 25 Christmas Day

The standard **closing days** are Sunday and Monday, and in small places you'll find everything except the odd boulangerie shut on both days. **Museums** aren't very generous with their hours, opening from around 10am to noon and again from 2/3pm to 5/6pm – opening hours from mid-May to mid-September are generally slightly longer than during the rest of the year. Museum closing days are usually Monday or Tuesday, sometimes both. Most **churches** are open all day; if you come across one that's locked, you can ask for the key at the local *mairie* (town hall).

Phones

To make domestic and international phone calls from any telephone box (*cabine*), you'll need a **phone card** (*télécarte*), available for €7.50 (50 call units) and €15 (100 units) from post offices and most *tabacs*. Alternatively, a more flexible option is one of the many pre-paid phone cards (*cartes téléphoniques*) on sale at post offices, *tabacs*, newsagents and many supermarkets, which can be used from both private and public phones. The post office, for example, sells €.Ticket pre-paid cards for domestic and European calls (€5 and €10)

and for international calls (€7.50 and €15); the €15 card buys up to 858 minutes to the US and Canada. You can also use credit cards in many call boxes. Coin-operated phones have almost completely disappeared except in cafés and bars.

Calling within Corsica

For **calls within Corsica** – local or long distance – simply dial all ten digits of the number. Numbers beginning ☎08.0 are free-dial numbers; those beginning ☎08.1 and ☎08.6 are charged as a local call; anything else beginning ☎08 is premium-rated. Note that none of these ☎08 numbers can be accessed from abroad. Numbers starting ☎06 are mobile numbers and therefore also expensive to call.

Calling home

One of the most convenient ways of phoning home from abroad is via a **telephone charge card** from your phone company back home, though check that France is covered. Using a PIN number, you can make calls from most hotel, public and private phones that will be charged to your account. Since most major charge cards are free to obtain, it's certainly worth getting one at least for emergencies; bear in mind though that rates aren't necessarily cheaper than calling from a public phone.

Mobile phones

SFR and Orange are the two main network providers in Corsica. Simply switch on your mobile when you arrive on the island and it should display one of the local networks (if it doesn't, you can search manually for one in "Settings"). French mobile phones operate on the European GSM standard, so US cellphones won't work in France unless you have a tri-band phone.

If you are going to be in Corsica for any length of time and will be making and receiving a lot of local calls, it may be worth buying a **French SIM card** and pre-paid recharge cards (*mobicartes*). You can buy a SIM card from any of the big mobile providers (Orange, SFR and Boygues Telecom), all of which have high-street outlets. They cost around €30, including a

Calling home from abroad

Note that the initial zero is omitted from the area code when dialling the UK, Ireland, Australia, New Zealand and South Africa from abroad. The international access code is 00.

UK international access code + 44 + area code
Republic of Ireland international access code + 353 + area code
US and Canada international access code + 1 + area code
Australia international access code + 61 + area code
New Zealand international access code + 64 + area code
South Africa international access code + 27 + area code

Useful telephone numbers within Corsica
Ambulance ☏15
Fire ☏18
Police ☏17
Mountain rescue ☏04 95 61 13 95
Weather For the coast ☏08 36 68 08 20; for the mountains ☏08 36 68 04 04; calls are charged at €0.34 per minute.
Time ☏36 99
Note that from a **mobile phone**, dialling ☏112 will get you through to the emergency services even in areas where your network may not offer coverage.
International operator For Canada and the US ☏00 33 11; for all other countries ☏00 33 followed by the country code.
International directory assistance For Canada and the US ☏00 33 11 12; for all other countries ☏00 33 12 followed by the country code.
French directory assistance ☏12

certain amount of credit, and you need to give an address in France to register – that of your hotel or a friend will usually suffice.

Time

French summertime begins on March 28 and finishes on September 26, and is therefore an hour ahead of Britain for most of the year, except in October, when times are the same. Corsica is six hours ahead of Eastern Standard Time, and nine hours ahead of Pacific Standard Time.

Toilets

Public toilets are virtually nonexistent, since Corsicans regard providing loos for visitors as a service to be paid for rather than a civic responsibility. Every bar has one – even if only a primitive, hole-in-the-floor affair – but you'll be expected to order a drink before using it. Ask for *les toilettes*, or *le WC* – pronounced "vay-say".

Tourist information

The foreign branches of the French Government Tourist Office give away maps and glossy brochures, including lists of Corsican hotels, campsites, sports facilities and public transport services. In Corsica every major town and large village has a tourist office, or Office de Tourisme (OT), usually open from May to September – addresses of these offices are detailed throughout the Guide. OTs give out specific local information, including free town plans, lists of leisure activities, bike rental and countless other things. Many OTs also publish hotel and restaurant listings, as well as driving and walking itineraries for their areas, and post daily weather forecasts, useful if you're hiking or sailing.

Tourist offices and government sites

Australia Level 13, 25 Bligh St, Sydney, NSW 2000 ☏02/9231 5244, ⓦau.franceguide.com.

Canada 1800 Ave McGill College, Suite 1010, Montréal, QC H3A 3J6 ☎514/288 2026, ⓦca-en.franceguide.com.

Ireland ☎1560 235 235, ⓦie.franceguide.com.

New Zealand Contact the office in Australia.

South Africa 3rd Floor, Village Walk Office Tower, cnr Maude and Rivonia, Sandton ☎11/523 8292, ⓦza.franceguide.com.

UK Lincoln House, High Holborn, London WV1V 7JH ☎09068 244123, ⓦuk.franceguide.com.

US 9454 Wilshire Blvd, Suite 210, Beverly Hills, CA 90212; 205 North Michigan Ave, Suite 3770, Chicago, IL 60601; 825 Third Ave, 29th Floor, New York, NY 10022; ☎514-288-1904, ⓦus.franceguide.com.

Useful websites

The following represent only a tiny selection of the thousands of Corsica-related sites on the web. For a more detailed rundown, go to ⓦwww.corsica-isula.com/hotlist.htm.

ⓦwww.corsica-isula.com The most comprehensive online guide to the island in English (though it's difficult to navigate), this unbelievably detailed English-language site is compiled and constantly updated by expatriate Corsicaphile Will Keyser. It's more than just a portal: you can download introductions to a wide range of subjects and browse reviews and useful links.

ⓦwww.corsematin.com Extracts – in French – from Corsica's bestselling daily paper.

ⓦwww.directCorsica.com Better-than-average Corsica portal set up by the founders of the travel agency Corsican Places after they retired to the island. Packed with useful practical hints, whether you're planning a holiday or looking to buy a house.

ⓦwww.corsicabus.org Up-to-date public transport timetables – a much more reliable source than most tourist offices.

ⓦwww.visit-corsica.com The Corsican tourist board's official website.

Guide

Guide

Bastia and northern Corsica

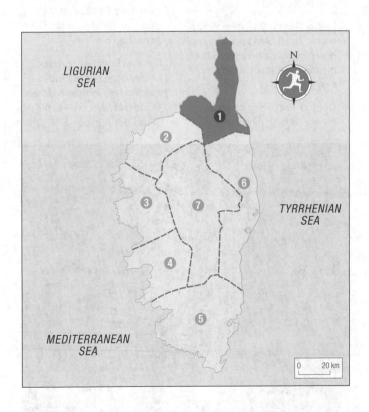

LIGURIAN
SEA

N

TYRRHENIAN
SEA

MEDITERRANEAN
SEA

0   20 km

CHAPTER 1 # Highlights

✳ **Dine in the Vieux Port, Bastia** Enjoy a quayside meal beneath the twin campaniles of L'Église St-Jean-Baptiste. See p.67

✳ **Muscat** The heavily scented dessert wine produced in Cap Corse is the ideal foil for Corsica's pungent ewe's cheese. See p.71

✳ **Le Sentier du Douanier** Wildly scenic coast path taking in deserted watchtowers and the marine reserve of Capandula. See p.79

✳ **Centuri-Port** Snug stone fishing harbour renowned for its seafood restaurants. See p.83

✳ **St-Florent** Hub of the fertile Nebbio region, fringed by kilometres of deserted coastline and mountains. See p.88

✳ **San Michele de Murato** The high watermark of Pisan church architecture on the island, made of polychrome stone. See p.97

✳ **Agriates beaches** Jump on a boat to the island's most spectacularly remote beaches – Loto and Saleccia – in the Désert des Agriates. See p.101

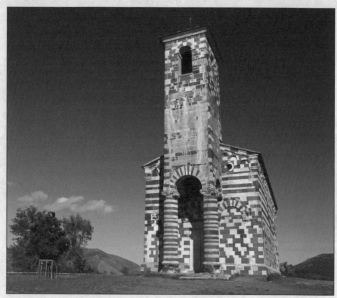

▲ San Michele de Murato

Bastia and northern Corsica

astia, nowadays capital of the *département* of Haute-Corse, was the capital of the entire island under Genoa's colonial administration, and it was the Genoese who laid the foundations of northern Corsica's prosperity by encouraging the planting of vines, olives, chestnut trees and other more experimental crops. The long-term result of this development was that the peasant farmers of the north tended to be not just better off than their southern counterparts, but also politically more ambitious. Thus, when Pascal Paoli recruited his rebel armies it was amongst this region's downtrodden rich that he concentrated his efforts, rather than amongst the downtrodden poor of the south. Even today there's a palpable difference in the political climate of the island's two halves, with northerners tending to see themselves as more radical, energetic and enterprising.

A thriving freight and passenger port, **Bastia** is the point of arrival for many visitors, though it can be a rather depressing experience at first, with industrial sprawl on the way into town from the airport, high-rise blocks stacked up the hillsides above town, and no decent beaches. Yet, while Bastia lacks the appeal of sleek Ajaccio, this is the town to visit if you want to get to grips with modern Corsica, for a quarter of the island's population lives and works here and in the immediate surroundings. Moreover, despite suffering considerable damage in World War II, the city has retained its Italian character, especially around the **Vieux Port**, a horseshoe of vertiginous buildings dominated by the towers of the Église St-Jean-Baptiste and the bulk of the Genoese citadelle.

The nearest beaches are to the south along the unremarkable stretch of coast known as **La Marana**, which adjoins the **Étang de Biguglia**, a huge lagoon that's a haven for migrating birds, and the beautiful Pisan church of **La Canonica**. To the north of Bastia, a single road follows the shore of the long rocky peninsula of **Cap Corse**, giving access to some exceptionally beautiful and unspoilt stretches of coast, as well as a string of diminutive ports, of which **Erbalunga** and **Centuri-Port** are the pick. At the base of the cape, on the western side, lies **St-Florent**, a compact little resort holding most of the north's accommodation outside the capital. The hinterland of St-Florent, the **Nebbio**, is famed for the wines produced near **Patrimonio**; for dramatically sited upland villages such as **Oletta** and **Santo-Pietro-di-Tenda**; and for the finest Romanesque **churches** on the island: Santa Maria Assunta, on the outskirts of

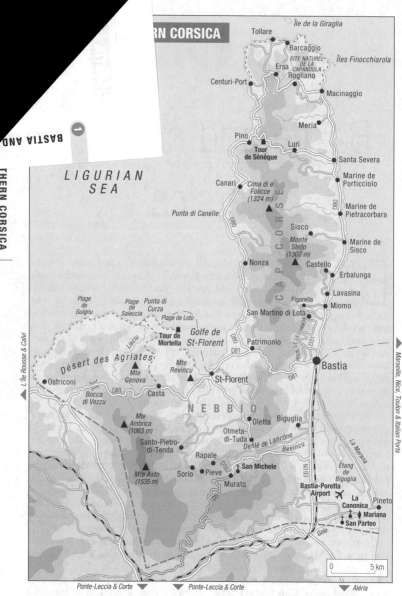

St-Florent; and the chapel of San Michele, near Murato. West of St-Florent lies the uninhabited **Désert des Agriates**, a vast, semi–barren expanse covered in massive clumps of rock, stands of cactus and the ruins of ancient stone granaries. The coast here is generally wild and inaccessible, though the beaches of **Saleccia** and **Loto**, reachable by excursion boat from St-Florent, are amongst the finest in Corsica.

Bastia

The dominant tone of Corsica's most successful commercial town, **BASTIA**, is one of charismatic dereliction, as the city's industrial zone is spread onto the lowlands to the south, leaving the centre of town with plenty of aged charm. This charm might not be too apparent from the vast **place St-Nicolas** and the two boulevards parallel to it, but south of here, in the old quarter known as the **Terra Vecchia**, lies a tightly packed network of haphazard streets, flamboyant Baroque churches and Genoese tenements, their crumbling golden-grey walls set against a backdrop of maquis-covered hills. **Terra Nova**, the historic district on the opposite side of the old port from Terra Vecchia, is a tidier zone that's now Bastia's yuppie quarter, housing the island's top-flight architects, doctors and lawyers.

As the sprawling light-industrial suburbs to the south remind you, though, Bastia is, first and foremost, a working city, and a highly political one at that. This is where the nationalist movement of the 1970s held its first big rallies, and where civil servants rioted in 1989 over the mysterious disappearance of local government funds – the disturbances culminated soon after with the razing of the local tax office by a nationalist-terrorist bomb. More recently, a strike called by the French transport union to oppose plans to privatize the ailing SNCM ferry company made national headlines after sailors commandeered the Pascal Paoli. The then interior minister, Nicholas Sarkozy, ordered in special forces to reclaim the vessel, though was later forced to capitulate, prompting widespread jubilation across the island.

Militant and busily self-sufficient, Bastia may make few concessions to tourism, but its grittiness makes it a more genuine introduction to Corsica than its longtime rival on the west coast, Ajaccio.

A brief history of Bastia

In the twelfth century, when Corsica was under Pisan control, wine was exported to the Italian mainland from **Porto Cardo**, forerunner of Bastia's **Vieux Port**. Moorish raids made the area too vulnerable to inhabit, however, and it wasn't until the Genoese ascendancy that the port began to thrive. At first the colony was governed from the former Roman base at Biguglia, to the south, but in 1372, when the fort was burned down by Corsican rebels, the Genoese abandoned the malarial site in favour of Porto Cardo, a spot close to Genoa and within easy trading distance of the fertile regions of the eastern plain, Balagne and Cap Corse. Before the end of the decade the governor, Leonello Lomellino, had built the *bastiglia* (dungeon) which gave the town its name; ramparts were constructed high on the escarpment above the port, and Genoese families, attracted by offers of free building land, began to settle within the fortifications in an area which became **Terra Nova**.

The sixteenth century saw the rise of a new class of merchants and artisans, who settled around the harbour on the site of Porto Cardo, the area now known as **Terra Vecchia**. The boom lasted until 1730, when Bastia was raided by an army of four thousand peasants. Provoked to desperation by the corrupt despotism of the Genoese republic, the *paesani* went on the rampage for three days, annihilating most of the population of Terra Vecchia, who lacked the protection of the upper-class inhabitants of Terra Nova. Peace was finally restored by the intervention of the bishop of Aléria, but the remaining Genoese merchants promptly left for the safer ports of Bonifacio and Calvi, and Bastia went into decline.

During the **Wars of Independence** (1729–96) Bastia became a battle-ground. Pascal Paoli coveted the town for its strong position facing Italy, but it took two attempts and the efforts of the British fleet to take the citadelle – the second assault was led by Nelson and Hood, who, though outnumbered by two to one, overcame the defenders in a long and difficult siege. In 1794, in the wake of this victory, Bastia became home to English viceroy Sir Gilbert Elliot, who lived here for the two years of the Anglo-Corsican alliance. Bastia's hour of glory was short-lived, however, as the French finally gained full control of Corsica in 1796, and the island was divided into two *départements*.

Despite the fact that in 1811 Napoleon appointed Ajaccio capital of the island, initiating a rivalry between the two towns that exists to this day, Bastia soon established a stronger trading position with the Continent. The **Nouveau Port**, created in 1862 to cope with the increasing traffic with France and Italy, became the mainstay of the local economy, exporting chiefly agricultural products from Cap Corse, Balagne and the eastern plain. During **World War II** Bastia was the only town on Corsica to be severely bombed – ironically, by the Americans: on the day after the island's liberation in 1943, a squadron of B52s belatedly launched an aerial attack against the nonexistent Germans, Von Senger und Etterlin's Ninth Panzer Division having already completed its withdrawal across the Ligurian Sea. With many people in the streets celebrating the retreat, civilian casualties exceeded the total sustained throughout the occupation and many buildings were destroyed, including much of the old governor's palace; the consequences of the bombing can still be seen in Terra Vecchia.

Today, Bastia's population has grown to forty thousand, with the long-standing industries of freight handling and small-scale manufacture providing most of the employment, augmented by the burgeoning bureaucracies of local government.

Arrival and information

Bastia's Poretta **airport** (℡04 95 54 54 54, Ⓦwww.bastia.aeroport.fr) is 16km south of town, just off the Route Nationale (N193); blue and beige **navettes** (shuttle buses) (℡04 95 31 06 65) into the centre coincide with flights, and enter town via Terra Nova, dropping passengers at the north side of the main square, place St-Nicolas, for €8.50 (one way). **Taxis** from the airport (℡04 95 36 04 65 or 06 13 24 72 66) cost €40/50 (day/night). The terminus for the *micheline* from Ajaccio, Corte and Calvi (via Ponte Leccia) is Bastia **train station** (*gare CFC*), on the north side of town off the rondpoint Leclerc (℡04 95 32 80 60). The smart **ferry dock**, or **Nouveau Port**, is a short way north of place St-Nicolas. The complex has two terminals – North (Nord) and South (Sud) – roughly 200m apart. Both have ticket hatches for the various ferry companies, in addition to **public toilets** (a rarity in Corsica).

There isn't a proper bus station in the town, which can cause confusion, with services arriving and departing from different locations around the north side of place St-Nicolas: see map opposite. A full rundown of routes and companies appears in Travel details on p.101.

Drivers should head for the large **car park** in the centre, beneath place St-Nicolas. It's expensive and often filthy, but is the only place you're guaranteed to find spaces; come armed with plenty of change for the ticket machine.

The **tourist office** (June to Sept 15 daily 8am–8pm; Sept 16 to May Mon–Sat 8am–6pm, Sun 9am–1pm; ℡04 95 54 20 40, Ⓦwww.bastia-tourisme .com) is at the north end of place St-Nicolas, but don't expect advice about other parts of the island – the staff are basically there to hand out glossy leaflets, bus timetables and free fold-out maps, and nothing more.

▲ Ⓐ Ⓑ , Camping Les Orangers & Cap Corse

BASTIA

North Ferry Terminal

Laundry

Objectif Nature

Nouveau Port

Préfecture

Airport Bus Stop

Cyber@Cyber

Train Station

Buses to Calvi

Bus Station (Gare Routière) Ⓒ

South Ferry Terminal

Ⓔ Buses to Aléria, Porto Vecchio & Bonifacio

Maison Mattei

Jetée St. Nicolas

PLACE ST-NICOLAS

Café des Palmiers ②

Chez Serge Raugi ③

Ⓕ

CyberTaz

Ⓖ

Album Bookshop

Oratoire St-Roch

Ⓗ

Le Regent Cinema

Theatre

Oratoire de L'Immaculée Conception

PLACE DU MARCHÉ

St-Jean Baptiste ④

⑤

Beith Meir Synagogue

Vieux Port

Ⓘ Studio Cinema

Église St-Charles

Palais de Justice

Jardin Romieu

Tunnel

Jetée du Dragon

Porte Louis-XVI

Palais des Gouverneurs ⑦

⑧

Jardin Romieu

PL. GUASCO

TERRA NOVA

Oratoire Ste-Croix

PLACE D'ARMES

Cathédrale Ste-Marie

Ⓓ St-Florent, San Martino di Lota (Via Route de la Corniche)

Oratoire de Monserato

EATING & DRINKING

A Casarelle	8
L'Apocalypse	9
Bar de la Citadelle	7
Le Bouchon	6
Café des Palmiers	2
Chez Serge Raugi	3
Le Palais des Glaces	1
La Table du Marché	4
U Tianu	5

ACCOMMODATION

Athéna	F
Best Western	D
Central	G
Cyrnea	A
L'Impérial	I
Pietracap	B
Posta-Vecchia	H
Riviera	C
Les Voyageurs	E

0   100 m

Camping San Damiano, Étang de Biguglia, ▼ Poretta Airport, La Marana, Corte, Porto Vecchio, Bonifacio, Ajaccio & ⑨

Accommodation

Bastia's passenger port receives twice as many visitors as Ajaccio's, but few linger in the city, preferring to head straight off to quieter corners of the island. This may in part explain the relative shortage of **hotel rooms**. Choice is particularly limited at the bottom end of the scale, so if you're on a tight budget think twice about spending a night here. Most of the classier places line the road to Cap Corse north of the port; the more basic ones are found in the centre of town, within striking distance of place St-Nicolas. Wherever you plan to stay, it's advisable to reserve well in advance.

Bastia's **campsites** are all located well outside the centre. The most convenient if you're relying on public transport is at **Miomo**, 5km north (buses every 30min Mon–Sat, hourly Sun, until 7.30pm, from the top of place St-Nicolas opposite the tourist office).

Hotels in the centre

Athéna 2 rue Miot ☎04 95 34 88 40. Modern hotel close to the ports and central *place*, with light, airy rooms at various rates. Go for the pricier ones if space is an issue (the cheaper ones are quite small). ❹

Best Western av Zuccarelli ☎04 95 55 05 10, ⓦwww.bestwestern-corsica-hotels.com. Hardly the most characterful option, but rates are highly competitive, the location (on the hill above town) attractive, and rooms spacious for the price. Central a/c. ❺–❻

Central 3 rue Miot ☎04 95 31 71 12, ⓦwww.centralhotel.fr. Eighteen pleasantly furnished rooms (plus a handful of larger studios), with textured walls and sparkling bathrooms, just off the southwest corner of place St-Nicolas. The welcoming *patronne*, Mme de la Paillonne, runs a tight ship, making this by far the most pleasant and best-value place to stay in the centre. Advance reservation essential. ❹

Cyrnea Pietranea ☎04 95 31 41 71. Congenial little two-star, 4km out of town beside the main road. All rooms are en suite, but only some overlook the water from balconies where you can take breakfast. You also get the run of a small garden, strewn with sun loungers, which runs down to a secluded pebble beach. Good value given the location. Secure parking. ❺–❻

L'Impérial 2 bd Paoli ☎04 95 31 06 94, ⓕ04 95 34 13 76. Central, efficient two-star on the south side of town; rooms aren't large, but acceptable for a short stay. ❹

Pietracap route de San Martino ☎04 95 31 64 63, ⓦwww.hotel-pietracap.com. Luxurious three-star set on a hillside overlooking the sea. The bright, white-painted rooms open onto flowery terraces, most have lovely views, and there's a large pool set amid old olive trees. Look for a signboard pointing right off the main road (if you're heading north). ❼–❽

Posta-Vecchia quai-des-Martyrs-de-la-Libération ☎04 95 32 32 38, ⓦwww.hotel-postavecchia.com. The only hotel in the Vieux Port, and good value, with views across the sea from the (pricier) rooms at the front. There are smaller, cheaper rooms in the old block across the lane, and all have a/c. ❹–❼

Riviera 1 bis, rue du Nouveau-Port ☎04 95 31 07 16, ⓦwww.corsehotelriviera.com. Basic and a bit noisy, but with pleasing rooms behind a period facade, but very near the harbour. ❺

Les Voyageurs 9 av Maréchal-Sébastiani ☎04 95 34 90 80, ⓦwww.hotel-lesvoyageurs.com. Smart three-star near the train station, done out in pale yellow and with two categories of rooms: the larger, pricier ones have baths instead of showers. No views to speak of, but fine for a night or two. Secure parking and central a/c. ❻

Campsites

Les Orangers Miomo, 5km north along the route du Cap ☎04 95 33 24 09. Tiny site crammed onto narrow terraces, just off the main road.

San Damiano Pineto, 10km south of Bastia ☎04 95 33 68 02. Huge (200-place) site, offering good value for money, with state-of-the-art facilities, including a pool and jacuzzi; take the road to the left across the bridge at Furiani roundabout (5km south on the N193). Hourly buses in summer from the *gare routière*, or you can jump on the train (the nearest station is Rocade).

The Town

The centre of Bastia is not especially large, and all its sights can easily be seen in a day without the use of a car. The spacious **place St-Nicolas** is the obvious place to get your bearings; open to the sea and lined with shady trees and cafés, it's the main focus, and social hub, of town life. Running parallel to it on the landward side are **boulevard Paoli** and **rue César-Campinchi**, the two main shopping streets. All Bastia's historic sights lie within **Terra Vecchia**, the old quarter immediately south of place St-Nicolas, and **Terra Nova**, the area surrounding the **Citadelle**. Tucked away below the imposing, honey-coloured bastion is the much-photographed **Vieux Port**, with its boat-choked marina and crumbling eighteenth-century tenement buildings. By contrast, the **Nouveau Port** area, north of the *place*, is bland and modern, with little of interest beyond some workaday restaurants and bars.

Place St-Nicolas

The most pleasant spot to soak up Bastia's Mediterranean atmosphere is **place St-Nicolas**. During the evening, with the Nouveau Port's gigantic white ferry boats forming a surreal backdrop, its cafés fill up with snappily dressed young Bastiais on their way home from work, while pensioners take leisurely *passeghiatas* under the trees. On Sunday mornings it hosts a busy **flea market** (*marché aux puces*), which is in full swing by 8.30am, attracting the usual mix of hardened antique dealers and townsfolk unloading family junk around the camp marble statue of Napoleon in Roman emperor's garb. Amid the row of cafés behind the statue stands the wonderful Art-Deco facade of the **Maison Mattei**, a long-established wine merchants (open till 10pm in July & Aug) which sells liqueurs from all over the island, including the famous local quinine-based aperitif, Cap Corse. The square's other sight of note, installed in pride of place on the northeast corner facing the ferry port, is the conning tower of the submarine **Le Casabianca**, famous for its role in supplying the Corsican resistance during the Axis occupation of World War II.

▲ Bastia

Terra Vecchia

From place St-Nicolas the main route south into Terra Vecchia is rue Napoléon, a narrow street with some ancient offbeat shops and a pair of sumptuously decorated chapels on its east side. The first of these, the **Oratoire St-Roch**, is a Genoese Baroque extravagance, built in 1604 to reflect the wealth of the rising bourgeoisie. Particularly remarkable are its walls, which are covered with finely carved wooden panelling. The chapel also possesses a magnificent organ, decorated with gilt and wooden sculpture, and hardly altered since it was built in 1750.

A little further along stands the **Oratoire de l'Immaculée Conception**, built in 1611 as the showplace of the Genoese in Corsica, who used it for state occasions such as the inauguration of the governor. In later years, the English viceroy, Sir Gilbert Elliot (see p.383), held parliamentary sessions here during the brief Anglo-Corsican interlude. Overlooking a pebble mosaic of a sun, the austere facade belies the flamboyant interior. The unusually narrow nave terminates at an elaborate polychromatic marble altar, over which hangs a copy of Murillo's *Immaculate Conception*. On the left stands a statue of the Virgin, which, on December 8, is paraded through the streets to the Église St-Jean-Baptiste.

If you cut back through the narrow steps beside the Oratoire de St-Roch, a two-minute walk will bring you to place de l'Hôtel-de-Ville, commonly known as **place du Marché** because of the fresh produce **market** that takes place here each morning (8am–1pm).

At the south end of the square is the **Église St-Jean-Baptiste**, an immense ochre edifice whose twin campaniles (covered for renovation work at the time of writing) loom dramatically above the Vieux Port – Bastia's most distinctive landmark. Built in 1636, the church was restored in the eighteenth century in a Rococo overkill of multicoloured marble. Decorating the walls are a few unremarkable Italian paintings from Napoleon's uncle, Cardinal Fesch, an avid collector of Renaissance art (see p.183).

Around the church extends the oldest part of Bastia, an enclosed zone of dark alleys, vaulted passageways and seven-storey houses locked in isolation from the rest of town. Hidden among them, on the rue Castagno, is one of Corsica's few remaining synagogues, the **Beth Meir**. A plaque on its wall alludes to the anti-Semitism that was rife in Bastia during World War II, after which all but a handful of the town's Jewish population left. Since then, families of North African immigrants have moved in to take their place as the district's underclass.

By turning right outside the Église St-Jean-Baptiste and following rue St-Jean, you'll come to **rue Général-Carbuccia**, the heart of Terra Vecchia. Pascal Paoli once lived here, at no. 7, and Balzac stayed briefly at no. 23 when his ship got stuck in Corsica on the way to Sardinia. Set in a small square at the end of the road is the **Église St-Charles**, an august Jesuit chapel whose wide steps provide an evening meeting place for locals.

The Vieux Port

The **Vieux Port** is the most atmospheric part of town: soaring houses seem to bend inwards towards the water, peeling plaster and boat hulls glint in the sun, while the south side remains in the shadow of the great rock that supports the citadelle. Site of the original Porto Cardo, the Vieux Port later bustled with Genoese traders, but since the building of the ferry terminal and commercial docks it has become a backwater, quiet by day, when the clinking of yacht masts echoes around the marina. It's livelier at night, with the glow and noise from the harbourside bars and restaurants. These continue round the north end of the port along the wide quai-des-Martyrs-de-la-Libération.

The best view of the Vieux Port is from the **Jetée du Dragon**, the quay that juts out under the citadelle. To build it, engineers had to destroy a giant lion-shaped rock, known as the Leone, which formerly blocked the entrance to the harbour. To reach the citadelle from the quai-des-Martyrs, you can walk through the **Jardin Romieu**, an eighteenth-century terraced garden adorning the cliff on this side of the harbour. The steps leading through it bring you out at a little green, huddled below the bastion walls, which makes an ideal picnic spot.

Terra Nova

The military and administrative core of old Bastia, **Terra Nova** – or the **citadelle** – lords it over the old port from its perch atop a sheer-sided rocky promontory. Beautifully restored over the past few decades, the quarter has a distinct air of affluence, and its lofty apartments and pastel-coloured houses are now largely the preserve of Bastia's affluent set. The area is focused on **place du Donjon**, immediately inside the main (north) gateway, which gets its name from the squat round tower that formed the nucleus of the town's fortifications and was used by the Genoese to incarcerate Corsican patriots – Sampiero Corso was held in the dungeon for four years in the early sixteenth century.

The Palais des Gouverneurs and Musée d'Éthnographie Corse

Facing the square is the impressive fourteenth-century **Palais des Gouverneurs**, Terra Nova's most prominent landmark. With its flamboyant facade, arcaded inner courtyard and peach-coloured paintwork, the building has a Baroque feel. During the Genoese heyday, the governor and the local bishop lived here with an entourage of seventy horsemen, entertaining foreign dignitaries and hosting massive parties. When the French transferred the capital to Ajaccio, it became a prison, and was then destroyed during Nelson's attack of 1794. The subsequent rebuilding was not the last, as parts of it were blown up by the allied bombard-ment in 1943, and today the restorers are trying to regain something of the building's former grandeur.

Part of the palace is given over to the **Musée d'Éthnographie Corse** (closed for renovation at the time of writing, but scheduled to re-open in 2009; daily: June 9am–6.30pm, July & Aug 9am–8pm, Sept–May 9am–noon & 2–6pm; last entry 45min before closing time; admission around €7), whose exhibition presents the history of Corsica from prehistoric times to the present day. Its vaulted chambers contain a motley collection of artefacts from rare rock specimens to Pascal Paoli memorabilia, an array that at first sight seems rather tired yet does include a lovely Roman sarcophagus decorated with hunting scenes. Thought to have belonged to a child, it was discovered in Bastelicaccia, near Ajaccio, where it was being used as a horses' drinking trough. The remaining exhibits illustrate the island's history with old maps, engravings and documents, along with cases relating to key figures such as Sampiero, King Théodore and Nelson. On your way around, look out for the replica of Napoleon's death mask, and for the original "Moor's Head" flag of Independ-ence, an emblem of obscure origins (see box, p.392).

The renovated Genoese **dungeons** below the governor's palace were where up to 350 inmates would be incarcerated, many of them chained to the wet walls for days on end. Resistance fighters were also held and tortured here by the Nazis during World War II.

Terra Nova churches

Back in place du Donjon, cross the square and follow rue Notre-Dame to come out at the **Cathédrale Ste-Marie**. Built in 1458 and overhauled in the seventeenth century, it was the cathedral of Bastia until 1801, when the bishopric was transferred to Ajaccio. Inside, the church's principal treasure is a small silver statue of the Virgin (housed in a glass case on the right wall as you face the altar), which is carried through Terra Nova and Terra Vecchia on August 15, the Festival of the Assumption.

A plaque on the wall to the south of the church marks the house where the French poet and novelist **Victor Hugo** lived as a young child between 1803 and 1805. His father, General (then Major) Leopold Hugo, was posted to Bastia after quarrelling with his commander-in-chief and spent just over a year here during the Napoleonic Wars, steeling Bastia's defenders against a feared British attack. While his wife remained in Paris to live "*une vie très libre*" with a certain General Lahorie, Leopold struck up an affair with the 18-year-old English governess of his three sons, Catherine Thomas. The experience of living above Bastia's Vieux Port is often cited by biographers as an important early influence on Hugo, much of whose poetry was inspired by the sea.

Immediately behind the Cathédrale Ste-Maire in rue de l'Evêché stands the **Oratoire Ste-Croix**, a sixteenth-century chapel decorated in Louis XV style, with lashings of rich blue paint and gilt scrollwork. It houses another holy item, the Christ des Miracles, a blackened oak crucifix, much venerated by Bastia's fishermen, which in 1428 was discovered floating in the sea surrounded by a luminous haze. A festival celebrating the miracle takes place in Bastia on May 3, when local fishing families carry it around Terra Nova. Beyond the church, the narrow streets open out to the secluded **place Guasco**, where a few benches offer the chance of a rest before descending back into the fray.

L'Oratoire de Monserato

One of Bastia's most extraordinary monuments, the **Oratoire de Monserato**, lies a pleasant two-kilometre walk from the town centre. From Terra Nova, leave the citadelle through its main (northern) gateway next to the Palais des Gouverneurs and follow the Chemin des Fillipines (a stepped lane starting on the opposite side of the main road) uphill for ten minutes. When you reach a road at the top, turn left and keep going for another 300m until you see a lane leading left to the Oratoire. The building itself looks unremarkable from the outside, but its interior houses the much revered **Scala Santa**, a replica of the Holy Steps of the Basilica of Saint John of Lateran in Rome. Penitents who ascend it on their knees as far as its high altar may be cleansed, or so it is believed, of all sins, without the intercession of a priest. Only Rome, Lourdes and Fatima enjoy such a privilege, an anomaly dating from the First Empire when bishops and other prominent clerics who refused to accede to Napoleon's Concordat of 1801 were imprisoned in the citadelle. The townsfolk of Bastia complained bitterly about this rough treatment of such high-ranking clergy and were granted permission to host the priests in their own homes instead. Following Napoleon's demise, the liberated clergy then petitioned Rome to grant the town a special favour in recognition of its generosity, whence the Scala Santa.

Eating, drinking and nightlife

Lively **place St-Nicolas**, lined with smart café-restaurants, is the place to be during the day, particularly between noon and 3pm, when the rest of town is deserted. Along **boulevard Paoli** and **rue César-Campinchi**, chi-chi *salons de thé* offer elaborate pâtisseries, local chestnut *flan* and doughnuts (*beignets*). Late-night clubbers can revive themselves with an early coffee and a pain au chocolat at one of the three cafés in **place de l'Hôtel-de-Ville**, which open at 4.30am for the market traders. There are also numerous **pizza vans** scattered about town until about 9pm. For additional reviews of restaurants in the Bastia area, see our account of **San Martino di Lota** on p.74.

Drinking is serious business in Bastia. The **Casanis** *pastis* factory is on the outskirts in Lupino, and this is indisputably the town's drink – order a "*Casa*" and you'll fit in well. The best place to buy wine is Grand Vin Corse at 24 rue César-Campinchi; the obliging proprietor will fill up plastic *vracs* of muscat and other Patrimonios from the barrels for you.

Bars and cafés

Bar de la Citadelle in front of the Palais des Gouverneurs, Terra Nova. Basically a sandwich and ice-cream bar that would have little to recommend it were it not for the superb location overlooking the Vieux Port.

Le Bouchon 4 bis, rue St-Jean, Vieux Port. Occupying a prime position on the quayside, this easy-going wine bar serves local and continental French wines by the glass (€5–6.50), as well as variously priced gastro-tapas on slate platters. Closed Wed & Sun.

Café des Palmiers place St-Nicolas. One of several cafés along this stretch, with comfy wicker chairs which catch the sun at breakfast time, plus delicious fresh pâtisseries and attentive service.

Chez Serge Raugi 2 bis, rue Capanelle, off bd Général Graziani, at the north end of place St-Nicolas. Arguably Corsica's greatest ice-cream maker, from an illustrious line of local *glaciers*. Tables on a cramped pavement terrace or upstairs on an even smaller mezzanine floor. In winter, they also do a legendary chickpea tart to take away.

Restaurants

A Casarelle 6 rue Ste-Croix ☎ 04 95 32 02 32. Innovative Corsican-French cuisine (lamb *noisettes* in Pietra beer and maquis-herbs sauce, for example) served on a terrace on the edge of the citadelle. The chef's specialities are traditional dishes of the Balagne, such as *casgiate* (nuggets of fresh cheese baked in fragrant chestnut leaves) or the rarely prepared *storzapretti* – balls of *brocciu*, spinach and herbs in tomato sauce. Menu at €29 for lunch, or €35 for dinner. Closed Sat lunchtime and all day Sun.

Le Palais des Glaces place St-Nicolas ☎ 04 95 35 05 01. One of the few dependable lunch spots on the main square, frequented as much by Bastiais as visitors. Their good-value €25 menu, served under swish awnings beneath the plane trees, often includes the house favourite: fish *bruschettas*.

La Table du Marché place du Marché ☎ 04 95 31 64 25. Offering far better value than most places on the nearby Vieux Port, this smart terrace restaurant serves a tempting €27.50 *menu regional* featuring local crayfish, east-coast oysters and fillets of St Pierre. The à la carte menu is dominated by fancier gastro seafood, and is much more expensive. For wine, try their very reasonably priced Clos Colombu. Closed Sun.

U Tianu 4 rue Rigo ☎ 04 95 31 36 67. Tiny, family-run restaurant with lots of atmosphere, hidden in a narrow backstreet behind the Vieux Port. Their limited but excellent-value menus (€22–27) change daily but feature typical country dishes such as *figatellu* pâté, blackbird terrine, chickpeas with anchovies, mutton and lentil stew, sardines stuffed with *brocciu*, and *fiadone* soaked in home-made eau de vie.

Nightlife

What there is of Bastia's **nightlife** centres around the bars, cafés and restaurants of the Vieux Port and place St-Nicolas. A couple of cheesy discos and cinemas offer some variety, but you'll have to search hard for a crowded venue, as the preferred entertainment of Bastiais seems to be a quiet night in front of the television. The best source of information about all events is the daily local paper *Corse-Matin*.

If there's a concert in Bastia it will almost certainly be held in the **theatre** in place Favalelli (☎ 04 95 34 98 00), west of rue César-Campinchi. Of Bastia's two **cinemas**, the triple-screen Le Regent, just off the south side of rue César-Campinchi, shows new films, always dubbed into French, whereas the Studio, in nearby rue Miséricorde, is a small outfit showing mostly subtitled foreign and arthouse movies.

Bastia's festivities

Bastia's summer **firework displays** are a regular occurrence, with the most spectacular show happening in place St-Nicolas on **Bastille Day** (July 14), when street parties are held all over town. Other annual events include the **Fête du Christ Noir** on May 3 (see p.37), a **regatta** in June and the **Foire de Bastia** in July, which has stalls – mainly promoting local businesses – and live music in the evenings. On August 15, a solemn procession heralds the **Fête de l'Assomption,** after which the Vieux Port becomes overrun by revellers.

The week-long **Festival du Film et des Cultures Méditerranéennes** takes place in the third week of November at the cinemas and the theatre, showcasing films, backed up by exhibitions, from all parts of the Mediterranean region. There's also a British film festival in the first two weeks in March, featuring fairly recent releases with French subtitles.

Nightclubs are few and far between in Corsica, and the only *boîte* of note in the Bastia area is *L'Apocalypse* (☎04 95 33 36 83, ⓦwww.apocalypse-bastia.com; closed Mon & Tues), 10km south of Bastia on the route de La Marana, Biguglia. It attracts a mainly teenage crowd, and you'll need a car to get there. Entry is free and drinks extortionate, at around €10 for a Pietra.

Listings

Airport enquiries ☎04 95 54 54 54, ⓦwww .bastia.aeroport.fr.

Banks and exchange Most of the main banks and cash machines are on place St-Nicolas, at the bottom of bd Paoli, and on rue César-Campinchi. The main branch of the Société Générale is at the bottom of the square on rue Miot. Crédit Agricole has a foreign-exchange counter in the arrivals hall of the *gare maritime* (terminal sud) in the Nouveau Port.

Bicycle rental Locacycles, behind the Palais de Justice (☎04 95 32 30 64), rents bicycles by the day (€18) or for longer periods, as does Objectif Nature, rue Notre Dame-de-Lourdes (☎04 95 32 54 34, ⓦwww.objectif-nature-corse.com).

Bookshops The best-stocked bookshop and stationer is Album Librairie, at the top of rue César-Campinchi, which has a great selection of titles on Corsica. More serious bibliophiles, collectors of rare prints and postcards, and anyone looking for out-of-print titles on the island shouldn't miss the Librairie Marzocchi, at 2 rue du Conventionnel Saliceti/41 bd Paoli (☎04 95 34 02 95).

Car rental ADA, 35 rue César-Campinchi ☎04 95 31 48 95, airport ☎04 95 54 55 44; Avis (Ollandini), 40 bd Paoli ☎04 95 31 95 64, airport ☎04 95 54 55 46; Europcar, 1 rue du Nouveau-Port ☎04 95 31 59 29, airport ☎04 95 30 09 50; Hertz, square St-Victor ☎04 95 31 14 24, airport ☎04 95 30 05 00; Rent-a-Car, Poretta airport ☎04 95 54 55 11. For central reservations and

website addresses of these and the island's other main rental companies, see Basics, p.25.

Diving Thalassa Immersion (☎04 95 31 78 90), 2km north of the centre (head past the marina and turn left at the Elf petrol station), or book through the shop of the same name, on rue Napoléon, just behind the Vieux Port; Club Plongée Bastiais, Vieux Port (☎04 95 33 31 28, ⓦwww.plongee-bastiais .com), work from their boat, moored on the north side of the harbour. Both outfits run trips to the famous Heinkel-111, just beyond the sea wall, and to the wreck of *La Cannonière*, about an hour's ride up the coast off Pietracorbara. Rates are around €35/41per equipped/non-equipped dive.

Ferry offices Corsica Ferries, 5 bis, rue Chanoine-Leschi ☎04 95 32 95 95, or at the *gare maritime* ☎04 95 32 95 94; Mobylines, Sarl Colonna D'Istria & Fils, 4 rue Luce de Casablanca, just behind the Nouveau Port ☎04 95 34 84 94; SNCM, Nouveau Port, BP 57 ☎04 95 54 66 99. For central reservations and website addresses, see p.22.

Hospital Centre Hospitalier, Furiani ☎04 95 59 11 11.

Internet Café Albert, 11 bd Général de Gaule.

Laundry Lavoir du Port (daily 7am–9pm), two doors down from the big Esso petrol station, opposite the ferry dock's north terminal.

Left luggage €3 per day at Objectif Nature, rue Notre Dame-de-Lourdes.

Pharmacies Plenty on bd Paoli, or try Ricci-Luciani (Mon–Sat 8.30am–12.15pm & 2.30–7pm), at the top of place St-Nicolas, near the tourist office. In an emergency, call ℡04 95 31 99 17.

Post office The central post office is on av Maréchal-Sebastiani, between the train station and place St-Nicolas.

Taxis There's a taxi rank at the northern end of place St-Nicolas, next to the *gare routière* (℡04 95 34 07 00). For airport taxis, call ℡06 13 36 04 65.

Train information ℡04 95 32 80 60.

Moving on from Bastia

Obtaining information about departure times and points can sometimes be difficult, mainly because most services are run by private companies with offices scattered across town. The only place that keeps up-to-date timetables for all public transport services operating out of Bastia is the tourist office on place St-Nicolas (see p.60).

By plane

Bastia's Poretta **airport**, 16km south of town, is served by direct flights from London (Gatwick), Birmingham and several major French cities. The cheapest way to get there from the town centre is on the beige and blue *navette* (€10 one way), which departs to connect with flights from the Leclerc roundabout, in front of the train station. For precise times of the service call ℡04 95 31 06 65. Taxis (℡04 95 36 04 65 or 06 13 24 72 66) charge €40–50 depending on the time of day.

By ferry

Regular car and passenger **ferries** operate all year round between Bastia and the French ports of Nice and Marseille, with a less frequent service to Toulon. There are also seasonal services (July to mid-Sept) to the Italian ports of Genoa, La Spezia, Livorno, Savona and Piombino. In summer, it's essential to reserve a place. For more on routes, fares and timetables see Basics, p.21.

By train

Corsica's famous narrow-gauge train, the **micheline** (see p.27), terminates in Bastia, and there are regular services from the town to stations along both branches of the line. For details see Travel details on p.101 or consult Ⓦwww .ter-sncf.com, Ⓦwww.corsicabus.org, or the station direct (℡04 95 32 80 60).

By bus

Roughly speaking, services to **Ajaccio**, **Corte** and smaller, rural destinations – including Patrimonio, Nonza, Cap Corse, Nebbio, St-Florent and Castagniccia – tend to operate out of the *gare routière*, at the north end of place St-Nicolas behind the Hôtel de Ville. Buses for **Bonifacio**, **Porto Vecchio** and services to the east coast can be picked up outside the Rapides Bleus office, at the roadside opposite the main post office on avenue Maréchal-Sébastiani. Services for **Calvi** via **L'Île Rousse** depart from outside the train station. Precise departure points are marked on the map on p.61. For a complete rundown of destinations reachable by bus from Bastia, see Travel details on p.101 or visit Ⓦwww .corsicabus.org. Tickets for all services are available on the bus from the driver.

South of Bastia

It's easy to be put off by the industrial sprawl **south of Bastia**, but amidst the built-up areas are hidden some ideal destinations for a half-day excursion – or as a scenic **alternative route to the airport**. At the Furiani junction, about 4km along the N193, you can turn off the main road to follow the stretch of coast known as **La Marana**, where holiday villages and villas back a sandy beach lined with pine woods. Between it and the N193 lies the **Étang de Biguglia**, a wildlife-rich lagoon named after the ancient capital of Corsica, now an unremarkable village on the slopes above the main road. The lagoon stretches as far as the Roman site of **Mariana**, 18km south of Bastia, where you can see the remains of a twelfth-century basilica and the superb Pisan church of La Canonica.

There is no public transport direct to Mariana. **Buses**, which leave from opposite the Bastia *gare routière* at 11.30am and 6pm in summer, take you along La Marana as far as Pineto. From here it's a good three-kilometre walk to the Roman site.

La Marana and the Étang de Biguglia

Traditionally the summer haunt of prosperous Bastia families, the 16km *littoral* known as **La Marana** (pronounced "la-mar*an*") is the beginning of the sandy stretch that continues more or less uninterrupted all the way down to Porto Vecchio in the south. Largely the preserve of joggers, rollerbladers and windsurfers, the beach offers shady pine woods, restaurants and bars and, even though the sea is quite polluted due to boat traffic and the proximity to the town, it makes an agreeable excursion from Bastia when the heat gets too much. All this part of the coast is divided into holiday residences or areas of beach attached to bars; the latter sections of beach are freely open to the public.

Fed by the rivers Bevinco and Golo, the **Étang de Biguglia** is the largest lagoon in Corsica and one of its best sites for **birdlife**, thanks largely to the reed beds bordering the water. Of the birds that nest in them, various species of warblers are most common – in summer you'll find reed warblers at the southern end of the lagoon, as well as moustached warblers and Cetti's warblers, with their distinctive loud repetitive cry. In winter, Biguglia is a stopoff point for migrating grey herons, kingfishers, great crested grebes, little grebes, water rails and various species of duck, such as the spectacular red-crested pochard, identifiable by its red bill, red feet and a bright red head.

Mariana

The Roman town of **Mariana**, just south of the Étang de Biguglia, can be reached either by taking the turning for the airport, 16km along the N193, or the more picturesque coastal route through La Marana.

Founded in 93 BC as a military colony, Mariana had become a Christian centre by the fourth century, when its basilica was built. The settlement was severely damaged by the Vandals and Ostrogoths in the fifth and sixth centuries, and by the time of the Genoese occupation Mariana had become so waterlogged and malarial that it had to be abandoned. Now the ruins and old Pisan church form an incongruous counterpoint to the space-age architecture of Poretta airport across the fields, whose constant traffic – both overhead and along the road – detracts somewhat from the forlorn beauty of the place. The houses, baths and basilica are now too tumbledown to be of great interest, but the square **baptistry** has a remarkable mosaic floor decorated with dancing dolphins and fish looped around a bearded Neptune – Christianized pagan images representing the Four Rivers of Paradise.

Adjacent to Mariana stands the church of Santa Maria Assunta, commonly known as **La Canonica**. Erected in 1119 close to the old capital of Biguglia, it is the finest of around three hundred churches built by the Pisans in their effort to evangelize the island. The perfectly proportioned edifice, modelled on a Roman basilica, is decorated outside with Corinthian capitals plundered from the main Mariana site and with plates of Cap Corse marble, their delicate pink and yellow ochre hues fusing to stunning effect. Carvings of animals and Celtic-like geometric bands also embellish the arch above the door. The interior has been restored in a very plain style, and is used for concerts and for Mass on religious festivals.

Marooned in muddy fields about 300m to the south of La Canonica stands **San Parteo**, built in the eleventh and twelfth centuries over the site of a pagan burial ground. A smaller church than La Canonica, it also displays some elegant arcading and stone sculpture – on the south side, the door lintel is supported by two writhing beasts reaching to a central tree, a motif of Oriental origins.

North of Bastia: Cap Corse

Until Napoleon III had a corniche coach road built around **Cap Corse** in the nineteenth century, the promontory was effectively cut off from the rest of the island, relying on Italian maritime traffic for its income – hence its distinctive Tuscan dialect. Ruled by feudal lords who retained substantial independence from the island's governors, it maintained a peaceful detachment that greatly influenced the character of the Capicursini, or **Cap Corsins**. For all the changes brought by the modern world, Cap Corse still feels like a separate country.

Forty kilometres long and only fifteen across, the cape is divided by a spine of mountains called the Serra, which peaks at **Monte Stello**, 1307m above sea level. The coast on the **east side** of this divide is characterized by tiny ports or *marines*, tucked into gently sloping river mouths, alongside coves that become sandier as you go further north. The villages of the **western coast** are sited on rugged cliffs, high above the rough sea and tiny rocky inlets that can be glimpsed from the corniche roads.

Cap Corse remains relatively unspoiled by tourism: wild flowers grow in profusion on the mountainsides in spring, goats graze freely, fishing villages are quiet and traditional, and many of the inland slopes are occupied by vineyards, producing the fragrant **muscat wine** that's one of the cape's few sources of income. Hotels are relatively thin on the ground, with the highest concentration at **Macinaggio** and **Centuri-Port**, on either side of the northern tip.

Even more numerous than the Genoese watchtowers dotted along the shore of the cape are the **convents**, **churches** and in particular **Romanesque chapels** overlooking it. Cap Corse harboured some of the first Christian centres in Corsica, and this was the only region of the island where the Franciscan movement had any real influence. Elaborate marble **mausoleums** are also a common feature, often occupying lonely places on the inland hill-slopes and standing out strikingly white in a sea of green maquis.

Many people tackle the 100km corniche in a one-day tour from Bastia or St-Florent. A shorter alternative is to cut across the peninsula at Santa Severa, thereby getting a taste of the interior and a look at the spectacular **Tour de Sénèque**, where, according to popular legend, the Roman poet-philosopher Seneca spent his exiled years. Best of all, of course, would be to spend a few days here breaking the journey in some of the cape's atmospheric little hotels or B&Bs, exploring off-track villages, hunting out Pisan chapels and hidden vineyards, and walking the wilder stretches of coast in the far north.

Cap Corse transport

The main villages on Cap Corse are connected to Bastia's *gare routière* by **bus**. Services are fairly frequent during the summer, but drop off considerably

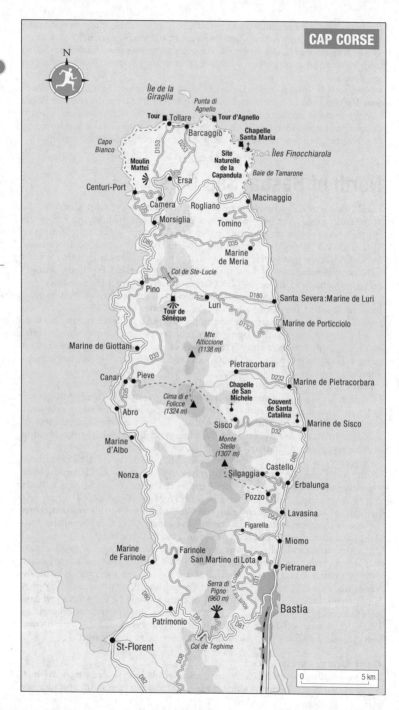

CAP CORSE

N

Île de la Giraglia

Punta di Agnello

Tour ■ Tollare
Tour d'Agnello
Barcaggio

Chapelle Santa Maria †

Capo Bianco

Moulin Mattei

Site Naturelle de la Capandula

Îles Finocchiarola

Baie de Tamarone

Centuri-Port

Ersa

Camera

Rogliano

Macinaggio

Morsiglia

Tomino

Marine de Meria

Col de Ste-Lucie

Pino

Luri

Santa Severa : Marine de Luri

Tour de Sénèque

Marine de Porticciolo

Marine de Giottani

Mte Alticcione (1138 m)

Pietracorbara

Canari
Pieve

Marine de Pietracorbara

Chapelle de San Michele †

Cima di e Folicce (1324 m)

Couvent de Santa Catalina †

Abro

Sisco

Marine de Sisco

Marine d'Albo

Monte Stello (1307 m)

Castello

Silgaggia

Erbalunga

Nonza

Pozzo

Lavasina

Figarella

Miomo

Marine de Farinole

Farinole

San Martino di Lota

Pietranera

Serra di Pigno (960 m)

ROUTE DE LA CORNICHE

Bastia

Patrimonio

St-Florent

Col de Teghime

0   5 km

Cap Corse driving tips

If you're driving on Cap Corse, bear in mind that **petrol stations** are few and far between, so fill up whenever you can: there are pumps in Bastia, St-Florent and Macinaggio. It's also worth noting that by heading in an **anti-clockwise direction**, you'll be on the outside lane of the road all the way around (local driving styles are especially perilous along the windy west coast, where there's little room for error if you're forced to suddenly *serrer à droite*). However, photographers may want to proceed in the opposite direction to benefit from the early-morning and late-evening light.

between October and May. Running up the east coast to Pietracorbara, the Bastia municipal bus company, SAB (℡04 95 31 06 65, Ⓦwww.bastiabus.com), lays on between six and nine services from Monday to Saturday in June–Sept, the first departing at 6.30am. Transports Micheli (℡04 95 35 14 64) also runs two daily services all the way to Macinaggio. Check all timings before departure at the Bastia tourist office or online at Ⓦwww.corsicabus.org.

A brief history of Cap Corse

Inhabited by various ancient civilizations – the Phoenicians, Greeks and Romans were all here – Cap Corse became significant in the tenth century, when the da Massa lords came over from Pisa and established fiefdoms across the region. By the following century Genoese settlers were being drawn to the cape's vineyards, and after Genoa's trouncing of Pisa at the Battle of Meloria in 1284, the feudal lords of Cap Corse became important – if intermittent – allies of the island's new rulers. Two local families shared most of the cape from this time – the da Mare clan held the north, whilst the da Gentile ruled the south, a situation that lasted into the late eighteenth century, when the French gained control of the island.

Although subject to the Genoese, the lords of Cap Corse were allowed a certain autonomy; largely ignored by the rest of the island, and well positioned for trading with the French and Tuscan ports, they were able to control their profits to a greater extent than their compatriots in the south. By the seventeenth century, Cap Corse was economically more successful than any other region in Corsica, but **piracy** was a huge problem for its tiny ports, which is why the coast is dotted with some thirty fortified watch-towers (see box, p.95).

The late eighteenth and early nineteenth centuries saw an upsurge in emigration from the cape, as a shortage of agricultural land (brought about by a sharp rise in population) forced thousands of Capicursini to seek their fortunes in the colonies of South America and the Caribbean. Many of the emigrants grew rich on gold prospecting and coffee or sugar planting, and in time returned home to live in large villas, or *palazzi*, erected on their ancestral land. Known as *les maisons d'Américains*, these ostentatious country mansions, with their colonial-style colonnades and arches, lend a distinctively Central or South American feel to villages such as Rogliano, Morsiglia and Pino. Most are still in use, and during the summer welcome families from Puerto Rico or Venezuela, where Corsican colonies still exist – indeed, one former Venezuelan president was a Corsican.

Today, although *capcorsin* wine is enjoying a minor revival, tourism has become the only real source of income. So far, however, it has been slow to develop, and there are few spots where concrete mars the views.

The eastern cape

The **east coast** of the cape progresses from tightly packed villas immediately outside Bastia to fishing villages such as **Erbalunga** and **Porticciolo**, and lonely *marines* such as **Pietracorbara** in the north. The D80, which winds all the way around Cap Corse to St-Florent along the course of the old Napoleonic cart track, is mostly built up within the first 5km or so of Bastia, although you can bypass the worst of the initial conurbation by following the wonderful **Route de la Corniche** (or Corniche Supérieure), which contours for 19km around the mountainside between the hamlet of Cardo (immediately above Bastia) and San Martino di Lota, rejoining the coastal D80 again at Miomo. From its average altitude of 350m, the route affords superb views over the town and Ligurian Sea out to the Tuscan islands of Elba and Monte Cristo. The easiest way to pick it up is to head west (left) from the top of place St-Nicolas, past the train station and straight up the hill; keep to the main road, bearing right onto the D231/D31 towards **Guaitella/Ville-di-Pietrabugno**.

San Martino di Lota

Once up on the corniche proper, the first village of note you pass through is **SAN MARTINO DI LOTA**, a typically *capcorsin* cluster of schist cottages stacked in terraces below a weathered church square. With your own transport, you might consider staying here rather than in Bastia: the village and its outlying hamlets hold a surprisingly wide choice of **accommodation**, from a no-frills Corsican *auberge* to an upmarket B&B in a splendid old *palazzo* – and there's a correspondingly broad selection of places **to eat**.

Château Cagninacci 2km west of San Martino di Lota (look for the sign) ☎06 78 29 03 94, ⓦ www.chateaucagninacci.com. One of the few bona fide *maison d'Américains* you can stay in as a paying guest, set in a seventeenth-century Capuchin chapel and friary which was converted in 1906 into a handsome *palazzo* by a local who had made his fortune in Venezuela. His descendants still live here, offering some upstairs rooms as *chambres d'hôtes*. The property, with its Tuscan arches, cloisters and grand interiors, oozes period charm. ❻–❼

Chez Elise & Gilles Medori in the hamlet of Figarella, 5km north along the corniche from San Martino ☎04 95 33 25 65, ⓦ www.medori.net. Simple B&B accommodation in one of the Cap's prettiest stone villages. The rooms (from €45 per night for two) have original chestnut wood beams and antique beds, with windows framing idyllic views down the mountain. Elise Medori is half English, so you get a decent cup of tea for breakfast. The family also let out well-equipped self-catering gîtes with lovely garden terraces at inexpensive weekly rates. ❸

La Corniche Sa Martino di Lota ☎04 95 31 40 98, ⓕ04 95 32 37 69, ⓦ www.hotel-lacorniche .com. Sunny rooms with superb vistas over schist rooftops and green hillsides to a pool and the sea. Part of the Logis de France chain, so rates are very reasonable (from €55 for a double in June). Bastiais drive out in droves for the restaurant's cordon bleu cooking – a mixture of old family recipes (on a €26 *menu Corse*) and classy Continental dishes (on the €45 *menu de découverte*). When booking, ask for a table on the terrace under one of the umbrella pines. ❺–❻

Maison Sainte-Hyacinth on the opposite flank of the valley from San Martino, 3km inland from Miomo on the eastern Cape ☎04 95 33 28 29. Bright, modern, comfortable en-suite rooms (€45–60, or bunk-bedded "box" dorms from €15) in a convent staffed by three friendly Polish nuns and their helpers. There's also a relaxing café-bar and refectory offering simple, inexpensive meals, all set in three acres of attractively landscaped gardens. Complimentary shuttle bus from Bastia available if you book in advance. Open all year. ❸–❹

Erbalunga

Built along a rocky promontory 9km north of Bastia, the small honey-pot port of **ERBALUNGA** is the highlight of the east coast, with its old stone buildings stacked like crooked boxes behind a cosy harbour and ruined

Genoese watchtower. A little colony of French artists lived here in the 1920s, perhaps drawn by the fact that the ancestors of the poet Paul Valéry came from the village, which has continued to attract a steady stream of admirers ever since. During the winter, well-to-do Bastiais frequent the harbourside restaurants, while in summer Erbalunga is transformed into a veritable cultural enclave, with concerts and art exhibitions adding a spark to the local nightlife.

A port since the time of the Phoenicians, Erbalunga was once a more important trading centre than Bastia or Ajaccio. With the increasing exportation of wine and olive oil in the eleventh century, it became the capital of an independent village state, ruled by the da Gentile family, who lived in the *palazzo* that dominates **place de Gaulle**. Its ascendancy came to an end in the 1550s, when long-running conflicts within the da Gentile camp finally broke the family's hold on this part of the cape, and in 1557 French troops destroyed the port, reducing the fifteenth-century tower to the ruined state it's in today.

Erbalunga is famous for its **Good Friday procession** known as the **Cerca** (Search), which has evolved from an ancient fertility rite. Starting at Église St-Érasme, at the entrance to the village, a procession of hooded penitents covers a distance of 14km, passing through the hamlets of Pozzo, Poretto and Silgaggia in the mountains and picking up people on the way. At nightfall, back in Erbalunga, the penitents form a spiral known as the *Granitola* (Snail); candles held high, they move to place de Gaulle and the spiral unwinds, while a separate part of the procession forms the shape of the cross.

Practicalities

Most of the village is closed to vehicles, but there's a **car park** on the left-hand side of the main road from Bastia, where the regular SAB **bus** from place St-Nicolas stops. From here, the harbour is reached through place de Gaulle, where the *mairie* and the *palazzo* Gentile stand side by side. On the quayside, a couple of **bars** shaded by an enormous chestnut tree look out across the water to the tower.

The village's one **hotel**, the gorgeous 🎕 *Castel Brando* (☎04 95 30 10 30, ⓦwww.castelbrando.com; April to mid-Oct; ❼–❾), stands at the entrance to the square, shaded by a curtain of mature date palms, like the backdrop to a classic Visconti movie. It's an elegant, old, stone-floored *palazzo* with a lovely pool and its own car park. Period furniture and antique Corsican engravings fill the rooms and apartments, which are all air conditioned; those on the top floor have great views. Rates soar in July and August, but at other times you can spend the night here for under €110. Filling buffet breakfasts (€12) are served al fresco in the courtyard.

Pick of the harbourside **restaurants** is the renowned 🎕 *Le Pirate* (☎04 95 33 24 20, ⓦwww.restaurantlepirate.com; Easter to Oct), for whose *haute gastronomie* well-heeled Bastiais flock here throughout the year. Local seafood and meat delicacies, such as braised *cabri* (suckling kid) or lobster tagliatelli served with wild asparagus, dominate their menu (€29–35/60–90 for lunch/dinner); fancier à la carte courses range from €26 to €75 and wind up with a choice of sublime desserts, while the wine list gathers together all the island's best *vignerons*. A more down-to-earth and affordable option is *A Piazzetta* (☎04 95 33 28 69), in the tiny square behind the harbour, which does quality pizzas, veal in Cap Corse liqueur, excellent *moules-frites* and possibly Corsica's best sorbets; count on €20–25 for three courses, plus wine.

Castello

The thirteenth-century castle at **CASTELLO**, one of the many bases of the da Gentile family, stands 2km inland from Erbalunga, beyond the hamlet of

Monte Stello

The starting point for the climb up **Monte Stello** (1307m), the highest peak on Cap Corse, is the medieval hamlet of **Pozzo**, 3km from Erbalunga. From the summit, a superb panorama extends west across Golfe de St-Florent to encompass the island's main peaks, and east across the sea to the Tuscan coast. To enjoy the views and avoid the worst of the heat, though, you'll have to set off early in the morning: cloud invariably obscures the top of Monte Stello from 11am onwards. Allow around five hours for the round trip.

From Pozzo's square, a sign marked "Monte Stello 3h" points the way through the houses into the maquis, where the trail starts off clearly marked by arrows and daubs of blue paint. The first section of the hike climbs steeply west into the deep Arega stream valley, via the **bergeries de Teghime**, reaching the windswept **Bocca di Santa Maria** pass, a distinctive niche in the Cap's watershed where you get your first hard-earned glimpse of the Golfe de St-Florent after around 1 hour 30 minutes. From here it's another 1 hour 40 minutes and a 169-metre haul to the summit. Return is by the same route.

For this walk we strongly recommend you take along IGN map #4347 OT Cap Corse. While most of the path is well waymarked, or cairned towards the summit, the maquis has overtaken some stretches, making it hard to follow in places.

Mausoleo. This ghostly village, dominated by the now-ruined castle, was the scene of a family feud that lasted a hundred years and split the da Gentile clan into two.

To the south of the village on the road to **Silgaggia** stands the Romanesque chapel of **Notre-Dame-des-Neiges/Santa Maria di e Nevi**. Dating from the tenth century, it contains the oldest known **frescoes** in Corsica, beautiful portraits of saints painted in 1386. Having been vandalized in 2001, the chapel is no longer open to casual visitors, but on Wednesdays in July and August you can book on to organized tours run by a local guide, M. Defendine (☎06 86 78 02 38; 2hr 15min; €12, children free), which start from Bastia or Erbalunga. Outside July and August, tours do run, but they're less regular – phone for more information (if your French isn't that fluent, ask the management of the *Hôtel Castel Brando* in Erbalunga for help).

Sisco

The landscape takes on a more desolate aspect as the coast road approaches **Sisco**, 6km north of Erbalunga, a *commune* made up of several hamlets scattered over the mountainside and the tiny seaside village of **MARINE DE SISCO**. The latter tumbles to a sandy beach, backed by a cluster of restaurants and two pleasant hotels. Of the pair, the old-fashioned *Hôtel de la Marine* (aka "*Chez Giuseppi*"; ☎04 95 35 21 04; Easter to Sept; ❸) is the less expensive, comprising rooms in terraced chalets that open onto a quiet garden behind the beach. There's no restaurant, but breakfast is served on the stone-floored veranda of the main house. If it's full, try the more modern *U Pozzu*, opposite (☎04 95 35 21 17, ⓦwww.u-pozzu.com; ❹–❻), some of whose (fully en-suite) rooms are darker and rather more cramped than others. Their restaurant offers a choice of two *menus fixes* (€16.50/20), with lots of fresh seafood à la carte (best accompanied by a bottle of rosé from the Lina Venturi-Pieretti vineyard at nearby Luri).

An altogether more authentically Corsican place **to eat** stands 200m up the lane running inland from *U Pozzu*. In a small no-frills ground-floor restaurant, *A Stalla Sischese* (☎04 95 35 26 34, ⓦwww.a-stalla-sischese.com), you can sample carefully prepared local specialities, including a succulent seafood salad, chestnut fritters, *ravioli al brocciu*, and a melt-in-the-mouth fresh *fiadone*. There's a choice of three menus (€18.50/22/28) at lunchtime, though only the pricier one is available in the evenings. Advance reservation is recommended. They also offer ten smart, though slightly overpriced, **rooms** (❺).

While in the area it's worth finding the time to visit the beautiful Roman-esque **Chapelle de San Michele**, hidden on a hillside inland. From the main road, head 7km west up the D32 past *A Stalla Sischese* as far as the large but unremarkable Église St-Martin, where a right-hand turn signposted to San Michele contours north to the start of a rocky track (on your left), at the end of which you'll find the chapel. Built in 1030 by Pisan masons, the tiny church occupies a spectacular windswept hillside overlooking the Marine de Sisco, with Pietracorbara a misty ridge of buildings stretching to the north. On September 29, the Festival of St Michael attracts pilgrims up from the surrounding hamlets to celebrate Mass here.

Pietracorbara

The next village along the cape is **PIETRACORBARA (Petracurbara)**, 18km north of Bastia, whose beautiful beach – the only one of fine white sand on the cape – marks the end of a broad river valley carpeted in shimmering reed banks. Overlooked by a ruined Genoese tower are a handful of houses, among them the *Hôtel-Restaurant Macchia e Mare* (☎04 95 35 21 26, ⓦwww .macchia-e-mare.com; ❺–❼), a modern two-star with panoramic views over the bay from its north-facing restaurant terrace, although only four of the eight rooms overlook the sea. For campers there's the pricey but very well set-up *Camping La Pietra* (☎04 95 35 27 49), 300m from the beach, which has a small shop and bar.

Santa Severa

At the little *marine* of **SANTA SEVERA**, 2km north of Porticciolo, the D180 cuts across the cape to Luri and the Tour de Sénèque. The village holds less appeal than nearby Macinaggio, but it does possess one of the island's finest vineyards, the 🌿 **Domaine Venturi-Pieretti**, which has the distinction of being run by a woman – a rarity indeed for Corsica. At the little roadside *cave* just outside Santa Severa (April–Sept daily 10am–noon & 4.30–7pm) you can sample Lina Venturi-Pieretti's muscat, white, rosé and red, which in 1999 was the only *rouge corse* to be given three Hachette stars.

The northern cape

Macinaggio, northern terminus of the road along the east side of the cape, is also the largest settlement north of Bastia, with a handful of hotels and restau-rants, and one of the cape's few petrol stations. The land between Macinaggio and **Barcaggio**, at the very tip of Corsica, forms part of a protected zone called the **Site Naturel de la Capandula** and is a wonderful area to explore on foot, boasting some glorious **beaches**. Known as the "holy promontory" in Roman times because of its Christian settlements, the tip of the cape also has many ruined chapels, such as **Santa Maria**, near Macinaggio. Five kilometres inland, the eight hamlets of **Rogliano**, spectacularly spread out over the slopes, were for a few centuries the fief of the da Mare family, whose castles and towers lie dotted over the hills. On the western side of the northern tip, the chief focus of interest is picturesque **Centuri-Port**, where the much-photographed horseshoe-shaped harbour shelters a string of seafood restaurants and the colourful boats that service them.

The only **bus** service to this somewhat isolated area is SAB's (☎04 95 35 06 65) service to Macinaggio, which runs two to three times daily from June to September and three times weekly from October to May from Bastia's *gare routière*.

Macinaggio

A port since Roman times, well-sheltered **MACINAGGIO** (**Macinaghju**) was developed by the Genoese in 1620 for the export of olive oil and wine to the Italian peninsula, and in later years played its part in the wider history of the island. **Pascal Paoli** landed here in 1790 after his exile in England, whereupon he kissed the ground and uttered the words "*O ma patrie, je t'ai quitté esclave, je te retrouve libre*" ("Oh my country, I left you as a slave, I rediscover you a free man") – a plaque commemorating the event adorns the wall above the ship chandlers. **Napoleon** also stopped here on his way to Bastia as he fled from the Paolists in 1793, and in 1869 the empress Eugénie was forced by a storm to disembark on her way back from the opening of the Suez Canal, before taking refuge in Rogliano – she had such a bad journey up the hill that on her return she ordered a new road to be constructed, known ever since as the "Chemin de l'Impératrice". There's not much of a historic patina to the place nowadays, but with its turquoise marina, line of seafront awnings and end-of-the-world feel, Macinaggio has a certain appeal; it also lies within comfortable walking distance of some of the island's most beautiful coastal scenery.

Another reason to linger here is to sample the superb **Clos Nicrosi** wines, grown in the terraces below Rogliano. Of all Corsica's top AOC labels, it's perhaps the hardest to find. But at their little shop on the north side of the Rogliano road, opposite the *U Ricordu* hotel, you can taste the *domaine's* famously distinctive white and reds, and heavily scented muscat, all of which benefit from the schist soil and proximity of the sea to the vineyards. It's also one of the few wineries on the island to still produce *rappu*, a ruby-coloured *aperitif* made in a similar way to muscat.

Practicalities

Macinaggio has a very helpful little **tourist office** (Mon–Sat 9am–noon & 2–7pm, Sun 9am–noon, Oct–May closed Sat pm & Sun; ☎04 95 35 40 34, Ⓦwww.ot-rogliano-macinaggio.com), on the first floor of a building on the harbourside, where you can pick up free map-leaflets for the Sentier du Douanier. They also keep timetables for the **boat trips** that run out to the nearby islands and beaches (see p.80). The village has two **shops**: the first, a small grocer's, opposite the tourist office, and the second, a much larger Spar minimarket, on the other side of Macinaggio, just off the Rogliano road (before the Close Nicrosi *cave*). On the opposite side of the road to the Spar, you'll also find a launderette, plus a cycle hire place, Loc' Ago (☎06 19 47 77 13).

The least expensive **accommodation** in Macinaggio is the *Hôtel des Îles*, opposite the marina (☎04 95 35 43 02; ❹), which also has a serviceable restaurant on its ground floor. All the rooms, though tiny, have showers and toilets; those at the front of the building overlook the port but get noisy at night, being above the most popular bar in the resort, so if you're a light sleeper ask for a room at the back. Otherwise try the more modern *U Libecciu*, down the lane leading from the marina to the plage de Tamarone (☎04 95 35 43 22, Ⓦwww .u-libecciu.com; April–Oct; ❺–❼); it occupies a modern building with no view to speak of, but the rooms are spacious. The pricier three-star *U Ricordu*, on the south side of the road to Rogliano (☎04 95 35 40 20, Ⓦwww.hotel-uricordu .com; March–Sept; ❻–❼), is the most luxurious option hereabouts, with a swimming pool, sauna and tennis courts.

Macinaggio's only **campsite**, *U Stazzu*, lies 1km north of the harbour and is signposted off the Rogliano road (☏04 95 35 43 76; May to mid-Sept). The ground is like rock, but it's cheap and there's ample shade and easy access to the nearby **beach**; the site's little café-pizzeria serves particularly good breakfasts and pizzas.

Besides the hotel **restaurants** listed above, decent places to eat in Macinaggio include the *Pizzeria San Columbu*, at the end of the port facing out to sea, which does a delicious seafood pizza for under €10. For a taste of local seafood, you won't do better than Le Vela d'Oro (☏04 95 35 41 46), tucked away down a narrow alleyway running off the little square opposite the marina. Offering menus from €15, they serve nothing but the freshest local fish – including crayfish in home-made spaghetti – in a cosy dining room decorated with old nautical maps. The other place worth trying is *Osteria di u Portu* (☏04 95 35 40 49; April–Sept), facing the marina. An offshoot of the excellent *A Stalla Sischese* in Sisco, it serves copious portions of finely prepared Corsican cuisine – fish off local boats, suckling lamb stew and tender free-range veal – at honest prices.

Site Naturel de la Capandula

Macinaggio's town beach tends to be inundated with smelly posidonia seaweed, but you can get to some stunning stretches of white sand and clear sea by following the track at the north end of the marina (past the campsite) to the **Site Naturel de la Capandula**. Covering 3.8 square kilometres of windswept maquis and pristine coast between Macinaggio and Bracaggio, the reserve, which encompasses the deserted Îles Finocchiarola and the Île de la Giraglia, can only be crossed on foot, via a coastal path that takes you through some wild scenery.

Although Capandula is off limits to motor vehicles, it is possible to drive the 2km from Macinaggio to the **Baie de Tamarone**, whose deep clear waters make it ideal for diving and snorkelling. There's a small *paillote* here serving overpriced meals and drinks, but no toilets or drinking water. Note that it's illegal to camp anywhere in the reserve; a warden hangs around outside the *paillote* to make sure no one tries.

The adjacent car park here marks the start of the popular coastal walk through the reserve, known as the **Sentier du Douanier** (see box below) after the Genoese customs officials who originally cut the path. For the less adventurous, there's a shorter **circular route** (1hr 30min–2hr), which begins at the Baie de

---

Le Sentier du Douanier

The roadless northern tip of Cap Corse is among the few stretches of coastline on the island crossed by a waymarked path, **Le Sentier du Douanier**. Following the yellow splashes of paint, it's possible to follow it all the way from Macinaggio to Centuri-Port (or vice versa) in seven to eight hours, taking in the picturesque Santa Maria and Agnello towers en route.

Although you can complete the *sentier* in a single long day, most walkers prefer to take their time, overnighting at Barcaggio (3hr) or Tollare (45min further on) before tackling the final, most spectacular stretch to Centuri-Port (3hr).

The **tourist office** in Macinaggio will furnish you with a free **map** and route description; otherwise get hold of a copy of IGN #4347 OT, which covers the entire path. Being mostly flat, the route presents no great physical challenges, although you should be aware of the force of the sun along this stretch of coast. In July and August, set off at dawn and aim to rest up in the shade (of which there's precious little) between 11.30am and 4pm. **Water** can also be a problem as there are no springs: take along at least three litres per person for each of the two *étapes*.

Tamarone and takes in most of Capandula's highlights. From the car park, follow the Sentier du Douanier along the line of the bay and around the headland to a second beach, **plage des Îles**. The sprinkling of barren islets offshore is known as the **Îles Finocchiarola**, after the wild fennel that grows in abundance over the rocks in the area. Hundreds of gulls and cormorants nest on this strip of coast, which during March and June also serves as a stopoff for migrating **birds** from North Africa. If you're here at this time, look out for the elusive Audouin's gull, with its distinctive red bill encircled by a black band. Only 2500 pairs still survive in the Mediterranean, and they are a protected species here. Other types you might expect to see are the more common herring gull; the black-headed Mediterranean gull; and perhaps a Manx or Cory's shearwater. The islets are a nature reserve, visitable only between March and August, and fires and camping are strictly forbidden. **Boat excursions** (€19.50) aboard the *San Paulu* (☎04 95 35 07 09) run from mid-June until early September from the marina in Macinaggio. The round trip includes a stop on the largest islet for a spot of birdwatching.

The boat also calls at a stunning arc of turquoise sea known as the **Rade de Santa Maria**, which can also be reached by a half-hour walk from the Baie de Tamarone. Just behind it, raised on the foundations of a sixth-century church, stands the **Chapelle Santa Maria**, a tenth-century and a twelfth-century chapel merged into one. Following recent acts of vandalism the building is now locked up and in dire need of renovation.

The bay's other distinctive landmark is the huge **Tour de Santa Maria**. Dramatically cleft in half and entirely surrounded by water, the ruined three-storeyed building was one of three *torri* built on the northern tip of the cape by the Genoese in the sixteenth century (the others are at Tollare and Barcaggio) as lookout posts against Moorish pirates (see box, p.95). As Macinaggio grew in importance, the towers were also used by health and customs officers, who controlled the maritime traffic with Genoa. Pascal Paoli established his garrison here in 1761, having failed in his attempt to take Macinaggio, and contemplated building a rival port. Six years later, to undermine Genoa's position in the area, Paoli sent two hundred men under the command of Achille Murati to capture the neighbouring island of Capraia, which had belonged to Genoa since 1507. Murati's relatively easy victory marked the beginning of the downfall of the Genoese in Corsica.

A short way beyond the tower lie two beautiful little beaches – **Cala Genovese** and **Cala Francese** – both shining turquoise and well sheltered, though prone to drifts of posidonia. If, instead of pressing on north, you turn south from the Chapelle Santa Maria and follow the track past a vine-covered hillside for around thirty minutes, you'll eventually arrive back at the Baie de Tamarone. Note that this circular walk can also be done in a clockwise direction by turning left out of the Tamarone car park instead of right at the start of the hike, and following the track inland to the chapel, and thence around the coast.

Rogliano

A cluster of schist-tiled hamlets scattered over a lush valley below the crags of Monte Poggio, **ROGLIANO** (Ruglianu), 7km up a series of hairpin bends from Macinaggio, ranks among the most picturesque *communes* in Corsica. Its constituent hamlets – Bettolacce, Olivo, Magna, Soprana, Vignale, Sottana and Campiano – were the base of the da Mare lords from the twelfth to the sixteenth century, and the ruins of their convents, towers and castles are distri-buted among them. However, the village's name, derived from the Latin Pagus Aurelianus, dates from the Roman era, when Rogliano presided over a busy trade with the Italian coast, while the oldest vines on the hillside are known to be of Carthaginian origin.

The easternmost and largest hamlet, **BETTOLACCE**, is dominated by the privately owned **Tour Franceschi**, an enormous round tower in remarkable condition. It also boasts an excellent **hotel**, the *Auberge Sant'Agnellu*, opposite (℡04 95 35 40 59, Ⓦwww.hotel-usantagnellu.com; mid-April to mid-Oct; ❼), whose terracotta- and blue-washed facades overlook the valley. There's a wonderful terrace making the most of the views, where you can enjoy fine

▲ Cap Corse watchtower

cuisine du terroir, prepared with ingredients from the farm of the *patron*, M. Albertini's, brother: home-made chestnut pâté, *cannelloni al brocciu* and fragrant *tarte aux herbes* for vegetarians.

Isolated in the valley some 500m beneath Bettolacce stands the ruined sixteenth-century **Église St-Côme-et-St-Damien**, accessible via the path leading opposite *Auberge Sant'Agnellu*. A curious rectangular bell tower stands separated from the nave, which is the oldest part of the church. **VIGNALE**, the hamlet above Bettolacce, is dominated by the crumbling ruins of the **Castello di San Colombano**, from where there's a magnificent view across the valley to Macinaggio. The castle was built in the twelfth century and became known as *U Castelacciu* (The Bad Castle) in the sixteenth, when Giacomo Santa da Mare abandoned the Genoese cause, switched his allegiances to Sampiero Corso and defected to the Franco-Turkish army. In 1553 the Genoese retaliated by destroying the castle, which was later restored, but then burned down in 1947.

Barcaggio

To get to the northernmost tip of Corsica, continue west along the D80 for about 5km until you reach **Ersa**, where the D253 twists off northwards to **BARCAGGIO**, giving breathtaking views of the Île de la Giraglia. The *marine* is tiny – just a jetty and a cluster of houses built from the greenish local schist – but the setting is sublime and the **beach** is wild and windswept, curving east of the village to a headland crowned by a Genoese watchtower and set against a backdrop of austere, maquis-covered hills which are oddly reminiscent of the Scottish Highlands. You can leave your vehicle in the village **car park** (also a park for camper vans), from where a track leads through the dunes to a crystalline sea.

The *La Giraglia* **hotel** (☎04 95 35 60 54, ⓕ04 95 35 65 92; April–Sept; no credit cards; ❺) occupies a fantastic location at the north end of the village overlooking the tiny harbour (rooms 25 & 26 have the best views), though it's expensive for what it offers. The same can't be said of the ♣ *U Fanale* **restaurant** (☎04 95 35 62 72, ⓦwww.u-fanale.com), next to the harbour, which serves sublime local seafood straight off the boats on a covered terrace looking out to the Île de la Giraglia. Run by a welcoming Anglo-Corsican family, it's the kind of place you dream of dining at but rarely encounter in Corsica: perfectly situated, genuinely friendly and with a creative menu. At lunchtime they do *grandes assiettes* of colourful Mediterranean salads (€15, including a drink), and *suggestions du midi* (€10–17.50) such as rockfish soup, *soufflé roulé* with red peppers and *brocciu*, and grilled fish with delicious chips made from polenta flour. The evening menu is more gastronomic (spider-crab and avocado tart; pears in Cap Corse liqueur with prunes marinated in green tea); count on €30–50 à la carte for three courses.

Tollare

The northern extremity of Corsica is marked by the **Île de la Giraglia**, a green islet whose bare, rocky slopes sport a lighthouse and a sixteenth-century Genoese tower. The nearest settlement is **TOLLARE**, a neglected little coastal village of squat grey fishing cottages clustered around a tiny harbour and watch-tower, where there's neither a hotel nor a restaurant, but which possesses a windswept charm. Apart from the handful of holidaymakers who rent houses in the summer, hardly anyone ventures out here. You can, however, park up and paddle on the hamlet's tiny pebble beach, or follow the footpath winding west along up the hillside to the lighthouse at Capo Bianco and on to Centuri-Port – the most dramatic stretch of the Sentier du Douanier coast path (see p.83).

Col de Serra

Further west along the main road, it's worth pulling over at the **Col de Serra** (365m) to admire the views and walk up to the famous **Moulin Mattei**, the round building with the coloured tiled roof on the hill above the road. Some considerate soul has installed a stone picnic table in the lee of this former windmill (restored in the 1930s by the Maison Mattei as a tasting place for their quinine-rich aperitif, Cap Corse), from whose terrace you can admire the impressive panorama along the peninsula's north and west coasts.

Centuri-Port

When writer James Boswell arrived here from England in 1765 (see box, p.208), the former Roman settlement of **CENTURI-PORT** was a tiny fishing village, recommended to him for its peaceful detachment from the dangerous turmoil of the rest of Corsica. Not much has changed since Boswell's time; despite the annual tourist influx, and the rows of seasonal cafés and restaurants that have sprung up to cater for them, the village's harbour still presents an arresting spectacle, its grey stone walls highlighted by the green serpentine roofs of the encircling cottages. The twenty or so boats bobbing around it are evidence of the village's ailing fishing industry. In years past, the local fleet was able to row to the fishing grounds just beyond the harbour wall and ceased work early in the autumn so as not to impinge on the lobsters' breeding season. But increased demand, modern nets and pollution from the asbestos mine at nearby Canari (see p.86) have all but wiped out inshore sea life, and these days the motorized boats are forced two or more hours further out, for ever-diminishing returns.

The only drawback to the settlement is that the small pebble-**beach** to the south is disappointingly grubby and not ideal for sunbathing. You can, however, reach some of the most pristine coast on the island if you're prepared to walk. Centuri-Port stands at the start of the wonderful **Sentier du Douanier** (see box, p.79), the former customs officers' path, which winds all the way to Macinaggio via Tollare and Barcaggio in seven to eight hours.

Practicalities

There are plenty of small hotels occupying the former fishers' cottages around the quay. Try the *Du Pêcheur*, the salmon-coloured building at the back of the harbour (☎04 95 35 60 14; Easter to mid-Nov; ❺–❼); its rooms, though showing signs of wear and tear, are agreeably cool, with thick stone walls and green shutters on the windows, and it has a popular restaurant on the ground floor. If it's full, try *Hôtel La Jetée*, to the left on the road as you arrive in Centuri (☎04 95 35 64 46, ⓕ04 95 35 64 18; April–Sept; ❸), whose rooms are more modern and for the most part without sea views, but the cheapest in the village during high season. The ⚜ *Vieux Moulin* (☎04 95 35 60 15, ⓦwww.le-vieux -moulin.net; March–Oct; ❼), opposite, is the most stylish option: a converted *maison d'Americains* with a wonderful terrace and attractively furnished en-suite rooms. For **campers**, choice is limited to the *Camping l'Isolettu*, 400m south along the D35 (☎04 95 35 62 81, ⓕ04 95 35 63 63; May–Oct), five-minutes' walk from Centuri's scruffy little pebble beach.

Among the many **restaurants** around the port, two stand out. Next door to the *Hôtel La Jetée*, the *U Cabalu di Mare* offers a cheap and cheerful selection of pizzas, omelettes, salads, sandwiches and three or four *plats du jour*, including the least expensive locally caught fish in town, which you can enjoy on a stone terrace above the harbour or indoors in a small bistro. The service is particularly friendly and you get a complimentary aperitif on arrival. For more serious *capcorsine* cuisine, *A Macciotta* (aka *Chez Sker*; ☎04 95 35 64 12), on the lane running uphill from the rear of the harbour (to the left if you're facing away from the sea), is the best choice. *Menus fixes* (€17.50–23) feature local delicacies such as anemones, squid salad and sea bass baked or pan-fried with fennel, but for the full monty, splash out on the €45 *menu langouste*, offering local lobster (cooked to perfection and served with home-made mayonnaise). Both their terrace and cavernous fisherman's cottage interior can be cramped, so get there early.

The western cape

An altogether more sombre and dramatic landscape takes over once you've reached the western cape, with maquis-covered mountainsides plunging at increasingly steep angles into a coastline that's indented with few accessible coves. Winding high above the shore, the corniche route around it has terrified travellers since the time of Boswell who, having just arrived by boat in 1765, wrote in his journal: "*such a road I never saw. I was absolutely scrambling along the face of a rock overhanging the sea, upon a path sometimes not above a foot broad.*" The road's narrowest stretches are being gradually widened and upgraded, but the route remains a challenging drive. Stacked up the cliffsides above small *marines*, a string of schist villages interrupt the road south. Just after **Morsiglia** you can take a detour inland to see the **Tour de Sénèque**, while further south **Canari** holds another remarkable Romanesque church and a terrace with a superb view across the gulf. Just a few kilometres north of St-Florent, **Nonza** is perhaps the most photographed of all the *capcorsin* villages, perched high above a black sandy beach.

Morsiglia

With its medieval *torri* and terraced vineyards tumbling down an amphitheatre of hills to the sea, **MORSIGLIA** (Mursiglia) typifies the stark beauty of the western cape. Having suffered more than its share of emigration since the 1950s, the village is hopelessly depopulated these days, but warrants a stop to admire its three splendid watchtowers (the last of six that originally stood here) and well-preserved eighteenth- and nineteenth-century *palazzi*. In 1765, Boswell spent the second night of his Corsican adventure in one of them. The pompous young dilettante was "much surprised" to find his host Signor Antonetti's house "quite an Italian one, with very good furniture, prints, and copies of some of the famous pictures". On a rainy Sunday morning, he was equally amazed that the locals seemed "afraid of bad weather, to a degree of effeminacy", until it was pointed out to him the reason for this was that most owned only one coat. Nowadays, with water shortages threatening to squeeze out the hundred or so remaining villagers who live here year round, the downpours that all too rarely sweep across this exposed tip of the peninsula are greeted with greater enthusiasm.

The droughts have been particularly tough on Eugène Paoli, one of Corsica's most famous *viticulteurs*, whose vineyards at Morsiglia have been cultivated continuously by the same family since 1768. Signposted from the corniche road, the **Domaine Pietri**, in the hamlet of Mucchieta (May–Sept Mon–Sat 10am–noon & 4–7pm; ☎04 95 35 60 93 or 04 95 35 64 79), produces equal quantities of white, rosé and red, but is perhaps most renowned for the latter, while the peach-tinted muscat warrants the stop alone.

Tour de Sénèque

At the first road junction south of Morsiglia, an east turn off the corniche in the direction of Luri winds through pine woods to the Col de Ste-Lucie and thence up a badly potholed lane to the **Tour de Sénèque**. Set atop a pinnacle of black rock, the tower was built in the fifteenth century by the da Mare family on the spot where Seneca is said to have lived from 41 to 49 AD, having been exiled for seducing the Emperor Claudius' niece. His rampant misconduct didn't stop there. During his exile, Seneca reputedly once came down from his rock in an attempt to ravage the Corsican women, for which he was attacked with nettles – hence, or so it is said, the profusion of the plants around the base of the tower. Whilst here he wrote a few appropriately bitter verses about the place:

What can be found so bare, what so rugged all around as this rock? What more barren of provisions? What more rude as to its inhabitants? What in the very situation of the place more horrible? What in climate more intemperate? Yet there are more foreigners here than natives. So far then is a change of place from being disagreeable, that even this place has brought some people away from their country.

It's a thirty-minute climb through the woods to the tower – well worth the effort for the views, which extend to both coasts of the cape and over the Monte Stello massif (see box, p.76). To pick up the trail, follow the motorable dirt track from the deserted school at the end of the *piste* towards the radio transmitter above you in the woods, then bear left along the path that peels from it after about five minutes. From here, it's a stiff ten-minute climb through the trees to the top, with the last 20m or so over exposed rocks.

Luri

Continuing south from the Col de Ste-Lucie, you soon come to the *commune* of **Luri**, surrounded by a delightful landscape of lemon trees and vineyards. At **PIAZZA**, Luri's central hamlet, the seventeenth-century **Église St-Pierre** houses a late sixteenth-century depiction of the life of St Peter against a background showing the local castles a hundred years or so before it was painted – the one on the left is the Tour des Motti, a precursor of the Tour de Sénèque; that on the right is the Castello di San Colombano, at Rogliano.

In early July, Luri is the venue for Corsica's biggest wine fair, A Fiera di u Vinu, attracting vignerons and enthusiasts from across the island. The group that organizes the event, A Cunfraternita (Ⓦ www.acunfraternita.com), also runs a small museum featuring displays on Corsica's chequered wine-growing history (June–Sept Tues–Fri 10am–4.30pm; €3.50). Equally worth a diversion are the nearby Jardins Traditionnels du Cap Corse (daily Mon–Fri 10am–noon & 3–6pm; €4), where local volunteers have created an organic garden dedicated to preserving flowering plants and kitchen-garden vegetables once common on the cape, but nowadays disappearing – many of them were originally brought back by sailors and emigrants from South America in the nineteenth century.

Pino

A sense of the tropics pervades the air at **PINO** (Pinu), some 2km south of the turning for Luri. Palm trees grow up the cliff, and the houses, coloured pale pink, orange and yellow, feature turreted roofs and verandas. Among the grander *maisons d'Américains* is one built by Antoine Liccioni, who, like many of his generation, left the village vowing not to return until he was rich. Liccioni struck lucky, discovering seams of gold in both Venezuela and Brazil, and by the time he died it is said he owned half of Guyana.

Boswell, his luggage having been carried along the corniche on the heads of "a couple of stout women", arrived here in 1765, and promptly committed an atrocious gaffe: mistaking the house he was shown to for an inn rather than the home of a local worthy, he barked orders for what he wanted "with the tone which one uses in calling to the waiters at a tavern". His host, however, responded with un-Corsican equanimity and, instead of dumping the young aristo's dinner on his head, or worse, merely "smiled, saying with much calmness and good nature, *Una cosa dopo un altra, Signore*. One thing at a time, Sir".

You could stop in the village for a drink under the shade of the chestnut and plane trees, or follow the steep road from just outside the village down to the *marine*, where a fifteenth-century **Franciscan convent** lies half-hidden amongst a jungle of bamboo. Although its outward appearance is grim, try to get inside for a look at the faded fifteenth-century frescoes above the entrance, featuring the Virgin flanked by saints Francis and Bernard.

Canari and around

Two corniche roads wind in tandem between Pino and Canari, along one of the most dramatic stretches of the Cap Corse coastline. The higher of the pair, the D33, is the more scenic, skirting through a string of isolated hamlets en route to **Canari**, this area's largest *commune*. **Buses** run out here from Bastia (daily in summer with Transports Micheli ☏04 95 35 64 02; Mon & Wed year round with Transports Saoletti ☏04 95 37 84 05), but even in high summer the villages remain well off the tour coach trail.

Reason enough to make the detour off either corniche is the Romanesque chapel of **Santa Maria Assunta**, in the hamlet of **PIEVE**. Built at the end of the twelfth century and in an astonishingly good state of repair, it is noteworthy for the primitive sculpture lining the cornice beneath the roof – weird mask-like faces alongside strange beasts and stylized geometric patterns – among which fragments of pre-Roman carving were incorporated. The chapel is opened only once each year, on Ascension Day (Aug 15).

Pieve's other claim to fame is the little white campanile in its square, from where the astounding **views** attract a trickle of picnickers in season. Standing on the east side of the *place*, the *Au Bon Clocher* (☏04 95 37 80 15; ❸–❹) is a

---

The White Hell of Cap Corse

Amianthus is a rare, fibrous rock with fire-resistant properties that were first discovered by the ancient Greeks. They are thought to have wrapped bodies with it for cremation, to prevent human ashes mingling with those of the wood. Unfortunately for the Cap Corse coastline between Canari and Nonza, where it is found in prodigious quantities, the pale grey mineral also used to be an essential ingredient in asbestos. During the 1950s and early 1960s, one million tonnes of the stuff were mined annually here, in a complex that would later be dubbed by its 320 ex-employees as "the White Hell".

For a while, the mining boom looked set to reverse the fortunes of this economically disadvantaged peninsula. But when cheap Canadian exports undercut the price of Corsican amianthus in 1965, the Canari mine was forced to close. It was then that the long-term costs of the project started to become apparent. With 98 percent of the extraction from the mine classed as *stérile*, or slag, untold quantities of pulverized toxic rock had been dumped via a vast silo into the sea. The impact on the local marine environment – including precious fish stocks – was catastrophic. Whole beaches, notably at **Marine d'Albo** and **Nonza**, were also ruined for decades by the pollution.

Another more sinister problem emerged in the years after the mine's closure, as former workers started to fall ill with a disease called *svetose*. Although similar to silicosis and linked to prolonged inhalation of toxic mineral dust, the condition is not officially recognized as an industrial disease, which meant that when former miners started to die from it their families weren't covered by insurance or entitled to any compensation. To this day, no one knows exactly how many people died.

modest but congenial **hotel-restaurant**, offering simple rooms with sea views, showers, balconies and shared toilets. The restaurant downstairs serves mainly seafood specialities, ranging from expensive Centuri-Port lobster to a delicious fish soup that comes with mountains of croutons.

This area's accommodation highlight, however, is ⚜ *I Fioretti* (☎04 95 37 80 17 or 04 95 37 13 90, ⓦwww.ifioretti.com; ❹), a low-key heritage hotel occupying a restored Franciscan friary at the top of the hamlet, next to an ancient oak wood. Six former monks' cells have been converted into comfortable en-suite *chambres d'hôtes*, while three well-equipped *gîtes* offer self-catering apartments for longer stays. Throughout, vaulted ceilings, exposed beams and windows opening on to a secluded inner courtyard preserve the building's original atmosphere.

The *I Fioretti* makes an ideal base for a couple of longish day **walks**. The best of these is along the waymarked track up to **Cima di e Folicce** (1305m), the second-highest mountain on the cape. Following old transhumant paths up on to the watershed of the peninsula, this stiff three hour forty-five minute climb should be attempted only in fair weather, starting early in the morning so as to avoid the convection clouds which mask the high ridges from 11am onwards most days. IGN #4347 OT covers the area and is widely available at local shops in Nonza, Macinaggio and St-Florent.

South of Canari, the main corniche road cuts across a sheer mountainside horrendously disfigured by the Dantesque terraces of an **amianthus mine**, whose workings resulted in the dumping of untold quantities of toxic dust on the surrounding hillsides and beaches (see box opposite).

Nonza

Set high on a black rocky pinnacle that plunges vertically into the sea, **NONZA** is one of the highlights of the Cap Corse shoreline. The village was formerly the main stronghold of the da Gentile family, and the remains of the **fortress** still cling to the furthest rocks of the overhanging cliff. Nonza has a shady square, behind which you twist your way through stone-tiled houses and bougainvillea bushes to reach the ruined fortress and the more impressive green **watchtower** nearby. In 1768 the tower, one of the few on the island built in Paoli's time and not by the Genoese, witnessed one of the greatest con tricks in military history. The French, having succeeded in taking over the rest of Cap Corse, closed in on the Nonza garrison, which was under the command of one Captain Casella. Fearing that Casella's tenacity would lead them to their deaths, the Corsican troops absconded, leaving him to defend the tower single-handed. This he did, using a system of cables to maintain constant fire from a line of muskets and a single cannon, until the disheartened French offered a truce. Old Casella demanded that his army be allowed to parade out in dignity, and duly emerged alone and on crutches, brandishing his pistol, to the amazement of the besieging army.

Nonza is also famous for **Santa Julia**, patron saint of Corsica, who was martyred here in the fifth century. The story goes that she had been sold into slavery at Carthage and was being taken by ship to Gaul when the slavers arrived. A pagan festival was in progress, and when Julia refused to participate she was raped, tortured and crucified; the gruesome legend relates that her breasts were then cut off and thrown onto a stone, from which sprang two springs, now enshrined in a chapel by the beach. To get there, follow the sign on the right-hand side of the road before you enter the square, which points to the **Fontaine de Ste-Julie**, down by the rocks.

Reached by a flight of six hundred steps, the long **beach** is grey coloured as a result of pollution from the asbestos mine up the coast. The local council has banned bathing here (allegedly because of the undertow). However, it's worth the walk down to the beach for the view of the tower alone, which looks as if it's about to topple over into the sea.

The village has two **accommodation** options, both very appealing. Note that neither of these have road access; you'll have to park just below the square and walk. Down a narrow alley off the main square, ⚘ *Casa Maria* (℡04 95 37 80 95, ⓦwww.casamaria-corse.com; ❺) is a B&B occupying an immaculately restored schist house. Two of its five comfy en-suite rooms enjoy sea views, and you can take your breakfast on a pretty stone terrace behind. Be sure to ask to see the hundred-year-old love letters the family came across while they were renovating the property.

Further down the hillside, at the bottom fringes of the village, the *Casa Lisa* (℡04 95 37 83 52, ⓦcasalisa.free.fr; ❸) has equally gorgeous rooms with exposed beams, original tiled floors and shuttered windows looking across the gulf to the Désert des Agriates. Considering the location and levels of comfort, it offers great value for money, with doubles starting at under €50 in June and September.

The Nebbio

Named after the thick mists that sweep across it in the spring and autumn, the **Nebbio** (Nebbiu) has for centuries been one of the most fertile parts of Corsica, producing honey, chestnuts and some of the island's finest wine. Officially, the region includes the barren **Désert des Agriates**, further west, but essentially the Nebbio comprises the amphitheatre of rippled hills, vineyards and cultivated valleys that converge on St-Florent, a region nicknamed *A Conca d'Oro* (The Golden Shell) by Pascal Paoli because it encompassed all the wealth of the area. Nourished by the headwaters of the **Aliso River**, its many beautiful villages, perched on pale green bluffs of schist that jut from the gently sloping sides of the basin, are swathed in greenery, with finger-thin bell towers pointing from their midst. In spite of their proximity to the coast, tourism has made little impact on these scattered settlements, which remain largely dependent on agriculture and EU subsidies. The one major development in recent times has been the shift to **viticulture**; some of the wines produced in the shadow of the chalk hills around the village of **Patrimonio** are world class, and *caves* offering wine tastings (*dégustations*) are a feature of the whole region.

St-Florent at the base of Cap Corse – a bishopric until 1790 and now a chic coastal resort – remains the Nebbio's hub and best base, while villages such as **Olmeta-di-Tuda** and **Oletta**, being close to Bastia, are lively and well-populated places, especially in the summer, when families move up to the cooler mountains from the city. The two most notable historic sites in this part of the island are the Pisan church of **Santa Maria Assunta**, just outside St-Florent, and the diminutive **San Michele de Murato**, close to the chapels strewn across the valley between **Rapale** and **Santo-Pietro-di-Tenda**.

The principal **public transport** serving the Nebbio is Transports Santini's bus from Bastia to St-Florent (see p.90 for details).

St-Florent

Viewed from across the bay, **ST-FLORENT** (San Fiurenzu) appears as a bright line against the black tidal wave of the Tenda hills, the pale stone houses seeming to rise straight out of the sea, overlooked by a squat circular citadelle. It's a

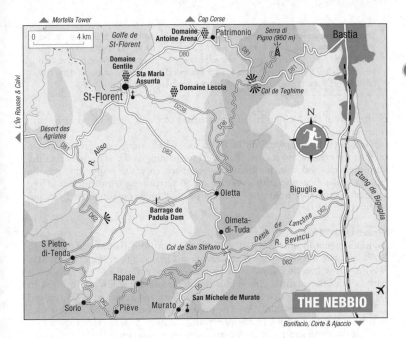

Mortella Tower ▲   ▲ Cap Corse

Golfe de St-Florent

Domaine Antoine Arena ▲ Patrimonio   Serra di Pigno (960 m)   Bastia

D80   D81

Domaine Gentile   Sta Maria Assunta

St-Florent   Domaine Leccia   Col de Teghime

L'Île Rousse & Calvi ◄

Désert des Agriates

D238

D36

R. Aliso

D82

Oletta   Biguglia

Barrage de Padula Dam

Olmeta-di-Tuda   Défilé de Lancône

Etang de Biguglia

D62

Col de San Stefano   R. Bevincu

D82

S Pietro-di-Tenda

Rapale

Sorio   Piève   Murato   San Michele de Murato

THE NEBBIO

0   4 km

N

Bonifacio, Corte & Ajaccio ▼

relaxing place, with a decent beach and a good number of restaurants, but the key to its success is the **marina**, which is jammed with expensive boats throughout the summer. Neither the tourists, however, nor indeed St-Florent's proximity to Bastia, entirely eclipse the air of isolation conferred on the village by its brooding backdrop of mountains and scrubby desert.

In Roman times a town called **Cersunam** existed on the site where Santa Maria Assunta stands today, 1km east of the present village, though few traces remain of this settlement. By the mid-fifteenth century a port had developed around the new Genoese citadelle and St-Florent proceeded to prosper as one of Genoa's strongholds, largely through the export of olive oil produced in its fertile hinterland, though it later went into decline as its population – ravaged by malaria, Moorish pirates, and continual battles between the Corsicans, the French and the Genoese in the mid-sixteenth century – dwindled to 65. The town was also fought over during the struggles for independence in 1769; and it was from here that Paoli set off for London in 1796, never to return.

There's not a great deal to see here, but there are plenty of tranquil cafés and restaurant terraces to laze in. **Place des Portes**, the centre of village life, has tables facing the sea in the shade of plane trees, and in the evening it fills with strollers and *pétanque* players. In **rue du Centre**, which runs west off the square, parallel to the seafront and marina, you'll find a string of inviting restaurants, shops and wine-tasting outlets – though to sample the area's best wines you should head out to the *domaines* themselves (see box, p.96).

To reach the **citadelle**, walk down rue du Centre and turn into place Doria, from the far side of which a lane runs up through the houses to the car park in front of the bastion. Unique in Corsica for its circular shape, the *torrioni*, as it's known locally, was built in 1439 for the Genoese governors, but was bombarded for two days by Nelson's fleet in February 1794 and reduced to a virtual ruin. Now renovated, it's worth a visit primarily for the beautiful views

Seasonal excursion boats run out of St-Florent marina to the superb beaches across the bay in the Désert des Agriates: the *U Saleccia* (Ⓣ04 95 36 90 78) and *Popeye* (Ⓣ04 95 37 19 07) leave at regular intervals throughout the day, returning around 4pm (or later in July & Aug); tickets cost €12 for the round trip and can be booked the day before from June to September (when there are two departures daily).

of the hills of the Nebbio and the mountains of Cap Corse, disappearing into mists up the coast.

The nearest beach, **plage de la Roya**, is a windy stretch of seaweed-strewn sand to the west of town – less than ideal for bathing as the sea is rather murky and often clogged with posidonia. To get there, cross the bridge through the marina and follow the path over the spit. Alternatively, jump on one of the seasonal **excursion boats** (see box above). For more on plages de Loto and Saleccia see p.101.

Practicalities

Transports Santini buses (Ⓣ04 95 37 02 98) run from Bastia's *gare routière* to St-Florent twice daily (except Sun), leaving at 11am and 6pm (except Oct–May Wed & Sat, when they leave at noon & 5.30pm), pulling into the village car park behind the marina. This is also the departure point for return buses to Bastia, which from June to September leave at 7am and 2pm, and at 6.50am and 1.30pm from October until May. The journey takes one hour. You can purchase tickets on the bus or book in advance from Transports Santini's travel agency on St-Florent's main street, rue du Centre, just below the post office.

Bus times may vary a little from year to year, but can be checked at the **tourist office**, at the top of the village (July & Aug Mon–Fri 8.30am–12.30pm & 2–7pm, Sat & Sun 9am–noon & 3–6pm; Sept–June Mon–Fri 9am–noon & 2–5pm, Sat 9am–noon; Ⓣ04 95 37 06 04, Ⓦwww.corsica-saintflorent.com). The **post office** next door has an ATM, as do the Société Générale and Crédit Agricole **banks**, off place des Portes (Mon–Fri 9–11.45am & 2–4.30pm).

The large Spar, next to the bridge in the marina, is the best-stocked **supermarket** in the area, and stays open on Sundays in the summer. Every other bit and bob you could possibly want for a beach, camping or watersports holiday is available at the cavernous Corse Plaisance next door.

For pottering around the idyllic coastline of the Désert des Agriates, **boats** – from pedalos and inflatable six-horse-power Bombards (which you don't need a licence to drive) to full-on 200-horse-power Glastons – are offered for rent at Sun Folies, at the far west end of plage de la Roya (Ⓣ06 13 07 39 83, Ⓦwww.sunfolies.com). Prices (which fluctuate according to the season) range from around €100 per day for the Bombards to €550 per day for the speedboats, and there are plenty of options in between. You can also rent **sea kayaks** – perfect for pottering around the Agriates coast in fine weather – from Cors'Kayak, on Plage de la Roya (Ⓣ06 12 10 23 27, Ⓦwww.corskayak.com), priced at €35–50 depending on the size of the canoe, and Dominique Plaisance (Ⓣ04 95 37 07 08, Ⓦperso.wanadoo.fr/dominiqueplaisance), down near the *gendarmerie* at the south end of the marina. The latter firm also has a range of powered inflatables and speedboats comparable to that offered by Sun Folies.

Accommodation

St-Florent is a popular resort and **hotels** fill up quickly, especially in the height of summer, when prior booking is essential. **Campsites** are strung along the length of plage de la Roya, and off the road running out towards Cap Corse,

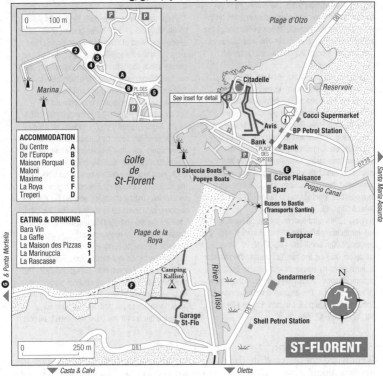

The map shows labels including:

- Plage d'Olzo
- Citadelle
- Reservoir
- Cocci Supermarket
- Avis
- BP Petrol Station
- Bank
- Bank
- Corse Plaisance
- Spar
- Poggio Canal
- Buses to Bastia (Transports Santini)
- Europcar
- Gendarmerie
- Shell Petrol Station
- Garage St-Flo
- Camping Kallisté
- Plage de la Roya
- River Aliso
- Golfe de St-Florent
- U Saleccia Boats
- Popeye Boats
- Marina
- PL. DES PORTES
- See inset for detail
- Santa Maria Assunta
- Casta & Calvi
- Oletta
- Camping U Sole Marinu, Camping A Stella, Patrimonio, Cap Corse & Bastia
- & Punta Mortella
- G
- **ST-FLORENT**

ACCOMMODATION

Du Centre	A
De l'Europe	B
Maison Rorqual	G
Maloni	C
Maxime	E
La Roya	F
Treperi	D

EATING & DRINKING

Bara Vin	3
La Gaffe	2
La Maison des Pizzas	5
La Marinuccia	1
La Rascasse	4

becoming less expensive the further they are from town; unless stated otherwise, they're open from May to October.

Hotels

Du Centre rue de Fornellu ☎04 95 37 00 68, ℻04 95 37 41 01. Refreshingly unpretentious, old-fashioned place of a kind that's fast disappearing on the island. The modest rooms, all en suite and with showers, are kept impeccably clean by the feisty Mme Casanova. Ask for "*côté jardin*". ④–⑤

De l'Europe place des Portes ☎04 95 37 00 33, ⓦwww.hotel-europe2.com. Simply refurbished old building in the village centre next to the square, with original flagstone floors and modern comforts. Rooms are on the small side, but all are en suite and well aired, and some overlook the marina. ⑤–⑥

Maison Rorqual at the far western end of plage de la Roya ☎04 95 37 05 37 or mobile 06 13 02 02 11, ⓦwww.maison-rorqual.com. The last word in high Mediterranean chic, this exclusive *chambres d'hôtes* huddles behind a screen of greenery on the far side of the bay. Scattered across an acre of flower-filled juniper scrub, its five luxury rooms and suites are

individually styled, incorporating local shells, river pebbles and wood; one even has a waterfall shower spilling over a schist boulder in its bathroom. Breakfast is served on stone terraces in the garden next to an overflow pool with dreamy views across the gulf, and there's a gastronomic restaurant. Starts at €250 in shoulder reason, rising to €400–450 in July/Aug. ⑨

Maloni on the Bastia road, 2km northeast of town ☎04 95 37 14 30, ⓦwww.malonihotel.com. Until EU regulations forced it to close its kitchen, this used to be the only Kosher hotel in Corsica, run by a welcoming Jewish family with pan-Mediterranean roots. It's now an excellent little budget hotel, especially popular with bikers, with simple but pleasant en-suite rooms opening on to a leafy garden. The whole place is slightly frayed around the edges, but the tariffs are the lowest for miles. ③

Maxime route d'Oletta, just off place des Portes ☎04 95 37 05 30, ℻04 95 37 13 07. Bright, modern hotel in the centre. The rooms, all with en-suite bathrooms and power showers, are on the small side but immaculate. Those to the rear of the building have French windows and little balconies overhanging a small water channel. No credit cards. ⑤

La Roya plage de la Roya ℡ 04 95 37 00 40, Ⓦ www.hoteldelaroya.com. Luxury three-star behind the town beach. The semi-open-air lobby, full of palms, Mediterranean pastels and plate glass, sets the tone. Beyond it, umbrella pines dot a huge lawn terrace and pool surrounded by a teak deck backing directly onto the sand. The thirty airy sea-facing rooms are spacious and quiet, and each has a large balcony. It's overpriced, however, unless you book through a tour operator. Doubles in the range of €210–320 in June & Sept. ⑨

Treperi 1.5km northeast on the Bastia road; turn left immediately after the Elf petrol station and continue 500m uphill ℡ 04 95 37 40 20. On a hilltop overlooking the bay, this smart little two-star is surrounded by vineyards and benefits from panoramic views across the gulf and Nebbio from its room terraces. The grounds have tennis courts and a decent-size pool. Doubles drop to €69 in May and June. ④–⑤

Campsites

Kallisté route de la plage de la Roya ℡ 04 95 37 03 08, Ⓕ 04 95 37 19 77. The priciest of the string of sites just west of town, but worth paying the extra for, since it's usually a lot less crowded, has cleaner *blocs sanitaires* than the competition and lies only 10min walk along the beach from town. There's also a café-restaurant and small shop.

U Sole Marinu Caldarelli, 7km northeast of St-Florent ℡ 04 95 37 12 20 or mobile 06 17 03 44 28. A good option if you're looking for a simple, natural site. Very basic by Corsican standards (there's only one small *bloc sanitaire* and very little shade), but superbly isolated down a long dirt track, next to a grey pebble beach that's backed by mountains and vineyards. The cove's great for snorkelling (swell permitting), and behind it an old customs path leads up to some spectacular cliffs. Look for the sign off the D80 just after it squeezes between two chalk escarpments.

A Stella Marine de Farinole ℡ 04 95 37 14 37. Slap on the beach in a remote spot, 10km northeast of St-Florent, with a shop and café. The proximity of a pebble beach ensures it's packed in high summer, but in May, June and Sept you'll have it virtually to yourself. A great base for exploring the area if you have your own transport.

Eating and drinking

Renowned for its crayfish (*langouste*) and red mullet (*rouget*), St-Florent has become popular with Corsican gastronomes over the past few years, largely thanks to the efforts of the establishments listed below. Dozens of other restaurants crowd the marina and its backstreets, enticing tourists with glossy photo menus and snazzy terraces, but as with most resorts, standards among them tend to vary widely from year to year. More consistent are the **cafés** lining the square, all of them with virtually identical prices, and terraces where visitors and locals alike gather to watch the *passeghiata* and *pétanque*.

Bara Vin place Doria. Popular tapas bar tucked away in a lively little square below the citadelle. Dishes run from €8.50 to €18 (for a full plate of *mezze*), and they do a great selection of Corsican AOC wines by the glass, served on stand-up barrel tops in the street.

La Gaffe on the harbourfront ℡ 04 95 37 00 12. French seafood classics, such as grilled salmon with a St-Jacques sauce, using only the freshest local fish. House specialities include sumptuous devilfish stew on a bed of tagliatelli and Cap Corse-style bouillabaisse (order a day in advance), offered exclusively à la carte. There are also menus at €30 & €40. Closed Tues, except July & Aug.

La Maison des Pizzas 1 place du Monument ℡ 04 95 37 08 52. Large red-and-white painted pizzeria on the main square, serving huge pizzas

(€7–13) and fresh Italian pasta dishes, as well as the usual range of *grillades* (€11–14), big salads and the house speciality, chestnut-flour crêpes (from €7). A dependable budget option, and it's virtually the only place open in winter.

La Marinuccia place Doria, below the citadelle ℡ 04 95 37 04 36. Traditional island seafood dishes – such as sardines stuffed with fresh ewe's cheese, local anemones or wood-baked sea bass – served on a gorgeous terrace jutting out into the sea off place Doria. The service is perhaps more formal than suits the setting, but their *menus fixe* (€18–24) are very good value, the *carte's* very classy and their wine list features the elusive Clos Nicrosi blanc.

La Rascasse on the quayside ℡ 04 95 37 06 99. One of the classiest addresses on the island, run by a talented chef who's a living legend among sybaritic Bastiais. His menu is unashamedly gastronomic, dominated by imaginative spins on local seafood: cream of ray's wing, mussel and chestnut fritters, and lobsters sautéed in cured ham with tartlets of warm *brocciu*. Menu €38.

Around St-Florent

The area around St-Florent offers plenty of opportunities for short excursions: the cathedral of **Santa Maria Assunta** is only a fifteen-minute walk from the town centre; also within easy reach are the **Tour de Mortella** and the wonderful **beaches** of the Agriates coast.

Santa Maria Assunta

Situated in a lonely spot 1km east of St-Florent on the original site of the Roman settlement of Nebbium, **Santa Maria Assunta** – the so-called "Cathedral of the Nebbio" – is a fine example of Pisan Romanesque architecture, rivalled only by La Canonica at Mariana, its exact contemporary (see p.70). The route to it east off place des Portes is clearly signposted. In theory the cathedral should be left open from 5pm to 8pm in July and August; at other times check opening hours at the tourist office. Entry costs €1.

Deprived of its bell tower, which was knocked down in the nineteenth century, and set among pastures next door to a farmyard, the cathedral has a distinctly barn-like appearance. Built of warm yellow limestone, it's a superlatively elegant barn, though, and a close look soon reveals an unexpected wealth of harmonious detail: gracefully symmetrical blind arcades decorate the western facade, and at the entrance twisting serpents and wild animals adorn

Walk to the Tour de Mortella and plage de Loto

Mortella point and its famous tower can be reached on foot from St-Florent – a wonderful, mostly flat walk (2hr 30min–3hr) along some of the island's most scenic coastline. Set off early enough, and you can continue past the tower to plage de Loto in the Désert des Agriates. The path is easy to follow, but you may want to take along IGN's #4348 OT (available at the Maison de la Presse newsagents on place des Portes in St-Florent).

The route begins at the far (west) end of plage de la Roya, from where you follow the surfaced lane running behind the beach. With transport, it's possible to cut short the dull first stretch of this walk (2km) by driving or cycling as far as **Anse de Fornali**, a narrow inlet overlooked by a cluster of luxury villas where there's a small car park (note that the last 2km of the drive is via a severely rutted *piste*). From the car park, a sign points the way through the maquis to the start of the **Sentier du Douanier** (Custom Officers' Path). This hugs a highly convoluted, rocky coastline, studded with a string of tiny bays below the Domaine de Fonaverte, to round the **Punta di Cepo** headland fifty minutes further on from the car park. From here onwards, the coast is very beautiful, with plenty of idyllic coves for swimming. The IGN map implies the river mouths are open, but you can cross them easily on seaweed-covered sand bars. Winding due north, the final stretch from the crystal-clear, white-bottomed **Fiume Santu Bay** to the tower takes around thirty minutes.

Most walkers turn around at the **Tour de Mortella**, but you can continue on to plage de Loto by heading around the next promontory and following the path west as it cuts inland beneath the lighthouse. At the top of the rise, just after the trail starts to give ground, another path peels right, but you should ignore this and go straight on. **Plage de Loto** is reached after another good hour from the tower. Time your arrival well, and you might be able to catch a ride back to St-Florent on one of the two excursion boats (see p.90).

the pilasters on either side of the door; the staring cherubs date from a more recent period.

In spite of some rather messy Rococo additions, the interior, too, is in essence plain. Carved shells, foliage and animals adorn the capitals of the pillars dividing the nave, at the back of which (to the left as you face away from the altar), you'll see a glass case containing the mummified figure of **St Flor**, a Roman soldier martyred in the third century for his Christian beliefs. Found among the catacombs of Rome with a vial of blood, signifying martyrdom, the soldier's remains were donated by Pope Clement XIV to the bishop of the Nebbio in 1771, and a gilded wooden statue stands as a further commemoration in the apse. The spacious nave also holds the tomb of **General Antoine Gentili**, a prominent supporter of Pascal Paoli during the struggles for independence.

Tour de Mortella

The ruined **Tour de Mortella**, isolated on the coast 7km west of St-Florent, is the most impressive piece of Genoese architecture hereabouts. Built around 1520 as an anti-piracy measure, the tower fell into disuse over time due to its inaccessibility, until the Corsican wars of independence, when it was reoccupied by French soldiers to guard the sea approach to the gulf. In February 1794, a British fleet under Lord Hood (which included the 64-gun *Agamemnon* commanded by the young Horatio Nelson) sailed in to blockade St-Florent, and was amazed when its two ships – a 74-gun and a 32-gun – were beaten off by the tower's three cannons, sustaining severe damage and suffering some sixty casualties. Only after two days of continual pounding from four guns placed on land (at a mere 137m from the tower), did the 38-strong French garrison surrender. As a result of the British bombardment, the tower was cleft in half, but its renovated ochre-washed walls still strike an impressive profile. More than two centuries later, towers modelled on this one still stand all over the world – from Key West in Florida to the islands of Mauritius – having been erected by the British as coastal defences. For more on "Martello Towers", as they were later renamed, see the "Pirates and watchtowers" box opposite.

Inland Nebbio

St-Florent may attract the bulk of visitors to the Nebbio, but the picturesque villages of its **hinterland** form the real heart of the region. Backed by a wall of sheer granite mountains, they cling to the sides of the spectacular **Aliso basin**, overlooking a vista of undulating vineyards that tumble to a cobalt-blue sea. Graffiti scrawled over any exposed rock face remind you that this is a staunchly nationalist area; the Nebbio witnessed some of the fiercest fighting during the wars of independence against the French in the eighteenth century, and the spirit of resistance has never diminished.

The villages of inland Nebbio can be visited in an easy day's drive from St-Florent. Aside from a handful of churches and **statue-menhirs**, they harbour few sights, but the constantly changing **views** make this round trip one of the most rewarding forays from the coast. Most people follow a loop from St-Florent, climbing through **Patrimonio**, epicentre of Corsica's most famous wine-growing area, to **Oletta** and the **Col de San Stefano**, then up to **Murato**, and down again to **Santo-Pietro-di-Tenda** before heading back to St-Florent. If you're driving into the Nebbio from Bastia, you can join this loop at the Col de San Stefano via the dramatic **Défilé de Lancône**.

Pirates and watchtowers

Crowning rocky promontories and clifftops from Cap Corse to Bonifacio, the 91 crumbling Genoese watchtowers that punctuate the Corsican coast have become emblematic of the island's picture-postcard tranquillity. Yet they date from an era when these shores were among the most troubled in Europe. During the early fifteenth century, some five hundred years after the Moors had been ousted from the interior, Saracen **pirates** from North Africa began to menace the coastal villages, descending suddenly from the sea and making off with any valuables – including people – that could be shipped back to the Barbary states.

Held for ransom or sold as slaves, Christians were prime plunder for the pirates, and hundreds of islanders were abducted each year. Some did eventually return to their homelands, though not to resettle. Taking advantage of a law that allowed a slave to claim his freedom if he converted to Islam, former captives would set themselves up as traders in their new countries, or, more often, turn to piracy as a means to amass a fortune. For some reason, the latter vocation appealed particularly to Corsicans: records illustrate that, of the ten thousand or so pirates operating out of Algiers in the mid-sixteenth century, some six thousand were from the island. It is a little-known fact that most of the raids on Corsica during the Genoese era were perpetrated by former natives. Pirate raids became so common by the end of the fifteenth century that many Corsicans left the coast altogether, retreating to villages in the hills. To protect those that remained, as well as the threatened maritime trade, the Genoese erected a chain of **watchtowers**, or *torri*, at strategic points on the island. Comprising one or two storeys, these squat, round towers measured 12–15m in diameter, with a single doorway 5m off the ground reached by a removable ladder. The towers were paid for by local villagers and staffed by watchmen, or *torregiani*, whose job it was to signal the approach of any unexpected ships.

Piracy more or less died out by the end of Genoese rule in the mid-fifteenth century, but the *torri* remained in use long after, proving particularly effective during the Anglo-Corsican invasions 250 years later. The British were so impressed with the system that they erected a chain of 103 similar structures along the south coast of England and Ireland to ward off attacks by the French. Over time the same system spread to the far-flung corners of the British empire: India, Australia, Mauritius, the West Indies and USA still have intact **Martello towers**, as they were re-christened (recalling the name of the one near St-Florent that held off Lord Hood and Nelson's fleet).

Patrimonio

Leaving St-Florent by the Bastia road, the first village you come to, after 6km, is **PATRIMONIO**, centre of the first Corsican wine region to gain *appellation contrôlée* status. Apart from the famous local muscat, which can be sampled at any of the *caves* along the route from St-Florent, Patrimonio's chief claim to fame is the sixteenth-century **Église St-Martin**, occupying its own little hillock and visible for kilometres around. Made of exposed brown schist and granite, it stands out vividly against the vineyards and weathered chalk outcrops to the north, but the interior was effectively ruined in the nineteenth century, when an elaborately painted ceiling and overdone marble altar were installed.

In a small clearing 200m south of the church, reached via the lane that drops sharply downhill from the crossroads, stands a two-metre-tall **statue-menhir** known as U Nativu, a late megalithic piece dating from 900–800 BC. The only limestone menhir ever discovered in Corsica, it was ploughed up in four fragments by a local farmer in 1964, restored and placed here under a small shelter. A carved T-shape on its front represents a breastbone, and two uncannily life-like eyebrows and a chin can also be made out.

The wines of Patrimonio

Thanks to its chalky soil and sheltered situation at the bottom of the Golfe de St-Florent, the Patrimonio region has long been Corsica's flagship wine-growing area. Since Roman times, vines have striped the slopes falling away beneath the dramatic white escarpments surrounding the village, and the church tower has become something of a symbol for the Corsican wine industry as a whole. This was the first region in the island to gain *Appellation d'Origine Contrôlée* (AOC) status (in 1968), and the hundred or so local vignerons struggled successfully to keep their reputations intact in the wake of the adulteration scandals that blighted the nearby eastern plain in the mid-1970s. That said, few of them these days can justifiably claim to produce wines of real distinction, and tastings (*dégustations*) advertised at the many roadside *caves* you pass en route through the village can be a hit-and-miss affair.

Three growers, however, stand out, producing wines of consistently high quality using a combination of modern New-World technology and labour-intensive, traditional (low-yield) techniques (such as harvesting by hand instead of with machines, and avoiding pesticides and herbicides). Their output is divided evenly between crisp, dry whites from the **Vermentino** grape, and pale rosés and robust, earthy reds from **Nielluccio** (*the* quintessential local vinestock). In common with most growers in the area, they also offer amber-coloured, sweet **muscat**, which the Genoese used to export from here as a dessert wine in vast quantities, but which nowadays is almost entirely unknown off the island.

The best way to buy wine hereabouts is to visit a *cave* in person, taste and purchase either a case or fill up *vracs* (plastic or glass containers) straight from the vats (which can work out costing half or less of what you'd pay for the same stuff bottled). The following Domaines are shown on the map on p.89. For more on Corsican wine, see p.34.

Domaine Antoine Arena Patrimonio ☎04 95 37 08 27. No set opening hours – ring ahead to arrange a visit, or call in person at the *cave*, which is situated on the junction of the D80 (Cap Corse) road and D81 (to Bastia via Patrimonio village).

Domaine Gentille ☎04 95 31 01 54 (Mon–Sat 8–11.30am & 2–6.30pm). The vineyards abut those of the Arena family, but the *cave* is on the outskirts of St-Florent, on the sea side of the D81.

Domaine Leccia Poggio d'Oletta ☎04 95 37 11 35 (Mon–Sat 9am–noon & 2–6pm). Follow the lane past Santa Maria Assunta in St-Florent and keep going towards Oletta for 3km until you see the *cave* on your left.

U Nativu takes pride of place next to the stage at Patrimonio's annual open-air **guitar festival** (ⓦwww.festival-guitare-patrimonio.com), held in the last week of July next to the church, when performers and music aficionados from all over Europe converge on the village.

An atmospheric **place to stay** in Patrimonio is the ⚘ *Château Calvello* (☎04 95 37 01 14; May–Oct, and by prior arrangement out of season; ❺), a wonderful seventeenth-century Corsican tower house offering a handful of vaulted *chambres d'hôtes* and apartments down a bumpy lane from the church. Period furniture and family oil portraits preserve the antique feel of its huge *salons*, and the château's shuttered windows look out across the gulf. Guests also get the run of a lovely garden, where breakfast is served.

For **meals**, you won't do better than the *Osteria San Martinu* (☎04 95 37 11 93), a simple Corsican place in the centre of the village (on the right of the main road if you're heading uphill), where *grillades* and *brochettes* are cooked on an open brazier of vine wood by the patron and served on a big covered terrace. The house menu costs €20.

Col de Teghime to Oletta

From Patrimonio the road climbs in a series of sharp switchbacks to the **Col de Teghime** (548m), where a memorial recalls the intense fighting that took place here prior to the withdrawal of the German army from Bastia in October 1943, and commemorates the troops who died here. Many of the fallen were North African *goumiers* from the Berber areas of the Atlas Mountains; a cemetery full of gravestones bearing Arabic inscriptions stands on the outskirts of St-Florent (2km northeast out of the town along the Bastia road).

From the col, it's possible to see the coastlines of both sides of the cape (when it's not swathed in fog), with a stunning panorama of St-Florent and Patrimonio spreading out to the west, while to the east you'll see Bastia, with the glistening Étang de Biguglia stretching south. It's not unusual for the weather to be entirely different on either side.

Oletta

The road south of the Col de Teghime leads after 10km to **OLETTA**, where the eighteenth-century **Église St-André**, in the centre of the village, has an ancient relief of the Creation (symbolized by a tree of life) embedded in its recently renovated facade – a relic from the church that occupied the site in the twelfth century. Inside, there's a graceful triptych dating from 1534, portraying the Virgin and Child flanked by SS John the Baptist and Reparata. This used to reside in a local peasant's house until the Madonna allegedly called out to the mother of the household to warn her that her baby's cot had caught fire. Thereafter the triptych was transferred to the church, and has been venerated as miraculous ever since.

The **square** outside the church witnessed one of the more gruesome episodes in the Paolist insurrections of the eighteenth century, when a daring rebel plan to seize Oletta from the French backfired. Eager to make an example of his Corsican prisoners, the French commander condemned the rebels to a horrible death, crushing them on a cartwheel.

Despite these gruesome past events, the **café** on the square is about as pleasant a spot as you'll find to soak up the village atmosphere of inland Nebbio; it doubles up as a *boulangerie-pâtisserie*, so the croissants are fresh. On the northern edge of Oletta, *A Maggina* (℡04 95 39 01 01; April–Sept) serves a good selection of local specialities such as veal and olives, grilled swordfish in lemon sauce and lamb *sauté*, with menus at €25–30. The main reason to eat here, however, is the stupendous panoramic views from its terrace.

Le Col de San Stefano and Défilé de Lancône

The crossroads at the **Col de San Stefano** (368m), 4km south of Oletta, marks the entrance to the **Défilé de Lancône**, a precipitous descent that hits the main coast road 10km south of Bastia – a good shortcut between St-Florent and the airport. Hewn out of the black rock, with nationalist graffiti adorning the rock face at every lurching bend, the road winds far above the River Bevinco, from whose bed the serpentine for the church of San Michele de Murato was quarried. The Défilé is a road to be treated with respect – numerous little shrines along the way testify to the fatal smashes that have occurred here, most of them in the small hours of Sunday mornings when local youngsters drive back to Bastia from the disco in Murato.

Murato

Continuing along the D5 instead of taking the Défilé, you soon pass the Pisan church of **San Michele de Murato**, which sits on a grassy bluff high above the Nebbio. Built around 1280, this late Romanesque building is notable for its asymmetrical patterning of dark green serpentine and off-white marble, a jazzy counterpoint to the simple lines of the single-naved church, though these were damaged in the late nineteenth century, when the disproportionate bell tower was added. Outside, there's some sophisticated carving on the arches of the blind arcades and immediately beneath the roof, depicting gargoyles, wild beasts and human figures – look out for a relief on the north wall, showing an ashamed Eve reaching out to take the huge apple proffered by the serpent.

MURATO, a kilometre or so south beyond the church, is one of the few well-populated villages in the Nebbio, with nearly 600 permanent residents. It played a prominent role in the wars of independence: Paoli established his headquarters here, and coins were minted in the local convent. Plenty of medieval charm lingers in the ancient streets around its pair of churches, but the reason most visitors venture up to Murato is because the village's outskirts harbour one of the island's top restaurants. Perched on the flank of a mountain, with superb views extending over the Nebbio, the *Ferme-Auberge Campu di Monte* (☎04 95 37 64 39; mid-June to mid-Sept daily; mid-Sept to mid-June Fri & Sat evening & Sun lunchtime) is renowned as much for its sublime location as the sumptuous mountain cooking of the *patronne*, Mme Juillard, whose specialities (many of them handed down from her grandmother) include traditional soft-cheese doughnuts, veal stews and fresh river trout. They offer a single set meal of unlimited portions for the all-in price of €45; reservations are essential, ideally at least a week ahead. Finding the *auberge* is something of a challenge: turn left at the *Victor Bar* in the village and follow the road down to the river at the bottom of the valley; shortly after the bridge, an unsurfaced track (indicated with a sign) turns right off the road, heading 1.5km to the farm.

On from Murato

To continue the Nebbio tour, backtrack to the D62, which hugs the side of the Tenda massif as it runs west, snaking through villages built precariously on the lip of a shadowy forested valley. At **RAPALE**, a tiny ancient hamlet with castle-like houses built of schist stone, you can see the Romanesque chapel of **San Cesareo**, a green and white ruin hidden in the woods south above the village – it's a twenty-minute walk, beginning up the lane behind the church.

Back on the main road, another 2km will bring you to **PIÈVE**. Set on a plinth in front of the church in the heart of this village are three well-preserved **stone menhirs**. Carved in the same minimalist style as the monolith at Patrimonio (see p.95), the 3000-year-old family group gazes out across the Aliso basin to the wall of cloud-fringed peaks to the west.

The Désert des Agriates

Bordered by 35km of wild and rugged coastline, the **Désert des Agriates** is a vast area of uninhabited land; a rocky moonscape interspersed with clumps of cacti and maquis-shrouded hills. Its limits extend eastwards to the Golfe de St-Florent, west to the mouth of the Ostriconi River and down as far south as Santo-Pietro-di-Tenda. Despite the landscape's inhospitable appearance, the area has a long agricultural history, as its name implies – *agriates* means "cultivated fields". During the time of the Genoese, it was a veritable breadbasket: the Italian occupiers even levied a special wheat tax on local farmers (most of whom came from Cap Corse) to prevent any build-up of funds that might have financed an insurrection in the area. Every winter until the early years of the twentieth century, shepherds from the mountains of Niolo and Asco would move down with their flocks here for the annual bartering of goat's and ewe's cheese, which they exchanged for olive oil and wheat cultivated on the Agriates. The grain was stockpiled in square stone storage huts known as *pagliaghju* or *paillers*, about twenty groups of which still exist and are nowadays used by hunters for shelter (one on the coast path has also been converted into a *gîte d'étape* – see box below).

In the course of the eighteenth and nineteenth centuries, fires and soil erosion reduced the region to desert, and it was a total wilderness by the 1970s, when numerous crackpot schemes to redevelop the area were mooted. These included a proposal to convert it into a test zone for atomic weapons, and a plan to transform the entire coast into a purpose-built Club-Med-style tourist complex, complete with concrete holiday villages and a giant marina. In order to block these schemes, the government gradually acquired the Agriates from its various owners (among them the Rothschild family), designating it a protected site. Wildlife, however, remains under threat, not least from trigger-happy hunters. Various ecologically sound projects are currently under discussion, such as plans to introduce controlled breeding of the Agriates' **wild boar**, the purest type on the island due to the isolation of the area, but now endangered by illegal hunting. Other rare species, such as the huge orange and brown Jason butterfly, are also under threat of extinction, largely because of the fires that increasingly devastate the maquis. The maquis also harbours many species of rare birds, including bee-eaters, red-backed shrikes and Celti's warblers.

The Désert des Agriates coast path

The old custom officers' path, **Le Sentier du Douanier**, along the coast of the Désert des Agriates has been resurrected to provide footpath access to this pristine shoreline, winding across wild headlands, crystalline coves piled high with bleached driftwood, and some of the most exquisite beaches in the western Mediterranean. The path is well waymarked throughout, but before attempting it you still need to be aware of the risk of sunstroke and dehydration; long stretches lack shade and there are very few sources of fresh water along the way (you'll need to carry at least three litres). Spring and autumn are the best times to walk; during the summer, temperatures are infernal.

The itinerary divides into three easy stages, which can be covered in two days or, at a more leisurely pace, in three. Most people begin the route at St-Florent (following the path described in detail in the box on p.93), but there's no reason why you shouldn't start it at Ostriconi and walk from west to east instead. In this case, simply reverse the outline below; the stage timings are the same. Whichever direction you head in, take along the two IGN maps covering the Agriates coast: #4347 OT (Cap Corse) and #4249 OT (L'Île Rousse).

Stage One: St-Florent to plage de Saleccia (4hr–4hr 30min). Key landmarks on this section include the Fornali lighthouse, the Tour de Mortella, and the famous beaches of Loto and Saleccia. The only source of water and permitted camping place is the *U Paradisu* site, behind plage de Saleccia (see p.101).

Stage Two: Saleccia to plage de Guignu (2hr 30min). The wildest leg of the route, with some very rough maquis and no water sources until you reach the old *bergeries* of Alga Putrica at Guignu, where there's a welcome little *gîte d'étape* just above the beach (reservation via the Syndicat Mixte des Agriates ☎04 95 37 09 86; April–Oct). Dorm beds cost €12 or you can pitch a tent for €7, for which you get the use of a small toilet block with cold showers.

Stage Three: plage de Guignu to Ostriconi (5hr 30min). The path hugs the mostly rocky shore until forced inland around the crags north of Ostriconi beach (covered on p.127).

▲ Wild cove on the Désert des Agriates

Practicalities

By far the most relaxed way to penetrate the Désert des Agriates is to jump on one of the excursion **boats** from St-Florent. From their moorings in the marina, the *Popeye* and *U Saleccia* shuttle passengers throughout the day to plage de Loto (see box, p.90). From plage de Loto you can walk back to St-Florent in a little over three hours, or press on along the coast for another hour to plage de Saleccia. For accounts of both beaches, see opposite.

Only one road, the D81, runs through the desert, skirting its southern limits between St-Florent and the junction with the N1197 *route nationale* near Ostriconi – the main artery between Bastia and L'Île Rousse/Calvi. In July and August, Autocars Santini's twice-daily L'Île Rousse **bus** covers the route, which passes the only **accommodation** on the eastern side of the Agriates area: at the village of **CASTA**, 12km west of St-Florent, *Le Relais de Saleccia* (℡04 95 37 14 60, Ⓦwww.hotel-corse-saleccia.com; Easter to Oct; ❸–❹) has ten simply furnished en-suite rooms with terraces looking across a sea of undulating scrub to Monte Genova, the highest point in the desert. The couple who run it are very welcoming and serve fresh local food in their roadside café-restaurant, which has a rear terrace that makes the most of the views.

The *Relais de Saleccia* stands near the start of the only motorable approach to the Désert des Agriates coast, an eleven-kilometre **piste** winding north to plage de Saleccia. Before venturing down it, enquire at the hotel about the state of the track, which even when it's in good condition can only be tackled by 4x4 vehicles and mountain bikes (the latter are available from the *Relais* for €20 per day). Allow around three hours to cover the route on foot, or one hour by car or bicycle; and be sure to leave early in the day to avoid the heat, taking plenty of water. The same advice applies if you attempt the popular trip along the desert's coast by **sea kayak** or **inflatable boat**; these can be rented by the day, or for longer periods, from three firms in St-Florent (see p.90).

On the far western side of the desert, 4km beyond the junction where the D81 joins the *route nationale* (RN1197), there's a good **campsite** and spectacular beach at **Ostriconi** (see p.127) – trailhead for the Agriates coastal walk described in the box on p.99. You can get there via any of the buses running between Bastia and L'Île Rousse/Calvi (see Travel details below), but not by train (the line approaches the Balagne further west). With your own transport, another good springboard for the area would also be the village of **Lama**, one of the most attractive in northern Corsica, 12km southeast.

Désert des Agriates beaches

The Désert des Agriates coast is strung with gorgeous beaches, but none is more spectacular than **plage de Saleccia**, 10km west along the coast from St-Florent – a kilometre-long curve of pearl-white sand and perfectly transluscent sea that's inaccessible by road. The majority of people who travel out to it (and be warned that there are lots of them in summer) do so in pleasure boats, or else via the horrendously pot-holed *piste* from Casta (see p.99), where you rent bicycles for the eleven-kilometre trip. It's also possible to walk via the coast path – a four to four hour thirty-minute trek from St-Florent (see box, p.99). The excursion boats don't sail this far, but from the jetty at plage de Loto it's only a gentle hour's walk around the headland. Just behind the beach, *Camping U Paradisu* (T04 95 37 82 51; mid-June to Sept) offers basic facilities in a scruffy site that's barely a notch better than bivouacking on the beach (which isn't allowed). Note that **swimming can be dangerous** off Saleccia; at certain phases in the tide, rips drag out unwary bathers – worth bearing in mind if you find yourself alone on the beach. In recent years, the famously white sand has also lain for much of the summer under drifts of rank-smelling posidonia.

The same isolation that makes Saleccia so alluring today was the main reason it was chosen during World War II as a landing stage by the commander of the submarine *Le Casabianca*. The beach's historic associations may in part explain why Saleccia was used as a location for the World War II epic *The Longest Day*, starring Robert Mitchum.

The other Agriates beach within easy reach, and thus deluged in summer by day-trippers, is **plage de Loto** (or plage de Lodo, as it's sometime spelt), to which the two excursion boats from St-Florent sail daily between June and September (see p.90). To see this magnificent site in all its deserted glory, therefore, you'll either have to get to it before or after the boats (a tall order in summer, when the first arrives by 10am and the last leaves around 7.30pm), or, better still, walk there out of season.

Following the **coast path**, you'll cross several other, even more isolated, coves and beaches, the most striking of which is **plage de Guignu**, two and a half hours west of Saleccia, where there's a small *gîte d'étape* (T04 95 37 09 86; €12 per bunk) run by the local nature conservancy council. Beyond the reach of all but the most tenacious trekkers and pleasure boaters, it's the most remote of the desert's large beaches and a perfect place to hole up for a few days (stays at the *gîte* are officially limited to four nights maximum).

Travel details

Trains

At the time of writing, Corsica's old *micheline* train service was in the process of being upgraded. By the spring of 2009 new track and locomotives should be fully operational, which will substantially shorten the journey times given below. The latest timetables are available at any Corsican station, and online at Ⓦ www.corsicabus.org. More details on the upgrade appear on p.27.

Bastia to: Ajaccio (2–4 daily; 3hr 10min–3hr 40min); Algajola (2 daily; 2hr 40min); Aregno-plage (2 daily; 2hr 40min); Belgodère (2 daily; 2hr); Biguglia (2–4 daily; 10min); Bocognano (2–4 daily; 2hr 25min); Calvi (2 daily; 3hr); Corte (2–4 daily; 1hr 30min); L'Île Rousse (2 daily; 2hr 30min); Ponte Novu (2–4 daily; 50min); Ponte Leccia (2–4 daily; 1hr); Sant'Ambrogio (2 daily; 2hr 40min); Venaco (2–4 daily; 1hr 45min); Vivario (2–4 daily; 2hr); Vizzavona (2–4 daily; 2hr 10min).

Buses

The listings below summarize which bus companies cover which routes, how often they run and how long journeys take. Start by looking up your intended destination in the first section; then, using the company's acronym (eg EV or RB), go to the second section for more detailed route and frequency information. Precise departure times can be checked in advance either via the bus companies direct, or (if your French isn't up to that) Bastia tourist office (☎04 95 31 81 34). A full rundown of Corsican bus services, including up-to-date timetables, also appears online at ⓦwww.corsicabus.org.

Bastia to: Ajaccio (EV; 3hr); Aléria/Cateraggio (RB; 1hr 30min); Algajola (BV; 1hr 40min); Calvi (BV; 2hr); Canari (TS; 1hr 30min); Corte (EV; 1hr 15min); Erbalunga (SAB; 30min); L'Île Rousse (BV & EV; 1hr 40min); Macinaggio (SAB; 2hr); Miomo (SAB;

1–2hr; 30min); Nonza (TS; 1hr 30min); Patrimonio (TST; 30min); Porto Vecchio (RB; 3hr); St-Florent (TST & TS; 1hr); Solenzara (RB; 2hr 10min).

St-Florent to: L'Île Rousse (TST; 1hr).

BV: Les Beaux Voyages ☎04 95 65 15 02 or 04 95 62 02 10, ⓦwww.corsicars.com. Bastia–L'Île Rousse–Algajola–Calvi; year round Mon–Sat 1 daily.

EV: Eurocorse Voyages ☎04 95 31 73 76, ⓦwww.eurocorse.net. Bastia–Corte–Ajaccio; year round Mon–Sat 2 daily.

RB: Rapides Bleues ☎04 95 31 03 79, ⓦwww.kallistour.com. Bastia–Aléria/Cateraggio–Ghisonaccia–Solenzara–Porto Vecchio; year round Mon–Sat (& Sun from mid-June to mid-Sept) 2 daily.

SAB: Société des Autobus Bastiais ☎04 95 31 06 65, ⓦwww.bastiabus.com. Bastia–Lavasina–Erbalunga–Sisco–Pietracorbara–Macinaggio; June–Sept Mon–Sat 2–3 daily; Oct–May Mon–Sat 2 daily. Bastia–Miomo–Erbalunga; Mon–Fri every 30min, Sat & Sun hourly.

TST: Transports Santini ☎04 95 37 02 98. Bastia–Patrimonio–St-Florent; year round Mon–Sat 2 daily. St-Florent–Casta–L'Île Rousse; July & Aug Mon–Sat 2 daily.

Ferries

For ferry details, see p.21 and p.69.

2

The Balagne

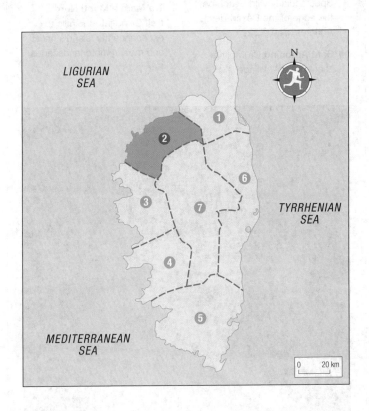

LIGURIAN
SEA

N

①

②

⑥

③

⑦

TYRRHENIAN
SEA

④

⑤

MEDITERRANEAN
SEA

0   20 km

CHAPTER 2 # Highlights

✳ **Quai Landry, Calvi**
Sophisticated Riviera-style cafés in the shadow of the Genoese bastion, with mesmeric views of the mountains. See p.113

✳ **Plage de Perajola, Ostriconi**
Spectacularly wild beach on the edge of the Désert des Agriates. See p.127

✳ **Sant'Antonino** Crumbling "eagle's nest" village surveying a vast sweep of the Balagne. See p.131

✳ **Pigna** The epicentre of the region's cultural revival holds numerous craft workshops and a dreamy café terrace, A *Casarelle*. See p.132

✳ **Tra Mare e Monti Nord trail** Climb into the hills to experience the island's finest and most remote landscapes. See p.141

▲ Plage de Perajola

The Balagne

M uch of Corsica's northwest is taken up by the **Balagne**, a region divided into Haute-Balagne – the coast between Calvi and L'Île Rousse, and its hinterland – and Balagne Déserte, the area south of Calvi. In the past the Haute-Balagne was the most fertile region of Corsica, famous for its prolific production of honey, fruit and wine, but nowadays – though it has its patches of lushness – a stark brightness characterizes the fire-devastated landscapes of the interior, with acres of gnarled olive trees and wavy vestiges of dry-stone walls intermittently breaking the pattern of pale orange rock. If you're approaching this region from the east, the first glimpse of its coast is an arresting sight, the turquoise and white stripes of sea and sand making a vibrant contrast with the mottled land.

Calvi, the Balagne's largest town and Corsica's third largest port, is also one of the most attractive places in Corsica, with its medieval citadelle rising majestically from a stark granite promontory. Six kilometres of sandy beach, backed by a dark ribbon of pines, ensures its popularity as a summer resort, the seasonal influx being served by numerous hotels and a string of campsites. Tourist development has got a little out of hand to the east of Calvi, where private marinas and expensive holiday villages occupy much of the Haute-Balagne coast, but the beaches are outstanding, none more so than that at the former Genoese stronghold of **Algajola**. A stunning white strand also forms the focal point of nearby **L'Île Rousse**, a beguilingly faded port built in the eighteenth century as a rival to Calvi.

Despite the widespread devastation wrought by fires in the summer of 2005, the hinterland of the Haute-Balagne is still a glorious landscape, with thousands of olive trees swathing the rocky slopes, and fortress villages such as **Sant'Antonino** and **Speloncato** crowning the hilltops, each one embellished with a Baroque bell tower. Many of these settlements are at the receiving end of government programmes aimed at reviving ancient industries and crafts, so you'll see functioning workshops in various places – indeed **Pigna** and **Feliceto** are practically run by their artisan communities. The area tourist office has included most of them on the so-called **Strada di l'Artigiani**, or Route des Artisans, which you can follow in easy day-trips from the coast; ask at any tourist office for the colour leaflet outlining the route.

The **Monte Grosso massif**, whose sheer granite spine dominates the horizon south of the Haute-Balagne, divides the coastal strip from the secluded **Vallée de la Tartagine**, a region of landlocked pine and chestnut forest known since ancient times as the **Giunssani**. With only a handful of depopulated villages hemmed in by towering peaks, this isolated valley system harbours some of the best hiking routes on the island. Its highest

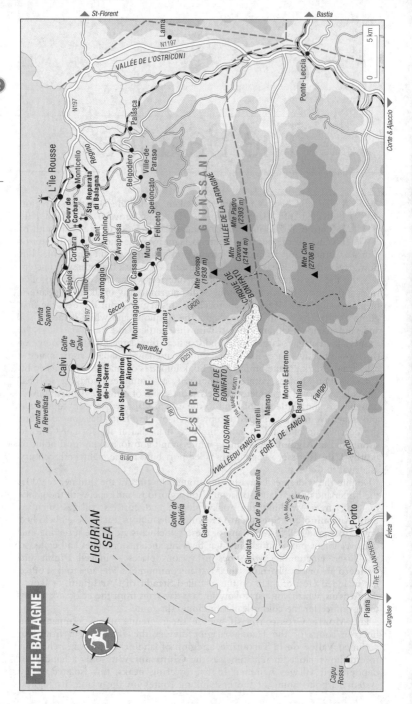

THE BALAGNE

ridges are accessible via sections of the **GR20**, which skirts the Giunssani and presses southeast along the Corsican watershed towards the interior. The official trailhead of the arduous ten- to fourteen-day route, however, is at **Calenzana**, in the hills southeast of Calvi. The village also marks the start of the gentler ten-day **Tra Mare e Monti**, which zigzags south to Cargèse through some of the Mediterranean's most dramatic scenery. For more on both routes, see Chapter 8.

Southwest of Calvi the terrain becomes increasingly grandiose, and the isolated coastal settlement of **Galéria** is well placed for excursions into some memorable landscapes. Inland, there's the **Vallée du Fango**, whose dense forests track the river to the base of towering Cinto and Paglia Orba Massifs, or the spectacular **Cirque de Bonifato**, a ridge of jagged peaks encircling another forested valley.

A brief history of the Balagne

Archeological digs in the Balagne have yielded evidence of settlements dating back to the sixth millennium BC. Early Neolithic peoples hunted and gathered along the coast, moving gradually inland during the late Neolithic period; by the Bronze Age, most settlements occupied more easily defensible hilltop sites. Tools and bones discovered in these suggest that their inhabitants both hunted (mainly a now-extinct species of mountain goat) and reared sheep for milk, establishing an agro-pastoral economy that would endure more or less unchanged for more than four thousand years.

Sweeping economic changes occurred in antiquity with the arrival of technologically advanced Phoenician and Etruscan traders, but the Balagne's agricultural potential was fully exploited only by the **Romans**, who began the cultivation of olives here in the fertile volcanic soil. Known since these times, and in various languages, as the "Pays de l'Huile et du Froment" (Land of Oil and Wheat), the region became the richest on the island, and a prime target for the Saracen raiders who menaced the Mediterranean in the medieval era. The attacks subsided under the rule of the **Pisans**, who constructed forts along the coast to keep the marauding Moors at bay, as well as erecting dozens of beautiful churches and chapels, whence the popular nickname "Balagna Santa". After the **Genoese** takeover in the thirteenth century, the citadelles at Calvi and Algajola were built, and these new ports did a steady trade with Tuscany, the chief cargo being the local olive oil, which for hundreds of years enjoyed a reputation as the best in the Mediterranean. Under the Genoese, the region was divided into semi-autonomous cantons ruled by the local nobility, or **Sgio**, many of whom were highly cultured men who had been educated in Italy – a remarkable contrast to the wild *Sgio* of Sartène. Furthermore, although class divisions were as strong as elsewhere in Corsica, the peasants of the Balagne were distinguished by their versatility, with many working as tailors or cobblers as well as farmers, and by their greater independence from their lords, in that they were allowed their own flocks. The result of this comparatively enlightened rule was that the people of the Balagne remained loyal to Genoa well into the eighteenth century.

The Balagne reached its apogee in the nineteenth century, but decline set in when emigration began in the early twentieth century and the small oil mills in the depopulated villages could no longer compete with industrialized producers. It wasn't until the 1950s, when Calvi and L'Île Rousse became popular tourist spots, that the local economy began to pick up, and hotels and holiday complexes mushroomed along the Balagne coast. More recently, the

Bushfires and the bovine connection

Each year, despite armies of volunteer firefighters and a fleet of water-carrying Canadair seaplanes, vast swathes of the Corsican countryside are devastated by fire. All kinds of people have been blamed for starting the blazes – from lone pyromaniacs to cigarette-butt-chucking tourists – but the real culprits have only recently been singled out: **cows and sheep** or, more accurately, their owners.

The link between the annual infernos and the skinny livestock roaming the island's interior leads back to Brussels and the European Union's Common Agricultural Policy. In the late 1970s, the EU, attempting to reduce its milk lakes and butter mountains, introduced grants for dairy farmers to convert to beef and veal. Although they had never in fact produced much milk, the Corsicans responded by developing a sudden passion for cattle husbandry: within twenty years, the number of cows on the island nearly tripled from 29,000 to 80,000, bringing in a shower of lucrative **subsidies** from Brussels. Ironically, few of the recipients of EU money actually own any land – proof that possessing cattle is enough to secure entitlement. The cows, meanwhile, wander freely across communal areas of maquis, which the *faux éleveurs*, or "fake livestock rearers", routinely burn so that fresh shoots of grass will grow to feed their neglected animals. This technique has been used by pastoralists for centuries to provide food for cattle and ewes in long, dry summers, but their careful control of the fires meant that the amount of land damage was always sustainable. The uncontrolled blazes started by the *faux éleveurs*, on the other hand, have been catastrophic.

In September 1994, when the bureaucrats in Brussels finally got wind of what was happening in Corsica, all EU aid to the island was suspended. The effects of the move were dramatic: bushfires fell to one tenth of the normal level that summer. Solving the problem in the long term, however, may be more difficult. EU subsidies bring in large sums of money for cattle owners, and any threat to their livelihood is bound to come up against stiff resistance. Nor is it only the farmers who benefit from the fires, but also builders (who restore damaged houses), foresters (to replant the trees) and, of course, firefighters (who welcome the overtime pay). Combine the financial disincentive with the customary Corsican mistrust of outside interference, and the future for the maquis looks black indeed.

A series of particularly destructive fires in recent years has demonstrated just how difficult the problem has been to snuff out. One of the more high-profile reactions to the phenomenon was the foundation by Jean-François Bernadini, frontman of the group I Muvrini (see p.418), of the pressure group **Vergogna à tè chi brusgi a terra** ("Shame on you who burn the land"), which has sought ways to break through the typically Corsican code of silence that protects the fire starters.

N1197 road, linking Calvi to Bastia via Ponte Leccia, has improved communications with the rest of the island, while maritime traffic and flights to mainland France have increased in the last couple of years. Nevertheless, the economy of rural areas continues to struggle, in spite of attempts to develop small-scale wine and olive oil production with a modern irrigation programme. The expensive new **Codole Dam**, inland from L'Île Rousse, has remained full to the brim since it was built because there has been so little demand for its water, while the planned resorts hereabouts, for which the reservoir was constructed, have failed to materialize due to unwieldy local bureaucracy and the complexities of nationalist politics. Further setbacks to rural development have been the fires that have repeatedly devastated the countryside in recent years (see box above).

Calvi

Seen from the water, **CALVI** is a beautiful spectacle, its three immense bastions topped by a crest of ochre buildings, sharply defined against a hazy backdrop of snowcapped mountains. Below the citadelle, a much-photographed strip of pastel-painted, red-roofed houses, belfries and spidery palm trees delineates the *basse ville*, with its yacht-crammed marina, from where the town beach sweeps in a graceful semicircle around the bay. Add a perpetually mild climate and Riviera-like atmosphere, and you can see why Calvi has been attracting tourists for quite a while.

A popular hangout for European glitterati since the 1950s, when *Tao's* nightclub kept the tangos playing till dawn, Calvi in high summer has the ambience of a ritzy Côte d'Azur resort, with expensive quayside cafés and a clientele drawn largely from the luxury yachts moored in the marina. A more down-to-earth holiday culture is never far away, though, thanks to the huge campsites that sprawl under the *pinède* (pine forest) to the east of the town, and the backstreets have their fair share of tacky souvenir boutiques.

Calvi's cultural life has been considerably enriched by the numerous **festivals** held here (see p.116).

A brief history of Calvi

Calvi began as a fishing port on the site of the present-day *basse ville*, but like many of Corsica's coastal towns it fell victim to relentless Vandal, Ostrogoth and Saracen raids between the fifth and tenth centuries. No more than a cluster of houses and fishing shacks existed on the site until the Pisans conquered the island, and it was only with the arrival of the Genoese that the town became a stronghold, in 1268, when the Corsican nobleman **Giovaninello de Loreto** built a huge citadelle on the windswept rock overlooking the port and named it Calvi.

The republic of Genoa granted the town special privileges, such as freer trading rights and tax exemptions, in order to ensure the fidelity of the population – who, in any case, were for the most part Genoese. This loyalty was tried in 1553 by a terrible combined siege of the Turks and French, earning Calvi its motto: *Civitas Calvis Semper Fidelis*. In 1758 Calvi refused to become part of independent Corsica, a stand for which it suffered in 1794, when Paoli made an alliance with the British. A fleet commanded by Nelson launched a brutal two-month attack, bombarding the walls from all sides and eventually forcing surrender. Nelson left saying he never wanted to see the place again, and nearly didn't, for during the attack he lost the use of one eye.

The nineteenth century saw a decline in Calvi's fortunes, as the Genoese merchants left and the French concentrated on developing Ajaccio and Bastia. One Victorian traveller described it as "a frowning fort with cracked, tottering ruins, worn and wasted by the rain". Later Calvi became primarily a military base, used as a point for smuggling arms and commandos to Occupied France in World War II, and has been a base of the **Légion Étrangère** (Foreign Legion) since 1962; you're bound to see groups of cropped-haired legionnaires in their characteristic white-peaked *képis* and immaculate khaki uniforms strolling up and down the marina, watched by couples of similarly attired military police. Tourism, however, is now the essence of Calvi; the town became fashionable right after the war and has enjoyed good business as a holiday resort ever since.

Nelson in Corsica

More than a decade before his death at the battle of Trafalgar, a young and ambitious **Horatio Nelson** was gaining valuable experience fighting the French in Corsica on behalf of Pascal Paoli and his patriots. The unlikely alliance came about following the fall of Toulon in 1793, when the British, under Lord Hood, chose the island as a base for their Mediterranean fleet. Several ships were dispatched to blockade Corsica, among them Nelson's 64-gun *Agamemnon*.

Arriving off Cap Corse in the middle of winter, the British picked off a series of easy targets along the north coast before laying siege to the watchtower at **Punta di Mortella** (see p.93) and, later, the citadelle at St-Florent, where they took a bloody nose before setting their sights on the tougher proposition of **Bastia**. In the course of the hard-fought 37-day siege that ensued, Nelson – who, during reconnaissance, had lied about the strength of the French defences in order to gain permission for an attack considered by his superiors as "most visionary and rash" – played a key role, overseeing the landing of cannon and manning of batteries. However, his small but resolute crew's contribution was never fully acknowledged. The army, whose commander had consistently refused to "entangle (himself) in any co-operation", stood by until the French surrender, whereupon it promptly marched on the town from St-Florent to steal Nelson's glory.

The bombardment began on July 4. It was during the concentrated French counter-fire that Nelson, eight days later, was struck in the face by stones and splinters thrown up after an enemy shell burst on the emplacement he was commanding. One laceration penetrated his eyeball, but the paragon of British stiff upper lip, writing to his senior officer that evening, reported only that he'd "got a little hurt".

Seemingly of more concern to Nelson at the time were the "shivering fits" bedeviling him and his men. The British hospital ship was by this stage crammed to the gunwales with malaria cases, stewed by the relentless mid-summer heat. Getting wind that the besiegers were succumbing to illness, the French sued for a short truce (time enough for the British to be further weakened and for reinforcements to arrive from the mainland) but their ruse didn't work. The cannonfire continued: in the four weeks preceding the surrender by a depleted and demoralized Gallic garrison on August 10, some eleven thousand cannon and around three thousand shells were launched at Calvi, reducing huge chunks of it to rubble (some of which has still not been cleared away). "The place is a heap of ruins," wrote Nelson.

On board the *Agamemnon* as it sailed back to Leghorn (Livorno), the future hero of Trafalgar finally wrote to his wife to inform her that the "slight scratch" he'd sustained three weeks earlier had resulted in the loss of sight in one eye. "(It) is grown worse, and is in almost total darkness, and very painful at times; but never mind, I can see very well with the other."

Among the many myths surrounding Britain's most illustrious admiral was that he wore an eye patch over his bad eye for the rest of his life. In fact, Nelson had a special shade made and fastened to his famous naval hat to protect his good eye from sun glare. In later years, he was able to put the bad one to good use. During the messy battle of Copenhagen in 1801, Lord Nelson, as he was by this time known, ignored orders from his Commander-in-Chief, Sir Hyde Parker, to discontinue action, saying to his colleague, "You know, Foley, I have only one eye. I have the right to be blind sometimes." Raising his spyglass to his damaged one, he uttered the historic words "I really do not see the signal", and went on to win the decisive victory of the Baltic campaign.

Arrival and information

Ste-Catherine airport (℡04 95 65 88 88, ⓦ www.calvi.aeroport.fr) lies 7km south of Calvi and is served by daily flights from mainland France and weekly charters from the UK and other northern European countries during the summer. **Taxis** (℡04 95 65 30 36 or 04 95 65 03 10) provide the only public transport into town; the trip shouldn't cost more than €17 during weekdays (or €22 evenings and on Sun). The **train station** is on avenue de la République (℡04 95 65 00 61), close to the marina and the air-conditioned **tourist office** on quai Landry (June 15–Sept 30 daily 9am–7pm, Oct 1–June 14 Mon–Fri 9am–noon & 2–5.30pm, Sat 9am–noon; ℡04 95 65 16 67, ⓦwww.balagne-corsica.com).

Autocars Les Beaux Voyages' **buses** from Bastia and towns along the north coast stop outside the train station on place de la Porteuse d'Eau; Autocars SAIB's minibuses from Porto pull in at the marina.

Ferries dock at the Port de Commerce, immediately below the citadelle. For details of companies offering **car** and **motorbike rental** in Calvi, see p.118.

Car parking is easiest (and free) in the large roadside lot next to the marina, to the right of the main road as you approach town; otherwise, try the Super-U car park further south (see map for directions).

Accommodation

There are a vast number of beds for tourists in Calvi, and **accommodation** is easy to find except from mid-July to August and during the jazz and choral festivals (see p.116), when you should book weeks ahead. Prices are generally reasonable, apart from during high season, when they go through the roof. There's a full rundown of places to stay in the tourist office's free handout – useful in the unlikely event that our recommendations are all fully booked.

Hotels

Les Arbousiers route de Pietra-Maggiore ℡04 95 65 04 47, ℉04 95 65 26 14. Large, fading pink place set back from the main road, 1km south of town and 150m from the beach, with rooms ranged around a quiet courtyard. A particularly good deal in shoulder season (€42 per double). ④

La Caravelle Marco Plage, 1km south of centre ℡04.95.65.95.50, ⓦwww.hotel-la-caravelle.com. An impeccably clean, modern hotel virtually on the beach, with ground floor rooms set around a garden; those on the first floor are more luxurious. Buffet breakfasts served on a sunny patio, and there's a nice bar-restaurant. Good value considering the location, quality of the property and service. ⑧–⑨

Casa Vecchia route de Santore ℡04 95 65 09 33, ⓦwww.hotel-casa-vecchia.com. Small chalets set in a leafy garden, 500m east of town, and 200m from the beach. In June and Sept doubles drop to €60; half board (€112 for two persons) is obligatory in July and Aug. Friendly management. May–Sept. ④–⑤

🏃 **Du Centre** 14 rue Alsace-Lorraine ℡04 95 65 02 01. Old-fashioned *pension*, with a welcoming owner, occupying a former police barracks in a narrow, pretty street near Église Ste-Marie-Majeure and harbourside. Its rooms are large for the price, but plain with shared WC. The cheapest option in town by a long chalk: from €33

per double June & Sept, rising to a mere €46 in July & Aug. June–Oct. ②–③

🏃 **Cyrnea** route de Bastia ℡04 95 65 03 35, ⓦwww.hotelcyrnea.com. Large budget hotel, a 20min walk south of town, and 300m from the beach. Good-sized rooms for the price, all with bathrooms and balconies (ask for one with "*vue montagne*" to the rear). Outstanding value for money, even in high season. April–Nov. ④–⑤

Grand Hôtel 3 bd Wilson ℡04 95 65 09 74, ⓦwww.grand-hotel-calvi.com. Elegant *fin-de-siècle* luxury hotel in the centre of town, with mostly period furniture and fittings. The rooms, though somewhat dowdy, are huge, and many have good views (as does the breakfast salon, which looks over the rooftops of the old quarter). April–Oct. ⑥–⑦

Relais International de la Jeunesse "U Carabellu" 4km from the centre of town on route de Pietra-Maggiore ℡04 95 65 14 16 or 04 93 81 27 63. Follow the N197 for 2km, turn right at the sign for Pietra-Maggiore, and the hostel is in the village another 2km further on (along a track that's impassable for cars). The dorms are mostly small (so you don't always have to share if you're in a couple or a small group), and the views from the terrace wonderful. €16 per bed, or €25 with breakfast and €32 for full board. April–Oct.

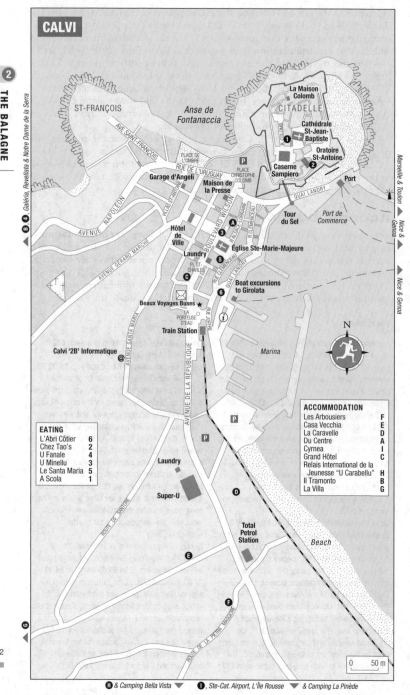

CALVI

ACCOMMODATION

Les Arbousiers	F
Casa Vecchia	E
La Caravelle	D
Du Centre	A
Cyrnea	I
Grand Hôtel	C
Relais International de la Jeunesse "U Carabellu"	H
Il Tramonto	B
La Villa	G

EATING

L'Abri Côtier	6
Chez Tao's	2
U Fanale	4
U Minellu	3
Le Santa Maria	5
A Scola	1

Il Tramonto route de Porto ☏04 95 65 04 17, ⓦwww.hotel-iltramonto.com. Excellent little budget hotel, with rates falling to €35 in low season. Its 1970s exterior is a bit unpromising, but the rooms are clean, comfortable and light (try for one with "*vue mer*") and there are little terraces and superb views over Punta della Revellata. On-site parking available. ❸–❹

La Villa 2km west of town along Chemin de Notre-Dame-de-la-Serra ☏04 95 65 10 10, ⓦwww.hotel-lavilla.com. Spacious cloisters, sunny mosaics, low terracotta roofs and arcades framing sea views give this luxury hotel on the hill above town, one of only a handful of four-stars on the island, the feel of a Balagne monastery fused with a Roman villa. You get the run of their Turkish baths, top-notch sports facilities and four pools (including one which seems to blend with the horizon), as well as an exclusive stretch of beach. And they've a helipad, should you need one. Rooms and suites from €230 to €700 per night. ❾

Campsites

Bella Vista 2km along the N197 from Calvi ☏04 95 65 11 76, ⓦwww.camping-bellavista .com. A large, quiet and friendly three-star site, 700m from the beach. Turn right at the sign to Pietra-Maggiore, and the campsite's another 1km along on the right-hand side. Open April–Oct.

La Pinède 2km east of Calvi between the beach and N197 ☏04 95 65 17 80, Ⓕ05 96 65 19 60. Popular site in a pine forest, with bar, restaurant, supermarket and tennis courts. Just far enough out of town to be quiet and only 5min walk from the beach, though you pay a bit extra for the prime locations and three-star facilities. Catch the train out here, and ask the guard to let you get off two stops after Calvi. April–Oct.

The Town

Social life in Calvi focuses on the restaurants and cafés of **quai Landry**, a spacious seafront walkway linking the marina and the port. This is the best place to get the feel of the town, but as far as sights go there's not a lot to the *basse ville*. At the far end of the quay, under the shadow of the citadelle, stands the sturdy **Tour du Sel**, a medieval lookout post once used to store imported salt. If you strike up through the narrow passageways off quai Landry, you'll come out at **rue Clémenceau**, where restaurants and souvenir shops are packed into every available space. In a small square opening out onto the street stands the pink-painted **Église Ste-Marie-Majeure**, built in 1774, whose spindly bell tower rises elegantly above the cafés on the quay but whose interior contains nothing of real note. From the church's flank, a flight of steps connects with boulevard Wilson, a wide, modern high street which rises to **place Christophe-Colomb**, point of entry for the *haute ville*, or **citadelle**.

The citadelle

Beyond the ancient gateway to the **citadelle**, inscribed with the town's motto – *Civitas Calvis Semper Fidelis* (see p.109) – a narrow alleyway twists past the enormous **Caserne Sampiero**, formerly the governor's palace. Built in the thirteenth century, when the great round tower was used as a dungeon, the castle is currently used for military purposes, meaning that it's now closed to the public. The best way of seeing the rest of the citadelle is to follow the **ramparts**, which connect three immense bastions from where there are magnificent views across the bay to the mountains of the Balagne and Cinto massif.

Within the walls the houses are tightly packed along tortuous stairways and cobbled passages that converge on the diminutive **piazza d'Armes**, next to the Caserne Sampiero. Dominating the square is the **Cathédrale St-Jean-Baptiste**, set at the highest point of the promontory. This chunky ochre edifice, founded in the thirteenth century, was partly destroyed during the Turkish siege of 1553 and then suffered extensive damage twelve years later, when the powder

White képis and winged daggers

Each year on April 30, ranks of immaculately dressed legionnaires from Calvi's Camp Raffali parade through town to celebrate "Camerone Day". The parade is the public face of a very private army unit: the enigmatic **2e Régiment Étranger de Parachutistes** of the French Foreign Legion, or **Légion Étrangère**.

The French Foreign Legion was formed in 1831 at the behest of King Louis Philippe as a way of offering gainful employment to the potentially troublesome hordes of economic migrants and excitable revolutionaries collecting in Paris at that time. Enticed by the promise of French citizenship in exchange for five years' service (an incentive that still exists today), the recruits were promptly packed off to fight in France's North African colonies. Expected to march 30km per day across soft sand carrying full packs, the first legionnaires were just as likely to perish from heat exhaustion and dysentery as battle wounds.

It was during this era that many of the clichés surrounding the Legion were coined; deserters were indeed buried up to their necks in sand to face the Saharan sun with their eyelids sewn open or dragged for days tied to mule carts. But in spite of the inhumane conditions, recruits continued to pour in. Many – like the American songwriter Cole Porter, English philosopher Arthur Koestler and the young Prince Aage of Denmark – did so for pure adventure; many more signed up to flee debt, prison or unhappy love affairs. Then, as today, the Legion offered **anonymity** for its recruits. For the first year of service, legionnaires are given a false name and there's an unwritten law that no one should be forced to answer questions about their past. Today, the Légion Étrangère comprises 8500 men from more than one hundred countries.

The muscle-bound, crew-cut Rambo lookalikes you'll see swaggering around Calvi's quai Landry in their knife-edge creases and white *képis* are members of the Legion's elite force, hand-picked from the cream of the recruits. Based at Camp Raffali, on the southeast edge of town, the 1300 crack paras get to wear the coveted green beret bearing the famous winged-hand-and-dagger emblem of the 2e REP. More often than not, however, it is the distinctive *képis* you'll encounter on the quai Landry, pulled more steeply over the eyes by Calvi's notoriously arrogant legionnaires than by those from regular regiments.

The Legion's headquarters at Camp Raffali opens its door to the general public twice each year: Camerone Day (April 30) and St Michael's Day (Sept 29).

---

magazine in the governor's palace exploded. Rebuilt in Greek cross form and surmounted by a black-tiled octagonal dome, the church became a cathedral in 1576, as the reconstruction was drawing to a close. The church's great treasure is the **Christ des Miracles**, which is housed in the chapel on the right of the choir; this crucifix was brandished at the marauding Turks during the 1553 siege, an act that reputedly saved the day.

North of piazza d'Armes, in a small patch of wasteland off rue du Fil, stands **La Maison Colomb**, the shell of the building that Calvi believes was Christopher Columbus's birthplace, as the plaque on the wall states. The claim rides on pretty tenuous circumstantial evidence. Columbus's known date of birth coincides with the Genoese occupation of Calvi, at which time a weaving family by the name of Columbo lived in the town. Papers left by Columbus's son state that Christopher was the son of weavers, that he had two relations in the navy (there was indeed a Corsican sea captain named Columbo), who "came from the sea" (which could be interpreted as coming from the island of Corsica). What's more, Columbus is said to have taken Corsican dogs on his voyage, and he placed his first New World ports under the protection of popular Corsican saints. Believers claim that the Genoese deliberately burned the town archives in 1580 and renamed the street, formerly rue Columbo, in order to cover up the truth. The house itself was destroyed by Nelson's army during the siege of 1794, but as recompense a statue was erected on May 20, 1992, the 500th anniversary of his "discovery" of America; his alleged birthday, October 12, is now a public holiday in Calvi, celebrated with fireworks and speeches.

On the east side of the citadelle, it's a quick walk along the ramparts to Maison Pacciola, where Napoléon spent a night in 1793. Close by is the **Oratoire St-Antoine**, an unremarkable building dating from the early sixteenth century but worth a look for the graceful grey granite **relief carving** above the door, featuring Anthony, patron saint of Calvi, flanked by St John the Baptist and St Francis.

The beach

Calvi's spectacular **beach** sweeps right round the bay from the end of quai Landry. Most of the first kilometre or so is owned by bars, which rent out sun loungers for a hefty price, but these can be avoided by following the track behind the sand for a kilometre or so to the start of a more secluded stretch. The sea might not be as sparklingly clear as at many other Corsican beaches, but it's warm, shallow and free of rocks. You can also swim and sunbathe off the rocks at the foot of the citadelle, which have the added attraction of fine views across the bay.

Eating, drinking and nightlife

Eating is a major pastime in Calvi and you'll find a wide selection of restaurants and snack bars, although few offer good value for money. This is particularly true of the **fish restaurants** lining the marina, where a three-course seafood supper fresh from the bay can cost upwards of €50. As a rule, it's cheaper to eat in the backstreets of the *basse ville*, whose stairways and cramped forecourts hide a host of buzzing, inexpensive pizzerias and Corsican speciality places. **Cafés** are strung along the marina, becoming more expensive the nearer they get to the Tour de Sel.

▲ Calvi beach

For **food shopping**, Calvi's two largest **supermarkets**, Casino and Super-U, are both south of the centre on the main road (avenue de la République). You can also buy groceries at the small self-service *alimentation* on the corner of rue Joffre and rue Georges, above quai Landry (open Sun during the tourist season), or at the daily fresh produce **market** in the hall between rue Clémenceau and boulevard Wilson. For artisanal local specialities and other authentic souvenirs, the best shop in town is *Chez Annie*, at 5 rue Clémenceau, which stocks a huge range of wines, honey, charcuterie, liqueurs and *canastrelli* biscuits.

Calvi's **nightlife** is livelier than you might expect, with clubs opening up all over town in the summer. There's also an open-air **cinema**, *Le Pop Cyrnos*, next to the Rallye supermarket on the N197, 1km out of town towards L'Île Rousse, which screens new releases (in French).

Restaurants

L'Abri Côtier on the quay, but entrance on rue Joffre. Mostly seafood dishes (such as sea bass with fennel and crayfish fresh from the gulf of Calvi) served on a terrace looking out to sea. Their set menus (€23–35) and *formules* are invariably the best deals; for vegetarians, there's a copious veggie *grande assiette*.

Chez Tao's rue St-Antoine, in the citadelle ☎04 95 65 00 73. Legendary nightclub (see box opposite) which has now been turned into an expensive piano bar offering fussy nouvelle cuisine and an outstanding view of the bay. The only hints of its unusual history are the striking black-and-white photos of Russian aristos on the walls. Count on roughly €40 à la carte. June–Sept daily 7pm–midnight; closed Oct–May.

U Fanale route de Porto, just outside the centre of town on the way to Punta della Revellata ☎04 95 65 18 82. It's worth the walk out here for the delicious, beautifully presented Corsican specialities – mussels or lamb simmered in ewe's cheese and white wine, a fine *soupe Corse*, and melt-in-the-mouth *fiadone*. Lovely views of the bay and Punta della Revellata too. Menu at €25 plus full à la carte choice. Closed Tues.

U Minellu off bd Wilson, near Ste-Marie-Majeure. Wholesome Corsican specialities served either in a narrow stepped alley or on a shady terrace. Their menu features local charcuterie, baked lamb, *cannelloni al brocciu*, wild boar with *pulenta*, and a cheese platter – great value at €20.

Le Santa Maria next to the Église Ste-Marie-Majeure, rue Clémenceau ☎04 95 64 04 19. A popular four-course tourist menu (€20) and paella (€23) are the main offerings here, served in an atmospheric little square in front of the church, with *pichets* of house wine or, if you can stretch to it, the wonderful Clos Culombu.

A Scola 27 Haute Ville. Delightful salon de thé-cum-pâtisserie opposite the entrance to the cathedral, serving salads, cakes, pastries and desserts freshly made on the premises, along with five blends of coffee and various speciality teas. It took the smiling proprietor a year of experimentation to perfect her lemon tart, and the chocolate and apricot sacher torte is equally sublime. A genuinely friendly address (a rarity for Calvi), and the view's great too.

Festivals and events

Over the last decade or so, Calvi has sought to reinvent itself as the island's culture capital through hosting a string of lively music **festivals** and **arts events** during the summer and early autumn. One of the chief instigators of this renaissance was Jean-Témir Kéréfoff, son of the famous nightclub impresario, Tao, who saw a festival scene as the ideal way to assert a new identity for a town whose inhabitants feel perennially outnumbered – by tourists in the summer and legionnaires in the winter. Specific dates and details, for all the events listed below, are available through the Calvi tourist office (see p.111).

La Passion Good Friday. One of the island's most sombre Easter celebrations revolves around a procession of hooded penitents called *La Granitola* ("The Snail" in Corsican), which takes place on Good Friday. Starting at 9pm in Calvi's *basse ville*, the line of penitents, barefoot and carrying simple wooden crosses, winds and unwinds itself through the streets to the citadelle, accompanied by an eerie chanting from the onlookers.

St-Érasme June 2. Fishermen's festival with firework displays in the harbour.

Rencontres d'Art Contemporain Mid-June to mid-Sept. Exhibitions by local artists at various galleries in the citadelle.

Festival du Jazz Third week of June; ⑩www .calvi-jazz-festival.com. One of the highlights of France's packed jazz calendar, featuring headline acts from all over the world. Tickets for the formal evening gigs (available at the marquee on the north side of the marina, immediately below the citadelle) cost around €25, but you can catch spontaneous free jam sessions, or *bœufs*, in the bars on quai Landry afterwards.

Le Feu d'artifice Ascension Day, Aug 15. Corsica's biggest firework display, celebrating the fête de Ste-Marie (the town's patron saint) and attracting upwards of fifty thousand people.

Rencontres de Chants Polyphoniques Mid-Sept; ⑩www.myspace.com/rencontrespolyphoniques. Corsica's principal festival of song is hosted by renowned Corsican singer Jean-Claude Acquaviva and his wonderful polyphonies group, A Filetta, who share the stage with top a cappella performers from around the world. Regular workshops run throughout the fortnight.

Festiventu Late Oct ☎04 95 65 06 67, ⑩www.lefestivalduvent.com. Calvi psyches itself up for winter with a feast of kite flying and microlight aircraft displays on the beach, as well as other weird attractions loosely connected to the theme of wind. Perfect for children.

Tao

A rare Dionysiac interlude in Dorothy Carrington's classic but rather staid portrait of Corsica, *Granite Island*, occurs in a club in Calvi in the late 1940s:

The night was gathering impetus … it carried us with the rising moon into dark, unexplored, fathomless places. The music was hypnotic. No one resisted it; the dancers moved with a taut, controlled violence, the men crouching over their partners as if kindling a fire.

When Dorothy Carrington was being whisked off her feet by dashing legionnaires and "unnaturally quiet men from Calenzana", *Chez Tao's* (see opposite) was still owned and run by its founder, Tao, a charismatic Russian whose life story reads like the plot from a lurid picaresque novel. A handsome Tcherkess Muslim from the Caucasus, Tao came to Calvi via a convoluted odyssey that began with him fleeing slaughter following the defeat of his White Russian cavalry regiment in the Crimea. He escaped to Constantinople and scraped a living as a dancer, performing for the sultan and his harem. From Turkey he danced through the vaudeville theatres and ballrooms of Europe to Paris and eventually New York where, in 1928, he met **Feliz Youssoupof**, a rich Russian nobleman believed to be one of Rasputin's murderers. The two became firm friends and together decided to return to Paris, and then to Calvi.

The arrival of the exotic pair, together with their musical entourage, must have cut a dash in the (then) sedate Corsican town. Before long, peasants and fishermen from all over the island were flocking in to watch Tao's show, and to dance with the foreign thespians on the quayside (at that time women dared not venture out at night, so men danced with them "sailor style", as Dorothy Carrington puts it). His popularity was still running high when his benefactor left, and the resourceful Tao, now married to a local woman, was able to open a nightclub in the former chapel of a bishop's palace in the citadelle.

Now run by Tao's son, *Chez Tao's* occupies the same sixteenth-century vault and still does a brisk trade during the season, though it's no longer a place where, in Dorothy Carrington's words, "masks and attitudes slip away". Far from it: posing and star-spotting these days preoccupy the majority of *Chez Tao's* summer punters. The local contingent, however, remain as "unnaturally quiet" as ever.

Around Calvi

Surveying Calvi and its mountainous hinterland from a picturesque hilltop south of the town, the **Chapelle de Notre-Dame-de-la-Serra** is a popular picnic spot, and an obvious target if you fancy a short hike inland. To reach it by car, follow the Ajaccio road for 3km, then take the signposted left turn up the hill. An alternative route is the steep and rather slippery path that starts above *La Villa* hotel: following the signposts off the main Calvi to L'Île Rousse road, drive or hike to the end of the lane running past the hotel, and follow the well-worn track that peels off left through the maquis for about twenty minutes until you see the chapel above you, set amid bulbous clusters of pale-pink granite.

Built in the 1860s over the site of a fifteenth-century sanctuary, the building boasts a fine parchment painting of the Immaculate Conception, but it's essentially the view that draws visitors – the great bastions of Calvi presiding over the perfect curve of the bay.

Boat excursions from Calvi

Catamarans, run by Colombo Line (℡04 95 65 32 10, ⓦwww.colombo-line .com), leave Calvi marina every day during the tourist season for Girolata, on the west coast, calling at **La Scandola** nature reserve and the **Calanches** rock formations of Piana en route (see p.153 & p.154). Much of this beautiful coast is off limits to visitors and can be seen close up only from the sea, which justifies the somewhat hefty ticket price. Full-day excursions, leaving at 9.15am and returning at 4pm, cost €55; the 2pm trip (return at 5.30pm) will set you back €45. Along the way, the boat chugs into gulleys, or *failles*, in the stark red cliffs, and you can occasionally glimpse marine life through the glass floor of the boat. It's a good idea to book the day before, and be prepared for last-minute cancellations if the weather looks unstable.

Listings

Airport enquiries ℡04 95 65 88 88; ⓦwww .calvi-aeroport.fr.

Ambulance ℡04 95 65 11 91.

Banks and exchange All the main banks and ATMs are on bd Wilson. The bureau de change on place de la Porteuse d'Eau, at the bottom of bd Wilson (June–Sept daily 9am–noon & 3–7pm), is one of several such places that change money outside normal banking hours (for a hefty commission fee).

Bicycle rental Garage d'Angeli, rue Villa-Antoine, on the left just west of place Christophe-Colomb (℡04 95 65 02 13, ⓦwww.garagedangeli.com). New mountain bikes (€15–17 per day). Take along your credit card, which they'll need for the €150 deposit, or your passport.

Bookshop Halle de la Presse, at the top of bd Wilson on the left as you're heading towards the citadelle, stocks a good selection of English titles.

Bus information Autocars Les Beaux Voyages, Résidence Le Vieux Chalet, place de la Porteuse d'Eau (℡04 95 65 11 35 or 04 95 65 15 02). Departure times can be checked at the tourist office (see p.111). Autocars SAIB ℡04 95 22 41 99 or 04 95 21 02 07; no office in Calvi; buy your ticket on the bus.

Car rental Avis, Port de Plaisance ℡04 95 65 06 74; Budget, at the airport ℡04 95 65 88 34; Citer, l'Orée des Pins ℡04 95 65 29 99 or at the airport ℡04 95 65 16 06; Hertz, 2 av Maréchal-Joffre ℡04 95 65 06 64 or at the airport ℡04 95 65 02 96; Rent-a-Car ℡04 95 60 08 07.

Diving Calvi is one of Corsica's diving hot spots, with a wrecked American B-17 bomber from World War II at the mouth of the harbour at a depth of 30m, and more challenging underwater corridors full of marine life around the Punta della Revellata. The town's five diving centres are: Calvi Plongée Citadelle, in the marina ℡04 95 65 33 67; Club de Plongée Castille, marina ℡04 95 65 14 05 or 06 07 89 77 63, ⓦwww.plongeecastille.com; Hippocampe, at the foot of the citadelle next to the fishing outfitters ℡04 95 60 57 74, ⓦwww .hippocampe2b.fr; École de Plongée Internationale de Calvi, next to the marina car park ℡04 95 65 42 22, ⓦwww.epic-plongee.com.

Internet Calvi 2B Informatique, av Santa-Maria (€3 per hr).

Laundry The cheapest self-service laundry is in the car park of Super-U supermarket, av Christophe-Colomb (daily 8am–9pm); the one on bd Wilson has newer machines but is expensive.

Pharmacy Pharmacie Centrale, next to the *Rex Café*, bd Wilson, opens on Sun during the tourist season.

Police Av de la République ☏ 04 95 65 33 30.

Post office At the lower end of bd Wilson (Mon–Fri 9am–noon & 2.30–5pm).

Taxis At the airport and place de la Porteuse d'Eau ☏ 04 95 65 03 10 or 04 95 65 30 36.

Train information Gare de Calvi ☏ 04 95 65 00 61.

Moving on from Calvi

Calvi is a busy **transport hub** during the summer, and is thus fairly well connected to mainland France and the rest of Corsica. However you travel, check departure times and points in advance with the tourist office, or directly with the operator by telephone, as these tend to alter slightly from year to year. Bear in mind that timetables change during the off-peak period (late Sept to early June).

By plane

Daily flights to Paris and Nice with Air France and Compagnie Corse Mediterranée (CCM) leave from Calvi's Ste-Catherine **airport**. Weekly charter flights to London Gatwick also leave from here during the summer, and you can sometimes pick up one-way tickets on these through local agents, or by telephoning one of the charter operators in England, listed on p.19.

By ferry

Superfast Corsica Ferries and SNCM ferries to and from Nice run five times per week in each direction from July until mid-September, three or four times per week in April and May, three times a week in June, and twice each week or less from mid-September through the winter. The journey on the NGV boats takes a mere two hour forty five minutes. To make a reservation (essential in peak season), go to SNCM's agent, Agence Tramar (aka CCR; ☏ 04 95 65 01 38), opposite the excursion boat stalls, or Corsica Ferries ticket counter (☏ 04 95 65 43 21) in the port de commerce. You can also buy tickets for all the ferry companies operating on the island from Autocars Les Beaux Voyages, in place de la Porteuse d'Eau ☏ 04 95 65 11 35. For more general information on fares and ferry company contact details, see Basics, p.21.

By train

See Travel details on p.142.

By bus

Buses from Calvi run throughout the year to **Bastia**. Autocars Les Beaux Voyages (see opposite) stop at Lumio, Algajola and L'Île Rousse, and there's a quicker *navette* (minibus) service to L'Île Rousse (mid-May to Oct only). Beaux Voyages buses also run to **Galéria**, and to **Calenzana**, trailhead for the **GR20** and Tra Mare e Monti hikes. The latter service (Mon–Sat only) departs at 2.30pm and 7pm from place de la Porteuse d'Eau. Corse Voyages Mariani also operates services on this route, leaving at 6.30pm (Mon–Sat) from the car park below the citadelle.

    Ajaccio is more difficult to get to – you can either take a bus from the car park of Super-U to Porto and then another bus from there the following day to the capital (both legs operated by Autocars SAIB, see opposite), or take Beaux Voyages' Bastia service as far as Ponte Leccia, from where a connecting bus runs the rest of the way. All in all, you'd be better off taking the train.

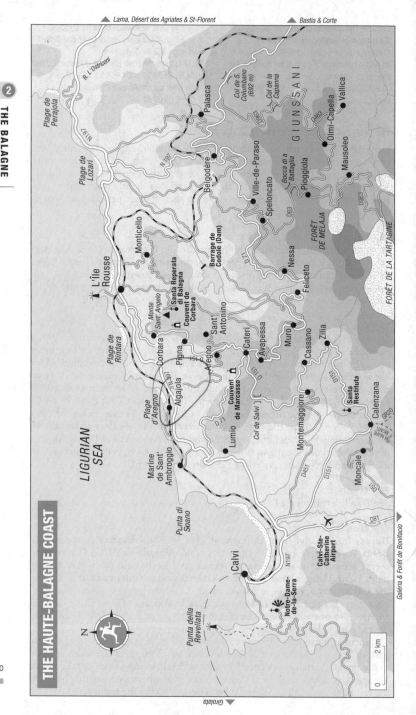

THE HAUTE-BALAGNE COAST

Lama, Désert des Agriates & St-Florent

Bastia & Corte

R. L'Ostriconi

Plage de Perajola

Plage de Lozari

N197

N197

Palasca

Col de S. Columbano (692 m)

D963

GIUNSSANI

Vallica

Olmi-Capella

D463

Belgodère

Ville-de-Paraso

Mausoleo

Bocca di a Battaglia

Ploggiola

Monticello

Speloncato

D63

FORÊT DE MELAJA

L'île Rousse

Santa Reperata di Balagna

Barrage de Codole (Dam)

Nessa

FORÊT DE LA TARTAGINE

Monte Sant' Angelo

Couvent de Corbara

D71

Feliceto

Plage de Rindara

Corbara

Pigna

Sant' Antonino

Cateri

Muro

Aregno

Avapessa

Zilia

Cassano

N197

Algajola

Plage d'Aregno

D151

Couvent de Marcasso

D151

Marine de Sant' Ambroggio

Lumio

Santa Restituta

D71

Col de Salvi

Calenzana

GR20

LIGURIAN SEA

Montemaggiore

D451

Moncale

D151

D151

D81

Punta di Soano

Galéria & Forêt de Bonifacio

Calvi-Ste-Catherine Airport

Calvi

N197

Notre-Dame-de-la-Serra

Punta della Revellata

N

0   2 km

Girolata

For a complete rundown of destinations reachable by bus from Calvi, see Travel details on p.142. Tickets for all services are available on the bus.

The Haute-Balagne coast

The **Haute-Balagne coast** may have been blighted in recent decades with purpose-built holiday villages and private marinas but there are many unspoilt places to spend a pleasant few days in this corner of the northwest. East of Calvi, the N197 cuts inland through **Lumio**, a terraced village overlooking the gulf that boasts both an exceptional Romanesque church and an excellent vineyard. One of the best places to stay in the area is **Algajola**, a few kilometres further along the coast road, a compact, relaxed resort with a golden half-moon beach. Beyond here, the distinctive red-tinged headland of La Pietra shelters the riviera-style resort town of **L'Île Rousse**, and a couple of outstanding beaches.

You can turn inland at regular intervals along the coast road to visit the beautiful Haute-Balagne hill villages, the pick of which are covered in the section beginning on p.128.

Lumio

Lining a sun-drenched hillside above the Golfe de Calvi, **LUMIO** was in ancient times the centre of a sun-worshipping cult, and was known to the Romans as *Ortis Culis*, or "Where the Sun Rises". Facing west, with spectacular views over the gulf, it's actually a more inspiring place to visit at sunset, when the honey-coloured **Chapelle San Pietro** is bathed in flattering light. Founded in the eleventh century and rebuilt in the eighteenth, the church retains some of its original Romanesque features, notably the palm-shaped capitals, geometric windows at the eastern end of the apse, and a pair of grinning lions jutting from the facade above the door (which are thought to have originally supported a porch).

Coming from Calvi, the easiest way to reach the church is to turn off the main *route nationale* where you see a lane veering right, just before the village. Park when you get to the monumental cemetery. Just beyond it, signs point the way to the **Clos Culombu** vineyard (Mon–Sat 9.30am–1pm & 4–7pm; ☏04 95 60 70 68), where traditional vigneron Etienne Suzzoni produces some of Calvi *appellation*'s finest wines, including a definitive Corsican red made from 100 percent Niellucciu grape.

Algajola

Roughly midway between Calvi and L'Île Rousse, **ALGAJOLA** is Balagne's third largest resort, but considerably quieter and less pretentious than either of its more famous neighbours. Although the village gets as swamped as anywhere else along this coast during July and August, out of season you can expect to have the beach, **Aregno-plage**, a kilometre-long curve of coarse sand beneath a picturesque Genoese citadelle, pretty much to yourself.

Because of its exposed situation, Algajola has suffered the frequent attentions of hostile forces; in 1643, the Turks devastated its Genoese citadelle, and in the 1790s Nelson assailed the town as a preliminary to the great Calvi siege. Despite such setbacks, the village did a steady trade in oysters and olive oil, and continued to be a major port on this part of the coast until L'Île Rousse developed towards the close of the eighteenth century. Its status was temporarily revived early in the twentieth century, when hotels were built over the old port, transforming it into a small but smart resort. However, decline set in after World War II, fuelled by the growing popularity of Calvi and L'Île Rousse.

Algajola consists of just one street, which begins alongside the beach and leads up to the **citadelle**. Beyond the gates, the dominant building is the **Castello**, raised on its small promontory in the thirteenth century then heavily restored in the seventeenth, when the fortifications were added after the Turkish attack. It's closed to the public, but you can walk around the ramparts behind the castle, from where a path leads back down to the beach.

Algajola lies on the main **bus** and **train** routes between Bastia and Calvi, with regular services in both directions throughout the year.

Accommodation

Virtually every **hotel** in Algajola overlooks the sea. **Campers** can stay at *Camping de la Plage* (℡ 04 95 60 71 76), sandwiched between the north end of the beach and *route nationale*.

Le Beau Rivage top of the beach ℡ 04 95 60 73 99, ⓦ www.hotel-beau-rivage.com. Panoramic views of the bay from light, airy and modern rooms with tiled floors; those on the second storey have more spacious balconies. Cheaper options in the hotel's annexe. ⑥

L'Esquinade next door to the post office by the citadelle gates ℡ & Ⓕ 04 95 60 70 19. The best budget choice: good-sized, impeccably maintained en-suite rooms (ask for one on the *côté jardin*), all with showers. No restaurant, but the downstairs bar's cheery enough. ③–⑤

De la Plage top of the beach ℡ 04 95 60 72 12, Ⓕ 04 95 60 64 89. An old-fashioned place, in the same family for seven generations and caught in a 1950s time warp. Very good value given the size of the rooms and the views, but often booked up (by groups of pensioners) in May, June & Sept. ⑥

Saint-Joseph at the entrance to the village if you're coming from Calvi ℡ 04 95 60 73 90. Good-value, modern, chalet-style rooms (with bathtubs instead of showers), close to the sea and castle, with turquoise shutters opening onto a breezy courtyard-terrace. Rates include breakfast. ⑤

Stella Mare above the train station ℡ 04 95 60 71 18, ⓦ www.stellamarehotel.com. Smart, friendly little two-star in its own garden on the hillside above the village. Lovely sea views, large rooms (with *loggias*) and a pretty Moroccan-style terrace with Berber rugs, lanterns and scatter cushions to lounge on in the evenings. The nicest option hereabouts, with a/c. ④–⑤

Eating

Le Padula Algajola beach. A great little *paillote* with fine views of the sunset, friendly service and tasty food, including delicious pizzas, rustled up by a Catalan chef.

La Vieille Cave just inside the arched entrance to the square, on the left ℡ 04 95 60 70 09. A range of different menus, most under €25 and with more imaginative dishes than usual (spinach and fromage frais soup, scorpion fish *aux herbes du maquis* and onions stuffed with *brocciu* and charcuterie). They also do a great seafood selection à la carte, and the location's very pleasant, especially in the evenings.

L'Île Rousse

Developed by Pascal Paoli in the 1760s as a "gallows to hang Calvi", the port of **L'ÎLE ROUSSE** (Isula Rossa) simply doesn't convince as a Corsican town, its palm trees, neat flower gardens and colossal pink 1930s hotel creating an atmosphere that has more in common with the French Riviera. Yet, for all its artificiality, the place has become unbearably popular in recent years, receiving more ferries and packing in more tourists than the larger port of Calvi. The proximity of three large white-sand **beaches** is the main reason for the resort's popularity, together with its ultra-mild **microclimate**; thanks to the amphi-theatre of hills that shelter the town from the cool winds blowing off the Haute

Balagne's mountains, temperatures here average two degrees higher than Bonifacio and Porto Vecchio, making this the hottest place in Corsica.

Pascal Paoli had great plans for his new town, which was laid out from scratch in 1758. He needed a port for the export of olive oil produced in the Balagne region, since Calvi was still in the hands of the Genoese, whose naval blockade was stifling the economy of the fledgling government. Originally the place was to be called Paolina, but the *Rubica Rocega* (Red Rocks) label had stuck from Roman times and L'Île Rousse it became. A large part of the new port was built on a regular grid system, featuring lines of straight parallel streets quite at odds with the higgledy-piggledy nature of most Corsican villages and towns. Thanks to the busy trading of wine and oil, it soon began to prosper and, two and a half centuries later, still thrives as a successful port, although these days the main traffic consists of holidaymakers. That the only town planned and built by Corsicans as a step towards self-reliance now makes its living from tourism as a classic French-style resort adds an ironic twist to Paoli's dream.

L'Île Rousse is connected by year-round **bus** services to Bastia and Calvi, with Autocars Les Beaux Voyages. The *micheline* **train** also stops here en route between Calvi and Ponte Leccia, where you can pick up connecting services to Ajaccio, via Corte and Vizzavona; and there are more or less hourly tramway services along the Balagne coast in the summer, starting at around 8am and

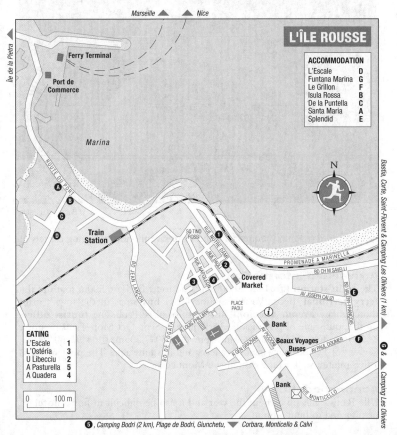

Marseille ▲　　▲ Nice

L'ÎLE ROUSSE

Île de la Pietra

Ferry Terminal

Port de Commerce

Marina

ROUTE DU PORT

Train Station

BD JEAN LANZON

BD DE FIGAJA

R GÉN GRAZIANI

L LOUIS PHILIPPE

RUE NAPOLÉON

RUE PAOLI

RUE NOTRE DAME

SQ TINO ROSSI

Covered Market

PLACE PAOLI

AV PICCIONI

PROMENADE A MARINELLA

BD CH M SAVELLI

AV JOSEPH CALIZI

BD VALÉRY-FRANÇOIS

AV PAUL DOUMER

RUE MONTICELLO

N

Bank

Beaux Voyages Buses

Bank

ACCOMMODATION	
L'Escale	D
Funtana Marina	G
Le Grillon	F
Isula Rossa	B
De la Puntella	C
Santa Maria	A
Splendid	E

EATING	
L'Escale	1
L'Ostéria	3
U Libecciu	2
A Pasturella	5
A Quadera	4

0　　100 m

Bastia, Corte, Saint-Florent & Camping Les Oliviers (1 km) ▶

G & ▶ Camping Les Oliviers

5 , Camping Bodri (2 km), Plage de Bodri, Giunchetu, ▼ Corbara, Monticello & Calvi

123

▲ U Babbu di u Patria

running until 6.30pm (frequent travellers can save money by buying carnets of ten tickets for €8).

Arrival and information

The **train station** (☎04 95 60 00 50) is on route du Port, 500m south of the **ferry terminal**. Beaux Voyages' Bastia–Calvi **bus** stops in the town's main thoroughfare, **avenue Piccioni**, just south of place Paoli. The **tourist office**, on the south side of place Paoli (April–June & Sept–Oct Mon–Fri 9am–noon & 2–5pm, July & Aug daily 9am–1pm & 2.30–7.30pm; ☎04 95 60 04 35, ⓦwww.ot-ile-rousse.fr), hands out ferry and bus timetables. The **post office** is a five-minute walk to the east, in rue Monticello.

Accommodation

L'Île Rousse fills up early in the year and it can be difficult to find a **hotel**, so be prepared to hunt around.

Hotels

L'Escale route du Port ☏ 04 95 60 27 08, ℻ 04 95 60 14 33. Two-star motel out near the port, with light a/c rooms, all en suite and with balconies. Plenty of parking. €60 off season. **❼**

Funtana Marina route de Monticello ☏ 04 95 60 16 12, ⓦ www.hotel-funtana.com. A modern hotel, 1km south of town (up the hill), with a pool and better-than-average views of L'Île Rousse and the bay from its rooms. Reasonable rates out of season, but very expensive in July & Aug. March–Dec. **❺**

Le Grillon 10 av Paul-Doumer ☏ 04 95 60 00 49, ℻ 04 95 60 43 69. The best budget hotel in town, 1km from the centre on the St-Florent/Bastia road. Nothing special, but quiet, immaculately clean and very cheap for the area (dropping to €40 in April–May). April–Oct. **❸**

Isula Rossa route du Port ☏ 04 95 60 01 32, ⓦ en.hotel-ile-rousse-isularossa.com. Smallish rooms with en-suite bathrooms (but no balconies) in a modern block on the seafront. The garden-side rooms are the least expensive; but no. 112 catches the sea breezes. **❹–❺**

De la Puntella route du Port ☏ 04 95 60 04 34, ℻ 04 95 60 40 87. Offering smart little "studios" (rooms with four beds, kitchenette and bathroom), which are usually booked on a weekly basis during Aug; particularly good value for families. There's ample parking, and a 10am checkout. **❺**

Santa Maria route du Port ☏ 04 95 63 05 05, ⓦ www.hotelsantamaria.com. Next to the ferry port, this is one of the larger and best-value three-star places in town. Their a/c rooms have small balconies or patios opening onto a garden and pool, and there's exclusive access to a tiny pebble beach. **❽**

Splendid 4 bd Valéry-François ☏ 04 95 60 00 24, ⓦ www.le-splendid-hotel.com. Well-maintained, 1930s-style building with a small swimming pool and some sea views from upper floors; very reasonable tariffs, given the location. April to mid-Nov. **❻**

Campsites

Camping Bodri 2km west on the Calvi Rd ☏ 04 95 60 10 86, ⓦ www.campinglebodri.com. Sprawling site separated from the beach by the train line, and well equipped with a large pizzeria and laundry. It's also marginally less cramped in peak season than others in the area. You can get here direct by train (ask the conductor for "*l'arrêt Bodri*"). June–Sept.

Les Oliviers 1km east of town ☏ 04 95 60 19 92, ℻ 04 95 60 30 91. Situated on a low hill overlooking the beach, but some pitches are a little too close to the *route nationale* for comfort, and the *blocs sanitaires* are inadequate in peak season. April–Sept.

The Town

All roads in L'Île Rousse lead to **place Paoli**, a shady square that's open to the sea and has as its focal point a fountain surmounted by a bust, **U Babbu di u Patria** (Grandfather of the Nation), one of many local tributes to Pascal Paoli. There's a covered *produits corses* market under the 21-pillared porch at the entrance to the square, while on the west side rises the restored facade of the Église de l'Immaculée Conception. Between the two, a row of quintessentially French terrace cafés does a steady trade under rows of old plane trees. It was here at breakfast time on August 7, 2000, that the prominent nationalist politician, Jean-Michel Rossi, was murdered by five gunmen. With former Cuncolta leader François Santoni, he had published a book blowing the whistle on corruption among Corsican paramilitaries, and his assassination was widely interpreted as the mob's response. Santoni was also gunned down the following year (for more background on these events, see "The Corsican Troubles", p.392).

To reach the **Île de la Pietra**, the islet that gives the town its name, continue north, passing the station on your left. Once over the causeway connecting the islet to the mainland, you can walk through the crumbling mass of red granite as far as the lighthouse at the far end. From here, the **view** towards town is spectacular, especially at sunset, when you get the full effect of the glowing red rocks.

The beaches

Immediately in front of the promenade, the town beach is a crowded, Côte d'Azur-style strand, blocked by ranks of sun loungers and parasols belonging to the row of lookalike café-restaurants behind it. With your own transport, you're better off heading 3km west up the N197, where a signpost pointing right off the main road (next to the turning for *Camping Bodri*) leads 300m downhill to a municipal car park from where you can walk to two of the most beautiful beaches on the north coast. To your right as you face the sea, **plage de Bodri** is the more sheltered, backed by soft white dunes in which is nestled a smart but overpriced *paillote* dishing up crêpes and unadventurous salads. The sand is clean and the water crystal clear, but from late June onwards this normally isolated cove is swamped by campers from the nearby *Camping Bodri* (see p.125). A short walk further west around the rocky Punta di Ginebre, **plage de Giunchetu** is a larger, though less picturesque, beach that gets even more inundated in summer.

You can reach both beaches by **train**: just behind plage de Bodri is a little request stop at which you can ask to be dropped by any service running between L'Île Rousse and Calvi.

Eating and drinking

Tourism has taken its toll in L'Île Rousse – hence the abundance of mediocre eating places. However, a few **restaurants** stand out, most of them in the narrow lanes of the old town. With your own transport, you might also consider heading inland to eat in one of the hill villages (see pp.128–138). The best **cafés** are those lining the south side of place Paoli, under a canopy of shady plane trees.

L'Escale rue Notre Dame ☎04 95 60 10 53. Giant fresh mussels, prawns and crayfish from the east coast *étangs* are the thing here, served in various *formules* and menus (€15–25) on a spacious terrace looking across the *micheline* line to the bay. Brisk, courteous service, copious portions and for once the house white (by the glass or *pichet*) is palatable. The *menu pêcheur* (a mixed platter) is especially good value.

U Libecciu rue Notre Dame, just behind the covered market ☎04 95 60 13 82. Trend-setting designer décor and gourmet cuisine to match, served in a little bar-restaurant just off the square. Specialities include king prawns in house pasta and seafood *feuillté* – and there's a chocolate fountain for the chocoholics. Count on €30–50 per head for three courses.

L'Ostéria place Santelli ☎04 95 60 08 39. Tucked away on a quiet backstreet in the old quarter, this established Corsican speciality restaurant offers an excellent menu (€18), featuring delicious courgette fritters, *soupe de nos villages*, tarragon-scented *gratin d'aubergines* and house specialities such as moray in flaky pastry parcels. You can sit in a vaulted room adorned with farm implements or on the shaded terrace.

A Quadera 6 rue Napoléon ☎04 95 60 44 52. Sunny Mediterranean salads, quality charcuterie and imaginative seafood dishes – such as king prawns flambéed in eau de vie and carpaccio of sea bass with Corsican figs – stylishly served inside an eighteenth-century town house with exposed stone walls. Their €19 menu offers great value for money, as does the legendary "*salade de M.Jo-Jo*", featuring local *panzetta* ham.

Listings

Banks Most of the major French banks have branches (with ATMs) around place Paoli.

Bicycle rental Mountain bikes (VTT) are available for rent at La Passion en Action, av Paul-Doumer ☎04 95 60 15 76.

Bus information Autocars Les Beaux Voyages (☎04 95 65 15 02 or 04 95 65 11 35) operates a year-round service connecting Calvi and L'Île Rousse with Bastia and Ajaccio, via Ponte Leccia (Mon–Sat 1 daily). Buses depart from in front of the *Bar Sémiramis*, on the junction of av Paul-Doumer

and av Picconi, at 7.10am, or at 6pm heading in the opposite direction to Calvi. In winter, the timetable changes slightly, so check in advance with the company or at the tourist office (see p.124), or go to www.corsicabus.org.

Car rental Filippi Auto, route de Calvi ☎04 95 60 12 63; Hertz, place Marcel-Delanney ☎04 95 60 12 63.

Diving One of Corsica's best-known dive sites, Le Naso, a colossal rock draped in colourful corals, lies in the bay and is a prime spot for moray and conger eels. The town has two dive schools: recommended for advanced divers is Beluga, at the *La Pietra* hotel near the ferry dock (☎04 95 60 17 36, ⓦwww.beluga-diving.com); the École de Plongée de L'Île Rousse, in a Portakabin near the ferry building (☎04 95 60 36 85, ⓦwww .plongee-ilerousse.com), caters particularly well for beginners and children.

Horse riding Arbo Valley, 5km east of town (signposted off the main Bastia Rd, N197; ☎04 95 60 49 49, ⓦwww.arbovalley.com), is an accredited riding centre offering short hacks and longer expeditions, including trips to the plage de Saleccia.

Internet access Movie Stores/Senso Media (Mon–Sat 10am–2am; €4 per hr), diagonally opposite the supermarket on the crossroads where the *route nationale* cuts through the centre of town.

Laundry rue Napoléon, one block down from *L'Osteria* restaurant (daily 7am–10pm).

Pharmacy On the corner of av Piccioni and rue Monticello.

Post office rue Monticello, on the south side of town (Mon–Fri 8.30am–5pm, Sat 8.30am–noon; ☎04 95 63 05 50).

Taxis Taxis Costa ☎04 95 18 84 40.

Train information Gare CFC, route du Port ☎04 95 60 00 50.

East of L'Île Rousse

Coastal development peters out almost immediately **east of L'Île Rousse**, with the *route nationale* (N197) hugging a low, rocky shoreline which is refreshingly devoid of building. Located only 3km out of town, on a sea-facing slope that was, only a few years ago, bare and fire-damaged desert, the **Parc de Saleccia** (July & Aug daily 9.30am–12.30pm & 4–8pm; April–June, Sept & Oct daily except Tues 9.30am–noon & 2.30–7pm; ⓦwww.parc-saleccia.fr; €7) is Corsica's only botanical garden, dedicated to vegetation from across the Mediterranean basin. Set over a seven-hectare site, walkways wind through beds and borders gathering together all the island's aromatic maquis herbs – from absinth and arbousiers (strawberry trees) to pungent cistus and myrtle bushes – together with a collection of various pines, cypresses, laurels, olives, wild oaks and roses from North Africa and the Levant. You can buy many of the plants in the nursery next door.

Two excellent **beaches** also indent this wild coastline. The first, the **plage de Lozari**, is a long, semicircular sweep of coarse white sand, 7km east of L'Île Rousse. A surfaced road signposted "Lozari" leads down to the shore and the discreet *Village de l'Ostriconi* holiday village, which pulls in the crowds in summer. Even more spectacular is the much-photographed **plage de Perajola**, at the mouth of the Ostriconi River, where the rocky hills of the Désert des Agriates ripple north against a backdrop of turquoise sea, forcing the *route nationale* east up the depopulated **Ostriconi Valley**. To reach it, you have to turn north off the N1197, 11km east of L'Île Rousse, and join the disused corniche road; head past the campsite and *village de vacances* and continue for around 500m until you see a couple of lay-bys on the right of the road where you can leave your car. From here, a steep path cuts down through the maquis to the southwest side of the beach. Tourists from the *Village de l'Ostriconi* spill over it in summer, but out of season this is a remote and windswept spot. The wilderness immediately to the north offers plenty of potential for **hiking**, although you'll need an IGN map of the area (#4249 OT) if you want to follow the waymarked **Désert des Agriates Coast Path** (see p.99).

Practicalities

The whole stretch described above is covered by Autocars Les Beaux Voyages' daily Calvi–Bastia–Calvi **buses**; ask for a ticket to Lozari or the *Village de l'Ostriconi*. Inexpensive **accommodation** is available at the *Village de l'Ostriconi* itself, 1km inland from Perajola beach (☎04 95 60 10 05, ⓦwww.village-ostriconi.com /camping.htm; ❷–❸), where simple bungalows cost €37–98 depending on the time of year (the pricier ones have bathrooms and kitchenettes). The same owners also have a large, well-shaded **campsite** (same phone; open Easter–Oct), within ten-minutes' walk of the beach: bring plenty of mosquito repellent, as the site borders a brackish lagoon, and be prepared towards the start of the season to wade through waist-deep water to reach the Perajola beach.

Lama

It's hard to picture the Ostriconi Valley, sweeping southwest from the edge of the Désert des Agriates into the mountains of the interior, as it must have looked three hundred or more years ago. Denuded by drought, overgrazing and repeated bush fires, its slopes now encompass some of the poorest agricultural land on the island. Yet in the seventeenth and eighteenth centuries the valley formed the centre of a booming trade in fine-quality olive oil, whence the profusion of Italianate *palazzi* at **LAMA**, an unexpectedly pretty village clinging to a granite spur high above the main road. Dozens of splendid *grandes maisons bourgeoises* still stand here, among them the Florentine **Casa Bertola**, with its distinctive arcaded belvedere, which belonged to the Corsican poet Paul Bertola in the last century.

Others have been renovated for use as holiday homes: the **tourist office** at the entrance to the village, which goes by the rather long-winded name of the Maison du pays d'accueil touristique de l'Ostriconi (Mon–Fri 9am–noon & 2–5pm, also Sat & Sun 2–5pm in July & Aug; ☎04 95 48 23 90, Ⓦwww .vacancesalama.com), keeps a list of fifty or more **gîtes** for rent, many of them modern villas with sunny terraces, pools and dramatic views down the valley towards the sea. There's also a fine **restaurant** here, the 🍴 *Campu Latinu* (☎04 95 48 23 83), set on the hillside at the top of the village on lovely inter-connecting stone terraces, shaded by ancient olive and oak trees with views over the rooftops; turn right before the church and follow the road until you see a sign on your right. The restaurant offers a sumptuous *menu corse* (€29), featuring local dishes such as lasagne with *brocciu* and mint, while entrées include a good choice of tempting vegetarian dishes, including delicate *beignets au fromage frais*, and tomato and mozzarella pâté.

Lama's cobbled, flower-filled lanes and arched passageways are ideal for a post-prandial stroll. Opposite the church, look out for the **U Stallo** (same timings as the tourist office), a photographic exhibition showing old images of the Ostriconi region. In summer, there's also a **swimming pool** (July & Aug noon–7pm, closed Thurs 3–7pm) on the far northern edge of Lama, while at the beginning of August the village hosts its own grandly titled **European Festival of Cinema and Rural Life**, featuring films set in or about the countryside.

Inland Haute-Balagne

The fortress villages of **inland Haute-Balagne** are among the most pictur-esque on the island, their higgledy-piggledy terracotta rooftops and belfries presiding over an idyllic Mediterranean landscape of cypress-studded olive groves, backed by a dramatic wall of pale-grey mountains. Many of the settle-ments are nearly a thousand years old, having been established during the Pisan occupation, when **Romanesque churches** such as San Trinita at **Aregno** and Santa Restituta near **Calenzana** were built. The rash of **Baroque churches** in the region was constructed during the prosperous years under the Genoese, and some of them, such as the church at **Corbara**, warrant a visit for the sheer flamboyance of their decoration, even if Baroque isn't your thing.

A government redevelopment programme has resulted in the revival of certain traditional practices, including the production of olive oil using old presses. Young people are being encouraged to settle in the villages by the introduction of special grants for artisans willing to live and work here, and several places have their own music and crafts societies – look out for posters advertising summer concerts in villages such as **Pigna** and **Belgodère**.

Another, less positive, feature of inland Balagne is the frequency and magnitude of **bush fires** (see p.108). In July 2005, a vast swathe of maquis between Calenzana and Sant Antonio was laid waste when a fire which had been started intentionally was fanned from the west by a strong Tramonto wind. People in Zilia, Montemaggiore and other villages fled for their lives to local churches; no one was killed, but thousands of ancient olive trees were destroyed and the landscape charred black.

The only **buses** in the area run daily between Calvi and Calenzana (with Autocars Les Beaux Voyages – see p.126). The **train** stops near Belgodère, but to make the most of this beautiful area you need to have your own vehicle and be prepared to walk.

Calenzana

Overshadowed by the great bulk of Monte Grosso and encircled by a belt of olive trees, the village of **CALENZANA** overlooks some of the most fertile land on the island. Historically an economic rival to Calvi, it's still an agricultural centre, renowned for its wine and honey, plus the village speciality, a little dry cake blessed with the tongue-twisting name of *cuggiuelli* (pronounced "koo-joo-*ell*-ee"), which you dunk in white wine before eating. There's a less pacific side to Calenzana as well: in the eighteenth century it was known as a refuge for Paoli's freedom fighters, who weren't welcome in the Genoese stronghold of Calvi, and more recently it has gained a reputation for harbouring French gangsters; with Marseille a quick hop across the water, prominent *milieu* members have retired here.

Lying close to the borders of the national park, Calenzana is the starting point for the famous **GR20 hike**, whose ten- to fifteen-day haul through the island's mountain spine starts just above the village at the Oratoire St-Antoine. The chapel and its adjacent spring are also the trailhead for the shorter **Tra Mare e Monti** walk, which traverses a section of the national park as far as Cargèse. Accounts of both routes feature in Chapter 8.

The lively core of the village, the **Piazza Communa**, is a pleasant tree-lined square dominated by the heavily Baroque **Église St-Blaise**. Founded in 1691, the church boasts a sumptuous but dusty interior. Its centrepiece is a marble altar (1750), to the right of which stands a seventeenth-century tabernacle with a particularly ghoulish painted border.

The bell tower beside the church, built in the 1870s, stands on the "**Cimetière des Allemands**", the burial place of five hundred Austrian troops dispatched by their king, Charles VI, to help his Genoese allies quell an uprising in January 1732. With no artillery to hand, the villagers are said to have hurled beehives, tiles and boiling oil from their windows, set flaming cattle loose in the alleyways, and then used makeshift weapons to pick off the Austrians as they fled through the old town. Only one hundred of the soldiers survived the massacre – a turnabout that played no small part in forcing the Genoese to capitulate at Corte the following May, three hundred years before the island's eventual independence.

Practicalities

Autocars Les Beaux Voyages (☎04 95 65 15 02; ⓦwww.corsicar.com) run buses between Calvi and Calenzana, departing services at 2.30pm and 7pm from their office at the Porteuse d'Eau intersection near the train station. **Taxis** (☎04 95 65 30 36) cover the route for €17–22.

There are only two **hotels** in Calenzana, neither of them particularly appealing – unless you've been roughing it on GR20 for ten days or so. At the bottom of the village on the left as you arrive from Calvi, the *Monte Grosso* (☎04 95 62 70 15, ⓕ04 95 62 83 21; ❹), 48 rue du Font, is basic, with mostly shared toilets, and suffers from traffic noise in the summer. A sunnier and quieter option is the *Bel Horizon* (☎04 95 62 71 72; ❹), further up the hill opposite the church, which has comfortable rooms with views over the square or down across the village. Most long-distance walkers check into the clean *gîte d'étape municipal* (☎04 95 62 77 13 or mobile 06 80 10 76 88; €14 per bed in a four-bed dorm; €10 camping), just off the main road on the southern side of the village. The rather impersonal complex has rudimentary self-catering facilities and bathrooms with power showers, but offers no meals. For **breakfast** you'll have to head back up the main street to the square, where *Café Le Royal*, right opposite the church's bell tower, opens at 7am. The village boulangerie, which also opens early, stands 400m east of the square on the left past the pharmacy. The famous *cuggiuelli* (see p.129) are sold at the Corsican speciality pâtisserie, *E Fritelle*, up a narrow alley called U Chiasu on the left of the road as you leave Calenzana in the direction of Calvi.

Of the handful of **restaurants** in the village proper, only one is worthy of mention: *Le Calenzana "Chez Michel"* (☎04 95 62 70 25; March–Dec) at 7 cours Blaise, opposite the church, which assuages the monster appetites of its predominantly hiker clientele with groaning platefuls of delicious mountain cooking. The house speciality, tender wild boar *aux herbes du maquis* with wheat-rolled potatoes, features on set menus (€17–23), and they also serve a fine *terrine de figatellu*, pan-fried veal and beans, and a serious Corsican soup which comes complete with the bones. Vegetarians will have to make do with wood-baked pizzas (€8–12).

With your own transport and a more flexible budget, this area's restaurant of choice, however, is the ⚹ *Ferme-auberge A Flatta* (☎04 95 62 80 38, ⓦwww .aflatta.com; ❻–❼), tucked away 3km above Calenzana in a hidden side valley at the foot of Monte Corona. To find it, bear right at the church and follow the signs until there's no more road. On an idyllic terrace beside a mountain stream, you can tuck into tasty local Corsican meat, game and fish dishes, grilled to perfection over a wood fire and accompanied by traditional sauces (veal in olive or foie gras, wild boar marinated in red wine, lamb sautéed in parsley and garlic, perch stuffed with *brocciu* and mint). They also offer a dreamy selection of home-made desserts. The **rooms** upstairs are on a par with the cuisine, individually styled with luminous drapes and exposed beams. Rates are high in peak season at €105 for a standard double, but drop to a more reasonable €90 in June and September. Advance booking (by phone or via their website) is essential.

Calenzana to Cateri

The D151, which winds beyond Calenzana, past the Romanesque church of **Santa Restituta**, across a spur of the Monte Grosso massif to **Cateri**, strings together several of the region's prettiest villages, in particular **Montemaggiore**, with superb views of the mountains to the south. Blackened stretches of maquis flanking the road recall the dreadful fire of July 2005, which scorched this area's olive orchards, destroying the livelihoods of dozens of farmers. Thankfully, it barely singed the famous vineyards of **Domaine d'Alzipratu** (daily 8am–noon & 2–7.30pm; ☎04 95 62 75 47), 1km past Santa Restituta, and Clos Culombu in Lumio (see p.121). The basin's other economic success story is the **mineral water** plant at **ZILIA** (Ziglia), from where some eleven million bottles of naturally sparkling water are exported annually.

Santa Restituta

One of the most important places of pilgrimage in Corsica, the church of **Santa Restituta** is set beside a shady grove of olive trees to the north of Calenzana, about 1500m along the D151. Dedicated to the martyred St Restitude, who was decapitated in Calvi for her Christian beliefs in 303 AD, during the reign of Diocletian, the Romanesque church has been rebuilt many times but retains its attractive eleventh-century single nave. In the crypt you can see the fourth-century **sarcophagus** of the martyr. Discovered in 1951, it's a magnificent marble tomb, decorated with a figure of Christ and adorned at each end with strikingly human faces. During the thirteenth century, the sarcophagus was covered by a cenotaph decorated with **frescoes** depicting St Restitude and her fate against a tableau of Calvi which is displayed nearby. The key to the church is kept by the owner of the *tabac*, just down from the village square, behind the church hall (*cazzasa*).

Montemaggiore

Fountains, arcaded houses and ancient streets characterize the village of **MONTEMAGGIORE**, which occupies a rocky pinnacle 3km north of Cassano. The **Église St-Augustin**, in the main square, has some interesting seventeenth-century paintings and an organ dating from the 1700s, but can't compete with the view from **A Cima**, the rocky outcrop at the eastern end of the village – from here you can see the ruins of the old village of Montemaggiore and right across to Calvi, with the gigantic granite cliffs of Monte Grosso on the opposite side of the valley.

In the third week of July each year, Montemaggiore plays host to the **Fiera di l'Alivu**, which brings together the *commune*'s olive producers for a weekend of exhibitions and tasting. For precise dates of the festival, contact the Calvi tourist office (see p.110).

Cateri

Seven winding kilometres after Montemaggiore, the D151 arrives at **CATERI**, which straddles the crossroads of the Balagne's principal routes. Tiny streets with overgrown balconies surround the requisite Baroque church, **Église de l'Assomption**, a seventeenth-century edifice dedicated to the martyr St Bernin, whose tomb is the principal feature inside. The hamlet of **SAN CESARIU**, just below the village, is worth visiting for its Romanesque sanctuary, while 1km west of the village lies the **Couvent de Marcasso** (☎04 95 61 70 21; ❷). Dating from 1621, the convent started life as a Franciscan friary, but was recently taken over by the Benedictine order. The monks provide simple, inexpensive **accommodation** for visitors seeking spiritual retreat (maximum 15 nights); meals are served on a half-board basis in the refectory.

Sant'Antonino to Monticello

The hazy silhouette of the oldest inhabited village in Corsica, **SANT'ANTONINO**, is visible for miles around, its huddle of orange buildings clinging like a crow's nest to the crest of an arid granite hilltop. The village was occupied in the ninth century, when the Savelli counts ruled from the now-ruined castle, and its circular layout of narrow cobbled lanes, vaulted passageways and neat stone houses has changed little over the past three hundred years. Thanks to its ancient architecture and 360-degree view of the Balagne, Sant'Antonino has become something of a honey-pot destination. Out of season, however, the place has a forlorn air, with most of its houses locked or boarded up; the 80 permanent residents are mostly retired small-holders or artisans.

You can't drive up into Sant'Antonino; there's a paying car park at the end of the road, just below the village. After a quick look at the sixteenth-century church, **Sant'Annunziata**, head uphill into the warren of alleys above, where sooner or later you'll stumble across the wonderful A Stalla shop, which sells local produce. Another good place for *produits corses* is Olivier Antonini's little Maison du Citron, at the entrance to the village just off the car park, where you can buy Balagne lemons, maquis-scented honey, village muscats, and citrus jams made according to recipes devised by the proprietor's mother twenty or more years ago.

For a good **meal**, try *La Taverne Corse* (℡04 95 61 70 15), overlooking the car park, whose €21 Corsican speciality menu includes five courses, served on a shady terrace with fine views of the hills inland. On the opposite side of the village, the more modest *La Belle Vue* (℡04 95 61 73 91) lives up to its name; the dishes on their superb-value €15 menu (charcuterie, mint and *brocciu* omelette, lamb or veal stew with beans, and local cheese) are all traditional and made with local ingredients by the *patronne*.

Kids, meanwhile, will enjoy the **donkey rides** (*promenades à dos d'âne*) offered from the car park.

Aregno

A kilometre further down the D151 lies the village of **AREGNO**, set amidst a swathe of fire-blackened olive, orange and lemon orchards that stretch down to the sea. The chief attraction here is the graceful Romanesque **Église de la Trinité et San Giovanni**, dating from the twelfth century and constructed, like San Michele de Murato in the Nebbio (see p.97), of chequered green, white and ochre stone. The triple-decker facade displays a fascinating diversity of stonework: an arch above the door is framed by two primitive figures; over these is a blind arcade decorated with geometric patterns and fantastic creatures; and right at the top there's a window surmounted by a couple of intertwined snakes and a crouching man holding his foot (believed to symbolize man paralysed by sin). Inside, on the north wall of the nave and to the right of the altar, are some arresting and well-preserved frescoes: the portraits at the top of the wall are the four Doctors of the Church, painted in 1458, and below them is St Michael lancing a dragon, from 1449.

Pigna

The tiny village of **PIGNA**, a compact cluster of orange roofs and sky-blue shutters set beneath the road 2km from Aregno, is home to one of the most successful restoration projects in the region. Combining the practical refur-bishment of buildings with a revival of traditional culture, the project's achievements so far include the building of a new *mairie* out of mud bricks and the construction of a Moorish-style auditorium with state-of-the-art acoustics. Pigna's success may have conferred on the place an air of artificiality and commercialism that's rare for interior Balagne (an overpriced *parking payant* nowadays greets visitors), but it's still an undeniably beautiful spot. Several **artisans' workshops** (June–Sept 10.15am–noon & 3–7pm) are good for browsing, with various craftworks for sale including ceramics, engraving (*gravure*), musical boxes and instruments (namely flutes and the rare sixteen-stringed Corsican cittern), furniture and traditional woodcarvings.

The village follows an architectural plan typical of the Balagne, known as a *chjapatta* (hedgehog), whereby the streets branch out from the centre like spines. Pretty piazza d'Olmu and piazza Piazzarella provide glorious views of the sea, but your first visit will probably be to the central **Église de l'Immaculée-Conception**, built in the eighteenth century on a Romanesque base. A squat building with a giant facade flanked by a pair of stumpy campaniles, the church houses a magnificent organ that was restored in 1991 by local craftsmen.

In summer, the nearby open-air theatre hosts **concerts**, often featuring the ancient Moorish dance, the Moresc, which was traditionally performed to celebrate victory over the Saracens. Pigna is especially lively in early July when the **Festivoce** festival provides a forum for performances of traditional and World music at various locations around the village. Concerts run by E Voce di U Comune, an association of artists and musicians dedicated to the promotion of Corsican literature, singing and art, are also held every Tuesday night in summer (or on Sat in winter) at the Casa Musicale, an old house at the edge of the village. These generally start at around 10pm and feature recitals by *polyphonies* singers, violins, harpsichord, citterns, and traditional percussion and wind instruments made from goats' horns; admission is free.

Practicalities

The *Casa Musicale* has pleasant and attractively decorated en-suite **rooms** (℡04 95 61 77 31, ⓦwww.casa-musicale.org; ❺–❻) with colour-washed walls and trompe l'oeil paintings, while "Sulana", on the first floor, has the added attraction of a huge terrace. Alternatively, ⚔ *U Palazzu* (℡04 95 47 32 78 or mobile 06 03 80 23 10, ⓦwww.hotel-palazzu.com; ❽), an eighteenth-century manor house on the edge of the village, offers posher **chambres d'hôtes** accommodation. The manor is the seat of the area's principal landowning clan, the Franceschinis, and is still occupied by members of the family. With exposed beams, terracotta-tiled floors, open fireplaces and antique furniture, its rooms and suites are elegant without being especially formal, and there's a sunny stone terrace boasting panoramic views where *table d'hôtes* meals are served.

Pigna is a great place to sample authentic local cuisine, made from locally grown produce. At the ⚔ *Casa Musicale*'s restaurant (℡04 95 61 76 57) you can enjoy the house speciality, local aubergine served with honey or grilled, fried, battered, stuffed and puréed, as well as quality Corsican charcuterie and main dishes such as *cabrettu a l'istrettu* (a kind of spicy kid stew) or delicious Cap Corse crayfish roasted in local olive oil and wild thyme, rounded off with home-made chestnut-flour desserts. Their terrace, with its panoramic view of the Balagne, is also an ideal spot for **breakfast**; non-residents pay €9 for a *petit-déjeuner complet* of coffee, fresh bread, *canastrelli* biscuits, local honey and home-made fig-and-walnut jam.

For a light snack or a sundowner, head through the winding alleyways at the bottom of the village to the wonderful ⚔ *A Casarelle* **café**, where you can order tapas made from organic local produce, washed down with *pichets* of chilled house rosé. The tiny terrace, with furniture fashioned from old olive wood, offers sublime views west across the Balagne to the coast at L'Île Rousse – especially fine late in the afternoon.

Le Couvent de Corbara

One kilometre down the road from Pigna stands the little chapel of **Notre-Dame-de-Latio**, which houses a beautiful painting of the Virgin dated 1002.

Opposite, a steep road leads up to the austere **Couvent de Corbara**, attractively framed by olive trees at the foot of Monte Sant'Angelo. Founded as an orphanage in 1430, it was transformed into a Franciscan convent in 1456, badly damaged during the revolution of the 1750s, abandoned soon after, then restored in 1857 by the Dominicans. During World War I the place was used as a prisoner-of-war camp. The Dominicans returned in 1927 and remain there today, running the place as a spiritual retreat. **Visits** are possible at set times (Tues–Sat: May 3pm, June 3pm, 4pm & 5pm, July & Aug 11.30am, 3pm, 4pm & 5pm; ☎04 95 60 06 65; free). Inside the adjoining white church, of which the oldest part is the eighteenth-century **choir**, you can see the **tombs** of the Savelli family (see opposite) bearing the family arms: two lions holding a rose.

Corbara

Fanning out over the Colline de Monte Guido, 2km beyond the convent road and 2km inland from the coast road, **CORBARA** is a quintessential Balagne town of small cubic houses clinging to a steep hillside. It served as capital of the region before the Genoese took over and founded the citadelle at Calvi, and it still boasts the largest of Balagne's parish churches, the **Église de l'Annonciation**, a glitzy Baroque edifice built in 1685. Inside, the most overblown feature is the enormous swirling main altar flanked by two cloud-borne angels, which was constructed from Carrara marble brought over in the 1750s. The painted panels and carved furniture in the sacristy date from the fifteenth century and are relics of the church that occupied this site before the present structure.

Two doors down from the church stands a grand house bearing the arms of the Franceschini family, who owned the village from the ninth to the nineteenth century. Known as the **Casa di Turchi**, it was built by Marthe ("Davia") Franceschini, a woman of Corsican decent who rose to become wife of the sultan of Morocco after being abducted by pirates in 1754. In a family house on the church square itself, the **Musée de Corbara** (Mon–Sat 3–6pm; free) holds a small collection of documents and artifacts put together over forty years by amateur local historian, M. Guy Savelli. Highlights of his hoard include a written history of Corsica dating from 1594 and a stick carved with the images of over one hundred historical figures.

Santa Reparata di Balagna

From Corbara you can head back inland along the D263, which climbs up the side of the Regino Valley for 3km before reaching **SANTA REPARATA DI BALAGNA**, a terraced village of crumbling ancient buildings and arcaded streets which yield spectacular glimpses of the sea. The best viewpoint is the terrace of Santa Reparata **church**, from where L'Île Rousse occupies the foreground. The church was built over a Pisan chapel and retains its eleventh-century apse, though the facade dates from 1590.

Monticello

Four kilometres higher up the D263 lies **MONTICELLO**, fief of the great warlord Giudice della Rocca, whose thirteenth-century **Castel d'Ortica** sits on a rocky hillock to the north of the village, surrounded by a belt of olive trees. In the centre, the sole sight is the imposing **Maison Malaspina**, formerly owned by descendants of Pascal Paoli's sister, and where Napoleon once spent a few days. One other famous former resident of Monticello was the English writer and comedian Frank Muir, who bought a house here called "A Torra" ("The Tower") with his wife, Polly, in the 1950s. In his autobiography, *A Kentish Lad*, Muir recalls many happy memories of the Balagne, among them "going on a tour and finding that we would rather be in Monticello than anywhere else on the island".

The village also boasts one of the Balagne's best **restaurants**, ⚜ *A Pasturella* (☎04 95 60 06 65), a stylish gastro-Corsican restaurant. Situated on the square, it has views and cooking of the highest order. There's an unusually international flavour to the menu (tandoori fish, prawns in satay sauce), and some imaginative gourmet takes on local classics (such as devilfish and saffron ragout). Menus at €35–60; pricier than average, but worth it.

Cateri to Belgodère

The area of inland Balgne between Cateri and Belgodère sustained some of the worst damage in the fire of 2005. At **Avapessa** the destruction of Corsica's most ancient olive groves was a bitter blow. Beyond here, however, the flames were kept at bay and the landscape shows few scars of the infernos that have regularly ravaged it over the past two decades. In fact, with the crags of the watershed looming to the south, and pale stone villages strung across the low mountain slopes, it remains one of the prettiest of Corsica's micro-regions, and among those most easily accessible by car.

Feliceto

Glass, wine and olive oil are the chief products at **FELICETO** (Filicetu), a village scattered over the banks of the River Regino. The settlement is also famous for the purity of its water – a couple of springs 200m west of the centre provide a refreshing halt along the way. The inevitable Baroque church is **Église St-Nicolas**, its crypt containing the lavish tombs of local bigwigs; the next-door **Chapelle St-Roch** has a beautiful seventeenth-century wooden statue of Roch, patron saint of shepherds and horsemen, in a chapel beside the altar.

In the village, next to the hotel, is the **Domaine Renucci cave** (June–Oct daily 9am–noon & 2.30–6pm), where you can taste a highly perfumed rosé and one of northern Corsica's most highly regarded AOC reds, made from grapes grown in vineyards spread out below Feliceto.

Feliceto has one of the few **hotels** in these parts, the elegant ⚜ *Mare e Monti* (☎04 95 63 02 00, ⓦwww.maremonti.c.la; April–Oct; ❼), an enormous nineteenth-century *maison d'Américain* with a faded facade and plain stone-floored interior, fitted out with furniture handmade by the owner, M. Renucci. Its eighteen rooms, gradually being restored in keeping with the building's period, are of modest size and have good views over the valley or rear garden, shaded by mature cedars.

Speloncato

Named after the caves and cavities that riddle the rocky prominence on which it sits, **SPELONCATO**, 6km from Feliceto and 33km east of Calvi, is one of the most appealing Balagne villages. A tight cluster of terracotta-red roofs crouched in the shadow of the Monte Grosso massif, it's dominated by the ruins of a convent of Santa Maria di a Pase, while the core of the place is a compact market square, **place de la Libération**. Opposite its café stands the stalwart **hotel** *Spelunca* (☎04 95 61 50 38, ⓕ04 95 61 53 14; April–Oct; ❺), former residence of Cardinal Savelli, an eighteenth-century papal minister whose corruption earned him the nickname *Il Cane Corso* ("The Corsican Dog"). All the hotel's comfortable rooms come with en-suite bathrooms, but it's worth shelling out the extra €10 or so for one of the pricier ones, which enjoy superior views. The hotel doesn't have a

▲ Speloncato

restaurant, but you can **eat** as well as anywhere on the island at the convivial ⚘ *Auberge de Domalto* (☎04 95 61 50 97; reservations essential), 6km below the village off the D71 (the final 2km of them down a badly rutted dirt track). Open only in the evenings, it serves sumptuous *cuisine corse* in the snug dining room of a stylish eighteenth-century house overlooking the valley. At €33 for a *menu fixe* plus wine, it isn't a cheap option, but quality is guaranteed. House specialities include a delicious wild boar terrine, sea bream in cream of lemon sauce and home-made chestnut ice cream; and the *patronne* leaves the bottle of eau de vie (made from peaches and wild violets) on your table at the end of the meal.

Belgodère

BELGODÈRE, fourteen winding kilometres northeast of Speloncato, lies at the junction of the main inland routes and provides a possible base for the beaches around L'Île Rousse (see p.125), 15km northwest. A typical Balagne village of orange granite houses clustered around a delightful square, it dominates a deep valley lined with olive orchards sweeping to the sea. The main Calvi–Ponte Leccia train stops here, though it's too far from the station to the village to walk, and there are no taxis. You can **stay** at *Hôtel Niobel*, 400m from the square on the edge of the village (☎04 95 61 34 00, ⓦwww.hotel-niobel-corse.com; April–Oct; ❺), a modern place with a good **restaurant**, whose large windows offer breathtaking views of the Balagne coast. Local specialities include pork in chestnut sauce and veal stew.

There are a couple of churches in and around the village worth a look: the **Église St-Thomas** (San Tumasgiu) dates from the sixteenth century and houses a magnificent painted panel of the Virgin and Child (ask for the key in the café opposite); and the **Oratoire de la Madonuccia**, 500m from the square along the Speloncato road, harbours Corsica's oldest statue of the Madonna, placed here in 1387 to seal a reconciliation between Speloncato and the rival village of San Columbano. The best **views** of the surrounding area are from the ruined **fort** on the edge of the village, reached via the archway between the two cafés on the square.

The Giunssani

The Giunssani is a spectacularly isolated part of the Balagne, enclosed by Monte Grosso (1938m) and Monte Padro (2393m), the northernmost high peaks of Corsica's mountainous spine. Rising in the cirque of Monte Corona, just south of Monte Grosso, the **River Tartagine** flows through its heart, fed on its northern flank by tributaries whose ravines are overlooked by four high-altitude villages and a scattering of more remote hamlets. Swathed in deep-green chestnut and oak forest, these are exquisitely picturesque but see surprisingly few visitors considering their proximity to the coast; most people who come here do so only for a day to take advantage of the **hiking trails** that thread around the lush sides and floor of the valley.

There are two **approaches** to the region. The first, giving an amazing view over the entire Balagne, is via the D63, which begins about 500m south of Speloncato, climbs up a high open route to the windswept Bocca di a Barraglia pass, and then plunges south, coming to a dead end in the base of the valley. The other route is along the D963, which branches off the N197 6km east of Belgodère, then drops down into the Tartagine Valley from the Bocca Capanna pass. If you're visiting the area as a day-trip from the coast, you could travel in on one road and out on the other, completing a loop that strings together the main settlements.

Pioggiola

Following the D63/D693 route in an anticlockwise direction, the first place you'll come to is **PIOGGIOLA**, a crown of yellow buildings nestled in a fold of hundred-year-old chestnut trees at an altitude of 1000m – which makes it one of the highest villages in Corsica. **Accommodation** is available in the ten-roomed ⚲ *Auberge l'Aghjola*, just above the village proper (☏04 95 61 90 48, ℉04 95 61 92 99; ❹–❺), which ranks among the loveliest country retreats on the island. Although equipped with modern comforts (including a pool), the building has retained its original rustic feel, with wood and stone walls, but the real attraction here is the food, served at a heavy wooden table next to an open fire. Menus range from the basic €23 *menu berger*, comprising a plate of charcuterie, a plate of cheese and dessert, to the *menu de résistance* at €35, which might include house specialities such as haunch of wild boar baked in Cap Corse muscat, quails in a cream of mint sauce, or veal with wild *cèpes*. The restaurant is open to non-residents, but you have to book ahead, preferably the day before.

Olmi-Capella

Beyond Pioggiola the road divides, one branch of the D963 descending to the region's principal village, **OLMI-CAPELLA**, a huddle of sharp red roofs and mellow stone overlooking the Tartagine. In past centuries, many of the inhabitants of this village used to make their living as itinerant traders, selling top-notch Giunssani olive oil and leather shoes throughout the island. The local tourist office, housed in a converted school on the edge of the village (April–Oct daily 9am–12.30pm & 4.30–6pm, ☏04 95 47 22 06), hands out leaflets detailing some of the best walking routes in the valley.

There's only one **place to stay**, *U Chiosu di a Pietra* (☏04 95 61 91 01; ❺), a pretty three-roomed *chambre d'hôtes* clinging to the mountainside with superb views of the valley.

Walks in the Giunssani

Cut off by two of the highest motorable passes on the island, the **Giunssani** is a walkers' and mountain bikers' paradise, with an extensive network of well-marked and well-maintained trails leading through acres of pristine pine, chestnut and oak forest. The regional tourist office at Olmi Capella (see p.137) produces a series of leaflets describing **three excellent routes** (in French), accompanied by extracts from the 1:25,000 Topo-map of the area (4249OT).

In addition to these relatively easy trails, Giunssani offers several **more challenging trails** that give access to the high ridges and peaks surrounding the basin. Deservedly the most popular of these is the six-hour climb up the head of the Tartagine Valley to Monte Corona (2144m), reached by following a chain of cairns through some rough alder scrub and boulders from the Bocca Tartagine (1852m). The final push to the summit, described in detail in our account of the GR20 on p.337, is rewarded with an astonishing view of Monte Cinto's north face and most of the northwest of the island besides. Other rewarding routes take you to the **Bocca di l'Ondella** (1952m), 10km south, from where you can drop down to the *bergeries* de la Tassineta in the Asco Valley. The paths to both these passes are ancient transhumant arteries used by shepherds and traders to reach the pastures of the west coast. They're fairly straightforward, though you definitely need to be equipped for altitude and sudden changes of weather (see p.334).

Vallica

Carry on 3km further east from Olmi-Capella and you'll come to **VALLICA**, a sleepy village, swamped in greenery, which looks out to Monte Padro on the other side of the valley. Apart from the spectacular views, there's little of note here other than the nineteenth-century church and a lovely little **farm campsite**, ⚑ *Camping à la Ferme l'Aghja* (☏04 95 63 36 13, ⓦwww.camping -ferme-l-aghja.com), which has three basic *blocs sanitaires* and space for a couple of dozen tents. Owners Mado and Christophe Piegelet also lay on simple but copious evening meals (€18 including wine) featuring local specialities such as veal with olives or wood-baked lasagne; nearly all the ingredients come from their own fields or are produced locally. Being a working farm, this is somewhere that is especially likely to appeal to kids.

Mausoleo

The other branch of the D963 from Pioggiola descends to a junction for the ancient village of **MAUSOLEO**, the last of the Tartagine quartet, which boasts a fifteenth-century church containing an olive-wood statue of John the Baptist. In the first week of August, the hamlet's population of fourteen is swamped by visitors for the annual **Rencontres Internationales de Théâtre en Corse**, a theatre festival featuring plays written and performed by local people under the directorship of Giunssani thespian Robin Renucci. The plays are all performed al fresco, out on the footpaths and under the stars in summer meadows, when the heat has subsided.

Past the Mausoleo turning, the D963 twists through the spectacular gorges of the River Melaja to the banks of the Tartagine, terminating at the *maison forestière* and the **Forêt de la Tartagine-Melaja**. For a brief taste of the forest, you can follow various short marked paths from here; the principal major hikes are detailed in the box above.

Le Filosorma

From Calvi, two routes run south to **Galéria**, a tiny fishing settlement and summer resort situated about 25km down the coast. If speed is your main concern, the inland D81 is the better, cutting diagonally across the **Filosorma** region. An area of rolling, empty maquis overshadowed by the imposing north wall of the Paglia Orba massif – or *Grande Barrière* as it's known locally – this is one of the most sparsely populated corners of the island, largely due to the ravages of Muslim pirates in the fourteenth and fifteenth centuries, who burned some ninety villages to the ground and carried off their inhabitants as slaves to ports of North Africa; later, a succession of malaria plagues took its toll, while fierce fighting with the Genoese during Paoli's war of independence ensured the area's terminal decline by wiping out virtually all of its few remaining menfolk.

The D81 veers southwest just beyond Calvi airport at the village of **Suare**, in the Figarella Valley, from where the D251 continues southeast to penetrate a large forest of Laricio pines and evergreen oaks enclosed by some of the highest mountains in Corsica: the **Cirque de Bonifato**. The alternative, coastal route to Galéria is the D81B, which snakes around a relentlessly rocky shore via Argentella, the remote bay where de Gaulle planned to conduct nuclear tests in the 1960s (the plans were blocked by the first act of Corsican armed resistance against the French state since Napoleonic times: see p.395). This road rejoins the D81 at the River Fango, where a right turn brings you to Galéria and a left leads to the **Vallée du Fango**, one of the least-traversed areas of the island, worth visiting for the dramatic views of the *Grande Barrière* rising to its south.

Public transport through the area is limited to Autocars Les Beaux Voyages' seasonal minibus from Calvi to Galéria and Autocars SAIB's seasonal service between Calvi and Porto (see Travel Details, p.142). Cycles and scooters can also be rented from Calvi (see p.118) and Porto, though these are more expensive than those available in Ajaccio. If you have the time, the best way to explore this beautiful region is on foot, via the Tra Mare e Monti Nord long-distance **footpath**, which runs from Calenzana, just south of Calvi, to Galéria, Porto and across the hills to Cargèse. For a full description of the trail, see p.367.

Cirque de Bonifato

A gigantic amphitheatre of red-grey crags and needles looming above a carpet of Laricio pines, the **Cirque de Bonifato**, 20km southeast of Calvi, forms an awesome gateway to the Corsican watershed. At few places on the island do the peaks surge so dramatically from the forest, rising from 200m to more than 2000m in only 7km. With the coast less than half an hour away, this is also among the most easily accessible mountain areas. The resulting traffic congestion can get unbearable in high summer, but at other times of year Bonifato provides an inspiring springboard for forays into the hills and woods.

The twisting road up the Figarella Valley comes to an abrupt end at a large **car park**, which costs a hefty fee unless you say you're en route to the *Auberge de la Forêt* (℡04 95 65 09 98; April–Oct; ❶), just above it. A *gîte d'étape* with a better-than-average **restaurant**, the *auberge* is an ideal place to steel yourself for the climbs ahead with sandwiches of local charcuterie, goat's cheese salad, *tarte aux herbes* and wild boar stews; the set menu costs €19–23. **Accommodation** is basic but cheap (€16 per head, or €34 for half board, obligatory in Aug), comprising a few spartan dorms with bunk beds. You can also camp or bivouac (on very uneven ground) in the pines behind for €8.

Galéria

The only coastal settlement in the Filosorma, **GALÉRIA**, is believed to have been first settled by the Phoenicians in the sixth century BC, possibly even before the rise of Aléria on the east coast. Numerous Roman artefacts found in the vicinity, including fragments of an anchor discovered by divers here during the summer of 1992, have helped archeologists identify this as the site of ancient Kalaris, named on Ptolemy's map of the Mediterranean and a major port in classical times. Later, the anopheles mosquito ruled supreme, ensuring that the village remained malaria-ridden until the advent of DDT in the 1940s.

Since its renaissance as a low-key resort and diving centre in the early 1980s, Galéria's old granite core and beach, a compact curve of coarse sand ending at a fishing jetty, has acquired a scattering of modern houses, hotels and restaurants. But even in high summer the place never feels too crowded. Plage de Riciniccia, a dramatic sweep of red shingle 500m further northeast, attracts a fair number of visitors in season (most of them German naturists), but at other times of year remains blissfully empty.

Practicalities

Galéria's **tourist office** (June–Sept daily 9am–noon & 2–6pm; ☎04 95 62 02 27, ⓦ www.ot-galeria.com) is inconveniently situated at Maison a Torra, 4km away east at the junction of the D81 and D351 by the Cinque Arcate bridge. Autocars SAIB's **buses** stop here en route between Calvi and Porto (see Travel details, p.142), while Autocars Les Beaux buses stop by the church in the village (daily July to mid-Sept). The **post office** next to the church doesn't have an ATM, but gives cash advances on credit cards.

Galéria has plenty of places to **stay**, the least expensive of them the municipal *gîte d'étape* (☎04 95 62 00 46), 1km out of the village on the Tra Mare e Monti trail, where dorm beds cost €14 (or €35 for half board). Advance reservation (by postal payment of twenty percent) is recommended in May, June and September. More comfortable options include *La Martinella*, behind the beach (☎04 95 62 00 44; ❹–❺), whose five immaculate rooms (all en suite and with fridges) open onto a small garden with tables and views of the bay, and *Stella Marina* further up the lane (☎04 95 62 00 03; ❺), which offers a dozen large, light en-suite rooms set in a pleasant garden, also with sweeping views over the bay. **Campers** have a choice between the rudimentary *Camping Idéal* (☎04 95 62 01 46), just behind the beach, and the better-equipped *Les Deux Torrents* (☎04 95 62 00 67, ⓦ www.2torrents.corsica-net.fr; June–Sept), 5km north on the Calvi road.

Of the restaurants and cafés, none offer quality comparable to the *L'Artigiana*, at the entrance to Galéria (☎04 95 60 64 00), which serves sumptuous home-baked flans and freshly cut sandwiches made with typically Corsican ingredients straight out of their own organic garden or from nearby farms.

La Vallée du Fango

Until the beginning of the twentieth century, the **Fango River**, which rises high on the flanks of Paglia Orba and flows west through a broad-bottomed valley into the sea at Galéria, served as a transhumant corridor between the winter pastures on the coast and the summer ones across the mountains in the Niolo Valley. The region's shepherds, known as the *Niulinchi*, would drive their flocks along the river banks and through the dense forests that still line the head of the valley to the famous Bocca di Capronale pass, ascending by means of a paved path that remains largely intact, although much less frequented these days.

Following in the footsteps of the *Niulinchi*, the **Tra Mare e Monti Nord** trail (see p.367) winds through the charred maquis and smooth boulders lining the Fango's right bank as far as the *gîte d'étape* of **TUARELLI** (see below), passing numerous *piscines naturelles* en route where you can pull over for a bracing swim. Traffic along the **D351** on the opposite bank tends to dry up once past the crossroads at **LE FANGO**, where a couple of hotels and restaurants serve travellers on the convoluted journey between Porto and Calvi. But with the *Grande Barrière* forming an awesome backdrop in the east, the scenery grows steadily more astounding as you progress up the valley towards **MANSO**, a scattering of a dozen or so houses where there's a working olive mill but little else – the locals claim this as the most remote village in Corsica.

Still more impressive views of the fin-shaped Paglia Orba and its adjacent peaks – the pierced Capu Tafonatu (2343m) and, to the left (north), Punta Minuta (2556m), part of the Cinto massif – lie in store if you continue past Manso to the tiny hamlet of **BARGHIANA**, above the confluence of the Candela and Fango rivers, site of an early twentieth-century church dedicated to San Pancraziu, patron saint of shepherds. On the opposite flank of the valley, a short drive beyond the river bridge, the hamlet of **MONTE ESTREMO** is the last in Filosorma, and the site of a *gîte d'étape* (see below), set up to accommodate walkers following the trail south towards the Bocca Caporale.

The trail starts back at Barghiana: the narrow lane running next to the church (not the road that drops down to the river bridge and Monte Estremo) swings southwards through the village's chestnut orchards, eventually coming to an end 5km later at **Ponte di e Rocce** (aka Pont de Lancone). From there on, you'll need sturdy footwear and IGN map #4150 OT to tackle the remaining rough forestry *piste* (not passable in a hire car) and footpath to **Bocca di Caporale** (1329m) – a superb three-hour climb through holm oak woods. The route, which lies in shadow early in the morning, zigzags up via an ancient paved mule path that's a marvel in itself, with some stretches actually chiselled out of sheer rock. Once at the ridgetop, you'll be rewarded with a magnificent panoramic view over Paglia Orba and the Lonca Valley, enjoyed by only a tiny number of hikers each summer; in spite of being well cleared and waymarked, this is among the least frequented high trails on the island, and a good place to spot mouflons. You can follow it down to the unstaffed **Refuge de Puscaghia** on the far side of the pass, and thence over the Bocca di Guagnerola (1833m) into the Golo Valley, or south over the Col de Cuccaveca and Bocca a u Saltu to Évisa. However far you venture up this trail, a dawn start is recommended to avoid the heat and clouds that build up by early afternoon. Bear in mind, too, our advice on trekking safety (see p.332).

Practicalities

Autocars SAIB's seasonal Porto–Calvi bus will get you only as far up the valley as Le Fango, where two run-of-the-mill **hotels** – the *A Farera* (aka *Chez Zézé*; ☎04 95 62 01 87, ⊛www.corsica.net.com/afarera; ❹–❺) and *Le Fango* (☎04 95 62 01 92; ❹) – offer modest en-suite rooms and Corsican speciality restaurants. Walkers following the Tra Mare e Monti invariably check in to the busy **gîte d'étape** at Tuarelli (☎04 95 62 01 75; April–Oct), another one-and-a-half-hour's plod along the river bank, which has a cramped, grotty **campsite**. Beds cost €14 per head, or €35 for half board. The restaurant offers good value for money given its remoteness, and has a lively atmosphere during the trekking season, with food served on a stone terrace overlooking the river.

The valley's other **gîte d'étape**, *A Funtana* (☎&⒡04 95 34 36 03), lies at Monte Estremo, probably the most remote spot reachable by road on the island.

It has bunk-bed dorms (€12) and a couple of double rooms (❷), and offers good-value half board for €34 per head. The *patron* is a local man and can advise you on walking itineraries through the *Grande Barrière*, including the GR20 Variant over the Bocca Caporale described on p.141.

Travel details

Trains

At the time of writing, Corsica's old *micheline* train service – including the Balagne Tramway – was in the process of being upgraded. By the spring of 2009, a new track and locomotives should be fully operational, which will substantially shorten the journey times given below. The latest timetables are available at any Corsican station, and online at ⓦ www.corsicabus.org. More details on the upgrade appear on p.27.

Algajola to: Ajaccio (2 daily; 4hr–4hr 30min); Bastia (2 daily; 2hr 30min); Belgodère (2 daily; 35min); Corte (2 daily; 2hr 30min); L'Île Rousse (2–10 daily; 20min).

Calvi to: Ajaccio (2 daily; 4hr 30min–5hr); Algajola (2–10 daily; 20–30min); Bastia (2 daily; 2hr 45min–3hr); Belgodère (2 daily; 1hr); Corte (2 daily; 2hr 30min); L'Île Rousse (2–10 daily; 30min); Ponte Leccia (2 daily; 2hr 40min).

L'Île Rousse to: Ajaccio (2 daily; 3hr 30min–4hr); Algajola (2–10 daily; 15min); Bastia (2 daily; 2hr 30min–3hr); Belgodère (2 daily; 20min); Calvi (8–10 daily; 30min); Corte (2 daily; 1hr 45min).

Buses

The listings below summarize which bus companies cover which routes, how often they run and how long journeys take. Start by looking up your intended destination in the first section; then, using the company's acronym (eg BV or SAIB), go to the second section for more detailed route and frequency information. Precise departure times can be checked in advance either via the bus companies direct, Calvi tourist office (ⓣ 04 95 65 16 67) or online at ⓦ www.corsicabus.org.

Calvi to: Bastia (BV; 2hr 15min); Calenzana (BV; 30min); Corte (BV; 2hr 15min); Galéria (BV/SAIB; 1hr); L'Île Rousse (BV; 40min); Lumio (BV; 10min); Porto (SAIB; 2hr 30min).

Galéria to: Calvi (BV; 1hr); Porto (SAIB; 50min).

L'Île Rousse to: Ajaccio (EV; 2hr 30min); Algajola (BV/EV; 10min); Bastia (BV; 1hr 50min); Calvi (BV/EV; 25min); St-Florent (TST; 1hr).

BV: Autocars Les Beaux Voyages ⓣ 04 95 65 15 02 or 04 95 65 11 35, ⓦ www.corsicar.com. Calvi–L'Île Rousse–Bastia; year round 1 daily Mon–Sat. Calvi–Galéria; July to mid-Sept 1 daily Mon–Sat. Calvi–Calenzana; July to mid-Sept Mon–Sat 2 daily; mid-Sept to June timetable coincides with school terms.

EV: Eurocorse Voyages ⓣ 04 95 31 73 76, ⓦ www.eurocorse.net. Calvi–L'Île Rousse–Ponte Leccia–Corte–Vizzavona–Ajaccio; year round 1 daily Mon–Sat.

SAIB: Autocars SAIB ⓣ 04 95 22 41 99 or 04 95 21 02 07, ⓦ www.autocarsiledebeaute.com; Calvi–Porto; July & Aug 1 daily, mid-May to mid-Oct 1 daily Mon–Sat.

TST: Transports Santini ⓣ 04 95 37 04 04. L'Île Rousse–St-Florent; July & Aug 2 daily.

Ferries

For ferry details, see p.21.

The northwest

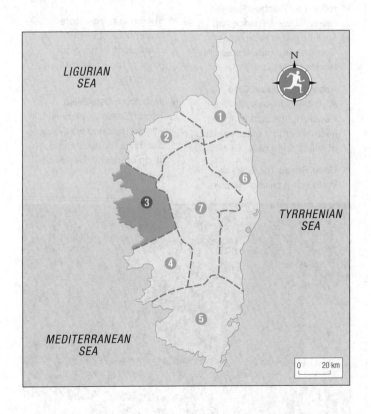

CHAPTER 3 # Highlights

✳ Girolata Extraordinarily picturesque village, set against red cliffs, and still unreachable by road. See p.152

✳ The Calanches Phantasmagorical rock formations in vivid red-tinged porphyry. See p.154

✳ Hôtel Les Roches Rouges *Fin-de-siècle* elegance and sublime vistas make this Corsica's top café-restaurant terrace. See p.156

✳ Ascent of Capo d'Orto Arguably Corsica's ultimate viewpoint, the summit falling away sheer to a massive vista of sea and red cliffs. See p.157

✳ Capo Rosso The Golfe de Porto's own pillar of Hercules is crowned by a lonely watchtower, which you can climb to – a superb walk. See p.157

✳ Plage d'Arone White sand, turquoise water and an undeveloped hinterland of dense maquis – the best beach in the area. See p.158

✳ Spelunca gorge More stupendous scenery culminating in the giant pines of the Forêt d'Aïtone. See p.159

✳ Walk from Ota–Évisa Two of Corsica's prettiest hill villages, reached via Genoese packhorse bridges and a string of natural river pools. See p.160

▲ The Calanches

The northwest

For sheer diversity of landscapes, nowhere else on the island compares with Corsica's **northwest** – the giant amphitheatre of mountains and valleys rearing up behind the gulfs of Porto and Sagone. Ringed by high peaks, this whole region is believed to have been formed by lava flows from the Monte Cinto massif, and its contorted rock formations retain a distinct air of cataclysm. The wild feel of the northwest, however, can be somewhat tempered by the volume of tourists who pour through from June until mid-September. Most of Corsica's two million annual visitors will spend a day or so here at some stage in their holiday, and your enjoyment of the scenery will probably depend on the extent to which you are able to escape the crowds.

Porto village, at the easternmost extremity of the **Golfe de Porto**, is the epicentre of the region's tourist scene, with a crop of hotels, campsites, restaurants and shops lining the narrow floor of a deep valley. Although a peaceful enough place out of season, its tiny harbour and approach roads can get congested in summer. Visitors pour through here en route to or from the **Calanches de Piana**, the vast mass of red pinnacles and cliffs rising to the west. An alternative base – closer to the rock formations, quieter and much more photogenic – is **Piana**, whose pretty stone houses stand on the lip of a sheer drop with breathtaking views across the bay. Beyond it, the *falaises* of the westernmost Calanches peak at **Capo Rosso**, a vertiginous lump of pink rock crowned by a solitary watchtower, overlook the least-exploited beach hereabouts, **Plage d'Arone**.

Clearly visible from Piana on the opposite shore of the gulf, the **Réserve Naturelle de Scandola** is this area's other prime attraction: a pristine red-granite promontory supporting a wealth of wildlife (both above and below the water level). The reserve is strictly off limits, but you can approach its fringes by boat or on foot, along one of the superb marked paths that wind high above the headland. The closest most visitors get to Scandola, however, is the spectacular corniche road (the D81) running from Porto along the northern shore of the gulf. Halfway along it, the **Col de la Croix** pass (269m) marks the start of the well-trodden trail to one of Corsica's most picturesque villages, **Girolata**, the only permanently inhabited settlement on the island still unreachable by road.

Inland from Porto, the D84 and an old paved Genoese mule path thread their way through the towering **Gorges de Spelunca** to **Évisa**, a compact hill village and hiking centre clustered on a spur below the **Forêt d'Aïtone**. The Genoese shipbuilding industry nearly finished this forest off four centuries ago, but the woodland has recovered and huge Laricio pines still loom over the main road to Corte, roamed by herds of semi-wild pigs. Temperatures drop as you

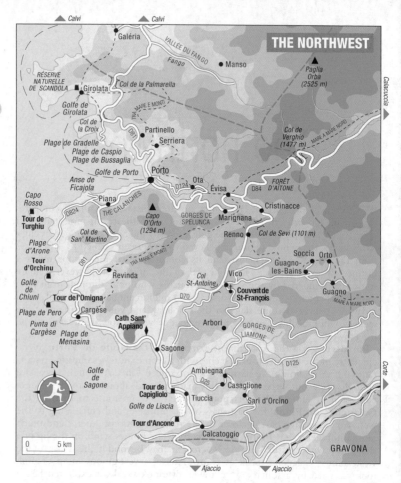

approach the **Col de Verghio** via the highest motorable road on the island – gateway to the hidden Niolo Valley (covered in Chapter 7).

Back on the coast, the corniche road climbs high above Piana to the Col de San, then cuts inland to reach the **Golfe de Sagone** at **Cargèse**, an enchanting village with an unusual history of conflict and immigration from Greece. Lying within easy reach of the gulf's best beaches and coast walks, Cargèse makes a much better base than **Sagone**, one of a string of minor resorts further down the coast which boast a good range of amenities but little character. In this area, **Vico** and its surrounding hamlets, scattered over the steep slopes inland from the Golfe de Sagone, are the most rewarding targets for day-trips to the interior, offering glimpses of the watershed peaks between forests of chestnut and pine trees.

Getting around the northwest

Public transport in the northwest region is limited to SAIB's daily **bus** service between Ajaccio, Cargèse, Porto and Ota, and Autocars R. Ceccaldi's daily bus from Ajaccio to Marignana, via Sagone, Vico and Evisa. In summer, SAIB runs an additional service beyond Porto to Galéria and Calvi, and you can catch buses inland from Porto over the Col de Verghio to Niolo and Corte with Autocars Mordiconi.

Barely a straight stretch of road exists in this area, and surfaces can vary as wildly as the scenery, so if you're driving take extra care, especially on the corniche road between Porto and Col de la Palmarella, which sees more than its fair share of accidents.

The Golfe de Porto

The coast of the **Golfe de Porto** is one of Corsica's classic landscapes, famed above all for the corroded beauty of its red cliffs. Soaring sheer from a lapis-blue sea, the famous red-granite escarpments give way to layer upon layer of shadowy ridges that culminate in the shark's-fin peak of **Paglia Orba**, dominating the horizon to the east.

Porto, hidden in a niche at the end of the gulf, serves as the area's main resort. Although rather boxed in and cut off from the best of the views, the village does boast plenty of amenities, and is perfectly placed for day-trips around the gulf. Northwest along the corniche road, a string of secluded coves punctuates the route to **Col de la Croix**, jumping-off place for wonderful walks to **Girolata**, an isolated fishing village on the edge of the **Scandola Nature Reserve**. Highlight of the southern gulf is the **Calanches**, 12km of dizzying pinnacles and ravines, ideally explored on foot, or at sea level by launch. A couple of superbly situated hotels make the nearby village of **Piana** a good alternative to Porto as a base, lying close to one of the island's most outstanding beaches, **plage d'Arone**.

Porto

Before the tourist boom of the 1950s, virtually the only building in **PORTO** was an old Genoese watchtower, erected in the sixteenth century on an outcrop of granite where the river debouches into the gulf. Now the tower presides over a straggling rash of hotels, restaurants and shops, serving the hordes of visitors who pass through en route to or from the nearby Calanches. Overdevelopment, however, has been effectively held in check by the steep mountain slopes that hem in the village, and it is still the dramatic landscape of the gulf and its hinterland, rather than traffic congestion and jammed campsites, that leave the most lasting impressions. That said, you'd do well to time your visit carefully. Porto is so small that it can become claustrophobic in July and August, when overcrowding is no joke. Off season, the place becomes eerily deserted; the best months are May, June and September.

Arrival and information

Autocars SAIB's **minibus** from Calvi pauses in front of the Banco supermarket car park at Vaïta, but terminates (and leaves for the return journey from) in front of the tourist office. Coaches to and from Ajaccio, also operated by Autocars SAIB, run all year round – again, stopping at the marina and opposite Banco supermarket. Note that the second departure to Ajaccio leaves one hour fifteen minutes earlier on Saturdays than during the week (ie at 10.45am). Tickets can be bought on the bus. From July until mid-September, an additional service runs to Corte, via Évisa, with Autocars Mordiconi. A roundup of these services appears in Travel details on p.170.

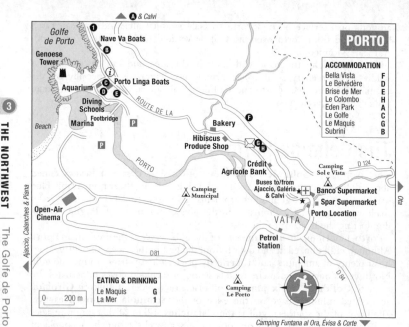

Camping Funtana al Ora, Évisa & Corte ▼

The **tourist office** is down in the little square behind the Genoese Tower (May, June & Sept daily 9am–6pm; July & Aug daily 9am–7pm; Oct–April Mon–Fri 9am–5pm; ☎04 95 26 10 55, ⓦwww.porto-tourisme.com). Among the many publications on sale here is the particularly useful *Balades & Randonnées dans le Golfe de Porto*, detailing the best day-walks in the area, with extracts from the relevant topo-maps.

Porto doesn't have a year-round bank, but during July and August a temporary branch of the Crédit Agricole opens on route de la Marine, opposite *Hôtel Cala di Sol*. You can withdraw cash against debit and credit cards from its **ATM**, but the one outside the **post office**, further down the road on the right, is more reliable.

Accommodation

Competition among **hotels** is more cut-throat in Porto than any other resort on the island. During slack periods towards the beginning and end of the season, most places engage in a full-on price war, pasting up cheaper tariffs than their neighbours to entice straggling tourists – all of which is great for punters. At this time, queues for the three main **campsites** often trail along the main road, forcing many visitors further north along the gulf, where a string of quieter villages and beaches – notably Bussaglia and Partinellu – harbour a handful of smaller hotels and campsites. In the unlikely event that all the places listed below are full, ask at the tourist office for their *Guide Pratique*, which for once is exactly what it's called, with up-to-date listings for dozens of hotels and rented properties in the area. You might also consider spending the night in nearby **Piana** (see p.155), an altogether quieter village with lots more character and better views. The price categories given below refer to rates in June and September.

Hotels

Bella Vista above the village on the Calvi Rd, just past *Le Maquis* ℡04 95 26 11 08, ⓦwww.hotel-bellavista.net. Pleasant, well-furnished rooms in an old pink-granite three-star with outstanding views of the mountains and sea. Also has fully equipped studios, and a good restaurant. Obligatory half board in Aug. April to mid-Oct. ❻

Le Belvédère Porto marina ℡04 95 26 12 01, ⓦwww.hotel-le-belvedere.com. This three-star is the smartest of the hotels overlooking the marina, with great views from its comfortable rooms and terraces of Capo d'Orto. Reasonable rates given the location, with full a/c. ❹–❺

Brise de Mer on the left of route de la Marine as you approach the tower from the village, opposite the telephone booths ℡04 95 26 10 28, ⓦwww.brise-de-mer.com. A large, old-fashioned place with very friendly service and a congenial terrace restaurant. Rooms at the back have the best views. April to mid-Oct. ❹

Le Colombo at the top of the village opposite the turning for Ota ℡04 95 26 10 14, ⓦwww.hotellecolombo.com. An informal, sixteen-room hotel overlooking the valley, decorated in sea-blue colours with driftwood and flotsam sculpture. ❻

Eden Park 4km north of Porto on the Calvi Rd ℡04 95 26 10 60, ⓦwww.hotels-porto.com. Porto's most luxurious hotel, this glam four-star is set in its own grounds above Busaglia beach, with a palm-lined pool, piano bar and gourmet restaurant. Doubles from €162 in June/Sept. April–Oct. ❾

Le Golfe at the base of the rock in the marina ℡04 95 26 13 33. Small, cosy and unpretentious; every room has a balcony with a sea view. Among the cheapest at this end of the village (falling to €40 in shoulder season). May–Oct. ❸

🏃 **Le Maquis** at the top of the village just beyond the Ota turning ℡04 95 26 12 19, Ⓕ04 95 26 12 77. A perennially popular budget hotel. Rooms are basic, but comfortable enough, and they give amazing discounts (falling to below €40) if business is slack. Advance booking recommended. ❸

Subrini opposite the tower ℡04 95 26 14 94, ⓦwww.hotels-porto.com. A very comfortable three-star right in the centre of things, but with peaceful, a/c rooms. Ideally placed for the sunsets behind Scandola. April–Oct. ❹

Campsites

Camping Funtana al Ora 2km up the Évisa road ℡04 95 26 11 65, ⓦwww.funtanaalora.com. Shady, well-managed site close to some quiet bathing spots in the river – although it's too far from the village if you're travelling without your own vehicle. Mid-April to Sept.

Camping Le Porto on the right as you approach Porto from Piana ℡04 95 41 98 69, ⓦwww.camping-le-porto.com. Small site a 5min walk from the supermarkets at Vaïta, but with plenty of shade. Mid-June to Sept.

🏃 **Camping Sol e Vista** At the main road junction near the supermarkets ℡04 95 41 98 69, ⓦwww.camping-sole-e-vista.com. A superb location on shady terraces ascending a steep hillside with a small café at the top. Great views of Capo d'Orto cliffs opposite, and immaculate toilet blocks. April–Nov.

The village

An avenue bordered by stately old gum trees, **route de la Marine**, links the two parts of the resort. A strip of supermarkets, boutiques, cafés and hotels 1km from the sea makes up the end of the village known as **Vaïta**, but the main focus of activity is the small **marina**, located at the avenue's end. Until the close of the nineteenth century Porto was used for exporting Laricio pines from the inland forests, and the route de la Marine was built to accommodate the great carts that used to haul the timber down from the mountains. Clustered around the great red rock that supports the tower, a nucleus of hotels and restaurants vie for views of the sea, while the rest of the buildings are crammed into what little space remains.

It's about a fifteen-minute walk from the marina up to the recently restored **Genoese Tower** (May–Sept daily 9am–8.45pm; €2.50, or €6.50 combined entry with the aquarium), a squat, square, chimney-shaped structure, built in 1549, that was cracked by an explosion in the seventeenth century, when it was used as an arsenal. Renovated in 1993, it offers the village's best view of the churning sea. The ticket price includes an audioguide (French only), outlining the history of towers such as this and their role in the defence of the island against Saracen and pirate raids in centuries past.

③

Diving and boat trips

The clear waters of the gulf offer superlative **diving**, with a string of outstanding sites along the Golfe de Porto from Capo Rosso to the tip of Scandola. There are two dive schools, both working out of the marina next to the footbridge: the École de Plongée Sous-Marine "Génération Blue" (☏04 95 26 24 88) and the Centre de Plongée du Golfe (☏04 95 26 10 29 or 04 95 26 19 58, ⓦwww.plongeeporto.com). Both run courses for beginners and will take out more experienced divers with their own equipment; you can also fill your gas bottles here. In addition, the Centre de Plongée du Golfe have unsinkable **canoes** for rent – ideal for paddling into the hidden coves around Porto.

Tickets for the daily **boat excursions** to the Réserve Naturelle de Scandola via Girolata, and to the Calanches de Piana, are available in advance direct from the operators (not from the tourist office), who have stalls outside their associated hotels in the marina. Working out of the *Hôtel Monte Rossu*, just off the square is J.B. Rostini's *Porto Linea* (April–Oct: for Scandola and Girolata, daily departures 9am & 2pm; €45; Calanches de Piana evening cruises five daily; €25; ☏04 95 26 11 50, ⓦwww.portolinea.com). One of their vessels, the Mare *Nostrum*, carries only twelve people. Its diminutive size can be a disincentive if there's a big swell, but allows the boat to enter narrow defiles and caves in the Calanches unreachable by the competition, plus you gain a more vivid sense of the sea. The rival Compagnie Nave Va has a much larger boat, which accommodates up to 150 people. They operate from the *Hôtel Cyrnée*, just behind the tourist office (April–Oct: Scandola and Girolata daily departures 9.30am, 1.30pm & 2.30pm, €37; Calanches de Piana daily 4.15pm & 5.30pm; €25; ☏04 95 26 15 16, ⓦwww.naveva.com). Both these boats leave from Porto marina. Finally, from the *Hotel du Golfe* at the foot of the tower, Via Mare (☏06 07 28 72 72, ⓦwww.viamare-promenades.com) run the largest boat of all, with daily trips to Scandola (9.15am & 2pm; €36) and the Calanches (5.45pm; €25), or longer tours combining both (3pm; €45). Reduced tariffs for children apply to all these excursions. Tickets should be booked at least a day in advance.

Occupying a converted powder house down in the square opposite the base of the tower is the **Aquarium de la Poudrière** (June–Aug daily 10am–10pm; €5.50 or €6.50 combined ticket with the tower), where you can ogle the various species of sea life that inhabit the gulf, including grouper, moray eels and sea horses. Kids under seven get in free, but might find the *Jaws*-style background music and light effects a bit unsettling.

The **beach** consists of a pebbly cove south of the massive rock supporting the tower. To reach it from the marina, follow the little road that skirts the outcrop, cross the wooden bridge over the River Porto on your left, then walk through the car park under the trees. Although it's rather exposed and the sea is very deep, the great crags overshadowing the shore give the place a vivid edge, and there's some great snorkelling to be had from the rocks to the south of the cove.

Eating and drinking

The overall standard of restaurants in Porto is pitiably poor, with overpriced food and indifferent service the norm, particularly during high season. There are, however, a handful of exceptions. If you're here during the summer and fancy eating somewhere less hectic than the busy pizzerias in the marina, head for *Chez Félix*, 4km up the road at Ota (see p.159). Porto also boasts one of the island's top artisanal food outlets, Hibiscus, on route de la Marine, where you can taste and buy a range of authentic charcuterie, cheese, jams and alcohol.

Le Maquis in the hotel of the same name, at the top of the village just beyond the Ota turning. Honest, affordable home cooking in a warm bar or on a tiny terrace that hangs over the valley. Their good-value €20 menu includes delicious scorpion fish in mussel sauce.

La Mer opposite the tower ☎ 04 95 26 11 27. One of the best seafood restaurants in the area, with fish fresh from the gulf, imaginatively prepared and served in an ideal setting beside the tower. Try the monkfish (*lotte*) *au Muscat corse* or mussels from the étang di Diane, flambéed in whisky. Set menus from €22.

The northern gulf

The D81 north of Porto – a 30km sequence of hairpin bends which has been substantially widened and resurfaced over the past few years – provides breathtaking views across the gulf to the Calanches and Capo Rosso, plus the opportunity to swim or dive at a string of coves along the way. Autocars SAIB's Calvi **bus** travels this route daily, passing **Col de la Croix** and **Col de la Palmarella**.

Bussaglia

An abrupt left turn off the D81 about 5km west of Porto leads to **plage de Bussaglia** (Bussaghia), the longest beach on this side of the gulf and the first you can get to by car. A sheltered curve of grey pebbles hemmed in by steep, scrubby headlands, it's flanked by a pair of seasonal pizzerias. The one on the left as you face the sea, *Les Galets* (☎ 04 95 26 10 49), is among the best places in the region for seafood, fresh pasta and wood-baked pizzas, with a breezy sea-facing terrace that's popular with locals and visitors alike. Count on €20–28 à la carte for a couple of courses.

You can also **stay** in Bussaglia, at the very pleasant *Hôtel L'Aiglon* (☎ 04 95 26 10 65, ⓔ hotelaiglon@tiscali.fr; April–Oct; ❹-❺), a large pink-stone building with a relaxing terrace, restaurant and comfortable rooms that overlook the valley; it's excellent value for the area, except in July and August, when half board is obligatory.

Plage de Gradelle

An enticing cove along this stretch is shingly plage de Gradelle, accessible via a narrow signposted road at a point where the D81 widens. The deep translucent sea and superb views of the Calanches and Capo d'Orto across the bay, which glow luminous red at sunset, make this one of the most attractive beaches in the area, though it's far from a well-kept secret and gets crowded in summer. Behind the beach, the *Bar-Restaurant Santa Maria* has a welcome shady terrace where you can order chilled Pietra beer and a range of salads, snacks and pizzas. Most of its clientele are drawn from the **campsite**, *E' Gradelle* (☎ 04 95 27 32 01), just up the lane, which is busy in season though all but deserted in June and September. Set on a steep hillside amid crumbling olive terraces, it's one of the most pleasant sites in the area, with a very friendly *patron* who keeps a modest stock of supplies, including quality wines and local cheeses, in his little shop. There's also a little restaurant on site serving pizzas and simple *grillades*.

The Cols de la Croix and Palmarella

A short distance beyond the Gradelle turning, the **Col de la Croix** (272m) has a strategically placed *buvette* with a wooden deck from which to enjoy the views west towards Scandola. It also marks the start of the **footpath to Girolata** via Cala di Tuara (see box, p.152). **Col de la Palmarella** (408m), a further 10km north along a gradually deteriorating corniche road, gives another panoramic view of the gulf and distant hills, and is a popular target for cyclists.

Girolata

Connected by a mere mule track to the rest of the island, the tiny fishing haven of **GIROLATA** has a dreamlike quality that's highlighted by its proximity to the sea and the vivid red of the surrounding rocks. For hundreds of years its few inhabitants lived a reclusive life, surviving on fishing and hardly communicating with the rest of the island. Then, in 1530, drama struck, when the notorious corsair Dragut was taken prisoner here by the Genoese general, Andrea Doria, who captured nine galleys. Dragut managed to bribe his way out of trouble, though, and returned eleven years later to wreak revenge by razing Girolata to the ground.

A sleepy place of only fifteen permanent inhabitants, Girolata comprises a short stretch of stony beach and a handful of houses overlooked by a stately seventeenth-century Genoese **watchtower**, built high on a bluff above the cove. For much of the year, this ranks among the most idyllic spots on the island, with only the odd yacht and party of hikers to disturb the settlement's tranquillity. From June through to September, however, daily **boat trips** from Calvi, Porto and Cargèse ensure that the village is packed during the middle of the day, so if you want to make the most of the grandiose scenery and peace and quiet, walk here in the evening when the weather's cooled down and the light is at its best, and stay a night.

Walk from Col de la Croix to Girolata: le Sentier de Guy le Facteur

The path from Col de la Croix to Girolata ranks among the most popular walks on the island, and with good reason. Apart from affording wonderful views of Scandola and the gulf, it takes you past a small pebble beach that's great for snorkelling and, ultimately, leads to the postcard-pretty village of Girolata, where you can steel yourself for the climb back to the pass with a drink at one of the café-restaurants catering for the day-trippers who travel out by excursion boat from Porto and Calvi.

The route is synonymous with the larger-than-life character of Guy Ceccaldi, the ex-legionnaire who, until his recent retirement, walked it six times each week to deliver the post from nearby Partinello. Two often repeated French television documentaries were made about the white-bearded "**Guy le Facteur**", conferring on him a celebrity status he little dreamt of when he took the job. Bus parties used to drive out to applaud his arrival at Col de la Croix. A special launch was laid on to carry Guy to Girolata for his last round, on May 13th, 2008.

Signposted from the *buvette* at the pass, the path is easy to follow. Having passed the Funtana de Spana **spring** after fifteen minutes (the last source of fresh water before Girolata), it drops steadily downhill to **Cala di Tuara** (45min), a flotsam-covered cove offering sheltered swimming. The water here is clear and, as it's near the Scandola marine reserve, rich in sea life.

From the north end of the cove, follow the path bearing left around the headland rather than the one striking uphill – it's more scenic. The trail keeps climbing for fifteen minutes or so to crest a low pass, and then more or less contours around the headland, revealing ever more impressive views of Scandola. Eventually you'll round a corner and catch your first glimpse of Girolata through the maquis, its Genoese tower and turquoise anchorage set against the red cliffs behind. Allow one and a half hours to reach the village.

You can either return by the same path, or follow a more frequented orange-waymarked route over the top of the hill. This drops down to Cala di Tuara in around one hour. Allow another hour for the rest of the climb from there back up to Col de la Croix. For details of buses passing the Col de la Palmarella, see p.170 at the end of this chapter.

▲ Girolata

There are no hotels in Girolata, but you can stay at one of two **gîtes d'étape** that cater for the steady flow of hikers through here in the summer. Located on the beach, *La Cabane du Berger* (☎04 95 20 16 98; June–Oct) offers a choice of accommodation in dorms (€36 per person half board) or small wood cabins in the garden behind (€110 for two half board); you can also put your tent up here. Meals are served in their quirky woodcarved bar, but the food isn't up to much. The same is true of the other *gîte*, *Le Cormorant*, among the houses at the north end of the cove (☎04 95 20 15 55; July & Aug; €36 half board), which has eighteen dorm spaces and a small restaurant overlooking the boat jetty. Unless you're staying at one of the *gîtes* (and thus obliged to pay for supper), you'll be better off spending a little extra to eat at one of the two restaurants just up the steps. With a teak terrace overlooking the beach, *Le Bel Ombra* is the pricier of the pair, offering local seafood specialities, including Scandola lobster fresh from the tank. *Le Bon Espoir*, next door, is marginally cheaper. Note that neither restaurant accepts credit cards.

Girolata also has a little **shop** (March–Oct) selling staples for the trekkers who pass through on the **Tra Mare e Monti Nord** (see p.367). Among the most memorable stages of this ten-day trail is the one leading north from Girolata to Galéria via the Bocca di Fuata; for more on this walk, which takes around three hour thirty minutes, see the account of Galéria on p.140.

Réserve Naturelle de Scandola

The 700-square-kilometre **Réserve Naturelle de Scandola** (Scandula) is thought to take its name from the wooden tiles (*scandule*) that cover many of the island's mountain houses, but the area's roof-like rock formations are only part of its amazing geological repertoire. The stacked slabs, towering pinnacles and gnarled claw-like outcrops were formed by volcanic eruptions 250 million years ago, and subsequent erosion has fashioned shadowy caves, grottoes and gashes in the rock. Scandola's colours are as remarkable as its shapes, the hues varying from the charcoal grey of granite to the incandescent reds and rusty purples of porphyry, striking a vivid contrast with the deep greens of the maquis and the cobalt-blue sea.

The headland and its surrounding water were declared a nature reserve in 1975, so **wildlife** is as varied here as anywhere in Corsica. Dolphins and seals thrive in the area, which also supports more than 450 types of seaweed and other subaquatic plants – including a rare type of photosynthesizing grass that grows at a depth of 35m due to the exceptional clarity of the water – as well as some remarkable fish, such as the grouper, a species more commonly found in the Caribbean. Colonies of giant gulls and cormorants inhabit the cliffs, and you might see the odd fish eagle (*Balbuzard pêcheur* in French) – there used to be only a handful of nesting pairs at one time, but careful conservation has increased their numbers considerably over the past two decades, and sightings are almost guaranteed. Rare plants native to Corsica grow freely, such as the sea daffodil (*Pancratium maritimus*) and the *Senecio cineraria*, with its distinctive furry silver leaves.

Unfortunately, however, the entire reserve is off limits to hikers and can only be viewed from the sea, which means taking one of the daily **boat trips** from Calvi or Porto (see p.118 & p.150). Among the prominent landmarks visited in the reserve is the **Baie d'Elbu**, last refuge in Corsica of Europe's largest bat. Two kilometres south of here lies the **Punta Palazzu**, so called because of the soaring rocky towers that spring from the sea like a giant palace. Over the course of the last thousand years or so, the seaweed here has formed a thick white band around the base of the cliffs just above the surface of the water – a rare phenomenon that provides invaluable information about the changing sea level.

The southern gulf

South of Porto, the D81 twists and turns through the Piana pine forest before entering the spectacularly eroded terrain of the **Calanches**. The village of **Piana** itself, 12km along the route, has this area's main concentration of cafés, restaurants and hotels, and lies within easy reach of several rewarding day-hikes, among them the ascent of **Capo d'Orto**, the mountain whose sheer northern crags tower above Porto. On the seaward side of Piana, the panoramic **route de Ficajola** connects with the D824, leading to **plage d'Arone**, the finest beach in the vicinity. En route, you pass the start of the footpath leading to **Capo Rosso**. Crowned by a Genoese watchtower, this distinctive sugar-loaf lump of pink granite marks the southernmost extremity of the Golfe de Porto, of which its summit affords a sweeping view.

The Porto–Ajaccio **bus** (see p.170) stops at Piana, and will drop you at the *Roches Bleues* café in the Calanches.

The Calanches

The **Calanches** derives its name from the Corsican word for "inlet" (*calanca*), but it is the vivid orange and red colours of the weathered porphyry, rather than the creeks in the base of the cliffs, that leave the most lasting impressions of this UNESCO-protected site. Liable to unusual patterns of erosion, the rock formations, some of which tower 300m above the water, were described by Maupassant as a "nightmarish menagerie petrified by the will of an extravagant god" and have long been traditionally associated with different animals and figures. The most famous is the Tête de Chien at the north end of the stretch of cliffs, but elsewhere you might come across a Moor's head, a monocled bishop, a bear and a tortoise. An old local legend holds that these fantastic forms were the work of the Devil, who created them in a fit of rage after a shepherdess refused his amorous advances. Unable to punish her pure soul, he conjured the forms of his enemies from the fiery rocks, among them the giant representations of the shepherdess and her fiancé that tower above the corniche road to this day.

Calanches walks

The rock formations visible from the road are not a patch on what you can see from the waymarked trails winding through the Calanches, which vary from easy ambles to strenuous stepped ascents. An excellent leaflet highlighting the pick of the routes against a colour segment of the IGN topo-map is available free from local tourist offices. Whichever one you choose, leave early in the morning or late in the afternoon to avoid the heat in summer, and take plenty of water with you.

The most popular walk is the one to the **Château Fort** (1hr), which begins at a sharp hairpin in the D81, 700m north of the *Roches Bleues* café (look for the car park and signboard at the roadside). Passing the famous **Tête de Chien**, it snakes along a ridge lined by dramatic porphyry forms to a huge square chunk of granite resembling a ruined castle. Just before reaching it you arrive at an open platform from where the views of the gulf and Paglia Orba are superb. This is one of the best sunset spots on the island, but if you do come out here late in the evening bring a torch with you to help find the path back.

For a more challenging extension to the above walk, begin instead at the **Roches Bleues café**. On the opposite side of the road, two paths strike up the hill: follow the one on your left nearest the stream (as you face away from the café), which zigzags steeply up the rocks, over a pass and down the other side to rejoin the D81 in around one hour fifteen minutes. A hundred and fifty metres west of the spot where you meet the road is the trailhead for the Château Fort walk.

A small oratory niche in the cliff by the roadside, 500m south of the *Roches Bleues*, contains a Madonna statue, Santa Maria, from where the wonderful **sentier muletier** (1hr) climbs into the rocks above. Before the road was blasted through the Calanches in 1850, this old paved path, an extraordinary feat of workmanship supported in places by dry-stone banks and walls, formed the main artery between the villages of Piana and Ota. After a very steep start, the route contours through the rocks and pine woods above the restored mill at Pont de Gavallaghiu, emerging after one hour back on the D81, roughly 1.5km south of the starting point. Return by the same path.

The Calanches have long been the west coast's top tourist site, and the road that winds through its granite archways en route to Piana gets jammed solid with coaches, cars and camper vans during July and August. One way to avoid the jams is to view the cliffs on a **boat excursion** from Porto (see p.150). Alternatively, get out on one of the marked trails that fan through the cliffs, crags and pine trees (see box above).

Piana

With its terracotta roofs and ochre granite houses huddled on a *belvédère* overhanging the gulf, **PIANA**, at 438m above sea level, is both arrestingly picturesque and optimally placed for explorations of this dramatic coast. Yet it sees only a fraction of the number of visitors who descend on Porto – a fact all the more apparent after the through traffic has died down at the end of the day. The village – or, more accurately, a long-defunct medieval castle 4km south – was the seat of the Seigneurs de Leca, whose rule came to a bloody end on March 29, 1489, when they revolted against Genoese occupation and were brutally massacred for their audacity, along with the entire male population. Two centuries elapsed before Piana recovered. Not until the decline of the Genoese was the settlement rebuilt and reoccupied. Most of the buildings that today crowd its narrow paved alleyways – including the picturesque **Église de Saints Pierre et Paul**, venue for an Easter *Granitola* procession – date from the settlement's late eighteenth-century renaissance, when nearly 800 people lived here, farming the vineyards, fruit orchards and *châtaigneraie* that formerly spilled down the hillside.

Practicalities

The views across to Scandola from the village are in a class of their own, and there's no more civilized a place from which to savour them than the terrace of ⚜ *Les Roches Rouges* (☎04 95 27 81 81, ⓦwww.lesrochesrouges.com; April–Oct; ❻–❼), an elegant old *grand hôtel* rising from the eucalyptus canopy on the outskirts. Having lain empty for two decades, the early twentieth-century building was restored with most of its original fittings and furniture intact, and possesses loads of *fin-de-siècle* style. The rooms are huge and light, with large shuttered windows, but make sure you get one facing the water (those on the opposite side overlook the car park). Non-residents are welcome to drop in for a sundowner on the magnificent rear terrace, or for a meal in the fresco-covered restaurant, whose *menus gastronomiques* (at €32, €36 & €68), dominated by local seafood delicacies such as Scandola lobster and crayfish, are as sophisticated as the ambience. On the hillside above, the more modern *Capo Rosso* (☎04 95 27 82 40, ⓦwww.caporosso.com; ❻–❼) boasts still more impressive views and all the trappings of a luxurious four-star (including a large pool and gourmet restaurant). It lacks the allure of the *Roches Rouges*, but still offers value for money considering the facilities and location.

Of the more modest places to stay down in the village proper, the faded *Hôtel Continental* (☎04 95 27 89 00, ⓦwww.continentalpiana.com; ❹), the old house with blue shutters opposite the supermarket near the square, is much the best deal. It's a little eccentric and the rooms, which have original stripped wood floorboards and creaky shutters, are frayed around the edges, with mostly shared bathrooms, but the management is friendly and there's a secluded garden to the rear where the *patronne* serves breakfast. You can stay either in the old house on the street, or in a more modern annexe around the back in the garden. If it's full, the best fallback in this bracket is the *Mare e Monti* (☎04 95 27 82 14; April–Oct; ❹–❺), on the Porto side of the village, which has good views from its sea-facing en-suite rooms, though be warned that the so-called "*vue montagne*" ones actually overlook the road.

If your wallet won't stretch to a meal at the *Roches Rouges*, the most dependable option among the many little **restaurants** clustered around the square is *Le Casanova*, on the east side of place de la Coletta opposite the church. Steps up the side of a little stone building lead to a snug dining room where the €19 *menu corse* features a delicious grilled *figatellu*. For dessert, try their melt-in-the-mouth nougat ice cream with raspberry coulis.

Full listings for everywhere to stay in the area, as well as the handy leaflet detailing the local footpaths, are available from Piana's **tourist office**, the *syndicat d'initiatif* (June–Sept Mon–Fri 9am–6pm, Sat & Sun 9am–1pm; Oct–May Mon–Fri 9am–4pm; ☎04 95 27 84 42, ⓦwww.sipiana.com), housed in the grand Neoclassical *mairie* above the square.

Around Piana

Piana serves as a convenient springboard for two of Corsica's benchmark **walks**. The ascent of **Capo d'Orto** (1294m) – the massive, sheer-faced horn of granite dominating the gulf – begins just east of the village. To scale the region's other Herculean pillar, **Capo Rosso**, you'll have to drive west along the D824. Just after the hamlet of **Vistale**, a winding side road (the D624) peels right off the main road, looping 350m downhill via a series of tight hairpins to the **Anse de Ficaghiola**. Reached after a five-minute walk down a stairway from the road's end, the tiny jetty here, hemmed in by the bottom of the Calanches tumbling almost vertically into the sea, serves as an anchorage for Piana's lobster fishermen. It's possible to snorkel from a minuscule pebble beach to explore the base of the surrounding cliffs, but keep an eye on the swell and passing excursion boats.

The main reason most people follow the D824, however, is to reach the beautiful **plage d'Arone**, at the end of the road, where there's a better-than-average campsite and a couple of well-situated beachside restaurants.

Capo d'Orto

From Porto, you have to crane your neck to see the tooth-shaped escarpments of **Capo d'Orto** (1294m), Corsica's most imposing coastal peak, which looms above the head of the Spelunca Valley. Its north and west faces, and those of the massif's subsidiary summits – Capo Vittellu and the Tre Signore – still harbour unexplored rock walls up which new climbing routes are opened every year. But the approach from the more gently shelving western side is a popular forest walk via an old paved mule track, with a final section following cairns over exposed rock. The main incentive to make the ascent is for the vast panoramic views from the summit, which even by Corsican standards are extraordinary, taking in the entire gulf and central watershed.

Free **maps** outlining the route are available from local tourist offices; otherwise, try to get hold of IGN #4150 OT. Don't rely on the **water** sources marked on either map, which can run dry in summer; bring at least three litres per person in warm weather. Highly exposed and largely treeless, the summit of Capo d'Orto is no place to be in a storm; even a light rainfall can render the easy scramble to the top tricky in places. In dry conditions, however, the route offers no technical obstacles.

The round trip from **Piana** takes about five to six hours. You can save yourself a dull thirty-minute plod at the start by driving 1.5km east along the D81: just after the sharp bend at the Pont de Mezzanu, look for a stony *piste* cutting off the road to the right, where you can park. Following the track along, you'll then arrive at a **football pitch**; walk diagonally across it to a little **footbridge**, on the far side of which you should turn right, as shown by a signpost. From here a well worn mule track presses east up the right bank of a stream under a dense cover of pine trees. After 45 minutes, it starts to zigzag more steeply northeast up a side valley, reaching a low saddle pass, **Bocca di Piazza Monica** (910m), where you meet another path (from the *Roches Bleues* café in the Calanches). Head right at this first junction and keep following the orange waymarks east around the line of the hill until you arrive at another signpost pointing the route left, over bare rock, towards the summit, visible shortly after. From the hollow on the far side of the pass, a long sequence of **cairns** threads a steepening route through the rocks to the top, reached after three hour fifteen minutes from the car park. Allow one hour thirty minutes to two hours for the descent by the same route.

Capo Rosso

The spectacular red mountain at the southern extremity of Porto's gulf, **Capo Rosso**, is crowned by a little Genoese watchtower, the **Tour de Turghiu**, reachable via a three-hour round trip on foot offering stupendous views. The waymarked trail begins 7km west of Piana along the D824, as indicated by a blue and yellow *conservatoire du littoral* panel. Passing deserted *bergeries* and stone terraces that until the 1950s were occupied in winter by shepherds from Piana, the path gradually steepens into a stiff climb on its approach to the summit, but involves no technical difficulties and should be accessible to anyone over the age of 9 or 10 in reasonable physical shape. The tower itself contains a small fireplace, which means you can bivouac in it and thus be up here for sunset,

▲ Plage d'Arone

when the panoramic views, encompassing the entire gulf and Paglia Orba massif, are at their most memorable.

Plage d'Arone

Continue along the D824 for another 6km after the start of the Capo Rosso path and you'll reach stunning **plage d'Arone**, where the submarine *Le Casabianca* (see p.63) made its first landings of arms and supplies for the Corsican maquis in February 1943. A memorial statue on the roadside recalls the names of the local *maquisards* and members of the mission from Algiers code-named **Pearl Harbour** who took part in the *débarquement*.

Behind the beach is a large, leafy and impeccably clean **campsite**, *Le Camping d'Arone* (℡04 95 20 64 54; June–Sept) with a shop and path leading through the maquis to the dunes. If it's closed, you can ask to pitch your tent in a grove to the rear of the *Casabianca* restaurant, on the far right side of the beach as you face the sea. On a terrace overlooking the sand, they serve inexpensive wood-grilled pizzas, *brochettes*, fresh salads and a full menu of Corsican specialities and seafood; count on €25–35 per head for three courses.

The **beach** itself can get crowded in summer, but tracks lead through the rocks on either side of it to secluded coves. Snorkellers and anglers should head right, where the surfaced road leading down to the *Casabianca* forks, then follow the dirt track that plunges into the maquis at a sharp left-hand bend; ten-minutes' walk further down this path brings you to a rocky promontory where the water is crystal clear and the sea bed shelves steeply down, giving glimpses of many kinds of fish and underwater plants.

Inland from Porto

The coast around Porto may be spectacular, but it's positively tame in comparison with the jaw-dropping scenery immediately **inland**. Slicing into the craggy spine of the island, the Spelunca Valley snakes from sea level to the **Col de Verghio**, draped in thick pine forests. Its defining feature, however, is the awesome **Spelunca gorge**, whose colossal granite cliffs can be approached either by the D84 or along the smaller D124, via the attractive village of **Ota**, the administrative centre for the area and the best base for hiking in the valley. From here you can ascend the gorge along an ancient mule track, pausing at the Genoese bridges and crystalline bathing pools en route to **Évisa**, a resort situated in the lap of the mountains, or less frequented **Marignana**, whose lively *gîte d'étape* is well sited for explorations of the wild country to the west. Both villages serve as bases for visits to the **Forêt d'Aïtone**, which borders the road to the windswept **Col de Verghio**, the highest point in Corsica traversable by road.

The Ajaccio–Porto **bus** passes through Ota. During July and August there's also a daily service to Corte that calls at Évisa before scaling the pass into the Niolo; timetables for these are available from tourist offices, or you can call the companies direct; see Travel details at the end of this chapter for more details.

The Spelunca gorge

Cleaving from the coast to the edge of the island's watershed, the **Spelunca gorge** is a formidable sight, its bare granite walls, 1000m deep in places, plunging into the green torrent created by the confluence of the rivers Porto, Tavulella, Onca, Campi and Aïtone. The sunlight reflecting off the rock walls creates a sinister effect that's heightened by the dark, jagged needles of the encircling peaks. Not surprisingly, local legend has it that the gorge was hewn by the Devil in a terrible rage.

The most dramatic part of the gorge is best viewed from the road, which hugs the edge for much of its length, but you can explore some beautiful side-valleys and riverbanks by striking out on foot along the old path between Ota and Évisa (see box, p.160).

Ota

Isolated on a verdant ledge 5km east of Porto, **OTA** is dominated by **Capo d'Ota**, a colossal domed rock whose overhanging summit looks like it's about to topple onto the village. Generations of kids here have grown up believing that the only reason it doesn't is because the rock is held in place by monks tugging on long chains. As a ploy to get them to eat their greens, the children are also told that the ecclesiastical strongmen are sustained in their task by spinach *bastelles*, or pasties, delivered to them each week by an old lady on a donkey.

If you're in the area to hike, this village makes a much better base than Porto. An overnight stage on the Tra Mare e Monti trail, it boasts two excellent **gîtes d'étape**: *Chez Félix* (☎04 95 26 12 92; open all year), where you can bed down in clean and cosy dorms in a large stone building next to the village; and *Chez Marie* (*Le Bar des Chasseurs*), just down the road (☎04 95 26 11 37), which is equally well maintained. Given the choice, however, the former has the edge thanks to its wonderful **restaurant**, whose terrace affords a sublime view of Capo d'Orto on the opposite side of the valley. The food is great, too – ranging from local specialities such as lamb stew and roast veal *à l'ancienne* or wild boar (featured on the €22 *menu corse*), to more adventurous couscous dishes – and

Walks from Évisa

The wild pine-covered mountains around Évisa and the Spelunca Valley offer inexhaustible walking possibilities, from leisurely streamside rambles to the dizzying ascent of Paglia Orba (described on p.303). Most of the routes are well waymarked and frequented, but to penetrate the more remote areas you'll definitely need a copy of the area IGN **map** #4150 OT.

An enjoyable half-day appetizer is the walk to neighbouring **Marignana**, which takes you in a sweeping loop across the Tavulella Valley, through some of Évisa's decaying chestnut forests. The trail, waymarked in orange, begins just under 1km southwest of the village centre along the D24, past the *gîte d'étape*: look for the *piste* heading straight on at a prominent bend in the road. From here, the clear orange waymarks will lead you down through the woods – which open intermittently to reveal great views of Capo d'Orto and the Tre Singore over the gorge – to cross the river via a somewhat precarious cable bridge. From here they climb up the opposite bank to the deserted village of **Tassu** and, once clear of the ruins, contour west around the hillside, passing some giant dead chestnut trees before emerging on the road next to the *gîte d'étape* at Marignana (see above). Allow around one hour thirty minutes for this walk, and the same for the return leg back to Évisa.

Much the most popular route in the area, however, is the one leading from **Évisa to Ota**, which drops down to the Spelunca gorge through dense forest of chestnuts and holm oak via a cobbled Genoese mule track. Clearly marked with orange splashes of paint, the route is basically easy-going.

To find the trailhead, follow the road west of the village as far as the **cemetery** next to the *Hôtel La Châtaigneraie*, where a path marked "Ota–Évisa" descends sharply over the lip of the gorge into thick maquis interspersed with pines and moss-covered oaks. About one third of the way down the valley, you pass a spring on the left where you can fill your bottle; from here, the path descends through an endless series of sharp switchbacks, emerging after around an hour and a half at the picturesque Genoese **Pont de Zaglia**, a row of alders leaning across the confluence of the Aïtone and Tavulella. This is a good place for a swim, and a side track heads northeast up the Spelunca from the bridge, giving access to less-frequented bathing spots. Hugging the left bank of the stream, the path then cuts through the rocks below the most spectacular cliffs in the gorge to the confluence of the Onca and Spelunca, reached after around two hours. You can either cross the road bridge here and head up the Onca Valley to a chain of beautiful deep-green pools that are perfect for swimming, or else turn left onto the road, follow it for five minutes, and then skirt the village football pitch on your right to pick up the onward trail to Ota. This keeps to the left bank of the river until it reaches another beautiful Genoese bridge, the **Ponte Vecchiu**, from where the path gradually ascends the north flank of the valley to the village.

their deliciously cool draught beer is more than welcome if you've just hiked up from the river.

Évisa

The bright-orange roofs of **ÉVISA** emerge against a lush background of chestnut forests about 10km from Ota, on the eastern edge of the gorge. Situated 830m above sea level, the village sees a steady stream of hikers passing through on the two long-distance trails that converge here, and makes a pleasant stop for a taste of mountain life – the sky is blue, the air crisp and clear, and the food particularly good.

Buses to Évisa leave Ajaccio up to three times daily except Sunday, travelling via Sagone and Vico; the service runs year round, with a slightly reduced schedule outside school terms. Timetables can be consulted at most tourist offices in the area, or by telephoning Autocars R. Ceccaldi (☎04 95 21 01 24 or 04 95 21 38 06).

The best place to **stay** is the rambling *La Châtaigneraie*, on the west edge of the village on the Porto road (☎04 95 26 24 47, ⓦ www.hotel-la-chataigneraie .com; April–Oct; ❸-❹). Set amid chestnut trees, this traditional schist and granite building has a dozen smart, cosy rooms (with and without toilets) in an annexe around the back of the main building; a pleasant little restaurant serves mountain cooking such as wild boar stew with *pulenta* made from local chestnuts. The *patronne* is Californian, so English is spoken. At the other end of the village, *Hôtel l'Aïtone* (☎04 95 26 20 04, ⓦ www.hotel-aitone.com; ❷-❻) is a large country hotel with a very wide range of differently priced rooms (ranging from boxed-in ones with shared bathrooms to fully en-suite rooms with balconies). You also get the run of a swimming pool, and relaxing bar-restaurant with fine views; the atmosphere here is best around early evening, when you can watch the sun set behind the gorge from the terrace.

Walkers overnighting on the **Tra Mare e Monti** or **Mare a Mare** long-distance routes tend to check into the cheerful *Gîte d'Étape Sarl u Poghju* (☎04 95 26 21 88, ⓔ gite-etape-upoghju@club.internet.fr; April–Oct; ❶), a prettier-than-average hikers' hostel at the bottom of the village, just off the waymarked path. Bunk beds in its clean, well-aired dorms cost €15, but most people opt for the half board as the food, grilled on an old oven in the garden, is excellent. If you're **camping**, however, you'll have to press on up the Col de Verghio road to the *Camping Acciola* (☎04 95 26 23 01), a small site with a café-bar and great views of the mountains and sunset. It's roughly 3km out of Évisa: take the D84 for 2km, and turn right at the T-junction towards Cristinacce; the site lies another 400m on your left.

Marignana

Eclipsed by more accessible Évisa on the opposite flank of the Spelunca gorge, **MARIGNANA** presides over one of the northwest's sleepier side valleys. The vast chestnut woods enfolding it give some indication of how well populated and prosperous the village was until the mid-twentieth century, but since then economic decline has squeezed out all but a hundred or so stalwarts. What little work there is here these days revolves around either pig rearing (this remains a famous charcuterie-making centre) or the trickle of walkers passing through on the Tra Mare e Monti and Mare a Mare trails.

In addition to the many footpaths winding out of Marignana to the high ridges above the valley, the main incentive to come here is the excellent 🍴 *Ustaria di a Rota* (☎04 95 26 21 21), on the village's northern outskirts. The **accommodation** – in large dormitories (€16 per person) or half a dozen double rooms (**④**) in a separate annexe up the lane – is a bit ragged around the edges and less appealing than the warm atmosphere of the downstairs bar and dining hall, where you can enjoy local charcuterie and specialities such as wild boar or kid stew and traditional *pulenta*. The views across the treetops from the front terrace over Capo d'Orto to the sea are great, too, and there's also a small concert hall where in summer the *gîte* hosts cultural shows and concerts.

The Forêt d'Aïtone

Thousands of soaring Laricio pines, some of them as high as 50m, make the **Forêt d'Aïtone** the most beautiful forest in Corsica. Incorporating the mountainous Forêt de Lindinosa, it reaches 1391m at its highest point – the Col de Salto – and extends over ten square kilometres between Évisa and the Col de Verghio. Well-worn tourist paths cross the forest at various points, but human disturbance is not yet great enough to upset the balance of local **wildlife**, even if the Aïtone foxes have become quite tame owing to visitors feeding them. Wild boar and stoats thrive here, while, high up in the remoter parts of Lindinosa, mouflon are sometimes seen. Birds sighted in the forest include eagles, sparrow-hawks and goshawks, and if you're lucky you may spot a Corsican nuthatch, a species endemic to Corsica distinguished by a black crown and a white stripe over the eye. The most exotic creature to haunt these parts is a rare, large and savage cat known as a **ghjattu volpe** – literally "cat-fox". Back in the late 1990s a haul of illegal game from Corsica was uncovered by French customs, amongst which one of these cats was discovered. However, sightings of the creature in the wild are extremely rare.

Some of the oldest pines in the forest are approaching five hundred years old. Fine-grained, strong and very resistant to weathering, the Laricio was highly valued by the Genoese for ships' masts and furniture, and it was they who first built a road down the valley to the coast, later upgraded by the French using convict labour. Throughout the nineteenth century, forests all over Corsica were regularly decimated, as the island has the very best specimens of this species, which only grows in forests higher than 1000m. When the British artist and poet Edward Lear came here in the 1860s, he noted with regret "the ravages of [the] hatchets: here and there on the hillside are pale patches of cleared ground, with piles of cut and barked pines … everywhere giant trees lie prostrate".

Théodore Poli: Roi des Montagnes

Théodore Poli was 20 years old in 1817, at a time when the French administration was conscripting young men all over the island in an attempt to curb banditry. A brigadier from Poli's village of Guagno, in an act of spite, neglected to inform Poli that he was due for national service, thereby making him a deserter – an offence on which the French were especially harsh. Poli shot the man in revenge and, in true outlaw tradition, took to the maquis, where his confederation of some 150 bandits soon elected him "**Roi des Montagnes**". A bandit constitution was drawn up, whereby Poli was named Théodore II, after Théodore I, who had briefly ruled Corsica some sixty years earlier. Hiding out in the Aïtone forest, Théodore and his gang proceeded to terrorize the neighbourhood, imposing a heavy "tax" on the rich and the clergy, while exempting the poor. Becoming ever more ambitious, these self-styled champions of the downtrodden poor whipped up anti-French feeling wherever they could, raiding the gendarmeries for arms and even gunning down the local execu-tioner of Bastia when he refused to participate in anti-French demonstrations. In 1827 the Roi des Montagnes' rule came to an abrupt end – lured into a forest glade by a beautiful woman, he was shot dead by one of his many enemies.

One of the most popular short **walks** goes to the **Belvédère**, a great natural balcony giving magnificent views across the copper-tinted rocks of the Spelunca gorge. To reach it, look for a wide lay-by on the left-hand side of the road, 5km northeast of Évisa. A signpost pointing left indicates the well-trodden route through the forest. Following the unsurfaced track that peels left a little further up the main road, you can also drop down to the **piscine naturelle d'Aïtone**, one of the more accessible bathing spots in the forest, where the river flows through a series of idyllic pools and falls.

Col de Verghio

Forming the northeastern limits of the Forêt d'Aïtone, **Col de Verghio** (1477m), gateway to the remote Niolo Valley, presents a bleak spectacle, its denuded hillsides scarred by centuries of deforestation and overgrazing. After the long drive up, along an endlessly winding road scattered with pine cones and foraging pigs, the pass comes as a bit of a disappointment (not least of all for the bus parties of pensioners who pour into the windswept car park to find there isn't a toilet). From the *col* you can, however, strike out on foot along the marked mountain trail leading north towards the bergeries de Radule, roughly an hour away. Minutes into the walk, the views improve dramatically, with vistas of Punta Licciola and the lower slopes of the red, wedge-shaped **Paglia Orba** opening to the north. Keep going long enough and you'll eventually hit the GR20, which winds past a succession of translucent turquoise natural pools up the Golo Valley to the **Refuge Ciottulu di i Mori**, springboard for the ascent of Paglia Orba and the adjacent giant rock archway, Capo Tafonata. For accounts of both this stretch of the path and the route up the mountain see p.303.

Immediately below the Col de Verghio is one of Corsica's few **ski stations**, an incongruously ugly concrete edifice that sees few visitors in winter, as these days there's rarely enough snow to keep it in use. Desperate for customers, the entrepreneurial owner "redirected" the GR20 through his establishment some years back with a couple of tins of red and white paint. His hotel-restaurant thrived briefly until the Parc Naturel Régional got wind of what he'd done and removed the misleading marks. Since then, the PNRC has rubber-stamped the re-route but, despite having been recently renovated, the *Hôtel Castel di Verghio* (☎04 95 48 00 01; May to mid-Oct) remains a blot on an otherwise beautiful landscape. Facilities here include a fenced enclosure where you pitch tents for €8 (make sure you close the gate to keep the pigs out at night); a **gîte d'étape** (dorm beds €14, or €34 half board); and simple **hotel** (④). The food served in the downstairs restaurant is nothing special, either, but the views over Monte Cinto and the Niolo from its huge fish-bowl windows are magnificent. Trekkers can restock from the modest selection of groceries and other basic supplies sold at the bar.

The Golfe de Sagone

Long curves of sandy beach characterize Corsica's largest gulf, the **Golfe de Sagone**, which stretches 40km from Capo di Feno up to the Punta di Cargèse. The gulf lacks the wild allure of much of the west coast, with new holiday villages, bungalows and campsites springing into existence every year, but its resorts make acceptable bases for a few days if you have your own transport. On the north side of the Golfe de la Liscia, **Sagone** is a thriving scuba diving and watersports centre, but it can't match the appeal of **Cargèse**, a lovely clifftop village at the northern tip of the bay.

Bounded by a curtain of pale grey peaks, the gulf's depopulated hinterland is among Corsica's least-explored areas. Once past **Vico**, its only sizeable settlement, the main road splinters into a network of narrow lanes winding to near-deserted hill settlements, several of which feature on the **Mare a Mare**'s variant footpath (see p.368). The region, however, is better known among Corsicans as a bastion of extreme nationalism. It was a separatist hit man from here who gunned down the island's Préfet, Claude Érignac, in 1998 while he was leaving the opera with his wife in Ajaccio (see p.400).

Cargèse

Sitting high above a deep-blue bay on a cliff scattered with olive trees, **CARGÈSE** (Carghjese) exudes a lazy charm that attracts hundreds of summer residents to its pretty white houses and hotels. The locals, many of them

The Greeks of Cargèse

Some 730 Greek settlers from Mani, in the southern Peloponnese, originally landed on Corsica in 1676, fleeing a vendetta between the Maniotes and Stephanopoli clan that was decimating their villages (a bitter irony, given that Corsica was itself riven by appalling vendettas at the time). They came as part of a Genoese plan to weaken Corsican resistance by colonizing the island with different nationalities; the deal involved the payment of a large sum of money in return for guaranteed protection from any hostile Corsicans who might object to their presence. The Greeks were allowed to maintain their own customs, including their Orthodox religion (though they had to recognize the supremacy of the pope), but were forced to Italianize their surnames: thus Papadakis and Dragakis became Papadacci and Dragacci, two prominent names in the village to this day.

The first settlement was 4km northeast of Cargèse at a place they called **Paomia**. Within a year they had built five hamlets, proving so successful as farmers that they began to incur the wrath of the locals, who resented Genoa's patronage. Peace came to an abrupt end in 1715, when Paomia was ransacked by Corsican patriots enraged by the Greeks' refusal to take up arms against their Genoese benefactors. After much bloodshed, the Greeks were forced to take refuge in Ajaccio, where they remained for forty years until the arrival of the French brought temporary peace to the island.

Their deliverance came in the form of **Count Marbœuf**, an ambitious French nobleman who in 1773 attempted to integrate the communities by forming a united regiment of Greeks and Corsicans, and offered the Greeks Cargèse as compensation for the loss of Paomia. Unfortunately, the building of 120 family houses and a castle for Marbœuf again provoked the locals, who in the same year descended from the hills to burn the castle and drive the Greeks into hiding in the towers of plage de Pero. In 1793 the Greeks were attacked once more: their village was burned to the ground and they had to flee to Ajaccio. Four years later, only two-thirds chose to return. Gradually the Corsicans came to join them in their reconstructed village, marking the beginning of an uneasy coexistence that, largely through intermarriage, eventually led to integration. In the nineteenth century the Corsicans built their own church, after which the Greeks built one opposite and adopted some Catholic rites as a gesture towards integration.

There are still three hundred Greek families in Cargèse, well assimilated into the Corsican way of life but still observing the Greek liturgy and conducting weddings in the traditional Greek style, with the bride and groom crowned with vine leaves and olive branches. Also distinctively Greek are the **festival** of St Spiridion on December 12, when fireworks light up the village, and the Easter Monday blessing of the village, when all the women dress in black, the lights in the village are extinguished and the villagers form a candlelit procession to the church.

descendants of Greek refugees from the Peloponnese in the seventeenth century (see box opposite), seem to accept this inundation and the proximity of a Club Med complex with generous nonchalance, but the best time to visit is September, when Cargèse empties and you can wander around its winding, flower-filled lanes, dripping with fig trees, bougainvillea and palms, in peace.

Arrival and information

There's an unusually helpful tourist **office** on rue Dr-Dragacci (daily: July–Sept 9am–noon & 4–7pm; Oct–June 3–5pm; ℡04 95 26 41 31, Ⓦwww.cargese.net), which will help you find accommodation; it also sells tickets for the **boat trips** up to the Calanches and Girolata (see p.152) run by Le Grand Bleu (℡05 95 26 40 24; departures daily at 8.45am & 3.30pm) and Nave Va (℡04 95 28 02 66, Ⓦwww.naveva.com; departures daily at 9.30am). Both companies charge €45 for the return trip.

Buses running between Ajaccio and Porto pull in for a ten-minute pit stop at the *Bar des Amis*, in the village centre. Timetables can be consulted at any tourist office, by telephoning Autocars SAIB (℡04 95 22 41 99 or 04 95 21 02 07), or online at Ⓦwww.corsicabus.org.

Cargèse is well stocked with **shops**, including a large Spar supermarket just off the place St-Jean at the top of the main street, rue Colonel-Fieschi, where you'll also find a handy ATM. There are other **ATMs** at the BPPC bank just past *Le Continental*, at the Crédit Agricole on rue Colonel-Fieschi, and at the **post office**, on the lane opposite the Spar down in the middle of the village.

Accommodation

Ranging from mountain refuges a day's walk into the hills to beachside villas with their own pools, accommodation in Cargèse is plentiful and, on the whole, good value – at least outside school holidays.

The nearest **campsite** is *Camping Toraccia*, 4km north along the main road (℡04 95 26 42 39; May–Oct). Well shaded under olive groves, its best pitches are at the top of the hill, looking inland towards Capo Vitullo (1331m); they also have simple wood cabins that can be rented on a daily basis out of season (❷), or by the week from late June to August.

Bel' Mare 400m south of the centre on the Ajaccio Rd ℡04 95 26 40 13 or 04 95 26 48 24, Ⓦwww .belmare.net. Twenty spacious en-suite rooms in a modern block, steeply stacked down the hillside on the edge of the village, with sweeping sea views from their "loggias"; the restaurant upstairs is also pleasant. ❹

🏃 **E'Case** near Revinda ℡04 95 26 48 19. Wonderful little *gîte d'étape*, converted from an old stone farm, high up in the hills behind Cargèse, with superb views and walking possibilities. A stop on the Tra Mare e Monti and Mare a Mare Centre, it's 10min walk from the nearest road but you can drive as far as the hamlet of Revinda: head north on the D81 and take the first turning right after the junction for the Club Med complex at Chiuni. From Revinda village, walk past the church and turn right at the crosspaths after 5min. Dorm facilities are spartan, but you can camp in the garden and use the self-catering kitchen. They also offer copious Corsican meals. Advance reservation essential. ❶

Le Continental top of the village, near the turning for plage de Pero ℡04 95 26 42 24, Ⓦhttp ://continentalhotel.free.fr. Mostly sea-facing rooms (not all en suite) overlooking the main road just past place St-Jean. Clean, efficient, and good value. ❸–❹

Cyrnos rue de la République ℡04 95 26 49 47 or mobile 06 08 42 03 17, Ⓦwww.torraccia.com. Simple hotel on the main street offering smallish and plain but clean rooms with mountain or sea views; the glass-partitioned balconies of the *vue mer* rooms look out over the church to the bay. The same family also has bargain wood chalets up the hill near *Camping Torraccia*. ❹

De France rue Colonel-Fieschi ℡04 95 26 41 07, Ⓦwww.infocorse.com/defrance. The rock-bottom option: a bit dark and noisy (the front rooms open onto the main road), but unbelievably cheap, even in Aug. ❷–❸

Les Lentisques plage de Pero ☎04 95 26 42 34, ⓦwww.leslentisques .com. Very congenial, family-run three-star with a large, breezy breakfast hall and ten simple rooms (fully en suite and sea-facing), set in the dunes just behind the beach. There's also a fair-sized pool. ⑥–⑧

Punta e Mare up the lane past the Spar supermarket ☎04 95 26 44 33, ⓦwww.corsica.net /punta-e-mare. Secluded, unpretentious hotel tucked away on the quiet outskirts of the village. There's ample parking, and the rooms, though on the small side, are well kept and have little loggias.

Handy if you're heading off on one of the trails. No credit cards. ④

St Jean overlooking the crossroads ☎04 95 26 46 68, ⓦwww.lesaintjean.com. Smart rooms, some with sea views, balconies and self-catering facilities. Rates fall to €50 per double off-peak. ⑤–⑥

Thalassa plage de Pero ☎04 95 26 40 08. ⓦwww.thalassalura.com. Among the oldest-established places in the area, this attractive hotel is set right on the beach, amid swaths of oleanders and tamarisk trees. Hospitable owners, but no credit cards. ⑦

The Town

Two **churches** stand on separate hummocks at opposite sides of the valley head: one Catholic and one Orthodox, a reminder of the old antagonism between the two cultures. Built for the village's Corsican families in 1828, the **Catholic church** is one of the latest examples of Baroque in Corsica and has a trompe l'œil ceiling, though it can't really compete with the view from the terrace. The **Greek church** is the more interesting of the two – a large granite neo-Gothic edifice built in 1852 to replace a church that had become too small for the congregation. Inside, the outstanding feature is the **iconostasis**, a gift from a monastery in Rome, decorated with icons painted by monks from Mount Athos and brought over from Greece with the original settlers in the late seventeenth century. Behind it, the graceful *Virgin and Child*, to the right of the altar, is thought to date from as far back as the twelfth century. The frescoes lining the side walls have been restored, giving the church a rather too vibrant look. Mass is held here once each fortnight by the local priest, Monseigneur Florent Martiano. A Greek-Albanian raised in Calabria and educated in Paris, Père Florent is the only Catholic priest in the world permitted, according to a papal decree, to pronounce both Greek Orthodox and Latin rites.

Eating

Le Cabanon de Charlotte in the marina ☎04 95 23 66 93. Local seafood (menus €15–40) served in a wooden cabin with a raised deck and teak furniture overlooking the jetty, or go for their fresh fish of the day. Starters include locally made charcuterie and Cargèse's only Greek salad.

A Piaghja plage de Pero. A well set-up *paillote* right on the beach, offering a range of moderately priced *menus fixes* and filling *bruschetta*.

U Rasaghiu in the marina ☎04 95 26 48 60. Slightly more competitively priced than its

neighbour, *Le Cabanon de Charlotte* (see above), and good value: local *specialties corses*, seafood dishes (including lobster in garlic sauce) and huge pizzas to eat in or takeaway (€8–13). They also lay on live polyphony music two or three evenings each week in season.

Le St Jean place St-Jean. Busy, dependable hotel restaurant at the top of the village serving a wide selection of island specialities, grilled seafood, pizzas and salads on a roadside terrace.

Around Cargèse

Much the most spectacular and easily accessible beach in the area is the **plage de Pero**, 1.5km north of Cargèse – head up to the place St-Jean roundabout and take the left fork down to the sea. Backed by a couple of seasonal cafés and terraces of holiday villas smothered in palm trees, it's large enough to absorb the crowds that descend here in summer and boasts a better than average *paillote*, *A Piaghja* (see above). An enjoyable **walk** leads west along the headland to the seventeenth-century **Tour de l'Omigna**, from whose ramparts you get a fine view up the coast to Capo Rosso. The path begins at the end of the road running behind plage de Pero: pass through the green gate and follow the orange waymarks along a broad *piste* until you reach a rather smelly sewerage treatment tank. Bear left here and then follow a narrower path through the maquis, past a little *bergerie* and its adjacent oven and threshing circle. The route takes around one hour thirty minutes there and back, and is easy to follow.

The other beach within walking distance of Cargèse is the **plage de Menasina**, a pretty cove with turquoise water 2km south along the main road. Although only a stone's throw from the highway, it's secluded, gently shelving and well sheltered.

Plage de Chiuni and Tour d'Orchinu

North around the headland from Pero lies another broad sweep of white sand enfolded by a pair of maquis-covered headlands, the **plage du Chiuni**, reached by turning off the main D81 6km north of Cargèse. The presence of a large Club Med campus behind it ensures the sand is usually crowded, but you can escape the watersports scene by heading along an old shepherds' track to the **Tour d'Orchinu**, which crowns the steep hill overlooking the bay. The quickest, though far from driest, way to pick up the trail is to wade at low tide across the stream at the west end of the beach and turn left onto the *piste* at its far side. With a car, however, you can drive the long way around: follow the lane back past the holiday village, taking your first left and then, 1km later, another left turn; ignore the *piste* running left 500m later, and instead bear right along the track following the stream bank, which brings you after another 1km to the far side of Chiuni beach. A green gate marks the **start of the path**, which is well cleared and waymarked throughout, although a stiff 172-metre climb. After thirty minutes of steady ascent through the maquis, you'll arrive at a col with a little ruined *bergerie*, just before which a narrower path continues up to the ruined tower.

Sagone

SAGONE, 13km east of Cargèse, was a bishopric and important fishing port until marauding Saracens destroyed the town in the sixteenth century. Today, however, the only evidence of its past glory is the cathedral of **Sant'Appiano**, a crumbling medieval ruin just off the main road 1km north of the village. The settlement proper comprises a string of tired-looking hotels and restaurants, slightly redeemed by the long sandy beach spread out in front of them. Despite its minimal charm, Sagone gets pretty crowded in high season, principally on account of the watersports facilities offered along the beach.

The resort is served by Autocars SAIB's buses between Ajaccio and Porto (see p.170 for details).

Practicalities

Accommodation is strung out along the main road through the centre of the village. *Hôtel Cyrnos*, next door to Immeubles Les Mimosa in the centre (☎04 95 28 00 01, Ⓦwww.chez.com/hotelcyrnos; ➎), is functional and nothing special – it is, however, the base for the Centre Subaquatique (same phone no.), whose staff can guide you to the excellent **dive** sites around the Ponte Leccia, a headland with a sheer underwater drop of 80m. A better option if you're looking for somewhere with more character close to the beach is *La Marine*, an attractive stone building with cheerful blue shutters on the side of the Ajaccio Road (☎04 95 28 00 03, Ⓦwww.hotellamarinesagone.com;

closed Jan; **④**–**⑤**). The best **campsite** in the area, *Camping Sagone*, lies 3km inland on the road to Vico (☎04 95 28 04 15, ⓦwww.camping-sagone.com; May–Oct).

There are plenty of seafood **restaurants** and pizzerias dotted along the highway, but for classier local cuisine, head 2.5km inland along the Vico road to *Le Ranch* (☎04 95 28 07 30), a country *auberge* where you can enjoy the best of local charcuterie and traditional dishes such as courgettes fritters with mint and *brocciu*, stuffed cabbage and meat dumplings made with fresh *herbes du maquis*; the *patronne* offers a single set menu, priced at €22.

Worth considering if you're staying in Sagone is a **boat trip** to Girolata and the Scandola reserve with Nave Va (ⓦwww.naveva.com). Departing from the *Ancura* restaurant at 9am, the trips cost €45; the boats are narrow enough to penetrate several of the most impressive breaches in the red cliffs and sea caves around Porto, and return via the Calanches at around 5pm. Tickets should be reserved the day before (☎04 95 28 02 66).

Vico and around

Vico, the old capital of the Sagone region, crouches in the mountains 15km northeast of the coast. Although there's not much to see in the village proper, its café-lined squares and authentically Corsican atmosphere may tempt you to pull over if you're heading inland, while the **Couvent St-François**, on its outskirts, is a low-key pilgrimage place. To the north, the **Col de Sevi** provides fine views across the mountains, or you can strike east and visit the thermal springs at **Guagno-les-Bains**. For a really vivid taste of the interior, however, press on up some of the island's most winding roads to the dramatically situated hamlets of **Soccia**, perched on a ledge in front of the crags of Monte Sant'Eliseo, from where you can walk to the popular beauty spot of **Lac de Creno**.

The only public transport in this region is Autocars R. Ceccaldi's **bus** between Ajaccio and Marignana (see p.170), which goes via Vico and the Col de Sevi.

Vico

Dominated by the domed rock of La Sposata, **VICO** lies at the base of a high wooded valley, remaining invisible until the final approach. For two hundred years the village was the residence of the bishops of Sagone after their settlement was destroyed by the Saracens in the tenth century. It went on to become the seat of the Da Leca clan, a Cinarchesi family who ruled the district in the fifteenth century. In 1456, 23 members of this rebel family were put to death by the Genoese governor Spinola, who had their throats cut out on the slopes east of town. Gian' Paolo da Leca escaped this massacre, and in 1481 founded the only surviving remnant of Vico's past, the **Couvent St-François**, a great white building encircled by vivid green chestnut woods and gardens, 1km along the road to Arbori. Worth a look here is the seventeenth-century church (daily 2–6pm), whose chief treasures are the carved chestnut furniture in the sacristy and the wooden figure of Christ above the altar, which predates the fifteenth-century foundation of the monastery and is thought to be the oldest in Corsica. The dozen or so resident monks also run a *gîte d'étape* (see below).

On the outskirts as you head out towards the convent, the *Hôtel U Paradisu*, (☎04 95 26 61 62, ⓦwww.hotel-uparadisu.com; April–Dec; **④**) is a serviceable, old-fashioned two-star that's part of the Logis de France chain. Its rooms are

Walk to Lac de Creno and Monte Sant'Eliseo

High up in the lap of the watershed, **Lac de Creno** (Lavu di Crenu in Corsican) is the only altitude lake on the island surrounded by Laricio pine trees. Screened from the winds off the surrounding hills, it forms an oasis of green, dotted with clumps of scarlet lotus flowers and surrounded by grassy banks that make perfect picnic places. In high summer, this idyllic spot sees a stream of visitors fleeing from the coastal heat, but at other times of year the path to it, from the village of Soccia, remains relatively empty.

From Soccia, the route takes one hour thirty minutes to two hours (allow 2hr 30min–3hr 30min there and back). You can drive as far as a car park above the village, overlooked by a large cross, where there's a seasonal *buvette* serving drinks and snacks. Waymarked with yellow paint blobs, the route rises gradually from the outset, arcing northeast above the *bergeries* de l'Arcate, visible on the valley floor.

After around an hour you pass the turning for **Monte Sant'Eliseo** (1511m), a pyramidal peak and superb viewpoint crowned by a little chapel that's the object of a mass pilgrimage in August. To reach the summit, follow the path that doubles back to the right of the Lac de Creno trail until it reaches the shoulder of the hill, where another path cuts more steeply up the ridgeline (on your left), drifting steadily off the ridge before switching southwards for the final steep climb to the top. This extension adds around one to two hours to the walk, but is well worth it for the extraordinary panorama, which encompasses a great sweep of the watershed peaks and west coast.

simply furnished but comfortable, and overlook the valley; there's a fair-sized pool and a restaurant on the ground floor. Rooms at the Couvent St-François (☎04 95 26 83 83; ❶) are offered on a *gîte d'étape* basis, principally to walkers and those wishing to spend time in retreat here.

Guagno-les-Bains

The inland route from Vico, the D23, crosses the Liamone River at the Pont de Belfiori and continues east through a densely wooded valley dotted with tiny hamlets and animal enclosures, finally reaching river level again after 12km at **GUAGNO-LES-BAINS**. A couple of hot springs were first exploited here in the eighteenth century, when illustrious personages such as Pascal Paoli made the trip by mule to take a thermal bath. The spa is open from May to October.

Soccia

A long climb up the side of the valley from Guagno-les-Bains via Poggiolo brings you to **SOCCIA**, one of western Corsica's most remote villages. Draped across a high wooded spur against a backdrop of blue-grey crags, it is one of the few settlements in the region with a sizeable permanent population, a fact attributable in part to the popularity of the walks to Lac de Creno and Monte Sant'Eliseo, which begin at a car park just above it. Even if you're not here to hike, Soccia's ancient stone houses, crisp light and sweeping views over the valley make it an ideal target for a trip inland.

Run by a welcoming young couple, *A Merendella* (☎04 95 28 34 91), in the centre of the village, is the perfect spot to stop for lunch. On a grassy rear lawn looking across the valley, you can enjoy plates of superb homemade charcuterie and cheeses, or go for their €23 menu, changed daily. The service is cheerful and the cooking careful and refined, using fresh local organic produce.

Travel details

Buses

The listings below summarize which bus companies cover which routes, how often they run and how long journeys take. Start by looking up your intended destination in the first section; then, using the company's acronym (eg ARC or SAIB), go to the second set of listings for more detailed route and frequency information. Precise departure times should be checked in advance either via the bus companies directly, at the tourist offices at Porto (☎ 04 95 26 10 55) and Cargèse (☎ 04 95 26 41 31) or online at ⓦ www.corsicabus.org.

Évisa to: Ajaccio (ARC; 1hr 45min); Sagone (ARC; 1hr 20min); Vico (ARC; 45min).

Porto to: Ajaccio (SAIB; 2hr); Calvi (SAIB; 3hr); Calacuccia (AM; 1hr 45min); Cargèse (SAIB; 1hr 15min); Col de la Croix (SAIB; 1hr); Col de Verghio (1hr 15min); Curzo (SAIB; 40min); Corte (AM; 2hr 45min); Evisa (AM; 45min); Galéria–Fango crossroads (SAIB; 2hr 20min); Ota (SAIB; 2hr); Partinello (SAIB; 30min); Piana (SAIB; 15min).

Vico to: Ajaccio (ARC; 1hr 15min).

AM: Autocars Modiconi ☎ 04 95 48 00 04, ⓦ www.hotel-des-touristes.com. Porto–Evisa–Calacuccia-Corte; July to mid-Sept Mon–Sat 1 daily.

ARC: Autocars R. Ceccaldi ☎ 04 95 21 01 24 or 04 95 21 38 06. Ajaccio–Sagone–Vico–Évisa–Marignana; Mon–Sat 2 daily.

SAIB: Autocars SAIB ☎ 04 95 22 41 99 or 04 95 21 02 07, ⓦ www.autocarsiledebeaute.com. Ajaccio–Sagone–Cargèse–Piana–Porto–Ota; July to mid-Sept 2 daily; mid-Sept to June Mon–Fri 2 daily. Porto–Partinello–Col de la Croix–Le Fango (near Galéria)–Calvi; mid-May to Oct 10 Mon–Sat 1 daily (daily in July & Aug).

The Ajaccio region

CHAPTER 4 # Highlights

✳ **Ajaccio market** Browse or buy top-quality fresh produce – cheese, charcuterie, wine and chestnut cakes – from around the island. See p.183

✳ **Musée Fesch** The most important collection of Renaissance art in France outside Paris, collected by Napoleon's step-uncle. See p.183

✳ **A Cupulatta** Tortoise sanctuary, that looks after many species of the loveable reptile, inland from Ajaccio – a must for kids. See p.189

✳ **Plage de Verghia** Silver sand and perfectly translucent water edged by pines. See p.193

✳ **Cala d'Orzu** Pristine beach on the remotest stretch of Ajaccio's gulf. See p.193

▲ Cheese at Ajaccio market

The Ajaccio region

A jaccio is Corsica's largest town, capital of the *département* of Corse-du-Sud and seat of the island's Assemblée Régionale; yet – with its palm trees, street cafés and yacht-filled marina – the image it immediately projects is that of the classic French Mediterranean resort. Modern blocks are stacked up behind the town, but they do little to diminish the visual impact of its warm, yellow-toned buildings and sturdy citadelle, set in a magnificent bay and framed by a shadowy mountain range. Unlike Bastia, Ajaccio makes most of its money from tourism thanks to its own attractions, to its proximity to the west coast's wonderful beaches, and to its having been the birthplace of Napoleon Bonaparte. The prime Napoleonic sites – the Maison Bonaparte and the Salon Napoléonien – are not, however, the best of Ajaccio's cultural assets: that distinction goes to the **Musée Fesch**, which boasts France's most important collection of Italian paintings outside the Louvre.

The **Golfe d'Ajaccio**, an ethereal vista of mist-shrouded mountains by day, is transformed at night into an equally evocative scene by the lights of the bay's sprawling tourist developments. Flung out at the northern tip of the gulf, beyond the hotels, the islets known as the **Îles Sanguinaires** are perhaps the most popular excursion from the town, rivalled by **Porticcio** on the gulf's southern shore, a ribbon resort popular with sporty Ajacciens. Of greater appeal to most visitors are the secluded beaches that punctuate this side of the bay towards **Capo di Muro**, ideal for a picnic and a swim. Inland from Ajaccio, the craggy **Gorges du Prunelli** edge the river as far as **Bastelica**, birthplace of Corsican freedom fighter Sampiero Corso but now an uninspiring village that owes its popularity to the nearby Val d'Èse ski station.

Apart from the train line to Bastia and a few long-distance bus connections, **public transport** in this region is confined to a few shuttle services past the holiday complexes of the Rive Sud, the gulf's southern shore.

Ajaccio

Edward Lear claimed that on a wet day it would be hard to find so dull a place as **AJACCIO** (Aiacciu in Corsican), a harsh judgement with an element of justice. The town has none of Bastia's sense of purpose and can seem to lack a definitive identity of its own. On the other hand, it's a relaxed and good-looking place, with an exceptionally mild climate (the average temperature is 17°C) and a wealth of cafés, restaurants and chic shops.

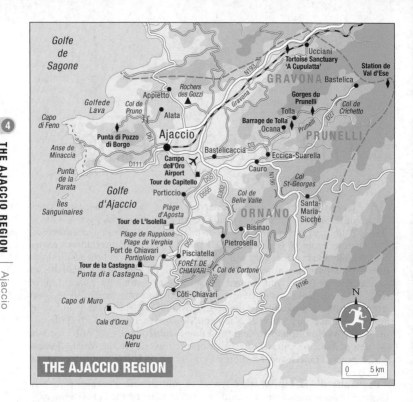

THE AJACCIO REGION

Golfe de Sagone

Golfe d'Ajaccio

THE AJACCIO REGION

0 5 km

N

Napoleon gave Ajaccio international fame, but though the self-designated Cité Impériale is littered with statues and street names relating to the Bonaparte family, you'll find the Napoleonic cult has a less dedicated following in his home town than you might imagine. The emperor is still considered by many Ajacciens as a self-serving Frenchman rather than as a Corsican, and from time to time their disapproval is expressed in a dramatic gesture – such as painting his statue yellow, as happened a few years ago. Napoleon's impact on the townscape of his birthplace wasn't enormous, either. Spacious squares and boulevards were laid out during Ajaccio's brief spell as island capital, but Napoleon's efforts did little to alter the intrinsic provinciality of the place, and Ajaccio remains memorable for the things that have long made it attractive – its battered old town, the pervasive scents of fresh coffee and grilled seafood, and the encompassing view of its glorious bay.

A brief history of Ajaccio

Although it's an attractive idea that Ajax once stopped here, the name of Ajaccio in fact derives from the Roman *Adjaccium* (place of rest), a winter stop-off point for shepherds descending from the mountains to stock up on goods and sell their produce. This first settlement, to the north of the present town in the area called Castelvecchio, was destroyed by the Saracens in the tenth century, and modern Ajaccio grew up around the citadelle that was founded in 1492 by the **Bank of St George**, a Genoese military organization that handled the administration of Corsica. Built to intimidate the local nobility,

174

who had been launching regular assaults on the oppressive Genoese, the citadelle was packed with Ligurian immigrants and remained off limits to Corsican settlers for half a century. In 1553, the Corsican patriot Sampiero Corso took control of the citadelle, having sided with the French, but within six years the former rulers had returned, inaugurating a period of expansion fuelled in part by an influx of people fleeing Moorish raids on the surrounding countryside. The town's population rose from 1200 to 5000 between 1584 and 1666, a period that saw the reinforcement of the citadelle, the construction of a new cathedral and the improvement of the **port**, which by 1627 was doing a better trade than Bastia, at that time a far more important military and political centre. Nonetheless, the infertility of the immediate hinterland kept many Ajacciens in extreme poverty and made the town reliant on imports of Genoese olive oil and wheat, while trading restrictions imposed on the town's merchants fostered resentment among the rising bourgeoisie.

Notwithstanding, when Pascal Paoli launched his first campaign for an independent republic in 1739, the Ajacciens stayed faithful to their Genoese masters. In 1796, however, the **French** finally prevailed, and the ramparts were demolished on the orders of Napoleon. In its new role as capital of Corsica, Ajaccio expanded more rapidly than ever before and maintained its economic momentum right through the nineteenth century, largely due to the success of the wine trade. Since World War II – when Ajaccio, a centre for Resistance fighters, was the first Corsican (and thus French) town to be liberated – the tourist industry has become the most important income-provider.

As the capital and seat of French government in Corsica, Ajaccio sustained its share of nationalist attacks during the troubled 1980s and 1990s. The most notorious was the murder in February 1998 of Préfet Claude Érignac, France's most senior representative on the island, who was gunned down while leaving the opera with his wife. However, separatist violence rarely (if ever) affect tourists. The only outward signs of the unrest you're likely to come across are the heavily armed CRS police who routinely patrol the port and streets around the gendarmerie and Assemblée Régionale, and the facade of the Palais de Justice, which is periodically sprayed with automatic gunfire.

Arrival and information

Served by regular direct flights from France, northern Europe, and North and West Africa, Ajaccio's **airport**, Campo dell'Oro (T04 95 23 56 56, Wwww.ajaccio.aeroport.fr), is 6km east around the bay. All the island's main car rental companies have offices lined up outside the terminal building (see p.186), and metered taxis queue up here at flight times, charging around €24–29 for the journey into town. In addition, *navettes* (shuttle buses; every 20min–1hr; 6.30am–10.45pm; T04 95 23 29 41; €4.50 one way) run into the centre via the train station and stop on cours Napoléon, the main street – buy your ticket on the bus and stamp it in the machine behind the driver's cab.

Long-distance buses pull in at the **terminal routière/gare maritime** (T04 95 51 55 45), next to the port de Commerce, a five-minute walk from the centre. **Ferries** from the mainland also dock in this gleaming modern complex, where you'll find a bureau de change and the cleanest **public toilets** in town. The **train station** (T04 95 23 11 03) lies almost 1km north along boulevard Sampiero, a continuation of the quai l'Herminier.

Car parking is a nightmare year round. You'll spare yourself a stressful tour of the town's one-way system by stumping up the fee for one of the large *parkings* on quai l'Herminier, close to the Hôtel de Ville, or under place du Diamant/place de Gaulle. Alternatively, head straight through the centre and west along the route des Îles Sanguinaires: there's nearly always plenty of (unshaded) space outside the cemetery, from where you can jump on a municipal bus back to the centre.

The **tourist office** is on place du Marché, behind the Hôtel de Ville (April, May, June & Sept Mon–Sat 8am–7pm, Sun 9am–1pm; July & Aug Mon–Sat 8am–8.30pm, Sun 9am–1pm & 4–7pm; Oct–March Mon–Fri 8.30am–6pm, Sat 8.30am–noon; ☎04 95 51 53 03, ⓦ www.ajaccio-tourisme.com). Anyone planning a long-distance hike should head for the office of the **Parc Naturel Régional Corse** (or PNRC), 2 rue Sergeant-Casalonga, around the corner from the *préfecture* on cours Napoléon (Mon–Fri 8am–noon & 2–6pm; ☎04 95 51 79 00, ⓦ www.parc-naturel-corse.com). They are also a good source of advice on how to combine different stages of their long-distance footpaths, and will help you sort out *gîte d'étape* accommodation and transport to the trailheads.

Accommodation

Ajaccio suffers from a dearth of inexpensive **accommodation**, but there are a fair number of mid- and upscale places scattered around town, chiefly along cours Napoléon and the coast road leading to the Îles Sanguinaires. Whatever your budget, it's essential to **book ahead**, especially for weekends between late May and September. All those places listed below are open year-round unless specified otherwise.

Hotels

Le Dauphin 11 bd Sampiero ☎04 95 21 12 94, ⓦ www.ledauphinhotel.com. No-frills place opposite the port de Commerce, above a bar that's straight out of a French crime flick, complete with wide-screen TV, pinball machine and old men sipping *pastis* under a cloud of Gauloise smoke. Various categories of rooms, some on the grotty side for the price, but their budget options in an adjacent building (with shared showers and toilets) are among the cheapest beds in town at €60 per double most of the year. Includes breakfast. ④

Fesch 7 rue Cardinal-Fesch ☎04 95 51 62 62, ⓕ04 95 21 83 36. One of the oldest-established hotels in Ajaccio, and famous as the site of a (bloodless) armed siege in 1980, when it was occupied by fugitive nationalist guerrillas and their French secret service hostages. All rooms are bright and modern, with repro antique furniture, a/c, sound-proofing and TVs; balconies cost extra. ⑤–⑥

Kallisté 51 cours Napoléon ☎04 95 51 34 45, ⓦ www.hotel-kalliste-ajaccio.com. Third-floor hotel right in the centre, with plenty of parking space. The sound-proofed rooms can sleep up to four people, and all come with cable TV and bathroom. There's free internet access in the lobby, a launderette on the ground floor, 24hr check-in, and the staff speak English. The best choice in this category by a long chalk. ⑥

Marengo 12 bd Mme-Mère ☎04 95 21 43 66, ⓦ www.hotel-marengo.com. A 10min walk west of the centre, up a quiet side street off bd Mme-Mère. Slightly boxed in by tower blocks, but a secluded, quiet and pleasant small hotel (with only 16 rooms) away from the city bustle. Best fallback if the *Kallisté* is full. Mid-April to mid-Nov. ④–⑤

Les Mouettes 9 cours Lucien-Bonapartere ☎04 95 50 40 40, ⓦ www.hotellesmouettes.fr. Luxuriously renovated nineteenth-century villa off the Routes des Sanguinaires, shaded by mature palms and pines, with direct access to its own private cove. The pricier rooms, facing the pool and sun terrace, enjoy expansive views of the bay and have well shaded balconies. Doubles from €150–250. ⑨

Napoléon 4 Lorenzo Vero ☎04 95 51 54 00, ⓦ www.hotelnapoleonajaccio.fr. Welcoming, a/c three-star tucked just off cours Napoléon. The rooms are dark and on the small side – a bit of a squeeze for three, but comfortable enough as doubles. ⑥

Du Palais 5 av Bévérini-Vico ☎04 95 22 73 68, ⓦ www.hoteldupalaisajaccio.com. Restful mid-scale place, a 10min walk north of the centre, within easy reach of the train station. The rooms are on the small side and most have shared bathrooms, but they're impeccably clean; count on €20 extra for en suite, and ask for one at the rear of the building if you want peace and quiet. ⑤

La Pinède route des Sanguinaires ☎04 95 52 00 44, ⓦ www.la-pinede.com. Most secluded and peaceful of the swish star hotels out towards Les Îles Sanguinaires, 4km west of the town centre. It's

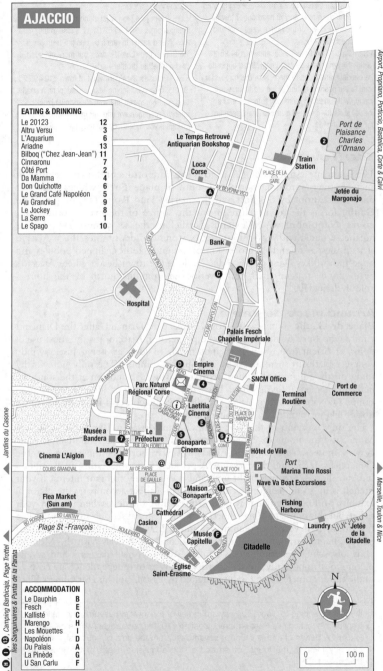

AJACCIO

EATING & DRINKING

Le 20123	12
Altru Versu	3
L'Aquarium	6
Ariadne	13
Bilboq ("Chez Jean-Jean")	11
Cinnaronu	7
Côté Port	2
Da Mamma	4
Don Quichotte	6
Le Grand Café Napoléon	5
Au Grandval	9
Le Jockey	8
La Serre	1
Le Spago	10

ACCOMMODATION

Le Dauphin	B
Fesch	E
Kallisté	C
Marengo	H
Les Mouettes	I
Napoléon	D
Du Palais	A
La Pinède	G
U San Carlu	F

Les Millelli & Camping Les Mimosas

Airport, Propriano, Porticcio, Bastelica, Corte & Calvi

Jardins du Casone

Camping Barbicaja, Plage Trottel
Îles Sanguinaires & Punta de la Parata

Marseille, Toulon & Nice

300m from the beach (up a narrow lane signposted right off the main road as you head out of town), but with great views of the gulf, a large pool and tennis court. ❽

U San Carlu 8 bd Danielle-Casanova ☎04 95 21 13 84, ⓦwww.hotel-sancarlu.com. Sited opposite the citadelle and close to the beach, this three-star hotel is the poshest option in the old town, with sunny, well-furnished rooms, all fully a/c, and a special suite for disabled guests in the basement – but no parking. ❼

Campsites

Le Barbicaja 4.5km west along the route des Sanguinaires ☎04 95 52 01 17. Close to the beach and easier to reach by bus (#5 from place de Gaulle) than Les Mimosas, but more crowded, and altogether grottier. April–Oct.

Les Mimosas 3km northwest of town ☎04 95 20 99 85, ⓦwww.camping-lesmimosas.com. A shady and well-organized site with clean toilet blocks, friendly management and fair rates – though a long trudge if you're loaded with luggage. May–Oct.

The Town

The most interesting part of Ajaccio is the core of the old town: a cluster of ancient streets spreading north and south of **place Foch**, which opens out onto the seafront by the port and the marina Tino Rossi. Nearby **place de Gaulle** forms the town centre and is the source of the main thoroughfare, **cours Napoléon**, which extends parallel to the sea almost 2km to the northeast. Lined with chi-chi boutiques, stores and brassy cafés, this is Ajaccio at its posiest – an endless procession of designer clothes, clipped poodles and huge motorbikes. West of place de Gaulle is the town beach where Ajaccio's beau monde top up their tans, overlooked from the north by the honey-coloured citadelle.

Around place de Gaulle

Place de Gaulle – otherwise known as place du Diamant, after the Diamanti family who once owned much of the property in Ajaccio – is the most useful point of orientation, even if it's not much to look at, being just a windy concrete platform surrounded by a shopping complex. The only noteworthy thing on the square is the huge **bronze statue** of Napoleon at the southern end: nicknamed *L'Encrier* (The Inkstand), the pompous lump was commissioned by Napoléon III in 1865 and shows Napoléon clad in Roman garb on horseback, surrounded by his four brothers.

The only museum in this part of town, the **Musée a Bandera** (May–Sept Mon–Sat 9am–noon & 2–6pm; Oct–April Mon–Fri 9am–noon & 2–6pm; ⓦwww.musee-abandera.fr; €4), is a short way north of the square, in rue Général-Levie, behind the *préfecture*. A privately run project, this small military museum houses few objects of note and is only likely to be of interest if your French is up to the lengthy written explanations that accompany the pictorial exhibits. An English guide may be borrowed from the desk when you buy your ticket, but this translates only a fraction of the material set out on the walls. The first room is devoted to prehistoric times, showing off bronze daggers and pottery fragments; the more interesting second room deals with the Moorish raids, displaying beautiful ivory-handled stilettos (small daggers) and several pictures of flamboyantly dressed corsairs. The Wars of Independence are covered in the third room, featuring statutes drafted by Pascal Paoli and Sir Gilbert Elliot

If you're intending to work your way around all of the town's museums and galleries, it's worth investing in a **Passemusée**. Costing €10, the pass covers all the museums (except A Bandera) and is valid for seven days from the time of your first visit; you can buy them at the tourist office and at the admission desks of the museums themselves.

▲ Napoleon monument

during the Anglo-Corsican alliance of 1794–96. The last room has a section on World War II and the Corsican Resistance.

Devotees of Napoleon should take a stroll 1km up cours Grandval, the wide street rising west of place de Gaulle and ending in a square, the **Jardins du Casone**, where gaudily spectacular son et lumière shows take place in summer. On the way you'll pass the **Assemblée Nationale**, an enormous yellow Art-Deco building fronted by a jungle of palms and a couple of armoured police vans. An impressive **monument** to Napoleon dominates the square – a replica of the statue at Napoleon's burial place, Les Invalides in Paris, standing atop a huge pedestal inscribed with the names of his battles.

Behind the monument lies a graffiti-bedaubed **cave** where Napoleon is supposed to have frolicked as a child.

Place Foch

Once the site of the town's medieval gate, **place Foch** lies at the heart of old Ajaccio. A delightfully shady square sloping down to the sea and lined with cafés and restaurants, it gets its local name – place des Palmiers – from the row of mature palms bordering the central strip. Dominating the top end, a fountain of four marble lions provides a mount for the inevitable statue of Napoleon, this one by Ajaccien sculptor Maglioli. A humbler effigy occupies a niche high on a wall south of the fountain, above a souvenir shop – a figurine of Ajaccio's patron saint, **La Madonnuccia**, her base bearing the text *Poserunt me custodem* ("They have made me their guardian"). The image dates from 1656, a year in which Ajaccio's local council, fearful of infection from plague-struck Genoa, placed the town under the guardianship of the Madonna in a ceremony that took place on this spot. Ajaccio was saved on that occasion and again in 1745, when *La Madonnuccia* was paraded around the ramparts to dispel the Anglo-Sardinian fleet bombarding the city – whereupon the enemy beat a miraculous, speedy retreat. If you're here on March 18 you can witness Ajaccio's big event, the **Fête de la Miséricorde**, in which the statue is conveyed through the old town as a prelude to a big party and firework display.

Taking up the northern end of place Foch, the **Hôtel de Ville**, with its impenetrable wooden doors, was built in 1826. The first-floor **Salon Napoléonien** (June 15–Sept 15 Mon–Sat 9–11.45am & 2–5.45pm; Sept 16–June 14 Mon–Fri 9–11.45am & 2–4.45pm; €2.30) consists of two rooms that are really only for dedicated Napoleon fans. A replica of the ex-emperor's death mask takes pride of place in a chamber bedecked with velvet, crystal chandeliers and a solemn array of Bonaparte family portraits and busts. Next door, the smaller medal room has a batch of minor relics – a fragment from Napoleon's coffin, some earth from his garden, and part of his dressing case – plus a model of the ship that brought him back from St Helena, and a picture of the house where he died.

South of place Foch

The **south side of place Foch**, the former dividing line between the poor district around the port and the bourgeoisie's territory, gives access to **rue Bonaparte**, the main route through the latter quarter. Built on the promontory rising to the citadelle, the secluded streets in this part of town – with their dusty buildings, bistros and bar fronts lit by flashes of sea or sky at the end of the alleys – retain more of a sense of the old Ajaccio than anywhere else. Of the families who lived here in the eighteenth century, one of the most eminent was the **Pozzo di Borgo** clan, whose house still stands at 17 rue Bonaparte, its facade adorned by trompe l'œil frescoes. Carlo Andrea Pozzo di Borgo was a distant cousin and childhood friend of Napoleon, but was later to become one of his bitterest enemies. A supporter of Paoli, he was elected to the Corsican legislature and became president of the Council of State under the short-lived Anglo-Corsican rule of 1794–96. Described as "a man of talent, an intriguer", Pozzo was not content with this domestic position and in 1803 he became the ambassador to Russia, later befriending Wellington, with whom he fought at Waterloo. He went on to become a favourite at the English court, where Queen Victoria referred to him affectionately as "Old Pozzo".

Maison Bonaparte

The Bonaparte family first appeared in the chronicles of Ajaccio in the fifteenth century, when they lived in a house that was demolished in 1555 by the French attack on the citadelle. Napoleon was born in the colossal **Maison Bonaparte**, on place Letizia, just off the west side of rue Bonaparte (May–Sept Mon 2–6pm, Tues–Fri 9am–noon & 2–6pm, Sat 9–11.45am & 2–6pm, Sun 9am–noon; Oct–April Mon 2–6pm, Tues–Sat 10am–noon & 2–5pm, Sun 10am–noon; €4). Soon after, in May 1793, Letizia and her children were driven from the house by Paoli's partisans, who stripped the place down to the floorboards. Requisitioned by the English in 1794, Maison Bonaparte became an arsenal and a lodging house for English officers, amongst whom was Hudson Lowe, later Napoleon's jailer on St Helena. Though Letizia subsequently paid for its restoration with an indemnity given to those Corsicans who had suffered at the hands of the English, her heart wasn't in the job – she left for the second and last time in 1799, the year Napoleon stayed here on his return from Egypt. Owned by the state since 1923, the house now bears few traces of the Bonaparte family's existence, and barely warrants the admission charge.

The visit begins on the second floor, but before you go up look out for the wooden sedan chair in the hallway – Letizia was carried back from church on it when the prenatal Napoleon started giving her contractions, and it's one of the very few original pieces of furniture left in the house.

Upstairs, an endless display of portraits, miniatures, weapons, letters and documents gives the impression of having been formed by gathering together anything that was remotely connected with the family and unwanted by anyone else. Amongst the highlights of the first room are a few maps of Corsica dating from the eighteenth century, some deadly "vendetta" daggers and two handsome pairs of pistols belonging to Napoleon's father. The next-door Alcove Room was, according to tradition, occupied by Napoleon in 1799, when he stayed here for the last time, while in the third room you can see the sofa upon which the future emperor first saw the light of day on August 15, 1769. Adjoining the heavily restored long gallery is a tiny room known as the Trapdoor Room, whence Letizia and her children made their getaway from the marauding Paolists.

The Cathedral

Napoleon was baptized in 1771 in the **Cathedral**, around the corner from Maison Bonaparte in rue Forcioli-Conti. It was built in 1582 on a much smaller scale than originally intended, due to lack of funds – an apology for its diminutive size is inscribed in a plaque inside, on the wall to the left as you enter. The interior is interesting chiefly for a few Napoleonic connections: to the right of the door stands the font where he was dipped at the age of 23 months; and his sister, Elisa Bacciochi, donated the great marble altar in 1811. Before leaving, take a look in the chapel to the left of the doorway (as you're facing the altar), which houses a gloomy Delacroix painting of the Virgin holding aloft the Sacred Heart.

Musée Capitellu

Opposite the citadelle, an elaborately carved capital marks the entrance to **Musée Capitellu** (May–Oct Mon–Sat 10am–noon & 2–6pm, Sun 10am–noon; €4), a tiny museum mainly given over to offering a picture of domestic life in nineteenth-century Ajaccio. The house belonged to a wealthy Ajaccien family, the Bacciochi, who were related to Napoleon through his sister's marriage, though he doesn't figure at all here.

Napoleon and Corsica

"M de Choisel once said that if Corsica could be pushed under the sea with a trident it should be done. He was quite right. It is nothing but an excrescence." This sentiment, expressed by Napoleon to one of the generals who had followed him into exile on St Helena, encapsulates his bitterness about his birthplace. Corsica's opinion of its most famous citizen can be equally uncomplimentary.

The year of **Napoleon's birth**, 1769, was a crucial one in the history of Corsica, for this was the year the French took over the island from the Genoese. They made a thorough job of it, crushing Paoli's troops at Ponte Nuovo and driving the Corsican leader into exile. Napoleon's father, **Carlo**, a close associate of Paoli, fled the scene of the battle with his pregnant wife in order to escape the victorious French army. But Carlo's subsequent behaviour was quite different from that of his former leader – he came to terms with the French, becoming a representative of the newly styled Corsican nobility in the National Assembly, and using his contacts with the French governor to get a free education for his children.

At the age of 9, Napoleon was awarded a scholarship to the Brienne military academy, an institution specially founded to teach the sons of the nobility the respon-sibilities of their status. The French were anxious to impress their values on the potential leaders of a now dependent territory, and with Napoleon they certainly appear to have succeeded. Give or take a rebellious gesture or two, this son of a Corsican Italian-speaking household used his time well, leaving Brienne to enter the exclusive École Militaire in Paris. At the age of 16, he was commissioned into the artillery. When he was 20, the Revolution broke out in Paris and the scene was set for a remarkable career.

Always an ambitious opportunist, he obtained leave from his regiment, returned to Ajaccio, joined the local Jacobin club and – with his eye on a colonelship in the Corsican militia – enthusiastically promoted the interests of the Revolution. However, things did not quite work out as he had planned, for Pascal Paoli had also returned to Corsica.

Carlo Bonaparte had died some years before, and Napoleon – though not the eldest son – was effectively the head of a family that had formerly given Paoli strong support. Having spent the last twenty years in London, Paoli was pro-English and had developed a profound distaste for revolutionary excesses (it was his determina-tion to keep the guillotine out of Corsica that, as much as anything else, led him into the later failed experiment of union with Britain). Napoleon's French allegiance and his Jacobin views antagonized the older man, and his military conduct didn't enhance his standing at all. Elected second in command of the volunteer militia, Napoleon was involved in an unsuccessful attempt to wrest control of the citadelle from royalist sympathizers. He thus took much of the blame when, in reprisal for the killing of one of the militiamen, several people were gunned down in Ajaccio, an incident that engendered eight days of civil war. In June 1793, Napoleon and his family were chased back to the mainland by the Paolists.

Napoleon promptly renounced any special allegiance he had ever felt for Corsica. He Gallicized the spelling of his name, preferring "Napoleon" to his baptismal "Napoleone". And, although he was later to speak with nostalgia about the scents of the Corsican countryside and to regret he did not build a grand house there, he returned only once more to the island (after being forced to dock here during his return voyage from Egypt) and put Ajaccio fourth on the list of places where he would like to be buried.

Watercolour landscapes of Corsica line the walls of the first room, which also contains a marble *Madonnuccia* whose head was cut off with a sabre during the French Revolution. A bust of Sampiero Corso, a common adornment of smart nineteenth-century households, dominates the second room. The glass display cases hold the most fascinating exhibits, however, which include a rare edition of the first history of Corsica, and the 1796 *Code Corse*, a list of laws set out by Louis XV for the newly occupied Corsica. The last room contains a bronze bust of a chubby-cheeked Pascal Paoli, and a striking painting titled *Sunrise over Bavella*, attributed to Turner's nephew.

The citadelle

The restored **citadelle**, a hexagonal fortress and tower stuck out on a wide promontory into the sea, is occupied by the military and closed to the public. Founded in the 1490s, the fort wasn't completed until the occupation of Ajaccio by Sampiero Corso and the powerful Marshal Thermes from 1553 to 1558. During World War II it was taken by the Italians and used as a prison, whose most famous inmate was a young paratrooper captain called **Scamaroni**. Dispatched to Corsica from North Africa by de Gaulle in January 1943, he set up radio posts in the Ajaccio area. But Scamaroni would never see the island's liberation. Betrayed by the forced confession of a fellow radio operator, he was captured and subjected to days of appalling torture in the citadelle, but did not divulge any names of his contacts, eventually slitting his throat and wrists with a length of electric wire. With his blood he wrote on walls of his cell the words, "*Je n'ai pas parlé, vive la France. Ajaccio, 19 Mars, 1943.*"

The citadelle overlooks the town beach, **plage St-François**, a short curve of yellow sand facing the expansive mountain-ringed bay. Several flights of steps lead down to the beach from boulevard Danielle-Casanova. A little further down the promenade, the parking lot in front of the municipal sports centre hosts a weekly **flea market** each Sunday morning, starting at around 9am.

For the nicest beach within easy walking distance of the town, press on past the exercise area and gendarmerie to **plage Trottel**, which is larger and much cleaner than plage St-François.

North of place Foch

Immediately **north of place Foch** behind the Hôtel de Ville, **square César-Campinchi** (aka **place du Marché**) is the venue for the island's largest **fresh produce market**, held here daily except Monday (6am–2pm), and an essential part of Ajaccien life. Alongside the usual array of cut flowers, vegetables and fruit laid out under colourful stripy awnings are stalls selling artisanal delicacies such as barbary fig jam, honey *aux fleurs du maquis*, wild boar sauces and ewe's cheese from the Niolo, as well as muscat wines and myrtle liqueurs. The cafés lining the west side of the square are among the liveliest breakfast spots in town – ideal for crowd-watching after you've finished browsing.

A stone's throw east of the square lies the **Quai L'Herminier**, the long harbourfront connecting Ajaccio's two pleasure ports, where ferries and cruise liners now dock. The harbour-front was the scene of Corsica's most glorious hour in World War II, when it became the first patch of Metropolitan France to be liberated from occupation by Axis forces. On September 14, 1943, the submarine **Le Casabianca**, under the command of **Capitain du Vaisseau Jean L'Herminier**, sailed into the harbour from Algiers with 109 troops.

Musée Fesch

Behind the market, the principal road leading north is **rue Cardinal-Fesch**, a delightful pedestrianized street lined with boutiques, cafés and restaurants. Halfway along the street, set back from the road behind iron gates, stands the **Palais Fesch**, home of Ajaccio's best gallery, the **Musée Fesch** (April–June & Sept Tues–Sun 9.30am–noon & 2–6pm; July & Aug Mon 2–6pm, Tues–Thurs

10.30am–6pm, Fri 2–9.30pm, Sat & Sun 10.30am–6pm; Oct–March Mon–Fri 9.30am–noon & 2–5.30pm; €5.35). Cardinal Joseph Fesch, whose bronze image presides over the courtyard, was Napoleon's step-uncle and bishop of Lyon, a lucrative position which allowed him to invest in large numbers of paintings, many of them looted by the French armies in Holland, Italy and Germany. A highly cultured man with an eye for a bargain, he bequeathed a thousand paintings to Ajaccio on the condition that an academy of arts was created in the town. His wishes were contested by Napoleon's brother Joseph, who turned a quick profit by dispersing much of the collection on the art market. Luckily for Ajaccio, however, Renaissance art was less highly regarded in those days than in later years, so many of the more valuable works remained here.

The collection is housed on four storeys; if you're pushed for time, skip the basement – which harbours an uninspiring assortment of Napoleonic memorabilia – and head, via the temporary exhibition room on the ground floor, to **Niveau 1** upstairs where the cream of the sixteenth- and seventeenth-century Italian works are displayed. In the first room hangs one of Fesch's greatest treasures, Sandro Botticelli's exquisite *Virgin and Child*, painted when the artist was just 25 years old. Dating from a later period, Titian's smouldering *Man with a Glove*, at the end of the corridor, is shown opposite Veronese's *Leda and the Swan*, an uncompromisingly erotic work for its time. **Niveau 2** is given over primarily to seventeenth- and eighteenth-century paintings, where the absence of the Dutch masters sold off by Napoleon's brother is most keenly felt. Highlights here include Poussin's *Midas à la Source du Pactole*, in the first gallery on the right after the stairs, and a vibrant array of still lifes, notably Giuseppe Recco's *Ray on a Cauldron with Fish in a Basket*. The largest gallery on this floor, **La Grande Galérie**, houses a collection of outsize canvases, of which Gregorio de Ferrari's *La Sainte Famille* is the most famous.

You'll need a separate ticket for the **Chapelle** (same hours; €1.50), which stands across the courtyard from the museum. With its gloomy monochrome interior the chapel itself is unremarkable; the interest lies in the crypt, which holds the remains of various members of the Bonaparte family. It was the cardinal's dying wish that all the Bonaparte family be brought together under one roof, so the chapel was built in 1857, and the bodies subsequently brought in – as recently as 1951, Charles Bonaparte was reburied here, alongside Letizia, Cardinal Fesch and half a dozen other Bonapartes.

Lucien Bonaparte laid the first stone of the adjacent **Bibliothèque Municipale**, which contains a huge collection of rare antique books. You're not allowed to handle any, but are welcome to browse and read periodicals and magazines on the long, polished table stretching down the middle of the chamber.

Eating and drinking

At mealtimes, the alleyways and little squares of Ajaccio's old town become one large, interconnecting restaurant terrace lit by rows of candles. All too often, however, the breezy locations and views of the gulf mask indifferent cooking and inflated prices. Stick to the places reviewed in the listings below, though, and you shouldn't go far wrong.

Cafés and **bars** jostle for pavement space all over town but especially along cours Napoléon, which grows more old-fashioned and sedate as it approaches the place de Gaulle. If you fancy sipping a drink with a view of the bay, try one of the flashy cocktail bars that line the seafront beyond the citadelle on boulevard Lantivy, but expect to pay for the privilege. For **breakfast**, you can't beat the row of workers' cafés along the west side of boulevard du Roi-Jérôme, which look onto the square César-Campinchi and the morning market place.

Cafés and bars

Le Grand Café Napoléon 10 cours Napoléon, opposite the *préfecture*. Allegedly the oldest café in town, with Second Empire decor and a *troisième âge* clientele, most of them in suits and shades. The bar inside was the scene of a famous shootout during World War II, when a cell of key Resistance members was disturbed by the Italian caribinieri and forced to flee with guns blazing.

Au Grandval 4 rue Maréchal Ornano. Lively neighbourhood bar that's famous for its collection of antique photos of Ajaccio (mostly evocative portraits). Only a couple of doors down from *Le Jockey*, which stays open later.

Le Jockey 1 rue Maréchal Ornano. An Ajaccien institution, renowned above all for its extraordinary list of wines, which you can order by the glass or bottle: Cantemerle, Morgon, Sancerre, Chasse-Spleen, Châteauneuf du Pâpe and all the local stars (including Arena, Leccia, Toraccia, Saparale, Abbatucci). The decor's a quirky but cosy hotchpotch of ephemera and old memorabilia, with a soundtrack to match. They also host very *rive gauche* literature and philosohy *soirées* on Thurs.

Restaurants

Le 20123 2 rue Roi-de-Rome ☎ 04 95 21 50 05, ⓦ www.20123.fr. Decked out like a small hill village, complete with *fontaine* and parked Vespa, the decor here is a lot more frivolous than the serious Corsican food (from charcuterie starter to chestnut-flour flan desserts) featured on a single €34 menu. Top-notch cooking, and organic AOC wine. Closed Mon except in July & Aug.

Altru Versu 2 rue Jean-Baptiste Marcaggi ☎ 04 95 50 05 22, ⓦ www.laltruversu.com. Classy Corsican speciality place hosted by Corsican celebrity chef David Mezzacqui. The menu's a mouth-watering array of traditional fare given a gourmet twist: seabass soufflé with *brocciu* and fresh mint, clams in flaky pastry and Muscat sauce, chestnut tagliatelle. À la carte only (count on €45–50 per head, plus wine). Live Corsican music Fri–Sat. Closed Sun.

L'Aquarium rue des Halles ☎ 04 95 21 11 21. One of the best places in town for *friture du golfe* and fresh baby red snappers, seabass or bream – everything comes straight from the adjacent covered market, and you get to pick your fish before it's grilled. Set menus €20–27; eau de vie on the house. Closed Mon except July–Sept.

Ariadne route des Sanguinaires, near *Barbicaja* campsite ☎ 04 95 52 09 63. The oldest and most cheerful of Ajaccio's many beachside *paillotes*, with a wooden *pied dans l'eau* terrace opening straight onto the sand, and a consistently lively ambience. World cuisine dominates the menu (dishes from Cuba, Morocco, Mali, the Caribbean and Laos) and there's usually live music (salsa/reggae/soukous) from 8.30pm. Most main courses €17–20. Open Easter–Oct Tues–Sun. You can get here from place de Gaulle on bus #5.

Bilboq ("Chez Jean-Jean") av des Glacis, just off place Foch ☎ 04 95 51 35 40. The eponymous *patron* (a former fisherman and boxer) of this legendary seafood joint is Ajaccio's undisputed "lobster king", and there's no point in coming here to eat anything but local *langouste*, served grilled with spaghetti. You can dine al fresco on a narrow alley terrace, or inside, regailed by Tino Rossi music (which, unlike the lobster, is definitely an acquired taste). Count on €32 per head for three courses, plus wine.

Cinnaronu rue Maréchal Ornano ☎ 04 95 21 49 37. Small backstreet restaurant that's a draw for charcuterie enthusiasts across the island. You won't eat better *figatellu*, *lonzu* or *coppa* anywhere, and they also do pizzas and succulent *grillades*. Closed Sun.

Côté Port Port Ornano ☎ 04 95 10 55 75. The nicest of the row of quayside places down in the marina, with bleached wood beams, decking and a giant anchor underlining the nautical ambience. It's run by a dynamic young couple and offers an eclectic mix of world cooking, using only fresh local produce. *Suggestions du jour* around €23. Closed Sun.

Da Mamma passage Guinghetta ☎ 04 95 21 39 44. Tucked away down a narrow passageway connecting cours Napoléon and rue Cardinal-Fesch. Authentic but affordable Corsican cuisine – such as *cannelloni al brocciu*, roast kid and seafood – on set menus from €14–29 served in a stone-walled dining room or under a rubber tree in a tiny courtyard.

Don Quichotte 7 rue des Halles ☎ 04 95 21 27 30. The only one along this line of terrace restaurants that enjoys a local clientele. Everyone comes for the steaks, but their fish dish of the day is invariably delicious (try the seabass grilled *au pastis* if it's available), the coffee is second to none and the wine list features Domaine Saparale.

La Serre at the north end of cours Napoléon. Eccentric self-service restaurant where you can eat a filling three-course meal for under €20. They usually offer half a dozen main courses (mostly French standards), plus a host of side dishes and desserts. It's great for crowd-watching, especially on Sun lunchtimes when locals pile in from the nearby workers' suburbs.

Le Spago 1 bis, Rue Emmanuel Arene ☎ 04 95 21 15 71. Thanks largely to its idiosyncratic designer decor, this funky little lounge restaurant has become one of Ajaccio's hippest places to eat. Live techno DJs and local bands frequently enliven meals, and the food – a mix of Corsican standards and innovative modern dishes – is reasonably priced. Try their tasty raclette, or Bonifacien-style baked aubergine; and leave room for one of the tempting desserts. Most mains around €20.

Nightlife and entertainment

What **nightlife** there is in Ajaccio consists chiefly of eating and drinking, though there are four **cinemas** (see below), a busy municipal **casino** on boulevard Lantivy (Pascal Rossini), and a few Eurotrashy **discos** with extortionate entrance charges. Of these, *Le Duplex*, on Ricanto beach out near the airport, is the most consistently lively and liberal, with a monthly gay night and visiting DJs.

North of the centre, in the district of Brasilia, the arts centre **A l'Aghja**, 6 chemin de Biancarello (☎04 95 20 41 15), hosts theatre performances, world-music gigs and Corsican polyphony singing, mostly on Friday and Saturday nights starting at 9pm. It's hard to find, but is the only venue in town where you can escape synth maestros and "club-style" crooners; head for Brasilia bus stop and ask the way from there, or take a taxi (€12 approximately). The tourist office posts details of forthcoming events.

Listings

Airport enquiries ☎04 95 23 56 56; ⓦwww .ajaccio.aeroport.fr.

Banks and exchange Most of the main banks have branches on place de Gaulle or cours Napoléon, while the BNP is near the market place, on bd du Roi-Jérôme.

Bookshops Maison de la Presse, 2 place Foch (☎04 95 25 81 18), stocks Ajaccio's best selection of new publications on Corsica, as well as a good range of international newspapers, including the *Guardian*, *Independent*, *New York Times* and *Washington Post*. Serious book, print and map collectors, and anyone with more than a passing interest in the island should also make time for the wonderful Le Temps Retrouvé, at 1 rue Ste-Lucie (☎04 95 20 17 30, ⓔapiazzola@wanadoo.fr). Its owner, Alain Piazzola (Dorothy Carrington's former editor), has amassed a huge collection of rare books and other printed memorabilia – well worth a browse even if you're not buying.

Bus information See Travel details (p.197) for specific bus companies and their routes, or visit ⓦwww.corsicabus.org.

Car rental Rent-a-Car, *Kallisté*, 51 cours Napoléon (☎04 95 51 34 45, ⓦwww.rentacar.fr), airport (☎04 95 23 56 36); ADA Location, airport (☎04 95 23 56 57, ⓦwww.ada.fr); Avis, 1 rue Paul Colonna d'Istria (☎04 95 23 92 50), airport (☎04 95 21 28 01, ⓦwww.avis.fr); Budget, 1 bd Lantivy (☎04 95 21 17 18, ⓦwww.budget-en -corse.com), airport (☎04 95 23 57 21); Citer, bd Lantivy (☎04 95 51 21 21, ⓦwww.corse-auto -rent.fr), airport (☎04 95 23 57 15); Europcar, 16 cours Grandval (☎04 95 21 05 49,

ⓦwww.europcar.com), airport (☎04 95 23 57 01); Hertz, 8 cours Grandval (☎04 95 21 70 94, ⓦwww.hertz.fr), airport (☎04 95 23 57 04).

Cinemas Ajaccio's four cinemas are dowdy old dinosaurs left over from the pre-war era, complete with fire screens, sagging seats and ice-cream-selling usherettes. Unfortunately, ticket prices do not reflect their generally shabby state, but they offer an alternative to café crawling if you've an idle evening to kill. Those on cours Napoléon – the Empire, at no. 18 (☎04 95 21 21 00), the Bonaparte, down the road at no. 10 (☎04 95 51 27 98), and Laetitia, opposite the post office at no. 48 (☎04 95 21 07 24), screen mainstream French and Hollywood blockbusters dubbed in French. The latter also has an annexe, The Aiglon, around the corner at 14 cours Grandval (☎04 95 51 29 46), which shows mainly art-house and foreign films.

Diving Popular dive sites around Ajaccio include Les Dentis, a shallow shelf 200m offshore near the citadelle; La Castagne, dramatic rock formations rich with underwater life on the southern extremity of the bay; and the Îles Sanguinaires, 12km west of town (see p.190). Winds and currents can be a problem at all three. For advice, transport and training, contact any of the following reputable diving clubs: Odyssée Plongée, Port de Plaisance Charles d'Ornano ☎04 95 20 53 51, ⓦwww .odyssee-plongee.fr; E. Ragnole, 12 cours Lucien Bonaparte, behind place Trottel at the west end of town ☎04 95 21 53 55, ⓦwww.eragnole.com; Isula, *Hôtel Cala di Sole*, route des Sanguinaires ☎04 95 52 06 39, ⓦhttp://jpvigno.club.fr.

Ferry offices SNCM, terminal maritime, quai l'Herminier (Mon–Fri 8–11am & 2–6pm, Sat 8–11.45am; ☎04 95 29 66 99). You can also access fares and timetable information via the ferry companies' websites at ⓦwww.sncm.fr and ⓦwww.corsicaferries.com.

Hospital Centre Hospitalier, 27 av Impératrice-Eugénie ☎04 95 29 90 90; for an ambulance, call ☎15.

Internet access Free in the lobby of the *Kallisté* on cours Napoléon.

Laundry Just down the road from the Musée a Bandera at the bottom of rue Maréchal-Ornano, off cours Grandval; and in the marina Tino Rossi, next to the harbour master's office.

Motorbike rental Cyrnos Location, *Kallisté*, 51 cours Napoléon ☎04 95 51 61 81 or 04 95 23 56 36, ⓦwww.cyrnos.net; Moto Corse Évasion, Montée St-Jean ☎04 95 20 52 05, ⓦwww.corsicamoto.com.

Pharmacies There are several large pharmacies on place Foch and cours Napoléon.

Police rue Général-Fiorella ☎04 95 29 95 29; emergencies ☎17.

Post office 13 cours Napoléon (June–Aug Mon–Fri 9am–4.45pm, Sat 9am–noon; Sept–May Mon–Fri 9–11.45am & 2.30–4.45pm, Sat 9–11.45am; ☎04 95 51 84 65).

Sports facilities The Complexe Municipal Pascal Rossi, on av Pascal-Rossini (☎04 95 21 08 30), is Ajaccio's largest public sports centre, with a pool, gym, weights room and running track. The municipal tennis courts are out of town, on route des Sanguinaires (☎04 95 52 00 25).

Taxis The main taxi ranks are: on the north side of place de Gaulle (☎04 95 21 00 87); and on av Pascal-Paoli (☎04 95 23 25 70).

Train information Gare CFC ☎04 95 23 11 03.

Moving on from Ajaccio

Ajaccio's ferry port is the second busiest on the island after Bastia, and its *terminal routière* on the quai l'Herminier forms the nexus of the region's long-distance bus network, so most independent travellers come here at some point to pick up onward transport.

By plane

Campo dell'Oro airport has daily scheduled **flights** to cities on the French mainland, including Marseille, Nice and Paris on Air France/Air Inter, as well as weekly EasyJet flights to London Gatwick and charter flights to many destinations in northern Europe between April and October. The cheapest way to get to the airport from town is on the shuttle bus (*navette* #8) that runs between one and three times per hour from the parking lot next to the *terminal routière* (☎04 95 23 29 41 20; €4.50 one way); taxis cost around €25.

By ferry

Most of the car and passenger **ferries** sailing out of Ajaccio go to Marseille, with less frequent departures to Toulon and Nice. Tickets are available up to two hours before departure time from SNCM's counter inside the arrivals hall of the *terminal maritime*, or in advance at their office directly opposite on the quai l'Herminier (see above). For more details, see p.21.

By train

Run by the Chemin de Fer de la Corse (CFC), the **micheline** trip from Ajaccio across the mountains to Bastia ranks among the island's most memorable journeys, taking in the wild valleys and pine forests of the interior around Corte, and a string of sleepy village stations. At the time of writing the line was being substantially upgraded with new track and trains, with timetables still under deliberation; the latest timings are posted on ⓦwww.corsicabus.org. A roundup of routes and stations reachable direct from Ajaccio appears in Travel details on p.197.

By bus

Ajaccio is well connected by bus to other towns on the island: the tourist office on boulevard du Roi-Jérôme keeps a set of up-to-date timetables, and you can also get information at the *terminal routière* on quai l'Herminier, where all the various operators have individual counters (open half an hour or so prior to departure). Their destinations and departure times are displayed on boards, and you can pay for tickets in advance as soon as the counter opens. This is a particularly good idea for services such as SAIB's Porto bus and others using minibuses, which tend to fill up quickly. They'll also look after your luggage for free. A full list of routes, along with telephone numbers for their operators, appears in Travel details on p.197.

Around Ajaccio

The maquis-carpeted ridge of hills north of Ajaccio, known as **Les Crêtes**, holds a few interesting possibilities for a half-day excursion if you have your own transport. Chief of these is the **Punta di Pozzo di Borgo**, which provides an excellent view of Ajaccio and its bay and is reached by a road that takes you close to **Les Millelli**, the country residence owned (but seldom visited) by the Bonapartes. Walkers can take the gentle stroll west of town to **Monte Salario** to see the **Fontaine de Salario**. Further out of town is the **Tortoise Sanctuary**, **A Cupulatta**, 17km northeast along the N193.

Les Millelli

Enveloped in old olive groves on the hillside above Ajaccio, **Les Millelli** (daily except Tues 9am–noon & 2–6pm; €2) was the much loved, though rarely used, country retreat of the Bonaparte family. Letizia, Napoleon's mother, was forced to hide out in the house with the future emperor's sisters and uncle during the Paolist uprising of May 1793, and Napoleon himself famously stayed here with Murat six years later on his return from Egypt – but that's about the extent of the site's relevance. Nonetheless, the house is a firmly established stage on the Napoleonic trail: a stolid, plain, eighteenth-century building whose real attraction is the surrounding terraced olive grove overlooking the gulf – a pleasant picnic spot. Inside, there's just a small and dreary ethnographical museum. To reach Les Millelli, follow the main drag north out of town for around 1km and turn left onto the D61, marked to "Alata". A sign on the far side of the first large roundabout you reach, just under 1km beyond the turn-off, indicates the route up the hill.

Punta di Pozzo di Borgo

If, instead of taking the turn to Les Millelli, you continue 6km further along the D61, you'll come to the Col de Pruno, where a left turn along a narrow twisting road will bring you after another 6km to the **Punta di Pozzo di Borgo** and its ruined **château**. Built by the Pozzo di Borgo family in 1886, the château was constructed with materials salvaged from the charred remains of Les Tuileries (Napoleon's residence in Paris), which burned down in 1871, and is the exact reproduction of one of its pavilions. An inscription on the wall states that it was built to preserve a precious souvenir of the home country; in reality, the Pozzo di Borgos – bitter enemies of the Bonapartes since the latter switched sides during Paoli's first exile – erected the replica to rub salt in their old rivals' wounds following the overthrow of Napoléon III. The village was razed by pirates in 1594, but the family held on to the land; a tower on the track up to the Punta is the sole vestige of the former settlement. From the terrace of the château you get fine **views** of the gulfs of Sagone and Ajaccio, and of Monte d'Oro and Renoso to the east.

A Cupulatta: the Tortoise Sanctuary

An essential destination for children and wildlife lovers is the **Tortoise Sanctuary**, **A Cupulatta**, at the hamlet of **Vignola**, 17km northeast of Ajaccio up the Vallée de la Gravona, on the N193, the main Corte road (daily: April, May & Sept–Nov 10am–5.30pm; June–Aug 9.30am–7pm; €7, children half price; Ⓦ www.acupulatta.com). This sensitively designed breeding and research centre is the largest of its kind in Europe, boasting 125 different species and around 2000 animals from five continents. All the island's indigenous tortoises, terrapins and turtles are represented, along with a number of exotic types such as the gargantuan Alligator tortoise (*Macroclemys temminckii*) and the unfeasibly ugly Matamata (*Chelus fimbriata*) from the Amazon region, which looks like a cross between a rotten log and a melting car tyre. The remaining species are considerably cuter, especially the newborns and the tiny terrapins you get to coo over on arrival.

The easiest way to get to A Cupulatta from Ajaccio by public transport is to jump on a train to **Carbuccia** station, a twenty-minute walk from the sanctuary (head left out of the station and follow the D129 until you reach the N193, where you should turn right; the site lies another 1km or so on your right). Alternatively, jump on any of the **buses** running between Ajaccio, Corte and Bastia.

The Golfe d'Ajaccio

Although Ajaccio's smart street life dominates most visitors' experiences of the town, it's the city's location, set against a grandiose sweep of mountains and blue water, which has most impressed travellers over the years. Frequent municipal bus services and boat trips provide an easy means of restoring your sense of geography. The quickest escape is to head 1km west along the route des Sanguinaires – the northern shore of the gulf (on the D111) – passing a string of tourist developments and sandy beaches en route to the road's end at **Punta della Parata**. This headland faces the cluster of crumbling granite islets called the **Îles Sanguinaires**, a miniature archipelago ideally seen from the sea. Although the **beaches** along this stretch don't rate as highly as the more secluded strands of the southern gulf, they're more easily accessible if you don't have your own vehicle. Regular **buses** from place de Gaulle follow the route: buses #1 and #2 go as far as Ajaccio's cemetery, whereas #5 will take you all the way to Punta della Parata, stopping at **Barbicaja**, **Scudo** and **Terre Sacré**.

The largest and most established resort along the southern arm of the Golfe d'Ajaccio – known as **La Rive Sud** – is **Porticcio**. Once a hangout for the rich and famous, the place nowadays has lost its elitist appeal and gets swamped by watersports enthusiasts as soon as summer sets in. Quieter spots are found beyond Porticcio, where the coast is less developed and the scent of the maquis takes over, the shrubland clearing at intervals to reveal superb sandy beaches such as **plage de Verghia** and **Portigliolo**. Genoese watchtowers again feature on every headland, the most prominent being the **Tour de la Castagna** and the enormous construction on **Capo di Muro**, the southern-most point of the gulf.

An alternative to the coast road is the inland route from Pisciatella, crossing a series of lovely mountain passes surrounded by maquis and dense woodland, through the belvedere village of **Côti-Chiavari** and then down to Capo di Muro.

Route des Sanguinaires

The first landmark along the coast west of Ajaccio, the **Chapelle des Grecs**, lies just beyond plage Trottel. Built in 1632 by Artilio Pozzo di Borgo, it was allocated for the use of the Greeks in 1733, who settled in Ajaccio after being driven out of their small colony at Paomia by Corsican rebels (see p.164)

Ajaccio's characteristically ostentatious **cemetery** lies another kilometre west, its miniature streets of Neoclassical tombs stacked up the hillside like a ghost town. Busloads of French pensioners pour through here during the holiday season to pay their respects at the **tomb of Tino Rossi**, France's most famous crooner, who was born in the town and warbled his way to superstardom between the 1940s and 1960s.

The **beaches** start about 1km beyond the cemetery with **Barbicaja**, a usually crowded sandy stretch close to a large campsite of the same name (see p.178). **Marinella** (aka "Palm Beach"), another 2km on, is the next cove and the most popular, backed by bars and restaurants. About 4km further, **Terre Sacré** gets its name from the one-metre-high stone urn, containing the ashes of soldiers killed in World War I, that stands on the beach. **Cala Lunga** is the last strand, stretching as far as **Punta della Parata**, the narrow, rocky headland that was once connected to the Îles Sanguinaires. Tremendous views of the gulf reward the ten-minute clamber up to the **Tour de la Parata**, a twelve-metre-tall watchtower built of dark grey granite in 1608. One of the last of its kind erected by the Genoese to guard the coast against Barbary pirates, it sports the rusting remains of Corsica's first aerial telegraph, installed by the engineer Claude Chappe in the latter half of the eighteenth century.

Les Îles Sanguinaires

Composed of four humps of red granite, the **Îles Sanguinaires** might be named after Sagone or after *Sagonarri* (Black Blood), from the colour they turn at sunset. A protected site, the islands harbour large colonies of gulls, and it's forbidden to pick flowers or disturb nests on them.

The largest islet, **Mezzo Mare** (or Grande Sanguinaire), is topped by a lighthouse where Alphonse Daudet spent ten days in December 1862. The experience marked him for life, inspiring one of his famous *Lettres de Mon Moulin*, in which he waxed lyrical about the islet's "reddish and fierce aspect", and instilling in him a preoccupation with the theme of isolation, which repeatedly resurfaced in his work. Tufts of gorse, a square watchtower (la Tour de Castellucciu) and crashing surf give the place a dramatic air, which is perhaps why Joseph Bonaparte wanted to be buried here, though his wish wasn't realized. In the nineteenth century, Mezzo Mare harboured a quarantine hospital for sailors and coral fishermen returning from the West African coast to protect from tropical infections a town already in mortal fear of malaria. The ruins of the building, including its distinctively high wall, can still be seen.

Without the luxury of your own vessel, the only way to get a close look at Mezzo Mare is to join the daily **boat excursion** from Porticcio and Ajaccio run by Nave Va (☎04 95 51 31 31, ⬤www.naveva.com). It leaves Ajaccio's Marina Tino Rossi at 2pm, and from Porticcio half an hour later. Tickets cost €28.

La Rive Sud

Capped with crumbling Genoese watchtowers, the three headlands of the Golfe d'Ajaccio's southern shore – the **Rive Sud** – separate a succession of sheltered

▲ Îles Sanguinaires

bays, each lined with large sandy beaches. Those closest to Ajaccio, grouped around the resort of **Porticcio**, are marred by modern holiday developments, but press on southwest down the D55, which keeps close to the convoluted coastline from its turning off the main N196 until the **Punta di a Castagna**, 22km south, and you'll soon escape the villa belt. Growing more spectacular at each bend in the road, the scenery culminates at **Capo di Muro**, the far south-western extremity of the gulf, where a particularly impressive tower stands within walking distance of some gorgeous coves.

The Rive Sud resorts have a year-round **bus** service, operated by Sarl Casanova Transport (☎04 95 25 40 37), which runs around the bay to Porticcio and then on via Isolella to its terminus at plage de Verghia (aka "Mare e Sole"). Six buses per day cover the route in summer (July–Sept), scaled down to just two (with one on Sat morning and none on Sun) from October. You can consult current timetables at the *terminal routière* and tourist office in Ajaccio, and at the bus shelters lining the route itself, or by phoning the company direct.

Porticcio can also be reached by **boat** from Ajaccio. A godsend in the summer when the main road around Campo dell'Oro gets very congested, the service, run by Nave Va, shuttles five times daily between Porticcio jetty and the Marina Tino Rossi; tickets cost €6 one way or €10 return.

There's no public transport to the more isolated headlands beyond Verghia, to which you'll need to drive or walk. The same applies to the sinuous inland route around Côti-Chiavari.

The Tour de Capitello

Overlooking the confluence of the Gravona and Prunelli rivers, the massive **Tour de Capitello**, 2km north of Porticcio, is one of the Golfe d'Ajaccio's defining landmarks. Before it was restored a few years ago, deep cracks in its side bore witness to the famous siege in 1793, when Napoleon and fifty men from the French fleet were stranded waiting for backup in preparation for an attack on Ajaccio. With only one cannon to protect them from the army of Corsican patriots, the defenders managed to hold out for three days – thanks to the same architectural design that so impressed Nelson when he was laying siege to the Mortella tower near St-Florent (see p.93). This was also the scene of Napoleon's reunion in 1793 with his mother, sisters and Cardinal Fesch, who, after travelling under cover of darkness from the Bonapartes' country house at Les Millelli, embarked here for Toulon as the Paolist mobs searched for them across the water. Renovated in 1998, the tower stands on the spit dividing Porticcio from the gay and nudist end of plage de Ricanto, close to the end of Campo dell'Oro's runway. It can be reached in an easy fifteen-minute walk; from the car park at the top of Porticcio beach, head right and skirt the edge of the Étang de Casavone until you see a path leading up to the tower from the end of the sand. The concrete ruins scattered around the building's base date from World War II, when it served as an important anti-aircraft battery, first for the Italians and, after September 1943, for the Allies.

Porticcio

PORTICCIO, 18km around the bay from Ajaccio, has curiously little Corsican character considering its location and the proximity of both the sea and maquis. This is due largely to the main road which scythes straight through the middle of the resort, and the greater than usual quantity of pastel-coloured concrete. Come summer, what little charm the place might possess evaporates altogether, as its beachside strip is overwhelmed by a constant stream of cars, gleaming motorbikes, joggers, rollerbladers, windsurfers and lapdogs. The reason so many Ajacciens drive out here is the **plage de la Viva**, a wide sandy cove with a full-on watersports scene and great views of the gulf and city across the bay. For the many foreign visitors who rent holiday properties in the area, however, Porticcio serves as a convenient hub for trips down the coast to quieter corners. Grouped around a large car park behind the beach is the tourist office (see below), the area's biggest supermarket, a petrol station, bank (with ATM), Les 3 Stars cinema (☏04 95 25 91 82), boulangerie and collection of shops which provide most essentials, as well as easy access to Ajaccio via the seasonal ferry and year-round bus link.

Practicalities

The small **tourist office** (May–Aug Mon–Sat 9am–1pm & 2.30–8pm, Sun 9am–1pm & 4–8pm; ☏04 95 25 01 01) has a patchy accommodation brochure for the Rive Sud, as well as public transport timetables and contact details for diving schools and other watersports facilities in and around the resort.

Porticcio's top **hotel** – in fact, one of the most luxurious places on the island – is the four-star *Le Maquis* (☏04 95 25 05 55, ⓦwww.lemaquis.com; ⑨), a terracotta-roofed campus grouped around its own exclusive cove. Old farm implements and exposed beams lend a rustic air, and each of the twenty individually styled rooms has panoramic sea views and large terraces. Tariffs range from €360 (for the *chambre classique*) to €1110 (for the *suite penthouse jacuzzi*). Mediterranean cuisine with a Corsican bias is served in their gourmet restaurant, *L'Arbousier*, against an appropriately exotic backdrop of the gulf and distant Îles Sanguinaires (set menu €45).

For **campers**, the four-star *Camping Benista* (☏04 95 25 19 30, ⓦwww.benista.fr; June–Sept), 2km north on the main road, is the swishest option, with a pool and footpath access to the beach. It's also handy for the airport. Much closer to town, and a good deal cheaper, is the *Camping Les Marines de Porticcio* (☏04 95 25 09 35; June–Sept), next to the Elf petrol station.

South of Porticcio

South of Porticcio the D55 narrows in its progress along the coast, a high bank of maquis screening expensive villas and private beaches from the passing cars. The best-value hotel in the area is the *Kallisté* (☎04 95 25 54 19, ℱ04 95 25 79 00; Easter to mid-Oct; ❹), which stands on a hillside behind plage d'Agosta at the end of a badly rutted track. Located in a quiet spot with sweeping views, its rooms are light and airy and, off season, inexpensive for the area. For a sundowner, you won't find a more spellbinding location than the *Bar Oasis* (June–Sept), down in Isolella village, whose beachside terrace enjoys superb views across the bay to the mountains inland.

Plage d'Agosta and plage de Ruppione

Some 5km along from Porticcio, you'll come to **plage d'Agosta**, a popular, wide, sandy beach sheltered in the south by the Punta di e Sette Nave, crowned by the **Tour de l'Isolella**. It's worth pulling over here to follow the gentle path through the maquis to the tower, a well-preserved structure of exposed yellow granite giving fine views of the gulf.

A still more spectacular beach is **plage de Ruppione**, a half-moon-shaped cove 8km south of Porticcio, with a sand bar that makes it especially safe for kids and snorkellers. Campers should make for the three-star *Le Sud* (☎04 95 25 40 51, ⓦwww.camping-lesud.com; May–Oct), one of the less expensive sites along this coast, situated on a pine-shaded terrace beside the main road. The quietest pitches lie at the top of the enclosure – an uphill trudge from the pizzeria, where you can tuck into huge pizzas for under €12.

Plage de Verghia and Anse de Portigliolo

From here onwards, the coast becomes gradually less developed, with folds of woodland backing onto rocky headlands and golden coves. At **PORT DE CHIAVARI**, some 5km south of Ruppione, the beautiful **plage de Verghia** is the scenic highlight of the Rive Sud, and a much less frequented beach with finer, whiter sand than its neighbours. Lying at the end of the Ajaccio bus route, it also boasts much the cosiest **campsite** in the district, the two-star *La Vallée* (☎04 95 25 44 66, ⓦwww.camping-la-vallee.com; May–Oct), set back from the main road under a long, narrow grove of eucalyptus trees. The shady terrace gets packed out in high summer, but at either end of the season remains pleasantly peaceful; the friendly *patron* and his family also run a well-stocked shop.

Once clear of Verghia, the D55 narrows and turns sharply inland towards Côti-Chiavari, deteriorating markedly on its approach to the **Anse de Portigliolo**, a delightful, almost circular, sandy cove.

Capo di Muro

The Rive Sud draws to a dramatic climax at **Capo di Muro**, on whose sheltered northern flank a particularly picturesque watchtower rises from a dense cover of maquis. Follow the signposts to *Chez Francis* and you'll drop down a rutted *piste* to a magnificent **beach** on the south side of the promontory called **Cala d'Orzu**. One of the two bar-restaurants behind it, *Chez Francis* (☎04 95 27 10 39, ⓦwww.chez-francis.com; April–Nov), made international headlines when it was destroyed in an arson attack – not by separatist or Mafia guerrillas, as is normally the case in Corsica, but by undercover French police acting, it turned out, under direct orders from the state's most senior official on the island (see p.401). Since Préfet Bonnet's subsequent imprisonment, the infamous *paillote* has been restored to its former condition and is rebuilding its reputation as one of the area's top seafood restaurants, with prices to match its notoriety. The neighbouring *Le Lago Bleu*, just up the beach, may not enjoy the same fame but offers far better value for money.

The inland route

Immediately behind plage de Verghia at Port de Chiavari, the **D55** swings inland to begin its tortuous climb through the old holm and cork oaks of the **Forêt de Chiavari** to the ridgetops. As an alternative route over the headland, it offers some of the best views of the region as well as the very pretty belvedere village of **Côti-Chiavari**, where a dramatically sited (and particularly good-value) hotel offers one of this area's more tempting pit stops.

En route up or down the hill, keep an eye out for the gloomy ruins on the roadside, roughly 3km from the coast. These are the remains of an old prison camp, **l'ancien pénitencier de Chiavari**, dating from the Second Empire. Throughout the latter half of the nineteenth century convicts were interred in this lonely, malaria-infested clearing, where they served their time labouring in the surrounding vineyards and cork forest. A massive stone barn, which was used as a wine cellar, encapsulates the sinister feel of the place.

Côti-Chiavari

A reminder of the Nazi occupation of the island stands in the centre of **CÔTI-CHIAVARI**, in the form of a bust mounted of Antoine Michel Bozzi, a Resistance radio operator who was captured and shot by the Italians only days before the liberation in 1943. Beyond the memorial in the shade of the roadside plane trees is the village's cheerful little **pizzeria**, *Les Platanes*, where you can refuel with copious wood-baked pizzas and fresh salads for €12–14, served on a terrace overlooking pale orange rooftops to the church and sea.

For the most imposing views of the gulf, however, press on another kilometre along the D55 to the lower edge of Côti-Chiavari and the *Hôtel-Restaurant Le Belvédère* (☎04 95 27 10 32, ℻04 95 27 12 99; ❺). The building itself, a pink concrete structure that's clearly visible even from Ajaccio, is a bit of an eyesore, but boasts what must rank among the most sublime terraces in the Mediterranean. The cuisine befits the location: phone ahead to book (essential) and you'll be offered a choice of four set menus for €23–28 per head (not including wine), which might feature house specialities such as local king prawns, guinea fowl with chestnuts, or wild boar. Their sunny, gulf-facing rooms cost €55–70 in February, March and November, but for the rest of the year are only available on a half-board basis (€50–60 per head depending on the level of comfort and time of year). This is deservedly among the most popular addresses on the island and is more often than not fully booked, so reserve your bed as far in advance as possible.

The Gorges du Prunelli

A drive up through the **Gorges du Prunelli** provides an easy but varied excursion inland from Ajaccio, as the landscapes change dramatically from gardens and orchards to the bare jagged granite of the gorges themselves. Two roads climb the opposite flanks of the valley for 20km before converging on the run-up to **Bastelica**, a mountain village with restaurants and hotels that is the main gateway to the **Val d'Èse** ski station. The road on the north side of the valley, the D3, passes through the villages of **Bastelicaccia** and **Ocana** on its way to the dam at **Tolla**, where the route becomes increasingly hair-raising. To view the gorges from the other side, you can descend from Bastelica along the

D27 via the **Col de Crichetto**. The first route affords the best views, while the second is more easily negotiable by car; no public transport reaches these parts.

Bastelicaccia to Tolla

Fully cultivated since the nineteenth century in order to feed the growing population of Ajaccio, the plain around **BASTELICACCIA** has an air of cornucopian opulence, with its overflowing orchards of orange and lemon trees mingled with flower gardens and deep maquis. This is among the most pleasant places to stay within a short radius of Ajaccio, and one of the best local hotels is *L'Orangeraie* (℡04 95 20 00 09, ⓦwww.infocorse.com/oranrivoli; ➍), situated 1km beyond the village amidst an orchard and a beautifully kept garden of palms and other Mediterranean plants (amid which there is also a small swimming pool). In addition to rooms, you can rent well-equipped studios here, sleeping two to four people, by the night or the week; advance booking is essential.

The scenery undergoes a dramatic change after Ocana, as high rock walls and pointed granite pinnacles begin to emerge from the greenery. **TOLLA**, a pretty village strung out on a ridge overlooking an immense reservoir of the **Lac de Tolla**, appears 2km further on. Before you reach the village you can stop at the **Col de Mercuju** (716m), dominated by two great pyramids of rock rising from the circular hollow of the gorges, where a **restaurant**, *Chez Baptiste*, overlooks the gorges. Opposite the restaurant, a path leads down to a platform above the dam, affording an impressive view across the lake, and various gentle forest paths thread through the woodland lining the banks. **Pedalos** and **canoes** are available for rent here.

Tolla itself is a lively place in summer, popular with Ajacciens who, returning to visit the family home, flock to the open-air pizzeria at the entrance to the village on the left. The only place to stay is a well-placed **campsite** down by the lake, *A Selva* (℡04 95 27 00 28; May–Oct), which also offers tasty Corsican cooking.

Once past Tolla, the landscape continues to be wild – rocky walls strewn with high maquis border the road, overlooked by the ragged crest of Punta di Forca d'Olmu to the south.

Bastelica

Set at 800m on the lower slopes of Monte Renoso, **BASTELICA** is a stark and unusually unprepossessing spot with a few rows of cold granite houses and an ugly modern church. It attracts a fair number of visitors, however, partly because of the nearby **Val d'Èse** ski station, and partly because it is the birthplace of **Sampiero Corso** (see box overleaf), whose statue, dating from the 1890s, stands in the village centre. To visit the spot where Sampiero was born, walk up the road east of the church towards the adjoining hamlet of Dominicacci; take a left turn at the *U Renosu* restaurant, and then the first right up the lane running behind this building, which brings you to a T-junction; head right here and follow the backstreet for 20m or so; the house is on your right. The original building was burned down by the Genoese in 1554, but the facade of its replacement (1855) is adorned with an inscription that extols "the most Corsican of Corsicans, a famous hero amongst the innumerable heroes that love of the country, superb mother of male virtues, has nursed in these mountains and torrents".

Bastelica has remained a hotbed of nationalism. In 1980, it witnessed one of the more dramatic encounters between Corsican activists and the state when, on January 6, a group of RPR militants discovered three undercover Secret Service agents operating in the village. The men were captured and taken at gunpoint to Ajaccio's *Hôtel Fesch*, where they were held to draw attention to the

French government's covert activities on the island. Paris, however, refused to negotiate with the Bastelica nationalists, whom they dubbed "racketeers and hostage takers", and ordered the storming of the hotel. On January 12, armed police liberated the three agents and seized the militants, who were subsequently tried and imprisoned on the mainland. Coming only a few years after the siege at Aléria (see p.272), the event enraged the FLNC and plunged the island into a period of spiralling violence during the early 1980s.

Accommodation and eating

A few **hotels** open in Bastelica in the summer. The most central is *Le Sampiero*, a large, modern two-star opposite the church (☎04 95 28 71 99, ℱ04 95 28 74 11; ➍–➎; closed Nov & Fri in winter), which enjoys uninterrupted views of the mountains from most of its rooms, and has a friendly bar on the ground floor. *Chez Paul*, 1km or so north (☎04 95 28 71 59; ➌–➍), is more modest, offering simple but impeccably clean apartments by the night or week; it also

Sampiero Corso

"The most Corsican of Corsicans", **Sampiero Corso** was born into a peasant family in 1498 and first took up arms in 1517, when he entered the service of the Medici as a mercenary – a career followed by many of his poorer compatriots. Gaining himself a reputation for audacious ambition – he is said to have put forward a plan to assassinate Charles V in 1536 – he arrived in France in the company of Catherine de' Medici, and went on to distinguish himself in several campaigns, becoming renowned as the most valiant captain in the French army. At Perpignan in 1543 he saved the life of the future Henry II, husband of Catherine de' Medici, thereby ensuring his promotion in 1547 to colonel of the Corsican infantry. He returned to Corsica a proud and popular figure, and promptly married a young noblewoman named Vannina d'Ornano. The match was not approved of by her brothers, who saw their inheritance about to slip from their fingers – and their enmity was to have dire consequences.

Around this time the Genoese, suspicious of Sampiero's prestige, decided to lock him up for a spell, accusing him of having plotted an uprising against the republic. Their action engendered a hatred of Genoa that Sampiero was to hold for the rest of his days. It was the French declaration of war against Genoa in 1553, and their attempt to "liberate" Corsica from the despotic republic, that established Sampiero's legendary status. Setting out with Marshal Thermes and an expeditionary force of seven thousand mercenaries, amongst them a Turkish contingent led by the notorious Dragut, he managed a rapid takeover of Bastia, Ajaccio and Corte. Bonifacio and Calvi weren't such an easy proposition, however, being populated primarily by Ligurian settlers and thus more firmly entrenched as Genoese strongholds. Long and relentless sieges ensued, with Turkish ships ruthlessly bombarding the towns in a prelude to massacre and pillage.

The subsequent Genoese alliance with the Spanish resulted in Sampiero's return to the continent in 1557, and two years later the treaty of Cateau-Cambresis gave Corsica back to Genoa. Sampiero passionately wanted independence for the island, but could not command the backing of France after strangling his wife, in Aix-en-Provence, after he found out she had betrayed him to the Genoese and sold most of his possessions. Escaping with some of her fortune, he returned to Corsica in 1564 to organize another revolt. He rapidly took over much of the island's interior but failed to take the ports, and enthusiasm for his cause soon diminished, a process doubtless hastened by the 2000-ducat price the Genoese put on his head. In 1567, Sampiero was decapitated in an ambush near Bastelica, a murder engineered by the Ornano brothers, who had never forgotten their grudge. His head was impaled on the town gate of Ajaccio, a warning to would-be rebels that ensured his martyr's status.

has an excellent little **restaurant** where you can enjoy home-made charcuterie and traditional local dishes such as courgettes suffed with *brocciu*, wild boar pâté and veal in *cèpe* sauce, on excellent-value menus (€15–22).

Bastelica to Santa Maria Sicché

On the way back down the main D27, there's the option of turning off the road 4km south of Bastelica to follow a parallel road which gives a stunning view of the gorges. If you're in a sturdy vehicle, you can enjoy even better views by taking the rough mountain track that branches off just before the junction at the **Col de Menta** (762m); this runs parallel to the D27, merging with it at the **Col de Crichetto**. The D27 is bordered by the **Forêt de Pineta**, whose carpet of Laricio pines, chestnut and beech trees makes it a good place for a picnic. From the *maison forestière*, 3km along the same road, it's a ten-minute marked walk to the **Pont de Zipitoli**, a single arc of Genoese stone spanning the River Èse.

After regaining the D27 at the **Col de Marcuggio** (670m), you descend through an increasingly pastoral terrain of vineyards interspersed by fields and folds of woodland to the roadside village of **Cauro**, on the main Ajaccio–Propriano *route nationale* (RN196). A left turn here brings you after 9km to the **Col St-Georges**, source of a famous local brand of mineral water, where there's an excellent little roadside **restaurant**. In a small dining room behind a bar, the 🍴 *Auberge du Col* (☎04 95 25 70 06) serves tasty traditional Corsican dishes such as cannelloni made with chestnut flour, and wild rabbit stew. It also offers smart **gîte d'étape** accommodation (€45 per person half board) for hikers on the Mare a Mare Centre trail (see p.370).

From the pass, it's an easy 13km detour south to **SANTA MARIA SICCHÉ**, set amid dense swathes of coastal maquis just off the main road. Dominating the southern Taravo Valley, the village would be a pretty but otherwise undistinguished place were it not for the fact that Sampiero Corso's wife, Vannina d'Ornano, was born here (see box opposite). The old stone house the couple lived in, the **Palazzo Sampiero** (1554), still stands; follow the lane leading left around the village church for about 500m and you'll see it on your left, marked with a plaque. Vannina's family home also still stands in the village, but it's unmarked and harder to locate: take the main road leading downhill past the church towards the highway for 300m – the house, a fifteenth-century tower, stands on the right, at the top of a black tarmac lane.

Travel details

Trains

At the time of writing, Corsica's old *micheline* train service was in the process of being upgraded. By the spring of 2009 new track and locomotives should be fully operational, which will substantially shorten the journey times given below. The latest timetables are available at any Corsican station, and online at ⓦ www.corsicabus.org. More details on the upgrade appear on p.27.

Ajaccio to: Bastia (4 daily; 3hr 15min–3hr 30min); Bocognano (4 daily; 50min); Calvi (2 daily; 4hr 25min–5hr); Carbuccia, for "A Capulatta" tortoise sanctuary (4 daily; 20min); Corte (4 daily; 1hr 45min–2hr); L'Île Rousse (2 daily; 4hr); Ponte Leccia (4 daily; 2hr 45min); Venaco (4 daily; 1hr 30min–1hr 45min); Vizzavona (4 daily; 1hr).

Buses

The listings below summarize which bus companies cover which routes, how often they run and how long journeys take. Start by looking up your intended destination in the first section; then, using the company's acronym (eg EV or RB), go to the second section for more detailed route and frequency information. Precise departure times can be checked in advance either via the bus companies direct, or (if your French isn't up to that) Bastia tourist office (☎ 04 95 31 81 34). A full rundown of Corsican bus services, including up-to-date timetables, also appears online at 🖥www.corsicabus.org.

Ajaccio to: Aullène (BE; 1hr 25min); Bastia (EV; 3hr); Bavella (AR/BE; 2hr 5min–3hr 15min); Bonifacio (EV; 4hr); Cargèse (SAIB; 1hr 10min); Cozzano (AST; 1hr); Corte (EV; 1hr 45min); Évisa (ARC; 2hr); Levie (AR; 2hr 45min); Olmeto (AR/EV; 1hr 35min); Porticcio (CA; 40min); Porto (SAIB; 2hr 10min); Porto Vecchio (BE/EV; 3hr 10min–3hr 45min); Propriano (AR/EV; 1hr 50min); Quenza (BE; 1hr 45min); Sagone (SAIB; 40min); Sartène (AR/EV; 2hr 15min); Ste-Lucie-de-Tallano (AR; 2hr 30min); Santa Maria Sicché (EV; 45min); Tiuccia (SAIB; 35min); Vico (ARC; 1hr 15min); Vizzavona (EV; 1hr); Zicavo (AST; 1hr 30min); Zonza (AR/BE; 2hr 15min–3hr).

Cargèse to: Ota (SAIB; 1hr 30min); Piana (SAIB; 30min); Porto (SAIB; 1hr); Sagone (SAIB; 15min); Tiuccia (25min).

AR: Autocars Ricci ☎ 04 95 51 08 19. Ajaccio–Olmeto–Propriano–Sartène–Ste-Lucie-de-Tallano–Levie–Zonza–Bavella; 1 daily Mon–Sat year round, with an additional departure weekday afternoons and Sun from July to mid-Sept.

ARC: Autocars R. Ceccaldi ☎ 04 95 21 01 24 or 04 95 21 38 06. Ajaccio–Tiuccia–Sagone–Vico–Évisa–Marignana; Mon–Sat 2 daily year round.

AST: Autocars Santoni ☎ 04 15 22 64 44, 🖥www.autocars-santoni.com. Ajaccio–Cozzano–Zicavo; Mon–Sat 1 daily year round.

BE: Balési Évasion ☎ 04 95 17 50 55, 🖥www.balesievasion.com. Ajaccio–Aullène–Quenza–Sonza–Bavella–l'Ospédale–Porto Vecchio; July & Aug Mon–Sat 1 daily; Sept–June Mon & Fri only.

CA: Casanova Autocars ☎ 04 95 21 05 17 or 04 95 25 40 37. Ajaccio–Porticcio–Isolella–plage de Verghia (Mare e Sole); Mon–Sat 2–6 daily.

EV: Eurocorse Voyages ☎ 04 95 21 06 30, 🖥www.eurocorse.net. Ajaccio–Bocognana–Vizzavona–Vivario–Venaco–Corte–Bastia/L'Île Rousse & Calvi; Mon–Sat 1–2 daily. Ajaccio–Propriano–Sartène–Ste-Lucie-de-Tallano–Levie–Carbini–Zonza; June–Sept Mon–Sat 1 daily. Ajaccio–Olmeto–Propriano–Sartène–Roccapina–Figari–Porto Vecchio; Mon–Sat 2 daily year round, with additional service on Sun June to mid-Sept.

SAIB: Autocars SAIB ☎ 04 95 22 41 99 or 04 95 21 02 07, 🖥www.autocarsiledebeaute.com. Ajaccio–Tiuccia–Sagone–Cargèse–Piana–Porto–Ota; July to mid-Sept 2 daily; mid-Sept to June Mon–Sat 2 daily.

Ferries

For ferry details, see Basics, p.21.

5

The south

LIGURIAN
SEA

N

TYRRHENIAN
SEA

MEDITERRANEAN
SEA

0   20 km

CHAPTER 5 # Highlights

✳ **Plage de Cupabia** Gem of a white-sand bay, hidden on the western arm of the Golfe de Valinco. See p.205

✳ **Filitosa** Standing stones with carved faces are the highlights of this unique, world-renowned prehistoric site. See p.206

✳ **Mountain cuisine** Sample definitive regional cooking at *Le Kiesale* near Calzola, *A Pignata* at Levie and *Le Chalet* in Aullène. See p.209, p.221 & p.223

✳ **Campomoro** One of Corsica's most picturesque coastal villages, with a fine beach, huge watchtower and kilometres of deserted coast to the south. See p.214

✳ **Pianu di Levie** Well-preserved megalithic remains, lost amid the gnarled oak woods of the Alta Rocca region. See p.221

✳ **Sartène** Quintessentially austere Corsican town, whose buttressed-walled *vieille ville* overlooks the dramatic Rizzanese Valley. See p.232

✳ **Wine** Full-bodied, spicy reds and whites with hints of maquis herbs are the speciality of the south's top vineyards: the Domaines de Torraccia, Fiumicicoli and Saparale. See p.237 & p.260

✳ **Baie de Roccapina** Stunning turquoise inlet overlooked by a lion-shaped rock formation. See p.239

▲ Filitosa standing stones

5

The south

S ome of the most enduring evocations of Corsica's varied landscapes and culture – from Edward Lear's eerie etchings to Prosper Mérimée's vendetta-yarn, *Colomba* – were inspired by **the south**, and this remains the most quintessentially Corsican corner of the island. Sparsely populated by comparison with the Ajaccio region, its rugged, inhospitable coastline and valleys support scattered villages where the old ways are never far from the surface. Vendetta may have been officially stamped out, but its roots still run deep. In the past decade, long-standing family rivalries have repeatedly erupted into bloodshed, hiding behind the guise of nationalist-separatist score-settling, while organized crime, too, is rife, from petty racketeering to high-level Mafia corruption.

The only evidence tourists tend to see of this malevolent undercurrent, however, is bullet-raked road signs, black graffiti and the odd bombed-out holiday home. It's the extraordinary landscapes that will leave the more lasting impression: the wild, maquis-backed coast beyond Campomoro, the striated chalk cliffs of Bonifacio, or the brooding, shadowy hinterland of Alta Rocca, with its vineyards, fragrant Laricio pine forests and backdrop of pale granite peaks.

The south is most famous of all, though, for its mysterious prehistoric standing-stone sites. **Filitosa**, a collection of carved menhirs strewn amid the ruins of three-thousand-year-old fortifications, is the best preserved of these. A good base from which to visit the site is **Porto-Pollo**, a secluded seaside village at the northern end of the vast **Golfe de Valinco**. Alternatively, there's **Propriano**, a livelier modern port in the centre of the bay, offering the widest choice of hotels, shops and restaurants in the area. From here you can also explore the southern section of the Golfe de Valinco as far as picturesque **Campomoro**, or roam into the island's richest wine-producing country, taking in **Fozzano**, famed for its blood feuds and stalwart granite tower houses. A bit deeper inland, the region of **Alta Rocca** has an abundance of historic villages and prehistoric sites: the architecture of **Sainte-Lucie-de-Tallano** pays testimony to the wealth of the area's former overlords, the della Rocca family, while a visit to the Bronze-Age ruins of the **Pianu di Levie** is an essential complement to the Filitosa trip. In the heart of Alta Rocca, the village of **Zonza** stands on the threshold of the south's major natural attraction, the granite *aiguilles*, or "needles", of **Bavella**.

Moving southwest, **Sartène** is in many ways the archetypal Corsican town, its history saturated with stories of vendetta and its stark, fortified buildings redolent of the harshness of life in the not-so-distant past. South of Sartène, a weird landscape of thick maquis and eroded rock outcrops makes an appropriate

THE SOUTH

0 ─── 5 km

Golfe d'Ajaccio

Capo di Muro

Bale de Cupabia

Porto Pollo

Campomoro

Golfe de Valinco

See map 'Golfe de Valinco'

Olmeto

Propriano

D157

Filitosa

Solfacaro

Bichisano

Fozzano

Petreto

D420

Col de Ste Eustache

Col de la Tana

Col de Celaccia

Taravo

N196

N196

Rizzanese

Sartène

Alignement de Palaggiu

Tizzano

Cauria Megaliths

Capo di Senetosa

Bocca Albitrina

D48

Otolo

Golfe de Roccapina

Ilots des Moines

N196

Pont de Curgia

San Gavino

Pianotoli-Caldarello

Poggiale

Figari

L'Uomo di Cagna (1217 m)

MASSIF DE CAGNA

Ermitage de la Trinité

Capo di Feno

Bonifacio

See map 'Around Bonifacio'

RÉSERVE NATURELLE DES ÎLES LAVEZZI

Île Cavallo

Îles Perduto

Île du Toro

Plage de la Rondinara

Golfe de Santa-Manza

Golfe de Santa-Giulia

Plage de Palombaggia

Punta della Chiappa

Golfe de Porto Vecchio

Porto Vecchio

Chera

Sotta

Cecia

Tappa

Ste-Trinité

Casteddu d'Arraggiu

Torre

Lecci

Ste-Lucie-de-Porto-Vecchio

See map 'Porto Vecchio'

Golfe de Pinarellu

Pinarellu

Conca

CÔTE DES NACRES

Anse de Favone

MASSIF DE L'OSPÉDALE

Ospédale

Cartalavonu

Ste-Lucie-de-Tallano

Carbini

Fiumicicoli

Levie

Planu di Levie/ Cucuruzzu

ALTA ROCCA

Quenza

Aullène

Col de la Vaccia

Zonza

Col de Bavella (1218 m)

FORÊT DE BAVELLA

AIGUILLES DE BAVELLA

Col de l'Arone (608 m)

MASSIF DE ZONZA EST

Monte Incudine

Zicavo

Bastia

Ajaccio

Ajaccio

N

background for the **megaliths of Cauria** and **Alignement de Palaggiu**, Corsica's largest arrays of prehistoric standing stones.

Marking the southern extremity of the island, **Bonifacio** is one of the most dramatically sited towns in the whole Mediterranean, its old quarter sitting atop vertiginous white cliffs and almost severed from the mainland by a deep natural harbour. It's a popular holiday centre for Corsica's wealthier tourists, as is **Porto Vecchio**, a former Genoese citadelle that's close to the island's most beautiful, and popular, beaches and to the majestic forest scenery of the **Massif de l'Ospédale**.

The Golfe de Valinco

The most southerly of the four great bays indenting Corsica's west coast, the **Golfe de Valinco** gives easy sea access to two deep valleys – the Taravo and Rizzanese – that were among the first regions on the island to be settled. Following in the footsteps of James Boswell, who travelled this way in 1765 to meet Pascal Paoli, most visitors enter the region via the **Col de Celaccia** before dropping down to **Sollacaro** (en route to Filitosa) or to **Olmeto** (on the main Propriano road, the N196). However, a much more scenic alternative is to take the coastal D155, which threads its way around Capo di Muro (see p.193) into the Golfe de Valinco. Aside from some amazing views of an unspoilt coastline, this quiet back road passes close to beautiful **plage de Cupabia** – the area's best beach.

Porto-Pollo

On the northwestern edge of the gulf is **PORTO-POLLO**, whose name derives from the Corsican *Porti Poddu*, meaning "troubled port" – a legacy of the pirate raids that ravaged the island's coast in former times. Today, the little harbour in this compact fishing village, 18km northwest of Propriano, provides sheltered moorings for yachts and the few fishermen who still venture out to supply the local restaurants with fresh lobster and crayfish from the gulf. Development here has been limited: barely a handful of hotels line the road behind the village's narrow beach and traffic is minimal, making this a peaceful base from which to visit Filitosa, the Alta Rocca and Sartenais. In addition, the Golfe de Valinco's particularly clear waters have made the village one of Corsica's prime **diving** centres.

Practicalities

Autocars Ricci (☎04 95 51 08 19) provides a year-round **bus** service to Porto-Pollo from Propriano and Ajaccio, stopping outside the *Hôtel L'Escale*. The village's only road runs behind the beach, dominated by a string of mid-range **hotels**. Of these, *L'Escale* (☎04 95 74 01 54, ✉hotel-skle@wanadoo.fr; April–Sept; ❹–❺), a bland modern place right behind the beach, is the least expensive, although its rooms lack sea views, and half board (€105 for two sharing) is obligatory between July and mid-September. Only slightly pricier, *Les Eucalyptus* (☎04 95 74 01 52, ⓦwww.hoteleucalyptus.com; April–Oct; ❹–❼), on the opposite side of the road, has three categories of rooms, from large sea-facing ones with little terraces to three dingy budget options around the back. They also offer plenty of off-road parking and a restaurant. Further along the main street, the smart, modern *Kallisté* (☎04 95 74 02 38, ⓦlekalliste.fr; ❺) has large rooms and a quality restaurant serving mainly fresh seafood.

Other places worth considering if you've your own transport are M. et Mme Tardif's lovely **bed and breakfast** in Sollacaro (see p.209) and the *Auberge U Mulinu* at nearby Calzola (see p.209), which lies just down the road to the area's most congenial **campsite**, the *Camping Kiesale* (see p.209). Closer to Porto-Pollo itself, the best option in this area for campers is the Camping Turraconnu, up in Serra di Feno (T 04 95 74 00 57, W www.propriano.net/turracconu) – a breezy site overlooking the bay, within walking distance of Cupabia beach.

Inland, the *U Mulinu* and *Kiesale* at Calzola (see p.209) are the best **places to eat** in the area, along with the wonderful *Abbartello* restaurant (see p.205), a ten-minute drive away down the coast road to Propriano. In Porto-Pollo itself, the most dependable option is *A Marina* (T 04 95 26 73 49), at the top end of the village. On a waterside terrace overlooking the bay, the affable, football-mad *patron* serves a tempting menu of traditional Corsican specialities (*terrine de figatellu*, veal *tripettes* and roast suckling kid) or Asian dishes (glazed duck, Peking shrimps, chicken with pineapple), rounded off with a great *fiadone* or chestnut-flour flan for dessert. Most main courses are reasonably priced at €15–22.

Beaches around Porto-Pollo

Staying in Porto-Pollo, you're spoilt for choice when it comes to **beaches**. Sandy southwest-facing coves scallop the entire north shore of the Golfe de Valinco, although getting to them can be tricky without some form of transport.

Watersports at Porto-Pollo

Surfing and **windsurfing** equipment can be rented at the Centre Nautique de Porto-Pollo, at the entrance to the village. **Divers** are catered for by Porto-Pollo Plongeé (T 04 95 74 07 46, W www.portopollo-plongee.fr), based in a Portakabin above the marina (accessible from the road). It runs dives to the spectacular Cathédrales, an underwater massif of rock pinnacles on the northern side of the gulf, as well as to some of the superb sites around Campomoro; rates start at around €45 per person for a guided dive (includes equipment hire). Full details are posted on their website.

Pick of the crop, and the least accessible, has to be gorgeous **plage de Cupabia**, a twenty-minute drive northwest. Lining the sheltered end of a deep blue bay against an amphitheatre of near-deserted hills, it's the most scenic of the Valinco region's beaches, yet sufficiently difficult to reach to have escaped development. To get there by car from Porto-Pollo, take the first left (the D155) off the Propriano road and follow the bends uphill through the hamlet of Serra di Ferro. Around 2km later you'll come to a junction, just after which a side road (signed) turns downhill to Cupabia. The *Cala di Cupabia* (☎04 95 74 04 38) offers basic camping, and there's a busy *buvette*.

Two kilometres east of Porto-Pollo lies a second enormous stretch of sand, **plage de Taravo** and the contiguous **plage de Tenutella**, separated by a narrow tidal creek. This beach is busier than Cupabia due to the presence of a couple of campsites behind it, but is large enough to absorb even the August deluge. You'll need a car to get there: the approach is via a kilometre-long *piste* which turns right (south) off the D757 2km out of Porto-Pollo – look for the sign for *Camping Cyrnos* (☎04 95 74 00 55; July to mid-Sept), a small site shaded by straggly poplars and lime trees, whose only plus is its proximity to the sand.

Abbartello

The stretch of coast between the mouth of the Taravo River and eastern extremity of the gulf, crossed by the main Propriano road (the D157), shelters a necklace of pretty beaches, all of them easily accessible. The coastal hinterland covers a rippling hillside littered with dozens of pastel-coloured holiday villas and a series of large, sheltered campsites strategically placed for easy access to the coves. In high season, the whole area, collectively known as **Olmeto-Plage**, becomes one large holiday centre, but outside school holidays you can expect to have most of the beaches to yourself.

The main agglomeration of shops, hotels and restaurants is at **ABBARTELLO**, a ribbon development that begins at the southeastern end of the plage de Tenutella and straggles along the main road, overlooking three small *criques* with lovely views across the gulf to Campomoro. Much the best-value **place to stay** here is the modern *Hôtel Abbartello* (☎04 95 74 04 73, ⓦwww.hotelabbartello.com; May–Sept; ❷), which offers some of the cheapest rooms in the area (falling to €27 in low season), most of them sea-facing, en suite and with breezy terraces; those on the "*côté montagne*" have shared toilets. They also offer breezy self-contained studios which can accommodate a family of four or five, and in May and June they rent out larger bungalows for maximum periods of three days.

On the opposite side of the road, *Camping Chez Antoine* (☎04 95 76 06 06) is a small, basic and inexpensive **campsite** – ideal if you're passing through, but a lot less comfortable than the swish three-stars you'll see further along the main road to Propriano. One of the largest of these, *U Libecciu* (☎04 95 74 01 28, ⓦwww.campingulibecciu.com), lining a small, dark side valley above a bend in the D157, stands opposite the track down to **Cala Piscona**, one of the gulf's most beautiful beaches, though one to be avoided in high season if you want to keep clear of the crowds.

Next door to the *Hôtel Abbartello*, the ⚜ *Abbartello* restaurant (☎04 95 74 04 74, ⓦwww.hotelabbartello.com) is the finest **place to eat** in the area, with a superb terrace overlooking the gulf and a gastronomic menu that does credit to the views. Only the freshest seafood is served on their menus (€17.50–30). If it's available, try the sea bass (*loup*) *croustillant* and snapper in sea-urchin butter on a bed of fresh lasagne, ideally with a bottle of Domaine d'Abbatucci's Cuvée Faustina *blanc*. À la carte, expect to pay €45–50 for three courses, plus wine: great value for money given the quality of the cooking, service and location.

Filitosa

Eight thousand years of history are encapsulated by the extraordinary **Station Préhistorique de Filitosa** (Easter–Oct daily 9am–sunset; Nov to Easter by prior arrangement only; ☎04 95 74 00 91; €5; see also *Traditional Corsica* colour section), 10km inland from Porto-Pollo. The site remained undiscovered until **Charles-Antoine Cesari** came upon the ruins on his farmland in 1948. He and **Roger Grosjean**, who was to become head of the centre for archeological research in Sartène, set about a full-scale excavation, discovering some menhirs lying face down in the maquis, others broken at waist level inside what is now known as the central monument (you can read an evocative first-hand account of the discovery in Dorothy Carrington's *Granite Island*; see p.422). When the digging was completed the menhirs were set into lines, and the site was opened to the public in 1954.

There's no public **transport** to Filitosa, but the Propriano to Porto-Pollo bus will take you as far as the D157/D57 junction, just before the Taravo bridge, from where you can hitch the remaining 6–7km; hitching is fairly reliable during the summer, when nearly all the traffic on these backroads is heading to or from the site.

A brief history of Filitosa

Filitosa was occupied from 6000 BC, when it was settled by **Neolithic** farming people who lived here in rock shelters. Flakes of obsidian, used to make arrowheads and only available from the Aeolian Islands and Sardinia, have been unearthed, indicating that the first Filitosans must have engaged in trade, but little else is known about them, other than the fact they were colonized some time between 3500 and 3000 BC by **megalithic** peoples from the East. Believed to have been missionary navigators, these early invaders came in search of converts to their faith, as well as land and metals, and were the creators of the first menhirs, the earliest of which were possibly phallic symbols worshipped by an ancient fertility cult. Later statues display stylized human features, making them quite distinct from nearly all other European menhirs of the megalithic period – such as those at Stonehenge and Avebury – which would seem to have been abstract expressions of devotion to a godhead rather than tributes to

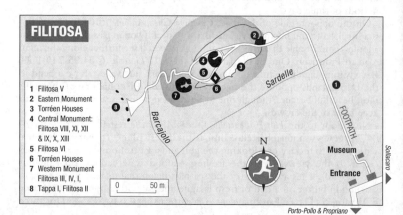

humankind. Most archeologists believe that the representational menhirs were memorials to dead chieftains and warriors. Grosjean, however, maintained that they were portraits of enemy **Torréens**, who – most people agree – arrived in the Golfe de Porto Vecchio from the eastern Mediterranean around 1700 BC. To back up his theory, Grosjean cites Aristotle, who claimed the ancient Iberians used to raise stones around the tombs of slain enemies; moreover, very few knives or daggers like the ones depicted on the menhirs have ever been found in megalithic sites on the island, nor, at the time of the invasions, did the farmers of Filitosa have the technology to make them.

The Torréens conquered Filitosa around 1300 BC and destroyed most of the menhirs, incorporating the broken stones into the area of dry-stone walling surrounding the site's three **torri** (towers). Conical structures such as these were built by the Torréens all over the south of Corsica. Again, no one is absolutely certain of their function; it's generally agreed that the smaller specimens are likely to have been used as places of worship to some divinity, though traces of ashes and bones found in some also suggest they could have been where the Torréens burned or buried their dead. Corsica's larger *torri* are thought to have served as stores for weapons or food, or perhaps as refuges or lookout towers.

Around the Filitosa *torri*, whose remains comprise the site's "eastern", "central" and "western" monuments, was constructed a village of Cyclopean stone shacks – a complex known as a **casteddu**. As such *casteddi* became more numerous, their inhabitants were forced into attacking neighbouring settlements in order to protect their land and livestock. Grosjean believed that competition between the *casteddi* forced Torréen expeditions to migrate to northern Sardinia, which would explain the existence on that island of **nuraghi**, larger and more technically advanced versions of *torri*. A rival theory, however, suggests that the Torréens were in fact indigenous Corsicans who simply acquired their technical expertise from the Sardinian *nuraghi* builders.

The site

Vehicles can be left for free in the small **car park** opposite the main entrance, from where it's a five-minute walk to the site proper, which includes a small **museum** (best seen at the end of your visit) and a workshop producing reproduction prehistoric ceramics. Intrusive trilingual listening posts are installed at key positions, so get here early in the day if you want to escape the annoying recorded commentaries, which can severely detract from the natural beauty and haunting atmosphere of the site.

Filitosa V looms up on the right shortly after the entrance. The largest statue-menhir on the island, it's an imposing sight, with clearly defined facial features and a sword and dagger outlined on the body. Beyond a sharp left turn lies the oppidum, or **Eastern Monument**, comprising the remains of one of the three *torri*, its entrance marked by the **eastern platform**, thought to have been a lookout post – this cave-like structure sculpted out of the rock is the only evidence of Neolithic occupation and is generally agreed to have been a burial mound.

Straight ahead, the Torréen **Central Monument** comprises a scattered group of menhirs on a circular walled mound, surmounted by a dome and entered by a corridor of stone slabs and lintels. Nobody is sure of its exact function. Nearby **Filitosa IX** and **Filitosa XIII**, implacable lumps of granite with long noses and round chins, are the most impressive menhirs on the site – indeed Grosjean considered Filitosa IX to be the finest of all western Mediterranean megalithic statues. Filitosa XIII, the last menhir to be discovered here (the Torréens had built it into the base of the central monument), is typical of the figures created

Boswell in Corsica

Dr Johnson's biographer courted men of genius as assiduously as he pursued women, and one of his early conquests was the Corsican patriot **Pascal Paoli**. In 1765, at the age of 25, **James Boswell** contrived to make the acquaintance of the great French philosopher Rousseau in Switzerland. The Corsicans, struggling to formalize their independence, had asked the author of *The Social Contract* to give them a new set of laws. In certain circles Corsica had something of the appeal that Greece was to offer Byron's generation sixty years later, and Boswell promptly suggested that Rousseau make him his ambassador to the Corsicans. He duly received a letter of introduction, which he was able to present to Paoli the following year.

The meeting was a far more nerve-racking experience for Boswell than his encounter with the philosopher. "I had stood in the presence of many a prince but I never had such a trial as in the presence of Paoli," he wrote. "For ten minutes we walked backwards and forwards through the room hardly saying a word, while he looked at me with a steadfast, keen and penetrating eye, as if he searched my very soul." A student of physiognomy, Paoli also feared an attempt on his life, so the close scrutiny was scarcely surprising, and it didn't hinder the development of a friendship that was to hold throughout Paoli's later exile in London.

The success of Boswell's book about his visit, *An Account of Corsica – the Journal of a Tour to that Island and Memoirs of Pascal Paoli*, helped launch his social and literary career in London, and commemorated a passion that endured throughout his life. In 1769, the year of the book's publication, he attended the first annual celebration of Shakespeare's birthday in Stratford-upon-Avon, an event organized by the actor David Garrick. Boswell appeared at the celebrations dressed in the Corsican national costume and wearing in his hat a card that read "Corsica Boswell".

just before the Torréen invasion, with its vertical dagger carved in relief; **Filitosa VII** also has a clearly sculpted sword and shield. **Filitosa VI**, from the same period, is remarkable for its facial detail. On the eastern side of the central monument stand some vestigial **Torréen houses**, where fragments of ceramics dating from 5500 BC were discovered; they represent the most ancient finds on the site, and some of them are displayed in the museum.

The remains of the third of the three *torri*, the **Western Monument**, a two-roomed structure built underneath another walled mound, is thought to have been some form of Torréen religious building. A steep flight of rough steps leads to the foot of this mound, where a tiny footbridge leads into the meadow, on the other side of which five statue-menhirs are arranged in a wide semicircle beneath a thousand-year-old olive tree. A bank separates them from a jumble of contorted, nobbly grey rocks – the **quarry** from which the megalithic sculptors hewed the stone for the menhirs. A granite block, marked ready for cutting, has been propped up on stakes to make a seat from which you can survey the site.

The **museum** is a shoddy affair, with poorly labelled exhibits and very little contextual information, but the artefacts themselves are fascinating. The major item here is the formidable **Scalsa Murta**, a huge menhir dating from around 1400 BC and discovered at Olmeto. Like other statue-menhirs of the period, this one has two indents in the back of its head, which are thought to indicate that these figures would have been adorned with headdresses like the horn that's been attached to Scalsa Murta.

Inland from Filitosa

The lower Taravo Valley, a wide sweep of sparsely populated land patched with olive groves and old walled pastures, funnels **inland from Filitosa** towards the

Traditional Corsica

Invasion and resistance are recurring themes throughout Corsica's history, and while its invaders have left a lasting imprint on the island, the Corsicans' own traditions have been jealously protected, and in recent years, vigorously renewed. From ancient statue-menhirs to traditional hilltop villages and polyphonic music, Corsica's wealth of unique customs sets it deliberately apart from the rest of the Mediterranean.

Religious procession at Casamaccioli ▲

Charcuterie at La fête du Porc Courant ▼

Festivals

To see Corsican traditions in action, try to take in one of the island's regular **festivals**. Aside from the nationally celebrated religious festivals, local saints' days are feted throughout the year. Many events are music- and art-based affairs, with outdoor concerts and film festivals boosting the local tourist industry. There are also local county fairs, where you can hear traditional Corsican singing and purchase regional specialities such as *brocciu* (soft ewe's cheese) and maquis-flower honey.

Of the innumerable Catholic feast days, the most fervently observed are the **Easter celebrations**, featuring a parade through town bearing a statue of the Virgin or of Christ, followed by Mass and a street party with fireworks and music. Many of these rituals also include a procession called a *granitola* (see below).

Top festivals

▶▶ **A Tumbera: La fête du Porc Courant** Renno, late January/early February Farmers celebrate the pig-slaughtering season in this remote village – quintessential *corse profonde* and a must for charcuterie fans.

▶▶ **Catenacciu**, Sartene. A spine-chilling Easter procession of hooded *cunfratelli* (lay brothers) led by a penitent dragging a cross through the streets, in imitation of Christ's walk to Golgotha. See p.231.

▶▶ **Granitola**, Calvi and Erbalunga. Another Easter procession, which involves spiralling slowly through the streets in formations thought to derive from pre-Christian traditions. See p.37.

▶▶ **Santa di u Niola**, Casamaccioli, Sept. A riotous folk festival involving much drinking, singing and gambling. See p.302.

Statue-menhirs

Carved with clearly defined facial features, daggers and swords, Corsica's prehistoric standing stones, or menhirs, are unique in Europe. The most vivid specimens rise defiantly from the meadows and olive groves of **Filitosa**, in the southwest of the island (see p.206). Discovered by a local farmer in 1948, the site holds remnants of three ancient societies – Neolithic, Megalithic and Toréen – who inhabited the spot from the sixth until the first millennium BC. Little is known about these peoples, which adds to Filitosa's air of mystery. Stone rows and burial chambers litter the coastal maquis elsewhere in the south, and at locations such as **Cucuruzzu** (see p.221) and **Araggiu** (see p.262) you can clamber over the vestiges of 2400-year-old fortresses whose gateways and ramparts remain astonishingly intact.

▲ Filitosa statue-menhirs

▼ Ghisoni, a traditional Corsican village

Arts and crafts

The revival of the Corsican language since the 1970s has been accompanied by a renaissance in the island's traditional arts, crafts and cuisine; and one of the hot spots for this cultural turnaround has been the Haute Balagne, in the far northwest of the island, where a chain of pretty hilltop villages have got together to form the so-called **Strada de l'Artigiani** ("Road of the Artisans"). At **Pigna** (see p.132), artisans' workshops produce ceramics, engravings, musical boxes and traditional instruments, while the famous Casa Musicale hosts recitals of folk singing and dance. Nearby **Feliceto** (see p.135) is renowned for its glass, olive oil and wine outlets, and at **Sant'Antonio** (see p.131) a small, crow's nest settlement overlooking the coast, you can sample fragrant lemon jams and cakes.

▼ Corsican bread

Polyphonies corses

Nothing evokes quite so vividly the essence of Corsica's troubled soul as its traditional choral music, **polyphonies corses** (see p.413). Bearing influences as diverse as Roman–Christian liturgy, Genoese madrigals, Islamic prayer and even, some musicologists have argued, prehistoric chanting, the spiralling harmonies evoke a sense of both the island's distant past and the passion with which Corsicans today identify with their homeland.

Virtually extinguished by the end of World War II, the flame of this ancient musical form, kept alive by a handful of elderly villagers in the interior, caught fire during the nationalist resurgence of the 1970s. Today it enjoys increasing popularity, providing inspiration for a new generation of composers and singers. Names you may come across while in Corsica include the hugely popular **I Muvrini**, **Isula** and **A Filetta**.

Polyphonic singing in Calvi ▲

Poster promoting I Muvrini ▼

Listen here

The summer tourist season (June to mid-Sept) is when you're most likely to catch live performances of Corsican polyphony: recitals are held in churches and cathedrals, while the island's main groups stage tours of the bigger towns.

▶▶ **Easter festivals**, Sartene, Calvi and Erbalunga. Hear Corsican polyphony in its original, sacred context. See p.414.

▶▶ **Festivoce**, Pigna, early July. Polyphonic singing and world music at various locations around the village. See p.132.

▶▶ **Santa di u Niolu**, Casamoccioli, early Sept. Features singing competitions. See p.302.

▶▶ **Rencontres de Chants Polyphoniques**, Calvi, mid-September. Four-day music celebration, hosted by A Filetta. See p.117.

shadowy profile of the watershed peaks. Its principal village, **Sollacaro**, sits high on the lip of the valley above the prehistoric site, while 8km northwards the hamlet of **Calzola** is worth a visit for its accommodation and places to eat. If you're relying on **buses**, the good news is that you can reach Calzola on Autocars Ricci's Propriano–Ajaccio service, which runs daily (except Sun) in July and August, and on Mondays, Wednesdays and Fridays the rest of the year.

Sollacaro

SOLLACARO (Suddacaru) boasts of having hosted the first meeting of James Boswell and Pascal Paoli on October 21, 1765 (see box opposite) – a plaque opposite the post office commemorates the occasion. The scene of the historic encounter, immortalized in Boswell's *Journal*, was a room in the top right-hand corner of a house which still stands above the main street: look for the prominently carved "1755" inscription on the wall. The house is still occupied by descendants of the same family who lived in it back in 1765.

There's a particularly good **bed and breakfast** place in the area: 🏃 M. et Mme Tardif's *chambres d'hôtes* (☎04 95 74 29 48 or 06 62 43 13 69; ❸), situated 3km back down towards Filitosa. Signposted off the road, their house occupies a magnificent belvedere overlooking the valley, with modest but immaculately kept rooms (all en suite) opening on to a communal terrace. You can breakfast outside or in the family dining room upstairs, while it's also worth sampling M. Tardif's "*grand assiette*" of local cheese and charcuterie, which is served with home-made bread and jam in a little garden gazebo. Back in Sollacaro, the **bar**, *U Paese*, is a pleasant and welcoming place to refuel, serving delicious *bruschetta* made with local cheese and charcuterie.

Calzola

Two still more remote places to **stay** and **eat** are tucked away on the floor of the valley, near **CALZOLA**, reachable via the D757 from Porto-Pollo, the D457 from just below Filitosa, or on the scenic D302, which turns inland below Sollacaro and then winds downhill to the **Pont de Calzola**. Just next to the bridge (on its south side) stands the renowned *Auberge U Mulinu* (☎04 95 24 32 14; ❹), a restored water mill on whose riverside terrace you can enjoy traditional Taravo cuisine (menus €20–30), notably wild river trout stuffed with *brocciu* and mint. They also have fourteen **rooms**: small and lacking character, but convenient if you decide to make the most of the wine list, which features the special Abbatucci *blanc*, produced just down the lane.

In addition to growing some of the area's finest wines, the neighbouring Abbatucci family run a deliciously down-to-earth **restaurant** and **campsite**, 🏃 *Le Kiesale* (☎04 95 24 35 81 or 04 95 24 36 30), 500m beyond the *Auberge U Mulinu*. Having pitched your tent on one of their secluded, well-shaded terraces, you can order wonderful *beignets*, grilled organic lamb or veal and olives at the family restaurant, washed down with the *domaine*'s own wines. Nearly everything on the menu comes straight from the farm, except the wood-grilled fish of the day, which provides the ideal compliment for the Abbatuccis' prize-winning white (splash out on the marvellous Cuvée Faustina if there's any left).

Olmeto

Coming from Ajaccio and heading south, your first glimpse of the Golfe de Valinco comes just below **Col de Celaccia** (583m), where a series of steep turns brings you down to **OLMETO**, situated 4km below the pass. With its grandstand view over Propriano, Olmeto was once a favourite spot with artists such as Edward Lear, and it remains a captivating place, close to the coast but far enough from Propriano to retain a village atmosphere, compromised only by holiday traffic clogging up the main road through the centre in summer. Once off the road, however, you're instantly hemmed in by lofty buildings and sleepy back alleys.

Contrary to appearances, life in Olmeto has not always been peaceful. The village was actually established on this high, easily defensible site to provide protection from the constant pirate raids that menaced the gulf from the fifteenth to seventeenth century; in 1617, fifty villagers were abducted and taken as slaves to North Africa. The village is also renowned for its bloody **vendettas**, some of which carried on well into the twentieth century; in *Granite Island*, Dorothy Carrington recalls meeting an old man who could name twenty people murdered there in his lifetime. Most famous of all the Corsican vendettas was the one instigated by **Colomba Carabelli**, the heroine of Mérimée's novel *Colomba*, who died here in 1861, aged 96, in the forbidding *palazzo* facing the *mairie*. Her reputation still attracts a few admirers, but what brings most tourists to Olmeto today are the views from the village's two main streets, which are linked by steep stairways, with the foundations of the houses vanishing into a valley whose olive groves once sustained the local economy.

Practicalities

Straddling the busy N196, Olmeto is served by Eurocorse Voyages' regular **buses** between Ajaccio and Porto Vecchio, which run via Propriano and Sartène, as well as Autocars Ricci's Ajaccio–Alta Rocca service. The **place to stay** here is *U Santa Maria – Chez Mimi* (℡04 95 74 65 59, 🖷04 95 74 60 33; March–Oct; obligatory half board in Aug, €85 for two sharing, ❹–❺), an old-fashioned inn next to the church with twelve bright and spotless rooms looking over the rooftops. It possesses loads more character than anything in Propriano and has a dependable little **restaurant** featuring locally reared lamb with wild mushrooms on its €24.50 menu.

Propriano

Bracketed by the promontory of Scogliu Lungu, the fine natural harbour of **PROPRIANO**, 71km southwest of Ajaccio, was exploited by the ancient Greeks, Carthaginians and Romans, but became a prime target for pirate raids and by the eighteenth century had been largely destroyed. The amount of building work going on here also bears witness to the pace of change in Propriano, which has, in a little under two decades, metamorphosed from a sleepy fishing village into the service centre for an area capable of accommodating 23,000 visitors in peak season. Chief among the architects of this rapid transformation was Émile Mocchi, who served as mayor for over twenty years before being imprisoned on embezzlement charges – appropriately enough for an area long renowned for its corrupt officialdom and Mafia connections.

Propriano's internal politics don't seem to deter the tourists, however, who come for the beaches, the sailing, diving and other watersports. The resort also provides passing visitors with useful amenities, including supermarkets and ATMs, midway between Ajaccio and Bonifacio.

Arrival and information

Ferries dock in the Port de Commerce, west of the town centre and ten-minutes' walk from rue Général-de-Gaulle, the town's main street, which runs at right angles to the water. **Buses** pull into the little square in front of the church, on a hill above the main junction in the village centre reached via a

PROPRIANO

ACCOMMODATION
Arcu di Sole   D
Beach Hôtel   B
Bellevue   C
Claridge   H
Gîte d'Étape U Fracintu   F
Lido   A
Loft Hôtel   G
Miramar Hôtel   E

EATING
Chez Charlot   4
U Famale   1
Terra Cotta   2
Le Tout Va Bien   3

G, D, E, F, plage de Baracci, Porto-Pollo, Ajaccio, Camping Colomba (3km), ▲ Camping Lecci e Murta (7km)

Marseille, Nice & Toulon

Plage de Valinco

Diving Schools & Boat Excursions

Marina

Harbour Master's Office

Mairie

Boat Excursions

QUAI ST-ÉRASME

Pharmacy

RUE P. CLEMENCEAU

RUE DU 9 SEPTEMBRE

★ Bus Stop

Laundry

RUE GÉNÉRAL-DE-GAULLE

RUE CAPITAINE CAMILLE PIÈTRI

AVENUE NAPOLÉON

RUE BONAPARTE

RUE J. PANDOLFI

Port de Commerce

RUE DE LA MARINE

Laundry

Gare Maritime

QUAI L'HERMINIER

SNCM Office

CHEMIN DE PLAGE

RUE J. PANDOLFI

plage du Phare

& plage de l'Arena Blanca

Sartène & Campomoro

100 m

0

flight of steps from the bottom of rue Général-de-Gaulle. The **tourist office** is down in the marina (July & Aug daily 8am–8pm; June & Sept Mon–Sat 9am–noon & 3–7pm; Oct–May Mon–Fri 9am–noon & 2–6pm; ☎04 95 76 01 49, ⓦwww.propriano.net).

Accommodation

Most of Propriano's plentiful accommodation is in rented villas, but the centre of town holds several good mid-range hotels. With a car you might also consider heading down the coast to Campomoro, or north around the gulf to more peaceful Olmeto-Plage and Porto-Pollo.

Hotels

Arcu di Sole route de Baracci ☎04 95 76 05 10, ⓦwww.arcudisole.fr.st. A large, modern pink building with green shutters, just off the main Ajaccio road, 3km west of town (turn inland by the Total petrol station). The ground-floor rooms have little balconies; those to the rear are pleasantly shaded. No views to speak of, but there's a garden pool, gourmet restaurant, tennis courts and mini-golf for the kids. April–Oct.

Beach Hôtel av Napoléon ☎04 95 76 17 74, ⓦperso.wanadoo.fr/beach.hotel. Spacious and comfortable en-suite rooms in a four-storey block overlooking the Port de Commerce and plage du Phare. ④–⑤

Bellevue av Napoléon ☎04 95 76 01 86, ⓦwww.hotels-propriano.com. The cheapest central hotel, halfway down av Napoléon and bang opposite the marina; all rooms have balconies with a view of the gulf and are cheerfully decorated. The bar is lively and popular with locals. ④

Claridge rue Bonaparte ☎04 95 76 05 54, ⓦwww.hotels-propriano.com. A newish building in the middle of town, with comfortable rooms (from €58 in shoulder season) but grim views. March–Oct. ④–⑤

Lido Between plage du Phare and plage de L'Arena Blanca, on the west edge of town ☎04 95 76 06 37, ⓦwww.le-lido.com. Dating from the 1930s, this low-rise hotel on the outskirts had a major face-lift a few years back but still possesses more character than most of the competition. That said, its rooms, ranged around a cool courtyard with rear terraces jutting on the sand behind, are ridiculously overpriced in high season. ⑧–⑨

Loft Hôtel 3 rue Capitaine, Camille-Piétri ☎04 95 76 17 48. Former wine and flour warehouse imaginatively converted into a gleaming hi-tech hotel, with bright, clean rooms overlooking a car park. Good value. Mid-April to Sept. ④–⑤

Miramar Hôtel rte de la Grande-Corniche (a continuation of route de Baracci), 3km towards Ajaccio ☎04 95 76 06 13, ⓦwww.grandhotelmiramar.com. Splendid four-star hotel with a huge swimming pool, sauna, gardens and sweeping sea views from the a/c rooms. Doubles from €250 in May, Sept & Oct; and from €300–490 June–Aug. May–Oct. ⑨

Gîtes d'étapes and campsites

Camping Colomba 3km northeast along the route de Baracci ☎04 95 76 06 42, ⓦwww.camping-colomba.com. Take the right-hand turning off the main road by the Total petrol station to reach this medium-sized, peaceful three-star with good facilities (including a pizzeria) and plenty of shade – the best of the sites within walking distance of town.

Camping Lecci e Murta Portigliolo, 7km west on the Campomoro road ☎04 95 76 02 67, ⓦwww.camping-lecciemurta.com. Large, well-shaded site up a small side valley from Portigliolo beach, with grocery store, tennis courts and pizzeria. Very quiet in shoulder season.

Gîte d'Étape U Fracintu 7km northeast of Propriano at Burgo ☎04 95 76 15 05, Ⓕ04 95 76 14 31. One of the largest hikers' hostels in Corsica, with sixty dorm beds and a couple of cheap double rooms (€39). Lovely views across the valley from its terrace, and right next to the Mare a Mare Sud trailhead. Advance booking essential. ②

Beaches and boat excursions

The nearest **beach** to Propriano, **plage du Phare**, lies a short way past the Port de Commerce. A steep crescent of yellow sand, it's patrolled by lifeguards during the summer and gets swamped at lunchtimes. Just around the headland, past the *Hôtel Lido*, **plage de L'Arena Blanca** is a much longer expanse of grey sand, backed by a big concrete hotel, which can seem pretty bleak in the heat. With more time, or your own transport, it's worth continuing around the coast to **plage de Capu Lauroso**, a vast golden curve that rarely gets too crowded, at least if you're prepared to walk south beyond the aerodrome towards the **plage de Portigliolo**, the beach's southern end.

North of Propriano, **plage de Baracci** is less than ideal; locals avoid it because of the strong undertow and unsightly heaps of rubbish littering the wasteland behind. For an account of the more appealing **Olmeto–Plage** and the beaches lining the north shore of the gulf, covered by daily minibus from Propriano during the summer, see p.210.

An alternative way of reaching some of the less accessible stretches of the gulf is to take a **boat excursion** from the marina. The firm U Paesi di u Valinco (☎04 95 76 16 78, ⓦwww.corsica.net/promenade) run two-hour trips in a glass-bottomed cruiser for €20, longer daytrips along the Sartenais coast or out to Bonifacio for €40, and night cruises for €25. Rival outfit Promenade en Mer Valinco (ⓦpagesperso-orange.fr/propriano/bigblue) offer a comparable range of excursions, only in large catamaran or twelve-seater speedboats that can slip into some of the narrower inlets on the coast to the southwest. Both work from Portacabins in the marina where you can check departure times.

Eating

Propriano has more than its fair share of duff **restaurants** – most of them lining the marina. The swish terraced establishments on the waterfront along avenue Napoléon can be relied upon for fresh croissants at breakfast and maybe a pizza, but few live up to their location when it comes to serious cooking. For that, you'll have to stick to the places reviewed below, or head inland to Sartène or down the gulf to Abbartello (see p.205).

Chez Charlot Viggianello, 4.4km east along the D19 ☎04 95 76 00 06. Down-to-earth village cuisine – Corsican soup, veal *bruschettas*, stuffed courgettes, roast pork, tripe, rabbit stew and pan-fried snapper – offered on a superb-value €20 menu. You can eat indoors or out on a narrow terrace next to the church which surveys the entire gulf.

U Famale plage du Phare ☎04 95 76 43 06. Occupying a great spot facing the beach and gulf, this pizzeria does a reasonably priced €24 menu featuring *mussels à la crème*, fish of the day and various *grillades* (or *croustillant d'aubergines* for veggies). They also stock the full range of Fiumicicoli wines and host live Corsican music every evening.

Terra Cotta 29 av Napoléon ☎04 95 74 23 80. The town's swankiest restaurant, with tables in a cool, Moroccan-style bistro, or out on a seafront terrace. The cooking is uncompromisingly sophisticated, using only the freshest local seafood, and the service smiling. *Formules* at lunchtime from €20; count on €50–60 à la carte; reservations recommended in the evenings.

Le Tout Va Bien ("Chez Parenti") 13 av Napoléon ☎04 95 76 12 14. *Haute gastronomie* on a terrace jutting over the marina. It's far from cheap, but they do offer affordable *formules* (€25–32) at lunchtime; otherwise, around €50–60 à la carte.

Listings

Banks There are ATMs at the post office on the western edge of town; at the junction of rue du 9 Sept and av Napoléon; and on rue Général-de-Gaulle.

Diving Valinco Plongée (☎04 95 76 31 01, ⓦwww.valinco-plongee.com) and U Levante (☎04 95 76 23 83, ⓦwww.plonger-en-corse.com), both in the marina. See also Porto-Pollo, p.203.

Ferries Services to Marseille and Toulon depart from the Port de Commerce between the last week of March and the end of Sept. Contact the SNCM, quai l'Herminier, for bookings ☎04 95 76 04 36.

Horse riding The Centre Équestre de Baracci (☎04 95 76 08 02), 3km northeast on the route de

Baracci, a 5min walk from the Total petrol station, offers guided rides for around €23 per hr on particularly beautiful horses especially bred for the island.

Hospital The nearest hospital with a casualty department is situated 6km southwest of Sartène, near Bocca Albitrina, just off the D21 (the back road to Belvédère).

Laundry Propriano has two self-service laundries (*laveries automatiques*): one just down from the tourist office on rue Général-de-Gaulle, the other opposite the Port de Commerce on av Napoléon.

Motorbike and mountain bike rental Mountain bikes (*VTT*) and 50cc or 125cc scooters can be rented through TCC, 25 rue Général-de-Gaulle (☎04 95 76 15 32, ⓦwww.ttcmoto.fr), and Location Valinco (aka JLV), 25 av Napoléon (☎04 95 76 11 84).

Pharmacy One on rue Général-de-Gaulle and another around the corner on av Napoléon.

Taxis There's a rank on rue Camille-Pietri, off the av Napoléon (☎04 95 76 11 03). Taxis charge €20 for the ride out to the trailhead of the Mare a Mare Sud at Burgo, depending on the time of day. Count on double that for Campomoro.

Campomoro

Isolated at the mouth of the Golfe de Valinco, **CAMPOMORO**, 17km southwest of Propriano, ranks among the most congenial seaside villages on the island. The main attraction here is the beach: 1km or so of gently curving golden sand and translucent sea, overlooked by an immense Genoese watchtower. In late July and August it's inundated with Italian families from the nearby campsites, but for the rest of the year Campomoro remains a sleepy place, with barely enough permanent residents to support a year-round post office. The village basically consists of one road, which turns left when it arrives at the beach and then runs in a curve around the bay, coming to a dead end below the promontory, which you can scale in ten or fifteen minutes to reach the **tower** (summer 9am–7pm; free), a lookout point surveying the entire gulf.

Practicalities

A word of warning for car drivers: **parking** in Campomoro is a nightmare in peak season as there's only one small car park and tight restrictions apply on the road (enforced by wardens).

Holiday cottages and swish villas with pools make up most of the village's limited accommodation, so book well ahead if you plan to stay in either of its two **hotels**. *Le Ressac* (☎04 95 74 22 25, ⓦwww.hotel-ressac.fr; April–Oct; ❽–❾), about 100m behind the chapel, is a friendly family concern, with simply

The Campomoro to Tizzano coastal hike

South of Campomoro stretches one of the wildest coastlines in Corsica: a windswept, sun-baked expanse of gently undulating maquis fringed by outlandish rock formations and empty beaches. The absence of a road into the area, nowadays officially protected as a regional nature reserve, means the only way to explore it fully is on foot, though there exist enough 4x4 tracks to make parts of it accessible to intrepid drivers, motorcyclists and mountain-bikers. This is also a stronghold of the Corsican wild boar, and a tangle of cartridge-strewn hunters' trails crisscrosses the deserted sea-facing slopes. Hikers, however, should stick to the **coastal path**, or *sentier littoral*, which begins below the Campomoro watchtower and winds south through a string of flotsam-covered coves around Capo di Senetosa, crowned with a much-photographed Genoese tower, to Tizzano in five hour thirty minutes to six hours. Before setting off, get hold of a copy of the official accompanying leaflet, **De Campomoro à Senetosa**, available free from tourist offices in the area (and from most hotels). Aside from giving a detailed rundown of the history, flora and fauna of the path, it includes a helpful pull-out map. The more detailed and dependable IGN **map** #4154 OT covers the area.

If you attempt to follow the route all the way to Tizzano, be prepared for some rough tussles with the maquis, which is made up of some particularly vicious gorse, mastic and juniper scrub. The path is cleared only once each year (by a lone Moroccan labourer) and gets muddled at several points with animal trails. You should also bear in mind the risks of **heat and dehydration**: there is only one spring before Tizzano and it shouldn't be relied upon. Lose your way once or twice and you could well find your water supply running dangerously low.

furnished, tiled rooms; those on the upper storey have balconies overlooking the bay or the olive groves behind. The other hotel, *Le Campomoro* (☎04 95 74 20 89, ⓕ04 95 74 20 89; ❺), overlooks the beach about 500m from the post office towards the tower. It's a bit bland, but the rooms are clean and well aired.

Much the more appealing of the two **campsites** in the village is *Camping Peretto Les Roseaux* (☎04 95 74 20 52; May–Oct), 500m from the post office down the lane running inland from the beach; it's fairly basic, but generally a lot more peaceful than *Camping Campomoro* (☎04 95 34 56 86), to the left of the road as you approach the village.

Campomoro's perennially popular lunchtime **restaurant** is *La Mouette*, opposite the church, which serves a selection of fresh salads, fish from the gulf and *plats du jour* from €15. Their busy terrace makes the most of its situation overlooking the beach, and towards the end of the day fills up with *pétanque* players and *pastis*-sipping spectators. For a more sophisticated meal, a better choice is *Le Ressac*'s, which offers various *menus fixes* at €25, offering Corsican standards such as *cannelloni al brocciu*, squid, and lamb stew. They also do pizzas (€8–10) and sumptuous *bouillabaisse* with half-a-dozen or more kinds of fish for €32 per person (order the day before).

For self-caterers, the store (summer daily till 8pm) in the middle of the village opposite the post office stocks a range of fresh fruit and veg, charcuterie, cheese, local wines, and other essentials (including bread, croissants and delicious *bastelles* from the baker's van).

The Alta Rocca

Winding inland from the Golfe de Valinco, the **Rizzanese River** dominates the varied geography of the **Alta Rocca**, a region of sprawling deciduous woods and deep valleys whose headwaters rise on the slopes of Monte Incudine, southern Corsica's highest peak. Together with the towering Aiguilles de Bavella, Incudine's domed summit forms the backdrop to one of the island's most distinctive micro-regions. From their trading posts on the coast, the Genoese were able to make little impression on its scattered villages, heartland of the rebellious Seigneurs della Rocca, who held sway over most of the south until the early 16th century. The readiness of its inhabitants to take up arms in defence of their independence, however, endured, and it was this area more than any other that fixed the Romantic image of Corsica in the minds of outsiders during the nineteenth century: Prosper Mérimée set his best-selling vendetta novel *Colomba* in **Fozzano**, an austere granite village in the hills overlooking Propriano, and some of the most notorious and fêted bandits of the era were the scourge of the maquis above Sartène. Later, in World War II, it was in the Alta Rocca that some of the fiercest Resistance fighting took place, as partisans armed with little more than pine-tree roadblocks and Sten guns inflicted terrible damage on German armoured divisions retreating towards the east coast.

The charms of the Alta Rocca's scattered villages today lie more in the pleasures of uplifting mountain views and café terraces on ancient stone squares than historic sights. But one monument merits a special excursion: the vestiges of prehistoric **Cucuruzzu**, near Levie, whose rock shelters and fortified towers rise from an extraordinary landscape of contorted oak forest and mossy boulders. It is easily reachable from the coast; you could nip there in a day-trip from Propriano, breaking the journey at the **Domaine Fiumicicoli** (see p.237), one of the island's top wineries, and picturesque **Sainte-Lucie-de-Tallano**, at the start of a lovely walk through the maquis to a deserted Pisan chapel.

Alta Rocca practicalities

Hotels are few and far between, concentrated mainly in the hill resort of **Zonza**, from where you can walk or drive to one of the island's defining landscapes, the massif of Bavella, with its soaring orange cliffs and pine forest. Further west, **Quenza**, huddled around its bare granite church, offers a more peaceful alternative, or you could base yourself in sleepy **Aullène**, high up on the edge of the Coscione Plateau, a grassy tableland in the lap of Monte Incudine to which shepherds formerly drove their flocks in summer.

It's possible to visit the most accessible of the Alta Rocca villages in a couple of days by car, but really to get to grips with this outstandingly beautiful region you should take to the **Mare a Mare Sud** hiking trail, which winds between Propriano and Porto Vecchio in four to five days. Sections of the route are highlighted as short walks in this chapter. For tips on how to tackle all five stages, see p.371.

The Corsican vendetta

Corsica has long been renowned for its vendettas, or **blood feuds**, which in the past affected nearly every family on the island, dividing dozens of villages and resulting in the kind of body counts normally reserved for civil wars. First alluded to by the Roman chronicler Diodorus Siculus, the institution probably predates the arrival in the early medieval era of the Vandals and Ostrogoths. The heyday of the Corsican feuds, however, was during the Genoese occupation, when an average of 900 murders were reported annually from a population of only 120,000 – a homicide rate triple that of modern Manhattan. Later, King Théodore tried to tackle the problem by decreeing that anyone found guilty of a vendetta killing be tortured to death and publicly quartered, while Paoli went further, executing murderers and levelling their family houses to erect special "pillars of national disgrace". Vendettas might be sparked off for all sorts of reasons, but rarely did the original offence bear much relation to the gravity of the ensuing feud. At Venzolasco in Casinca, for example, the Sanguinettis and the Paolis committed 36 murders after an argument over a chestnut tree; fourteen deaths resulted from the theft of a cock in Castagniccia; and one of the most notorious and long-lasting feuds in the south was provoked by a stray donkey.

To understand how such seemingly trivial incidents could unleash years (or centuries) of violence, it's necessary to appreciate the traditional importance in Corsica of family honour. In close-knit peasant communities, the respect shown to members of a family depended less on its material wealth than on how closely its members adhered to unwritten codes of conduct and morality. Essential for basic survival, unsullied honour ensured the goodwill and economic cooperation of others. Without it, life could be miserable, as one individual's personal dishonour necessarily implicated his or her entire family.

The most common way of shaming a family was through its women, who, while they rarely committed violent acts themselves, often played a seminal role in vendettas. Rape, seduction or elopement were extreme causes, but a feud could easily result if a man merely went for a walk with a girl without the permission of her father. More often, however, vendettas were started on purpose, usually with an act of clear provocation, such as the public humiliation of a female family member outside the village church. In what became known as the **attacar**, a young woman's headscarf would be torn off while she was leaving Mass to cries of "Dishonorata!" from onlookers; this would be met with an on-the-spot stabbing or shooting.

Lost honour was not irredeemable, and could be atoned for with a revenge killing. Thus, following an *attacar,* a solemn vow to avenge the injury would be made before the assembled family. If a murder had been committed, the victim's shirt would be

A rundown of the three bus routes running through the region is featured in Travel details on p.263.

Fozzano

East of Propriano, the north flank of the Alta Rocca region is scattered with old stone villages, of which the best known is **FOZZANO**, 12km inland from Propriano and something of a tourist attraction due to its former reputation as a hotbed of vendetta. Its notoriety dates from the early eighteenth century, when the whole village became politically divided over the Corsican uprising against the Genoese, the lower village lining up behind the Carabelli and Bartoli families, the upper behind the Durazzo and Paoli clans. **Colomba Bartoli**, born a Carabelli, was a driving force within her faction and the most infamous example of the central role played by women in Corsican vendettas (see box below).

removed, smeared with blood from the wound and nailed to the wall of the house, to be left there until revenge had been exacted. Meanwhile, all windows would be boarded up – both a defensive and symbolic gesture – and the men would allow their beards and hair to grow to indicate their involvement in the feud. From this moment on, no member of either family could live in safety, for the declaration of a vendetta implicated all the relatives of any victims, from brothers and fathers to in-laws and third cousins.

Among the most emotionally persuasive means of inciting the menfolk to avenge the death was the **voceru**, an impassioned funerary rite in which close female relatives of the deceased would gather around the corpse, stretched out on the family table, to sing. While the chorus wailed and tore their hair and faces, the chief singer, or *voceratricci*, would improvise four- or six-line verses mourning the loss and stirring up vengeful zeal among the men, seated in a back room banging their gun butts in time with the dirge. Often, the *voceru* would be followed by a dance called the *caracolu*, in which the women would process around the table in darkness. And woe betide any of the men who failed to heed their wives' and daughters' call to arms. Cowards were subjected to **ribeccu** – cast out of their families and treated with looks of scorn and derision until they had settled scores with the enemy. In this way, vendettas could smoulder on indefinitely, only coming to an end if the murderer fled to the maquis to become a bandit (see box, p.219), or if a peace was brokered by the parish priest.

During the mid-nineteenth century, the Corsican vendetta excited the imagination of the French literary establishment, fuelled by a stream of lurid novels on the subject. The first of these was **Balzac**'s *La Vendette* (1830), but it was **Prosper Mérimée**'s phenomenally successful *Colomba*, inspired by the author's stay in the village of Fozzano (see above), that brought the subject to a mass reading public. Thereafter, a series of even more romanticized depictions of vendettas was penned by prominent writers – including **Alexandre Dumas** (*La Vendetta*; 1846) and **Guy de Maupassant** (*Un Bandit Corse*; 1877) – which over time actually provided role models for feuding Corsican villagers.

Officially, vendettas no longer exist in Corsica (the last one ended in a village near Ajaccio during the 1950s), but old habits die hard and family reputation and old rivalries still influence almost all major business deals, not to mention marriages and socializing in rural areas. Nationalist politics, too, have become increasingly vendetta-ridden. Reading the local press, you'll often come across the phrase *règlement de compte* ("settling of scores") to explain the politically motivated assassinations that have spiralled over the past decades.

In 1830, tension in Fozzano intensified after a quarrel outside the church culminated in three murders, with two victims coming from the Carabelli clan. When, a year later, a confrontation led to the death of another Carabelli, Colomba plotted an ambush in the maquis to murder three of the enemy, but the plan backfired and her son was killed. The result of the mayhem was that Fozzano was thrown into a state of siege: houses were barricaded up and children kept from school. When **Prosper Mérimée** came here in 1839, he talked to the ageing but fiercely rancorous Colomba, who had become something of a celebrity – Flaubert also paid homage to her. The Mérimée novel that came out of their encounter, *Colomba*, made the gang leader famous throughout France as a youthful, cold-hearted and beautiful heroine, a character far removed from the more brutal and ugly reality.

Fozzano's exceptionally high granite buildings and narrow streets are dominated by two towers: the fourteenth-century **Torra Vecchia**, on the left as you come from Arbellara, was the heavily fortified home of the Carabelli; **Torra Nova**, a Genoese construction built in 1548, was home to the Durazzo faction.

At the edge of the village, south of Torra Nova, you'll find **Colomba's house** – the upstairs balcony is supposed to be where she heard the fatal gunshots far below in the maquis. Believing it to be only her enemies who had died, she gloated to the passing Durazzo "there's fresh meat for you down there", and received the retort that there was some for her, too. The tombs of Colomba and her murdered son, Francescu, are in the nearby chapel.

Sainte-Lucie-de-Tallano and around

One of the most celebrated spectacles in the Alta Rocca is the view over the jigsaw roofscape of **SAINTE-LUCIE-DE-TALLANO**, perched on a green spur high above the Rizzanese Valley. Settled since pre-Roman times, the village was in the late fifteenth and early sixteenth century the stronghold of **Rinuccio della Rocca**, who, in addition to being a fearsome thorn in the side of the Genoese, was an eminent patron of the arts, donating many paintings and pieces of Renaissance sculpture to the parish church in between his repeated, and increasingly desperate, attempts to oust the Italian occupiers. Graceful balconied houses remain as a legacy of the wealthy families who once resided here, but Sainte-Lucie's chief treasures are housed in the Baroque **Église Paroissiale** next to the square. Attached to a column on the left inside the entrance, a finely worked marble bas-relief of the *Virgin and Child* was commissioned by Rinuccio della Rocca in 1498. There's also a marble font in the form of a hand, dating from the 1490s and bearing the della Rocca arms.

To reach the classic viewpoint over the village, walk north for five minutes to the **Couvent St-François**, founded by Rinuccio in 1492 and set squarely on a plateau overlooking the valley. It was here that Dorothy Carrington, guided by a descendant of the della Roccas, rediscovered the art treasures collected by Rinuccio in the decade leading up to his death in 1510. Her initial hunch that the dust-covered canvases rotting in a ruined side chapel were the work of a master artist proved correct, although it took a "quest as intricate and stormy as any I undertook in Corsica", involving trips to Spain and Sardinia, to identify their creator.

Sainte-Lucie's other claim to fame is a rare kind of rock called **diorite orbiculaire** – a greyish-blue stone with concentric rings of black and white, like a leopard pelt – which used to be quarried close by. The friendly *Bar Ortoli* opposite the war memorial at the bottom of the square displays some polished samples, but you can buy rough-cut lumps direct from the owner of the now-defunct quarry: head down the street from the bar and look for a sign saying

Les bandits d'honneur

The most romantic of all Corsican folk heroes is the bush bandit, or **bandit d'honneur**. Coined during the nineteenth century, the term was used to distinguish between common highway robbers and men who had taken to the maquis after committing a vendetta killing. Protected by impenetrable scrub and granite, these fugitives could survive for years in caves, ruins or makeshift shelters accessible only by a labyrinthine network of game trails.

The true *bandit d'honneur* never stole or murdered anyone except his sworn adversaries, and could rely on the support of local villagers in times of need. Wandering the maquis in a broad-brimmed hat, a gun slung over his shoulder and a dog at his heels, he was felt to epitomize the *âme corse*, or "Corsican soul" – the spirit of rugged defiance, pride and separateness with which islanders had traditionally engaged their colonial rulers. As such, the *bandits* were respected, and even revered: travellers, artists and famous authors would seek them out in their camps, wealthy women fell in love with them, and a spate of nineteenth-century novels romanticized their footloose lifestyles. During a visit to the Lauretti brothers in their Fiumorbo hideout, for example, Flaubert wrote the following: "Great and valiant heart that beats alone in freedom in the woods … purer and nobler, no doubt, than most people in France."

While some *bandits* lived up to this ascetic ideal, many more took to drink, robbery, rape and murder, safe in the knowledge that they were beyond the reach of the *gendarmes*. In time, a new breed of outlaw emerged; one who adopted the wild life as a means to personal gratification rather than to escape the stringent ancestral code of vendetta. Playing on their reputation for ruthlessness, the new *bandits* – dubbed *bandits percepteurs*, or "tax-collecting bandits" – began to racket businesses and wealthy landowners. Far from being Corsican Robin Hoods, however, they are these days regarded as the precursors of the modern Mafia.

Around the turn of the century, the atrocities committed by *bandits* such as the Bellacoscia brothers (an account of whose career appears on p.320) spurred the police to mount a sweeping crackdown. Hideouts were raided, outlaws rounded up and imprisoned and their protection rackets rumbled. Today, there are no longer any bona fide *bandits d'honneur* remaining in the Corsican maquis, but their racketeering tactics, heroic self-image and hold over the local population have become distinguishing traits of the FLNC paramilitaries, who regularly invite journalists to their hideaways in the dead of night to be photographed wearing black jumpsuits and balaclavas, brandishing automatic weapons. (For more on the FLNC, see p.394.)

A biography of one of the first, and most notorious, Corsican *bandits*, Théodore Poli ("Le Roi des Montagnes"), appears on p.162, while the story of Muzarettu, among the only traditional *bandits d'honneur* to have lived in the postwar period, is featured in the account of Sartène on p.232.

"*Pierre Corse*" hanging from one of the houses on the right. It's the home of Mme Renucci who, before sealing the family shaft a decade or so ago, extracted four final tonnes of diorite, which she sells to tourists for whatever she can get.

Chapelle St-Jean-Baptiste

From the edge of Sainte-Lucie's square, you can just make out the red-tiled roof of the Pisan **Chapelle St-Jean-Baptiste**, nestled in the maquis a couple of kilometres down the hillside. The path to it, a section of the Mare a Mare Sud, makes a pleasant thirty-minute walk: follow the lane from the bottom of the square (the one running directly opposite the church) to the adjacent hamlet of **Poggio**, turning right (onto the D320) when you reach a T-junction; marked by a PNRC signboard for Fozzano, the orange-waymarked path starts shortly after on the left. The early eleventh-century chapel, perched on a high bluff jutting over the valley, is one of Corsica's prettiest medieval parish churches, dating from the start of Pisan occupation. Its interior today serves as a cattle shed, and is usually left open.

Les Bains de Caldanes

Hidden away deep in the Fiumicicoli Valley, the thermal **Bains de Caldane** (April–Oct daily 9.30am–8pm, Aug to mid-Sept until midnight; €3.50) are one of the great natural curiosities of the Alta Rocca. First exploited by the Romans in the fourth century AD, they have long been prized for their curative powers, especially for skin and nervous disorders, and after a period of obscurity in the twentieth century are enjoying a renaissance.

The sulphurous water emerges from the spring at a temperature of 40°C, flowing through a small pool barely large enough to accommodate a dozen bathers if they sit shoulder to shoulder in the tank. A rather comical sight it might be, but locals and visitors alike swear by the healing properties of the waters. In summer the baths stay open until midnight and many people combine a twenty-minute dip (the maximum time you're allowed to stay in because of the high temperature of the water) with a meal at the adjacent restaurant. The food is excellent: try the *plats Caldanes* (€14.50), a *grande assiette* comprising mixed mezes of aubergine caviar, courgettes with *brocciu*, sundried tomatoes and houmous.

The Bains de Caldanes are situated 6.5km from Sainte-Lucie-de-Tallano (via the D268/148). You can also approach them on the D69, which cuts inland between Propriano and Sartène (past the Domaine Fiumicicoli vineyard): follow the signs to Sainte-Lucie on the D268 and then turn right on to the D148.

Practicalities

Eurocorse Voyages' bus calls at Sainte-Lucie en route between Ajaccio and Zonza via Levie and Propriano, or you could catch Autocars Ricci's Ajaccio–Bavella bus. Tourist offices in the region have timetables for you to consult; in Sainte-Lucie, ask at the *Bar Ortoli*.

The village sees few overnight visitors and has just two places to **stay**, one of which is the attractively converted *gîte d'étape U Fragnonu*, on the north edge of the village (T04 95 78 82 56; half board €40 per person; ②), which serves copious, traditional food.

For a **meal**, try the *Pizzeria Santa Lucia*, next to the monument, which does inexpensive pizzas, salads and local dishes such as rabbit in myrtle sauce and stuffed leg of lamb (menus from €20–26), and whose terrace is the best place to watch the *pétanque* players next to the fountain. The street-side tables outside the *Bar Ortoli* provide another good vantage point from which to follow the comings and goings in the square, and they serve fresh croissants for breakfast.

Levie

In the eighteenth century, **LEVIE** (Livia) was the capital of Alta Rocca, its Genoese families prospering from the fertile riverine countryside below. Today the village is rather dour, its main attraction being the proximity of the **Pianu di Levie** (see opposite), whose prehistoric sites provide much of the substance of the **Musée Départementale** (July & Aug daily 10am–6pm; Sept–June Mon–Sat 10am–noon & 2–4.30pm; €2), in the Quartier Pratu, below the main street on the north side of the village. The star exhibit is the so-called *Dame de Bonifacio*, a human skeleton discovered near Bonifacio and dated around 6570 BC, making this the oldest found in Corsica. The remains are those of a woman in her mid-thirties whose legs were badly crippled by old fractures; to have lived to such an age, she must have been cared for by her community. The other noteworthy artefact on display here is a beautiful ivory statue of Christ by a pupil of Donatello, given to Levie in the 1580s by Pope Sixtus V.

Practicalities

The only **accommodation** here is in the institutional *Gîte d'Étape Bienvenue à l'Alta Rocca* (☎04 95 78 46 41; April–Oct; €34 per person B&B, €40 for half board), below the village centre beyond the gendarmerie; run by the local municipality, it's an untypically charmless place serving mediocre food.

You'll eat a lot better at the moderately priced *La Pergola* **restaurant** opposite the post office on the main street, which serves plain home cooking and will make charcuterie sandwiches on request. There's also a decent pizzeria, *Sorba*, a little further up the main street, serving the usual range of inexpensive wood-baked pizzas plus plenty of salads.

Lovers of quality regional cuisine, however, should head for one of the island's finest gourmet restaurants, ★ *A Pignata* (☎04 95 78 41 90; April–Oct). It's hidden deep in serene countryside near Cucuruzzu, 5km west. Head 3km out of the village on the Sainte-Lucie road, turning right at the signpost for the Pianu de Levie archeological site. Roughly 1.5km further on the left you'll see a narrow, unsignposted lane marked by a couple of large wheely bins; the gateway to the *auberge* lies a short way further up the lane (don't look for a signpost – there isn't one). *A Pignata* earned its reputation through the cooking of its *patronne*, Lily de Rocaserra; her sons and daughter-in-law have since taken over the reins, but mum and dad still keep a careful eye on proceedings. On a serene covered terrace looking out across the Alta Rocca, the family serves a single set menu (€37 for seven courses and eau de vie); the food is traditional *cuisine du terroir*, with virtually all the ingredients from the farm or its garden. Advance reservation is essential, especially if you want to stay in one of their very pleasant **rooms**, which are rented out on a half-board basis (€65–73 per person).

The Pianu di Levie

The most interesting prehistoric site on Corsica after Filitosa, the **Pianu di Levie** (daily: July–Aug 9.30am–8pm; April–June & Sept–Oct 9.30am–7pm, last admissions 2hr before closing; €5.50), is reached by taking the signposted road off the D268, 3km west of Levie. A further 4km will bring you to a field where you can park and buy your ticket; the entrance price includes a ninety-minute audioguided tour (or a printed booklet in English if you prefer).

A fifteen-minute walk through a Tolkienesque tract of gnarled old oak trees brings you to the **Casteddu di Cucuruzzu**, the remains of a Torréen habitation dating from 1400 BC. Emerging from the forest and integrated into the chaos of eroded, moss-covered granite boulders, this is the best example of a *casteddu* in Corsica. The complex, dominated by a circular *torre* and surrounded by a thick high wall, was inhabited by Bronze-Age artisans and farmers, who lived in the chambers surrounding the *torre* and in dry-stone shacks close by. The *casteddu* is entered by a steep and narrow stairway. Storerooms are ranged on the right, opposite a series of chambers with openings above to let the light in and the smoke out. Straight ahead, the *torre* has retained its vaulted roof of wide granite slabs, below which stones jutting out sideways from the walls suggest the existence of another floor. Stone tools, bronze belt links and domestic utensils, found in the course of excavations here, all point to the tower's having a functional rather than religious purpose. From the top you get a magnificent panoramic view of the region, from the needles of Bavella to the gulf of Propriano.

Another twenty minutes through the woods brings you to **Capula**, a site occupied from the Bronze Age until 1259, when its so-called **castle**, an impressive circular monument, was partly destroyed. Just below the entrance, look out for a headless menhir; other pieces of Bronze- and Iron-Age stonework are incorporated into the monument, mixed with hundreds of small granite bricks from the medieval period. About 200m beyond the castle, **Chapelle San Lorenzu**, a tiny thirteenth-century Romanesque building extensively restored in World War I, stands beside the ruins of an even older apsidal-ended chapel.

Carbini

South of Levie, the D59 runs 8km around the flank of a twisting valley to **CARBINI**, a tiny, depopulated village at the foot of the Ospédale massif. Heralding your arrival, a lone, square campanile, decorated with three storeys of graceful pierced arcades, is all that remains of the Église St-Quilico, which historians believe was the birthplace of the **Giovannalani**, a heretical off-shoot of the Third Franciscan Order that emerged midway through the fourteenth century in the wake of the Black Death. Popular belief has it that the sect used to end their services with mass orgies in front of the altar, but Dorothy Carrington, who visited the village in the late 1940s, showed this to be a scurrilous gloss added by biased chroniclers in later centuries. In fact, the Giovannalani espoused a far more pious way of life than the order they sprang from. Fearing the spread of their popularity across the island, Pope Urban V resolved to stamp them out and dispatched a punitive expedition to Corsica in 1362. The papal troops were joined by local reactionaries who hunted the Giovannalani down and massacred them in two mass burnings – one here, at a rocky eminence above the village, and another near Ghisoni, further northeast. Carbini then had to be repopulated by families from Sartène, which explains why in subsequent centuries it was overtaken by a bloody vendetta.

The Romanesque **San Giovanni Battista**, next to the bell tower, was the precursor of St-Quilico (whose floor plan is discernible nearby); beautifully restored in the nineteenth century under instructions from Prosper Mérimée, the then inspector of historic monuments, it is decorated with geometric patterns, human forms and various odd beasts typical of the Pisan era. Crowned with a crucifix, the rocky hilltop rising above the houses to the south was where

Walk from Carbini

A stiff **walk** of around one hour forty five minutes takes you east from Carbini to a splendid viewpoint surveying the entire Alta Rocca. Look for the orange waymarks leading east off the main street towards the hamlet of Supranu. Once clear of the last houses, the route follows a *piste* for a short while before peeling left into the woods. Having crossed the *piste* again further on, it then starts to climb more steeply via an ancient paved mule track that zigzags through the forest at a comfortable gradient. Gradually, chestnut trees, beech and mountain oak start to give way to maritime pines, whose massive cones litter the path as you approach the ridge. At the point just before the *sentier* veers around a sharp bend, around one hour from Carbini, keep an eye out for a large flat-topped boulder on your right – the views from it west encompass most of southern Corsica, from the Golfe de Valinco to Monte Incudine.

Return by the same route, or press on for another hour past Foce Alta (1171m) – from where you get an even more impressive panorama across the Straits of Bonifacio to Sardinia – to **Cartalavonu**, where you'll find *Le Refuge* (see p.261). IGN **map** #4254ET covers the route.

the Giovannalani were murdered in 1362; a path leads to the spot, from where the views across the valley extend to Bavella – especially evocative at sunset.

No trace remains of the eccentric *Hôtel des Nations* where Dorothy Carrington spent a lurid sojourn in 1948, but you can stop for a drink at the *Café du Centre*, under the limes on the main street, which has changed little since then. Other than that, the only facility for visitors is a small tap dispensing spring water – a welcome sight for hikers ambling through on the Mare a Mare Sud trail.

Aullène and around

Set midway between the east and west coasts, at a crossroads of four main inland routes, **AULLÈNE** (Auddé), 40km northeast of Sartène, is a typical Alta Rocca hill village, its hub of weathered granite houses swathed in chestnut trees – the source of the village's long-gone prosperity. Pastoralism was the other traditional mainstay, and a network of old shepherds' paths still threads through the surrounding woods to the Plateau de Coscione, making this a prime spot for hikers.

Wonderfully old-fashioned **accommodation** is offered by the ⚸ *Hôtel de la Poste* (☎&℗04 95 78 61 21; May–Oct; ❸), on the main street just above the square. Occupying a late nineteenth-century coaching inn, its rooms overlook the village rooftops and valley; they're basic, with toilets *à l'étage*, but impeccably clean and comfortable, and great value. Ask for one on the top floor (*deuxième étage*) – these have stripped wood floors and exposed beams.

Further up the lane, the *Chambres d'Hôtes San Laurenzu* (☎04 95 78 63 12; ❹) is a smarter, more modern alternative, offering good-sized, en-suite rooms with mod cons for only €55. Next door, the mother of its young *patron* runs the best **restaurant** in the village, ⚸ *Le Chalet* ("*Chez Mireille Chiaroni*"; ☎04 95 78 63 12). Locals drive up from the coast for her unbeatable €23 menu, featuring wonderful charcuterie and traditional dishes such as pork and chestnut stew (ideally accompanied by a bottle of Domaine Saparale red).

Apart from a meal at *Le Chalet*, another reason to pause in Aullène is the seventeenth-century **Église St-Nicolas**, at the very top of the village, which harbours an unusual wood-carved pulpit supported by twisting sea monsters emerging from a Moor's head. Two theories account for this sculpture: the first holds that it symbolizes the defeat of the Saracens and Moorish pirates who penetrated deep into the interior of Corsica in the late-medieval era; the second is that the work depicts the migration of souls, carried (according to an image dating from antiquity) on the backs of dolphins. If (as is likely) the church is locked, ask at the *mairie* for the key.

Around Aullène

Two spectacular mountain roads wind over the ridges beyond Aullène, one connecting the village with **Petreto-Bicchisano** on the main Ajaccio–Propriano road (N196), the other striking north towards **Zicavo** and the deep interior of the island. They're adventures in themselves by car, and offer arguably two of the best long-distance **cycling** routes in Corsica due to the relative absence of traffic, even in summer.

Heading west towards Petreto-Bicchisano, the D420 crosses the Chiuvone River just north of the village at the **pont d'Arina** and then rises through a dramatic rocky landscape, with enormous boulders dominating the road as far as the **Col de la Tana** (975m), 7km along. Beyond this pass, the route contours around the mountainside at the edge of a fire-damaged belt of pinewood overshadowed by the pink granite bulk of the Punta di Taccۦlaja (1330m).

At the **Col de St-Eustache** (995m), a further 3km, a fantastic view opens up north over the mountains to the Vallée du Taravo and beyond.

North of Aullène towards Zicavo, an even wilder backroad, the D69, skirts the fringes of the Plateau de Coscione, passing a string of converted *bergeries* and streams on its winding climb to the **Col de la Vaccia** (1193m). From the pass, you can look across the entire upper Taravo Valley to the grey summits of the watershed in the distance. A perfect place to enjoy the panorama is the rarely frequented *Auberge du Col de la Vaccia* (☎06 84 75 70 27, ℗04 95 25 04 74; May to mid-Oct; ❹). Seated outside on the terrace, or indoors next to an open fire if the weather's chilly, you can tuck into copious local cuisine on four- or five-course €22–30 menus. Upstairs, half a dozen smart rooms provide the last **accommodation** before Zicavo. Priority is given to guests opting for half board (€57), so book ahead.

From Aullène to Quenza

At the head of the Rizzanese Valley, two charming hill villages straddle the main road between Aullène and Quenza, covered by Autocars Ricci's bus, but visited by surprisingly few outsiders. Hikers following the Mare a Mare Sud trail make up the majority of visitors to the first, **SERRA DI SCAPOMENA**, whose well-run **gîte d'étape** (☎04 95 78 64 90; April–Oct; €35 per person obligatory half board) enjoys glorious views across the pale blue Bavella, Zonza and Ospédale massifs from its terrace and dorms. If you're driving, a small car park in the middle of the village, facing the magnificent panorama, makes a good picnic stop. Stock up beforehand with the best of local cheeses, wines and charcuterie at the village shop, Funtanedda, below the *gîte*.

The only other **accommodation** hereabouts is a lovely **B&B**, *Chez Marie-Claire Comiti* (☎04 95 78 73 64; ❸) in the minuscule village of **ZERUBIA**. It's fiendishly difficult to find: look for the signpost off the D420, 2km west of Serra di Scapomena, and when you reach the church follow the lane steeply uphill until you see the house on your left. The situation is superb – Corsica does not get any *plus profonde* than this – and Mme Comiti's cooking (evening menus €19), based on old family recipes using only fresh local produce, is traditional and delicious.

Quenza and around

Set on a rocky *belvédère* smothered in pines and chestnut groves, with Bavella as a spiky backdrop, **QUENZA** – 13km east of Aullène, at an altitude of 820m – enjoys a spectacular location at the high end of the Alta Rocca and a refreshing climate. Its inhabitants have traditionally been a mixture of shepherds from Conca on the coast (whence the denuded slopes above the village) and malaria-plagued Porto Vecchiens. If you're merely passing through, make time for a visit to the fine Romanesque chapel of **Santa Maria**, located 300m southwest down the Serra di Scapomena road (D420). Built on a single-nave plan with a rounded apse in the year 1000, the building retains an ancient granite-tiled roof and some traces of fifteenth-century frescoes inside. It was founded long before Quenza had sprung up, perhaps because of the spot's remoteness from the pirate-ravaged coast. A further echo of Corsica's medieval struggle with North African raiders appears in the more modern **Église de St-Georges**, next to the *fontaine* in the centre of the village, whose pulpit is supported by twisting sea serpents and a Moor's head similar to the one in Aullène (see p.223). If the church is locked, ask at the bar opposite for the key.

Practicalities

Quenza lies along the route of Balési Évasion's Ajaccio–Porto Vecchio bus, which passes through daily in both directions. The village's only **hotel**, the *Sole e Monti*, lies just past the centre along the road to Zonza (☎04 95 78 62 53, ⓦwww.solemonti.com; ❺). It's a large granite-fronted place whose spacious en-suite rooms have small balconies overlooking the valley. The extrovert *patron*, M. Balési, claims to have accommodated two British prime ministers over the years, and his kitchen is regarded as one of the best in the Corsican mountains. On the small triangular garden out the front, you can enjoy menus (from €32) featuring local trout and free-range pork or lamb, rounded off with fiery home-made *vin de myrthe*.

Hikers passing through on the Mare a Mare Sud tend to check into the more modest **gîte d'étape**, 🏕 *Corse L'Odysée* (☎04 95 78 64 05 or mobile 06 16 26 01 46, ⓦwww.gite-corse-odyssee.com; April–Oct; ❸), 1km north of the village at the end of a badly rutted dirt track (follow the signs just beyond the *Sole e Monti*). It's one of the most pleasant *gîtes* on the island, with attractive Morrocan-style decor, a sunny terrace overlooking the Alta Rocca and a better-than-average kitchen. There are no dorms, however, only double rooms (€50–55). The cooking is Corsican with a North African twist: roast pork with plums, carrot and mint salad or wild trout tagine; half board costs €50 per head.

Alta Rocca round walk: Quenza–Zonza–Quenza

Forest walks don't come much more varied than this four to five hour **round route**, which can be begun at either Zonza or Quenza. It follows the Mare a Mare Sud and its less often walked variant routing in a broad triangle through a succession of remote stream valleys where you can swim and enjoy secluded picnics. Marked at regular intervals with orange blobs of paint, the itinerary is easy to follow. Don't bother with an IGN map as the route roams over two separate sheets. The tourist office in Zonza hands out free leaflets with the relevant extracts.

The waymarks begin to the right of the lane running behind Quenza's Église de Saint-Georges, emerging shortly after at another lane, which they follow for around 100m before turning right again. From here the route meanders due south at a largely level gradient to an estate known as **Campu di Bertu**, where tall fences enclose a twenty-acre site set aside by the PNRC for the regeneration of a rare species of deer, *Cervus elaphus corsicanusi*. Indigenous to the island, the deer was almost wiped out after World War II, and breeding pairs were imported from Sardinia in the 1970s to repopulate the Alta Rocca's woods.

Once past the deer enclosures, with the Aiguilles de Bavella rising to the north, bear left at a fork in the path and follow the waymarks steeply downhill to the **Rizzanese** (1hr 30min), turning right at the far side of the bridge. Having crossed a side stream on the left shortly after, the route then climbs steadily uphill to a **junction**, where you should **turn left** towards Zonza, as indicated by a PNRC signboard (if you head straight on here instead you'll arrive after twenty minutes at the Romanesque Chapelle de San Lorenzu and Bronze-Age site of Capula, part of the Cucuruzzu pre-historic complex, described on p.222). Forty-five minutes beyond the junction, after a steady descent through thick mixed deciduous forest, the path meets a second river, the **ruisseau di Pian di Santu**, which the waymarks follow for a while before crossing to the right bank to begin a sustained climb to **Zonza**, reached two hour thirty minute into the walk.

To pick up the onward trail from the village, head 1km down the D420 from the centre (past the *Hôtel Le Tourisme*), keeping an eye out for the start of the path on the left of the road. Crossing the **rau de St-Antoine** stream twenty minutes later, the path begins to climb steadily again, emerging on the D420 500m east of Quenza.

To explore the country surrounding Quenza on **horseback**, head up the hill to Pierrot Milanini's stables (☎04 95 78 63 21 or 04 95 78 61 09), in the nearby village of **Jalicu**, 5km northwest. A day's riding will set you back €120 (including picnic); the horses are in tip-top condition and the landscape's ideal for a good hack. Pierrot also runs an independent 🏡 **gîte**: a combination of budget dormitory accommodation and better-than-average half-board cooking for the excellent all-in price of €40 per head. With a little advance warning, nonresidents can drop in for a meal (€25), served in the *gîte*'s cavernous dining room with an open fire. A block of more comfortable **rooms** (④) – with cool terracotta floors, kitchenettes and tiled bathrooms – is at the rear of the *gîte*.

One of the best *ferme-auberges* in this area – the *Funtana Bianca* – stands a few hundred metres beyond the riding centre in a converted stone *bergerie*. Owners Marie-France and Pierre Poli rustle up staunchly traditional mountain cuisine (ranging from free-range charcuterie, grilled veal and chestnut fritters to melt-in-the-mouth *fiadone*) using ingredients straight off the plateau. Count on €30–40 per head. They also have a tiny granite cottage behind to accommodate guests (④) – more were under construction at the time of writing.

The Plateau de Coscione

The **Plateau de Coscione**, known as U Pianu (The Tableland) in Corsican, is the rugged road-less region north of Quenza, west of the mighty Monte Incudine Massif (2136m). For centuries, this wilderness of rolling grassland and bog, which remains well watered throughout the summer by thousands of mountain streams, provided rich grazing for the pastoralist communities of the coast, who used to drive their immense flocks of sheep and goats up here each year after the spring snow melt. Between June and September, up to seven hundred men and their animals would live here in seasonal settlements of ramshackle stone huts. With the demise of transhumance, however, Coscione became a total backwater. Nowadays, barely a handful of shepherds follow in their forebears' footsteps, and those that do drive their animals up here in trucks for the summer, leaving them to their own devices until the autumn.

The rutted 4x4 tracks used by today's shepherds and cattle rearers crisscross Coscione from north to south, but to experience the region properly you'll have to leave your car behind and set out on foot. Comprising areas of lumpy green marshland where mist and cloud frequently sweep in from the surrounding granite ridges, the landscape of the plateau will feel oddly familiar to British visitors. This is somewhere you'll want to walk more for the atmosphere than the views, although approaching the region via the GR20, which traverses Coscione en route between Zicavo and Bavella, affords some fine panoramas of the interior mountains and Alta Rocca. Probably the easiest way to get a quick taste of the plateau is to drive in **from Quenza**. A narrow single-track lane winds north along the west side of an otherwise road-less valley, around the flanks of Punta Grossa to a deserted outdoor pursuits complex that was built in the 1980s as a service centre for skiers; in winter, Coscione's undulating hills can be carpeted in deep snow for months – ideal for cross-country skiing. From the car park, you can set off on foot to follow a clearly defined jeep track into the heart of the plateau.

Zonza

Framed against the craggy *aiguilles* of the Bavella massif, **ZONZA** looks like something off the top of a chocolate box, and its prominence on postcard racks and brochure covers ensures that this picturesque granite village is transformed during summer by the annual influx of tourists – hikers, climbers and horse riders, as well as a steady stream of motorists and backpackers. Its most illustrious visitors, however, were probably Muhammed V, Sultan of Morocco, and his son, who turned up here with three limousines in October 1952 after the family had been deposed in a coup d'état. The French Ministry of the Interior had requisitioned the village's now-defunct *Mouflon d'Or* hotel to accommodate the royals during their two-year exile. But the winter snow and rain got the better of them, and after only five months the sultan demanded that the government find him a place on the coast. Another hotel was subsequently occupied: the palatial *Napoléon Bonaparte* in L'Île Rousse.

Situated within easy striking distance of the most dramatic mountain scenery in the south, Zonza is well placed to use as a base for day-walks in the Alta Rocca (try the round route described in the box on p.225, beginning it here instead of Quenza). The village, which owes its sudden expansion in the nineteenth century to its strategic position straddling the region's main roads, is well served by daily bus connections to Porto Vecchio, Ajaccio and the rest of the Alta Rocca.

Practicalities

Timetables for the three bus services running through Zonza (see Travel details, p.263) may be checked at the **tourist office**, Information Tourisme Alta Rocca (Mon–Fri 8am–6.30pm, daily in July & Aug; ☎04 95 78 56 33, ⓦwww.alta -rocca.com), just below the crossroads at the centre of the village behind the war memorial; the office also hands out leaflets for various Alta Rocca walks, including the one described on p.225. Topoguides for the **Mare a Mare Sud**, whose variant passes through, are sold at the nearby *tabac*.

Hotels and campsites

L'Aiglon on the main road ☎04 95 78 67 79, ⓦwww.aiglonhotel.com. Some of its rooms are on the small side and lack en-suite bathrooms, but all are beautifully decorated with local tapestries and collected textiles from around the world. Families should request the lovely wood-lined suite on the top floor, which has its own rooftop terrace. Also has an excellent restaurant (see opposite). ④–⑤

Camping La Riviere 2km out of Zonza on the Quenza Rd ☎04 95 78 66 33, ⓦwww.hotel dutourisme.fr/camping.htm. A clean, green, well-shaded site spread beneath large pines next to a mountain stream.

Clair de Lune Zonza ☎04 95 78 56 79, ⓦwww .hotelclairdelune.com. Bright rooms (all en suite) in a small, welcoming hotel; most have little balconies. Handy for the village, and there's a comfy living room to lounge in with an open fire off season. ④–⑤

Hameau de Cavanello 2km from village on Bavella Rd ☎04 95 78 66 82, ⓦwww.location zonza.com. Modern B&B with conteporary decor and a pretty kidney-shaped pool set next to a teak sundeck, tucked away on the outskirts of the village. Rates include the run of a much larger (25m) pool and tennis courts at the Mouflon d'Or chalet complex in Zonza. ④–⑤

L'Incudine on the southern edge of the village ☎04 95 78 67 71. Pleasantly old-fashioned, down-to-earth country inn with fourteen smart, modern rooms with a/c, en-suite bathrooms and views. There's a good restaurant here too (see p.228). April–Oct. Half board, €130 for two sharing, obligatory in Aug. ❸

Le Tourisme north side of the village, on the Quenza Rd ☎04 95 78 67 72, ⓦwww.hoteldutourisme.fr. A notch pricier, and correspondingly more spacious, than the competition, with a heated pool. Their top-of-the-range rooms have the best views over the valley, but the smaller standard ones are comfortable enough for a night or two. April–Oct. ⑤

Restaurants

L'Aiglon on the main Rd ☎04 95 78 67 79. This hotel-restaurant boasts one of the region's more original menus. Their *plat de résistance*, "La Muntanela", is a groaning selection of special mountain delicacies given a special twist by the chef. Vegetarians are well catered for with *charlotte d'aubergine*, and they serve a choice of dreamy desserts (try the *tarte à la farine de châtaigne* with walnuts, raisins and chestnut ice cream, or English-style wild-berry cheesecake). Menus cost €19.50–30. April–Dec.

Auberge du Sanglier centre of the village on the crossroads ☎04 95 78 67 18. Dominated by the head of a massive stuffed boar. Predictably, *sanglier* (boar) stew with chestnuts on a bed of tagliatelle is the signature dish (featured on their €24 menu), and they've a better-than-average wine list including Domaine Gentile and Domaine Torraccia.

L'Incudine on the southern edge of the village ☎04 95 78 67 71. The busy restaurant on the ground floor of this country inn (see p.227) is renowned above all for its home-made mountain charcuterie, cheeses and succulent *grillades*, prepared on a wood fire in front of you by the *patron-chef*.

The Col de Bavella

Immortalized in the etchings of Edward Lear, the serrated *aiguilles* (literally "needles") of the Bavella massif dominate the landscape of the Alta Rocca. The spot where you get closest to them by car is the famous **Col de Bavella**, the southernmost road crossing of the Corsican watershed, between Solenzara and Zonza. Overlooking the pass, a statue of **Notre-Dame-des-Neiges**, rising white above a pile of granite stones and votive plaques, stares beneficently across

---

Walks and outdoor adventure around the Col de Bavella

The vast escarpments towering above the Col de Bavella are riddled with waymarked **footpaths**, catering for all levels of fitness and competence. The three most spectacular walks are outlined below in order of difficulty. They're well marked and accessible to all – you'll only need a copy of IGM **map** #4253 if you want a fuller picture of the area. For thrill seekers, the crags also hold some of Corsica's most exhilarating canyoning routes, as well as a great adventure park. Car drivers should note that parking is limited at the *Auberge du Col*, starting point for two of the routes; leave your car instead at the large car park up at the col itself, next to the Notre-Dame-des-Neiges statue.

Trou de la Bombe and Calanca Murata

The most popular of the walks beginning at the *Auberge du Col* goes to the **Trou de la Bombe**, a circular hole in the Paliri crest of peaks between Punta Velaco (1483m) and Calanca Murata (1407m). From the spring next to the *auberge*, follow the GR20 for 800m, then take the first path to the right, signposted "Trou de la Bombe". The track rises through a wood as far as a ridge, then drops gradually before beginning a short climb to the hole, which emerges to the right. Those with a head for heights should climb right into the *tafoni* for the dizzying view down the sheer 500m cliff on the other side.

Foce Finosa

The distinctive red-and-white waymarks of the **GR20** skirt the *Auberge du Col* and can be used to explore some of the more rugged terrain flanking the pass. A varied three-hour return route leads via an ancient transhumant artery to the **Refuge de Paliri**, a mountain hut hidden on the far side of the Crête de Punta Tafonata. Paved for much of the way and keeping to manageable gradients, it's one of the less challenging sections of the GR20. From its bifurcation with the waymarks leading to Trou de la Bombe, the path plunges quite steeply downhill to join a *piste forestière*, then crosses a stream (whose banks you can follow uphill for five minutes to a wonderfully secluded **bathing spot**) before leaving the *piste* to start the stiff twenty-minute climb to **Foce Finosa** (1206m). The effort is rewarded with fine views over some desolate terrain to the south from the pass. Dropping downhill on the other side, it's another 45 minutes of easy walking to reach the refuge, which has a water source, camping and bivouacking space and bunk beds for twenty people. From the rock platform behind it, scan the vast cliff to the north for the **Punta Tafonata di Paliri** (1331m), a large hole high up near the ridge line that's a popular target for rock climbers. Return by the same route.

an amazing panorama of wind-twisted maritime pines and orange cliffs. The area can seem as eerie as it is serene, especially in winter, but the proximity of the mountains and long-distance trails (the GR20 makes one of its rare descents to road level here) makes this an ideal place to base yourself for **hikes** in the area (see box below).

Immediately below the col lies the hamlet of **BAVELLA**, a cluster of neatly painted tin- and stone-roofed cabins, 9km northeast of Zonza, which was built in the early nineteenth century for the inhabitants of the Conca *commune*, who were granted the land by Napoléon III as a refuge from the summer heat of the lowland. Since then, the *commune* has washed its hands of the settlement, which as a result lacks basic amenities, including electricity and mains water – the source of an ongoing dispute.

Practicalities

Accommodation around the pass caters primarily for walkers. Next to the car park, *Les Aiguilles de Bavella* (☎04 95 72 01 88; ❶) gets overwhelmed with bus

Le Variant Alpin

Starting from the main car park at the col proper (not the *Auberge du Col*), a more taxing route takes you via a famous high-level **variant of the GR20** into the heart of the **Aiguilles de Bavella**, the giant rock towers looming above the road. Waymarked with yellow paint spots, the itinerary is sheer and physical from the outset, and should only be attempted by adequately equipped, experienced walkers – and never in bad weather (the granite gets very slippery after even a light shower). Some simple hand holds are required on the tough initial ascent, which takes you from the col to the Bocca di u Truvunu, at the base of Tower I. For the next hour and a half or so you'll be climbing and descending across a mixture of pine-covered boulder fields, scree and steeply inclined slabs below Towers II and III, one section of which requires the use of a fixed stanchion cable. The waymarks then begin their final ascent to **Bocca di u Pargulu** (1622m), high point of the Variant Alpin, from where a magnificent view of the Incudine massif is revealed. Return by the same. For further advice on the kind of gear and precautions you'll need to take if you attempt the Variant Alpin from Bavella, see Chapter 8.

Bavellaventure

Just below the *aiguilles* on the main Zonza road stands the entrance to a great little **adventure park**, **Bavellaventure** (mid-June to mid-Sept daily 10am–6pm; ☎06 22 29 38 84; ⓦwww.jpquilicimontagne.com). It's hard to think of a more dramatic location on the island for such a course: the tyrolian slides, cable bridges, fixed ladders and other features lead around old pine forest and some of the most spectacular cliffs in the Mediterranean. Admission costs €10–20 depending on your chosen route.

Via Ferrata enthusiasts should note that a challenging rock circuit has been installed at the opposite end of the route de Bavella, inland from Solenzara. For more information, see p.269.

Canyoning

Bavella is the island's canyoning hotspot, boasting two top-drawer routes – le Canyon de la Vacca and Canyon de la Purcaraccia – in addition to one suitable for beginners, the Canyon de la Pulishcella. However, access to all of them is controlled by local guides, who charge anything up to €60 per person. Dependable outfits worth contacting include: Canyon Corse (☎06 22 91 61 44, ⓦwww.corsicacanyon.com) and Corsica Madness (☎04 95 78 61 76, ⓦwww.corsicamadness.com).

▲ The Notre-Dame-des-Neiges

parties during the day, but has a good 24-bunk **gîte d'étape** (€15 per dorm bed, €30 half board), with a pleasant rear terrace and self-catering facilities. Menus range from €14–20 for traditional Corsican meals such as wild boar stew with myrtle or ravioli-*brocciu*, local cheeses and charcuterie. Five-minutes' walk down the Solenzara road from the col, the *Auberge du Col* (℡04 95 72 09 87, Ⓦwww.auberge-bavella.com; April–Oct; ❶) is in much the same mould, only slightly cheaper (€13 per dorm bed or €30 half board). It's also got a bit more atmosphere, with a wood-lined bar displaying old photos of the area. *Le Refuge* (℡04 95 72 08 84, Ⓕ04 95 71 05 77; ❶), 50m further down the road, has four very basic rooms with shared toilets, and rough camping space under the pines around the back. Their homely little road-side restaurant offers simple but copious menus (€13–21, plus wine) of local specialities.

The route de Bavella

The **route de Bavella**, connecting Solenzara on the east coast with the Col de Bavella, is perhaps the most dramatic road in Corsica. Vast cliffs tower on all sides as it winds through a landscape reminiscent of the American Wild West, with dizzying drops to the River Solenzara, full of smooth white rocks and turquoise pools. The road was widened to alleviate the terrible traffic congestion, but the work seems only to have compounded the problem by enabling large RVs and coaches to make the trip. It's therefore best to undertake the journey at quieter times of day. Travelling southwest, from Solenzara up the valley, the scenery shifts a gear at the **Col de Larone**, where a grandiose 180-degree panorama of the watershed is revealed. You can pull over at the car park here and wander up several *pistes* and paths for still better views. The glorious **Forêt de Tova** carpeting the valley below has been destroyed several times since World War II by bushfires, but still holds some of Corsica's tallest Laricio pines.

For a review of the **campsite** and **places to eat** at the bottom of the valley, see p.269.

The Sartenais

The **Sartenais**, in Corsica's far southwest, is the wild tract of dense maquis fanning seawards from the district's main town, **Sartène**, which the French novelist Prosper Mérimée famously dubbed "*la plus corse des villes corses*" ("the most Corsican of Corsican towns"). Scattered with **standing-stone sites** and ghoulish rock formations, this is a region rich in folklore, much of it fragmented transmissions from ancient times, when the weird granite outcrops looming above the scrubland sheltered communities of hunter-gatherers and, later, Neolithic farmers. The settlements retained a healthy population until Saracen pirates made off with most of their inhabitants between the fifteenth and seventeenth centuries. Since then, the area has remained depopulated and desolate, save for the vineyards of the Fiumicicoli and Ortoli valleys, which produce a number of fine AOC wines – the last vestiges of a once thriving industry that in the nineteenth century employed hundreds of workers.

The writings of Dorothy Carrington did much to fix popular impressions of the Sartenais as a mysterious and somewhat forbidding corner of the island. Many of her most valuable informants – traditional healers, bards and *mazzeri* ("dream hunters") – were old folk from the region's most remote villages. Life has moved on since Lady Carrington first travelled here in the late 1940s, but this remains an area with a peculiarly loaded atmosphere, heightened by the shadowy forms that emerge from the rocks around sunset time. Crossed by comparatively few roads, it is also one of the least developed parts of Corsica. You can literally walk for days along the **Sartenais coast**, between Campomoro and Roccapina, and not see a single inhabited building.

U Catenacciu

Sartène's Good Friday ceremony of **U Catenacciu**, generally considered to be the most ancient ritual in Corsica, is a sombre enactment by hooded and masked brotherhoods of Christ's walk to Golgotha. The nocturnal procession through candlelit streets is headed by the **Grand Pénitent** or Pénitent Rouge, dressed in a scarlet hooded robe, who carries a heavy wooden cross and is chained on the ankle – *u catenacciu* means "chained one". In former times the volunteer was usually a bandit whose identity was officially known only to the priest. Anonymity is still guaranteed, and there's a waiting list of twelve years to take part, which means that some of the penitents are very old men. If the Grand Pénitent is too frail to shoulder the cross alone, he's helped out by the **Pénitent Blanc**, who follows behind, representing Simon of Cyrene. Behind him marches a troop of **Pénitents Noirs** bearing the statue of Christ on a bier. Accompanied by the continuous unearthly chanting of an ancient Corsican prayer, *Perdonu miu Diu*, the procession passes slowly from Église Ste-Marie through the streets of the *vieille ville*, ending up three hours later in place Porta, where they receive benediction at midnight.

In the past it was a dangerous event, as the penitents were often known murderers at whom onlookers would fling stones – though this was one time of year when a truce was observed between sworn enemies, so nobody got killed. It's still a rough affair, with a lot of pushing and shoving to get the best view among the throng of tourists, and shots are often fired into the air at the end of the ceremony, by which time excitement is running high.

▲ Sartène

Sartène

A "town peopled by demons" is how German chronicler Gregorovius described **SARTÈNE** (Sartè) in the nineteenth century, and the town hasn't shaken off its hostile image. Located near the coast and therefore vulnerable to foreign invaders, it was persistently attacked by pirates in the Middle Ages, and from the twelfth to the sixteenth century became the seat of the ferocious **Sgio** (from *signori*), feudal lords who preferred to implement justice without interference from the island's rulers and who thus turned Sartène into an asylum for refugees from the law of the state. A bloody **vendetta** in the nineteenth century sealed the town's reputation and left a legacy of tall, grim fortress houses. An insular outlook continues to this day, and outsiders can be put off by the implacable ambience of the place. On the other hand, it's a smarter, better-groomed town than most in Corsica, with a perfectly preserved medieval heart that's largely free of ferro-concrete.

Despite its turbulent history, the town doesn't offer many diversions once you've explored the enclosed **vieille ville**. The only time of year Sartène attracts more than a trickle of visitors is at Easter for **U Catenacciu**, its highly charged Good Friday procession (see box, p.231).

A brief history of Sartène

Sartène was formed in the tenth century, when the inhabitants of the region's scattered hamlets were forced to congregate in one place by Saracen raids. In the twelfth century the **della Rocca** family held sway over the area with the consent of its Pisan governors, but when the Genoese took over in the thirteenth century, Sartène became a centre of discontent. The laws giving Genoa a monopoly on Corsica's trade were anathema to the local nobility, the **Sgio**, who continued to resist the Genoese until the final stand of Rinuccio della Rocca, defeated after a long struggle in 1510.

It was not until early in the sixteenth century that Sartène became a Genoese administrative centre, and even then their tenure was deeply troubled. In 1565 Sampiero Corso's army destroyed the town after a 35-day siege, then the Genoese took it back, only to lose it again in 1583 to **Hassan Pasha**, the mad king of Algiers, who ransacked the town and abducted four hundred of its inhabitants, a third of the population. Thereafter Sartène remained faithful to

Genoa, so much so that Paoli had a struggle to win its inhabitants to his cause in the fight for a Corsican republic.

The nineteenth century saw the re-emergence of the Sgio. Recognized as members of the nobility by the French monarchy, these powerful aristocrats prospered under privileges granted by Napoléon III; and, whereas other parts of Corsica suffered depopulation and decline, the Sgio oversaw the development of a wine industry that formed the backbone of the local economy until its vines were decimated by the phylloera louse in the late-nineteenth century. Today, the Roccaserras and della Roccas continue to dominate the political life of the town, now the *sous-préfecture* of southern Corsica – France's second-largest *commune* – and the most important regional capital in the south after Ajaccio.

Arrival and information

If you're arriving in Sartène by **bus** you'll either be dropped at the bottom of avenue Gabriel-Péri (Eurocorse Voyages) or in the main square (Autocars Ricci). **Car parking** can be tricky, thanks to the one-way system: the easiest place to leave your vehicle is in the free municipal lot halfway up the hill between the *vieille ville* and the Couvent de San Damiano; free parking is also available at the Super U supermarket at the bottom of cours Soeur-Amélie/Gabriel Petri (but check what time the gate closes).

The **tourist office** is on cours Soeur-Amélie (May to mid-Sept daily 9am–6pm; mid-Sept to April Mon–Fri 9am–noon & 4–6pm; ☎04 95 77 15 40). The Crédit Lyonnais on the main square has an **ATM**, as does the post office, next

to the Echaugette. ADSL **internet access** (a rarity in this area) is available at the *Cyrnros Cyber Café*, on the northeast corner of place Porta, for €3/hr.

Accommodation

Sartène holds little tourist accommodation in its medieval core, most of the town's **hotels** being dotted along the main Propriano road, outside the old ramparts. **Campers** are catered for with a pair of sites – one close to town and one out towards the Fiumicicoli vineyard. Better still, consider driving 15km south along the *route nationale* to the wild Vallée de l'Ortolo, where 🏕 *Camping à la ferme U Cavaddu Senza Nome* (see p.239) enjoys a wonderfully tranquil spot deep in the most rugged corner of the Sartenais.

Hotels and B&Bs

🏃 **Domaine de Croccano** 3km down the D148, direction "Granace" ☎04 95 77 11 37. Gorgeous little B&B, hidden in a fold of the Rizzanese Valley, with panoramic views over the Sartenais from its vine-covered terraces. Exposed stone walls and whitewashed wood beams set the tone of the three en-suite rooms, which occupy a converted eighteenth-century farmhouse, furnished in a mixture of period and contemporary styles. The welcoming hosts also offer horse riding and guided walks. ❻

U Listincu 3km down the N196 ☎04 95 77 17 51. Simple but immaculate rooms in a modern building on the main road. Hardly the most appealing spot in the area, but fine for a night, and one of the cheapest options for miles in peak season. ❹

Les Roches av Jean-Jaurès ☎04 95 77 07 61, ⓦwww.sartenehotel.fr. A large 1970s-style hotel on the edge of the old town, most of whose sunny, en-suite rooms command panoramic views of the Vallée du Rizzanese from their balconies. It's invariably block-booked by coach parties, so reserve well ahead. ❺

Rossi Hôtel (Fior di Riba) 1km west of town on the Propriano Rd ☎04 95 77 01 80, ⓦwww .hotelfiordiribba.com. Plain, modern place next to *La Villa-Piana*, with smart rooms and furnished studios for longer stays. Tariffs vary according to room size and proximity to pool; good value. April to mid-Oct. ❻

U San Damianu Quartier San Damianu ☎04 95 70 55 41, ⓦwww.sandamianu.fr. Swiss-run three-star occupying a plum spot just below the convent. There are superb views over the *vieille ville* and valley from private balconies, and with all the comforts and courtesies you'd expect in this class, but it's a bit souless. ❼–❽

La Villa-Piana 1km west of town on the Propriano Rd ☎04 95 77 07 04, ⓦwww.lavillapiana.com. Smart three-star offering lovely views from spacious front terraces, plus a tennis court and a pool overlooking the Rizzanese. April to Oct 15. ❻

Campsites

Camping Olva (Les Eucalyptus) 5km out of town towards Castagna on the D69 ☎04 95 77 11 58. Three-star site, much larger and better equipped than *U Farrandu*, and in a more inspiring location – though correspondingly pricier and busier. May–Oct.

U Farrandu 2.5km down the Propriano road on the right-hand side ☎04 95 73 41 69. This cheap, spotlessly clean and friendly place is the nearest campsite to Sartène – a small site carved into the banks of a mountain stream under a dense canopy of deciduous trees. Facilities are basic, but rates are very low for the area. The only catch is the proximity of the main road. April–Sept.

The Town

Place Porta – its official name, place de la Libération, has never caught on – forms Sartène's nucleus. Once the arena for bloody quarrels, it's now a well-kept square opening onto the valley. Somnolent by day, place Porta comes alive for the early-evening *passeghiata*, when it fills with snappily dressed townsfolk.

Flanking the south side of place Porta is **Église Ste-Marie**, built in the 1760s, but completely restored since. The chief interest here is historical – it was in this church that the warring families of nineteenth-century Sartène were forced to make their peace, though the truce often lasted only until they got outside again. Inside you can see the weighty wooden cross and chain used in the *Catenacciu* procession (see p.231), but otherwise the only notable feature is the Baroque altar, a present from the town's now-vanished Franciscan monastery.

Formerly the palace for the Genoese governor, the nearby **Hôtel de Ville** serves as an archway into the Santa Anna district of the *vieille ville*; the building is not open to the public and its archives have been closed since the 1880s, due to the endemic corruption of local politicians, it's said.

The vieille ville
A flight of steps to the left of the Hôtel de Ville leads past the Maison de la Culture and cinema to the post office, behind which stands the ruined **Échauguette**, a small lookout tower which is all that remains of the town's twelfth-century ramparts. This aside, the best of the **vieille ville** is to be found behind the Hôtel de Ville in the **Santa Anna** district, a labyrinth of constricted passageways and ancient, fortress-like houses reached via the archway directly beneath the Hôtel de Ville. Featuring few windows and often linked to their neighbours by balconies, these houses are entered by first-floor doors, a necessary measure against unwelcome intruders; dilapidated staircases have replaced the ladders that used to provide the only access. The main "road" across Santa Anna is rue des Frères-Bartoli, to the left of which are the strangest of all the vaulted passageways, where outcrops of rock block the paths between the ancient buildings. Just to the west of the Hôtel de Ville, signposted off the tiny **place Maggiore**, you'll find the **impasse Carababa**, a remarkable architectural puzzle of a passageway cut through the awkwardly stacked houses. A few steps away, at the western edge of the town, **place Angelo-Maria-Chiappe** offers a magnificent view of the Vallée du Rizzanese.

Musée de la Préhistoire Corse
Sartène's only other cultural attraction is **Musée de la Préhistoire Corse** (closed at time of writing, pending a move to new premises across town, scheduled for 2009; check with the tourist office for timings), Corsica's centre for archeological research. If the old museum was anything to go by, the exhibits will comprise mostly Neolithic and Torréen pottery fragments, with some bracelets from the Iron Age and painted ceramics from the thirteenth to sixteenth centuries.

Couvent de San Damiano
A ten-minute walk along the road to Bonifacio will take you to the **Couvent de San Damiano**, the building in which the *Catenacciu* penitent spends the night before the procession, when he has to be guarded from curious outsiders by police. One of the last of the old-style bandits, a formidable character called **Muzarettu**, died here in the 1940s at the age of 90, having been given refuge by the monks. Cast out from his village for killing a nephew who had slapped his face, Muzarettu took to the maquis, then proceeded to terrorize the neighbourhood from his cave hideout near Propriano, where he hosted wild parties for the fishermen who brought him food and drink. A few more murders along the way kept him outlawed for many years, but as an old man he developed cancer and came to this convent to die; repenting his sins right at the very end, he was visited by the chief of police on his deathbed. The convent is now home to a brotherhood of Belgian monks and is out of bounds to the public, but there's a fine view of the valley from the outside.

Eating and drinking
There's no shortage of great **restaurants** in Sartène, most of them cosy, traditional places in old stone buildings. A handful of inexpensive snack bars and pizzerias also line the main square, ideal for a light lunch or ice cream.

Auberge Santa Barbara 2km out of Sartène on the main Propriano road ☎04 95 77 09 66. One of the gastronomic highlights of the Sartenais: fine, authentic local cuisine from the mountains and coast, served in a well-tended garden. Seafood lovers should try the sea bream *à la ratatouille* with aubergine caviar, shrimp soufflé or cuttlefish in red wine – and leave room for the famous *flan grande-mère*. Menus at €29–32; €35–60 à la carte.

La Cave Sartenais place de la Libération. Directly beneath the Hôtel de Ville, and the most congenial place in town to taste and buy quality local wines. The two top *domaines* – Saparale and Fiumicicoli – are well represented, and there's a great selection of cheeses and charcuterie. June–Sept Mon–Sat 9am–8pm. Closed lunchtimes Oct–May.

Restaurant du Cours "Chez Jean" 20 cours Sainte-Amélie ☎04 95 77 19 07. Wholesome, honest *cuisine sartenaise* (filling veal or pork stews, tripettes, stuffed courgettes, as well as pizzas) served in a stone-walled inn to a mostly local clientele. This is a particularly good address in winter, when *patron* Jean prepares his Pantagruellan *grillades* and *figatellu* over an open fire. Menus around €25 – excellent value.

Le Jardin de l'Echaugette next to the Échaugette in the *vieille ville* ☎06 20 40 71 49. Delightful garden restaurant on a shade-dappled terrace, tucked away on the edge of the medieval ramparts (get here early for a table with the best valley views). The food's refined *gastro corse* at friendly prices: grouper *croustillant* with almonds in red wine sauce; chicken liver with fresh mint; Sartenaise veal stew on a bed of creamy polenta. Count on €32–40 à la carte (plus wine); menus from €20 (at lunchtime) to €30 (evenings).

A Madunnina between Sartène and Propriano, at the turning for Fiumicicoli/Ste-Lucie/Levie (the D268) ☎04 95 77 16 22. Rough-and-ready road-side restaurant that looks a bit grim from the outside, but which turns out to be one of the liveliest and best-value places to eat for miles. It's famous for its vast wood-baked pizzas, but it also does superb Moroccan tagines, Portuguese calamari and *grillades* (the *merguez* and *brochettes* are particularly scrumptious), served with perfect *frites*. Seafood lovers should try the sea bass in anemone butter on lasagne leaves. Most mains €20–35.

Around Sartène

Littered across the southwest Sartenais is an extraordinary crop of **megalithic sites** around **Cauria**, ranging from the flat-topped **Dolmen de Fontanaccia**, the best-preserved prehistoric tomb on the island, to the enigmatic alignments of **Stantari** and **Renaggiu**, an impressive congregation of statue-menhirs close by. Further northwest, 258 standing stones of various sizes lie strewn amid the maquis at **Palaggiu**.

The coast hereabouts, most easily accessible via the D48 to **Tizzano**, is among the least developed on the island, with remote coves providing some excellent spots for diving and secluded swimming.

The megaliths of Cauria

To reach the **Cauria** megalithic site you'll need to pick up the **D48**, 2km southwest of Sartène at the **Bocca Albitrina**, and follow it south towards Tizzano. Four kilometres along the route a left turning brings you onto the D48A, which winds through empty maquis for another 5km. Park up where you see a sheltered lay-by on either side of the road; a *piste* nearby leads to the sites (it's possible to drive a further 800m down this track, though you might end up regretting it without a 4x4).

The first group of monuments you come to is the striking **Alignement de Stantari**, a group of 22 standing figures dating from the second phase of the megalithic era, around 2000 BC. All are featureless except the two distinctly phallic stones, which both have roughly sculpted eyes and noses, with diagonal swords on their fronts and sockets in their heads where horns would probably have been attached.

A footpath leads south from the Stantari enclosure across open scrub to the **Alignement de Renaggiu**, a gathering of forty menhirs standing in a small shadowy copse below the enormous granite outcrop of Punta di Cauria. Some

Sartenais wines

Wine buffs shouldn't leave the area without a visit to the **Domaine Fiumicicoli**, 7km north of Sartène on the D69, whose distinctive label design derives from the nearby **Spin'a Cavallu**, an immaculately preserved Genoese bridge spanning the Rizzanese. Made from a blend of traditional Corsican grapes (Nielluccio and Sciacerello) augmented by twenty-percent Syrah, the Fiumicicoli red is a perennial prize-winner – a light- to mid-weight wine with a crisp acidity that make it a perfect accompaniment for the kind of simple, rustic cuisine favoured hereabouts. Derived from pure Vermentino, the white is refreshing, with citrus aromas. And be sure to try their unique ruby Muscat ("Muscateddu"), sold in chic little half bottles.

The area's other noteworthy winery, Phillipe Farinelli's **Domaine Saparale**, is hidden away in the wild Vallée de l'Ortolo (see p.239), 5km southwest on the Bonifacio road. It isn't open for tastings, but you can pick up their full range at shops in the area. As the wines are made from relatively young vinestock, they're still establishing their reputation and are thus better value for money than some from more famous domaines. Made from hundred-percent Vermentino, the Saparale white has a distinctive bouquet of lemon and wild herbs, while the red is full of wonderful cherry flavours. They also do a fine rosé – an ultra-pale *vin gris* – and more expensive special *cuvée*, "Casteddu", a distinctive, New World-style wine aged in young oak barrels.

of the menhirs have fallen, but all face north to south, a fact that seems to rule out any connection with a sun-related cult.

The third point in this triangle of sites, the **Dolmen de Fontanaccia**, crowns the crest of a low hill five-minutes' walk from Renaggiu (double back towards the Stantari site and bear left after 20–30m when you come to a fork in the path). Known to the locals as the Stazzona del Diavolu (Devil's Forge), the dolmen is in fact a burial chamber. The late megalithic period it dates from was marked by a change in burial customs; bodies which had previously been buried in stone coffins in the ground were instead placed above, in a mound of earth enclosed by a stone chamber. What you see today is the great granite table, comprising six huge blocks nearly 2m high topped by a slab, which remained after the earth rotted away.

Alignement de Palaggiu

The **Alignement de Palaggiu**, the largest concentration of menhirs in Corsica, lies further south down the D48; 1500m past the Domaine la Mosconi vineyard (on your right, 3km after the Cauria turn-off), there's a turning on the right. From here a badly rutted dirt track leads another 1.2km through to the stones, lost in the maquis, with vineyards spread over the hills in the half-distance. Stretching in straight lines across the countryside like a battleground of soldiers, the 258 menhirs include three statue-menhirs with carved weapons and facial features – they are among the first line you come to. Dating from around 1800 BC, the statues give few clues as to their function, but it's a reasonable supposition that proximity to the sea was important – the famous Corsican archeologist Roger Grosjean's theory is that the statues were some sort of magical deterrent to invaders.

The plage de Tralicetu and plage d'Argent

Almost opposite the turning for the Palaggiu menhirs, a cutting in an earth bank marks the start of a rough four-kilometre *piste* leading to a string of spectacularly remote beaches. It's just passable in a hire car (though bear in mind you'll be breaking your rental agreement by venturing off the sealed road). Having wound down the west flank of a stream valley via a series of isolated farmsteads, the *piste* emerges at a clearing behind the impressive **plage de Tralicetu**, where a handful of locals' hideaway huts nestle in the maquis. The gleaming white sands stay empty most of the year, even in high summer. But for total tranquillity, you can walk south and continue via the coast path to the still more secluded **plage d'Argent**, lining the Cala Barbaria – one of the most scenic stretches of the Campomoro–Tizzano trek. There are no facilities, so take food and water.

Tizzano

TIZZANO (Tizza), the only permanently inhabited settlement on the Sartenais coast, brings the road to an end 3km south of Palaggiu. A scruffy collection of half-built holiday houses stacked around the sides of a steep headland, the village presents a much less arresting spectacle than its beach, **Cala di L'Avena**. Around the corner to the north, a narrow cove fitted with a jetty provides sheltered anchorage for a dozen or so fishing boats and yachts. It's overlooked from the opposite shore by the ruins of an intriguing fifteenth-century **fort**, built by the Genoese but destroyed in World War II, when it was used for explosives practice by trainee commandos (led, ironically, by a British SOE agent).

Aside from Cala di L'Avena, the main reason you might want to venture down here is **walking**. Interrupted by some of the island's most stunning shell-sand beaches and watchtowers, the coastlines in both directions are gloriously stark, road-less and unspoilt, although you need to be resilient to maquis scratches to explore them. For advice on how to set about the routes, see the box on p.214 (for the stretch between Campomoro and Tizzano).

Practicalities

The smartest of Tizzano's two **hotels** is the *Lilium Maris* (☎04 95 22 02 51, or 04 95 77 23 34; Easter–Oct; ⑥–⑨), a three-star in a prime beachside location and with ambitious tariffs. Most of its rooms and suites overlook the water and are decorated in light, white textiles and teak furniture. Nearby, the *Du Golfe* (☎04 95 22 02 51, ℻04 95 77 23 34; Easter–Oct; ⑥) is a less stylish option, also overlooking the bay, with seventeen rooms. For campers, *Camping L'Avena* (☎04 95 77 02 18; late-May to Sept) sprawls up the valley behind the beach, complete with rows of plastic bungalows.

The cream of the day's catch landed on Tizzano's pint-sized jetty is hauled straight up to the *Restaurant Chez Antoine* (☎04 95 77 07 25), just along the lane from the *Du Golfe*, whose terrace stands beside its own tiny beach. Depending on what the boats have brought in, their menu might include wood-grilled snapper, ray's wing in lemon sauce, or lobster, and given a day's warning they'll knock up a *bouillabaisse* with every edible kind of fish and crustacean available off the Sartenais coast. For more basic snacks, salads and pizzas there's the *Café Escale*, opposite which a seasonal **shop** (June–Aug daily 8.30am–12.30pm & 4–7pm; May & Sept Mon–Sat 9am–noon & 4–7pm) stocks essentials.

Sartène to Bonifacio

The far southwestern corner of Corsica, between Sartène and Bonifacio, is the island's least populated coastal lowland – a rolling expanse of archetypal Mediterranean scrub dotted with the odd vineyard and roadside *auberge*, but little else. Emblematic of its eerie grandeur, the **Uomo di Cagna** – a giant boulder eroded by the sea winds into the form of an old man wearing a hat – surveys the plain from the summit of the far south's highest mountain. Fishermen from the village of **Monaccia-d'Aullène**, at the foot of the hill, once used "u Uomo" as a beacon, turning back towards land whenever they lost sight of the figure.

The region's main artery is the **N196**, which wriggles south from Sartène past the mouth of the **Vallée de l'Ortolo**, and then veers eastwards at the col above **Roccapina**, one of Corsica's most arresting beaches. From there, the main road arcs across the low-lying coastal belt to **Figari**, centre of an upcoming wine region and site of southern Corsica's international airport. The rough swathe of maquis south of the main highway is edged by a string of hidden beaches, the best of them accessible via **Pianotolli-Caldarello**.

The Vallée de l'Ortolo

Fifteen kilometres southeast of Sartène an inconspicuous turning plunges east, via a surfaced road, into the most rugged and sparsely populated corner of the Sartenais. Until the phylloxera louse wiped out its vines around the turn of the century, the **Vallée de l'Ortolo** was a major wine-growing region, and a couple of vineyards survive here – notably the renowned **Domaine Saparale** (see p.237). Despite this, the valley's wild, somewhat forbidding ambience remains undiminished, not least because most of it lies in the hands of big landowners who resolutely refuse to grant rights of way. You can, however, get a good feel of the area at the farm **campsite**, *U Cavaddu Senza Nome* (☎04 95 77 18 47, mobile 06 10 39 14 29). It's owned and run by a welcoming Austrian-German couple, Heidi and Harkmut, who have lived in the area for years. They know all the best trails and hidden beaches in the Sartenais, and rustle up delicious pizzas from a giant stone oven in peak season. The campsite itself is simple, but well laid out over terraces beneath a dramatic grey escarpment – all in all, an idyllic spot which will appeal particularly to kids, thanks to the friendly dogs, cats, chickens and rabbits running around.

Roccapina

The great landmark of the journey around Corsica's southwest coast is the **Lion de Roccapina**, a lump of roseate granite weathered into the shape of a recumbent lion. Visible from a lay-by on the roadside, it presides over a dazzling turquoise-blue bay, the **Golfe de Roccapina**, a protected site whose dunes harbour nothing apart from a desultory municipal **campsite**. The only way to reach it is via a rutted *piste*, which winds 2.5km downhill from the *Auberge Coralli* on the N196 (a request stop for Eurocorse Voyages' bus) to the *Camping Arepos-Roccapina* (☎04 95 77 19 30; June–Sept), an inexpensive, well-shaded site, though it's plagued by particularly rapacious mosquitoes in summer. It only really gets crowded from early July, but the shallow bathing, soft white sand and crystal-clear water of the bay beyond are only too visible from the highway, so don't expect to have Roccapina to yourself unless you come off-season.

To reach the old Genoese **watchtower** on the hilltop above, head up the stony path that leads right off the main approach to the beach, and bear left when you reach a fork five minutes later (the right fork of this path will take you to the Lion de Roccapina, which is extremely dangerous to climb, regularly claiming lives in spite of the warnings posted around it). From the ridge, the views south across the cove, north up the wild Ortolo Valley and along the Sartenais coast, are superb. Immediately below the ridge, the immense white-sand beach around the headland from Roccapina, **plage d'Erbaju**, can be accessed via a stony path from the ridgetop in around twenty minutes. The

▲ Plage de Roccapina

dunes behind it, patrolled by a herd of stray cows, are strewn with bushes of cinqfoil and twisted pines – the only shade for kilometres. Backed by the private estate of **Murtoli**, whose isolated houses you can just about discern on the far side of the bay, this beach is inaccessible by road and thus sees only a scattering of (mostly German nudist) visitors, even in high summer.

Pianottoli-Caldarello

Back on the main road, the first sign of civilization comes at **PIANOTTOLI-CALDARELLO**, the largest settlement between Sartène and Bonifacio. Two hamlets make up the village, and their names tell you everything about the locale: Pianottoli, the northern half straddling the highway, is derived from the word for "plain", and Caldarello, 1.5km south, means "extreme heat". There's nothing much to see in either, but a handful of unfrequented coves lie within easy reach, and if you're catching a plane from nearby Figari airport, a couple of **campsites** provide convenient places to spend your last night on the island. Three kilometres down the road towards the sea, *Camping Le Damier* (T04 95 71 82 95, Wwww.camping-le-damier.com; open all year) is a large three-star site with a pizzeria and bungalows that are a steal (②-③) in low season. It charges more or less the same rates as the rival *Kevano Plage* (T04 95 71 83 22, Wwww.camping-kevano.com; April to mid-Oct), a short way down the lane and marginally the better of these two sites. Both lie within easy walking distance of the secluded **plage de Chevano**, a narrow sandy beach spread around a shallow turquoise bay, 500m further south.

To escape the campers who spill across it in season, head down the road directly opposite the entrance to the *Kevano Plage* campsite and turn onto the second *piste* on your left (after around 1500m). This splits into two at a bend: take the right fork and follow the track through the maquis to a small car park, from where it's a brief walk along the footpaths which run the rest of the way to a gorgeous string of little **coves**.

The only **hotel** in this area is the luxury *U Libecciu* (T04 95 71 87 93, Wwww.hotellibecciu.com; ⑧-⑨), a swish three-star backing onto its own exclusive beach, with a pool, tennis courts and eighty air-conditioned rooms. From the small jetty behind it you can rent sailing boats, windsurfers and waterskis. The hotel stands 2km south of Caldarello village; follow the signposts from the main road.

Pianottoli also has a couple of decent **B&B** places, the most secluded and appealing of which is 🌱 *Chez M Labbé* (☎04 95 71 86 18; ❸), signposted south off the main N196 (to the right of the road if you're coming from Sartène). Follow the winding dirt track for 500m or so and you'll arrive at a small organic plant nursery with two peaceful rooms (one of them in a tiny detached house). Evening meals feature local dishes (on a €24 menu) using only seasonally available ingredients from the property, such as veal fillet baked with herbs, red onions and ewe's cheese.

Figari

Cut in half by the main Porto Vecchio-to-Ajaccio highway, the village of **FIGARI** sees a disproportionate amount of traffic thanks to its proximity to south Corsica's civil **airport**, spread over the floor of the valley below. Most charter and scheduled flights to northern Europe leave at civilized times, and visitors generally drive here on the day of their departure. If, however, you're travelling without the luxury of your own vehicle you'll have to get here via Eurocorse Voyages' Ajaccio bus or one of the *navettes* that run to the airport from opposite the marina in Porto Vecchio to meet flights (for more details of this service, see p.257).

Overlooking the airport from the isolated village of **SAN GAVINO**, 6km off the main road, *L'Orcu* (☎04 95 71 01 27; ❺) is a quirky little **B&B** offering simple, clean rooms in an old granite house. The *patronne*, Mme Bartoli, cooks traditional family dishes, offered on a €27 menu which changes daily. Breakfast and dinner are served in the shade of an ancient tree outside. San Gavino is marked on the Michelin map (just): follow the signs to Poggiale from the main road and turn uphill at a sharp bed just southwest of the village church.

Even more tucked away is a great little boutique B&B, *Les Bergeries de Piscia*, (☎04 95 71 06 71, 🌐corse-chambres-hotes.com; ❻–❽), hidden deep in the olive groves and maquis above Figari. From the outside, its rustic granite shepherds' cottages look typical of the far south, but the interior decor of moulded plaster, wood and coloured tiles combine to create a romatic feel to the rooms. Plus you get to slosh around in a glorious overflow pool. Head for Tarrabuceta via the D22/D522, then follow to D22 west towards Poggiale until you see a sign for Piscia on your right. The B&B lies a few twisting kilometres further up the mountain.

Roccapina and the Queen-Emperor's jewels

The Baie de Roccapina witnessed one of the most notorious **shipwrecks** of the nineteenth century when, on the night of April 17, 1887, the luxury P&O steam liner *Tasmania* ran aground onto the treacherous Des Moines rocks a short way out to sea. En route to Southampton from Bombay, she was carrying in her holds a trunk containing precious gems sent by the rajahs of India to Queen Victoria on her jubilee – worth an estimated eight times the value of the entire ship itself. Once they learned of the nature of the cargo, rescuers began to search for the trunk, but it was eventually picked up by crew members of a salvage vessel, the *Stella*, three weeks later. Local legend has it, however, that some of the jewels found their way into the possession of the bandit **Barrittonu**, who used to hide out in the hollows around the Lion de Roccapina. No one has ever proven this rumour to be true, though it is known that a purse of Indian diamonds sent as part of the gift to the Queen-Emperor was never recovered; its whereabouts are still the subject of speculation.

Bonifacio and around

BONIFACIO (Bonifaziu) enjoys a superbly isolated situation at Corsica's southernmost point, a narrow peninsula of dazzling white limestone creating a town site unlike any other on the island. The **haute ville**, a maze of narrow streets flanked by tall Genoese tenements, rises seamlessly out of sheer cliffs that have been hollowed and striated by the wind and waves, while on the landward side the deep cleft between the peninsula and the mainland forms a perfect natural harbour. A haven for boats for centuries, the anchorage is nowadays dominated by a swish marina which attracts yachts from all around the Mediterranean.

Separated from the rest of the island by an expanse of maquis, Bonifacio has maintained a certain temperamental detachment from the rest of Corsica, and is distinctly more Italian than French in atmosphere. It has its own dialect based on Ligurian Italian, a legacy from the days when it was practically an independent Genoese town. The *haute ville* retains Renaissance features found only here, and, with Sardinia just a stone's throw away, much of the property in the area is owned by Mafiosi and smart Italians.

Such a place has its inevitable drawbacks: exorbitant prices, overwhelming crowds in July and August, and a commercial cynicism that's atypical of Corsica as a whole. However, the old town forms one of the most arresting spectacles in the Mediterranean, and warrants at least a day-trip. If you plan to come in peak season, try to get here early in the day well before the bus parties arrive at around 10am.

A brief history of Bonifacio

It could be that Bonifacio's first documented appearance is as the town of the cannibalistic Laestrygonians in **The Odyssey**; Homer's description of an "excellent harbour, closed in on all sides by an unbroken ring of precipitous cliffs, with two bold headlands facing each other at the mouth so as to leave

▲ Bonifacio

only a narrow channel in between" fits the port well. The unploughed land that Odysseus comes across inland of the harbour could be a reference to the plain beyond the Bonifacio promontory, and it's also possible that the Neolithic tribes that once lived in this area were the barbaric attackers of Odysseus's crew.

In Roman times there was a village on this site, but the town really came into being in 828 AD, when Count Bonifacio of Tuscany built a castle on the peninsula. Like other settlements on the Corsican coast, this one suffered continuous pirate raids, but its key position in the Mediterranean made various powers covet the port. Subject of a dispute between Pisa and Genoa in 1187, Bonifacio eventually fell to the Genoese, who then proceeded to massacre the local population and replace them with Ligurians, to whom they offered exemption from tax and customs duty in their ports. Two hundred and fifty families duly settled here, and soon the town developed into a mini-republic with its own constitution and laws, governed by elected magistrates called Anziani.

In 1420 **Alfonso V** of Aragon set his sights on Corsica, and for five months his fleet blockaded the port, hoping to starve the Bonifaciens into submission. Every citizen joined in the defence of the citadelle, with clergymen, women and children flinging wooden beams, rocks and blinding chalk dust down on the attackers – they even tried to demoralize the enemy by pelting them with cheese, an action masterminded by one Marguerita Bobbia, whose ingenuity is commemorated by a street named after her in the old town. Eventually, a boat was built inside the citadelle by the famished defenders, lowered onto the sea from the clifftop and dispatched to seek help from Genoa. Seven galleons were immediately sent to help the Bonifaciens, but they were delayed by contrary winds. Only by donning the armour of their dead soldiers, ringing all the church bells and parading around the town ramparts, were the last survivors of the siege able to buy the time needed for their Genoese rescuers to arrive. When the ships finally appeared, shortly after Christmas, the resolve of the Aragonese was decidedly weakened; they decamped shortly after. The Bonifacien bluff had turned the battle.

Another celebrated siege occurred in 1554, when the town was recovering from an outbreak of plague that had claimed two-thirds of the population. **Henri II** of France arrived with the Turkish fleet, led by the fearsome corsair Dragut. The town held on through eighteen days and nights of cannon fire, and then a member of the eminent Cattacciolo family was dispatched to Genoa to raise help. He was seized on his return by the Turks, who forced him to carry a forged letter refusing them the assistance of the republic, a ploy that brought about Bonifacio's surrender. The invaders pillaged the town, which was then rescued by Sampiero Corso. There followed a brief period of French rule, which came to an end when the Treaty of Cateau Cambresis returned Corsica to Genoa in 1559.

Thereafter the Genoese port enjoyed relative prosperity until the late eighteenth century, when the French gained control of the island. No longer permitted their special autonomy, the merchants moved away and the town suffered a commercial decline that was reversed really only with the advent of tourism.

Arrival and information

To get from **Figari airport**, 17km north of Bonifacio, you'll have to take a taxi into town – around €45–50. Eurocorse Voyages' **buses** to and from Ajaccio and Porto Vecchio stop in the car park by the **marina**. Drivers can either pay to park here or at one of the other *parking payants* dotted further up the valley; there are

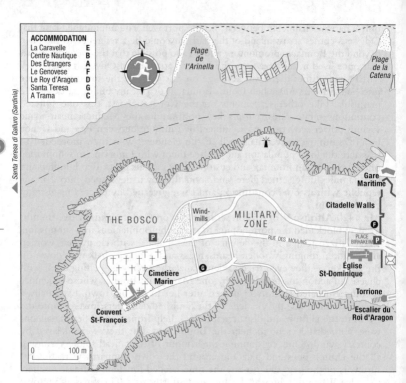

also four more municipal car parks up in the Bosco, at the west end of the *haute ville*, reached via avenue Générale-de-Gaulle. The **tourist office** (July–Sept daily 9am–8pm; Oct–June Mon–Fri 9am–12.30pm & 2–5.15pm; ☎04 95 73 11 88, ⓦwww.bonifacio.fr) is at the bottom of rue Fred-Scamaroni.

Accommodation

Finding accommodation can be a chore, as Bonifacio's few **hotels** are quickly booked up in peak season; if you want to stay centrally, ring well in advance. Be prepared, too, for higher-than-average tariffs. With the exception of the *Araguina*, the nearest campsites are all a drive away along the road to Porto Vecchio.

Hotels

La Caravelle 35 quai J. Comparetti ☎04 95 73 00 03, ⓦwww.hotel-caravelle-corse.com. Old-established place in a prime location on the quayside, though rooms (spread over five floors) are small for the price. Secure parking is available – if you're driving, turn right up the road past the hospital (towards the citadelle), and look for the rear entrance to the hotel on your right. ➐–➑

Centre Nautique The marina ☎04 95 73 02 11, ⓦwww.centre-nautique.com. Chic but relaxed hotel on the waterfront, fitted out with mellow wood and nautical charts. All rooms are tastefully furnished and consist of two levels connected by a spiral staircase. The best upmarket option in town, although prices reflect the hotel's popularity among wealthy Americans. ➐

Des Étrangers 4 av Sylvère-Bohn ☎04 95 73 01 09, ⓦhoteldesetrangers.ifrance.com. Simple double-glazed rooms (the more expensive ones have TV and a/c) facing the main road, just up from the port. Nothing special, but pretty good value for Bonifacio. April–Oct. ➌–➍

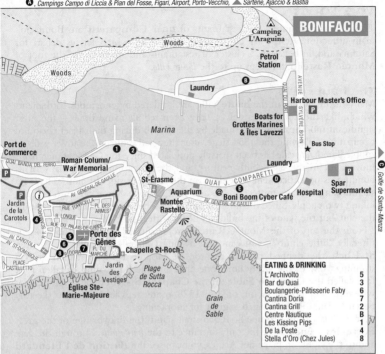

Le Genovese The citadelle ☎ 04 95 73 12 34, ⓦ www.hotel-genovese.com. The only luxury hotel in the *haute ville*, hence the sky-high rates (from €190–210 per double in April–June & Sept). There are views over the marina from some rooms, and a pool with teak deck (for which they controversially demolished parts of the old town walls). ⑨

Le Roy d'Aragon 13 quai J. Comparetti ☎ 04 95 73 03 99, ⓦ www.royaragon.com. Three-star overlooking the marina with better-than-average off-season discounts. Some of the rooms are small, but the pricier ones have sunny interconnecting terraces looking across the port. ⑦

Santa Teresa quartier St-François ☎ 04 95 73 11 32, ⓦ www.hotel-santateresa.com. Large three-star on the clifftop overlooking the Cimetière Marin, worth a mention for its stupendous views across the straits to Sardinia. Not all the rooms are sea-facing, though, so ask for "*vue mer avec balcon*" when you book. ⑧

A Trama 1.5km from Bonifacio along the route de Santa Manza ☎ 04 95 73 17 17, ⓦ a-trama.com. Discreet three-star, hidden behind a screen of maquis, palms, pines and dry-stone chalk walls. The rooms, all with private terraces, are grouped around a garden and pool, and there's a classy restaurant (*Le Clos Vatel*). Expensive (€161 per double) in high summer, but more affordable off-season. ⑧–⑨

Campsites

L'Araguina av Sylvère-Bohn, opposite the Total petrol station ☎ 04 95 73 02 96, ⓦ www .campingaraguina.fr. The closest place to town, but unwelcoming, horrendously cramped and with inadequate washing and toilet facilities. Avoid unless desperate. April–Sept.

Campo di Liccia 3km north towards Porto Vecchio, opposite *U Farniente* ☎ 04 95 73 03 09, ⓦ www.campingdiliccia.com. Well shaded and large, so you're guaranteed a place. April–Oct.

Pian del Fosse 4km out of town on the route de Santa Manza ☎ 04 95 73 16 34, ⓦ www .piandelfosse.com. Big three-star site with a pizzeria-restaurant, shop and nice pool. Very clean, peaceful and quiet in June & Sept, and well placed for the beaches. April to mid-Oct.

The Town

The lively cafés, hotels and restaurants of **quai Comparetti** are Bonifacio's main attraction. At the far end lies the port, from which ferries depart for Sardinia and, in between, a cluster of restaurants and shops lies at the foot of **Montée Rastello**, the steps up to the *haute ville*.

The haute ville

Many of the houses in the **haute ville** are bordered by enormous battlements which, like the houses themselves, have been rebuilt many times – the most significant modifications were made by the French during their brief period of occupation following the 1554 siege, after they had reduced the town walls to rubble. The *haute ville* has been sparsely populated since the Genoese merchants moved out in the eighteenth century, and the precariousness of many of its buildings is no enticement to settle – on the southeast side the houses have no surrounding wall to protect them, and in 1966 one house fell into the sea, killing two people. Since then, various plans have been put forward to reinforce the cliff, but the state of the buildings is still a great problem.

From the top of the Montée Rastello steps, dubbed locally as the *grimpette* (literally "little climb"), you can cross avenue Général-de-Gaulle to **Montée St-Roch**, the stepped path at the top of Montée Rastello, which gives a stunning view of the white limestone cliffs and the huge lump of fallen rock face called the **Grain de Sable**. At the **Chapelle St-Roch**, built on the spot where the last plague victim died in 1528, more steps lead down to the tiny beach of Sutta Rocca, which is great for snorkelling.

At the top of the Montée St-Roch steps stands the drawbridge of the great **Porte des Gênes**, once the only entrance to the *haute ville*. Through the gate and to the right, on place des'Armes, you can see the **Bastion de l'Étendard** (July & Aug daily 10am–9pm; April–June & Sept Mon–Sat 11am–5.30pm; €2.50), sole remnant of the fortifications destroyed during the siege of 1554. Inside is a small museum whose only noteworthy exhibit is a facsimile of the Dame de Bonifacio, a remarkably intact prehistoric skeleton of a woman found in a cave shelter near the town (the original is housed at the Musée Départementale in Levie: see p.220). You can also climb over the battlements to the tiny **Jardin des Véstiges**, which affords the *haute ville*'s best views of the cliffs to the east.

Back in the square, a few paces from the bastion lies **rue des Deux-Empereurs**, where at no. 4 you'll see the flamboyant marble escutcheon of the Cattacciolo family, one of many such adornments on the houses of this quarter. In 1541, the emperor Charles V, having been caught in Bonifacio by a storm, stayed in this house as a guest of Filippo Cattacciolo; after the departure of his illustrious visitor, Cattacciolo shot the horse he had loaned to him, on the grounds that nobody else was worthy to ride the poor beast after it had supported the ruler of half the known world. Opposite stands the house in which Napoleon resided for three months in 1793.

Cutting down to rue Palais-du-Garde brings you to **Église Ste-Marie-Majeure**, originally Romanesque but restored in the eighteenth century, though the richly sculpted belfry dates from the fourteenth century. The facade is hidden by a **loggia** where the Genoese municipal officers used to dispense justice in the days of the republic. If you look up you can see buttresses connecting the houses in the adjoining streets to the roof of the church – these were vital not just as support but also for draining rainwater into a huge cistern underneath the porch, which provided the town with water in times of siege and during the dry summers. The church's treasure, a relic of the **True Cross** said to have been brought to Bonifacio by St Helena, the mother of Constantine, was saved from a shipwreck in the Straits of Bonifacio; for centuries after, the citizens would take the relic to the edge of the cliff and pray for calm seas whenever storms raged. It is nowadays kept in the sacristy, along with an ivory cask containing relics of St Boniface. In the main body of the church the highlight is the marble **tabernacle** to the left of the door; decorated with a bas-relief carving of Christ supported by eight glum-faced cherubs, it's thought to have been created by a north Italian sculptor in 1565. The holy water stoup below it is a third-century **sarcophagus**.

Rue du Palais-de-Garde, which runs alongside the church, is one of the most handsome streets in Bonifacio, with its closed arcades and double-arched windows separated by curiously stunted columns. The oldest houses along here did not originally have doors; the inhabitants used to climb up a ladder, which they would pull up behind them to prevent a surprise attack, while the ground floor was used as a stable and grain store.

South of here, rue Doria leads towards the Bosco; at the end of this road a left turn down rue des Pachas will bring you to the **Torrione**, a 35-metre-high lookout post built in 1195 on the site of Count Bonifacio's castle. Descending the cliff, the **Escalier du Roi d'Aragon**'s 187 steps (June–Sept daily 11am–5.30pm; €2) were said to have been built in one night by the Aragonese in an attempt to gain the town in 1420, but in fact they had already been in existence for some time and were used by the people to fetch water from a well.

The Bosco

To the west of the tower lies the **Bosco**, a quarter named after the wood that used to stand here in the tenth century. In those days a community of hermits dwelt on the spot, but the limestone plateau now lies open and desolate. The only sign of life comes from the military barracks – home of the IIième REP Foreign Legion Parachute Regiment until it decamped to Calvi – where a couple of hundred youngsters now sweat out their national service. The entrance to the Bosco is marked by the **Église St-Dominique**, a rare example of Corsican Gothic architecture – it was built in 1270, most probably by the Templars, and later handed over to the Dominicans.

Beyond the church, **rue des Moulins** leads onto the ruins of three mills dating from 1283, two of them decrepit, the third restored. Behind them stands a memorial to the 750 people who died when the troop ship *Sémillante* ran aground here in 1855, on its way to the Crimea, one of the many disasters wreaked by the straits.

The tip of the plateau is occupied by the **Cimetière Marin**, its white crosses standing out sharply against the deep blue of the sea. Open until dusk, the cemetery is a fascinating place to explore, with its flamboyant mausoleums displaying a jumble of architectural ornamentations: stuccoed facades, Gothic arches and classical columns. Next to the cemetery stands the **Couvent St-François**, allegedly founded after St Francis sought shelter in a nearby cave – the story goes that the convent was the town's apology to the holy man, over whom a local maid had nearly poured a bucket of slops. Immediately to the south, the **Esplanade St-François** commands fine views across the bay to Sardinia.

Eating, drinking and nightlife

Eating possibilities in Bonifacio might seem unlimited, but standards rarely befit the locations, especially when it comes to the chintzy restaurants down in the marina, few of which merit their exorbitant prices – the places in the *haute ville* generally offer better value for money. For much of the day and in the evening, the **bars** and **cafés** lining the quai Comparetti are the social focus of town, but for serious nightlife you'll have to head for *Via Notte* near Porto Vecchio (see p.256).

For a definitively Bonifacien **breakfast**, you can buy a *pain de morts* warm out of the oven at the *Patisserie Sorba* (follow the smell of baking bread to the bottom of the Montée Rastello steps) and take it to *Bar du Quai* a couple of doors down.

Restaurants

L'Archivolto rue de l'Archivolto, just off the place de l'Église ☏ 04 95 73 17 48. With its candlelit, antique- and junk-filled interior, this would be the best place to eat in the *haute ville* were the cooking a little less patchy. But it still gets packed out for its aubergines with goat's cheese and other Bonifacien specialities: reservations recommended. Menus €16–20; or around €35 à la carte. Easter–Oct.

Boulangerie-Pâtisserie Faby 4 rue St-Jean-Baptiste, *haute ville*. Tiny local bakery serving Bonifacien treats such as *pain des morts* (sweet buns with walnuts and raisins), *fugazzi* (*galettes* flavoured with eau de vie, orange, lemon and aniseed) and *migliaccis* (buns made with fresh ewe's cheese), in addition to the usual range of spinach and *brocciu bastelles*, baked here in the traditional way – on stone.

Cantina Doria 27 rue Doria ☏ 04 95 73 50 49. Huge portions of down-to-earth *plats corses* at down-to-earth prices, served in an old vaulted dining hall. Their popular three-course €18 menu – which includes the house speciality, aubergines *à la bonifacienne* – offers unbeatable value for the *haute ville*, though you'll soon bump up your bill if you succumb to the temptations of the excellent wine selection, featuring Domaine Toraccia (available in half bottles) and the zesty Abbatucci Cuvée Faustina.

Cantina Grill Quai Banda del Ferro ☏ 04 95 70 49 86. Same *patron* as the popular *Cantina Doria* in the citadelle, but down in the marina and with a better choice of seafood (octopus risotto, swordfish steaks, fish soup). They also do succulent *grillades* with a selection of

different sauces. The food is dependably fresh, well prepared and presented, and the prices great value.

Centre Nautique The marina, in the hotel of the same name. Bonifacio's most chic breakfast venue: coffee, hot croissants, baguettes and freshly squeezed orange juice on a cool wood deck, with optimal views of the bastion across the marina. Well worth splashing out €10 for, but get here early for the best tables. Menus from €19.

De la Poste 6 rue Fred-Scamaroni. A cheap and cheerful pizza place serving oven-baked lasagne, spaghetti *al brocciu*, stuffed mussels and delicious pizzas (€9–12). Particularly good-value *formules* and *menus fixes* from €13.50.

Stella d'Oro (Chez Jules) 23 rue Doria, near Église St-Jean-Baptiste ☏ 04 95 73 03 63. Top-notch Corsican dishes including definitive *merrizzane* (stuffed aubergine) – the local speciality. They also do a famous spaghetti in lobster sauce and ravioli *brocciu*. Most main courses €20–25; menu at €23 (not available July & Aug).

Bars

Bar du Quai Marina. Run-of-the-mill café that's popular with locals, and an excellent spot for a croissant and coffee breakfast, as its terrace catches the morning sun and breeze off the water.

Les Kissing Pigs Quai Banda del Ferro ☏ 04 95 73 56 99. Curiously themed wine bar boasting the world's largest collection of kissing pig photos and other snout-related ephemera. They serve all the island's top wines (by the glass and carafe, as well as bottle), accompanied by fragrant *charcuterie maison* (try the pungent two-year-old *figatellu*), *grillades*, flans and salads. Open late.

Listings

Airport Figari, 17km north of town, off the D859 ☏ 04 95 71 10 31, 🌐 www.figari.aeroport.fr.

Banks and exchange Societé Générale, 2 rue St-Érasme, at the foot of the steps to the *haute ville*, has an ATM (as does the post office; see below). Avoid the bureaux de change dotted around town – they charge extortionate commission rates.

Bookshops There are a couple on the quai Comparetti, of which the Librairie-Papeterie Simoni is the largest, selling a range of imported newspapers, pulp fiction and guidebooks.

Car rental Avis, quai Banda-del-Ferro ☏ 04 95 73 01 28; Citer, quai Noel-Beretti ☏ 04 95 73 13 16; Hertz, quai Banda-del-Ferro ☏ 04 95 73 06 41.

Ferries to Sardinia

Ferries for **Santa Teresa di Gallura**, Sardinia, leave the *gare maritime* at the far southern end of the marina. Mobyline (☎04 95 73 00 29, ⊛www.mobylines.it) and Saremar (☎04 95 73 00 96, ⊛www.saremar.it) operate ten to twelve daily crossings between mid-July and September, reduced to between four and seven daily from March to mid-July and September, with only two or three daily (with Saremar) the rest of the year. The one-hour crossing costs €8–10, plus €21–37 per (small) car. You can get tickets for both operators from Agence Gazano, Port de Bonifacio ☎04 95 73 02 47.

All of the above also have branches at Figari airport.

Diving Full information about the superb diving possibilities in the south of Corsica – including the famous "Mérouville" site, where you're guaranteed a close encounter with huge grouper fish – is available from Bonifacio's two accredited schools: Barakdouda, av. Sylver Bohn, (☎04 95 73 13 02, ⊛club.barakouda.free.fr); and Dolinfu Biancu, Pinarollu (☎06 21 46 71 49, ⊛pagesperso -orange.fr/dolfinu.biancu).

Hospital 1 route de Santa-Manza, at the entrance to town ☎04 95 73 95 73. For an ambulance,

phone ☎04 95 73 06 95 or 04 95 73 06 94.

Laundry Laverie Automatique, northeast side of the port.

Motorbike and mountain-bike rental Corse Moto Services, quai Nova, on the north side of the port ☎04 95 73 15 16, ⊛www.corse-moto -service.com.

Pharmacy 17 quai Comparetti.

Police Route de Santa-Manza ☎04 95 73 00 17.

Post office On place Carrega in the *haute ville* (Mon–Fri 9am–noon & 2–5pm, Sat 9am–noon).

Taxis Louis di Meglio ☎04 95 73 02 86 or Nicole Horrach ☎06 62 35 79 50.

Around Bonifacio

The views of the citadelle from the cliffs at the head of the Montée Rastello (reached via a pathway running left from the top of the steps) are impressive enough, but they're not a patch on the spectacular panorama to be had from the sea. Throughout the day, a flotilla of excursion **boats** ferries visitors out to the best vantage points, en route to a string of caves and other landmarks only accessible by water, including the **Îles Lavezzi**, a scattering of small islets where the troop ship *Sémillante* was wrecked in 1855. The whole experience of bobbing around to an amplified running commentary is about as touristy as Bonifacio gets, but it's well worth enduring just to round the mouth of the harbour and see the *haute ville* perched atop the famous chalk cliffs, or to experience the translucent waters around the islands offshore.

With more time, you can sidestep the crowds completely by heading off on one of the wonderful coast walks from the town: southeast towards the lighthouse on **Capo Pertusato**, Corsica's southernmost point; or west to **Ermitage de la Trinité**, an old convent with fine views across the straits to Sardinia.

With the notable exception of the horseshoe-shaped plage de Rondinara, midway between Bonifacio and Porto Vecchio, the **beaches** along this part of the coast are generally smaller and less appealing than most in southern Corsica, although those fringing the Golfe de Santa Manza, to the north, are set amid some fine scenery. Over the past two decades, this whole area has become the preserve of an international jet set, whose luxury villas, golf courses and helipads are sometimes the only blots on otherwise unspoilt islets and coves.

Ermitage de la Trinité

The **Ermitage de la Trinité**, 7km west of Bonifacio off the N196, stands on a site that has been inhabited since prehistoric times and was a hermitage right

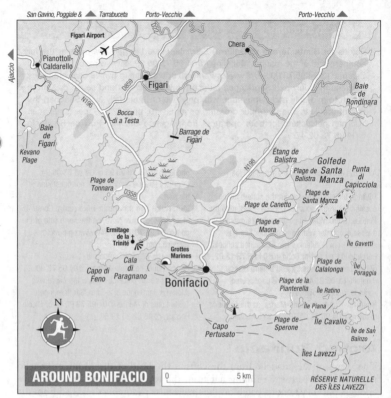

AROUND BONIFACIO

| 0 | 5 km |

RÉSERVE NATURELLE
DES ÎLES LAVEZZI

at the beginning of the Christianization of the island. Heavily restored in the thirteenth century, the convent sits beside a terrace of olive trees against a backdrop of gigantic eroded outcrops. There's a fine view of Bonifacio from here, and an even better one if you follow the track to the left before you reach the building, which arrives at the **Mont de la Trinité** after about fifteen minutes' gentle climbing.

Capo Pertusato

The deeply scored limestone cliffs southeast of Bonifacio culminate in the wide headland of **Capo Pertusato** (Pierced Cape), a steepish climb of about 45 minutes from Bonifacio. At the end of the walk you'll be rewarded with an incredible seascape embracing Sardinia, the rocky islands of Lavezzi and Cavallo, and Bonifacio itself, just discernible to the west. Leaving town along the D58 almost immediately bear right along the D260, a narrow road hugging the cliffside as far as the **Phare du Pertusato**, the lighthouse at the edge of the point. Drivers should take extra care as the road out here is very narrow, with no room for passing and no barriers to protect your car from the chalk walls.

Beaches around Bonifacio

Visible from the north side of the *haute ville*, the nearest accessible beach coves to Bonifacio, **plage de la Catena** and **plage de l'Arinella**, are small and picturesque but catch a lot of flotsam and oil pollution from the passing maritime traffic. The **walk** to them is very pleasant, however, beginning at a track just before *Camping L'Araguina* (see map, p.244).

On Corsica's southernmost tip, reached via a narrow but easily motorable road, a trio of small coves are the most popular beaches in this area. The first, **plage de Sperone**, is a tiny turquoise cove overlooked by luxury villas. Walk south around the headland for fifteen minutes and you'll reach the larger **plage de Pianterella**, a pearl-white lagoon with calm water that's ideal for children (and shallow enough at low tide to allow you to walk to the tiny Île Piana just offshore). It's overlooked by the remains of a **Roman fort** and villa complex, as well as the island's top eighteen-hole **golf course** (Ⓦwww .sperone.net), 72 hectares of immaculate turf installed with the help of huge subsidies from the regional assembly.

Boat trips to the grottes marines and Îles Lavezzi

From the moment you arrive in Bonifacio, you'll be pestered by touts from the many boat companies running excursions out of the harbour. There are more than a dozen of these, but they all offer more or less the same routes, at the same prices.

Lasting between thirty and forty-five minutes, the shorter trips take you out along the cliffs to the **grottes marines** (sea caves) and *calanches* (inlets) below the old town; tickets cost €12–15 depending on the demand and how well you can haggle. The largest of the three caves, the **Grotte du Sdragonatu**, is worth the money on its own – a magnificent grotto where the water takes on an extraordinary violet luminosity and the rock walls, encrusted with stalactites and arches, glitter with the colours of amethyst, indigo and gold. Guides like to point out that when viewed from directly below, the hole in the roof of the chamber resembles the shape of Corsica.

Longer excursions out to the **Îles Lavezzi**, part of the archipelago to the east of the straits of Bonifacio, cost around €23–27. Most companies offer a shuttle (*navette*) service, allowing you to spend as much time as you like on the islands before returning. Boats go out past the Grain de Sable and Phare du Pertusato and then moor at the main island of **Lavezzi**, beside the **cimetière Achiarino**. Buried in two walled cemeteries are the victims of the *Sémillante* shipwreck of 1855, in which 773 crew members and soldiers bound for the Crimean War were drowned after their vessel was blown onto the rocks. The bodies were washed ashore over the following fortnight, but so disfigured were they that only one (that of the captain) could be identified; the rest are interred in unnamed graves. A stone pyramid on the western tip of the isle commemorates the tragedy, the worst ever shipwreck in the history of the Mediterranean.

Classified as a nature reserve since 1982, the islets are home to several rare species of **wild flower**, such as the yellow-horned poppy, the white sea daffodil and the stonecrop, distinguished by its fleshy red leaves beneath heads of small blue flowers. The islands also offer some fabulous **snorkelling**, and there are some exquisite shell sand **beaches** to swim off. A network of footpaths runs between them, well waymarked, as you're not permitted to wander off into the fragile vegetation.

Further north, **Cavallo** island is jammed with heavily guarded private villas belonging to tycoons, film stars and royalty (among them Princess Caroline of Monaco). Both it and its adjoining islet, **San Bainzo**, were the sites of Roman quarries, which feature on most of the boats' half-day excursions; huge monolithic columns lie at the water's edge, cut from horizontal trenches in the rock nearby and discarded, seemingly in haste. The stone quarried here was not used in Corsica, but transported to the mainland to fuel the decadent building boom at the end of the Roman Empire. Most touching of the remains here is an image of Hercules Saxanus, the patron saint of hard labour, carved by slaves on the face of a large boulder.

A better place to escape the summer masses lies further around the coast at **plage de Calalonga**. To get there, head east of town on the D58 and take the first turning right after around 3km. Passing a series of heavily guarded military communications complexes, this narrows rapidly, deteriorating into a badly rutted *piste*, at the end of which lies a tiny, roughly made car park.

For details of **hotels** in this area, see p.244.

The Golfe de Santa Manza

A bit more off the beaten track are the beaches lining the **Golfe de Santa Manza**, northeast of Bonifacio along the D58. The first of these, **plage de Maora**, lies at the far west end of the gulf, reached by a lane running north off the crossroads of the D60 and D58. A narrow curve of pink granite grit with a small *buvette*, it's frequented mainly by tourists from the surrounding *villages de vacances*. Further around the bay, the views improve and the coves, backed by the road, attract increasing numbers of watersports enthusiasts as you approach the **plage de Santa Manza**, where the route ends. Again, the beach itself is a bit of a disappointment, but it does give access to a wild stretch of coast that has plenty of potential for walking.

Plage de Canetto and plage de Balistra

Two of the least-frequented beaches in the Bonifacio region line the north coast of the Golfe de Santa Manza. With a backdrop of weathered chalk cliffs, **plage de Canetto** is the most picturesque, but hard to reach. Heading north on the main Porto Vecchio road, turn right directly opposite the *Camping di Liccia*, 3km out of town, and follow the signs for the luxury four-star *Hôtel Capu Biancu*, until you reach a fork after 4.5km. Bear left here (not right, which will take you to the hotel) and drop down the south bank of a stream; the beach lies 500m further on.

Plage de Balistra is the next beach up the coast, 5km north of the Canetto turning down a very rough four-kilometre *piste* that's barely passable in a regular car – look for the hand-drawn signpost on the main road (though bear in mind you'll probably be contravening the terms of your rental agreement if you attempt it in a hire vehicle). The largest and least crowded in this area, the beach has nothing more behind it than a small *buvette* and brackish lagoon, flanked by low hills. From its southern end, you can swim through a jumble of colossal chalk outcrops that have collapsed into the sea from the cliffs behind and shelter diverse sea life – a fine **snorkelling** spot.

Rondinara

A perfect shell-shaped cove of turquoise water enclosed by soft dunes and a pair of twin headlands, **Rondinara** looks like most people's idea of a paradise Pacific lagoon. It's sufficiently off the beaten track to remain relatively peaceful (outside school holidays). Facilities are minimal, limited to a smart wooden beach restaurant and paying car park. There's also virtually no shade, so if you intend to spend much time here in summer, come armed with a parasol.

Set only 400m behind the bay, a large **campsite**, the *Camping Rondinara* (☏04 95 70 43 15, ⓦ www.rondinara.fr; mid-May to Sept), ensures the beach gets quite crowded in high summer. It's one of the area's better sites – spacious and well equipped, with flat, terraced pitches and an enormous pool – and tariffs are low considering the location. Above it, a scattering of beautiful holiday villas nestles on maquis-covered hillsides, looking out over the bay.

The Porto Vecchio region

Nowhere on the island has been so thoroughly given over to tourism as the area around **Porto Vecchio**, thanks to the wealth of white-sand beaches and turquoise bays that indent the coastline around this former Genoese port. Shaded by a canopy of pines, thousands of manicured holiday villas and *villages de vacances* carpet the headlands and hills behind the beaches, while the town itself, a seasonal ferry harbour, seems entirely populated by Italians in summer.

If you've wondered where those Seychelles-style beach shots might be that shine from every postcard rack on the island, head south from Porto Vecchio to **Palombaggia**, Corsica's most-photographed beach, or to the translucent waters of **Santa Giulia**. Bear in mind, though, that these photos tend to be taken in winter, when the beaches are deserted, and that during the summer you won't be able to slot a postcard between the sun worshippers crammed onto them. The same goes for the bays north of Porto Vecchio – **San Ciprianu** and **Pinarellu** – preludes to the near unbroken beach running from here all the way up the eastern plain to Bastia.

While you're in the area, make time for some of the **prehistoric sites** dotted around Porto Vecchio: the Bronze Age Casteddu d'Araggiu to the north, and the Torréan monument of Tappa near Ceccia. Inland, the **Massif de l'Ospédale** holds plenty of pine-shaded walks with fine views over the plains to Sardinia – the perfect antidote to the heat and bright light of the coast.

Porto Vecchio

Set on a hill in the most sheltered corner of a deep gulf, **PORTO VECCHIO**, in the southeast of the island, was rated by James Boswell as one of "the most distinguished harbours in Europe". Pleasure boats, yachts and international ferries still crowd the port, but trade has long given way to tourism as the town's *raison d'être*. Its popularity as a holiday centre derives more from the proximity of the island's most spectacular beaches, but you could do worse than spend an afternoon or evening here. Once beyond the unpromising outskirts – marred by roundabouts, light industry and patches of insalubrious marshland – things improve considerably as you approach the old **citadelle** that still forms the hub of the town, with its leafy church square and picturesque backstreets, lined by restaurant terraces and designer boutiques.

Porto Vecchio was founded in 1539 as a second Genoese stronghold on the east coast, Bastia being well established in the north. The location was perfect: close to the unexploited and fertile plain, the site benefited from secure high land and a sheltered gulf. Unfortunately, however, the Genoese hadn't counted on the mosquito problem, and within months malaria had wiped out the first Ligurian settlers. Sampiero Corso occupied the port for a brief period in 1564, having failed to take Ajaccio, but Genoa got it back a few months later, and things began to take off soon after, mainly thanks to the cork industry, which thrived until the twentieth century. Today a third of Corsica's wine is exported from here, but most revenue comes from the rich tourists who flock to the town each year.

There's not much to see around the centre of town, apart from the well-preserved **fortress** and the small grid of ancient streets backing onto the main **place de la République**. East of the square you can't miss the **Porte Génoise**, which frames a delightful expanse of sea and through which you'll find the quickest route down to the modern **marina**, lined with cafés and restaurants. Visible on the southeastern fringes, a grid of shallow basins comprises what remains of the town's **salt pans**, now disused.

Arrival and information

Porto Vecchio doesn't have a **bus** station; instead, the various bus companies arrive and depart from outside their agents' offices on the edge of the old town. Coming from Bastia or the eastern plain (Solenzara or Aléria) with Rapides Bleus, you'll be dropped at the Corsicatours office at 7 rue Jean-Jaurès. Rapides Bleus also runs shuttle buses to and from plage de Santa Giulia four times daily in the summer. Eurocorse Voyages operates fast services to Ajaccio via Bonifacio, Sartène and Propriano; its buses stop outside the Trinitours office on rue Pasteur, just north of the citadelle; they also have a seasonal *navette* to Palombaggia (2 or 3 daily July & Aug). There are also two daily departures from the same place to **Pinarellu** via Cala Rossa with Autocars Bradesi. Île de Beauté Voyages, at 13 rue Général-de-Gaulle, act as agents for Balési Évasion, whose minibus connects Porto Vecchio with Ajaccio via Bavella and Alta Rocca. For

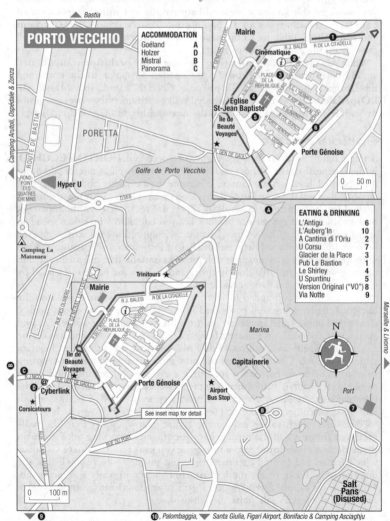

PORTO VECCHIO

ACCOMMODATION
Goéland	A
Holzer	D
Mistral	B
Panorama	C

Bastia ▲

Camping Arutoli, Ospédale & Zonza

ROUTE DE BASTIA

PORETTA

Golfe de Porto Vecchio

ROND-POINT DES QUATRES CHEMINS

Hyper U

Camping La Matonara

RUE DES OLIVIERS

RUE GÉNÉRAL LECLERC

Trinitours ★

Mairie

R. J. BALÉSI

PLACE DE LA RÉPUBLIQUE

Île de Beauté Voyages ★

Porte Génoise

RUE PASTEUR

Cyberlink ★

@

RUE NICOLA

RUE GÉN DE GAULLE

Corsicatours ★

R DE LA CITADELLE

Mairie

Cinématique
ⓘ

PLACE DE LA RÉPUBLIQUE

Église St-Jean Baptiste

Île de Beauté Voyages ★

R. GEN DE GAULLE

Porte Génoise

0   50 m

Marina

Capitainerie

Marseille & Livorno ►

N

Port

Airport Bus Stop ★

See inset map for detail

RUE DUPORT

Salt Pans (Disused)

EATING & DRINKING
L'Antigu	6
L'Auberg'In	10
A Cantina di l'Oriu	2
U Corsu	7
Glacier de la Place	3
Pub Le Bastion	1
Le Shirley	4
U Spuntinu	5
Version Original ("VO")	8
Via Notte	9

0   100 m

⑩, Palombaggia, ▼ Santa Giulia, Figari Airport, Bonifacio & Camping Asciaghju

more on services to and from Porto Vecchio, see Travel details on p.263 or visit
ⓦ www.corsicabus.org.

The town's efficient **tourist office**, just north of place de la République (July
& Aug Mon–Sat 9am–8pm, Sun 9am–1pm; June & Sept Mon–Sat 9am–1pm &
3–6pm; Oct–May Mon–Fri 9am–noon & 2–6pm, Sat 9am–noon; ☎04 95 70
09 58, ⓦ www.ot-portovecchio.com), is the best place to check transport
timetables. Its glossy brochure, *Destination Corse Sud*, is more thorough than
most such offerings, featuring aerial photographs of all the region's beaches in
addition to the usual listings.

Accommodation
Finding somewhere to stay in Porto Vecchio is only a problem during peak
season, when prices approach those of neighbouring Bonifacio. **Hotels** are
grouped around the old town, with a handful of more expensive places down
in the marina and out of town on the coast (shown on the map, p.259), while
campsites line the route north of the centre towards Pinarellu beach and
Bastia, and along the road to Palombaggia.

Hotels in the town
Goéland Port de Plaisance ☎04 95 70 14 15,
ⓦ www.hotelgoeland.com. Very pleasant hotel, with
large rooms, a convivial atmosphere and welcoming
owners, set in an excellent seaside location on a tiny
peninsula looking across the gulf, ensconced amid
pine trees and oleanders. Includes breakfast. ⑧–⑨
Holzer 12 rue Jean-Jaurès/rue Jean-Nicoli
☎04 95 70 05 93, ⓦ www.corse-eternelle.com.
Labyrinthine place with airless, boxed-in rooms, but
immaculately clean and very central. ⑤
Mistral rue Jean-Nicoli ☎04 95 70 08 53, ⓦ www
.lemistral.eu. Comfortable mid-range two-star, slightly
removed from the noisy centre of town. Classier than
the *Panorama* opposite, and fully a/c. ⑤
Panorama 12 rue Jean-Nicoli ☎04 95 70 07 96.
Basic pension-style place just above the old town,
with parking spaces and various types of rooms
(nos. 8 and 9 on the top floor are the cosiest,
though without toilets). Not all that well maintained,
but usually the cheapest in town. ③–④

Hotels around Porto Vecchio
Grand Hôtel de Cala Rossa Cala Rossa, near Lecci
di Porto Vecchio ☎04 95 71 61 51, ⓦ www.cala
-rossa.com. Beautifully designed luxury hotel
occupying a secluded cove lined by turquoise water
and a fine-sand beach, at the breezy northern end of
the Golfe de Porto Vecchio. Wooden decks, driftwood
beams and traditional terracotta tiles set the tone,
and the 52 a/c rooms, spread under the shade of
umbrella pines across a 72-hectare site, are bright,
private and modern. Extras include a large pool,
good childcare facilities, fitness centre, Michelin-
starred restaurant and 35-foot yacht. From €430 per
double low season, rising to €1000 and up from
May–Sept, when half board is obligatory. ⑨

Roc e Fiori Bocca dell Oro, 4km south ☎04 95 70
45 20, ⓦ www.rocefiori.com. Ersatz Mediterranean-
style "village" of fifteen-luminous rooms, suites and
apartments, painted in pretty lemon, pink and ochre
pastels amid rock gardens on the hillside above the
Palombaggia–Santa-Giulia strip. Very chic, but not
child-friendly. Doubles from €190–250 in season. ⑨
San Giovanni 2km southwest of the centre
along the D659, towards Arca ☎04 95 70
22 25, ⓦ www.hotel-san-giovanni.com. Thirty
comfortable chalet rooms in extensive landscaped,
flower-filled gardens. There's a good-sized pool,
plus complimentary mountain bikes, Jacuzzi,
sauna, tennis courts and table tennis. Good value
at this price, and peaceful. ⑥

Campsites
Arutoli 2km northwest along the D368 (route de
l'Ospédale) ☎04 95 70 12 73, ⓦ www.arutoli.com.
Large, well-equipped site. The enormous swimming
pool makes this a good option for families, and it's
handy for hikers arriving off the nearby Mare a
Mare Sud. June–Sept.
Asciaghju Bocca di l'Oro, 4km from Porto
Vecchio ☎04 95 70 37 87, ⓦ www.camping
asciaghju.com. Pick of the bunch within striking
distance of the beaches to the south. The ground is
rock hard, but there's plenty of shade, clean toilet
blocks and, due to the slope of the hillside, great
views over the secluded plage de Asciaghju, a 3min
walk away. Mid-June to mid-Sept.
La Matonara Carrefour des Quatre-Chemins
☎04 95 70 37 05, ⓦ www.lamatonara.com. Large
site shaded by cork trees, with clean *blocs sanitaires*
and washing machines. By far the best choice if you
don't have your own vehicle, as it's within walking
distance of the centre, but don't come here without
mosquito repellent. April–Oct.

Eating and drinking

With a few exceptions, most of Porto Vecchio's eating establishments are substandard tourist traps, but there are a few decent places where you can enjoy quality seafood and local specialities at affordable prices, and cheap and cheerful pizzerias and pasta places are dotted around the centre. Cafés line place de la République and cours Napoléon, which runs along the east side of the square.

L'Antigu rue Borgo ☏04 95 70 39 33. The row of restaurants along the east side of this medieval lane all boast wonderful *terrasses panoramiques* with exceptional views of the gulf, but none can match the quality of the cooking served here. The menu is Corsican gastronomy, but doesn't stray too far from its roots, using carefully sourced *produits du terroir*. For vegetarians, there's delicate *milliefeuille d'aubergines* with warm goat's cheese. Lunch menu €18, or €23 and €38 evenings. Closed Sun lunchtime.

L'Auberg'In 3km out of town along the route de Picovaggia ☏04 95 72 21 07. Housed in a converted *bergerie* up a dirt track on the eastern shore of the gulf, this popular little *auberge* serves great Moroccan food (chicken and lamb tagines, *harira* and mezes), in addition to a full Corsican menu. It's only 10min drive from the centre of town, but a world away from the bling and bustle. Count on €40–45 per head, plus wine.

A Cantina di l'Oriu 5 cours Napoléon. Essentially a Corsican produce shop selling top-quality cheese, charcuterie, wine, honey, jams and other local delicacies, with a small terrace tacked on the side where you can order various *formules*. Get there for "Happy Hour" (6.30–7.30pm), when they offer plates of strong mountain ham, bread and a glass of wine for €8. At other times, count on €13–16 for plates of assorted cured meats and olives.

U Corsu Port de Commerce ☏04 95 70 13 91. The best pizzas in town (€9–13.50), with finely baked bases, luscious home-made tomato sauces and dependably fresh ingredients; they also do a special *assiette végeterienne*. The location, down on the quayside of the ferry dock with a waterside terrace, is perfect too.

Le Shirley rue Joseph Pietri. Fast-food joint just off the place de l'Eglise offering the cheapest, most filling sit-down meals in the citadelle: copious salads, local pies, quiches and crêpes. Frequented as much by locals as tourists.

U Spuntinu place de l'Eglise ☏04 95 72 28 33. Corsican speciality deli, whose famous *assiette gourmande* (€15) – a selection of quality charcuterie, cheese, spinach pasties (*chaussons herbes*), savoury fritters (*migliacciu*) and mint omelettes – is served on *faux rustique* wooden tables opposite the church. Authentic and good value.

Version Original ("VO") Marina ☏04 95 70 38 75. Next to the port, this good-looking café, complete with polished steel tables and a wooden deck, serves designer sandwiches (€7) and salads (€12–14) named – somewhat arbitrarily – after film stars and directors.

Bars and nightlife

Apart from when the Italians swamp the town in August, **nightlife** is fairly low-key, revolving around the cafés in the square.

Glacier de la Place place de l'Eglise. Classiest of the cafés lining the square, offering a huge selection of beers and lagers from around the world, and *chocolat chaud* you can (literally) stand your spoon in. A good spot for breakfast, as they serve warm pastries. Prices inflate by thirty percent in July and Aug, but at other times aren't unreasonable given the location.

Pub Le Bastion rue de la Citadelle. Claiming to serve three hundred varieties of beer, this bar has one of Corsica's only dartboards, and stages live music – cheesy local rock bands – most weekends.

Via Notte on the south edge of town ☏04 95 72 02 12, ⓦwww.vianotte.com. Corsica's number-one nightspot: a full-on Italian-oriented place that stages internationally famous DJs in July & Aug (when admission charges and drink prices go through the roof) – about as sophisticated as the island's nightlife gets. To find it, head south of town on the Bonifacio road, cross the bridge and pass the Palombaggia turning, then take the second left after that, signposted for Bocca di l'Oru; the club is 500m further on. Women free before midnight.

Listings

Banks and exchange All the big banks have branches in the town centre and will change traveller's cheques. ATMs accepting Visa and other credit cards can be found at the post office; the

Société Générale on the Quatre-Chemins cross-roads near the Super U supermarket; and on the south wall of the Super U itself.

Car rental Europcar, route de Bastia ☎04 95 70 14 50; Hertz, in the marina ☎04 95 70 32 05; Rent-a-Car, route de Bonifacio ☎04 95 70 03 40.

Cinema Porto Vecchio holds the honour of being the site of Corsica's centre for cinematic arts, Cinémathèque, aka Casa di Lume, situated on the lane between the *mairie* and the post office, in the Espace de JP Rocca-Serra. It screens a regular programme of art-house movies, many of them about, or filmed in, Corsica. You can consult their listings onine at Ⓦwww.casadilume.com. Ruscana, an open-air cinema on route de Pinarellu, Ste-Lucie-de-Porto Vecchio (☎04 95 71 5 42), 11km north along the main highway, is the place to catch the summer blockbusters. Look for the posters at the tourist office in Porto Vecchio.

Diving Aztech, plage de Santa Giulia ☎04 95 70 22 67, Ⓦwww.divecorsica.com; CIP La Palanquée,

Les Marines, 500m south of town on the Bonifacio Rd ☎04 95 70 16 53, Ⓦvincent.caillier.free.fr; Club Plongée Kallisté, plage de Palombaggia ☎04 95 70 44 59. All can arrange trips to dive sites around the Îles Cerbicale, off Palombaggia, and the wreck of the *Pecorella*, lying 12m down at the north end of the gulf.

Internet access Cyberlink, rue Jean-Jaurès.

Mountain bike rental Années Jeunes, av Georges-Pompidou (between the port and Hyper-U) ☎04 95 70 36 50. VTTs from €18 per day.

Pharmacy Corner of rue Général-de-Gaulle and rue Général-Leclerc.

Taxis Campagnoli Corsi ☎06 07 21 88 39; Euro Sud Corse 06 22 78 04 87.

Theatre The Théâtre d'Été, a small open-air stage down behind the marina, hosts choral concerts and plays during the summer. Forthcoming events are advertised on posters around town, and in the tourist office.

Moving on from Porto Vecchio

Porto Vecchio's proximity to Figari airport means it is the first port of call for many independent travellers. Thankfully, it's well served by **public transport**, so you shouldn't have to spend more time here than you need.

By plane

Figari airport, 28km southwest, is served by weekly charter **flights** to various destinations in northern Europe, including London Gatwick, and by domestic departures to several cities on the French mainland. **Getting to Figari** without your own vehicle is straightforward during the summer, when a bus leaves three or four times daily from the marina; tickets cost €9 single. Timetable information appears online at Ⓦwww.corsicabus.org, or contact Transports Rossi direct on ☎04 95 71 00 11. At other times of year, you'll have to take a taxi (€45–50 depending on the time of day) or catch the Ajaccio bus to Figari village (see p.241) and arrange onward transport there.

By ferry

Car and passenger **ferry** services from Porto Vecchio to Marseille and Livorno operate from mid-June to September only. For more on ferry routes to and from Corsica, see p.21.

By bus

Buses to **Ajaccio** via **Figari**, **Sartène** and **Propriano** are operated by Eurocorse Voyages (Ⓦwww.eurocorse.net), leaving two to three times daily (except Sun) from in front of the Trinitours travel agents on rue Pasteur. From June through to September you can also travel to the capital via a longer and more convoluted mountain route that takes you through **Ospédale**, **Zonza**, **Quenza** and **Aullène**; this service is run by Balési Évasion (Ⓦwww.balesievasion.com) and leaves from outside Île de Beauté Voyages, 13 rue Général-de-Gaulle, at 7am. For **Bonifacio**, there are one to four buses each day with Eurocorse Voyages, taking thirty minutes. Rapides Bleus (Ⓦwww.kallistour.com) also run coaches up the east coast to **Bastia** (3hr) from outside the Corsicatours office, 7 rue Jean-Jaurès.

Bus tickets can be bought on the day from the driver. For outlines of frequencies and journey times, see Travel details on p.263.

Around Porto Vecchio

Much of the coast of the **Golfe de Porto Vecchio** and its environs is charac-terized by ugly development and marshland, yet some of the clearest, bluest sea and whitest beaches on Corsica are also found around here. The most frequented of these can be reached by bus from town in the summer (see p.257, or Travel details on p.263); at other times of year you'll need your own transport.

South of Porto Vecchio

A golden semicircle of sand edged by short twisted umbrella pines and red rocks, the **plage de Palombaggia** is south Corsica's trademark beach, and indisputably one of the most beautiful bays in Europe. Come here outside the school holidays and you'll find it hard to resist the striking colours and serene, clear water. But in summer the crowds can be simply overwhelming; and you'll also find it hard to find anywhere to leave your car if you're driving. One possible compromise is to press on south to two other smaller, less famous beaches just beyond Palombaggia – **Cala di la Folaca** and the **plage d'Acciaju** – where the sand is just as white and the water equally translucent. Narrow access lanes and *pistes* drop down to them from the main road at regular intervals, but the best way to enjoy this exquisite string of coves is by walking along them.

Immediately south of Palombaggia, **Cala di la Folaca** (also known as the Baie de Tamaricciu) is a beautiful bay harbouring what is probably the smartest *paillote* on the island. With a deck and huge supporting beams made entirely from teak, the *Tamaricciu* (☎04 95 70 49 89) serves food that's a cut above your average beach-shack fare (salads, fresh pasta, wood-baked pizzas, *grillades* and chargrilled seafood), although its prices reflect its exclusive location. The third and final cove in this stretch, just around the next headland, is known as the **plage d'Asciaghju** (pronounced "A-shaa-djoo", also spelled "Acciaju"), and tends to be swamped by (mostly Czech and German) campers from the site behind it.

A few kilometres further south along the same road takes you over the **Bocca di l'Oru** to the **plage de Santa Giulia**, a spectacular white-sand beach and turquoise bay that looks like something out of a Bounty advert (minus the palms). The presence of several sprawling holiday villages and facilities for windsurfing and other watersports ensure large crowds from early in the season, but the colours alone warrant a detour. Shallow and crystal clear, the water is especially good for little ones.

North of Porto Vecchio

North of Porto Vecchio, the coast has been intensively developed, much of it for upmarket tourism, with self-contained *villages de vacances* and large villa complexes shielded from view by screens of pine trees. The first beach along this stretch, **plage de Stagnolu**, is the least appealing, backed by a large campsite, *Camping Golfo di Sogno* (☎04 95 70 08 98, ⓦ www.golfo-di-sogno .fr; April to mid-Oct).

Just around the headland, **Cala Rossa** is a picturesque sweep of reddish sand and turquoise water whose most secluded cove is annexed by the glamorous *Grand Hôtel de Cala Rossa* (see p.255). Large modern villas line up behind it, some of them very swish indeed, with landscaped gardens running right down to the beach, leaving little room for outsiders.

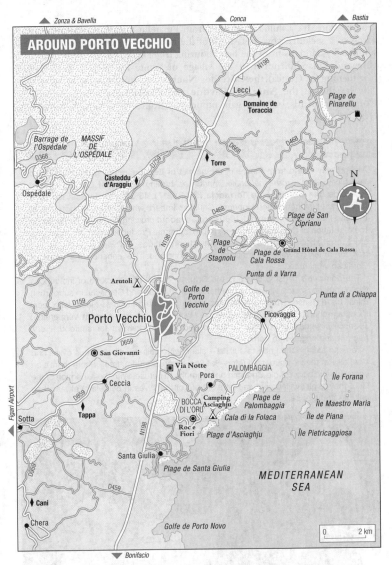

AROUND PORTO VECCHIO

▲ Zonza & Bavella   ▲ Conca   ▲ Bastia

N198

● Lecci
Domaine de Toraccia

Plage de Pinarellu

Barrage de l'Ospédale
D368

MASSIF DE L'OSPÉDALE

D758

D668

D468

▼ **Torre**

Casteddu d'Araggiu ♦

● Ospédale

D368

D468

Plage de San C">C04 Cipri
Plage de San Ciprianu

N198

Plage de Stagnolu

Plage de Cala Rossa ◉ Grand Hôtel de Cala Rossa

Arutoli ⚊

Golfe de Porto Vecchio

Punta di a Varra

Punta di a Chiappa

D159

Porto Vecchio

D659

● **San Giovanni**

■ **Via Notte**

● Picovaggia

Île Forana

PALOMBAGGIA

● **Ceccia**

Pora

D859

Figari Airport

BOCCA DI L'ORU
◉ **Camping Asciaghju** ⚊

Plage de Palombaggia

Île Maestro Maria

● **Sotta**

♦ **Tappa**

Roc e Fiori ◉

Cala di la Folaca

Île de Piana

Plage d'Asciaghju

Île Pietricaggiosa

N198

● **Santa Giulia**

Plage de Santa Giulia

MEDITERRANEAN SEA

D459

D859

♦ **Cani**

● **Chera**

Golfe de Porto Novo

0   2 km

▼ Bonifacio

Development is rather less obtrusive at the **plage de San Ciprianu**, a half-moon of white sand reached by turning right off the main road at the Elf garage. The FLNC blew up one of the largest holiday complexes here several years ago, having removed all the residents in minibuses during the middle of the night. The most promising beach for day-trips in this area, however, is the **plage de Pinarellu**, 7km further up the coast, with a long sweep of soft white sand overlooked by a Genoese watchtower and a dramatic hinterland of mountains. Hidden among the pine forest and lagoons at the far eastern end of the bay, *Camping Le California* (☎04 95 71 49 24, ⓦwww.camping-california .net; April to mid-Oct) is a swish three-star site with tennis courts, pizzeria and grocery store. It's a dull 1.5km plod from Pinarellu village, but enjoys private access to a secluded cove just south of the main bay (exclusively colonized in summer by naturists from the neighbouring *centre nudiste*).

Beyond Pinarellu, north of the village of Sainte-Lucie-de-Porto Vecchio (the turning for Conca), the **Côte des Nacres** runs from Favone to Solenzara. The beaches at the **Anse de Favone** and **Canella** are pretty average by Corsican standards, but they gain immensely from the backdrop of towering crags behind.

The Domaine de Torraccia

A short way inland from Pinarellu, the hamlet of **Lecci**, straddling the main Porto Vecchio-to-Bastia *route nationale*, marks the turning for one of Corsica's finest vineyards, the **Domaine de Torraccia** (℡04 95 71 43 50). It was founded by a flamboyant first-generation vigneron, Christian Imbert, who spotted the potential of the land hereabouts in the mid-1960s and set about growing grapes at a time when the reputation of Corsican wine was in the doldrums. Produced with traditional vine stock and labour-intensive organic cultivation methods, his wines have blazed a trail for other growers on the island and done much to enhance the name of Corsican viticulture.

The domaine's flagship *cuvée* is the **Oriu**, produced from a blend of indigenous Niellucciu and Sciacarellu grapes, with a splash of Syrah and Grenache in supporting roles. It's a dense, smoky *vin de garde* with dark fruit flavours – ideal with local mountain charcuterie and ewe's cheese. Made from hundred-percent Vermentino, Torraccia's white, by contrast, is the perfect accompaniment for seafood – dry, fragrant and tinged with herbs.

You can sample the Imberts' full list – along with their equally delicious olives and olive oil – at the vineyard itself (Mon–Sat 8am–noon & 2–6pm; free), where there's an engaging exhibition of old Corsican photographs to peruse. With the exception of the Oriu, they're all availabe *en vrac* (straight out of the *cuves* in demi-jars) at less than half the bottle price.

▲ Grape harvesting at Domaine de Torraccia

Conca

The largest village inland from Pinarellu bay is **CONCA**, renowned among hikers as the traditional finishing (or starting) point of the **GR20** (see p.337). Scattered over a broad amphitheatre of maquis, with the crags of Punta d'Orto towering behind, it is livelier than most villages in Porto Vecchio's depopulated, fire-scarred hinterland but holds nothing of sufficient interest to warrant a diversion from the nearby *route nationale*, beyond its role as a walkers' gateway to the interior mountains.

Footsore GR20 veterans stagger straight to the **gîte d'étape**, *La Tonnelle* (☎04 95 71 46 55, ℮latonnelleconca@hotmail.com), at the bottom of the village. Beds here cost €16–20, depending on the size of the dorm; you can also camp in the garden for €6. Half board (€40 per person, or €26 per person if you're camping) is obligatory from June to September. They also lay on minibuses to and from Pinarellu beach (€8), Sainte-Lucie-de-Porto Vecchio on the main *route nationale* (€5), Porto Vecchio (from €8) and Ajaccio (€30 for two people minimum) – you can phone ahead to ask them to pick you up.

A short walk up the street into the village proper, the *U Chjosu* **restaurant** (☎04 95 71 52 96), is a pleasant little Corsican speciality place, run by a chatty grandmother. Featuring stuffed aubergines, cannelloni *brocciu*, wild-boar-and-white-bean *ragoût*, their €23 *menu corse* is much better value than the rather indifferent food dished up at *La Tonnelle*.

Massif de l'Ospédale

Broadly covering the hinterland of the Golfe de Porto Vecchio, limited in the northwest by the Massif de Bavella and in the southwest by the Montagne de Cagna, the **Massif de l'Ospédale** is a forested upland studded with enormous granite boulders. Although much of its forest was devastated by fire seven or eight years ago, enough remains on the higher slopes to make this a rewarding area for short hikes, with spellbinding views across the gulf through the trees.

Leaving Porto Vecchio by the D368 northwest of town, a twisty drive of 19km up the slopes will soon get you to **OSPÉDALE**, a village that has long been used as a summer retreat by inhabitants of the coastal belt. Plumb in the middle of the forest, enclosed by a backdrop of massive granite clumps, it has a superb view over the Golfe de Porto Vecchio to Sardinia. An ideal place to enjoy the panorama is the rear terrace of the *Le Vieux Lavoir* **café** on the bend in the road at the top of the village. Next to it, Ospédale's **spring** – famous locally for its delicious, minerally water – has loaned its name to the adjacent **restaurant** *U Funtanonu* (☎04 95 70 47 11), where you can enjoy Corsican specialities such as Porto Vecchien-style stuffed aubergines or braised leg of lamb (€17–20). They also serve delicious salads based around locally produced charcuterie and cheeses (€12–14), and an exceptionally comprehensive (though very pricey) list of quality Corsican wines.

You can sidestep the bus parties that tend to congregate in Ospédale by heading out of the village along the **Mare a Mare Sud** footpath, which peels left off the main road, 500m beyond the last houses (look for the PNRC signboard). Winding at a gentle gradient under the maritime pines, the orange waymarked path cuts southwest up the mountainside to the former *bergeries* of **CARTALAVONU** in around 45 minutes. The route offers no views to speak of, but concludes at the welcoming **gîte d'étape-restaurant** *Le Refuge* (☎04 95 70 00 39; mid-April to Oct), where you can enjoy traditional Alta Rocca cooking – home-made charcuterie, *porcelait* (suckling piglet), wild-boar pâté, stuffed courgettes and lamb stew – served in a rustic dining hall around an open fire. Count on €30–35 for four courses à la carte (there's no *menu fixe*).

Most of the people who eat here are walkers, for whom basic dormitory **accommodation** is provided in four- to six-bed dorms (€14 per bed, or €40 per person half board).

Continue uphill from Cartalavonu, following the waymarks for another 45 minutes or so, and you'll walk clear of the forest across a rocky hillside to **Foce Alta** (1171m), one of southern Corsica's finest viewpoints. From one side of the pass unfolds the wild, spectacular Caracutu Valley and northern flank of the Cagna massif, while on the other the col overlooks the **Barrage de l'Ospédale**, a large reservoir supplying Porto Vecchio with water.

Prehistoric sites around Porto Vecchio

Sometime around 1500 BC, the megalithic people responsible for carving Corsica's famous figurative standing stones were displaced by more techno-logically advanced invaders. No one can say for sure where they came from, but the band of rolling maquis between the hills and coast around Porto Vecchio is where most experts agree the warlike incomers first settled. Known by archeologists as the **Torréens**, they quickly colonized the southeast, erecting fortresses of Cyclopean proportions – large dry-stone towers with corbel-vaulted roofs covering weirdly shaped curved rooms – over the vestiges of their Stone Age predecessors. The most fully preserved of these *torri* stands north of Porto Vecchio at **Casteddu d'Araggiu**, a Bronze Age settlement high on the mountain slopes above the gulf. To complete a prehistoric tour you should go south of Porto Vecchio to **Tappa**, an impressive remnant of the civilization that first brought metal-working and knife-making skills to the island. Finally, a worthwhile side-trip from the main Porto Vecchio to Figari road takes you south to the tiny hamlet of **Chera**, where a couple of enigmatic natural rock formations, known as **orii**, have become the objects of much local folklore.

The Casteddu d'Araggiu

Follow the N198 north of Porto Vecchio for 8km to reach the turning for **Casteddu d'Araggiu**, the path to which begins 3km up the D759. From the site's car park, you double back through the hamlet, past the *Orée du Site* café-restaurant, and follow the route indicated down the side of a house on your left – it's a twenty- to thirty-minute stiff climb from the stream below through tall maquis to the monument.

Erected around 1500 BC, the *casteddu* consists of a complex of chambers built into a massive circular wall of pink granite. The site is entered via a ten-metre-long corridor covered in stone slabs. Immediately to the left you'll see a small triangular enclosure, in the centre of which would have been a clay fireplace, a forerunner of the *zidda* (hearth) found in traditional Corsican households. Continuing in a clockwise direction you come to the *torre* itself, comprising a central chamber of which only the foundations remain. Past the tower, the next enclosure – measuring 10m across – also harbours the remains of a fireplace, while a little further on it's possible to make out a well built into the thick walls, beyond which stands another small hut with fireplace.

Tappa

About 1km southwest of Ceccia down the D859, the impressive **Tappa** *casteddu* is signposted south off the main road, opposite a farm. Set on a granite mound about ten-minutes' walk away, the site is encircled by a wall that's considered to be more recent than the rest of the *casteddu*, which was developed in the half-millennium prior to 1000 BC. A large *torre* at the southern end of the complex consists of several small rooms around a central chamber. A ramp leads up to the main structure, entered by a narrow corridor, inside which another ramp winds up to a second level. The excavation of various clay pots, pounding implements and grindstones here has led archeologists to propose that this building was used for milling as well as storage.

The orii of Chera and Cani

Amidst the chaos of rocks by the side of the roads in southern Corsica, you occasionally come across large boulders whose overhanging crevices have been bricked in with masonry. Known as **orii** (*oriu* in the singular), these distinctive rock formations, whose name is thought to derive from the Latin for "granary", *horreum*, have been used for centuries to store grain and hay, and to provide shelter for animals. They crop up with surprising frequency in old folk songs and legends, suggesting they were at one time central to the life of rural communities; some have even been "Christianized" and are the focus of religious rituals.

One such *oriu* stands in the far-flung hamlet of **CHERA**, roughly midway between Porto Vecchio and Bonifacio (turn south off the D859 at Sotta). The most famous of its kind, it overlooks the village from the top of a rocky outcrop, crowned by a crucifix. Local people believe the artificial cave sheltered their pastoralist ancestors when they fled here centuries ago to escape a vendetta in the mountains, since when it has been revered as a kind of guardian spirit of the Culioli clan. Dorothy Carrington – who was shown the *oriu* by one of the island's most renowned bards, the long-white-bearded Jean-André Culioli – was told it was haunted by a phantom goat whose hoofs could occasionally be heard trotting over the rock in the dead of night.

Even spookier is the *oriu* of **CANI**, 4km north down the valley from Chera (look for a hand-painted sign on the right, or east, side of the road). Pull over outside the farmhouses where the road ends and follow the track as it bends right; once over two stiles, you come to a breach in a wall, from where a faint trail cuts uphill through the woods to the *oriu*, perched on a rock platform above the tiny hamlet. An improbably contorted lump of granite with a strange high-pitched "roof", the structure looks like one of Salvador Dalí's visions, and it's not hard to see why local people believe it was once inhabited by a witch. In fact, the last recorded resident was one Vinceguerra Pietri, the local landowner, who lived here until a ripe old age at the end of the nineteenth century.

Travel details

Buses

The listings below summarize which bus companies cover which routes, how often they run and how long journeys take. Start by looking up your intended destination in the first section; then, using the company's acronym (eg EV or RB), go to the second section for more detailed route and frequency information. Precise departure times can be checked in advance either via the bus companies direct, or (if your French isn't up to that) Bastia tourist office (☎ 04 95 31 81 34). A full rundown of Corsican bus services, including up-to-date timetables, also appears online at ⓦ www.corsicabus.org.

Bonifacio to: Ajaccio (EV; 3hr 30min–4hr); Olmeto (EV; 2hr 20min); Porto Vecchio (EV; 30min); Pianottoli (EV; 30–50min); Propriano (EV; 2hr 10min); Roccapina (EV; 1hr 10min); Sartène (EV; 2hr).

Levie to: Ajaccio (AR & EV; 2hr 45min); Bavella (AR; 30min); Sainte-Lucie-de-Tallano (EV & AR; 15min); Zonza (EV & AR; 15min).

Olmeto to: Ajaccio (EV & AR; 1hr 20min); Bonifacio (EV; 2hr 30min); Porto Vecchio (EV; 2hr); Propriano

(EV; 15min); Roccapina (EV; 55min); Sartène (EV; 35min).

Porto Vecchio to: Ajaccio (EV, BE & AR; 3hr 30min); Aléria/Cateraggio (RB; 1hr 15min); Aullène (BE; 1hr 40min); Bastia (RB; 2hr 45min); Bavella (BE; 1hr 15min); Bonifacio (EV; 30min); Figari (EV; 15min); Ghisonaccia (RB; 1hr); Olmeto (EV; 1hr 45min); L'Ospédale (BE; 30min); Moriani (RB; 2hr 10min); Poretta (for Bastia airport; RB; 2hr 35min); Propriano (EV, BE & AR; 1hr 45min); Sainte-Lucie-de-Porto Vecchio (for Conca; RB; 20min); Quenza (BE; 1hr 25min); Roccapina (EV; 50min); Sartène (EV; 1hr 25min); Serra di Scapomena (BE; 1hr 35min); Solenzara (RB; 40min); Zonza (BE; 1hr 5min).

Porto-Pollo (Marinca stop) to: Ajaccio (AR; 1hr 30min); Calzola crossroads (AR; 20min).

Propriano to: Ajaccio (EV & AR; 1hr 35min–1hr 50min); Bonifacio (EV; 2hr 15min); Olmeto (EV & AR; 15min); Porto Vecchio (EV; 1hr 45min); Roccapina (EV; 40min); Sartène (EV & AR; 20min).

Roccapina to: Ajaccio (EV; 2hr 40min); Bonifacio (EV; 50min–1hr 35min); Olmeto (EV; 55min); Porto Vecchio (EV; 1hr); Propriano (EV; 50min); Sartène (EV; 35min).

Sainte-Lucie-de-Tallano to: Ajaccio (EV & AR; 2hr 30min); Bavella (AR; 45min); Levie (EV & AR; 15min); Zonza (EV & AR; 45min).

Sartène to: Ajaccio (EV & AR; 2hr); Bonifacio (EV; 1hr 10min–1hr 55min); Olmeto (EV; 20min); Porto Vecchio (EV; 1hr 10min–1hr 25min); Propriano (EV & AR; 15min); Roccapina (EV; 20min).

Zonza to: Ajaccio (BE & AR; 3hr); Bavella (BE & AR; 15min); Levie (EV & AR; 15min); Sainte-Lucie-de-Tallano (BE, EV & AR; 30min).

AR: Autocars Ricci ℡ 04 95 51 08 19 or 04 95 76 25 59. Ajaccio–Olmeto–Propriano–Sartène–Sainte-Lucie-de-Tallano–Levie–Zonza–Bavella; July & Aug 1 daily; Sept–June Mon–Sat 1 daily. Ajaccio–Calzola–Porto-Pollo–Propriano; July & Aug Mon–Sat 1 daily; Sept–June 3 weekly (Mon, Wed, Fri).

BE: Balési Évasion ℡ 04 95 70 15 55, ⊛ www .balesievasion.com. Ajaccio–Aullène–Serra di Scapomena–Sorbollano–Quenza–Zonza–Bavella–l'Ospédale–Porto Vecchio; July–Aug 1 daily; Sept–June Mon & Fri 1 daily.

EV: Eurocorse Voyages ℡ 04 95 70 13 83 or 04 95 21 06 3, ⊛ www.eurocorse.net. Ajaccio–Olmeto–Propriano–Sartène–Roccapina–Pianottoli–Figari (village)–Porto Vecchio/Bonifacio; July to mid-Sept 2 daily; mid-Sept to June Mon–Sat 2 daily. Ajaccio–Propriano–Sartène–Sainte-Lucie-de-Tallano–Levie–Zonza; Mon–Sat 1 daily.

RB: Rapides Bleus ℡ 04 95 31 03 79 or 04 95 70 10 36, ⊛ www.kallistour.com. Porto Vecchio–Sainte-Lucie-de-Porto Vecchio (for Conca)–Solenzara–Ghisonaccia– Moriani–Poretta (village, not airport)–Bastia; mid-June to mid-Sept 2 daily, mid-Sept to mid-June Mon–Sat 2 daily.

Ferries

For ferry details, see Basics, p.21, and the box on p.249.

6

Eastern Corsica

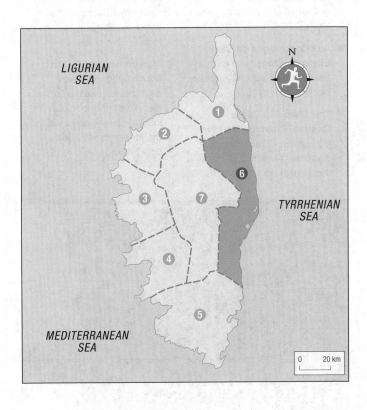

CHAPTER 6

Highlights

✳ **Via Ferrata, Solenzara and Chisá** Adrenalin-fuelled explorations of rock outcrops on the watershed's eastern spur. See p.269

✳ **Musée d'Archéologie Jérôme Carcopino, Aléria** Home to a hoard of Greek and Roman artefacts, unearthed at the nearby ruins. See p.274

✳ **Aux Coquillages de Diane, Étang de Diane** Dine on fresh oysters straight from the lagoon. See p.276

✳ **The Chapel of Santa Cristina, Cervione** Medieval frescoes in vibrant colours decorate the twin apses of this remote church. See p.279

✳ **Ascent of Monte San Petrone** Hike to the summit of Castagniccia's holy mountain for superb views across the Tyrrhenian Sea and the peaks of the interior. See p.283

✳ **Église de St-Jean-Baptiste, La Porta** The island's most celebrated Baroque church, with a resplendent Rococo facade. See p.284

✳ **Maison de Pascal Paoli, Morosaglia** Evocative memorabilia relating to the founding father of Corsican independence, collected in the former family home. See p.285

▲ The Via Ferrata

Eastern Corsica

Comprising 150 square kilometres of vine-striped plains backed by rippling mountains, the landscape of Corsica's **east coast** is restrained in comparison with the rest of the island. If you do visit the region it'll probably be to take advantage of the smooth, straight N198, the main north–south artery, from which windier side roads penetrate the more varied and rugged interior. That said, the *littoral oriental* – rebranded in recent years by its respective local tourist authorities as the Côtes des Nacres, **Costa Serena** and **Costa Verde** – does have its attractions, not least of which are several vast sandy **beaches**, where scattered resorts and a string of large self-contained campsites offer plenty of inexpensive accommodation.

Of the small seaside towns strung along the highway, **Solenzara**, at the head of the spectacular road leading to the Col de Bavella, is arguably the most appealing. North of here, beyond the desultory agro-town and budding resort of **Ghisonaccia**, the hills recede and you move into the eastern plain proper, an enormous malaria-ridden swamp until the Americans sprayed it with DDT after World War II. Now enclosing kilometres of clementine orchards and vineyards, this patchwork of fields is punctuated by shimmering lagoons, of which the **Étang d'Urbino** and **Étang de Diane** are the largest, supplying plentiful oysters and mussels for local restaurants. Set on a rise between these *étangs* – where Corsica's longest river, the Tavignano, debouches into the sea – is the Roman capital of **Aléria**, whose ruins have yielded a spectacular collection of ancient ceramics, jewellery and weapons. The small museum where they're now housed, in a converted Genoese fort, is reason enough to pull off the highway, and there's also a decent beach close by and a few hotels straddling the main road.

Inland, the terraced villages of the **Fiumorbo** region afford sweeping views of the plain and the Tuscan islands offshore. A still more fascinating region to explore is **Castagniccia**, further north, its tunnelled roads twisting past waterfalls and through an enormous forest of chestnut trees which shelters the highest concentration of highland settlements in Corsica. There's only one hotel in the area, at **Piedicroce**, on the slopes of Monte San Petrone, scaled by an ancient pilgrimage path that makes the best hike in the area. North of Castagniccia lies the **Casinca**, a more compact region of delightful villages such as **Vescovato** and **Venzolasca**, which could feasibly be seen on a day excursion from Bastia.

Since the German army sabotaged the Bastia–Porto Vecchio railway in 1943, **transport** around the east coast has been limited to the main highway. Rapides Bleus **buses** pass twice daily along it, stopping at Solenzara, Ghisonaccia and Aléria (Cateraggio), but to penetrate the hinterland you'll need your own transport.

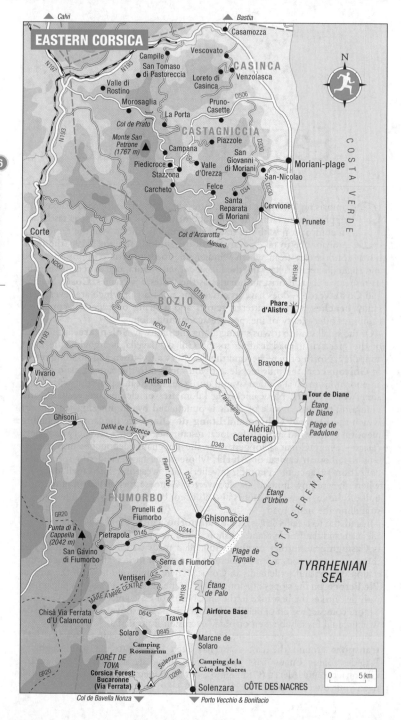

▲ *Calvi*　　　　　　　　　▲ *Bastia*

EASTERN CORSICA

Casamozza

Vescovato

Campile　　　　　　　CASINCA
San Tomaso　　Loreto di　Venzolasca
di Pastoreccia　Casinca

Valle di
Rostino　　　　　　　　　　D506
Morosaglia
　　　　　La Porta　　Pruno-
Col de Prato　　　　　　Casette

CASTAGNICCIA

Monte San　　　Piazzole
Petrone　　Campana
(1767 m) ▲　　　　San
Piedicroce　　Valle　Giovanni　　Moriani-plage
Stazzona　　d'Orezza　di Moriani
　　　　　　　　　San-Nicolao
Carcheto　　Felce
　　　　　　　　Santa　Cervione
　　　　　　　Reparata
　　　　　　　di Moriani　　Prunete

Corte

Col d'Arcarotta
Alesani

COSTA VERDE

BOZIO

Phare
d'Alistro ⛯

Vivario

Antisanti

Bravone

Ghisoni
Défilé de L'Inzecca

Tour de Diane
Étang
de Diane

Aléria/
Cateraggio　　Plage de
　　　　　　Padulone

FIUMORBO

Prunelli di
Fiumorbo
Pietrapola　D145

Ghisonaccia

Étang
d'Urbino

COSTA SERENA

Punta di à
Cappella
(2042 m) ▲
San Gàvino
di Fiumorbo

Serra di Fiumorbo

Plage de
Tignale

TYRRHENIAN
SEA

Ventiseri

Étang
de Palo

Chisà Via Ferrata
d'U Calanconu

✈ Airforce Base
Travo

Solaro

Marcne de
Solaro

Camping
Rosumarinu

FORÊT DE
TOVA
Corsica Forest:
Bucaronne
(Via Ferrata)

⛺ Camping de la
Côte des Nacres

Solenzara　　CÔTE DES NACRES

0 ———— 5 km

▼ *Col de Bavella Nonza*　　　▼ *Porto Vecchio & Bonifacio*

Solenzara and around

SOLENZARA might not be the most glamorous coastal resort in Corsica, but its endless sandy beach, hidden behind a strip of shops and busy marina, lies at the junction of the **route de Bavella** (see p.230), one of the island's most spectacular mountain roads. There are a few decent **hotels** here as well. If you don't mind sharing a dorm, the rock-bottom option is the *gîte d'étape* U Saltu, 8km west (☎04 95 56 32 70), where bunks only cost €19. The owners also run a low-key restaurant serving a limited *menu corse* for an additional €18, served on a terrace boasting superb views over the coastal strip. To reach it, turn left off the N198 at Marine de Solaro (3.5km north of Solenzara), and head west along the D845 for another 5.5km. On the main street just past the tourist office in Solenzara, the family-run *Orsoni* (☎04 95 57 40 25, ⓦ www.hotelorsoni.com; ⑤) has plain but impeccably clean mid-price rooms and a pleasant little restaurant on the ground floor. The most stylish place in this area, however, is *La Solenzara*, above the beach north of the village (☎04 95 57 40 25, ⓦ www.lasolenzara.com; ⑥), housed in a period mansion on the roadside with high stucco ceilings, gilt candelabras and a gorgeous pool overlooking the sea; considering the location, facilities and atmosphere, it offers good value for money.

The **tourist office** is on the main street opposite the Prisunic supermarket in the centre (June–Sept daily 9am–noon & 5–7pm; ☎04 95 57 43 75, ⓦ www .cotedesnacres.com). **Campers** have a choice between *Camping de la Côte des*

Via Ferrata circuits around Solenzara

Five minutes up the road from *Camping U Rosumarinu*, around a spectacular bend in the Solenzara river, is the entrance to an extensive outdoor adventure park, **Corsic⊐ Forest: Bucaronne** (June–Sept daily 9am–6pm; ☎06 16 18 00 58, ⓦ www .corsica-forest.com), featuring a great **Via Ferrata** circuit (for more on which, see p.40 & p.294). With an altitude gain of around 250m, the itinerary includes 25 fixtures, four tyrolean slides and a vertical net, culminating in a magnificent viewpoint over the valley and its surrounding crags. Allow between two and three hours to complete it, depending on your level of fitness and head for heights. The admission fee of €19 includes equipment hire (harness, gloves, helmets, karabiners, shock-absorbing ropes, etc), as well as a crash course on how to use it all.

Spectacular and heart-stopping though some sections of it are, Bucaronne is positively tame by comparison with the larger **Via Ferrata d'U Calanconu** (June–Sept daily 9.30am–6pm), near the village of **Chisá**, 20km northwest of Solenzara (take the D645 inland just south of the airforce base at Travo, 5.5km north of Solenzara, and follow the road to the valley's end). Equipped with Himalayan bridges, monkey walks, cable nets and vertical ladders, the route and its variations are all strenuous and vertigo-inducing – the main one winds up with a 250-metre tyrolean slide over a sixty-metre drop. The admission fee for adults is €10, including rental of all the kit you'll need. For a full description of U Calanconu (in French), complete with photos and topo maps, go to ⓦ www.communedechisa.com and click on "Activités" then "Via Ferrata". Out of season (Oct–May), opening hours can be checked with the *mairie* on ☎04 95 57 31 11.

Chisá holds a couple of simple accommodation options if you haven't the energy to rush off after a day on the rock. Climbers tend to bunk down in the *Bocca Bé* (☎04 95 56 36 61), a basic *gîte d'étape* on the outskirts offering dorm beds for €17, or €32 half-board; for some bizarre reason, prices drop slightly in peak season. For more comfort at only a fraction more, try the *U Chisá*, bang opposite the entrance to the Via Ferrata (☎04 95 57 31 06; ①), where rooms are a snip at €25 per double.

Nacres, set amid eucalyptus trees 1.5km north of Solenzara next to the river and beach (℡04 95 57 40 65, Ⓦwww.campingdesnacres.com; May–Oct), and the cheaper *U Rosumarinu* (℡04 95 57 47 66, Ⓦwww.urosumarinu.fr; June–Sept), 6km up the Bavella road in the middle of nowhere. If peace, quiet and scenery are more of a priority than sea and sand, this latter site, overlooking the stream and well placed for a bracing dip, definitely has the edge.

For a **meal**, head 1km north of town to the bridge, where the *A Mandria* (℡04 95 57 41 95; closed Mon Oct–March & Sun eve) serves succulent Corsican specialities – such as roast kid, veal escalope and stuffed pancetta and Bonifacien-style aubergines – in a rustic restored *bergerie* filled with old farm tools and memorabilia. The set menu is priced at a reasonable €22. It's a particularly fun place off-season, when locals flock in for filling evening roasts over an open fire.

Ghisonaccia

The one sizeable village between Solenzara and Aléria is dusty **GHISON-ACCIA**, whose pejorative *"accia"* suffix (meaning "bad") seems just as applicable today as it was when the town was a malarial bog. That said, the place has enjoyed a certain prosperity ever since the late 1950s, when *pieds-noirs* from Algeria bought much of the hitherto useless agricultural land in the area to plant vineyards. The wine they eventually produced became France's leading brand of cheap *vin de table*, stimulating a boom that lasted until the 1970s, when it was discovered that most of Ghisonaccia's farmers had been mixing sugar and dodgy chemicals into their wine to bump up production. Since then, the vines have been replaced by orchards of clementines, kiwis and other soft fruit, picked by the low-paid Arab agro-workers you'll see hanging around the main crossroads. The village's other main source of revenue, after tourism and farming, are the close-cropped national service lads from the nearby air-force base who fill the bars on weekends.

The nearest beach, **plage de Tignale**, lies 4.5km east; it's clean and broad for the east coast, but gets inundated during the summer by thousands of Germans and Italians from the enormous **campsites** behind it. These are all flashy four-star places complete with restaurants, shops, coin-operated fridges and the like. The most homely of the bunch is the *Arinella Bianca*, reached via a signposted turning off the main beach road (℡04 95 56 04 78, Ⓦwww.camping-corse.fr; May–Oct). A pleasant and relatively inexpensive place to **eat** at plage de Tignale is *Les Deux Magots*, where you can enjoy locally caught seafood such as mussels and *loup de mer* on a breezy beach-side terrace.

Fiumorbo

The little-explored region of **Fiumorbo** (or Fium'orbo), immediately inland from Ghisonaccia, has been renowned for the independent spirit of its inhabitants ever since 1769, when a group of shepherds who had refused to submit to French laws were struck down in an ambush along the road to Corte. Thirty years later a coalition of royalist, Paolist and pro-British Corsican exiles organized another anti-French rebellion, which spread as far as the Sartenais before it was crushed by the French authorities. This tradition continued into the early nineteenth century, when an insurrection broke out and five thousand troops hired by Louis XVIII's government were unable to suppress the hordes of mountain people who seized control of the region. Eventually the ringleaders were either gunned down or deported to the French mainland by Général Morand, who was nevertheless obliged to accede to them an area of coastal land.

By the end of the century the Fiumorbo had become notorious bandit country, ruled by outlaws who terrorized the villages, untouched by the police, but today this is one of the quietest, and most untroubled, parts of Corsica.

The region is reached by following the D244 west off the highway 2km south of Ghisonaccia, then turning onto the D145, a route that winds into the valley of the **River Albatesco**, a tributary of the River Fium'orbu ("Blind Waters") and location of the chief settlements of the region. Running between them, the old inter-village mule tracks have been exploited to create the **Mare a Mare Centre** long-distance footpath, which starts at the Pont de l'Abatesco, just south of Ghisonaccia, and penetrates the interior of the island via the Col de Laparo, a major landmark on the GR20.

Marking the end of the first stage of the walk, the **gîte d'étape** (℡04 95 56 74 97; obligatory half board €32 per person) in the village of **SERRA DI FIUMORBO** provides basic dormitory accommodation in a converted hydro-electricity station, with fine views over the eastern plain. To get there, you have to turn left off the D145.

Head straight on instead and you'll press up the Abatesco Valley to **PIETRAPOLA**, whose **thermal baths** attract sufferers from arthritis and rheumatic disorders throughout the year. The village is also thought to have been the site of an encounter between local bandits and a detachment of Roman soldiers en route from Sardinia in 231 BC. Ambushed and relieved of their booty, the Romans pursued the Corsican robbers into the hills, only to nearly die of hunger and thirst trying to find a way down again. Eventually they discovered a spring at Pietrapola and survived, consecrating a special "Temple of the Spring" at the gates of Rome on their return. The facade of the village church, Santa Maria, sports a remnant of this era: an incongruous four-metre column salvaged from a Jupiter-Saturn temple that once stood in a now deserted forest glade above the village.

Another column from the same ruin has been incorporated into the tower of the church at **PRUNELLI DI FIUMORBO**, 7km northeast uphill from Pietrapola along the D45. Approached along an avenue of oak trees, with the austere peaks of Monte Renoso looming behind, this beautiful village perches like an eagle's nest on top of a hill. Again, the views are superb, but an additional reason to make the drive up here is a little **museum** set up by local amateur historians (Mon–Fri 9.30am–noon & 3–5.30pm, Sat 9.30am–12.30pm; free). Housed in the *mairie*, it comprises a modest but fascinating collection of Roman and other archeological artefacts, displayed alongside photographs of the ruined temples and Pisan chapels lost in the surrounding forest. In another room is an array of World War II memorabilia, including evocative photos of the liberation. If there's no one at the *mairie* to let you into the museum, ask at the *Café Buttéa* next door for the key.

The Défilé de l'Inzecca

Northwest of Ghisonaccia, the D344 scythes straight across a broad tract of fruit orchards and vineyards towards a narrow niche in the wall of coastal mountains. Formed by the fast-flowing River Fium'orbu, the **Défilé de l'Inzecca** is a sheer granite trench bounded in the south by the needles of the Kyrie peaks, and in the north and west by the grey, snow-flecked east face of the Renoso massif. The road that winds through the gorge, leading from the coast to the village of **Ghisoni** (see p.320), provides one of the most spectacular approaches to the interior, cutting across dramatic pale green serpentine cliffs speckled with stunted trees. Below, colossal boulders choke the river, which has been dammed to form a reservoir for a small hydroelectricity station.

Aléria and around

Built on the estuary at the mouth of the River Tavignano, **ALÉRIA** was the capital of the Corsican province during the Roman era, remaining the east coast's principal town and port right up until the eighteenth century. Little is left of the historic settlement except the **Roman ruins** and the **Genoese fortress**, which stand high against a background of chequered fields and vineyards. A sizeable proportion of the local population is employed in farming oysters and mussels in the neighbouring **Étang de Diane**, formerly the Roman harbour. To the south, a strip of modern buildings flanking the main road makes up the modern village of **Cateraggio**.

A brief history of Aléria

This area was first settled in 564 BC by a colony of Greek Phocaeans who had been chased from their home by Persian invaders. Calling their new port Alalia, these Greeks initiated the island's trade routes around the Mediterranean, selling the copper and lead they mined from the land, and the wheat, olives and grapes farmed here. In 535 BC the settlers managed to survive a battle with the Carthaginians, but were left considerably weakened as a colony. Eventually

The Aléria siege

It may look like just another derelict, graffiti-covered ruin at the roadside, but the bombed-out Depeille wine cellar, 1.5km north of Aléria, was the site of the **Aléria siege**, a seminal event in the modern history of Corsica. On August 21, 1975, it was occupied by a group of armed nationalists, angry at its owners' part in a wine-adulterating scandal that threatened the livelihoods of many small-scale Corsican *viticulteurs*. Few of the militants, however, could have foreseen the violent outcome of their action, nor the dramatic impact it would subsequently have on the island's relations with the French government.

The **Depeilles** were one of around six hundred *pied-noir* families that settled on the east coast after Algerian independence in 1962, and who made sizeable fortunes from the vines they planted on newly reclaimed land in the area, helped by generous government subsidies. This and their North African origins made them unpopular with many locals, but the resentment never went beyond the odd piece of racist graffiti until it was discovered that many of the *pied-noir* farmers were doubling their wine output by illegally adding sugar and other chemicals to the grape juice. Frustrated by the government's apparent inability to stamp out the practice, armed commandos from the hitherto moderate nationalist organization the ARC (l'Action Régionaliste Corse), led by **Edmond Simeoni**, marched on the Depeilles' *cave*. With President Giscard d'Estaing on holiday, it fell to Michel Poniatowski, the minister of the interior and – unfortunately for the nationalists – a close associate of the Depeille family, to mount a response. Two days later, on August 23, 1250 police, four armoured cars and a couple of helicopters descended on the building. In the ensuing shoot-out two police officers were killed. Afterwards Simeoni was arrested and imprisoned in Paris (the campaign for his release would become the cause célèbre of the nationalist movement for decades to come), and riots erupted in Bastia, where another gendarme died.

The Aléria siege, the first direct confrontation between armed nationalists and the French authorities, marked a turning point in the struggle for Corsican autonomy, leading to the inauguration of the **FLNC** (Fronte di Liberazione Naziunale di a Corsica) in May 1976, and the first bombing campaign on the mainland. A full account of the nationalist armed struggle with the French state is featured on p.392.

▲ Bust of Jupiter Ammon, Musée d' Archéologie Jérôme Carcopino

fleeing to the mainland, the Phocaeans established a new capital at Massiglia (Marseille), retaining Alalia as a trading link between their colonies in southern Italy, Greece, Carthage and Spain.

In 259 BC the Romans arrived and conquered what was left of the port, which was by that time controlled by Carthaginians. It wasn't until around 80 BC, however, that a naval base was built on the site they rechristened Aléria, which re-established its importance in the western Mediterranean. As the only town of significant size on the island, Aléria was named administrative capital of the province, and before long boasted a population of some thirty thousand. Under the orders of the emperor Augustus a fleet was harboured in the Étang de Diane and public buildings were constructed, including baths, a forum and a triumphal arch, the remains of which are visible today. Light industries also flourished during this period as Aléria developed into a thriving crafts centre, producing jewellery, ceramics and clothes. Honey and wax were also marketed, and seafood from the Étang de Diane was traded with the Continent.

Aléria's Roman days came to an end in 410 AD, when the city was devastated by fire. Malaria epidemics put paid to many of the survivors and the town was all but finished off by Vandals later that century. Only at the start of the Genoese occupation in the thirteenth century was Aléria redeveloped, eventually becoming the seat of a bishopric with its own bastion, **Fort Matra**.

The Musée d'Archéologie Jérôme Carcopino and ancient Aléria

The best place to begin your visit is the **Musée d'Archéologie Jérôme Carcopino** (May 16 to Sept 30 daily 8am–noon & 2–7pm; Oct 1 to May 15 Mon–Sat 8am–noon & 2–5pm; €2), housed in Fort Matra. Pending the completion of building work on the ground floor, the collection – comprising remarkable finds from the Roman and Greek sites – is crammed into three interconnected rooms on the first storey of the fort, with ceramics, metal objects and jewellery forming the bulk of the exhibits.

The **first room** contains magnificent evidence of ancient Aléria's importance as a trading port. Hellenic and Punic rings and belt links are ranged alongside elaborate oil lamps decorated with Christian symbols, amphorae and some fragments of water pipes. In the first case on the left, a large Attic plate, depicting a faded red-grey elephant against a black background, takes up the middle of one display case, with various glazed dishes and jugs using the same painting method (red and black) ranged beneath. The real highlight of this first room, however, is a second-century marble bust of **Jupiter Ammon**, which was discovered near the forum.

Moving clockwise, the **second room** houses painted earthenware, Etruscan goblets, a number of exquisite Cretan-style vases from the fourth to third century BC, and more fine red-and-black ceramics in near-perfect condition. Most notable of the exhibits in the **third room** is a shallow-stemmed Attic bowl featuring a masturbating Dionysus, with twisting erotic figures on its rear face. Thought to date from 480 BC, this piece is attributed to master artist Panaïtos and ranks among the museum's most treasured exhibits (although you won't get to see its famous rear face as the curator recently removed the mirror formerly placed behind it, presumably in order to spare teachers accompanying school groups embarrassment).

Two remarkable drinking vessels, or "rhytons" – one representing the head of a mule and the other the head of a dog – feature in the longer **fourth room**, where you can also see finely worked Etruscan bronzes and delicate jewellery from the fourth to the second centuries BC. Encased here, too, are objects discovered in the tombs of ancient Aléria, one of which, uncovered in 1966, revealed a priceless collection of elegantly curved Greek swords, lances and daggers from the fifth century BC. Iron weapons, armour and hundreds of finely painted cups (called "craters"), one with a picture of *Hercules and the Lion* and another showing Dionysus, this time overseeing the grape harvest, are also housed in this end room, near a ground plan of a fourth-century BC tomb.

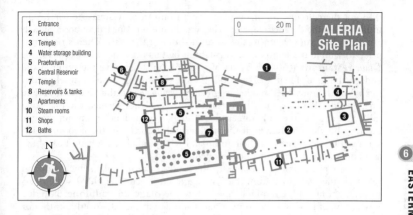

1	Entrance
2	Forum
3	Temple
4	Water storage building
5	Praetorium
6	Central Reservoir
7	Temple
8	Reservoirs & tanks
9	Apartments
10	Steam rooms
11	Shops
12	Baths

ALÉRIA
Site Plan

0   20 m

N

The Roman site

The proximity of the sea, the strong scent of wild tarragon and the arresting view of snowcapped mountains and Fort Matra create an appropriately epic backdrop to the **Roman site** (closes 30min before museum; admission by same ticket), a short way up the hill from the fort. It's believed that the core of the ancient capital would have extended from this ridge crest down to the Tavignano estuary and port, located east of the modern highway. Mérimée noticed signs of the Roman settlement here during his survey of the island in 1830, but it took over a century before systematic excavation work was undertaken. Begun in the late 1950s, this yielded the extraordinary finds now housed in the museum, but has since ground to a virtual halt. The fact that the bulk of the city remains buried, however, serves only to accentuate the site's romantic appeal.

First of the major discoveries at Aléria was Augustus's triumphal **arch**, which formed the entrance to the governor's residence – the **praetorium** – on the western edge of the **forum**, and which now dominates the ruins. In the adjacent **balneum** (bathhouse), a network of reservoirs and cisterns, the **caldarium** bears traces of the underground pipes that would have heated the room, and a patterned mosaic floor is visible inside the neighbouring chamber. To the north of the site lie the foundation walls of a large house, while at the eastern end of the forum the foundations of **shops** and the **temple** can be seen, alongside the ground plan of the apse of an early Christian church. Some vestiges of the Greek settlement – including an acropolis – have been discovered further to the east.

L'Étang de Diane and plage de Padulone

During his exile on Elba, Napoléon kept in contact with his homeland by ordering boatloads of oysters from the **Étang de Diane**, the large saltwater lagoon just north of Aléria. Flushed daily by the mingling of tidal currents and inflow of fresh water via the River Arena, the *étang* is freer of pollution now than it was two thousand years ago, when boatloads of oysters stacked in jars used to leave the teeming port for Rome. Prodigious quantities of the celebrated **Nustale oysters** are still hauled from the water here: seventy tonnes per year, plus four hundred tonnes of mussels. For visitors, the unusual landscape and vivid light of the lagoon, fringed on its eastern flank by a long sandy beach, make it a pleasant place to break the journey up the coast.

To get there, follow the main road north from Aléria/Cateraggio for 1.5km until you see the derelict Depeille wine warehouse on your left, opposite which a narrow lane runs down to the western shore of the *étang*. There's no better place to sample the famously strong-tasting oysters than the *Aux Coquillages de Diane* **restaurant** (☏04 95 57 04 55), resting on stilts above the water at the end of the lane. Their €23 seafood platter – featuring clams, mussels and a terrine made from dried mullet's eggs called *poutargue* – is the kind of food one imagines the Romans must have feasted on when they farmed the *étang* two millennia ago. Yet the only discernible evidence of ancient occupation here is the tiny **Île des Pêcheurs**, at the northernmost corner of the lagoon, which was used for centuries as a shell dump and whose lonely house and boat sheds as a consequence stand on a brittle calcified crust.

The best places for swimming are the sandy eastern banks, which you can reach via the main road from the Cateraggio crossroads, the N200, which cuts in a straight line though rolling vineyards to the **plage de Padulone**, 3km due east. A row of modest seafood restaurants and downbeat cafés overlooks the car park. Follow the beach north for 3.5km and you'll reach the Genoese **Tour de Diane**, which overlooks the mouth of the lagoon. Directly opposite, the **Île de Santa Maria** holds a tiny chapel and the ruins of an ancient quayside – all that remains of the port that formerly sprawled from the shores of the lagoon, now long since submerged. Just south of the tower, a waymarked **footpath** peels along the eastern shore of the *étang*, skirting the Domaine de Marestagnu vineyard to rejoin the beach a little under a kilometre from the roadhead – a round walk of about two hours.

Practicalities

Aléria has a handful of good-value **hotels**. *Les Orangers*, just off the crossroads on the road to the beach (☏04 95 57 00 31, ⓕ04 95 57 05 55; ❹), offers the best value, with fully en-suite rooms from €56 in season (or from €44 during the winter). Alternatively, *L'Empereur* (☏04 95 57 02 13, ⓦwww.hotel -empereur.com; ❺), a big hotel around the corner just north of the crossroads on the highway, is clean and comfortable, with large motel-style rooms opening onto a central garden. Top of the range is the three-star *L'Atrachjata*, a little further north (☏04 95 57 03 93, ⓦwww.hotel-atrachjata.net; ❾), which is plush, fully air-conditioned, and fitted with most mod cons. One of the most pleasant **campsites** on the east coast lies 3km east of the Cateraggio crossroads: the *Marina d'Aléria* (☏04 95 57 01 42, ⓦwww.marina-aleria.com; Easter–Oct) backs onto the beach and is well equipped, with facilities including washing machines and refrigerated lockers.

For **food**, you won't do better than ⚶ *Aux Coquillages de Diane* (see above). The same owners also run the *Auberge Le Chalet*, on the roadside at the turning off the main highway for the lagoon, which serves an identical menu but lacks the atmosphere of its floating sister concern.

Castagniccia

Castagniccia, pronounced "Castaneetch", takes its name from the dense forests of chestnuts (*castagna*), first cultivated here by the Genoese in the fifteenth century, which later made this the richest and most densely populated part of the island. Today, many of the beautiful grey-green and silver schist hamlets perched on its ribbon-thin ridges lie virtually deserted or derelict, but the region remains a rewarding one to explore – particularly during the autumn, when whole valleys are carpeted in vivid gold and russet, and in wet weather, when wisps of mist and cloud cling to the lush canopy.

Castagniccia covers roughly a hundred square kilometres, extending south of the River Golo as far as the Bozio, and westwards just beyond the shadowy crest of Monte San Petrone (1767m), its highest mountain. Fuelled by a lucrative trade in chestnut flour and fine woodcarving, the region's golden era occurred during the Genoese peace between 1569 and 1729, when the majority of its opulent Baroque churches, convents, chapels and lofty stone houses were built. In the eighteenth century the arms industry thrived here as well, and its products found a ready market during the Corsican Revolution, during which Castagniccia was a bastion of support for Pascal Paoli (see box, pp.284–285), a native of **Morosaglia**. Decline set in only towards the end of the nineteenth century, with the completion of the railways through the interior of the island. Easing the transport of timber to the coast, this hastened the process of **deforestation**, which ultimately undermined the area's traditional agro-pastoral economy, and stimulated an exodus to the coastal towns and French mainland. These days, Castagniccia comes alive only during August, when families return from Marseille to visit elderly relatives.

Exploring the Castagniccia requires a vehicle and some caution: although there's a larger concentration of roads here than anywhere else in the interior of the island, routes are extremely winding and narrow, with the added hazard of roaming pigs, cows and goats. Daily **trains** from Bastia stop in Casamozza and Ponte Leccia, but unless you're prepared to walk or hitch this isn't much help for exploring the area. Furthermore, hotels and restaurants are to be found only at **La Porta**, **Piedicroce** and **Cervione** – though you could always stay on the coast at Moriani-plage and see the Castagniccia on a day's tour. There's a choice of routes into the region: from the east coast via Prunete

Porto Vecchio & Bonifacio ▼

or Moriani-plage; from the north, via Casamozza; or, from the west, through Ponte Leccia and Morosaglia.

Moriani-plage

One of a string of virtually indistinguishable resorts along the coast north of Aléria, **MORIANI-PLAGE** is a bland strip of souvenir shops and cafés huddled around a crossroads on the N198. The one old building left standing is a tiny schist cottage facing the beach from where, as a plaque on its peeling wall recalls, a 14-year-old Pascal Paoli left for exile in Naples with his father in 1739. For a foray into Castagniccia, however, this is a convenient base, boasting the last decent beach before Bastia, a reasonable choice of accommodation, a large Champion supermarket (300m south of the crossroads), a Société Générale ATM (the only one for miles if you're heading inland), a self-service laundry (on the road leading to the beach) and a small, helpful **tourist office** (Mon–Fri 9am–noon & 2–5pm; ℡04 95 38 41 73, Ⓦwww .costaverde-corsica.com).

A pleasant place to stay is the *Casa Corsa* (℡04 95 38 01 40, Ⓦwww.casa -corsa.net; ❹), a small, homely **bed and breakfast** 6km south of Moriani on the highway; just north of the Cervione turning (D71) look for a sign on the roadside indicating a lane running to the west off the main road – the guesthouse is 150m along it. The hospitable owners have five large en-suite rooms, all lovingly decorated with home-made quilts and family photos, and a flowery patio where breakfast is served.

For somewhere **to eat**, look no further than the excellent ♨ *Chez Ernesto* (℡04 95 38 49 07), down the lane running parallel with the beach (head towards the main beachfront area and take your first right; the restaurant is on your right 30m further on). It serves mainly Italian specialities (including gourmet pizzas from €11) and local seafood. Everything that comes out of the kitchen, from the charcuterie to the chestnut-based desserts, melts in the mouth, and the prices are very restrained, with lunchtime menus from €16.

For **campsites**, there's a choice between the flashy four-star *Camping Merendella*, 700m south of the crossroads (℡04 95 38 53 47, Ⓦwww.merendella.com; May–Oct), or the more modest *Camping Calamar*, 6.5km south at **Prunete** (℡04 95 38 03 54, Ⓦwww.campingcalamar.com; May–Oct). The latter is situated right next to the beach amid an old olive grove; it's small, with only simple facilities, but is kept immaculately clean, and has a sociable little snack bar that stays open late.

Inland from Moriani-plage

A great place to make the most of the views from the east-facing flanks of the coastal hills lies a short way **inland from Moriani-plage** along the D34. Signalled by the prominent bell tower of its church, the village of **SAN NICOLAO** emerges after 6km of tight bends and dense chestnut woods. You can pull over here to admire the colourful decor and trompe l'œil in the seventeenth-century parish church, or continue 4km further uphill to the hamlet of **SAN GIOVANNI DI MORIANI**, where the wonderful *Bar-Restaurant Cava* (℡04 95 38 51 14; June–Sept) serves wholesome Castagniccian specialities – terrine de foie gras with figs and muscat, chestnut-flour cannelloni – on a €23 menu. Their terrace overlooks the Tyrrhenian Sea, with views of all the Tuscan islands; on a clear day you can even make out the Italian coast.

One of the most isolated villages in Castagniccia, **SANTA REPARATA DI MORIANI**, lies at the end of the D34, which winds southwest from

San Giovanni di Moriani into a thick chestnut forest. A good reason to venture up here is the superb *auberge-gîte d'étape Luna Piena* (☎04 95 38 59 48), which makes a perfect base from which to explore a network of **waymarked trails**. Three excellent round **walks** of between two-and-a-half and five hours begin at the village, taking in the old chapels, springs and *bergeries* dotted about the surrounding forests and steep hillsides. Glossy leaflets giving details of the routes on a simple contour map are available free from the *gîte*. Beds in their two- or four-person dorms cost €14, or €33 for half board, which is a bargain considering the quality of the food served – Castagniccian specialities made entirely from local produce. Non-residents can also eat here by prior arrangement; menus are priced at €15 and €24.

Cervione

From San Nicolao, it's 5km south to the largest, busiest and most welcoming village of the Castagniccia, **CERVIONE**, whose houses, spread in an amphitheatre around the lower reaches of Monte Castello, tower over a small, sloping medieval square that's linked to the surrounding streets by a labyrinth of alleys and archways. Flanking the south side of the square is one of the first Baroque churches on Corsica, the **Cathédrale St-Érasme**, founded in 1578 by St Alexander Sauli, who was ordained bishop of Aléria in 1570 and soon transferred the bishopric to Cervione to escape the malaria-ridden swampland of the plain. Reached via an arcaded entrance immediately behind it, the **Bishop's Palace and Seminary**, once the residence of King Théodore (see box, p.280), houses an ethnographical **museum** (June–Sept Mon–Sat 9am–12.30pm & 2–7pm; €2) exhibiting various farm implements and religious statuary.

While in the area, it's worth making a short detour to visit the elegant Romanesque chapel of **Santa Cristina** – take the road from Cervione down towards Prunete (the D71) for about 600m, where a signpost shows the way left down a narrow, twisting lane. The key should be in the door. Marvellous **frescoes** dating from 1473 decorate the twin apses inside: on the left side Christ is depicted with the Virgin, St Cristina and a kneeling monk; on the right, Christ is surrounded by the symbols of the Evangelists; and over the arch between them is a portrayal of the Crucifixion.

There is no hotel in the village, but the friendly *Les 3 Fourchettes* **restaurant** (☎04 95 38 14 86), in the square, does a great-value four-course menu featuring local charcuterie, *soupe corse*, pork fillet with aubergines and cheese, plus dessert, all for €15 (including wine). Advance booking is recommended.

Cervione to Carcheto

West of Cervione, after about 12km of hairpin bends (many with dizzying drops and no barriers), comes **Vallé-d'Alesani**, from where a short detour down the D217/D317 leads to the **Couvent d'Alesani**, near the hamlet of **Piazzali**, where **King Théodore** (see box overleaf) was crowned. Founded in 1236, the Franciscan monastery is mostly a ruin, but its church holds a beautiful fifteenth-century Sienese painting known as the *Virgin and the Cherry*. The site is also associated with the Giovannali sect, who sheltered here after the destruction of their monastery at Carbini (see p.222).

Back on the main road it's not long before you reach **FELCE**, whose Baroque church is decorated with simple yet arresting frescoes – on the ceiling you'll see the artist, palette in hand, floating among the clouds. Also of interest is the **tabernacle** above the altar, carved by a penitent bandit. Ask for the key at the

Théodore von Neuhof

Scorned by Corsican historian Chanoine Casanova as an "operetta king", **Théodore von Neuhof** was crowned king of Corsica on April 15, 1736, a unique title he was to hold for just eight months.

Théodore was an ambitious nobleman with a very colourful past. Brought up in the court of France where he was page to the duchess of Orléans, mother of the Prince Regent, he travelled around England, Holland and Spain, killed his best friend in a duel, and acquired a fortune through some rather dubious financial speculations. Captured by Moors in Tunis in the early 1730s and put into slavery in Algiers, he managed to bribe his way to freedom, and was soon sending word to a group of Corsican exiles in Livorno that he would provide them with aid in return for the crown of their troubled island. Impressed by his royal connections and fancy talk, and desperate for money and arms, the Corsicans agreed. Soon after, Théodore landed at Aléria, decked out in full Turkish regalia with a retinue of French, Italian and Moorish attendants, and was taken in state to the Couvent d'Alesani to be crowned King Théodore I of Corsica. His powers were severely constrained – a council of 24 men was appointed to advise him, and he was answerable to a Corsican parliament – but Théodore had plenty of opportunities for kingly behaviour. Living it up at the bishop's palace in Cervione, he distributed titles among the wealthier Corsicans, made increasingly exaggerated promises of arms for the liberation of his people, and organized a few ineffectual sieges and pointless military manoeuvres against the Genoese.

Mistrust amongst his ministers increased as the emptiness of his promises became obvious, and in November 1736 the king was forced to flee the island via Solenzara, disguised as a priest. Théodore didn't give up entirely on the Corsicans, however – in 1739 he returned with a small fleet but was deterred from landing by the French. Eventually Théodore returned to England, where he died in 1756 having accumulated massive debts. A plaque in London's Soho Square commemorates him: "Fate poured its lessons on his living head, bestowed a kingdom and denied him bread."

mairie. Another reason to pull over here is the fragrant local-produce shop, A Coualina, run by Christine Bereni, on the outskirts of the village, where you can buy home-grown chestnut-pollen honey, free-range eggs, charcuterie, jams, tasty goat's and ewe's cheese and locally made baskets.

Beyond Felce, the road winds slowly up to the **Col d'Arcarotta**, dividing the Alesani Valley from the Caldone basin, the heartland of Castagniccia. The distinctive green marble that crops up hereabouts was once much sought after, being used in the construction of the Paris Opéra and Medici chapels of Florence. Straddling the pass, a local speciality **restaurant**, the *Auberge des Deux Vallées* (☎04 95 35 91 20; June 15 to Sept), has the best of the views, with Monte San Petrone dominating the skyline to the northwest. Its convivial wood-lined bar makes a good place to sample typical Castagniccian cuisine (such as *figatellu*, roast pork or trout in cream cheese, suckling kid and chestnut-based desserts). Served indoors or al fresco on the terrace (for a ten-percent surcharge), menus (€15–25) all feature pork with *brocciu* and chestnut-flour fritters.

Standing at a nexus of some enjoyable local footpaths, the *Auberge* is also well placed for **walks** in the area. Ask in the bar for the *Sentiers de Pays* leaflet (*dépliant*), which gives you a rough idea of the routes and distances of the various paths. From the col, much the most rewarding option is the five-hour round walk to Stazzona and the mineral-water hamlet of Eaux d'Orezza (see p.282), taking in some of the region's best viewpoints and tracts of old chestnut forest.

The first sizeable settlement below the pass is **CARCHETO**, set amidst an ocean of chestnut trees and giving a good view of Piedicroce across the valley. Carcheto's dilapidated **Église Ste-Marguerite**, set by a wood on the edge of the hamlet, is an eighteenth-century edifice packed with decaying examples of local work – luridly painted stucco covers the walls, portraying scenes from the Crucifixion, with an alabaster statue of the Virgin and Child providing a restrained counterpoint. If the church is locked, you can pick up the key from the *Refuge* hotel in Piedicroce (see below). Outside the church, a sign for "La Fontaine" directs walkers through the wood to a **waterfall**, **Cascade La Struccia**, which crashes through an opening in the trees – a fine spot for a dip and a picnic: follow the track indicated, heading straight on where the main (motorable) trail switches sharply to the right (ignore the orange splashes of paint), passing a cemetery, followed by a spring.

Piedicroce

The cluster of hamlets comprising the commune of **Orezza** lies to the north of Carcheto, strung along the lower slopes of Monte San Petrone. During the mid-nineteenth century, this was the most densely populated *commune* in the whole of France, with 91 inhabitants per square kilometre. Today, however, barely two hundred permanent residents live in **PIEDICROCE**, the area's principal village, whose **hotel**, *Le Refuge* (℡04 95 35 82 65, ℻04 95 35 84 42; May–Oct; ❸), is the sole place to stay in the valley. Perched on a steep terrace, the building itself is a pink monstrosity, but its **restaurant** (open all year) does

---

A Castagna

The **chestnut tree** (*la chataîgnier* in French, *a castagna* in Corsican) grows in most areas of the island between 500m and 800m, but only in Castagniccia – whose mild, moist climate and schist soils create the optimum environment – does it form such extensive forests. Planted in the fifteenth century by the Genoese, these forests were the linchpin of the local economy for more than four hundred years, providing fuel, carving and building material, pollen for bees and, most importantly of all, a ready source of food.

The first chestnut pods, or *pelous*, appear on the trees in mid-August, but the harvest doesn't usually start until two months later, while the leaves are falling. Removed from their spiky pods, the nuts are shelled and stored in special double-storey stone sheds called **séchoirs**, where they dry over the winter. Traditionally, the largest and most succulent were eaten whole, while the rest were taken to watermills and ground into flour (*farina*). This formed the mainstay of the peasant diet in many areas of upland Corsica, where it was mixed with salt and water to make **pulenda**, a kind of polenta, or, on special occasions, baked into cakes and biscuits. Any surplus was bartered for olive oil and wine from the coastal villages.

During the late nineteenth century, the "chestnut economy" of regions such as Castagniccia went into freefall as acres of forest were felled for timber and to provide tannin for leather production. Still more trees died due to neglect as rural populations dwindled, while a virulent fungal disease has also taken its toll over the past decade. These days, *pulenda* and chestnut-flour cakes, served as gourmet specialities in expensive restaurants and souvenir boutiques, have become more a symbol of the islanders' traditional identity than eaten as daily staples; emigrants, for example, are still often sent parcels of flour from their family land by older relatives. The only apparent beneficiaries of the chestnut's decline are Corsica's wild pigs, who gorge themselves on the ungathered windfalls.

excellent Corsican food (menus €18–27), including Castagniccian specialities such as chestnut fritters with *brocciu*.

Piedicroce's **Église de Saints de Pierre et Paul**, built in 1691, harbours a handful of mediocre sixteenth- and seventeenth-century paintings, and a restored organ that is reputedly the oldest in Corsica. A short way further north on the D71, the forlorn ruins of **Couvent d'Orezza** have profound historic resonance for Corsicans. A centre of resistance to the Genoese republic in the eighteenth century, the building hosted several *consulte* (rebel meetings): on April 20, 1731, twenty representatives of the clergy gathered to discuss whether violent rebellion was against the fundamental principles of Christian morality, and it was here that Paoli was voted commander-in-chief of the Corsican National Guard. Paoli also met Napoléon at the church in 1793 during an unsuccessful attempt to achieve a truce between their respective armies. The Germans finally destroyed the convent in 1943 after discovering it had been used as a Resistance arms dump.

Piedicroce's **tourist office** (mid-June to mid-Oct daily 9am–noon & 2–6pm; ☎04 95 35 82 54), opposite the spring in the middle of the village, stocks an impressive selection of books on Corsica, as well as the handy *Sentiers de Pays* detailing the area's footpaths. Nearby, the *Café Oimeauz* serves fresh sandwiches and ice creams on a lovely terrace overlooking the valley; the baker's van passes by at around 10am in time for a late breakfast.

The Orezza Valley: Stazzona to the coast

STAZZONA, 2km downhill along the D506 from Piedicroce, was the centre of arms manufacture during the War of Independence – its name means "forge" in Corsican. From the 1850s onwards, however, it has made its money from the naturally sparkling **Eaux d'Orezza** spring: as the faded old hotel signs indicate, people used to come up here for the curative waters, among them Pascal Paoli, Napoléon Bonaparte, English aristocrats and colonialists from French Indochina. The gradual decline in the water's popularity in the twentieth century was mainly attributable to its foul metallic taste; but a new bottling plant has been set up to reduce the iron content (and the size of the bubbles) and Eaux d'Orezza is once again a popular brand, available in most restaurants and bars on the island.

While you're on this side of the valley, you could follow the D46 past the spring for another 4km to **VALLE D'OREZZA**, where traditional smoking pipes and boxes are carved from olive and chestnut wood. Formerly this hamlet exported crafted wood objects all over Corsica, France and Italy; now only a handful of elderly artisans still live here, selling their work to visitors direct from tiny cottage workshops.

Somewhat grander Castagniccian wood carving adorns the door of the church at **PIAZZOLE**, reached by following the D506 down the valley for 4km until you see a sign pointing uphill to the right. One of Corsica's finest examples of **naïve folk art**, the door, painted in terracotta, peppermint and blue, is believed to have been the work of a repentant bandit as an act of atonement and gratitude to the villagers for sheltering him from the gendarmes. An interpretative display nearby unpacks the elaborate symbolism of the carved panels, one of which features a self-portrait by the artist.

Back down on the main road, a right turn leads north along the D506 down an imposingly deep valley towards the coast. At a tiny hamlet called **Rumitoriu** is the region's most pleasant **campsite**, the *Camping à la Ferme Les Prairies* (☎04 95 36 95 90). Spread over grassy terraces under stands of magnificent old chestnut trees, it's a rough-and-ready place with only basic facilities, but the

The Monte San Petrone hike

Visible all over Castagniccia and central Corsica, the craggy summit of **Monte San Petrone** (1767m) is one of the most thrilling viewpoints on the island, accessible on a comfortable four-hour round-hike (2hr 30min ascent, 1hr 30min descent) along a clearly marked trail. Each year in August, hundreds of local villagers, including a fair number of old folk, climb to the top for a special Mass, so the route is relatively easy-going. That said, you'll definitely need sturdy footwear and a good pair of lungs, as the path gets steep and rocky towards the top.

The trailhead for the hike is at **Campodonico**, about 2km west of Couvent d'Orezza up a side road. Park your car in the lay-by at the entrance to the hamlet and head down the lane through the houses, turning right along the mule track that leads up the valley. From here, the trail – marked at regular intervals with splashes of orange or red paint – zigzags up to a scattering of **bergeries** (1hr 30min), where you should briefly quit the path and follow the hillside around to the north to get the best views of the mountains inland. All of northern Corsica's principal peaks are visible at this point, from the Cinto massif down to Monte Rotondo.

Once you've rejoined the marked trail, it takes around one hour to reach the summit, passing through beautiful birch woods and mossy boulders. The final thirty minutes are tough going, but the 360-degree panorama from the top, marked with a crucifix and a serpentine-stone carving of St Peter, is breathtaking. In clear weather you can see from the coast of Tuscany to Cap Corse, and across the swath of dramatic snowcapped mountains to the east.

Note that if you have the use of two vehicles or are happy to hitch, a good alternative descent leads north from the *bergeries* mentioned earlier along a clearly marked trail to the **Col de Prato**, a short way east of Morosaglia. Some hikers use this gentler, more shaded trail as an approach, but it isn't nearly as rewarding a route as the one described above, since the beech cover obscures the views for most of the way.

views up the valley are lovely and the *patrons* very welcoming; they also have a handful of simply furnished **rooms** in a new block on the edge of the site, costing around €55 in peak season.

Campana

CAMPANA, 4km west of Piedicroce, merits a stop for its Baroque church of **Sant'André**, which houses a fine *Adoration of the Shepherds* attributed to the Spanish seventeenth-century painter Zurbarán. Renowned for its beautiful light (and, bizarrely, for the faintly demonic expression on the face of the boy carrying the eggs), the painting was given to the parish by a wealthy local resident in 1895. The key to the church is kept by an old lady who lives in the last house on the left as you face the village.

There's a great little **place to eat** here: the *Restaurant Sant'Andria* (☎04 95 35 82 26; closed Sun out of season). The menus (€17–21) are definitively Castagniccian – local charcuterie or pâté, veal and olive stew, potatoes *au gratin* with wild mushrooms, *chard* spinach with mint, strong ewe's cheese and chestnut flan for dessert – and the interior full of warm wood colours from the carved furniture and light streaming in through large windows overlooking the valley.

La Porta and Col de Prato

Thanks largely to the gigantic five-storey bell tower rising from its terracotta and grey schist rooftops, **LA PORTA** is the most distinctive village in Castagniccia. Swathed in lush chestnut forest, with the granite crags of Monte San Petrone

Pascal Paoli

"He smiled a good deal when I told him that I was much surprised to find him so amiable, accomplished and polite," wrote Boswell on first meeting **Pascal Paoli** in 1765, "for although I knew I was to see a great man I expected to find a rude character, an Attila king of the Goths, or a Luitprand king of the Lombards." By this time Paoli was 40 years old and famous throughout Europe, widely admired by the liberal intelligentsia of the time, among them Jean-Jacques Rousseau.

Paoli was born in **Morosaglia** (see below) with the cause of Corsican independence in his blood – his father, Giacinto, a doctor, was a first-generation rebel, one of the three primates elected in 1731 by the independent assembly. At the age of 14, Pascal accompanied his father into exile in Naples, where the boy became a keen student of political enlightenment. At the time of Gaffori's assassination, Pascal was a 29-year-old sub-lieutenant in a Neapolitan regiment, but his brother Clemente was in the thick of the rebellion. Appointed one of four regents after Gaffori's death, Clemente invited his younger brother to take over the position of **General of the Nation**, a title he accepted in **1755** and was to hold for the next fourteen years.

Paoli's intention was to drive out the Genoese by force of arms, but despite his military background he wasn't an experienced soldier, and was anyway always short of the necessary supplies. However, he proved to be adept in the art of government, giving the island a **democratic constitution** that anticipated that of the United States of America; founding the university at Corte; building a small navy that was strong enough to break the Genoese blockade; and establishing a mint, a printing press and an arms factory. Furthermore, the system of justice instituted by Pascal Paoli was effective enough to bring about a decline in vendetta killings.

Then in **1768** everything collapsed. The French moved in once more, this time intending to stay after having bought out the Genoese under the terms of the Treaty of Versailles. Determined to crush the rebels for good, the French overwhelmed the Corsican troops at Ponte-Nuovo, whereupon Paoli went into exile in London. However, his political life was not over.

looming behind, its centrepiece is the spectacular **Église St-Jean-Baptiste**, erected in 1720 and widely regarded as the high watermark of Baroque architecture in Corsica. The church's grand facade gracefully unites all the principal features of Rococo. Inside the building are several noteworthy art treasures, including a resplendent trompe l'oeil ceiling, a gory depiction of the beheading of St John the Baptist (to the right as you face the altar) and, opposite this (on your left as you enter), *The Martyrdom of Sainte Elaulie* by Detouche, a student of Delacroix.

There is nowhere to stay in La Porta, but the ✣ *Restaurant de L'Ampigignani* (*Chez Elizabeth*; ☎04 95 39 22 00), down the road through the centre of the village from the church, is a good **place to eat**, with a light and airy dining hall offering magnificent views down the valley. The food is consistently good, too, and reasonably priced considering the quality; everything comes from the immediate vicinity and is prepared according to traditional Castagniccian recipes (menus €16–27; pizzas €8–12).

Heading uphill on the D205 out of La Porta will bring you to the **Col de Prato** (985m), the highest point on the roads of Castagniccia. It was here in 1948 that musicologist Félix Quilici and his team made some historic recordings of *chiami e rispondi* polyphony singing at the annual **Fiera di a bocca di u Pratu** agricultural fair, which is still held here at the end of July.

In **1789**, at the start of the French Revolution, the people of Corsica were declared to be subject to the same laws as the revolutionary state, and it was in this changed political climate that Paoli returned triumphantly to the island in the following year. Initially he sympathized with the new republicanism, but the Corsican Jacobites – the Bonaparte family amongst them – owed too much to France to have much sympathy with separatist politics. Disagreements came to a head with Paoli's arraignment in June **1793**. His response was dramatic. Setting up an independent government in Corte, he approached the British government for help, who, having been driven out of Toulon by the French, were in search of a naval base in the area; and so there followed one of the more curious episodes of Corsican history.

The British sent **Sir Gilbert Elliot** to evaluate the situation, and agreement was quickly reached. English troops and naval forces moved in, and after some fighting – during which the future Admiral Nelson lost the sight in one eye – the French moved out. A new constitution was drawn up that gave Corsica an attachment to the English Crown, but with a large degree of autonomy. It's questionable whether Paoli was ever entirely happy with the course of events, but he was in a difficult situation, as the guillotine was waiting for him if France ever regained control. There seems no doubt that he expected to be appointed viceroy of the island, and when Elliot was given the job things began to turn sour. The parliament of 1795 elected Paoli as president, but Elliot objected; soon after, rioting was provoked by a rumour that Paoli's bust had been deliberately smashed at a ball given in the viceroy's honour. When the English began talking again to the republican French, the game was over. In 1796 Paoli was persuaded to return to London, shortly before Elliot withdrew as Napoléon's army landed to secure the island for France.

Given a state pension, Paoli died in London in **1807** at the age of 82, a revered figure. He was initially buried in his place of exile – there's a bust of him in Westminster Abbey – but his ashes now lie in his birthplace.

Morosaglia

MOROSAGLIA, a short way north of Col de Prato on the edge of Castigniccia, is renowned as the birthplace of Pascal Paoli. The family home, still owned by a descendant of the man Corsicans call U Babu di a Patria ("Father of the Nation"), has been given over to a small but interesting museum, the **Maison de Pascal Paoli** (daily except Tues: April–Sept 9am–noon & 2.30–7.30pm; Oct–March 9am–noon & 1–5pm; €2), signposted east of the village in the hamlet of Stretta. A video primes you for the tour of the house, whose exhibits comprise a small collection of letters, maps (by cartographers such as Thomas Jeffries), books (among them a first edition of Boswell's *Journal*) and other memorabilia, including the very first Corsican newspaper, printed in 1794, and the original Moor's head flag. Over the past decade or so, the museum has also acquired an impressive array of Paoli-related works of art: the famous portrait painted during his exile in London by Sir Thomas Lawrence (formerly housed in the British Museum); a contemporary copy of a bust sculpted by Chapman for the memorial at Westminster Abbey; and Bainbridge's 1769 battlefield scene. Paoli's ashes, brought back from England in 1807, are entombed in a marble-lined chapel next door, revered by Corsican nationalists.

Paoli was baptized in the Pisan-founded but extensively rebuilt church of **Santa Reparata**, reached via a path that starts 400m down the hill, behind the large house on the right side of the road. His brother Clemente, described by Dorothy Carrington as "a matchless marksman who prayed for his enemies' souls as he shot them down", lived out his retirement here, in the large mansion that's now the village school.

A charming little Corsican-speciality **restaurant** here is the *Osteria di U Cunventu* (℡04 95 47 11 79), on the main street. It serves simple but refined versions of local standards, using seasonal ingredients sourced in and around the village – including kid with polenta, *blettes* (chard spinach) stuffed with proper (ie sheep's) *brocciu* and a sublime, Castagniccian-style tiramisu. Count on €35–40 à la carte; the specials board offers plenty of light mains and salads.

Alternatively, press on to the splendid *A Stella di Rustino* (℡04 95 38 77 09) in the village of **Valle di Rostino**, reached via the windy back road that turns right off the D71 at the Bocca a Serna, 2km below Morosaglia. Follow the D15B for 2km, and turn left at the first fork. The **restaurant**, occupying a new building at the entrance to the village, has two signature dishes: Corsican lasagne with six kinds of meat (including pigeon and wild boar) cooked in wine and flavoured with strong ewe's cheese; and *tripettes* of veal. Two menus are offered: one at €28 and the other at €37, both including wine, coffee and *digestif*.

The Casinca

Bounded by the Golo and Fiumalto rivers, the **Casinca** covers the eastern slopes of Monte Sant'Angelo, an area swathed in olive and chestnut trees and embellished with stately villages. It's less popular with tourists than the Castagniccia, but is easier to get into if you haven't got your own transport, as a **bus** runs daily (except Sun) from Bastia to **Vescovato** and **Venzolasca**, many of whose inhabitants earn their living in the city. There's **no accommodation** on offer, but it's a small area and can be easily covered in half a day.

The Casinca villages

CASTELLARE DI CASINCA, just 1km up the D6 from the main coast road, about 15km north of Moriani-plage, affords a wonderful view of the eastern

▲ A Casinca village

plain and has a beautiful tenth-century church, **San Pancrazio**, notable for its triple apse and for housing the mummified remains of St Pancrace, who was martyred in Rome in 304 AD and later became the patron saint of Corsican bandits. About 1km further along the D206, a road off to the left leads to **PENTA DI CASINCA**, the second-largest village in the region. Its dark streets, crammed with lofty schist buildings dating principally from the fifteenth century, open out onto a large square, which gives another fine view across the plain.

Heading east for 1km along the D206 will bring you to a junction where an abrupt left turn leads onto the spectacular road flanking Monte Sant'Angelo. **LORETO DI CASINCA**, the next halt and the area's most appealing village, perches on a spur overlooking all the villages of the Casinca, its long main street affording a panorama right across to Bastia – the terrace to the left of the church is the best place to make the most of it.

Some 500m north of the Loreto you can cut back east by taking a right turn and following the road across a ridge for 2km until you hit the D237 again. A right here will bring you to **VENZOLASCA**, a remote and lofty village whose slender, lance-like church spire is conspicuous from a long way off. This is one of the few places in Corsica where you still occasionally see men dressed in traditional black corduroy, complete with silver studs and gun belt. From here it's a short drive down to **VESCOVATO**, set amongst chestnut trees and olive groves. Capital of the Casinca, this was an important place in the thirteenth century when the bishopric of Mariana was transferred here in a move to escape the malaria-ridden plain (*vescovato* means "bishopric" in Corsican). The bishopric remained here until 1570, when it was relocated to the more important town of Bastia. The village is livelier than most places in the region – its busy central square, shaded by lines of ancient plane trees, even has an outdoor **café**, a rare find in these parts.

Eating

L'Ortu Venzolasca, 1km further down the same road as *U Fragnu* (see below) ☎04 95 36 64 69. One of Corsica's very few organic-vegetarian restaurants. It's a homespun kind of place, slightly ramshackle and swathed in greenery, but offers a tempting (and extremely healthy) €20 menu with sprouted seeds and root vegetables fresh out of the garden. The family also sell their own honey, walnuts and medicinal maquis herbs.

U Fragnu Venzolasca, 100m from the centre of the village along the road to Vescovato ☎04 95 36 62 33. *Patronne* Mme Ninou Garelli prides herself on reviving long-forgotten recipes, such as her fragrant *soupe de berger*, made with wild onions, nettle buds, maquis herbs,

pasta *maison* and a string of secret ingredients. At €38 per head, the single set menu isn't cheap, but quality is guaranteed.

U Radaghju Loreto di Casinca ☎04 95 36 30 66. People travel from Bastia to eat at this delightfully olde-worlde restaurant where you can enjoy copious home cooking in a stone-walled dining room filled with antiques. Corsican hot pots, chestnut and *brocciu* fritters, wild-boar with pasta, local ewe's cheese and wine all on feature on their great-value €24 menu. If you can live without the farm implements as a backdrop, try the less rustic dining room across the road, which has far better views over the coastal plain.

Travel details

Buses

The listings below summarize which bus companies cover which routes, how often they run

and how long journeys take. Start by looking up your intended destination in the first section; then, using the company's acronym (eg EV or RB), go to the second section for more detailed route and frequency information. Precise departure times can be checked in advance either via the bus companies direct, or (if your French isn't up to that) Bastia tourist office (℡04 95 31 81 34). A full rundown of Corsican bus services, including up-to-date timetables, also appears online at ⓦwww .corsicabus.org.

Aléria (Cateraggio) to: Bastia (RB; 1hr 30min); Corte (ACT; 1hr 25min); Ghisonaccia (RB; 25min); Porto Vecchio (RB; 1hr 20min); Solenzara (RB; 40min).

Cervione to: Bastia (TP; 1hr 30min).

Ghisonaccia to: Aléria (RB; 15min); Bastia (RB; 1hr 45min); Porto Vecchio (RB; 55min); Solenzara (RB; 15min).

La Porta to: Bastia (TAP; 1hr 30min).

Loreto di Casina to: Bastia (TA; 1hr 15min).

Moriani-plage to: Bastia (RB; 35min).

Solenzara to: Aléria (RB; 35min); Bastia (RB; 2hr 5min); Ghisonaccia (RB; 20min); Porto Vecchio (RB; 40min).

Venzolasca to: Bastia (AC; 50min); Vescovato (AC; 10min).

Vescovato to: Bastia (AC; 40min); Venzolasca (AC; 10min).

AC: Autobus Casinca ℡04 95 36 70 64. Bastia–Vescovato–Venzolasca Mon–Sat 1 daily.

ACT: Autobus Cortenais ℡04 95 46 22 89. Aléria–Corte July 15–Aug Tues, Thurs & Sat 1 daily.

RB: Rapides Bleus ℡04 95 31 03 79 or 04 95 70 10 36, ⓦwww.kallistour.com. Porto Vecchio–Solenzara–Ghisonaccia–Aléria (Cateraggio)–Prunete–Moriani-plage–Bastia mid-June to mid-Sept 2 daily; mid-Sept to mid-June Mon–Sat 2 daily.

TA: Transports Albertini ℡04 95 36 310 10. Loreto di Casinca– Bastia (Palais de Justie) Wed 1 daily.

TAP: Transports Ampugnani ℡04 95 36 90 33. La Porta–Barchetta–Bastia Mon–Sat 1 daily (Tues & Fri only in school holidays).

TP: Transports Peri ℡04 95 33 71 82. Cervione–Bastia Mon–Sat daily.

Central Corsica

CHAPTER 7

Highlights

✳ **Mountain hikes from Haut'Asco** Climb to the summit of Monte Cinto, Corsica's rooftop, or try the ascent of Punta Muvrella for the ultimate view of the island's highest peak. See p.296

✳ **Niolo cuisine** Eye-wateringly strong ewe's cheese and mountain charcuterie – perfect picnic fodder. See p.300

✳ **Lac de Nino** Scenery reminiscent of Tibet, with wild horses and snow peaks fringing the horizon. See p.301

✳ **Santa di u Niolu** The interior's major religious festival, celebrated with ritual and polyphony singing. See p.302

✳ **Corte citadelle** Perched atop a twisted pinnacle of rock – the perfect emblem for *l'âme corse*. See p.309

✳ **Gorges du Tavignano** Neck-craning cliffs and ancient pine forest, crossed by a medieval mule track. See p.310

✳ **Hotel Monte d'Oro** Hotel oozing period charm, with creaking floorboards, the smell of bees' wax and *fin-de-siècle* decor. See p.319

✳ **Santa-Lucia-di-Mercurio** Jewel in the crown of the Bozio's wild schist *villages perchés*, framed against a vast sweep of snow and granite. See p.313

▲ Lac de Nino

Central Corsica

W hen the FLNC (Fronte di Liberazione Naziunale di a Corsica) decided to stage a show of force – or *nuit bleue* – to underline its ceasefire in 1996, it was no coincidence that the location they chose lay deep in the centre of the island. Although thoroughly depopulated and at an all-time low ebb economically, the interior, with its granite mountains, swirling mists and dark tracts of pine forest, is far more expressive of Corsica's essence than the pastel and turquoise colours of the coast. Ajaccio and Bastia (or Paris and Marseille) may be where most islanders live these days, but it is to the villages of the mountain valleys that most return in August, and which they consider home.

For visitors, it's the stupendous **landscapes** that are the big attraction of the island's core, and the best way to explore them is to get onto the region's ever-expanding network of marked trails and forest roads. The ridge of mountains lining the watershed is closely tracked by the epic **GR20**, a route that can be picked up from various villages and is scattered with refuge huts. Other marked trails wind off the watershed to the surrounding summits. Of these, the island's two highest peaks – Monte Cinto and Monte Rotondo – provide the most compelling routes. For less experienced trekkers, there are also plenty of lower-altitude trails to exquisite glacial lakes and viewpoints over the valleys, while the region's roads, though often in disrepair, penetrate deep into the forests that carpet the mountain slopes.

Corte, set in a broad valley at the centre of the island on the main road between Ajaccio and Bastia, provides the perfect, most central base to begin exploring, and has the bulk of the region's accommodation – elsewhere, it's rare to find more than one basic hotel or *gîte d'étape* per village. Capital of independent Corsica in the eighteenth century, Corte is a fortress town *par excellence*, with its walled citadelle, set atop a twisted pinnacle of rock, piercing the landscape of overlapping mountains and forests. Despite being the second-ranking town of Haute-Corse, it's a peaceful, slow-moving place where old traditions die hard, making it a fascinating introduction to the mentality of the interior.

Around Corte the chief attractions are the spectacular **Vallée de la Restonica** and the parallel **Gorges du Tavignano**. A dramatic road scales the former, giving access to the beautiful Lacs de Melo and Capitello, as well as one of the most famous stretches of the GR20, but you can escape the crowds by following the time-worn medieval mule path bordering the Tavignano River deep in the mountains.

There are some astounding views from the Via Romana, the old Roman route which threads across the mountainsides of the **Bozio** region, a string of depopulated, time-worn villages southwest of Corte. Aside from a smattering of medieval chapels (many of them holding frescoes), the area has some of the most charismatic rural architecture on the island – ancient, labyrinthine hamlets of tower houses, crammed onto rocky spurs, with collapsing slate roofs and overgrown vegetable gardens spilling over their terraces below.

Further north, a hi-spec, euro-funded road penetrates a region of soaring peaks and wild forest that only a century ago was the domain of transhumant shepherds and the toughest alpinists. Dominated by the rugged north face of Corsica's

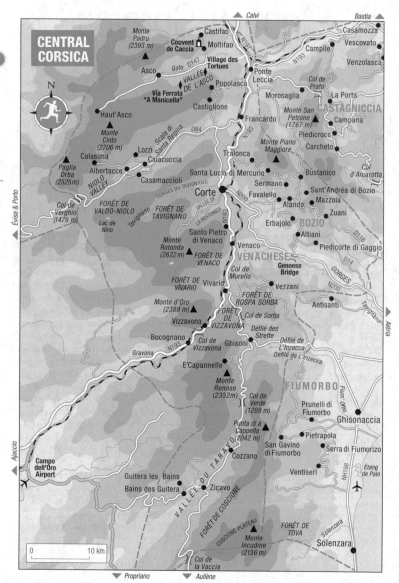

Évisa & Porto

Ajaccio

Propriano ▼   Aullène ▼

▲ Calvi   Bastia ▲

highest mountain, **Monte Cinto**, the higher reaches of the **Vallée de l'Asco** are encircled by a ring of 2500m mountains, many of which – including Cinto itself – may be approached via technically undemanding routes.

A gentler path up Monte Cinto begins in the adjacent valley of the **Niolo**, a sheep-rearing region that was isolated for centuries until legionnaires gouged a road up it a hundred years ago. Like Corte, the Niolo is an essential visit for anyone eager to understand *l'âme corse* – "the soul of Corsica" – so you might want to linger for a night or two in the main settlements of **Calacuccia**, **Albertacce** and **Casamaccioli**, not least to sample the region's famous mountain charcuterie and ewe's cheese, still made according to traditional methods.

The valleys to the south of Corte attract far fewer visitors than those to the north, but there's some great walking in the **Venachese**, where villages such as **Vivario** and **Vizzavona** stand amid some of the island's best-preserved forest. Edward Lear's trademark Gothic etchings perfectly captured the intense sense of verticality generated by **Monte d'Oro**, whose vast pyramidal summit dominates this part of the watershed. At its foot, the **Cascades des Anglais**, a sequence of turquoise pools and falls set amid some glorious old-growth forest, have been attracting tourists since the *belle époque* of the late nineteenth century, when aristocratic British expats used to catch the newly inaugurated railway up here to escape the heat of Ajaccio.

The *micheline* train still provides a convenient way to penetrate deep into the Monte d'Oro area, but to reach the high country further south and east you'll need a car. As a base camp for explorations of the whaleback Monte Renoso massif, the village of **Ghisoni**, at the head of the Fiumorbo Valley, is the obvious candidate, with the only hotel for miles. High above it, a decaying ski station, **E'Capannelle**, presides over the trailhead for the ascent, its lively *gîte d'étape* and refuge crammed with footsore GR20 hikers during the summer.

Pressing on south from Ghisoni, you cross the watershed at aptly named **Col de Verde** to enter the head of the magnificent Taravo Valley. Nestling amid the swathe of unbroken chestnut and pine forest spreading below the pass, the villages of **Zicavo** and **Cozzano** both retain plenty of Corsican character, with ancient stone houses and a handful of congenial places to stay and eat. While lacking the alpine feel of Asco and the Restonica Valley, the scenery of the **Haut Taravo** is nonetheless imposing, while the trails through it have the advantage of being less frequented.

The Vallée de l'Asco

The **Vallée de l'Asco**, the northernmost (and wettest) of the interior's great valleys, was once a region of intensive pastoral farming, whose scattered population lived for centuries off small-scale cheese and wool production, supplemented by crops such as wheat, tobacco, linen and hemp. During the Genoese era, the *poix*, or pitch, made by the Aschesi from pine sap, caused the wholesale destruction of the area's forests, and today much of the landscape is denuded and bleak. Ringed by a string of 2000-metre peaks, the valley remains among Corsica's most remote enclaves; only in 1937 was Asco village connected to the road network, which was extended as far as the ski station by the French Foreign Legion in 1968. Today, the Aschesi, like most mountain communities, rely on the seasonal influx of hikers to make ends meet, along with modest sales of cheese and charcuterie and their famously fragrant **honey**, produced in the ranks of ramshackle hives stacked up the hillsides.

The River Asco starts life as the Stranciacone, which rises at an altitude of 2556m on the lower slopes of **Monte Cinto**, Corsica's highest mountain, then flows through the village of Asco and on through a fantastic **gorge** before reaching the River Golo close to **Ponte Leccia**. In the upper valley, beyond Asco, the scenery is most alpine – up here mouflon roam in carefully protected zones, and bearded vultures and royal eagles can sometimes be spotted in the magnificent **Forêt de Carozzica**. The road comes to an end 15km west of Asco at the semi-operational ski station at **Haut'Asco**, from where trails lead into the surrounding mountains.

No buses run to Haut'Asco, so you'll need your own transport to make a tour of the valley. Starting at Ponte Leccia, it's a good idea to detour up to the delightful village of **Moltifao** before returning to the gorge and the road up to Haut'Asco.

Ponte Leccia

Lying 19km north of Corte at the junction of road and rail routes to Bastia, Corte and the Balagne, **PONTE LECCIA** has little to recommend it beyond its supermarkets and service stations, where you may want to refuel before pressing on into the Vallée de l'Asco or Castagniccia. Outdoor sports enthusiasts might also wish to pay a visit to the office of In Terra Corsa, next to the village train station, which manages (and rents equipment for) the nearby **Via Ferrata** (see below) in the Asco Valley, and can also kit you out for kayaking and canyoning trips in the area.

Moltifao and around

The road up the Vallée de l'Asco, the **D147**, begins 2km north of Ponte Leccia, past the train station on the main Calvi *route nationale*. A right turn after 5km (on to the D47) will take you up the hillside to **MOLTIFAO**, an amphitheatre of old stone buildings set on a spur above the Asco Valley. Moltifao's church

Via Ferrata

In 1998, an entrepreneurial team of Corsican outdoor instructors installed a superb Via Ferrata route in the Asco Valley, "**A Manicella**", 14km west of Ponte Leccia. Encompassing some 1700m of fixed cables (including a total ascent of 200m), the route is classed D+ according to the French scale, which means that only experienced enthusiasts can tackle it unaccompanied. In Terra Corsa, based next to Ponte Leccia station (☎04 95 47 69 48, ⊛www.interracorsa.fr), provides fully qualified guides to lead you through the succession of high rock ledges and weird *tafoni* formations. Under instruction, inexperienced climbers can follow the route in around two hours thirty minutes, rounding off the adventure with a celebratory dip in the natural pools of the Asco river afterwards. As with all Via Ferrata, a head for heights is essential: the route involves some hair-raising traverses of exposed monkey bridges, long tyrolean slides and vertigo-inducing ladder climbs. For those wishing to work into the sport more gradually, In Terra Corsa also manages three easier beginners' routes, among them "**A Torra**", conceived for absolute beginners.

All four itineraries last around two hours thirty minutes. Access is strictly controlled, with first-timers accompanied by In Terra instructors. Rental of all the necessary **gear** (gloves, helmet, harness, karabiners, lanyards and dynamic ropes to break falls) and the services of a guide are included in the cost of admission (around €35–60 per half day depending on the circuit followed). For more on these routes, which are open year round, visit In Terra Corsa's website, which lists various *forfaits* packages bundling together Via Ferrata with canyoning, hiking and "tyrotrekking" tasters.

houses a beautiful sixteenth-century triptych and some sacristy furniture, including a wooden retable incorporating a fine primitive painting of the Virgin on a gold background.

Presiding over the pass above is the ruined **Couvent de Caccia**, a former Franciscan monastery built in the late Gothic style. Partially derelict, it nowadays serves as a cemetery for the nearby villages; the crucifixes, marble tombs, candles and flowers create an extraordinary atmosphere amid the exposed brickwork and lofty Gothic arches. Some of the tombstones outside the building bear the name "Stuart", which historians believe may have been brought to the area by Scottish mercenaries during the Wars of Independence.

On the side of the main D147 below Moltifao, near the hamlet of **Tizarella**, the PNRC (Parc Naturel Régional Corse) have set up the **Village des Tortues de Moltifao** (mid-June to Aug daily 9.30am–noon & 3–6pm, Sept Mon–Fri 9.30am–noon & 3–6pm; ℡04 95 47 85 03; €4.50, children under 10 €1), a breeding sanctuary for the indigenous species of tortoise, which is under severe threat from forest fires, habitat destruction and competition from aggressive, non-native Florida turtles. The cheerful little centre will appeal in particular to kids and the admission charge includes an obligatory tour (you're not allowed to wander around unsupervised), during which visitors get to handle tortoises from age 30 right down to newborns (no bigger than a two-euro coin). The tours last around an hour, with the first kicking off at 10am and the last at 4.30pm.

Asco village and around

The valley proper begins at the **Gorges de l'Asco**, where overhanging rock faces of orange granite soar to 900m. There isn't much to **ASCO** itself, an austere little place 22km west of Ponte Leccia, famed in the eighteenth century as home of the *paceri* (peacemakers), a tribunal of locally elected magistrates who mediated between families involved in vendettas. Its location, however, couldn't be better: built up the left bank of the river, the village lies at the base of a grandiose crest of mountains, with the crags of Monte Padro immediately to the northwest and the Monte Cinto massif and Capo Bianco to the southwest.

A wonderful – if well-known – **swimming spot** can be found on the riverbank below Asco, at the renovated fifteenth-century **Genoese bridge**; follow the narrow one-way road west through the village until you reach a potholed lane running sharply downhill. The water on either side of the humpbacked stone bridge is transparent green and deep, but freezing cold even in midsummer. On its far side, an ancient, paved mule track strikes up the **Pinara Valley** towards the Col de Serra Piana – formerly the main line of communication with the Niolo Valley to the south. Twenty minutes into the walk, you find yourself deep in a wilderness of scrub and towering rock, with only semi-wild goats for company; press on for another couple of hours and you'll arrive at the disused **bergeries de Cabane**, ancient shepherds' huts clinging to the foot of Capu Biancu (2562m), the northeasternmost summit of the Cinto massif and a prime spot for sighting mouflon.

Haut'Asco

Beyond Asco village, the D147 widens as it passes through the **Forêt de Carozzica**, a magnificent forest of maritime and Laricio pines which extends up the valley walls as far as the 2000m contour line. Hugging the river, the road passes clearings and pools ideal for a picnic and a swim, then becomes

The road up the Asco Valley takes you right into the heart of the mountains, and the ski station is a popular springboard for some exceptional high-altitude hiking, most notably the ascent of Monte Cinto. Nearly all the trails in the area are well frequented and marked every 10m or so with paint splashes, but you should be prepared for sudden and dramatic changes of weather, particularly in August, when electric storms rip across the ridges most afternoons. IGN **topo-map #4250** is also useful, although you could get by with the Parc Naturel Régional's topo-guide of the GR20, which passes within a stone's throw of the roadhead.

Monte Cinto

A line of broken crags marking the high point of the crest dividing the Niolo and Asco basins, **Monte Cinto** (2706m) is the loftiest, if not the most handsome, mountain in Corsica, and as such attracts greater numbers of hikers than any other peak on the island. Even so, it's a long hard slog to the summit, and you need to be in good shape to complete the ascent in a day. The route from Haut'Asco, winding up the massif's wilder north face, is more varied and dramatic than the approach from the south (via the Niolo Valley), and is a much better option except in May and early June, when patches of eternal snow clinging to sheltered crevices can be treacherous. A spray-painted rock and regular red spots indicate the way from the ski station car park, from where the trail crosses the Stranciacone torrent, hugging the true right bank before peeling left into the Cirque de Trimbolaccio. Once across the little footbridge, the ascent steepens as the waymarks zigzag up the side of a spectacular ravine via a flank of steep, slabby rock. Once you've reached a spur at 2100m, look across the gorge to the "Leaning Tower", one of the Cinto Massif's most famous formations. From here, a sustained climb across a long scree field brings you to a saddle known as **Bocca Borba** (2207m), where there's a walled shelter under a prominent boulder. At this point, the path fragments into numerous trails which all lead southwest across the névé-encrusted cwm below the summit. Having skirted the semi-frozen **Lac d'Argentu**, you then press up a dramatic, steepening moraine to a ridgetop revealing for the first time superb views south over the Niolo Valley and west coast. However, another 45 minutes of stiff walking still lies ahead as the route drops down the far side of the ridge and then bends left (east), eventually cutting into a final steep climb to the summit across open boulders.

Allow at least **seven hours** for the trip to the top and back (4hr 30min of ascent and 2hr 30min of descent); and bear in mind the advice on mountain safety in Chapter 8 (see p.332). The weather on Monte Cinto can be treacherous at any time of year: a few years ago, seven hikers died on the mountain in a freak snowstorm in July, one of them only a few hundred metres from the ski station at Haut'Asco. Always check the latest weather report before you set off (see p.332) and carry enough warm, waterproof clothing to see you through a sudden deterioration.

Punta Muvrella

After Cinto, the most popular option for a day-hike is the strenuous ascent of **Punta Muvrella** (2148m), reached after a climb up a rocky ravine running west from the ski station (2hr 30min). The route follows that of the GR20 and is thus impeccably waymarked with red-and-white flashes of paint as far as the pass, **Bocca a i Stagni** (2010m). From here you have to follow a straightforward cairned route leading to the right (northeast) up the ridgeline to the summit of the mountain, which offers unrivalled views of the Cinto massif's spectacular north face and, in the opposite direction, distant Calvi. In clear weather it's even possible to see the southern Alps rising from the French and Italian rivieras.

increasingly steep as it climbs to **HAUT'ASCO**, a ski station set amid acres of denuded meadows and lightning-stunted pines. Paid for largely by government grants, the unsightly chalet blocks and rusting ski lifts would be more tolerable if they were used regularly, but the valley sees too little snow to keep the station open regularly. During the summer, however, the place is popular with hikers, who come to tackle the ice-flecked crags of the Cinto massif, looming to the south, while it also serves as a major reprovisioning stop for long-distance walkers following the **GR20**.

While you're here, keep your eyes peeled for a tiny bird scurrying up and down the trunks of the giant Laricio pines on the far side of the road from the station. Unique to the island, the Corsican nuthatch (*sitelle corse* in French) ranks among the rarest species of bird in Europe, with only an estimated 2000 breeding pairs left in the high pine forests of the Corsican interior. It was first discovered to be a separate species in 1883 by a British ornithologist, whence its Latin name, *Sitta whiteheadi*.

No-frills **accommodation** is available at the large and impersonal *Le Chalet* (℡04 95 47 81 08, ℻04 95 30 25 59; May–Sept; ❹), which, in addition to standard chalet-style rooms with balconies, offers budget *gîte d'étape* dorm beds (€9 per bed, or €30 half board). If you can ignore the dusty car park in front of it, the downstairs terrace, where GR20 hikers nurse their aches and blisters, offers an inspiring view of Monte Cinto's forbidding north face. Worth a look in the wood-lined bar behind is the collection of evocative old black-and-white photos showing the Asco Valley's turn-of-the-twentieth-century explorers, among them **Félix Von Cube**, the Austrian doctor who pioneered the first ascent of Monte Cinto, and several other of the island's major peaks, between 1899 and 1904. The food served in the adjacent **restaurant** is nothing to write home about, unless you've just staggered in from the hills, in which case forget their €17 menu in favour of the *carte*, which includes great steak and chips.

Still more basic dormitory accommodation is offered at the PNRC **refuge** (€11 per bunk), behind the hotel, which also has a well-equipped kitchen and communal dining hall centred on a huge wooden table. Campers and bivouackers (€6) pitch amid the scant shelter of the pines and juniper bushes outside. A couple of kilometres back along the valley, the two-star *Monte Cintu* **campsite** (℡04 95 47 85 88; May–Oct) is a popular option with drivers, offering more comfort on fairly level riverside pitches under the pine trees, plus clean toilet blocks and electricity hook-ups.

The Niolo

The Niolo – homeland of Corsican freedom, inviolable citadelle from which the island's invaders have never been able to expel its mountain folk. This wild trench is unimaginably beautiful.

Guy de Maupassant, *Un Bandit Corse* (1892)

The **Niolo** is the glacial basin of the upper reaches of the **Golo**, a river that rises on the flank of Paglia Orba and debouches to the south of Bastia, 80km from its source. The region's name – a corruption of the Corsican *niolu*, meaning "sombre" or "afflicted" – is now more appropriate than ever, for fire has destroyed much of its forested land, leaving bleak landscapes of granite and shrivelled vegetation dotted with megalithic remains and weird boulders. Conifers and chestnut trees scatter the lower slopes of Monte Cinto, but of the great dark forest that once blanketed the whole basin all that remains is the **Forêt de Valdo–Niolo**, a swathe of Laricio pines.

The forest extends east of the frequently snowbound Col de Verghio, the highest motorable mountain pass in Corsica and one of two routes into the Niolo. The other one is the rocky corridor known as the **Scala di Santa Regina**, a vertiginous ravine some 21km long and 300m high, through which a road was built in the late nineteenth century. Until then, people had used hazardous goat and mule tracks (the *scala*) to get into this region, whose isolation and consequent inbreeding perpetuated the singularly tall, blond and blue-eyed appearance of the Neolithic tribes known as the Corsi, from whom the Niolins claim direct descent.

The Niolins have always made their living from the breeding of goats. Shepherds formerly lived a solitary, harsh existence, trekking over the mountains with their herds to the milder coastal plains for winter – mainly to Galéria on the west coast, but sometimes as far as Cap Corse – and returning to the high ground with their flocks in summertime. Some of the old, bare stone dwellings still litter the higher hillsides, but are mostly abandoned these days. The Niolo's craft industry has all but disappeared, too, though the production of local gastronomic specialities survives: a sharp goat's cheese and some renowned charcuterie, which cures particularly well at this altitude. Ancient traditions, however, have an extra vitality in the Niolo, and some of the finest polyphony singing can be heard here (for more on Corsican music, see p.413).

These days tourism is making itself felt at the far-flung capital of the Niolo, **Calacuccia**, an exposed little place whose (albeit limited) accommodation makes it the most promising base from which to explore the area. Apart from a trip to **Casamaccioli**, you could pause for a definitive Niolin meal at **Albertacce**, climb the southeast side of **Monte Cinto** or hike up the southern flank of the valley to Corsica's most exquisite altitude lake, **Lac de Nino**. To the north, the distinctive shark's-fin summit of **Paglia Orba** offers perhaps the most compelling of all mountain ascents on the island, the spring-board for which is a tiny mountain refuge at the head of the magnificent Golo Valley, a paradise of translucent pools and Laricio pine forest.

Calacuccia

CALACUCCIA, main village of the Niolo region, benefits from its unusual location high on a south-facing slope at the heart of the valley's head. Looming behind, the Cinto massif forms a grandiose backdrop, while below stretches the Lac de Calacuccia, a large reservoir built in 1968 to supply Bastia and the eastern plain. Bathing and sailing on the lake are forbidden, and locals insist the water has caused undesirable climatic changes in the valley – notably an increase in mist and humidity – but its rippled surface, shimmering with reflections of the surrounding peaks, is undeniably beautiful.

Most visitors come to Calacuccia en route between Porto and Corte, pausing to sample its famous charcuterie and ewe's cheese before embarking on the long drive down the Scala di Santa Regina. But the village makes a good base for **walks**, not least the ascent of Monte Cinto and the coast-to-coast **Mare a Mare Nord**, which winds through on its way to the Col de l'Arinella and Tavignano gorge over the ridge to the south.

Aside from a scattering of inaccessible menhirs, the most notable historic monument here is the white-painted **Église de St-Pierre**, at the western exit of the village near the petrol station; inside, a seventeenth-century wooden statue of Christ forms the principal attraction. A kilometre further west on the

By far the most popular mountain hike in the area is the ascent of **Monte Cinto** (2706m), Corsica's highest mountain, via its southeast face. Although not nearly as dramatic as the approach from the Asco Valley (see p.293), this route, boulder-strewn for much of its length, ranks among the island's most frequented trails between mid-June, when the snow melts, and mid-October, when it returns with a vengeance on the high ridges.

To drive as far up the mountain as possible, take the D218 north out of Calacuccia, then turn right along a cement road at the hairpin bend just beyond the hamlet of **Acquale-Lozzi**, some 6km along. A short way above the village lie two campsites (see p.300), where you should leave your vehicle. From there, an unsurfaced *piste* (passable only in a 4x4) winds via another series of sharp switchbacks to the **bergeries de Petra Pinzula**, and on for another 35 minutes to the **refuge de l'Ercu** (1600m), which is open all year but not staffed. If you're hiking all the way from Lozzi, allow around two-and-a-half hours to reach the refuge. This is where the ascent proper starts, and you should aim to be here shortly after dawn, particularly during the summer, when electric storms and rain frequently force hikers off the mountain by mid-afternoon. The climb to the summit takes between three and four hours, depending on how fit you are, and the views are sublime, taking in both coasts, the Tuscan islands and even, on very clear days, the Côte d'Azur and Alps. Descend by the same waymarked route, or via the beautiful **Lac de Cinto** (which adds one hour to the walk). From the campsites to the summit and back takes an average of **ten to eleven hours** of steady walking – a long, tough day by anyone's reckoning.

For the best views of the Cinto massif itself, however, you have to scale the opposite, southern, side of the Niolo Valley. A broken mule track beginning at the Calacuccia dam cuts up the mountainside to the **Col de l'Arinella** (1592m), a pass separating the Golo and Tavignano valleys, from which there's a magnificent vista of the valley. To pick up the trail – a section of the **Mare a Mare Nord** long-distance footpath – cross the dam and follow the waymarks as they cut uphill across the switchbacks on an unsurfaced *piste*. Allow two hours for the climb to the col from the dam. Descend via the same route back to Calacuccia, or continue down the other side for an hour to the **Refuge a Sega**, where you can camp or bunk down in a swish steel-and-wood chalet by the side of the stream. From here, the trail follows the Genoese paved mule path down the Tavignano all the way to Corte, reached in around four hours from the refuge.

Gentler walks

If you feel more like a leisurely **low-altitude walk** than a full-on mountain hike, call in at the Calacuccia tourist office for a free copy of the Parc Naturel Régional's excellent *Balades en Corse: Niolu* leaflet (*dépliant*), which outlines five routes (of between 3hr 30min & 7hr) on a monochrome topo-map. Some, like the excellent "Tour des Cinque Frati" (beginning at Calasima; see p.302), involve stiff ascents, but most are leisurely ambles taking in some of the many prehistoric sites littering the valley floor.

Whichever route you choose, bear in mind the advice regarding mountain safety and equipment in Chapter 8. For getting to and from the trailheads around the Niolo region, a recommended **taxi** service, based in Calacuccia, is offered by M. Jean-Charles Antolini (℡06 10 60 55 24).

7

main road, the **Couvent St-François-di-Niolu** houses an excellent *gîte d'étape* (see p.300). The convent is infamous as the scene of a Massacre in 1774, when eleven local men (one of them only 15 years old) were crushed on cart wheels and hanged for their part in a rebellion against the French. The event is commemorated by a memorial, while on the anniversary of the atrocity, June 23, a special Mass is held in the church.

Practicalities

From July to mid-September, Calacuccia is served by one daily **bus** from Corte (with Autocars Mordiconi; ☏04 95 48 00 04), which continues over the Col de Verghio to Evisa and on to Porto, then returns via the same route. Timetables are available at the helpful village **tourist office**, 200m east of the centre on the Corte road, adjacent to the fire station (May–Sept Mon–Fri 9am–noon & 2–6pm, July & Aug daily 9am–7pm; ☏04 95 47 12 62, ⊛www.asniolu.com). This is also a good place to get advice about local walking routes (see box, p.299).

For **eating**, the popular little *L'Auberge du Lac* restaurant (☏04 95 48 02 73), 2km west of the village along the road that skirts the lakeside, in the hamlet of Sidossi, enjoys a perfect location on the water's edge (though there are no views from it over the lake), and serves authentic *Niolin* cuisine at reasonable prices; menus (€17–25) feature home-made charcuterie, free-range lamb, wild mushrooms and local cheeses.

Accommodation

L'Acqua Viva next to the petrol station as you leave the village on the road to Col de Verghio ☏04 95 48 06 90 or 04 95 48 00 08, ⊛acquaviva-fr.com. Modest, modern two-star on the roadside. The rooms are well furnished (all en suite) and have balconies – those to the rear of the building enjoy the best views (and escape the petrol fumes). ❹

Auberge Casa Balduina opposite the convent, 1km west on the Albertacce road ☏04 95 48 08 57, ⊛www.casabalduina.com. Smart little two-star on the village outskirts. The *patronne*, who speaks good English, does a quality *table d'hôtes: charcuterie maison*, a delicious white-beans-and-ham soup, free-range veal steak with olives, and chestnut *fiadone*. ❹

Couvent St François di Niolu 1km west of the village on the main road ☏04 95 46 11 73. Housed in an old convent (the site of a famous massacre – see p.299), this is an atmospheric place to bunk down if you're walking, with large, well-fitted dorms, some double rooms and a refectory that's fully equipped for self-caterers. The only catch is that they don't offer evening meals, for which you'll have to plod back into Calacuccia or over to the *Auberge du Lac* (see p.299). Dorm beds €15. Rooms ❸

Hôtel des Touristes ☏04 95 48 00 04, ⊛www.hotel-des-touristes.com. A large, grey, granite building slap in the village centre, close to the cafés. The interiors and ambience are little changed since the 1920s, and popular mainly with hikers. As well as standard hotel rooms (with or without attached toilets), they offer budget *gîte d'étape* accommodation in an annexe down the road for €15 per head. May–Oct. ❸

Campsite

Camping U Monte Cintu ☏04 95 48 04 45, ⊛www.camping-montecintu.com. Situated on a natural balcony overlooking the valley in the hamlet of Acquale-Lozzi, 4km west (steeply uphill) on the D218, and well-placed for early morning departures. There are also a handful of inexpensive rooms (❷), as well as a basic pizzeria. Mid-May to Sept.

Camping L'Arimone ☏04 95 48 05 51, ⊛www.camping-larimone.com. The just slightly inferior neighbour to *Camping U Monte Cintu*. Mid-May to Sept.

Albertacce and around

The row of low granite cottages comprising **ALBERTACCE**, 3km west of Calacuccia, makes an interesting contrast with the fortress houses found throughout the rest of the island – people hereabouts thought the mountains were protection enough against uninvited guests. For walkers, the village's modest **gîte d'étape** (☏04 95 48 05 60 or 04 95 48 08 05; €15 per person), on the side of the main road on the eastern edge of the settlement, provides adequate dorm beds and self-catering facilities, though you'd do better to eat at the informal and hugely hospitable 🍴 *Restaurant U Cintu* ("*Chez Jo Jo*"; ☏04 95 48 06 87; May–Oct, and out of season with a couple of hours' notice),

Two of the best hikes in central Corsica begin southwest of Calacuccia, at the head of the Niolo Valley. Crossed by the D84 on its way to Col de Verghio, this area is covered by the extensive **Forêt de Valdo-Niolo**, which comprises some of the island's finest Laricio pines, some of them more than 500 years old and 40m tall. To get to or from the trailheads for these routes, you could either jump on Autocars Mordiconi's daily Corte–Porto–Corte **bus** (see Travel details, p.323), or book a taxi from Calacuccia with M. Jean-Charles Antolini (℡06 10 60 55 24).

Lac de Nino hike

The classic trail hereabouts leads from the *maison forestière* at Poppaghia, 10km southwest of Calacuccia, to **Lac de Nino**, an exquisite high-altitude lake reached after a strenuous three-hour climb from the road. The path is well waymarked and frequented, but it's a good idea to get hold of the IGN topo-map 25, #4251 OT. The trail, marked with yellow splashes of paint, follows a mountain stream up to the **bergeries de Colga**, a gathering of stone shacks just above the tree line (1411m), then on more steeply through a boulder-strewn landscape dotted with stunted elms, up to the **Col de Stazzona** (1762m), between Monte Tozzu (2007m) and Punta Artica (2327m). At the top of the pass there's a weird scattering of black, pointed rocks known as the **Devil's Oxen** – the story goes that the Devil was challenged by St Martin to plough a straight line and, upon failing, his oxen were turned to stone. The Devil hurled his ploughshare in a rage through the distinctively shaped red peak known as **Capu Tafonatu** ("Pierced Mountain"), the vast *tafonu* visible on the opposite side of the valley. It's only fifteen minutes further to the lake, which from June to September is home to herds of wild horses and pigs; in autumn, with a dusting of snow on the peaks, the scenery is reminiscent of Tibetan plateau pasture-land. The surrounding marshy turf declivities, known as *pozzi* ("wells"), are the remnants of lakes gouged by glaciers, which subsequently filled up with sediment.

Cascades de Radule hike

The other recommended hike in the forest is a much easier two-hour return trip to the **Cascades de Radule**, where the River Golo, which has its source high up on Paglia Orba, plunges through a series of waterfalls, forming perfect natural pools. Although it is marked with red-and-white splashes, it's worth taking the IGN topo-map 25, #4250 OT. The trail (one of the rare easy stretches of the GR20) starts at the hairpin bend in the D84 known as Fer à Cheval ("Horseshoe"), 4km below the Col de Verghio. After around thirty minutes you emerge from the pine trees at the **bergeries de Radule**, a collection of shepherds' huts from where the path descends to the river and falls. The GR20 proper continues north, winding up the stream valley, and is well worth following for another couple of hours as far as the **refuge Ciuttulu di i Mori** (1962m), the usual night halt for mountaineers attempting Paglia Orba (for a description of this ascent, see box, p.303).

a short walk west. In a small family dining room, complete with TV in the corner, you can enjoy definitive Niolo home cooking – *charcuterie maison*, *ravioli-brocciu*, locally reared veal in a rich stew, chestnut flan, cheese from a nearby *bergerie*, and *eau de vie* – on a superb-value €21 menu; they also do a simpler three-course €17 menu.

A pleasant **short walk** leads west of Albertacce via the **Mare a Mare Nord**, which begins directly opposite the large roadside crucifix on the edge of the village, to the locals' favourite **picnic spot**. Follow the orange-waymarked path for twenty minutes or so and you'll round the hillside to reach the **Pont de Muriccioli**, where a small chapel and restored water mill overlook a particularly beautiful stretch of river (the Rau de Viru). You can swim in a series of deep natural pools and enjoy the dramatic spectacle of Paglia Orba's rugged summit rising at the head of the valley to the northwest.

With a car, another worthwhile foray from Albertacce is the seven-kilometre drive up the D318 to **CALASIMA**, which is as remote as you'd expect for a settlement at 1100m. With the bulk of Paglia Orba's summit looming to the north, the views over the Niolo improve if you press on through the village and follow the *piste* as it winds below the distinctive needles of the **Cinque Frati** ("The Five Brothers"; 1986m). The tarmac ends 4km west of the Calasima, but the track is motorable for another 2km, where it stops in a clearing wide enough to turn around. From there you could follow the forestry path north into the spectacular **Ravin de Straciancone**. Another hour will take you through some majestic Laricio pine forest to the ⚜ *Bergeries de Vallone*, a remote café serving wonderful home-made Niolo charcuterie, cheese and wholesome soups. The hut, re-provisioned each day by mule, serves as a stopover on the GR20 and makes an ideal target for a walk into this magnificent roadless area. For a fuller review, see p.345.

Casamaccioli

Occupying the greenest part of the Niolo, **CASAMACCIOLI**, 5km from Calacuccia, lies south of the lake on the edge of a large *châtaigneraie*. Its small square, edged by enormous chestnut trees, is the setting for the **Santa di u Niolu**, when thousands of pilgrims and expatriate natives descend on the village to celebrate the Nativity of the Virgin. The focal point of the event is a statue of the Madonna, **Santa Maria della Stella**, which miraculously transported itself here by mule in the fifteenth century after the convent in which it originally resided was burned down by Turkish pirates. Now venerated for her miracle-working powers, she is carried in procession through the village, but the most visually striking feature of the festival is the famous **Granitola**, when dozens of white-robed and white-hooded penitents, drawn from the village's various religious brotherhoods, or *Cunfraternita*, wind and unwind in spirals around a cross (a similar procession takes place in Calvi; see p.116). La Santa has a strongly secular aspect, too. The event, held at the end of the first week in September, formerly provided the main opportunity of the year for Niolins from remote villages to buy, sell and barter; in exchange for wool, meat, milk, cheese and charcuterie, they would obtain hardware, hats, horse tack, woodcarving, textiles, shoes and anything else that could not be manufactured in the mountains. Gambling was also central, and remains so to this day, with serious round-the-clock card sessions held in unlicensed home casinos. Afterwards, the participants celebrate, or drown their sorrows, in the village bar – one of the few places in Corsica where you can still hear traditional improvised singing, or *chiami e rispondi* (see p.413). Outside festival time, however, the only noteworthy sight here is the small **Église de la Nativité**, where you can pay your respects to the crudely repainted and gold-crowned Santa Maria della Stella herself, and enjoy magnificent views of the Cinto massif to the northwest.

Dorm beds in Casamaccioli's tiny **gîte d'étape** (℡04 95 48 03 47), beside the church, cost €15 per night. You can use their self-catering facilities or, if you book in advance, opt for an evening meal (€19). There's also a very congenial *chambres d'hôtes* here, ⚜ *Casa Vanella* (℡04 95 48 69 33, ⓦwww.vallecime .com; ❺), in a modern house overlooking the village boasting fabulous views over to Paglia Orba. It's run by trekking guides Pascale and Jean-François Luciani, who have four sunny guest rooms, plus a family suite on the ground

The ascent of Paglia Orba

The great red wedge of **Paglia Orba** (2525m), rising like a giant dorsal fin beside the pierced peak of **Capu Tafonatu** (2343m), is the Corsican watershed's most distinctive mountain. Thanks to the dizzying drops into the Fangu Valley and Filosorma from its vast northwest face, it is also a more challenging proposition than nearby Cinto. In fine, dry weather you don't need ropes or any technical expertise to attempt the ascent, but a good head for heights is essential, as some sections are notoriously vertigo-inducing.

The traditional **approach** to the mountain via the **Cascades de Radule** at the head of the Golo Valley (described on p.303) is itself a wonderful walk, passing stands of old Laricio pines, deep bathing pools, and eventually high alpine-style pastureland where you can usually spot mouflon grazing on inaccessible ledges. However, you'd have to be a strong climber indeed to cover this, the ascent to the summit and descent back to the roadhead afterwards, in a single day. Instead, most people bivouac at the **refuge Ciuttulu di i Mori**, perched on a natural balcony at the head of the Golo, and set off for the top the following morning (thereby increasing the chances of clear skies and good views).

The **route** begins immediately behind the refuge, climbing steeply up a huge rock choke towards a ridge known as **Col de Maures**. A short way before the pass, cairns rising to your right (north) up a deep corridor indicate the way through a series of huge granite blocks. Once you've arrived at a large ledge after around twenty minutes, the route steepens, progressing through some tight chimneys as far as a false summit, the western edge of the giant Paglia Orba tabletop. From here you drop into a little hollow known as "La Combe de Chèvres", before tackling the final haul to the top. Because the sides of Paglia Orba fall away so steeply, the views from the summit are even more dramatic than those from Monte Cinto, extending far out to sea and across the entire northwestern watershed. Allow a good three and a half hours for the ascent from the refuge, and don't attempt the route if the rock is wet.

floor, and offer evening meals of quality mountain cooking (€75 per double, or €120 for two half-board). Jean-François is something of a living legend in Corsica: in 2000, he covered the famous GR20 trekking route in just over 37 hours – a record no one has got near since (it takes most fit walkers at least ten days to cover the 185km route). The couple also run another, equally pleasant B&B in the Bozio (see p.314).

Corte (Corti) and around

Stacked up the side of a wedge-shaped crag, against a spectacular backdrop of brooding granite mountains, **CORTE** (Corti) epitomizes the spirit of dogged defiance and patriotism which is never far from the surface of Corsican life. This has been the home of island nationalism since the first National Constitution was drawn up here in 1731, and was also where **Pascal Paoli** (see p.284) formed the island's first democratic government later in the eighteenth century. Self-consciously insular and grimly proud, it can seem an inhospitable place at times, although the presence of the island's only **university** lightens the atmosphere noticeably during term time, when the bars and cafés lining its long main street fill with students. For the outsider, Corte's charm is concentrated in the tranquil **haute ville**, where the forbidding **citadelle** – home to the island's premier museum, the **Museu di a Corsica** – presides over a warren of narrow cobbled streets.

Immediately behind the citadelle, the Restonica and Tavignano gorges afford easy access to some of the region's most memorable mountain scenery, best enjoyed from the marked trails that wind through them.

A brief history of Corte

Corte's reputation for belligerent independence was born in the ninth century, when the occupiers of a strategically positioned fort allegedly saw off a group of Saracen raiders. Later on, the Genoese rulers were constantly harried by the local nobles, culminating in 1419 with the takeover by **Vincentello d'Istria**, the king of Aragon's viceroy. After Vincentello's execution in 1434, Genoa ruled relatively undisturbed until the French expedition of 1553, when Corte happily succumbed to Sampiero Corso, though within six years the Genoese were back in charge, and were to stay in control for a long time.

By the early eighteenth century, Corsican nationalism was on the rise in Corte, its success due in part to the town's isolation from the occupied coastal towns. Following a local insurrection in 1731, a National Constitution was drawn up here at the first National Assembly, and in 1752 Gaffori was elected head of state in Corte. After Gaffori's assassination in 1753, Pascal Paoli returned from exile and from 1755 to 1769 made Corte the seat of his revolutionary government, which set up the first Corsican printing press and the **Università di Corsica**, the first university to be established on the island.

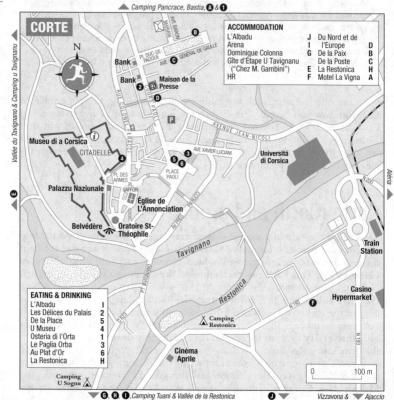

CORTE

Camping Pancrace, Bastia, **A** *&* **1**

N

Bank

Bank

Maison de la Presse

Museu di a Corsica

CITADELLE

Palazzu Naziunale

PL DES ARMES

PL GAFFORI

Belvédère

Oratoire St-Théophile

Église de L'Annonciation

PLACE PAOLI

Universitá di Corsica

AVENUE JEAN-NICOLI

AVE XAVIER LUCIANI

AVE BARON MARIANI

PL DUC DE PADOUE

AVE GENERAL-DE-GAULLE

RUE COLONEL FERACCI

RUE ST-PAUL

Vallée du Tavignano & Camping a Tatoni

Aleria

N200

Tavignano

Restonica

N193

N190

N200

PT AUVIGNANO

N623

Train Station

Casino Hypermarket

Camping Restonica

Cinéma Aprile

ACCOMMODATION
L'Albadu	**J**	Du Nord et de	
Arena	**I**	l'Europe	**D**
Dominique Colonna	**G**	De la Paix	**B**
Gîte d'Étape U Tavignanu		De la Poste	**C**
("Chez M. Gambini")	**E**	La Restonica	**H**
HR	**F**	Motel La Vigna	**A**

EATING & DRINKING
L'Albadu	**1**
Les Délices du Palais	**2**
De la Place	**5**
U Museu	**4**
Osteria di l'Orta	**1**
Le Paglia Orba	**3**
Au Plat d'Or	**6**
La Restonica	**H**

Camping U Sognu

0   100 m

G, **H**, **I**, *Camping Tuani & Vallée de la Restonica*   **J**   *Vizzavona &* ▼ *Ajaccio*

Wild Corsica

An astonishing landscape made up of over 200 beaches, dramatic mountain peaks and thick forest, Corsica is relatively untouched by concrete development. And while it's very tempting to just grab your sunscreen and head for the beach, the variety of landscapes makes Corsica an ideal place to indulge in exciting outdoor pursuits, from canyoning and snorkelling to horseriding and hiking.

The Route de Bavella forest ▲

Forests

In spite of the extensive Genoese timber trade from the fourteenth to the eighteenth centuries, as well as the fires that periodically devastate large swathes of the island, the interior still retains some of the Mediterranean's richest and largest forests. Between altitudes of 700m and 1500m, Laricio pines, some of them growing to staggering heights of over fifty metres, carpet the mountainsides. Lower down, old chestnut woods (which in wetter regions such as Castagniccia still form an unbroken cover) and other deciduous trees such as beech and holm oak give way to more temperature-sensitive maritime pines – the twisted orange trees you'll come across on sea-facing slopes.

Mountains

Responsibility for making sure the mountain areas remain as unspoilt as they are today is the job of the Parc Naturel Regional Corse, or PNRC, which encompasses nearly forty percent of the island's total area. Aside from preserving the natural environment and livelihoods of those people who live in it, the park's chief task is to maintain the waymarked footpaths that provide access to the most remote areas. Nowhere else in the entire Mediterranean boasts such a diverse, well-supported trail network, and tens of thousands of visitors come to the island each year to enjoy it – 18,000 alone to walk the legendary GR20, the high-level route following the line of the Corsican watershed (the *partage des eaux*). Corsica's highest mountain peak is Monte Cinto (2706m), and it's consequently the most popular hiking spot. See p.296 for more on how to tackle it.

Restonica valley, near Corte ▲

GR20, Bocca a Reta ▼

Coast

You can explore the last three roadless areas of the island's shoreline on foot – thanks to the efforts of the Conservatoire du Littoral, which has gradually converted the old Genoese customs officers' paths (known as *Sentiers des douaniers*) into long-distance waymarked paths.

• **The Désert des Agriates**, between St-Florent and the Balagne. It can be covered in two days, with a night stop at a refuge. See p.99.

• **Cap Corse**, from Macinaggio to Centuri-Port. It's possible in one day but take your time and book into a hotel mid-way, or camp. See p.79.

• **Sartenais**, from Campomorro to Roccapina. It can be covered in two days, passing a string of deserted white-sand turquoise coves along the way. See p.238.

▲ Walking the Désert des Agriates

▼ Cycling round Capo D'Orto

Activities

▸▸ **Canyoning** Popular sport that involves following the course of a river or stream on foot, with the aid of ropes and harnesses. Head for Calanches de Piana; Faile de Revinda between Piana and Cargese; Falcone and Ladroncellu gorges around Bonifacio; the Fangu Valle; the Spurtellu ravine near Porto; and the Fiumicelli and Polischello gorges in Bavella. See p.40.

▸▸ **Hiking** The island is home to the famous GR20, along with many other gentler walks and hikes. See Chapter 8.

▸▸ **Horseriding** This has been revived over the past decade or two by the appearance of several excellent *centres équestres*, within reach of the main tourist areas, which offer half-day, full-day or even longer treks. See p.41.

▸▸ **Mountain biking** Corsica is inundated with keen mountain bikers. The best routes are mostly in the south – around the Forêt de l'Ospedale, Bavella and the Coscione Plateau. See p.40.

Underwater Corsica

With visibility extending to 40m in good conditions, Corsica boasts some of the clearest and least-polluted seas in all the Mediterranean. Underwater, the island's topography is as varied and dramatic as it is above the surface, with mountains and sheer cliffs running down to the sea floor. Along the way, pinnacles, plateaux and other distinctive rock formations support an astonishing wealth of subaquatic wildlife, from tiny, multi-coloured rainbow wrasse to giant grouper measuring well over a metre.

With the help of local guides, experienced divers can descend deep enough to Corsica's legendary red coral, which grows at depths of between 70m and 300m. Controlled by strict quotas, a small number of licensed harvesters still collect this rare treasure, most of which is sold in Naples where it is transformed into expensive jewellery.

You don't, however, have to be a fully qualified diver to appreciate the wonders lurking under Corsica's seas. Snorkelling off the beaches, particularly in the far south between Porto Vecchio, the Îles Lavezzi and Bonifacio, you'll be amazed by the variety of sponges, spiky anemones and brightly coloured fish, along with shoals of silver dentex, snapper and turbot.

Preparing for a scuba dive ▲

Fighter bomber wreck ▼

Top 3 diving spots

▶▶ **Méerouville**, off Bonifacio. The best spot to sight a group of tame, chubby-lipped grouper. See p.249.

▶▶ **B-17 American bomber**, Calvi Bay. The bomber crashed into the bay in World War II. See p.118.

▶▶ **German Heinkel 111**, Bastia harbour. Another World War II casualty. See p.68.

However, in 1768, under the terms of the Treaty of Versailles, France bought Corsica from the Genoese, and after the Battle of Ponte Nuovu the following year the period of Corsican independence was at an end. Under the French the town became insignificant, and it's only recently that it has acquired a slightly more exalted status as *sous-préfecture* of Haute-Corse and as the seat of the revived university, whose aims are to re-establish the value of Corsican culture, partly through the compulsory teaching of the indigenous language.

Arrival and information

Buses from Ajaccio and Bastia stop in the centre of town on cours Paoli, the main street, and halfway along avenue Xavier-Luciani. The **train station** is at the foot of the hill near the university, from where it's a ten-minute uphill walk into town. If you're **driving**, the best place to aim for is the **free car park**, to the left at the top of avenue Jean-Nicoli, the road leading into town from Ajaccio and Aléria.

Corte's **tourist office** is situated inside the citadelle, opposite the museum (July & Aug daily 9am–8pm; June & Sept Mon–Sat 9am–1pm & 2–7pm; Oct–May Mon–Fri 9am–noon & 2–6pm, plus Sat in May; ℡04 95 46 26 70, Ⓦwww.corte-tourisme.com). In the same office you'll also find the desk of the Parc Naturel Régional Corse (same hours and telephone number), the best place in Corte for walkers' information.

Accommodation

Accommodation in Corte is plentiful and, with the exception of the smarter hotels hidden 2km southwest of town amid the lower reaches of the Restonica Valley, costs a lot less than on the coast. One reason is that the majority of visitors to the area come here equipped for the outdoors and prefer to **camp**. If you do have trouble finding a room, try *Le Torrent* in Santo-Pietro-di-Venaco (see p.315), which usually has vacancies.

Hotels

If you're travelling without a vehicle, bear in mind that most of the hotels and guesthouses situated out of town will provide a complimentary pick-up from the station if you let them know the day before.

L'Albadu ancienne route d'Ajaccio, 2.5km southwest of town ℡04 95 46 24 55, Ⓕ04 95 46 13 08. Simply furnished rooms with showers (shared toilets) on a working farm-cum-equestrian centre. Warm family atmosphere, beautiful horses, fine views and good Corsican food, served *en famille* so you get to practise your French (at €42 per person, the half board is a bargain). Easily among the most congenial, and reasonably priced, *ferme-auberges* on the island. If you're driving, the easiest route is via the main Ajaccio road for 1500m, where a red-and-white sign points to the right (around the side of a building). Advance reservation essential. ❷–❸
Arena Vallée de la Restonica, 2.5km southwest of town ℡04 95 46 09 13, Ⓦwww.hotel-arena -lerefuge.com. Cosy, unpretentious hotel-restaurant at the roadside, with a sunny terrace and rooms

overlooking a stream (the ones at the back are a touch noisy in spring, when the snowmelt raises the water level, but fine in summer). April–Sept. ❻
Dominique Colonna Vallée de la Restonica, 2km south of town ℡04 95 45 25 65, Ⓦwww .dominique-colonna.com. The more modern of this pair of luxury *auberges*, set amid pine woods next to a stream. It has less character than its neighbour (see *La Restonica* overleaf), but is smart and efficient and with all the mod cons you'd expect of a three-star. Rates include use of the *Restonica*'s pool. Half board optional. Mid-March to Oct. ❺–❽
HR allée du 9-Septembre ℡04 95 45 11 11, Ⓦwww.hotel-hr.com. This converted concrete-block gendarmerie, 200m southwest of the SNCF train station, looks grim from the outside, but its 125 rooms are comfortable enough and its rates

rock-bottom; bathroom-less options are the best deal. No credit cards. ②–③

Du Nord et de l'Europe 22 cours Paoli ⚲04 95 46 00 33, ⓦwww.hoteldunord-corte.com. Pleasant, clean place right in the centre. The rooms are huge and the building has oodles of charm, with a marble-floored entrance hall and high stucco ceilings. Reception is in the *Café du Cours* next door. ⑥

De la Paix 1 av Général-de-Gaulle ⚲04 95 46 06 72, ⓔsocoget@wanadoo.fr. Set in an elegant part of town, this large, smart and central hotel is pitched primarily at tour groups. The pricier rooms have large balconies and TVs. No credit cards. ③–④

De la Poste 2 place du Duc-de-Padoue ⚲04 95 46 01 37. The cheapest rooms in the centre (from €40 for WC *à l'étage*), in a huge old building that opens onto a quiet square just off the main drag. Comfortable enough, but on the gloomy side. ③

La Restonica Vallée de la Restonica, 2km southwest from town ⚲04 95 46 09 58, ⓦwww.aubergerestonica.com. Sumptuous comfort in a wood-lined riverside hotel set up by a former French-national footballer, Dominique Colonna, who bought it after winning the lottery. Hunting trophies, old paintings, salon with open fireplace and leather upholstered furniture create an old-fashioned atmosphere, and there's a large pool and garden terrace. Good value in summer, but not such a great deal in winter, since rates are the same year round. ⑤

Motel La Vigna chemin de Saint-Pancrace ⚲04 95 46 02 19. Tucked away on the leafy edge of town, this small but rather swish students' hall of residence is vacated between early June and the end of Sept and converted into a motel. The rooms are simple and lacking character by Corte standards, but clean and all en suite, with balconies. June–Sept. ④

Gîtes d'étape and campsites

Camping Pancrace 2km north of town, past Saint Pancrace's chapel. Basic, and ultra-secluded, with plenty of shade under ancient olive trees – though quite a plod from town.

L'Albadu 2.5km southwest of town ⚲04 95 46 24 55. Perfect little *camping à la ferme*, situated on a hillside above Corte. No-frills, but much nicer than any of the town sites, and well worth the walk up here (the owners will show you a short cut that'll get you to the centre in 15min). For directions by road, see p.305.

Gîte d'Étape U Tavignanu ("Chez M. Gambini") behind the citadelle ⚲04 95 46 16 85. Scruffy hikers' hostel with small dorms and a garden terrace overlooking the valley. Peaceful, secluded, and the cheapest place to stay after the campsites. Follow the signs for the Tavignano trail (marked with orange spots of paint) around the back of the citadelle. €17 per person (includes breakfast).

Restonica 500m south of the town centre. Middle-sized site on the riverside, close to town, with low terraces, plenty of shade and its own café-bar.

U Sognu route de la Restonica ⚲04 95 46 09 07. At the foot of the valley, a 15min walk from the centre. Has a good view of the citadelle, plenty of poplar trees for shade, and toilets in a converted barn. There's also a small bar (in summer) and a small restaurant (pizzas *au feu de bois* June–Sept).

U Tavignanu chemin de Balini, Vallée du Tavignano ⚲04 95 46 16 85. The hiker's option: a tiny campsite next to the *gîte d'étape* of the same name (see above), accessible only on foot. Follow the road around the back of the citadelle, cross over the river bridge and bear right; the site lies another 10min walk up a path.

Tuani 7km southeast, Vallée de la Restonica ⚲04 95 46 11 62. The wildest and most atmospheric of the campsites around Corte, overlooking a rushing stream, deep in the woods (although too far up the valley without your own car). Ideally placed for an early start on Monte Rotondo. Facilities are more basic than most, although they do have a cheerful little pizzeria-restaurant where locals flock in summer.

The Town

Corte's very compact centre effectively consists of one long street – **cours Paoli**. Lined with shops, banks, restaurants and cafés, this busy thoroughfare runs alongside the **haute ville**, which is reached by climbing one of the cobbled ramps on the west side of the *cours*, or by taking the steep rue Scoliscia from place Paoli.

At the north end of the *cours* lies **place du Duc-de-Padoue**, an elegant square of nineteenth-century buildings that's strangely out of place in this rough mountain town. Its statue, a grim bronze lump by Bartholdi, designer of the

Statue of Liberty, is of Arrighi di Casanova, a general whose service under Napoleon earned him the title of duke of Padua; his ancestral home can be seen in **place Poilu** in the *haute ville*. Apart from this square, there is only one spot where you might want to hang around: **place Paoli**, at the southern end of the main street in the lower town – a more tourist-friendly zone lined with relaxing cafés and restaurants. Its centrepiece is a cumbersome statue of a rather self-satisfied-looking Pascal Paoli.

Place Gaffori

Place Gaffori, the hub of the old **haute ville**, is dominated by a statue of General Gian'Pietru Gaffori pointing vigorously towards the church. On its base a bas-relief depicts the siege of the Gaffori house by the Genoese, who attacked in 1750 when the general was out of town and his wife Faustina was left holding the fort. Faced with weakening colleagues, she is said to have brandished a burning torch over a barrel of gunpowder, threatening to blow herself and her soldiers to smithereens if they surrendered, a threat that toughened them up until Gaffori came along with reinforcements. The house stands right behind, and you can clearly make out the bullet marks made by the besiegers.

Opposite the house, the **Église de l'Annonciation**, built in 1450 but restored in the seventeenth century, is where Joseph Bonaparte, Napoleon's brother and future king of Spain, was christened. Inside, there's a delicately carved **pulpit** and a wax statue of St Theophilus, patron of the town, on his deathbed. The saint's birthplace – behind the church in place Théophile – is marked by the **Oratoire St-Théophile**, a large arcaded building which commands a magnificent view across the gorges of Tavignano and Restonica. Born in 1676, Blaise de Signori took the name of Theophilus upon entering the Franciscan brotherhood, and went on to study in Rome and Naples, then to found numerous hermitages in Italy. In 1730 he returned to Corsica, where, after a few years' activity in the fight for independence, he died on May 9, 1740. He was canonized in 1930, the only Corsican to achieve sainthood, and on the anniversary of his death a commemorative Mass takes place in the oratory, followed by a procession from the Chapelle Ste-Croix, carrying a huge figure of Christ.

For the best view of the citadelle, follow the signs uphill from place Gaffori to the viewing platform, the **Belvédère**, which faces the medieval tower, suspended high above the town on its pinnacle of rock and dwarfed by the immense crags behind. From here you can also admire the vista of the converging rivers and encircling forest – a summer bar adds to the attraction.

Just above place Gaffori, left of the gateway to the citadelle, stands the **Palazzu Naziunale**, a great, solid block of a mansion that's the sole example of Genoese civic architecture in Corte. Having served as the seat of Paoli's government for a while, it became the **Università di Corsica** in 1765. Run by Franciscan monks, the island's first university offered free education to all (Napoleon's father studied here), and the monks taught the contemporary social thought of philosophers such as Rousseau and Montesquieu as well as traditional subjects such as theology, mathematics and law. The university closed in 1769, when the French took over the island after the Treaty of Versailles, and wasn't resurrected until 1981. Today several modern buildings have been added and the *palazzu* houses the Centre du Recherches Corses, dedicated to the study of Corsican history and culture.

The Museu di a Corsica

The monumental gateway just behind the Palazzu Naziunale leads from place Poilu into Corte's Genoese Citadelle, whose lower courtyard is dominated by

▲ The Corte citadelle

the modern buildings of the **Museu di a Corsica** (June 20 to Sept 19 daily 10am–8pm; April 1 to June 19 & Sept 20 to Oct 31 daily except Tues 10am–6pm; Nov–March Tues–Sat 10am–6pm; €5.50). This state-of-the-art museum, designed by Turin architect Andréa Bruno, was inaugurated in 1997 to house the collection of ethnographer **Révérend Père Louis Doazan**, a Catholic priest who spent 27 years amassing a vast array of objects relating to the island's traditional transhumant and peasant past. Gifted to the state in 1972, the three thousand pieces he collected remained in storage for nearly a quarter of a century until a suitable site could be found to exhibit them. With its huge tinted windows and sweeping views, the building certainly makes the most of the location, but ultimately upstages the somewhat lacklustre exhibits inside it. On the first floor, old farm implements and peasant dress are the mainstay of the **Louis Doazan Gallery**, while the adjacent **Musée en train de se faire** (Museum in the Making) gallery explores aspects of contemporary Corsican society, including industry, tourism and religious brotherhoods. In addition, a couple of rooms at the head of the main staircase house themed temporary exhibitions of Corsica-related art and photography.

The citadelle

The entry ticket to the museum also includes admission to the adjacent **citadelle**. The only such fortress in the interior of the island, it was founded in the fifteenth century and served as a military base for the Foreign Legion from 1962 until 1984. Reached by a huge staircase of Restonica marble, a medieval tower known as the **Nid d'Aigle** (Eagle's Nest) forms its highest point. The tower is the only original part of a complex built by Vincentello d'Istria in 1420; the barracks (*caserne*) were added during the reign of Louis-Philippe. These were later converted into a prison, in use as recently as World War II, when the Italian occupiers incarcerated Corsican resistance fighters in the tiny cells. Adjacent to these is the **Échauguette**, a former watchtower which, at the time of Paoli's government, was inhabited by the hangman. This was a job no Corsican would take – accustomed to killing with guns and knives, they found the practice of hanging someone to death too demeaning and dishonourable. A Sicilian duly volunteered, and in 1766 James Boswell visited the poor reprobate: "a more dirty rueful spectacle I never beheld", he wrote of the wretched specimen he found cowering in the turret, with a "miserable bed and a little bit of fire" as his only comfort.

Eating and drinking

Corte has only a handful of **restaurants** worthy of note (see below), plus the usual pizzerias and crêperies. Cortenais specialities are stuffed trout, and lasagne with wild-boar sauce, but if you just want a hot snack try the pizza van parked opposite *Café de France* in place du Duc-de-Padoue. The **bars** along cours Paoli are patronized mainly by locals, while tourists hang out in those lining place Paoli.

Cafés and bars

Les Délices du Palais cours Paoli. Frilly little crêperie-cum-*salon-de-thé* whose bakery sells a selection of delicious Corsican patisserie: try their *colzone* (spinach pasties) or *brocciu* baked in flaky chestnut-flour pastry.

De la Place place Paoli. On the shady side of the main square, this is the place to hole up for a spot of crowd-watching over a *barquette de frites* and draught Pietra.

Restaurants

L'Albadu 2.5km southwest of town ☏ 04 95 46 24 55. Bargain €20 menu – muscat, *brocciu* fritters, soup, main meat course, cheese, dessert, coffee and as much wine as you like – with most ingredients straight off the farm. Everyone sits together around long tables, which makes for a lively atmosphere. Advance booking essential.

U Museu rampe Ribanelle in the *haute ville* at the foot of the citadelle, 30m down rue Colonel-Feracci. Congenial and well situated on an atmospheric terrace, with lots of choice on its mixed menus. Try the €17 *menu corse*, featuring wild boar and myrtle stew, trout, and *tripettes* (imaginatively translated as "trip"). Their hot goat's cheese (*chèvre chaud*) salad, filling enough for two, comes on a groaning bed of richly flavoured potatoes. Great value for money, and the house wines are local AOC.

Osteria di l'Orta Casa Guelfucci, Pont de l'Orta, on the northern edge of Corte ☏ 04 95 61 06 41, ⓦ www.osteria-di-l-orta.com. Served in a stone-walled annexe tacked on to the family's eighteenth-century mansion, the food here is honest, fragrant and traditional. House specialities include veal with figs, chargrilled lamb fillets and – the dessert *de résistance* – chestnut mousse. All meals also include hosts Marina and Antoine's delicious home-made apéritifs and liqueurs. *Formules* from €20–35. Head 500m north of the place du Duc de Padoue, and take the first right after the Pont de l'Orta – it's the grand, five-storey house painted bright blue.

Le Paglia Orba 1 av Xavier-Luciani ☎ 04 95 61 07 89. Quality Corsican cooking at very reasonable prices, served on a raised terrace overlooking the street. Most people come for the succulent pizzas (€7–10), but they also offer plenty of choice à la carte, particularly for vegetarians (baked aubergine with chestnuts or stuffed onions), and do some imaginative salads (such as chicken in Cognac), plus pan-fried veal served with *stozapreti* (nuggets

of *brocciu* and herbs) as their *plat de résistance*. Menus from €15.

Au Plat d'Or place Paoli ☎ 04 95 46 27 16. One of the classier options in Corte: Corsican specialities made from locally produced ingredients, and served under awnings on the shady side of place Paoli. Meat and seafood dishes (such as *brochettes* of beef with fragrant wild mushrooms or river trout in Cap Corse liqueur) are their forte, but they also do pizzas, pastas and home-made desserts. Menu for €22 (four courses). Closed Sun.

La Restonica *Hotel La Restonica*, Vallée de la Restonica, 2km southwest of town ☎ 04 95 45 25 25. Warm-toned riverside dining salon attached to Corte's most stylish mountain *auberge*. Go for their €21 *menu du terroir* featuring *Cortenais* specialities such as trout stuffed with garlic and *brocciu*. The best eating option if you're staying in either of the Dominique Colonna-owned hotels.

Listings

Banks All the main banks on cours Paoli have ATMs which accept the usual cards.
Bookshop Maison de la Presse, 22 cours Paoli, has a good selection of books about Corsica, and occasional English-language newspapers.
Bus information Corte is the midway point for Eurocorse Voyages' Ajaccio-to-Bastia bus, which runs twice daily except Sun; tickets can be bought at *Bar Colonna*, av Xavier-Luciani. From July 15 to the end of Aug you can get to Bastia with Autocars Cortenais, 14 cours Paoli, which also operates services to Aléria from outside the train station on Tues, Thurs & Sat. From July to mid-Sept, Corte is connected to Porto via Calacuccia and Évisa by Autocars Mordiconi's service, which leaves from in front of the train station at 8am. See Travel details, p.323.

Car rental Europcar, 9 cours Paoli ☎ 04 95 46 06 02.
Horseriding Centre Équestre l'Albadu, ancienne route d'Ajaccio, 2.5km southwest of town – among the best of riding centres on the island, and the rates are rock-bottom for Corsica.
Hospital av du 9-Septembre ☎ 04 95 46 05 36.
Internet access Cyber Snack, in the *Café du Cours* on cours Paoli.
Pharmacies Several on cours Paoli.
Police 4 av Xavier-Luciani ☎ 04 95 46 04 81.
Post office Av du Baron-Mariani, off place du Duc-de-Padoue.
Taxis Michel Salviani ☎ 04 95 46 04 88 or 06 03 49 15 24; or Thérèse Feracci ☎ 04 95 61 01 17 or 06 12 10 60 60.

Around Corte

The gorges of the **Vallée du Tavignano**, virtually on the town's doorstep, are accessible only on foot and offer an exhilarating hike from Corte. The less energetic can simply drive southwest to the **Vallée de la Restonica**, where the road closely follows the river's torrent of jade-green water to within striking distance of the stunning **Lac de Melo**, the **Lac de Capitello** and **Monte Rotondo** – a superb sight close up, with its ring of crags encircling a cluster of blue glacial lakes.

Vallée du Tavignano

The medieval cobbled path winding up the **Vallée du Tavignano**, Corsica's deepest and most spectacular gorge, offers one of the island's classic walks. You can pick up the trail, a stage of the Mare a Mare Nord long-distance footpath (covered on p.368 and marked in orange paint flashes), from the bottom of rue col-Feracci, below the citadelle, and follow it for two days as far as the source of the river at Lac de Nino (see p.298). There's a very well set up **refuge**, *A Sega* (dorm beds €11, bivouac €5; ☎06 10 71 77 26), situated at the halfway point, which serves filling breakfasts and evening meals (half board €30 to bivouac or €52 in a dorm), and can supply packed lunches (€7). From there the orange waymarks peel north up the side of the Tavignano into the Niolo Valley. Yellow paint flashes, meanwhile, continue west towards the watershed and Lac de Nino – a key stage on the GR20 and as idyllic a trekking destination as you could wish for.

From the trailhead in Corte, the old mule track steadily climbs the steep left bank of the river across a bare hillside scarred with the remains of old farming

Hike to Monte Rotondo and the Lac d'Oriente

A jagged-topped arc of granite splashed with small blue lakes, **Monte Rotondo** (2622m), Corsica's second-highest mountain, looms southwest of Corte at the head of the Restonica Valley. The peak can be scaled from two directions, but the most common approach is from the north, via the beautiful Lac d'Oriente. Though technically straightforward between July and late September, this route is a long hard slog involving 3360m of ascent and descent, much of it across steep boulder-choked terrain. Don't consider attempting it unless you're in good shape and properly equipped (see p.332), and check the weather forecast carefully before you set off. Of the many hikers that tread the Rotondo trail during the summer, most only aim to reach the lake, a rewarding return trip (4hr 30min) in itself.

The **trailhead** lies 11km up the Restonica Valley, 700m beyond the Tagone bridge (where the road crosses from the north to the south side of the gorge) – look for the red spray-painted sign on a rock to the right. From here, a wide forestry track strikes steeply up the side of a stream valley, zigzagging through fragrant pine woods to the **bergeries de Timozzo** (1hr 15min), where it levels out briefly before climbing a long ridge. Follow the red-and-yellow splashes of paint rather than the cairns (which mark a less well-defined path that gets lost in maquis), crossing the stream near the head of the valley.

Enfolded by the Rotondo massif, the **Lac d'Oriente** (2hr 30min) is a great place to picnic before pressing on to the summit. From here, the trail, which restarts at the south side of the lake, is marked every 10m or so by cairns; as long as you keep close to these, the ascent across the moraine that follows is safe and enjoyable. However, things get a little trickier towards the top, where patches of snow and ice can be hazardous, particularly during early summer (an ice axe or snow stick is recommended if you're attempting this route before Aug); keep an eye out, too, for loose rocks, as these can be lethal for anyone ascending below you. The last stretch of the climb is a very steep clamber up a narrow corridor; patches of ice are more common on the left side of this, so pick a route up the right (sunnier) side. From the **ridge** (4hr 15min), drop down slightly to the left and follow the cairns to a cleft that leads up the crow's-nest **summit** (4hr 30min). On a clear day, the views from the top are sublime, taking in all of the island's major peaks, both coasts, the shores of Tuscany and, if you're lucky, the distant Alps. If you have an all-season sleeping bag, it is possible to bivouac in the tiny tin-roofed **Helbronner refuge** just below the summit and enjoy the spectacle at dawn.

Return by the same route, or down the south side of the mountain, via the beautiful **Lac de Bellabone**, to the **Petra Piana refuge**. Note that times given do not take into account rest breaks; allow a total of eight hours for the return trip to the top from the Restonica Valley and back (5hr 15min ascent and 2hr 45min descent), and aim to start walking by 7am, which will get you to the summit well before the clouds blister up at around 2pm.

terraces. Massive rocks border the river below, which you can scramble down to in places for a secluded swim. Some 5km into the walk, the gorge proper begins and the scenery becomes wilder. Passing through patches of dense maquis interspersed with evergreen oak and chestnut trees, you gradually rejoin the river, crossed at the **Passarelle de Rossolino** footbridge after around two and a half hours. Once on the true right bank, the mountainside grows steeper as the path skirts the **Ravin de Bruscu**, swathed in forest that was severely damaged by fire in 2000, then winds gently above the stream to the refuge, reached after five and a half hours from Corte.

Vallée de la Restonica

Dividing the barren wastes of the Rotondo massif and the cloud-swept plateau d'Alzo, the **Vallée de la Restonica** is lined with spectacular gorges – a riot of twisted granite cliffs covered in thick Laricio pine forest. Unfortunately, it is one of the few motorable routes into the heart of the Corsican watershed, a fact which, along with its proximity to Corte, means the entire fifteen-kilometre stretch from town to the *bergeries* de Grotelle can get hideously congested in high summer. To alleviate the peak season traffic, there's a shuttle bus service between July 15 and August 15, which runs from the information point at the bottom of the valley to the *bergeries*. Heading uphill, services depart hourly 8am–1pm; in the other direction, they run 2–5pm; tickets cost €2.

The **gorges** begin after 6km, just beyond where the route penetrates the **Forêt de la Restonica**, a glorious swathe of chestnut, Laricio pine and the tough maritime pine endemic to Corte, recognizable by its conical shape. Not surprisingly, it's a popular place to walk, picnic and bathe – the many pools fed by the cascading torrent of the Restonica River are easily reached by scrambling down the rocky banks.

The **bergeries de Grotelle**, 15km from Corte, mark the end of the road, with a large car park that barely accommodates the summer crowds. From here, a well-worn path winds along the valley floor to a pair of beautiful glacial lakes. The first and largest, **Lac de Melo**, is reached after a fairly strenuous hour's hike through the rocks. Particularly steep parts of the path have been fitted with stanchion chains and vertical iron ladders, causing some visitors to freeze with vertigo halfway up. If you're attempting this walk in early spring, you should also expect to encounter deep snow patches in places, especially once you're past Lac de Melo, where a steeper trail over a moraine climbs up to the second lake, **Lac de Capitello** – the more spectacular of the pair. Hemmed in by vertical cliffs, the deep, turquoise blue pool affords fine views of the Rotondo massif on the far side of the valley, and in clear weather you can spend an hour or two exploring the surrounding crags, scoured by tame choughs (*chocards* in French).

East of Corte: The Bozio

Scattered across the bare ridges dividing the Vallée du Tavignano and Castagniccia, the **Bozio**, just east of Corte, comprises a wild, depopulated necklace of schist villages strung over spurs and rocky *belvédères* on the northern shoulder of the lower Tavignano. A major crossroads in Roman times, when it formed a trade link between the mountains and coastal plains, the region today sees fewer visitors than perhaps anywhere else on the island. Yet as a route between Corte and Aléria, it holds considerably more appeal than the faster highway on the valley floor. Romanesque churches, many of them decorated with original medieval frescoes and stone carving, lie scattered around the villages, and the views across the valley to the central range are magnificent. An additional incentive to spend time in the area is the **Mare a Mare Nord** (for more, see p.368) long-distance walking trail, which contours in tandem with the D14, roughly following the course of the old paved Via Romana, between Poggio in the east and Santa Lucia di Mercurio in the west.

The route outlined below progresses from west to east, starting at the village of Tralonca, which is most easily reached by heading north on the *route nationale* towards Bastia, then turning right on to the D41 after 3km. Alternatively, you can pick up the narrow D14 corniche road at various points along the *route nationale* (N200) running southeast along the valley floor towards Aléria. Either way, a good map is essential, as those in this book do not include every backroad and may thus not be much help if you make a wrong turn.

Tralonca to Sermano

Overgrazed hillsides and derelict *bergeries* mar the approaches to **TRALONCA**, but the village itself, a wonderfully cuboid cluster heaped on the top of a conical hill, epitomizes the defiant nationalist spirit that has always been synonymous with the region, from the uprisings of the medieval era to the present day. It was on the outskirts of Tralonca in 1996 that the FLNC staged its most infamous show of force of recent decades, when six hundred paramilitaries – wearing black balaclavas and armed to the teeth with automatic pistols, rifles, flame-throwers and rocket launchers – staged a *nuit bleue* to declare a cessation in hostilities against the French state (for more on this event, see p.400).

Perhaps the finest view of the whole Bozio, however, is past the next village along the road, **SANTA LUCIA DI MERCURIO**: framed by a dramatic 2500m wall on the far side of the valley, the village's tiny campanile looks southwest up the Restonica and Tavignano gorges to the snowcapped peaks of the watershed. The spectacle is best viewed from the road 1km beyond Santa Lucia.

SERMANO, 6km east around the spur from Santa Lucia, is famous primarily for its polyphonic singing (see p.413). One of the island's finest singers, Petru Guelfucci, comes from here – the most recent in a long line of renowned singers the village has produced – and still resides in his traditional family home, earning his living partly as a beekeeper, and partly through his polyphonic ensemble, Voce di Corsica. The group forms the backbone of the male-voice choir that sings Mass for the annual **Jour des Morts** festival, held at the Pisan chapel of **San Nicolao**. The chapel, which holds naïve fifteenth-century frescoes, stands fifteen-minutes' walk from the centre: follow the footpath descending from behind the houses on the opposite side of the road from the church. The key is kept at the *gîte d'étape* (see below).

Back up in the village centre, the **Église de l'Annunziata** incorporates fragments of a much older Romanesque chapel, which formerly stood on the hillside above – look for the strange mythical animals on the lintels of the north door. Sermano also holds the area's only accommodation: the tiny **gîte d'étape** *U San Firenzu* (☏04 95 48 68 08), overlooking the main road at the western edge of the village, with only 26 dorm beds and no camping space. Obligatory half board costs €34 per person.

Bustanico to Piedicorte di Gaggio

The overgrazing of the Bozio's hillsides takes on apocalyptic proportions as you wind along the D441 to **BUSTANICO**. A tight cluster of troglodyte-style dwellings huddled into a stream valley, the village is said to be the source of the

War of Independence. Conflict errupted in 1729 when an old man named Lanfranchi, or "Cardone", sparked off a local rebellion against the Genoese after a tax collector threatened to carry off all his possessions. Outraged at such injustice, fellow villagers rose up in his defence, triggering riots and raids all over eastern Corsica, culminating in the sack of Bastia in 1730. The village church has a graceful polychrome wooden figure of Christ, sculpted by a local craftsman in the eighteenth century.

A kilometre or so south of Bustanico, the tiny **D339** peels off the D39 to begin its climb through beech and chestnut forests to one of this region's highest villages, **SANT'ANDRÉA DI BOZIO**. Aside from the superlative views, the main reason to venture up here is to stay at the ⚶ *Casa Capellini* (☎06 15 75 16 37, ⓦwww.vallecime.com/chambres.htm; ⑤), a charming **B&B** run by mountain guides Pascale and Jean-François Luciani (see p.303). The house holds five pleasant guest rooms overlooking the valley. Evening meals are available by request.

From Sant'Andréa, you can either follow the D16 east to the **Col de Casardo** for a stupendous panorama of the region, or else drop back down to the D39, the old Via Romana, as it winds through one of the last remaining stretches of greenery on this side of the valley to reach **ALANDO**. The village is thought to be the birthplace of **Sambucuccio d'Alando**, a legendary fourteenth-century leader of a popular movement against the region's despotic nobility. Alando is credited with the invention of the "Terra del Commune", an organization that between 1359 and 1362 united villages all over Corsica under one administrative body of elected magistrates. If you fancy stretching your legs, you can **walk** along the Mare a Mare Nord west from Alando to Sermano. Waymarked in orange, the old path drops down into the chestnut woods from the road (look for a PNRC signboard at the trailhead), crossing a series of pretty streams before climbing to Sermano, reached after one hour thirty minutes.

At **FAVALELLO**, where the Romanesque church of **Santa Maria Assunta** harbours fifteenth-century frescoes, the road begins its sharp descent to the Zingaio River, at which point the D14 turns south and zigzags all the way back up to the corniche. **ERBAJOLO** (Erbaghjolu), the next major village along the route, offers another fantastic view of the Rotondo massif on the far side of the Tavignano. From the end of the lane behind the church, you can walk a kilometre or so along a mule track to the remote Pisan chapel of **San Martino**, a gentle thirty-minute hike through the maquis. Erbajolo boasts a spanking new three-star hotel-cum-*chambres d'hôtes*, the *Armonia* (☎04 95 48 80 07, ⓦwww.hotel-armonia-corte.com; ❸); the B&B side of the business is called *L'Altipratu* (☎04 95 48 80 07, ⓦwww.altupratu.com; ❸). Accommodation is in a modern building, with immaculate en-suite rooms and superb views over the valley; there's even a pool. Moreover, the wine and food are both organic, and great value.

A little under 9km of narrow twisting lanes separate Erbajolo from the crumbling tower houses of **ALTIANI** (a contraction of *alti piani*, or "high pine trees"), grouped around a huge lump of grey granite. The village's focal point, the place Mauresque, is said to be so named because of a fierce fight that took place on the spot in medieval times with an army of Moorish raiders. After a long and bloody siege, or so the story goes, the Corsicans flew a white flag to seek terms. But the surrender would only be accepted on condition that all the women and girls of the village, then sheltering in the church, were handed over to the pirates. This insult only seems to have stiffened the resolve of Altiani's menfolk to fight on, because somehow the encounter ended with a massacre of the Moors in the square.

At Altiani, two onward routes are possible. You can drop straight down to the Tavignano on the D314, where the river is spanned by a fine triple-arched **Genoese bridge** nicknamed "Pont Laricio" because it was once nearly washed away by a giant pine tree swept down in the spring floods. Opposite stands the tenth-century **chapelle San Giovanni Battista** – a tiny Romanesque edifice built of patterned stones alternating with plain blocks of granite.

Alternatively, continue along the more scenic Via Romana (D14) for 4km to **PIEDICORTE DI GAGGIO**, whose central square opens onto a panorama of the eastern plain. In the thirteenth century, while the island was being disputed by the regional superpowers Genoa and Pisa, this was the fief of the powerful de Gaggio family, the ruins of whose castle mingle with those of the Chapelle de Santa Maria on the Punta Gaggio (1189m), rising steeply above the village to the north.

South of Corte

The main road south of Corte, the N193, slices into the heart of the Corsican mountains, tracked by the railway through Venaco and Vivario – a region of deep, forested valleys known as the **Venachese** – to Vizzavona and Bocognano. East from **Vivario** a memorable drive takes you southeast over the Col de Sorba to **Ghisoni**, a mountain base dominated by the peaks of Kyrie-Eleison and the craggy Monte Renoso. You have a choice of spectacular exits from Ghisoni: east through the Défilé de l'Inzecca, a shortcut down to the eastern plain; or south along the zigzagging route to Col de Verde, offering incredible views of the peaks. South of the pass, the villages of the Haut Taravo Valley, **Zicavo** and **Cozzano**, make ideal bases for trips into the hills, including **Monte Incudine**, the southernmost high summit of the island.

Back on the N193 and the rail line, **Vizzavona**, a scruffy cluster of rail buildings and hikers' hotels, lies just below the highest point of the road before its descent to Ajaccio. A beautiful forest spreads one side of the settlement up the flanks of mighty Monte d'Oro, but for the best views of this giant pyramidal peak you should head down to **Bocognano**, about 7km from the Col de Vizzavona.

Aside from the handful of hikers' refuges and *gîtes d'étapes* that punctuate the region's footpaths, **accommodation** is very limited in these parts except for a couple of hotels in Vizzavona and Santo Pietro di Venaco.

The Venachese

"My journey over the mountains was very entertaining. I past [sic] some immense ridges and vast woods. I was in great health and spirits, and fully able to enter into the ideas of the brave rude men whom I found in all quarters," wrote James Boswell in 1765 as he made his way south of Corte to his meeting with Pascal Paoli. These days the same journey through the Venachese tends to be conducted at a brisker pace via the high-grade *route nationale* or narrow-gauge railway, but the route is punctuated by a succession of large, well-populated villages from where you can strike into the hills.

Swathed in chestnut forest, the first one you come to along the main road is **SANTO PIETRO DI VENACO**, 7.5km south of Corte, where there's an old-fashioned **hotel**, *Le Torrent* (☎04 95 47 00 18; ❸–❹), former manor of the Count Pozzo di Borgo (see p.188). Its rooms are basic and a bit frayed around the edges but possess some charm, and there's a shady terrace under the lime trees outside. Also in the village, up a steep, narrow, potholed lane, the welcoming **gîte d'étape** ⚐ *Chez Antoinette et Charles* (℡04 95 47 07 29, ⓦwww .antoinette-et-charles.fr.st), a night halt on the Mare a Mare Nord (*variant*) footpath, offers beds in four-person dorms (€30 per person for obligatory half board) or more comfortable en-suite **chambre d'hôte** accommodation (half board €68 for two sharing). The rooms are spotless and good value, and the hosts very hospitable. Evening meals are served around a communal table.

Both places provide inexpensive bases from which to complete the wonderful round walk to the **Chapelle Sant'Eliseo** (1555m), a tiny shrine set against the massive east wall of Monte Cardo, from where you can begin a high-level traverse of the valley head via old shepherds' *bergeries* or strike further up the mountain to the more exposed Arête de Cardo – one of Monte Rotondo's spurs. The owner of the *gîte d'étape* is a qualified mountain guide and can advise you on the various routes in the area.

Venaco

A couple of kilometres south of Santo Pietro, the *route nationale* squeezes through **VENACO**, an elegant village emerging from the verdant lower slopes of Monte Padro. You might want to halt here to admire the views – there's a spectacular panorama of the lower Vallée du Tavignano to the east from the terrace of the beautifully restored **Baroque church** – or enjoy a meal at the *Restaurant de la Place* on the main square (℡04 95 47 01 30), which offers a good-value €15 *menu fixe* at lunchtime featuring spinach pie and red mullet, river trout or sardines stuffed with *brocciu*, rounded off by home-made walnut flan.

Venaco also harbours one of the area's few good **campsites**, the *Camping Peridundellu* (℡04 95 47 09 89; April–Oct) – take the D43 towards the Tavignano Valley and you'll see it after 4km on your right. It's very cosy, with room for a couple of dozen tents, and the farmhouse doubles up as a simple **restaurant** (fixed four-course menu at €19) serving home-made charcuterie, goat's cheese in flaky pastry and *fiadone*.

Vivario

Gustave Eiffel (of Eiffel tower fame) built the dizzying **Pont de Vecchiu** railway bridge at the foot of Monte Rotondo, 5km south of Venaco. Alongside it, the even more impressive road bridge, opened in 1999, spans the 222-metre-wide gorge at a height of 137.5m. A series of tortuous switchbacks beyond here heralds your arrival at **VIVARIO**, located at the junction of the routes to the Forêt de Rospa-Sorba and the Col de Verde. Straddling the main highway and surrounded by fire-scarred forest and maquis, the village makes a less appealing place to spend the night than most hereabouts, but if you're following the Mare a Mare Nord its excellent little **shop** is particularly handy.

The grandiose Manganello Valley, tracked by the Mare a Mare as far as the refuge de l'Onda, once supported its own **wild man**, dubbed by folk chroniclers as *un Mowgli corse*. In 1800 a 10-year-old boy went missing here after an argument with his parents, and stayed missing for twenty years until a group of hunters ensnared him by the Vecchiu. The unfortunate soul was carted off to be reunited with his parents but, unable to adapt to his new life, perished after a few months. The only traversable spot across the Gorge du Vecchiu, a three-hour walk west of Vivario, is a three-metre jump still known as the **Saut du Sauvage**, or "Wild Man's Leap". Vivario's other claim to fame is as the birthplace of the infamous **Bartolomeo brothers**, who were abducted by pirates here in the sixteenth century and went on to lead highly eventful lives. Shipwrecked off the coast of Italy, they escaped the clutches of their Saracen captors and swam to safety at Talamona on the Tuscan shore, where they subsequently settled. The elder of the two, later known as Bartolomeo de Talamona, rose to become an admiral in the local navy, and used his position to exact revenge on the pirates who had kidnapped him in his youth, ruthlessly pillaging the Mytilena region of Algeria, home of the dey of Algiers – the Red Beard, or Barbarossa, of pirate legends. It is said that the sultan was so incensed at Bartolomeo's behaviour that he attacked Talamona in 1544, only to find his adversary dead and buried, whereupon he exhumed the Corsican's corpse and burned and scattered what was left by way of retribution. The other brother, Bartolomeo de Vivario, eventually returned home from Talamona and worked for the Genoese for a while, before defecting to Sampiero Corso's side in the Wars of Independence, in the course of which he was mortally wounded.

If you feel like a **short walk** from Vivario, head 1km south of the village to a stony car park on the side of the main road, from where a clear path leads to the **Fort de Pasciolo**, an evocative ruin set high on a rounded hilltop 1km or so west of the N193. Facing a great circle of peaks above the deep gorge of the Vecchiu, the fort was built around 1770 by the French, and later transformed into a prison to incarcerate the rebels of Fiumorbo (see p.270).

Practicalities

There are two pleasant sites just south of the village: the quieter of the pair, set up primarily for walkers, is the *Camping de Savaggio* (℡04 95 47 22 14; open year round) in an out-of-the-way spot close to the Mare a Mare Nord trail 3km south along the N193 (look for a sign pointing west off the highway). Occupying a small field next to the rail line, the site has around thirty pitches for tents, a café and basic provisions store, plus a 22-bed **refuge** (open all year; €11). A couple of kilometres further south down the highway, just after the point where the main road crosses the railway, another sign points to *Camping Le Soleil* (℡04 95 47 21 16; May–Oct), an equally congenial site directly opposite **Tattone** station in an old chestnut glade. The fine views up the valley to Monte d'Oro are only slightly marred by the proximity of a large and rather grim sanitorium just down the road. The useful **shop** here is near the fountain in the centre, a convenient place to stock up on supplies before heading into the pristine country to the west.

Vizzavona and around

Monte d'Oro dominates the route south of Vivario to **VIZZAVONA**, 30km beyond Corte. Shielded by trees, the village, a cluster of mostly tin-roofed forestry huts and old station buildings, is invisible from the main road, so keep your eyes peeled for a couple of lanes dropping down on the right, one of them signposted for the **gare de Vizzavona** – the place where the bandit Bellacoscia famously surrendered to the police at the age of 75 (see p.320). Marking the midway point of the GR20, Vizzavona is always crowded with walkers during summer, and those on a modest budget are well catered for by the handful of *gîtes d'étape*, hotels and hikers' cafés grouped around the railhead. The station building also houses the best-stocked **shop** on the GR20, the Épicerie Rosy, which keeps a supply of stove fuel and blue camping gas canisters as well as overpriced food supplies.

The smartest **place to stay** here is *I Laricci* (℡04 95 47 21 12; ⓦwww.ilaricci .com; April–Oct; ❹), a well-maintained red-and-white alpine-style building with pitched roofs and Moroccan carpets decorating the walls of its dining room. Rooms here (from €86 for two half board) are invariably booked up well

The fifth-highest peak on Corsica, **Monte d'Oro** (2389m) stands on the edge of the island's interior range and thus affords superb views not only of the other four big mountains – Cinto, Rotondo, Renoso and Incudine – but also of Ajaccio and the southwest coast. The route up it is well frequented, but involves some exposed scrambling towards the top; be prepared to cross the odd névé (patches of deep ice or snow) until late June. The exposed position of the peak also means it's particularly vulnerable to sudden and extreme changes in weather, so check the forecast before you set off and make sure you follow the advice on clothing, equipment and mountain safety on p.332.

There are two ways to the summit from Vizzavona. The **conventional route** is to ascend via the Cascade des Anglais and the main route of the GR20 along the River Agnone, and then follow the variant of the GR20 over the summit and down the east flank of the mountain via the *bergeries* de Pozzatelli – a fine round walk that takes about eight hours. Take along a copy of the FFRP's topo-guide for the GR20, which clearly maps the route, or IGN Top 25, **#4251 OT**.

From Vizzavona, follow the red-and-white waymarks of the GR20 for thirty minutes until you reach the **Cascade des Anglais**. Once across the ruisseau d'Agnone, the path climbs northeast along the left bank of the stream, zigzagging steeply up pastureland strewn with elms and, later, denuded rocky terrain towards the **Crête de Muratellu** (2020m). Just below the ridge, you leave the waymarked section of the GR20 and follow its variant (cairned and waymarked in yellow) northeast towards **Bocca di u Porcu** (2159m). The final leg to the summit involves some climbing for which you'll need a head for heights but not ropes.

The **descent** to Vizzavona is well cairned. You have to head north and northeast from the summit, past a small grassy plateau known as **Bratu Scampicciolo**, and down the steep zigzags of **La Scala** to the distinctively shaped rock dubbed **La Cafetière**. Shortly after, the route veers due east and drops down the side of a stream gulley, penetrating the treeline just above the **bergeries de Pozzatelli**. The last section of the walk keeps to the forest, much of it damaged by fire and clear cutting. Allow at least two and a half hours to reach Vizzavona from the summit – and at least double that for the ascent.

in advance, but you can nearly always get a bed in one of their six-person dorms (€33 per bed for half board). Weather permitting, meals and authentic Moroccan tea are served in the flower-filled garden outside, which has fine views of Monte d'Oro. More conventional *gîte d'étape* accommodation is offered at *Resto-Refuge-Bar de la Gare* (☎04 95 47 22 20; May–Oct; €16), directly opposite the station. When full, the dormitories here are stuffy and cramped; half board (€36) is available, but the food isn't up to much.

La Foce

If your budget can stretch to it, head 3km further south along the main road to the hamlet of **LA FOCE**, near the col proper, where the venerable old ☘ *Monte d'Oro* (☎04 95 47 21 06, ⓦ www.monte-oro.com; ❺) occupies a prime spot overlooking the valley. With its period furniture and fittings, *fin-de-siècle* feel and magnificent terrace looking out onto the mountain, this ranks among the most congenial hotels in Corsica. Originally built in 1880 as a guesthouse for government engineers, it has altered little since and offers good value considering its location and character, and it provides a free transfer to and from Vizzavona if you phone ahead. The hotel's charming **restaurant**, ☘ *L'Eddera*, is locked in a charismatic time warp, with starched white napkins and tablecloths, old prints of cruise liners on the walls and ivy growing from the wood ceiling. The menu

(€23) features trout from the mountain streams around Ghisoni, lamb with morelle mushrooms, or wild boar in myrtle-berry *eau de vie* sauce.

Immediately behind the *Monte d'Oro* stands the tiny **Chapel de Notre-Dame-des-Neiges** ("Our Lady of the Snows"), to which travellers traditionally paid their respects while crossing the pass. The shrine was the centre of a dispute during World War II when it was used by Italian troops billeted in the hotel to stable mules. The protests of the owner, Mme Plaisant, had no effect, but when the Italians' High Chaplain happened to be passing and noticed the act of sacrilege, he had the offending soldiers pull down the chapel and rebuild it from scratch as an act of purification. Masonry for the job came from the ruins of the old French **fort**, whose vestiges can still be seen on a forested ridge 1km southwest – look for the wide path running north into the woods from the picnic tables and car park at the col.

Cascades des Anglais

The glorious forest of beech and Laricio pine carpeting the valley below the pass, the **Forêt de Vizzavona**, is among the most popular walking areas in Corsica, thanks to the easy access by main road or train. A lot of people come here to tackle the ascent of Monte d'Oro (see box opposite), but there are many less demanding trails to follow. One of the most frequented of these is the **walk to the Cascades des Anglais**, which can be reached from Vizzavona via an uncharacteristically gentle section of the GR20 but is more commonly approached from La Foce. Some 200m down the main road from *Hôtel Refuge Monte d'Oro* (in the direction of Vizzavona/Corte), opposite the *Auberge Muntagera* (see p.320), look for the roadside car park from where a *piste* plunges through the woods to the river; follow the green waymarks for a little over a quarter of an hour until they merge with the red-and-white ones of the GR20, which passes a stone's throw from the falls, where the River Agnone crashes into emerald-green pools. These are perfect for bathing, but the site is far from a secret. Its popularity dates from the late nineteenth century, from which time it became a favourite summer picnic spot of British aristocrats residing in Ajaccio (whence the falls' name).

▲ Cascades des Anglais

One titled visitor who did a lot to raise the profile of Vizzavona around this time was Prince Roland Bonaparte, grandson of Napoleon's younger brother, who spent a night at an inn next to the pass in the autumn of 1887 prior to an early-morning ascent of Monte d'Oro. Among his entourage was the writer **Emile Bergerac**, whose account of the prince's tour of Corsica became a classic travelogue of its era. Bergerac was enraptured by the scenery, the mountain food, and by the hospitality the party received. You can read extracts from his book, *La Chasse Au Mouflon*, and enjoy a meal similar to the one Prince Roland would have tucked into here at the charming 🍴 *Auberge A Muntagera*, on the roadside opposite the start of the path to Les Cascades des Anglais. The food, served on wooden tables scattered over a pretty garden terrace, is proper farmhouse cooking: filling bean stews in rich, home-made tomato sauces, local charcuterie, rocket salads and pungent mountain cheeses.

Bocognano

From the Col de Vizzavona, the route winds southwards for 6km before reaching the appealing ochre cottages of **BOCOGNANO** (Bucugnanu). Set on a plateau amidst a chestnut forest, the village gives a perfect panorama of Monte d'Oro's pale-grey needles, and is well placed for walks to the **Cascade du Voile de la Mariée**, where the River Gravona crashes from a height of 150m in a series of cascades. The approach to the falls is via the D27, which turns southwest at an inconspicuous junction on the western edge of the village. Follow the winding road to its end, roughly 3km later, from where a path winds up through the forest to the falls.

Bocognano is indissolubly associated with **Antoine and Jacques Bellacoscia**, born here in 1817 and 1832, fathered by a man who earned the family surname – meaning "beautiful thigh" – by also fathering eighteen daughters by three sisters with whom he lived simultaneously. Antoine, the elder son, took to the maquis in 1848, having killed the mayor of the village after an argument over some land. With his brother he went on to commit several more murders in full view of the hapless gendarmes, yet remained at liberty thanks to the support of the local population. In 1871 Antoine and Jacques managed to gain a safe pass into Ajaccio to organize an expedition to fight for the French in the war with Prussia. They returned from the war with their reputations restored, and took up residence in the family home, from where they continued to flaunt the law. In 1888 the police finally succeeded in ousting them from their house, which was converted into a prison. Antoine eventually surrendered when he was 75, at Vizzavona station on June 25, 1892, whereupon he was acquitted and exiled to Marseille in true Corsican tradition. The fate of Jacques is unknown.

Ghisoni and around

Nestling in a huge hollow at the head of the Vallée du Fiumorbo, **GHISONI** is separated from the Venachese by a 1500-metre-high ridge crossed at the **Col de Sorba**. The D69, which wriggles south from the pass to the village, affords tantalizing glimpses of the Renoso massif, and the majority of the people who come here do so to climb the peak (see opposite), or en route between **Zicavo** and the east coast via the Col de Verde.

Ghisoni's only **hotel** is the unsightly mustard-coloured *Kyrié*, close to the centre of the village (☎04 95 57 60 33, ℻04 95 57 63 15; ④–⑤). It's an unexciting place, but the rooms are clean (the cheaper ones on the top floor enjoy the best views of the valley). The **bar-restaurant** on the ground floor is currently the only place to eat – it does a filling and tasty *soupe corse*, but otherwise the food isn't anything to write home about. For a pitstop, there's always the dingy *Bar Jacques*, whose street-side terrace sits next to a rusting statue of Neptune, seemingly misplaced this far into the mountains. In fact, the work was originally destined for a coastal *commune* in Cap Corse, but when it came to paying for the thing the council in question declared itself broke and Ghisoni snapped it up instead.

Hugging the sinuous Fium'orbo River, the road running **east from Ghisoni** plunges steeply downhill through the **Défilé des Strette** gorge, giving spectacular views of the two peaks on the far side of the valley: **Kyrie Eleison** (1535m) and **Christe Eleison** (1260m). It was at the foot of these mountains that the last group of **Giovanalanis**, devotees of a breakaway Franciscan sect whose rituals were falsely rumoured to include mass orgies, were massacred at the behest of Pope Urban V in 1362. Hounded to this remote spot, they were captured and bound for burning, but just at the point when the wood was to be set alight an old priest took pity on the heretics and administered their last rites. The assembled crowd is then said to have taken up the last line of the prayer – *Kyrie eleison, Christe eleison* – which echoed through the gorge and across the mountains, giving the peaks the names by which they are known to this day.

Further east, the main road skirts the Sampolo reservoir before penetrating the spectacular **Défilé de l'Inzecca**, a sheer trench slicing the coastal range. The gorge offers a little-used shortcut from the interior to the fertile eastern plains, and after the shattered rock formations, cuttings and tunnels of the road, the lush orange groves and vineyards around Ghisonaccia come as something of a shock.

E'Capannelle

An endless series of tight switchbacks wind 17km up the flank of the Fiumorbo Valley from Ghisoni to **E'Capannelle** (1586m), a little-used ski resort on the lower slopes of the Renoso massif. As a target for a drive into the mountains, the ski resort – a port of call on the **GR20** – is a dud: the once grassy slopes surrounding it have been badly carved up by a decade of skiers struggling on inadequate snow, while the restricted views of the peaks are marred by decaying chair lifts and *téléphérique* pylons. The one reason you might wish to venture up here is to get yourself into position for an early start up Monte Renoso. Dormitory **accommodation** is offered by the *gîte d'étape "U Fugone"* in the station itself (℡04 95 57 01 81, ⒲www.gite-ufugone.com; obligatory half board €32 per person). There's also a **refuge** just up the hill, with **camping** and bivouacking space around it.

Monte Renoso

E'Capannelle stands at the beginning of the standard route up **Monte Renoso** (2352m), the most southerly of Corsica's 2300-metre-plus summits. With a light pack and an early start, you can reach the top and return by lunchtime, or else press on south along the summit ridge, dropping down the far side via the GR20's superb high-level variant (waymarked) towards Col de Verde (as outlined on p.322) and then hitch back. Either way, take note of the advice on equipment, clothing and mountain safety in Chapter 8: exposed to coastal weather, this can be a treacherous route at any time of year, even in summer, when electrical storms may descend with little warning.

From the station, waymarks lead you steeply uphill, zigzagging between the chair-lift pylons to gain a ridge at 1725m (in only half a kilometre). Cairns then flag the route across a more gentle grassy hollow, at the end of which you'll crest a bouldery rise at the 2000m mark for your first sight of **Lac de Bastiani**

(2092m), a grey expanse of water framed intermittently by snowdrifts. Skirting the northern shores of the lake, the path then steepens considerably as it traverses a scree-covered cwm to reach the summit ridge – a vast, rocky crest, falling away steeply on both sides to reveal magnificent views of southern Corsica to Sardinia. Allow around two and a quarter hours to reach the summit proper from E'Capannelle, and a good hour for the descent afterwards by the same path.

If you carry on south along the waymarked route past the **Punta Orlandino**, you'll reach the **Col de Pruno** (2262m) in another thirty minutes or so. From here the path descends sharply across boulders and alder scrub to the **bergeries des Pozzi**, then strikes east across lush alpine meadows to the Plateau de Gialgone, after which it joins the **GR20**. At this point, you can either follow the GR20 north, hugging the contours of Renoso for another three and a half hours to get back to the E'Capannelle refuge, or take the quicker and easier route east to the D69 where it crosses Col de Verde (see below).

Col de Verde and around

Dividing the Fiumorbo and Taravo valleys, **Col de Verde** (1289m) provides a convenient springboard for walks up into the high country of the watershed, the best of them via the red-and-white waymarks of the GR20, which makes another of its infrequent drops to road level here. Right on the pass, the privately run *Refuge San Petru di Verdi* (☏04 95 24 46 82, Ⓦwww.boccadiverdi .com; late May to mid-Oct) has a relaxing, shady little terrace café serving quality snacks and drinks, and a cluster of wood-lined bunkhouses around the back with clean dorms (€13 per bed, or €34 half board). Campers are welcome to pitch up in the garden for €7 per person, which includes the use of solar-heated showers.

The two most obvious **walks** from the col are both well-marked and well-frequented stretches of the GR20. Starting at the forestry *piste* on the far side of the road from the refuge, the first strikes southeast into the woods, emerging after 45 minutes or so to begin a long, sweeping traverse of the valley head to **Bocca d'Oro** (aka Col de Prati) – an ascent of roughly 550m which should take a little under two hours. From there you can press on for another ten minutes to the **refuge de Prati** (1820m), a wonderfully sited hut from which the mountain falls away to the hazy eastern plain and Tyrrhenian Sea.

Alternatively, the GR20 can be followed west from Col de Verde through the **Vallon de Marmano**, site of some immense pine trees, the largest of which towers to 55m and is thought to be the tallest in Europe. Around one and a half hours into the walk, the red-and-white waymarks reach the **Plateau de Gialgone**, where you should turn left off the GR20 and follow the orange waymarks for another hour or so up to the bucolic **bergeries des Pozzi**. A short way beyond here the trail reaches **I Pozzi**, patches of lush marshy ground scattered with lakes and winding watercourses interconnecting at different levels – a veritable Shangri La that more than warrants the two-and-a-half-hour uphill walk to reach it. The essential IGM **map** #4252 OT covers both the above routes.

Haut Taravo

From its mouth on the Golfe de Valinco, the **Vallée du Taravo** cleaves diagonally inland, narrowing and deepening as it approaches the watershed at Col de Verde. Ringed by jagged blue-grey granite ridges, the valley's upper reaches, known as the **Haut Taravo**, form a fertile basin of lush chestnut, beech and pine forests fed by meltwater streams tumbling from the mountains. The region's villages, many of them linked by the **Mare a Mare Centre** long-distance footpath (see p.370), are definitive *Corse profonde*, where the ageing human population is far outstripped by the number of semi-wild pigs, and where you're almost guaranteed not to meet another tourist.

Zicavo

The main village of the Haut Taravo is **ZICAVO**, a handsome village famed for its charcuterie and, according to local folklore, vampires (*streghe*) and zombies (*acciacciatori*), said to emerge from the forest to feed on the crushed skulls of unwary travellers. The generic term for these mythical horrors is *grammanti*, which probably harks back to the Saracen raids of the fourteenth-century corsair d'Agramante, who plagued the area from his stronghold on the gulf.

Autocars Santoni's daily **bus** service from Ajaccio connects the village with the coast, providing one of the most convenient and dependable public transport options to the deep interior of the island. Zicavo has a couple of pleasant **places to stay**, both with satisfying little **restaurants**. The most welcoming of them is the **gîte d'étape** ⚐ *Le Paradis* (☎04 95 24 41 20; ❸), run by a friendly former schoolteacher and her family, which offers dorm beds for €15 per person or smart little double rooms. You can also camp here (€7 per head) and eat home-cooked food on a flowery stone terrace. Otherwise, there's the more established *Le Tourisme* in the centre of the village (☎04 95 24 40 06; ❹), which has fifteen rooms, the best with en suite and terraces. Two menus (€16 and €21) are served in the bar downstairs featuring quality local charcuterie, free-range meat from the mountains and cheeses made up on the nearby Coscione Plateau.

Cozzano

The next village up the valley from Zicavo, **COZZANO** makes a better base for extended walks in the Haut Taravo, not least because of its excellent **gîte d'étape**, the *Bella Vista* (☎04 95 24 41 59, ✉renucciauberge@aol.com; March–Oct), on its northern outskirts. Advice on the most rewarding itineraries to follow, backed up with loans of maps and unfailingly warm hospitality, is doled out by father and son, Pierre and Baptiste Pantalacci, while Madame takes care of the cooking. The food (€16 for an evening meal or €31 half board) is superb, the wine beguilingly spicy and the hillsides riddled with enough trails to keep you here for at least a couple of days. Beds cost around €10 per person and they've three bargain doubles (❶).

For more comfort, try the good-value *Auberge A Filetta* (☎04 95 24 45 61, ⓦwww.pour-les-vacances.com/filetta; May–Sept; ❸), down on the other side of the village, where optional half board costs €80 for two sharing.

Travel details

Trains

At the time of writing, Corsica's old *micheline* train service was in the process of being upgraded. By the spring of 2009 new track and locomotives should be fully operational, which will substantially shorten the journey times given below. The latest timetables are available at any Corsican station, and online at ⓦwww.corsicabus.org. More details on the upgrade appear on p.27.

Corte to: Ajaccio (4 daily; 1hr 30min); Bastia (4 daily; 1hr 10min); Bocognano (4 daily; 1hr); Calvi (2 daily; 2hr 30min); L'Île Rousse (2 daily; 1hr 55min); Ponte Leccia (4 daily; 30min); Venaco (4 daily; 13min); Vivario (4 daily; 20min); Vizzavona (4 daily; 40min).

Venaco to: Ajaccio (4 daily; 1hr 20min); Bastia (4 daily; 1hr 35min); Bocognano (4 daily; 40min);

Calvi (2 daily; 3hr 50min); Corte (4 daily; 15min);
L'Île Rousse (2 daily; 2hr 20min); Ponte Leccia
(4 daily; 45min); Vivario (4 daily; 15min); Vizzavona
(4 daily; 30min).

Vivario to: Ajaccio (4 daily; 1hr 5min); Bastia (4 daily;
1hr 50min); Bocognano (4 daily; 30min); Calvi
(2 daily; 3hr 5min); Corte (4 daily; 30min); L'Île
Rousse (2 daily; 2hr 35min); Ponte Leccia (4 daily;
1hr); Venaco (4 daily; 10min); Vizzavona (4 daily;
15min).

Vizzavona to: Ajaccio (4 daily; 55min); Bastia
(4 daily; 2hr); Bocognano (4 daily; 15min); Calvi
(2 daily; 4hr); Corte (4 daily; 1hr); L'Île Rousse
(2 daily; 2hr 50min); Ponte Leccia (4 daily;
1hr 10min); Venaco (4 daily; 35min); Vivario
(4 daily; 15min).

Buses

Corte to: Albertacce (AM; 10min); Ajaccio (EV; 2hr);
Aléria (ACT; 1hr); Bastia (EV/ACT; 1hr 15min);
Calacuccia and the Niolo (AM; 1hr); Col de Verghio

(AM; 1hr 30min); Évisa (AM; 2hr 15min);
Ghisonaccia (ACT; 1hr 10min); Porto (AM; 3hr).
Cozzano to: Ajaccio (AST; 1hr); Zicavo (AST; 30min).
Ponte Leccia to: Calvi (ABV; 1hr).
Zicavo to: Ajaccio (AST; 1hr 30min).
ACT: Autocars Cortenais ☎ 04 95 46 02 12 or
04 95 46 22 89. Corte–Aléria;1 daily Tues, Thurs &
Sat; Corte–Bastia; Mon, Wed, Fri.
AST: Autocars Santoni ☎ 04 95 22 64 44,
Ⓦ www.autocars-santoni.com. Ajaccio–Cozzano–
Zicavo; Mon–Sat 1 daily.
AM: Autocars Mordiconi ☎ 04 95 48 00 04,
Ⓦ www.hotel-des-touristes.com. Corte–
Calacuccia–Albertacce–Col de Verghio–Évisa–
Porto; July to mid-Sept Mon–Sat 1 daily.
EV: Eurocorse Voyages ☎ 04 95 21 06 30,
Ⓦ www.eurocorse.net. Ajaccio–Bocognano–La Foce
(Col de Vizzavona)– Vivario–Venaco–Santo-Pietro-
di-Venaco–Corte– Ponte Leccia–Bastia; Mon–Sat
2 daily.Lut lam verilit dunt dipit wismodit alit
auguercinit aciduisl utem erosto commy nullutat,

8

Long-distance walks

* **Monte Corona** One of the most spectacular viewpoints in all Corsica, most easily accessible via Ortu di u Piobbu refuge. See p.341

* **Cirque de la Solitude** Stanchion cables, fixed ladders and chains ease the crossing of this, the most vertical and compelling stretch of the GR20. See p.345

* **Golo Valley** Deep turquoise pools, Laricio pines and alpine meadows, with Pagia Orba as a backdrop. See p.346

* **Lac de Nino** Serene glacial lake ringed by turf *pozzines* and jagged, snow-streaked mountains, where wild horses and pigs graze in summer. See p.349

* **Arête a Monda** A razor-sharp ridge high above the Haut Taravo Valley, lined with pinnacles, tilting slabs and wind-sculpted buttresses. See p.360

▲ Hiking along the Cirque de la Solitude

8

Long-distance walks

Corsica is virtually unique in the Mediterranean for offering both superb mountain scenery and a world-class outdoor infrastructure. The thousand kilometres of waymarked trails that crisscross the island, backed up by a network of well set-up refuges and hostels, enable you to explore some spectacular wilderness regions without the hassle of having to carry excessive amounts of gear and supplies. Couple this with weather that's dependably warm and sunny from early May until the middle of October and you'll appreciate why Corsica ranks among Europe's top trekking destinations.

Since it was first inaugurated in the late 1970s, the single most compelling attraction for serious walkers has been the **GR20**, regarded as one of the most challenging of Europe's *haute routes*. For extreme mountain environments, awesome landscapes and pure physical challenge, it's in a class of its own. Of the thousands of people who attempt it each season, less than half manage to complete all sixteen stages. Those that do, however, are invariably as amazed by the scenery they encounter along the way – the colossal pine trees, glacial lakes and massive granite peaks – as by the ingenuity of the path itself, which penetrates terrain which is normally the exclusive preserve of rock climbers.

Although well deserved, the GR20's reputation tends to eclipse the existence of Corsica's other long-distance paths. But the lower-altitude coast-to-coast routes – known as the **Mare a Mare** and **Tra Mare e Monti** trails – offer some superlative walking in their own right. In addition to gorgeous scenery from start to finish (much of it within sight of the sea), they pass at regular intervals through hill villages, allowing you to experience traditional island life at close quarters. This means you not only get to walk through miles of oak-, chestnut- and pine-forested river valleys, but can also break your days with leisurely lunches or coffee stops on shady squares.

The **best periods to walk** depend on the route you're aiming to follow. For the GR20, summer – from early June until mid-October – is the only season when you can be sure of avoiding snow on the highest passes. The lower-altitude routes, by contrast, can be hard going from mid-June until mid-September because of the extreme heat along their exposed coastal sections. To enjoy fully any of the routes that drop to sea level, you should come in the spring or autumn when temperatures are bearable and the flora at its most abundant.

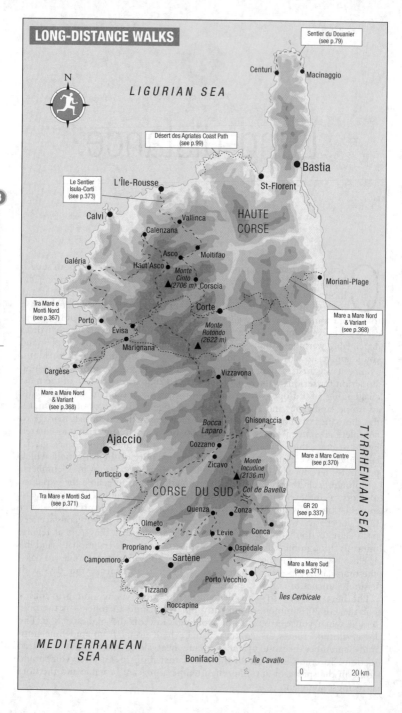

LONG-DISTANCE WALKS

Sentier du Douanier
(see p.79)

LIGURIAN SEA

Centuri
Macinaggio

Bastia

Désert des Agriates Coast Path
(see p.99)

St-Florent

Le Sentier
Isula-Corti
(see p.373)

L'Île-Rousse

HAUTE
CORSE

Calvi

Vallinca

Calenzana

Asco   Moltifao

Galéria

Haut'Asco

Monte
Cinto
(2706 m)   Corscia

Moriani-Plage

Tra Mare e
Monti Nord
(see p.367)

Corte

Mare a Mare Nord
& Variant
(see p.368)

Porto

Évisa

Monte
Rotondo
(2622 m)

Marignana

Cargèse

Vizzavona

Mare a Mare Nord
& Variant
(see p.368)

Bocca
Laparo

Ghisonaccia

Ajaccio

Cozzano

Zicavo

Monte
Incudine
(2136 m)

Mare a Mare Centre
(see p.370)

Porticcio

CORSE DU SUD

Col de Bavella

Tra Mare e Monti Sud
(see p.371)

Quenza   Zonza

GR 20
(see p.337)

Olmeto

Levie   Conca

Propriano

Ospédale

Campomoro

Sartène

Mare a Mare Sud
(see p.371)

Porto Vecchio

Tizzano

Íles Cerbicale

Roccapina

MEDITERRANEAN
SEA

TYRRHENIAN SEA

Bonifacio   Île Cavallo

0   20 km

The paths: waymarks and maps

Well conceived and well waymarked, Corsica's long-distance footpaths are a dream to follow. Every ten metres or so a blob of coloured paint or tape on a rock, tree, lamppost or wall reassures you that you're on the right track. Up

Coastal walks

Lots of walkers come to Corsica expecting the kind of multi-stage coastal paths common in Britain and Ireland, and are disappointed to find most headlands swathed in impenetrable maquis or blocked by rocks. There are, however, some notable exceptions. Exploiting the old Genoese custom officers' footpaths (*sentiers des douaniers*) that formerly encircled the whole island, three waymarked routes have been set out along some of Corsica's most unspoilt shorelines.

Winding around the far northern tip of **Cap Corse**, the oldest-established of them is the one- to two-day route between Macinaggio and Port-Centuri, which passes through the Site Naturelle de Capandula, a reserve encompassing the deserted islets of Finocchiarola and Giraglia. Other landmarks encountered include the watchtowers of Agnello and Santa Maria, an ancient chapel and a string of sheltered sandy coves. For more on this path, see p.79.

Further southwest, a longer three-stage itinerary skirts the edge of the **Désert des Agriates**, Corsica's largest coastal wilderness, between St-Florent near Bastia and plage de Perajola at the mouth of the Ostriconi Valley. Crossing two of the island's most spectacular beaches, the plages de Loto and Saleccia, the first stage of this walk is well frequented in season, but once beyond the midway point you'd be unlikely to encounter another walker. In addition to the beaches, the path also winds past the famous Tour de Mortella, on the Golfe de St-Florent, which took a pounding from Nelson in the eighteenth century. A fuller account of the route appears on p.93.

The path along the **Sartenais coast** in the far south of the island presents another exciting prospect. Starting at Campomoro, at the far west end of the Golfe de Valinco, you can head southwest to Tizzano via the Tour de Senetosa and a chain of exquisite white-sand coves in around six hours. The second day is shorter, but passes some even larger beaches that remain accessible only by 4x4, as well as some memorable rock formations. Ending at beautiful Roccapina, with its distinctive Rocher du Lion and views across the straits to Sardinia, this is probably the most varied of the three coastal paths. Plans are afoot to extend it all the way to Bonifacio, which would make a superb four-day itinerary. For more details on the Sartenais coast path, see p.214.

Don't be fooled by the absence of serious gradients into underestimating the potential rigours and **dangers** of these coastal walks. **Route finding**, in particular, can be a problem, especially early in the spring before the paths have been properly cleared. Waymarkers do exist but they're far less frequent than those up in the hills and cannot be relied upon without the aid of an IGN **map** (see p.330). Spiny maquis is another attendant hassle, tearing your clothes, rucksacks and sleeping mats to shreds. Perhaps the biggest risks of all, though, are **dehydration** and **heatstroke**. None of the three paths have much shade, and from June until the end of September the sun can be merciless. Nor are there many water sources along the way, which means you have to carry between three and five litres with you, topping up wherever possible. Bear in mind, too, that if you injure yourself you'll probably have a very long walk out to reach help: some sections of the above paths may remain deserted for days on end, even at the height of the trekking season in late spring and the autumn.

More specific tips on how to tackle each coastal route, with information on reaching the trailheads and where to sleep and eat along the way, are to be found in the relevant chapters.

on the GR20, the *balisage* (sometimes called *flèchage*) comprises flashes of red and white; on all other coast-to-coast routes, you'll be following single orange spots.

With the aid of the waymarkers you should easily be able to find your way between stages. For a fuller picture of the route's topography, however, some kind of **map** is essential. The most detailed on the market are the IGN's (Institut Géographique National's) splendid Séries Bleues TOP maps which, in addition to helpful shading to emphasize the contours, pick out footpaths in easy-to-read red. At a scale of 1:25,000 (1cm = 250m), they're beautifully drawn, but cost €10 each, which can considerably bump up the overall cost of your trek; a full set for the GR20, for example, will set you back around £45/US$90.

A cheaper alternative is to invest in the FFRP (Fédération Française de la Randonnée Pédestre) **Topo-guide** for your chosen itinerary. These basically consist of extracts from the relevant IGN Séries Bleues maps, reduced in size and interspersed with helpful route information and background on the region (in French only). You'll find them on sale at most bookshops and newsagents in Corsica, and in your home country at the specialist outlets listed on p.49.

Useful hiking vocabulary

balisé/balisage (m) waymarked/ waymarking
berger (m) shepherd
belvédère (m) viewpoint
bifurquer (à gauche/à droite) to bear (left/right)
boussole (f) compass
bergeries (f) high-altitude shepherds' huts
brêche (f) pronounced gap in a ridge or seam of rock
bocca* (f) pass
châtaigneraie (f) chestnut wood
chemin (muletier) (m) (mulepackers') path
cascades (pl) waterfall
cirque (m) steep-sided amphitheatre of cliffs at valley head
col pass
courbe (f) bend
crête (f) ridge
défilé (m) gorge, ravine
descente (f) descent
ébouli (m) boulder choke
étape (f) stage (of a hike)
fleuve (m) river
fontaine (f) spring
franchir to cross
gardien/nne warden (of refuge)

gîte d'étape (m) hikers' hostel
hébergement (m) accommodation
IGN Institut National Géographique
lacets zigzags
longer to follow (eg a river)
météo (f) weather forecast
montée (f) ascent
névé (m) patch of eternal snow
passerelle suspendue (f) rope bridge
pente (f) slope
partage des eaux (m) watershed
pozzines* (pl) rivulets in spongy turf
piste (f) unsurfaced road
PNRC Parc Naturel Régional Corse (Corsica's National Park Authority)
raide steep
randonnée (f)/**randonneur** hike/hiker
ravitaillement (m) provisions
refuge (m) bothy, hikers' shelter
rive (gauche/droite) (f) (left/right) bank (of a stream or river)
ruisseau (m) stream
sac à dos (m) rucksack, backpack
sentier (m) path
sommet (m) summit (of a mountain)
torrent (m) mountain stream
vallée (f) valley
variant (m) alternative route

*Corsican words

Accommodation

Among the great plus factors of Corsica's trekking routes is the quality of accommodation laid on by the PNRC. Although they frequently struggle to keep up with demand in peak season, the island's refuges and *gîtes d'étape* provide inexpensive shelter (and often meals) at the end of each stage, enabling you to walk unencumbered by a heavy pack if you choose.

Along the GR20, **refuges** mark the start and finish of virtually every *étape*. Whether simple wooden shepherds' huts or more ambitious glass-and-steel structures, they all offer basic bunk beds, the use of a well-equipped kitchen, dining room, deck and shower-toilet block for around €11 per night. You can also pitch a tent or bivouac in designated areas around them for €5–7, which sometimes includes the use of an exterior gas-fuelled stove and access to the toilet block (but not to the utensils and interior kitchen).

From June until late September, all of the refuges on the GR20 are staffed by wardens (*gardiens*), most of whom provide expensive supplies and rustle up simple meals in the evening. Kitted out with radios, they are also the best source of advice on impending weather conditions and can summon a rescue helicopter if required.

At those occasional points on the GR20 where the path dips to road level, and at the end of each waystage on lower-altitude routes, accommodation is offered by **gîtes d'étape**. More comfortable than refuges, these are essentially hostels providing bunk-bed accommodation in communal dormitories (for around €11 per head), along with breakfast and evening meals (around €30–35 for half board, or *demi-pension*). Standards of cooking and hospitality vary between establishments, but most *gîtes* are very congenial places to rest up after a day on the trail. The only catch is that they tend to get booked well in advance, so if you intend to rely on them be sure to reserve (by telephone or letter) as far ahead as possible, and reconfirm a day or two before your expected arrival date.

Eating and drinking

Food is likely to comprise most of the weight in your backpack. Aim to carry at least two or three days' worth of supplies with you; during July and August, refuges stock basic provisions (*revitaillement*), but you can't bank on them in June or September/October. The food is always sold at inflated prices, but paying them buys you the luxury of not having to carry so much heavy food in your rucksack – a godsend given some of the gradients. Where the path descends to road level (as at Haut'Asco, Col de Verghio and Vizzavona), you'll always find a shop or bar selling supplies for hikers but, again, they'll be pricey. Dehydrated and dried food is obviously best: pasta, couscous, rice or "boil-up" powder meals (widely available in Corsican supermarkets, where they're much cheaper than at specialist outdoor shops). The one thing to avoid while hiking strenuous routes is **alcohol**, which gives you a short burst of energy but will demand it back with interest the following day. As anyone who's nursed a hangover after an evening's premature celebrations along the GR20 will tell you, wait until you've finished before popping any corks.

You can expect to get through between three and four litres per day – or four to five on the GR20 in summer. On Corsica's low-altitude routes, a couple of litres should see you through: the paths regularly cross villages, streams and springs where you can top up (note that "*Non Potable*" signs on fountains and springs mean they're not safe to drink). Our route descriptions indicate the location of reliable springs along the paths, as do IGN topo-guides and maps. Even at altitude, however, all torrents, streams and rivers in Corsica should be regarded as being contaminated with animal waste, or dead animals themselves, and treated accordingly; if you do need to drink any, boil or clean it first with water **purification tablets** (chlorine-based ones are fine, and healthier over long periods than iodine) or a specialist **filter**.

Equipment

In the light of the potential dangers posed by the volatile weather and tough terrain of the mountains, it is essential to be properly equipped for any hike. Your top priority should be a good pair of **boots**, preferably leather ones with plenty of ankle support. These days, lightweight boots made from synthetic waterproof and breathable fabrics such as Gore-Tex are popular, especially in summer, and although they may be fine for Corsica's low-altitude hikes you should think twice about using them on the GR20, much of which crosses long expanses of broken boulders and granite scree that can be merciless on your ankles. Don't, whatever you do, attempt anything more ambitious than an hour-long amble along level ground in trainers, no matter how comfortable they may feel. Unless you're planning some hard-core winter adventure sports activity, you won't need to hike with a **tent** in Corsica, although many hikers regard the additional weight as a worthwhile trade-off for a bit of extra privacy (refuge dormitories can be very stuffy and noisy). All of the footpaths are well served by *gîtes* and refuges. It is technically forbidden to **bivouac** within the Parc Naturel (except in the purpose-built *aires de bivouac* outside the GR20 refuges), but in practice no one is likely to stop you as long as you don't light fires and leave rubbish behind. An army-style poncho or large plastic bivvy bag can come in handy for this, and you'll need at least a three-season sleeping bag to bivouac at altitude along the GR20, especially during the first and last months of the trekking season – June and September – when freezing temperatures are not uncommon.

As for **clothing**, expect to have to add and remove layers constantly. During ascents, shorts and vest are usually adequate, even at altitude, while on the way downhill you may need long sleeves and long trousers. A good fleece can also prove invaluable, as can a lightweight coat of some kind, ideally one made of waterproof breathable fabric such as Gore-Tex. Anyone attempting the GR20 might also consider shelling out on some kind of underwear made of wicking fibre, which prevents the build-up of sweat that can cause sudden drops in body temperature when you stop moving; they're not cheap, but over a fortnight on the GR20 you'll easily get your money's worth. In summer, however, you should take along a sun hat and high-factor sun cream – sunstroke, caused by prolonged dehydration and exposure to strong sunlight, is a big problem if it hits you three or four hours from the nearest refuge.

Health and safety

Serious injuries are rare on Corsica's trails, but any foray into the mountains implies an element of risk and you should be equipped accordingly. Its exposed position means that the island is prone to sudden and dramatic changes in **weather**, which can transform a leisurely ramble into a battle with the elements

Essential checklist

There are no hard and fast rules about what to pack. The following lists summarize the most useful items for trekking in varied weather conditions during the summer season.

Kit

Adjustable (telescopic) trekking poles Knee-savers on those crunching GR20 descents.

Bivouac bag An ideal weight-saving alternative to a tent, a bivvy bag will provide an additional insulating layer if you're sleeping under the stars; dry nights are the norm through the summer, and you can get by without a tent, bedding down inside refuges (or *gîtes*) if the weather looks dodgy.

Body wallet

Boots Two- to three-season for the GR20; or two-season/multi-activity shoes on lower-level routes. Choose ones with Vibram soles and solid ankle support.

Fleece

Gloves

Hats A sunhat and a warm hat.

Head torch

Jacket Lightweight wind- and waterproof, ideally made of breathable fabric such as Gore-Tex.

Penknife

Shorts and long trousers (both loose or made of four-way stretch material).

Sleeping bag Three- to four-season, or comfort down to –5°C minimum for the GR20; two-season for lower routes.

Sleeping mat If you're camping or bivouacking.

Slippers or outdoor "Teva"-style sandals – great for resting your feet at the end of the day.

Soap The biodegradable liquid kind.

Socks Purpose-made trekking socks that wick out sweat are best.

Stove Multi-fuel burners are best; Bleuet Camping Gas canisters and methylated spirit (known as *alcool à brûler* in French) are the only fuels routinely available in Corsica.

Sunglasses

Thermal T-shirts Made of modern wicking textiles.

Toilet paper

Water bottle or "Platypus-Hoser"-style reservoir.

Water purification tablets

Medical supplies

Antiseptic cream or spray

Deep heat spray or balm

Glasses or contact lenses Bring spare pairs.

Hypodermic needles For piercing blisters.

Insect repellent

Nail scissors or file

Painkillers Anti-inflammatory, Ibroprufen-based.

Plasters

Prescription drugs Bring a supply of any you might need.

Silicone blister pads

Sterilized gauze

Sun cream High-factor.

Zinc tape

with little warning. This is particularly true of the GR20's high ridge sections, where electric storms are near daily occurrences during hot periods. Just how lethal the interior mountains can be was vividly demonstrated in the mid-1990s when seven people died on the lower flanks of Monte Cinto on a single night, after being overtaken by a freak blizzard in July.

As a base requirement, therefore, carry waterproof clothing and a change of kit in your pack. Ensure, too, that your sleeping bag is stored in a plastic bag (or purpose-made waterproof stuff sack) to stop it getting wet, and that you have enough warm gear, food and water to survive a night outdoors if you have to. Take into account the terrain ahead and assess how exposed to the elements you'll be should conditions take a sudden turn for the worse. **Forecasts** (in French) can be obtained by telephone on ☎08 36 68 02 20, but your best source of advice are the refuge and *gîte* wardens, who receive meteorological bulletins by radio each day.

In the summer months, the **sun** is more likely to pose a threat than storms. When walking on hot, exposed trails, always wear a hat and drink plenty of fluids. Nothing saps your energy faster than **dehydration**, which can be easily avoided by gulping down as much water as you can before setting off and then keeping topped up at regular intervals throughout the day. Use our route descriptions and maps to gauge how long you'll have to walk before reaching a water source and never run low; remember that when it comes to liquid, "little and often" is the golden rule. Early symptoms of sunstroke include dizziness, headaches, acute fatigue and nausea. The only remedy is to rest up, cool down and drink lots of fluid.

Sunstroke may set you back a day or two at worst, but the most common reason trekkers abandon the trail altogether is **blisters**. Caused by rubbing from ill-fitting or stiff boots, these can also be avoided by making sure your footwear is well worn in before the start of the trek. A good sock combination will also help: take along a thin inner pair and a thicker outer one, both made from wicking textiles that ensure your feet stay dry, and remove them during rest breaks. If blisters do begin to build up, the worst thing you can do is ignore them. At the first hint of rubbing deploy a Compeed-style silicone blister pad and some zinc tape. Should this fail you'll have no option but to burst the blister

Low-impact walking

Corsica's natural environment comes under intense pressure from the hundreds of thousands of visitors who enjoy it each summer. You can, however, **minimize your impact** on the island's wilderness areas by observing a few common-sense dos and don'ts.

Don't pollute water sources: never defecate or use detergents within 25m of a stream or spring; if there's a toilet and wash block within reach, use it.

Don't defecate on or near the paths: if you get taken short, dig a hole somewhere discreet and well away from the path for your faeces, which will attract flies and cause a health hazard if left unburied.

Dispose of your toilet paper hygenically: bury it; never leave it in the open to rot.

Don't light fires or leave cooking stoves unattended.

Don't leave litter behind you: refuges and *gîtes d'étape* all have trash bins which are emptied regularly throughout the summer (by helicopter on the more remote stretches of the GR). Remember that some organic refuse such as orange peel can take weeks or months to degrade.

Don't pick wild flowers, even those that grow in abundance.

with a hypodermic syringe or sterilized needle (essential components of any trekker's medical kit). Allow the wound to breathe afterwards and then apply antiseptic cream and a plaster to keep it clean.

In the event of a serious, life-threatening accident, or if you need to be evacuated by helicopter for any reason, contact the local **mountain rescue** service, the Peloton de Gendarmerie de Haute Montagne (PGHM) in Corte on ☏04 95 61 13 95. They can also be reached via the police ☏17 or fire brigade ☏18. Note that from a **mobile phone**, dialling ☏112 will get you through to the emergency services even in areas where your network may not offer coverage. Bear in mind that the gendarmerie, who operate the PGHM, are entitled to charge a large sum for their help, and will almost certainly do so if they feel you have been imprudent in any way – another good reason to arrange dependable **insurance** cover before leaving home (see p.48).

Costs and money

Helicopter evacuation excepted, the cost of trekking in Corsica is surprisingly low, especially for the GR20 where opportunities to spend are few and far between. Resist the temptation of cold beers from the *gardiens'* refrigerators and you should be able to get by on very little indeed. Allowing €12 per day for food and €9 for refuge accommodation, it would be theoretically possible to complete all sixteen stages without spending much more than €200–250. In practice, however, most walkers get through double that. Take your time, splash out on hotel beds and restaurant meals, catch taxis to and from the trailhead, and you'll be looking at more like €560–750 for the fortnight.

On lower-level routes, which pass through villages at regular intervals, café, restaurant and hotel bills tend to put greater strain on wallets. But you can economize considerably by sleeping and eating in *gîtes d'étape*, where a dorm bed costs around €12–15 per night, or €30–35 for half board (*demi-pension*). Add in the cost of supplies, and a typical five-day trek wouldn't have to set you back more than €250–300. With a budget of €375 or above, you could afford to stay in comfortable hotels and eat out most days.

Note that once away from the main towns on the coast, banks and ATMs are a comparative rarity (and on the GR20 they're nonexistent), so be sure to **take enough cash** on your trek to see you through.

Organized walking holidays

It's perfectly possible to arrange your own **walking holiday** and navigate your chosen route with no more help than the PNRC's waymarks and the information in this book. All the same, plenty of firms are on hand to take care of the practicalities on your behalf. Some supply little more than travel tickets and detailed route descriptions which you use to get between *gîtes* or hotels (the so-called "self-guided" option); others organize baggage transfer between stages (*sac allegé*), lay on experienced guides and generally pamper clients with slap-up picnic lunches and posh hotels.

Deciding on what level of support you require means thinking hard about how much of the graft and logistical hassle you'd prefer to spare yourself, and what route would best suit you. Bear in mind that in addition to UK- and US-based outfits, there are plenty of local Corsican guides and walking holiday

▲ Hiking the GR20

firms who'll provide much the same services, sometimes for a lot less money and with a greater degree of local expertise. The following contacts represent a good cross-section of the kind of services available.

Corsica

Alti Piani Ⓦwww.altipiani-corse.com. Various guided and self-guided options, staying in *gîtes* or smart hotels.

Altre Cime Ⓣ04 95 35 32 59, Ⓦwww.altre-cime .com. Association of guides who have put together an inspired choice of less-frequented mountain and valley routes, including the rarely attempted ridgetop traverse of Cap Corse.

Couleur Corse Ⓦwww.couleur-corse.com. All-women team operating more than twenty routes, which they combine with canyoning, kayaking, climbing and mountain-biking extensions.

In Terra Corsa Ⓣ04 95 47 69 48, Ⓦwww .interracorsa.fr. From their base at Ponte Leccia

station, this group of young guides leads well-honed *via ferrata*, canyoning, "tyrotrekking" (routes using Tyrolean slides) and sea kayak trips. You can mix and match packages of adventure sports, or opt for more conventional guided walks in the Asco–Niolo regions.

Rando Ane Corse Ⓦwww.rando-ane-corse.com. Guided low-level walks with donkeys to carry your bags.

Vallecime Ⓣ04 95 48 69 33, Ⓦwww.vallecime .com. A selection of carefully chosen routes, ranging from sections of the GR20 to lower-level hikes around the west coast, guided by Pascale and Jean-François Luciani (Jean-François holds the record for the fastest completion of the GR20).

In the UK and Ireland

Explore Ⓣ0870 333 4001, Ⓦwww.explore.co.uk. "Village trek" from Calacuccia in the Niolo Valley over the Col de Verghio to Porto.

Exodus Ⓣ0870 240 5550, Ⓦwww.exodus.co.uk. Centre-based walking from the village of Boconagno.

HF Holidays Ⓣ020/8905 9556, Ⓦwww .hfholidays.co.uk. Seven-night trek covering the best bits of the Tra Mare i Monti between Col de la Palmarella and Cargèse.

Nature Trek Ⓣ01962/733051, Ⓦwww.naturetrek .co.uk. Eight-day birdwatching, botanical and natural history walks by an established UK outfit.

Sherpa Ⓣ020/8577 2717, Ⓦwww.sherpa -walking-holidays.co.uk. Self-guided routes through the Niolo to Porto, or a guided GR20 option.

World Walks Ⓣ01242/254353, Ⓦwww .worldwalks.com/corsica.htm. Guided and self-guided walking holidays along the Mare a Mare Centre or GR20.

Adventure Center ℡ 1-800/228-8747, ⓦ www
.adventure-center.com. US hiking and "soft
adventure" specialists offering Corsican village
treks.

World Expeditions ℡ 1-888/464 TREK, ⓦ www
.worldexpeditions.net (US) or 1-800/567 2216,
ⓦ www.worldexpeditions.ca (Canada). Fully
supported trekking holidays.

The GR20

Although it has only recently begun to attract the attention of North American
and British walkers, the GR20 has long been France's most illustrious *Grande
Randonnée*. The trans-Pyrenean GR10 may be longer, and the Tour de Mont
Blanc may scale higher mountains, but "*le Grand GR*", as it's colloquially known
in Corsica, still tops most French trekkers' hit lists. Some 17,000 people travel
to the island each year expressly to walk the route, many of whom have never
ventured on foot to such altitudes before. If you're one of them, the landscapes
awaiting you over the first few stages alone – not to mention the experience of
hauling yourself and your gear up and down a succession of mighty slopes –
may come as a revelation. In very few places on the globe do mountain ranges
nudging 3000m surge straight from the sea, and none is so well served by
marked trails and refuges as this.

Even for experienced mountain walkers, though, the wild granite peaks and
high ridges of the Corsican watershed cannot fail to impress. All of the island's

Warning: weight and water

One sure-fire way to improve your chances of finishing, and actually enjoying, the
GR20 is to **minimize the weight of your pack**. With two big bottles of water and
three days' worth of food to carry on top of your equipment, this can be difficult,
but a heavy rucksack can place a critical amount of strain of your knees and feet,
and generally make life uncomfortable – especially during ascents and descents.
The majority of people who bail out of the route over the first three days do so
because of problems related to overweight sacks: blisters; knee or ankle strain; or
excessive fatigue.

Before setting off, therefore, weigh your gear carefully (you can do this at any
hunting and fishing store on the island). As a rule of thumb, men shouldn't carry over
15kg, and women 10kg. Any more than that and you ought seriously to consider
ditching some stuff. Go through your rucksack and remove anything you can live
without – even excess toothpaste, antiseptic cream and shampoo. Consider, too,
replacing heavy cotton clothes with lightweight purpose-made ones. Aside from
being more comfortable, wicking garments can also be washed and dried more
quickly, which allows you to make do with a single spare shirt, for example, rather
than several.

One thing you shouldn't scrimp on, however, is **water**. Springs are few and far
between up on the watershed. Run out and you'll be risking dehydration, which can
precipitate severe tiredness and sunstroke. Plan ahead: always keep at least half a
litre in reserve and stash a strip of chlorine purification tablets in your kit in case you
need to fill up with stream water.

major summits – névé-encrusted until well into the summer – lie within reach of the path, and there are numerous alpine-style alternative routes, scrambles and multi-pitch climbs to distract the more adventurous.

Devised by the alpinist Michel Fabrikant in the early 1970s, the GR20 boasts some impressive **vital statistics**. Between the starting point at **Calenzana**, near Calvi in the northwest of the island, and **Conca**, near Porto Vecchio in the southeast, sprawl 170km of relentlessly rugged country. To cross it, you have to negotiate a total of 19,000m of ascent and descent, climbing to a maximum altitude of 2225m (or 2706m if you climb Monte Cinto as a side trip). Some particularly steep and exposed sections – such as the notorious Cirque de la Solitude – involve pitches fixed with ladders, chains and stanchion cables, while early in the season patches of melting snow can impede progress towards the highest passes.

Don't, however, let the GR20's somewhat exaggerated reputation put you off. Strenuous though it undoubtedly is, the route is perfectly manageable for anyone in reasonable shape. No technical expertise is required, and even walkers with a poor head for heights usually manage the trickier pitches with ease.

Nevertheless, the GR20 should always be approached with respect. Fatalities and serious accidents do occur – albeit very rarely – usually because of recklessness in poor conditions. Be aware that the weather at altitude can change dramatically and if it does you need to be prepared, with solid equipment and adequate supplies (see p.332). Above all, **never lose sight of the waymarks** unless you know exactly where you are and what you're doing, and have the necessary navigation skills to find your way back to them again if the rain or mist sweeps in. This applies especially to **solo trekkers**. On the GR20 you're seldom alone for long, but wander only a short distance off the path and you'll find it difficult to call for help in the event of an injury.

Supplies along the route

These days, every refuge on the GR20 – with the exception of Paliri on the penultimate stage – stocks a considerable range of **trekking supplies**, ranging from chocolate, biscuits, pasta and dehydrated food, to fresh fruit, bread, dried sausage and local ewe's cheese. Most also prepare hot meals, usually filling bowls of *soupe corse* and a hunk of bread (for which they'll typically charge around €10). In fact, if you're prepared to pay the prices to spare you the trouble of carrying a heavy pack, you can safely rely on refuges to supply you along the route, at least in peak season, although towards the beginning and end of the summer, the *gardiens* tend not to make daily trips to restock.

How long will it take?

Most walkers take between ten and twelve days to complete the GR20 from start to finish. It's possible to cover the ground more quickly than that (the record, held by Jean-François Luciani from Sant'Andréa di Bozio, is a superhuman 37hr), but to do so you'll have to double or triple up stages most days, which can alter the whole complexion of the route (especially if you're not very fit).

Also worth bearing in mind are the tempting **side trips** and **alternative routes** you can make from the main GR itinerary, notably the ascents of Corsica's highest peaks, which all lie within reach of the path. Such detours can add a few days to your overall time, but they're well worth the extra effort, taking you into terrain that's in every way a notch above what you cross on the red-and-white waymarked route.

In short, try not to rush your trek. Far too many people treat the GR20 like some kind of assault course, to be completed as fast and aggressively as possible. But ultimately it's more important that you walk at whatever pace you feel most comfortable with. As long as the weather is fine make the most of it: stay at altitude for as long as you can and take plenty of rest breaks to enjoy the scenery. It's amazing how many trekkers scramble out of the refuges into the pre-dawn darkness only to arrive at the end of the *étape* by lunchtime, spending the afternoons lazing around the huts instead of amid the very landscapes they've travelled so far to experience.

The GR20 is described below in sixteen stages. Within those stages, times given are always from the start of that stage.

Stage one: Calenzana to refuge d'Ortu di u Piobbu

Taking you from the coastal maquis belt to the rocky heights of the watershed, stage one provides a stark introduction to both the pains and pleasures of the GR20. With virtually no let-up in the gradient and three days' worth of

> **Stage summary**
> Walking time: 5hr 30min
> Distance: 21km
> Total ascent: 1610m
> Total descent: 300m
> Highest point reached: Refuge d'Ortu di u Piobbu (1570m)
> IGN Map reference: #4149 OT & #4250 OT

supplies in your pack, you'll probably find yourself taking lots of breathers to gaze at the progressively more spectacular views across the Balagne and interior range that unfold as the path progresses. This is one day when advance fitness preparation will definitely pay dividends. In all, the stage involves 1610m of altitude gain – more than one and a half times the height of Ben Nevis – much of it over ground exposed to the full glare of the mid-morning sunshine. With a dawn start, the first long climb of the day (to Bocca a u Saltu) can be tackled in cool shadow, but once beyond the pass the only shade comes from wind-blown pines as you enter an archetypal Corsican landscape of green-tinged granite interspersed with alder bushes and shimmering silver birch coppices.

Water is short on this stage. Some seasonal streams may be found in early summer, but don't rely on them. Carry at least three litres.

The official trailhead of the GR20 at **Calenzana** (see p.129) stands at the top of the village, as indicated by numerous PNRC signboards. Flanked on one side by the tiny **Oratoire Sant'Antoine** and on the other by a covered spring (the first and last convenient water supply on the *étape*), the path strikes immediately uphill via a sunken cobbled mule track, emerging shortly after to open pasture dotted with solitary pines and chestnut trees. Scratchy maquis closes in as you approach the first ridge of the day, just below which a signboard indicates the **junction** (50min) of the GR20 and orange-waymarked Tra Mare e Monti. Bear left here to begin a gradually ascending traverse to the

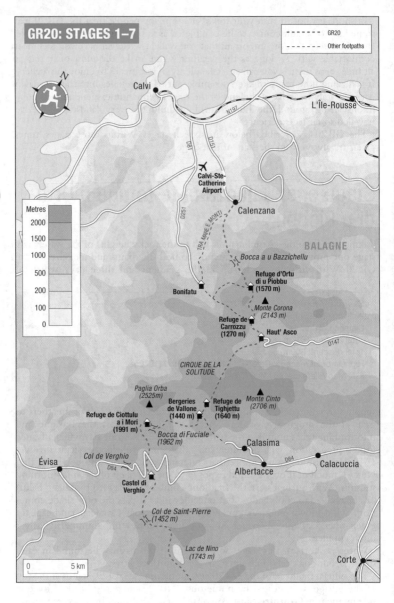

GR20: STAGES 1–7

- – – – – – GR20
- – – – – Other footpaths

Metres
- 2000
- 1500
- 500
- 200
- 100
- 0

Calvi

L'Île-Rousse

N197

D81

D1510

Calvi-Ste-Catherine Airport

Calenzana

TRA MARE E MONTI

BALAGNE

Bocca a u Bazzichellu

Bonifatu

Refuge d'Ortu di u Piobbu (1570 m)

Monte Corona (2143 m)

Refuge de Carrozzu (1270 m)

Haut' Asco

D147

CIRQUE DE LA SOLITUDE

Paglia Orba (2525m)

Bergeries de Vallone (1440 m)

Refuge de Tighjettu (1640 m)

Monte Cinto (2706 m)

Refuge de Ciottulu a i Mori (1991 m)

Bocca di Fuciale (1962m)

Calasima

Évisa

Col de Verghio
D84

Castel di Verghio

Albertacce

Calacuccia

D84

Col de Saint-Pierre (1452 m)

Lac de Nino (1743 m)

Corte

0   5 km

promontoire d'Arghioa (2hr), a rock outcrop where the path cuts decisively into the line of the hill and starts a long, steep ascent culminating at the **Bocca a u Saltu** (1250m; 3hr 15min).

The tone of the route changes abruptly on the far side of the pass as the waymarks plunge into old-growth pine forest. With the bulk of Monte Corona looming above, you then start to climb again into a long, convoluted traverse across a rocky slope that's steep in places. In early summer, clumps of spotted orchid enliven this enjoyable scramble, whose trickiest pitch is made easier by a fixed stanchion cable that you'll be glad of in wet weather.

Having climbed out of the valley to a second pass, the **Bocca a u Bazzichellu** (1486m; 4hr 30min), the GR20 continues uphill in an easterly direction, emerging from the forest to a superb view of the interior mountains. From here on, the going gets a lot easier. Sweeping around the head of the Melaghia Valley, the route then winds at a mostly even gradient to a boulder-choked spur, over which a short climb leads you to the **refuge d'Ortu di u Piobbu** (1570m; 5hr 30min; some basic supplies).

Monte Corona

With an early departure from Calenzana, strong walkers can expect to arrive at Ortu di u Piobbu by midday, leaving plenty of daylight left for the enjoyable – if somewhat strenuous – **ascent of Monte Corona**. Given the length, extreme gradients and water shortages of the second *étape* to Carrozzu, the climb, which yields a spectacular panorama of the watershed's big peaks to the south, affords a more sensible way to pass the afternoon than pressing on. You'd have to be very fit, fully acclimatized to the sun and altitude, and travelling light to double up the GR's first two stages.

The round trip to the summit of Monte Corona and back takes around two hours and thirty minutes; leave mid-afternoon as the views from the summit are best towards sunset (you'll also stand a better chance of spotting mouflon in the early evening). If you're heading off alone, it's also a good idea to inform the *gardiens*.

Immediately behind the hut, yellow paint blobs mark the path, which zigzags steeply uphill through birch woods to the windy **Bocca Tartagine** (1852m), gateway to the remote Giunssani region (see p.137). From here, look for cairns striking steeply up to the right along a ridgeline cluttered with alder scrub and boulders. Eventually, after a frustratingly slow half hour or so, you'll emerge at open scree, across which the path to the summit is well trodden and easy to follow. Extending as far as the tip of Cap Corse, south to the snow-tinged massif of Monte Cinto and over the entire Balagne coast, the views are magnificent. Descend by the same route; you might need a head torch.

Stage two: Refuge d'Ortu di u Piobbu to refuge de Carrozzu

Some of the longest, hardest climbs and descents of the entire GR20 occur on stage two, but as recompense you have a correspondingly memorable traverse to look forward to midway through the day, affording one of the route's definitive panoramas. Once again, water sources are virtually nonexistent and you'll

Stage summary
Walking time: 6hr 15min
Distance: 13km
Total ascent: 670m
Total descent: 975m
Highest point reached: Ladroncellu traverse (2030m)
IGN Map reference: #4250 OT

need to carry plenty of liquid to get you through the last section of the *étape*, a knee-crunching drop down a steep, south-facing slope that's a veritable furnace in sunny weather.

The stage gets underway with a short ascent through the woods and over a rounded spur, on the far side of which the **bergeries de la Mandriaccia** huddle beneath a dense pine canopy. Beyond the old shepherds' hut, a boulder-covered rise heralds the start of a hefty two hour thirty-minute climb across a mixture of smooth-backed slabs and large boulders. Its steepest section comes after you pass an arrowed turning to a **spring** hidden in the rocks just off the path, with the gradient only easing off as the waymarks approach the **Bocca Piccaia** (1950m; 3hr 15min), a superb little col from where a wild vista extends southwards to Paglia Orba.

A further short climb through the rocks overlooking the pass takes you over the 2000m mark for the first time. Skirting the southern flank of Capu Ladroncellu, the ensuing traverse is the day's highpoint in every sense. Most people kick back for an hour or two here to enjoy the amazing views, which encompass a huge chunk of the watershed and rugged northwest coast. Dominating the horizon, the distinctive profile of Paglia Orba marks the route you'll be following over the coming days.

From the level path around the summit of Capu Ladroncellu, an entirely different kind of traverse opens up to the south. After a sheer drop, the red-and-white waymarks guide you up a narrow curving ridgetop to the **Bocca d'Avartoli** pass (1898m; 4hr 15min), where they switch repeatedly from one side of the *crête* to the other to navigate a route through a dramatic sequence of wind-eroded outcrops and pinnacles.

At **Bocca Carrozzu** (1865m; 5hr) – or Bocca Inuminata as it's marked on some maps – you get your first sight of the refuge far below on the valley floor. However, a relentlessly steep, hot and slippery descent across loose scree has to be tackled before you can sun yourself on the hut's deck. On the way down,

▲ Rope bridge near Bonifatu

look out for lammergeiers soaring around the spectacular red crags of the Cirque de Bonifatu, which looms above the hut.

Thanks to its sheltered situation deep in the pine forest, the **refuge de Carrozzu** (1270m; 6hr 15min; good range of supplies and hot food, but very expensive) used to be one of the most congenial stops on the GR20, but in recent years the hut and its camping-bivouac area have strained to cope with the summer influx. Toilet facilities are particularly inadequate, so brace yourself for some unpleasant mess and queues if you come here in July or August.

Congestion becomes marginally less of a problem beyond Carrozzu, largely because this is the point where most of those for whom the first two days of the GR have been too much drop out: a **liaison path** leads in around one hour thirty minutes from the refuge to the roadhead at **Bonifatu**, from where you can catch a bus or hitch to Calvi, or head off on the less arduous Tra Mare e Monti route towards Galéria.

Stage three: Refuge de Carrozzu to Haut'Asco

The crux of stage three – and the cause of more dropouts than any other stretch of the GR20 – is the ascent of the Spasimata Valley, which begins just over the rise from Carrozzu. Although no more taxing than anything on the previous two days' terrain, the giant staircase of smooth-backed granite slabs leading to the Lac de la Muvrella comes as a rude shock to tired legs first thing

> **Stage summary**
> Walking time: 5hr
> Distance: 6km
> Total ascent: 860m
> Total descent: 715m
> Highest point reached: Bocca a i Stagni (2010m)
> IGN Map reference: #4250 OT

in the morning, and many walkers turn tail while they are still able to beat an easy retreat to Calvi. Those that prevail, however, can look forward to the route's best views of Monte Cinto's north face, which holds a fair splattering of snow until well into July.

The climb begins as soon as you've crossed the swaying cable bridge ten minutes or so beyond Carrozzu (one of the GR's classic photo opportunities). Although straightforward enough in dry conditions, it should nevertheless be approached with caution in wet weather, when the stanchion cables attached to some of the more steeply inclined pitches come into their own.

Depending on how early you set off from the refuge, you should emerge from the valley shadow into bright sunshine shortly before arriving at the **Lac de la Muvrella** (2hr 45min), a tiny lake cradled in a hollow just below the pass. The grassy banks around it provide perfect spots from which to admire your morning's work stretched out below, and contemplate the remaining short but steep pull to the col ahead, which early in the season can be complicated by a fair-sized névé. On setting off for the couloir leading to the pass, look out for the famous rock formation to its left, known for obvious reasons as "**The Red Indian's Head**".

Reached after around three hours, the **Bocca di a Muvrella** (1860m) reveals another sweeping vista across the hinterland of Corsica's west coast, but for an uninterrupted view of Monte Cinto you'll have to press on to the second pass of the day, which the GR20 approaches after a short zigzagging drop and a more gentle traversing climb. Once at the **Bocca a i Stagni** (2010m; 3hr 30min) you can either linger to admire the spectacle of the Cinto massif in all its glory or else get stuck into the abrupt 588-metre descent to the old ski station at **Haut'Asco** – one of the sheerest on the route. Winding over a steeply piled chaos of sharp-edged boulders, this descent is another that should be undertaken with particular care in rainy conditions.

For a full account of Haut'Asco – including reviews of its limited accommodation and eating options and a route description for the **ascent of Monte Cinto** – see p.296. A Portakabin just below the refuge stocks a good range of supplies at reasonable prices.

Stage four: Haut'Asco to refuge de Tighjettu/bergeries de Vallone

No stretch of the GR20 is approached with quite as much trepidation as the Cirque de la Solitude, the defining feature of stage four. A sheer-sided amphitheatre enclosed by the gloomy west wall of the Cinto massif, it's the passage GR veterans love to talk up, mainly because of the famously long sequence of

> **Stage summary**
> Walking time: 5hr/5hr 30min
> Distance: 7km/8km
> Total ascent: 1000m/1000m
> Total descent: 740m/840m
> Highest point reached: Bocca Minuta (2218m)
> IGN Map reference: #4250 OT

chains, ladders and cables lining it. The gradients are certainly the steepest of the whole route, but Via Ferrata this certainly isn't and most people end up wondering what all the fuss is about. In any case, bottling out isn't an option: to skip the next couple of stages would require a long and expensive taxi ride or unpredictable hitchhike to Col de Verghio, which would, quite apart from the time spent travelling up the Niolo Valley, also mean missing out on the magnificent Golo River section of stage six.

The cirque aside, stage four is a case of *plus ça change, plus c'est la même chose*: another long climb to start the day and a boot-jamming descent to wind things up. The initial section of the *étape*, however, begins with a fairly leisurely, but extremely scenic, ascent of the Asco Valley's head, in the course of which you get some spectacular views of the Cirque de Trombolacciu's peaks through the charred pines to the south.

If you're covering this stretch early in the morning, look out for mouflon scouring the crags high above the river as you approach the **ancien refuge d'Altore**, a former GR20 hut which was firebombed by "nationalists" back in the 1980s. From the concrete rubble where the refuge used to stand, an impressive névé usually lines the steep climb up to **Bocca Tumasginesca** (aka Le Col Perdu 2183m; 2hr 15min), which should take around thirty minutes. On fine, clear mornings you can sometimes see the snowcapped Alps floating above the distant horizon from here.

The view north, however, tends to be overshadowed by your first sight of the **Cirque de la Solitude** plummeting from the far side of the pass. Get here early in the day before the queues build up around the chain and ladder-pitches and you can expect to complete the sheer two-hundred-metre descent and correspondingly steep climb up the other side of the chasm in around one hour thirty minutes. But hold-ups are par for the course unless you're comfortable on steep, exposed rock, in which case bypass some of the climbing aids, many of which are essential only in wet weather (when you'd be foolhardy to wander away from the waymarks without ropes and harnesses).

From **Bocca Minuta** (2218m; 3hr 45min), take one last look at the magnificent view over the cirque before beginning the long descent to Tighjettu. Funnelling you down the side of a broad south-facing moraine, the **Ravin de Stranciacone**, this stretch can be hot going in warm weather, and tough on the knees, with the waymarks dropping sharply down inclined boulders.

Many trekkers are happy enough to call it a day at the **refuge de Tighjettu** (1640m; 5hr; good range of supplies), perched on a spur overlooking the valley, but a more congenial place to rest up lies a short way further down the trail. Run by a local family from the Niolo Valley (see p.302), the **bergeries de Vallone** (1440m; 5hr 30min; very good range of supplies and hot meals) comprise a cluster of old shepherds' huts recently converted to service walkers. Large canvas tents provide basic dormitory shelter, or you can camp and bivouac. Included in the €5 fee is the use of a flush toilet and access to a water tap and spring. Tasty Niolin specialities – from ewe's cheese omelettes to full-blown four-course meals – are also served up on their wooden deck, along with hot and cold drinks, and the views are great.

Stage five: bergeries de Vallone to Ciottulu a i Mori

Stage five of the GR20 is comparatively short and easy, with only one significant ascent – the climb up Bocca di Fuciale to enter the Golo Valley. Most people combine it with the previous stage from Haut'Asco, which makes for a long day but leaves you in a prime position to scale Paglia Orba – Corsica's third-highest mountain – the following morning.

A gentle forest walk gets the *étape* underway as the path winds around the base of Paglia Orba via a series of side ravines. Giant Laricio pines shade most

Stage summary
Walking time: 3hr
Distance: 6km
Total ascent: 550m
Total descent: 200m
Highest point reached: Refuge Ciottulu a i Mori
IGN Map reference: #4250 OT

of the route until it bends decisively westwards to begin the assault of **Bocca di Fuciale** (1962m; 2hr 30min), reached after a long clamber across steadily steepening, exposed rock. A broad saddle coated in red scree, the pass itself is bleak, snow-patched and scoured by strong winds, but it is worth hanging around for a while on the off chance of spotting the herd of mouflon that habitually grazes above.

The waymarks then continue uphill to the right of the pass, before dropping down through juniper scrub to the GR20's highest refuge, **Ciottulu a i Mori** (1991m; 3hr; very good range of supplies and cooked food). Overlooking the beautiful Golo Valley from a natural balcony on the base of Paglia Orba, the stone-built hut is smaller than most on the route, with only 29 beds inside and little shelter for campers and bivouackers around it, but the location is superb.

Paglia Orba

8

With its awesome fin-shaped summit, **Paglia Orba** is Corsica's most spectacular massif, even if not its highest. The two-hour ascent from Ciottulu a i Mori presents no technical difficulties in fair, dry weather, but you'll most definitely need a head for heights to enjoy some of the scrambling involved, which exposes you to the full dizzying drop of the north face – one of the Mediterranean's most challenging rock-climbing locations. Allow three to four hours for the round trip from the refuge, and leave early in the morning to catch the best views, which are as amazing as you'd expect for a mountain that peaks only 19km from the sea. Confirmed scramblers might also consider the rewarding side trip to **Capu Tafonatu**, an extraordinary natural arch said to have been created by the Devil in a fury (see p.303), which can be reached by following a well-cairned route from the Col des Maures (see below).

From immediately behind the refuge, a clearly marked path picks its way up the side of the scree-covered ravine to the **Col des Maures** (2335m), a rocky saddle in the ridge separating Paglia Orba from its sister peak, Capu Tafonatu. Turn left and follow the sequence of small cairns to reach the latter, but be warned that the two-hour round trip requires some hairy scrambling across very steep and exposed rock. Even competent climbers should think twice before attempting it if there's even a hint of rain.

The same applies to the next section of the ascent up Paglia Orba, which begins to the right of Col des Maures. Although not especially difficult, it includes a couple of pitches that are a notch trickier than any on the GR20, including a narrow ledge passage above a vast cliff. Once atop Paglia Orba's forepeak, though, it's plain sailing through the Combe des Chèvres, a hidden dip encrusted in eternal snow, and thence across the windy ridgetop to the summit proper. Allow one hour thirty minutes for the ascent, thirty to forty minutes for the descent, and a good hour to take in the stupendous view from the top.

Stage six: Ciottulu a i Mori to Castel di Verghio

By the standards of the GR20, stage six is a rest day – a chance to recover from the travails of the previous five *étapes* with regular dips in the Golo River, which flows through a series of deep turquoise pools, waterfalls and stands of magnificent Laricio pines. Presided over by the red bulk of Paglia Orba to the north,

LONG-DISTANCE WALKS | The GR20

Stage summary
Walking time: 2hr 15min
Distance: 8km
Total ascent: 0
Total descent: 580m
Highest point reached: Refuge Ciottulu a i Mori
IGN Map reference: #4250 OT

the valley rising from it also ranks among the most beautiful in Corsica, and in fine weather the grassy banks, old-growth forest and paved Genoan mule track that usher you towards the stage end make a blissful change from the uncompromising terrain now behind you.

From Ciottulu a i Mori there's a choice of routes down the head of the Golo basin: either follow the cow track that plunges steeply downhill from in front of the hut; or else stick to the red-and-white waymarks as they sweep around a grazed spur to the west and then cut downhill to the **bergeries de Tula**. From this junction on the valley floor, a well-worn track then winds south alongside the Golo, which it crosses a couple of times. Lying only a couple of hours' gentle walk from the main road at Col de Verghio, the beautiful natural pools passed on this stretch are popular day-trip destinations, so expect plenty of company from midday onwards.

After the second and last river crossing, the next landmark on the stage is the **bergeries de Radule** (1hr 15min), a cluster of restored dry-stone huts which are these days among the few working sheepfolds on the GR20. Camping is prohibited here, but you're welcome to refill your bottles from the spring nearby and, at times when the shepherds are in residence with their flocks, strong goat's and ewe's cheese is available.

The *bergeries* stand more or less at the midway mark of the *étape*, but the remaining half is largely a dull plod through dense pine forest. You'll know when you're nearing the end (2hr 15min) when you start to hear the unfamiliar sound of traffic drifting through the trees.

A full account of **Col de Verghio** and the Niolo Valley appears on p.297.

Stage seven: Castel di Verghio to Manganu

Stage seven is essentially a transitionary section of the GR20, connecting the high mountains of the northwest with the Rotondo massif in the deep interior. Your first good sight of the serrated ridges that will dominate the trail ahead comes on reaching Lac de Nino – Corsica's most photographed altitude lake and the undisputed highlight of this *étape*. Many trekkers are tempted to double

Stage summary
Walking time: 5hr 30min
Distance: 17km
Total ascent: 670m
Total descent: 475m
Highest point reached: Bocca a e Rete (1883m)
IGN Map reference: #4251 OT

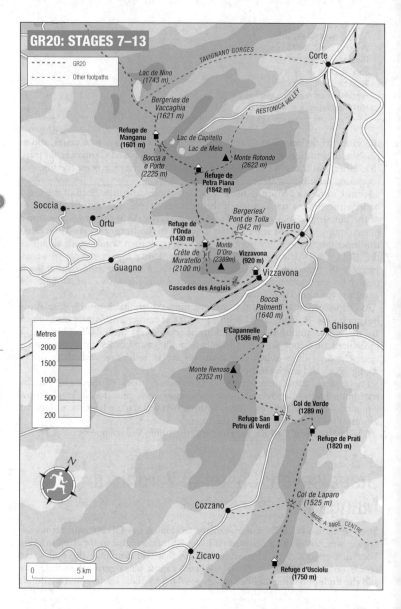

GR20: STAGES 7–13

- - - - - - - GR20
- - - - - - - Other footpaths

Lac de Nino (1743 m)

TAVIGNANO GORGES

Corte

Bergeries de Vaccaghia (1621 m)

RESTONICA VALLEY

Refuge de Manganu (1601 m)

Lac de Capitello
Lac de Melo

▲ *Monte Rotondo (2622 m)*

Bocca a e Porte (2225 m)

Refuge de Petra Piana (1842 m)

Soccia ●

● Ortu

Bergeries/ Pont de Tolla (942 m)

Vivario

Refuge de l'Onda (1430 m)

Monte D'Oro (2389m) ▲

Vizzavona

Vizzavona (920 m)

Crête de Muratello (2100 m)

● Guagno

Cascades des Anglais

Bocca Palmenti (1640 m)

● Ghisoni

Metres

2000
1500
1000
500
200

E'Capannelle (1586 m)

Monte Renoso ▲ *(2352 m)*

Col de Verde (1289 m)

Refuge San Petru di Verdi

Refuge de Prati (1820 m)

N

Col de Laparo (1525 m)

Cozzano ●

MARE A MARE CENTRE

0   5 km

● Zicavo

Refuge d'Usciolu (1750 m)

up such an easy stage, but it's a shame to rush past the lake, which makes as serene a spot to spend an afternoon as you'll encounter on the GR20.

At Castel di Verghio, a PNRC signboard on the right-hand side of the D84, 20m below the ski station's bivouac area, marks the re-start of the red-and-white waymarks, which veer immediately into cool pine forest. Having levelled off, the path then winds at an uncharacteristically even gradient for an hour or so through beech and pine woodland until it reaches the start of the day's main ascent. Compared with the rigours of the preceeding *étapes*, the climb to the **Col de Saint-Pierre** (or Bocca San Pedru in Corsican; 1452m; 1hr 15min) is a gentle one. This whole portion of the route follows paths originally set down for horses and flocks of sheep, so it keeps to easy slopes. All the same, the views – of Paglia Orba and the Niolo Valley on one side, and down to the west coast on the other – are wonderful, improving gradually as you progress southeast along the ridgetops towards the **Bocca a e Rete** (1883m).

Once over the pass, **Lac de Nino** (1743m; 3hr 15min) is revealed for the first time in all its glory. Despite the hordes of walkers, joggers and trout fishermen who pour through here in summer, the eleven-metre-deep lake still exudes an air of sublime tranquillity. Herds of wild ponies and pigs graze its banks, which are sliced by winding watercourses known as *pozzi* in Corsican (or *pozzines* in French). Concerns about the fragility of this unique spot, and its delicate turf shores in particular, have led the PNRC to install a *gardien* to ensure the ban on camping and lighting of fires is respected. You can, however, fill up your water bottles at the spring on the lake's southern shore, followed by the GR20 waymarks.

Having crossed the grassland plateau enfolding Lac de Nino, the route strikes gently downhill again along the banks of the Tavignano River, which it leaves soon after to cross a rocky area dotted with gnarled beech trees and alder bushes. One and a half hours after leaving the lake you arrive at the **bergeries de Vaccaghia** (1621m; 3hr 45min; very good range of supplies), whose stone huts enjoy a spectacular view south over the next stretch of the GR20. This is the point at which the yellow- and orange-waymarked route from the Refuge *A Sega* (described on p.311) intersects with the GR20, and some trekkers peel left here to follow the lower route down the Tavignano Valley to Corte.

The shepherds at Vaccaghia welcome groups of four people or more for supper, and provide tent space, bunk beds and breakfasts, as well as picnic lunches on a half-board basis (€40 per person; one week's advance warning essential; ☏04 95 48 02 57). You can also buy their cheese, as well as other supplies, for the onward leg over the **Pianu di Campotile**, the giant, trian-gular-shaped plain spread out below. It takes 45 minutes or so to cross the plateau, on the far side of which, at the **Bocca d'Aqua Ciarnente**, the GR20 crosses another yellow-waymarked route: this one drops off the opposite side of the watershed towards Soccia via the Lac de Creno (another beautiful altitude lake; see p.169) in around two hours and thirty minutes – the quickest route to a roadhead between here and Vizzavona.

The **refuge de Manganu** (1601m; 4hr 30min; good range of supplies and cooked food) is another beautifully situated hut, with fine views of the surrounding peaks from its deck and a rushing stream to splash around in if the weather's hot. Basic supplies are sold during the evening, in addition to chilled beers and soft drinks. There's not much space inside, but the *gardien* has erected a dozen or so tents to provide additional shelter.

Stage eight: Refuge de Manganu to refuge de Petra Piana

With its panoramic views across the watershed and intense sense of verticality, this *étape* perfectly epitomizes the GR20, and many rate it as the most memorable of the route. After a hefty initial ascent, the waymarks squeeze through a niche in the ridge high above Manganu to enter a spectacular world of bare granite cliffs and pinnacles that tower above the head of the Restonica Valley, famed for its twin lakes, Melo and Capitello. Keeping close to the watershed, the route remains above 2000m for most of the day, so check the weather forecast before you set off – some of the exposed ridge sections you'll be crossing are no places to be stuck in during an electric storm. Take plenty of water along, too, as springs are few and far between.

After the gentle slopes of the previous two stages it's back to business as usual, with the route heading uphill from the time it crosses the bridge beside Manganu. A couple of open, flatish areas of *pozzi* provide brief respites, but basically you're climbing for the first two hours and thirty minutes or so up a picturesque valley head lined by slabs, alder scrub and a small lake. Eventually the waymarks reach the foot of a shadowy moraine from which the pass is clearly visible.

At an altitude of 2225m, the **Bocca a e Porte** (or Brêche de Capitello, as it's marked on some maps; 2hr 30min), is the highest point attained by the GR20. Appropriately enough, it also marks one of the route's most dramatic changes in landscape, revealing not only the lakes of the Restonica Valley but also a panoramic sweep of peaks stretching south along the line of the watershed. Care should be taken crossing the two névés immediately below the pass, and throughout the steep section that follows, which requires some simple scrambling.

A messy, steep descent across mostly bare rock brings you after thirty minutes or so to the ridge. Look out for a second *brêche*, flanked by a pair of pinnacles, where yellow waymarks plunge left towards Lac de Capitello (see p.312), the smaller and higher of the two lakes visible below. Winding along the ridge, the GR20, meanwhile, presses on to **Bocca a Soglia** (2052m; 3hr 45min), where a second yellow-waymarked route drops sharply downhill, this time to Lac de Melo (see p.312).

At this point the GR switches suddenly northeast and contours across the mountainside for a while before beginning a steep 210-metre climb to **Bocca Rinosa** (2170m; 4hr 45min), from where you get a magnificent view north across the watershed to Monte Cinto and Paglia Orba. The last pass of the day, **Bocca Muzzella** (2206m), affords another spectacular view south to Monte d'Oro and Monte Renoso, and you may well want to lounge around in the rocks here for a while to steel yourself for the short, sharp descent to follow.

With its back against the sheer south wall of Monte Rotondo and its front opening onto a hypnotic expanse of ridges and peaks, the **refuge de Petra Piana** (1842m; 5hr 45min; basic supplies only, but cooked meals available) is a fine place to soak up the atmosphere of the high watershed. Resisting the temptation to press on southwards, many trekkers linger here for an extra day or two, taking the opportunity to scale Monte Rotondo (Corsica's second-highest mountain), whose summit can be reached in an unforgettable two hour forty-five minute climb from the hut. The one downside of the site, at least for anyone bivouacking, is its comparative lack of shelter; aside from a few straggly alder bushes and piles of stones there's little to break the chilly wind that blows up the valleys most nights. A small range of basic provisions is available from the *gardienne*, but a better place to stock up on supplies is the *bergeries* de Tolla, midway through the next stage.

Monte Rotondo

Petra Piana forms the base camp for the southern approach to **Monte Rotondo** (2622m) – an ascent that's far less daunting than it looks from below. Only 780m – an average GR20 climb – separates the hut from the summit, which can be reached in around two hours and forty five minutes (3hr 30min–4hr there and back). Moreover, the route is well cairned, free of technical obstacles and a joy to walk: aside from the astounding 360-degree panorama from the top, you pass a large glacial lake that stays frozen for most of the summer, and get an unsurpassed view over the remaining portion of the GR20. However, the weather can change suddenly and in the wet the boulders of the granite moraine you have to traverse to reach the summit become very slippery. Waterproofs, emergency warm gear, food and water are essential, and if you're going it alone make sure you leave your name with the *gardienne* (and inform her when you're back safely).

The trail follows the course of the stream flowing past Petra Piana. Having crossed a grassy hollow, you ascend across rough bouldery ground and rock bands to a ridge from where the south face of the mountain and lake are fully revealed for the first time. The cairns then lead around the southeast shore of the **Lake Bellavone**, from where they strike across the huge scree- and boulder-covered cirque below the summit, reaching the ridgetop at a rock pinnacle called "Le Fer de Lance" on IGN maps after around two hours and fifteen minutes. Approached via a short chimney, the **Helbronner Shelter** (named after the first person to climb Rotondo) is a tiny hut that's left open year round in case of emergencies. A five-minute scramble, some of it involving one or two exposed but straightforward moves, takes you from there to the summit.

For a full account of the much longer **northern approach** to Monte Rotondo, see p.311.

Stage nine: Refuge de Petra Piana to refuge de l'Onda

A change of tone marks stage nine of the GR20, at least if you take the softer, conventional route: a long meandering descent through pine forest along the banks of a rushing torrent, followed by an equally gradual climb to just above the treeline again. Numerous opportunities to swim and lounge in the sun punctuate this stretch, and you can reprovision at the picturesque *bergeries* de Tolla halfway along.

Alternatively, a more challenging, high-level **variant** runs between the two refuges via the ridges. Truer to the spirit of the GR, it takes you along one of the narrowest sections of the watershed, offering great views down to both coasts and back across the central range. In terms of time, there's little to choose between the two, with the low route only shaving around thirty minutes off the total walking time. The one thing that might deter you from following the yellow-waymarked variant is bad weather; the exposed ridgetops are no fun at all in misty or wet conditions.

Petra Piana to Onda via the bergeries de Tolla: low-level route

> **Stage summary**
> Walking time: 4hr
> Distance: 11km
> Total ascent: 500m
> Total descent: 910m
> Highest point reached: Refuge de l'Onda (1430m)
> IGN Map reference: #4251 OT

The trailhead for both routes stands just west of the refuge, at a junction marked by a PNRC signboard. Follow the **red-and-white waymarks** southeast steeply downhill to the **bergeries de Gialgo** and thence across a succession of streams at a more leisurely gradient. On reaching the confluence of the Rotondo and Manganello torrents, the path, by this point paved and worn by centuries of transhumant traffic, follows the stream bank down through a mixed forest of beech and Laricio pine where you'll encounter plenty of tempting pools and smooth rocks to swim from.

A better-than-average choice of food – from staple supplies and local cheese to full-blown cooked meals – is available at the **bergeries de Tolla**, reached after roughly three hours near the end of this long descent. Make the most of the laid-back atmosphere. Spanning the beautiful **confluence** of the Manganello and Grotaccia, the **cable bridge** (942m) ten minutes or so below heralds both a change in direction and gradient.

From the **path junction** of the Mare a Mare Nord Variant and GR20, on the far side of the cable bridge, the red-and-white waymarks lead southwest to begin the ascent to Onda. Gentle to start with, the slope steepens gradually the higher through the woods you climb, emerging from the trees to open mountainside again after around one hour.

Petra Piana to Onda: high-level route

Start by following the red-and-white GR20 waymarks as far as the path junction marked by a PNRC signboard; from here, yellow paint flashes lead to the right ("*par les crêtes*", or "via the ridges") for the high-level variant to Onda. This is an immensely enjoyable stretch (at least, in fine weather), and far less of a straightforward ridge walk than it might look from the hut. Some simple scrambling is required to navigate around the lumpy outcrops that periodically block the ridgeline. But, once again, clever waymarking makes light of these and most of the time you'll be striding along clear paths with 360-degree views.

> As indicated by a prominent PNRC signboard, a **GR20 liaison path**, routed along the Mare a Mare Nord Variant and waymarked in **orange**, leads downstream (east) from the cable bridge just below the *bergeries* de Tolla to the hamlet of Canaglia, three-hours' walk away, where it joins the tarmac road to **Tattone**, a little village on the main Bastia–Ajaccio train line. For more on the village, which has a small campsite and station, see p.317.

Stage summary
Walking time: 3hr 30min
Distance: 8km
Total ascent: 390m
Total descent: 800m
Highest point reached: Onda (1430m)
IGN Map reference: #4251 OT

Although little of the variant follows level gradients, there's only one prolonged descent: the final drop to the **Bocca d'Oreccia** (1427m), where the route intersects first with the orange-waymarked **Mare a Mare Nord Variant** and, after a short climb, the red-and-white flashes of the main GR20 arriving from the east. If you're intending to stop over at Onda, drop left (west) off the ridge here. Otherwise, follow the main route onwards for the long haul up to the Crête de Muratello.

Refuge de l'Onda

Clinging to a shadowy ledge just below the ridgetop, the **Refuge de l'Onda** (1430m; 4hr/3hr 30min) is far from the most enticing hut on the route, but it does enjoy great views east over the tree tops to Monte Rotondo. Campers and bivouackers are somewhat cooped up in a fenced enclosure below the refuge proper, where a toilet block and spring provide basic amenities. For supplies and payment, go to the *bergeries* nearby, which stock essentials such as cheese, charcuterie and even fresh fruit during the season.

Confronted with the uninspiring prospect of a sleepy afternoon at Onda, many trekkers elect to press on across Monte d'Oro to Vizzavona. If you're one of them, be warned that this makes for a long, tough day. In addition to the 600-metre haul to the Crête de Muratello, you'll have to contend with the gruelling 1100-metre descent down the Vallée de l'Agnone on the other side. Bear in mind, too, that the most compelling approach to Vizzavona is via the summit of Monte d'Oro – a longer, high-level variant outlined below – which would require loads of stamina to complete on the back of the *étape* from Petra Piana.

Stage ten: Onda to Vizzavona

Comprising a short, sharp climb followed by a long descent, stage ten can seem a deceptively easy one. But take a closer look at the map and you'll see a disconcerting number of contour lines stacked up between Onda and Vizzavona, and those who've walked the *étape* will certainly know all about it by the time they arrive at the railway line.

The payoff for the unrelenting gradients is more breathtaking vistas as the GR20 scales the shoulder of mighty Monte d'Oro, the peak whose imposing profile has dominated the route since leaving Petra Piana. Rather than follow the conventional path down the Vallée de l'Agnone, intrepid trekkers can peel off the main path to pursue the more challenging *haute route* over the summit of the mountain, which winds down to Vizzavona via an even longer, steeper track. Either way, a superb day's walking is guaranteed. A full account of **Vizzavona**, including accommodation and places to eat, appears on p.317.

Stage summary
Walking time: 5hr
Distance: 11km
Total ascent: 670m
Total descent: 1100m
Highest point reached: Crête de Muratello (2100m)
IGN Map reference: #4251 OT

Onda to Vizzavona via the valley

Stage ten kicks off in typically uncompromising fashion, with a lung-busting two-hour ridge ascent to the **Crête de Muratello** (2100m). You'll be heading steeply uphill right from the start and there's no let-up in the gradient until the pass, a rocky doorway from where you get your last dramatic view of northern Corsica. On the far side, the more subdued mountains of the island's southern watershed rise above Vizzavona, still hidden by a fold in the valley.

Don't be lulled into thinking that the day's hard work is done: the long, arcing descent down the Vallée de l'Agnone takes a good three hours in dry conditions. The first hour, across a messy combination of boulders, steeply tilting slabs and alder scrub, is particularly taxing on the knees. The going gets easier only once you've crossed the river for the first time, where the leafy beech woods begin to yield to the mature pines of the Forêt de Vizzavona proper.

Enclosed by an awesome cirque of crags, this valley has been a popular leisure destination for as long as there has been tourism in Corsica. At roughly the two-hour mark, the **Cascades des Anglais** (see p.319), a sequence of pictur-esque waterfalls and deep turquoise pools, recalls the era when wealthy British aristocrats used to travel up here to picnic away from the summer heat of Ajaccio. Today, it remains a well-frequented spot, visited in large numbers by day-trippers from the car park on the nearby *route nationale*.

Beyond the falls, the now well-beaten path drops steeply through the woods and then hugs the river as far as a **footbridge**, which you should ignore and head past if you're making for the *Hôtel-Refuge Monte d'Oro* at La Foce (see p.319). To reach the Gare de Vizzavona, cross the bridge and follow the *piste* around to the right. The station lies roughly 45-minutes' walk further down the trail.

Onda to Vizzavona: high-level variant

Roughly ten minutes into the descent from the **Crête de Muratello**, a line of yellow waymarks strikes left off the main GR20. These mark the start of a high-level variant which, instead of plunging down the head of the valley, traverses the top of it to scale **Monte d'Oro** (2389m). If you've the legs for it and are not perturbed by the prospect of some exposed scrambling, the ascent of Corsica's fifth-highest peak offers a more enjoyable route to Vizzavona than the somewhat monotonous descent of the Vallée de l'Agnone. The one catch is its

Stage summary
Walking time: 7hr
Distance: 12km
Total ascent: 1000m
Total descent: 1500m
Highest point reached: Monte d'Oro (2389m)
IGN Map reference: #4251 OT

overall length. Although you've only 300 additional metres to cover between the pass and the summit, the spectacular drop down the far eastern flank of the mountain involves nearly 1500m of combined ascent and descent. While perfectly manageable as a single *étape* from Onda, you'd have to be fit to tackle this after trekking all the way from Petra Piana. Note, too, that due to its proximity to the sea, Monte d'Oro gets more than its fair share of high winds, rain storms and generally murky conditions, which can sweep in very suddenly and make progress down the steep summit ridges slow going.

The route (basically a reverse version of the one described on p.318) is fairly well marked with a mixture of paint flashes and cairns. It follows the main western spur up to **Bocca di u Porcu** (2160m) and thence southeast towards the summit, accessed via a steep boulder-choked couloir running off a gully. The last stretch involves a bit of scrambling which, although straightforward enough in dry weather, is tricky in the wet. Allow one hour thirty minutes for the climb.

The **descent** drops down the same gully by which you approached the summit, but at the bottom the waymarks and cairns peel left (east). Having crossed a grassy hollow, you then penetrate a dark and windy ravine, known as "La Scala" ("the Staircase"), where there are nearly always large névés. Beyond it, a rock pinnacle called "La Cafetière" flags the start of a zigzagging descent down a stream channel towards the tree line.

The famous Forêt de Vizzavona closes in below the **bergeries de Pozzatelli** (1500m), which you should reach in roughly one hour thirty minutes from the summit. Following a well-marked path from there, the remaining two hours to Vizzavona cut between the corners of a giant forestry *piste* before turning left to cross the Agnone just below the station.

Stage eleven: Vizzavona to E'Capannelle

With the most rugged portion of the watershed now behind you, the GR20 takes on a more subdued quality beyond Vizzavona. There's plenty of excitement still in store – especially if you opt to follow the more sporting high-level variants over Monte Renoso and the Aiguilles de Bavella – but for the next

> **Stage summary**
> Walking time: 4hr 30min
> Distance: 16km
> Total ascent: 1000m
> Total descent: 340m
> Highest point reached: Bocca Palmenti (1640m)
> IGN Map reference: #4252 OT

couple of stages at least, shady forest, gushing streams and verdant mountain flanks take the place of bare granite.

After a stiff but steady climb out of Vizzavona to the Bocca Palmenti, stage eleven of the GR20 settles into a long traverse through mostly wooded terrain that rarely strays far from contour level. Coverable in an easy four hours and thirty minutes, it is the obvious one to double up if you're keen to push on quickly to Conca, although by doing that you'd be forsaking the chance to scale Monte Renoso – the last big peak of the central range – en route to Col de Verde.

With your back to Vizzavona station, turn right and follow the road uphill, past the shrine dedicated to Notre Dame de la Forêt, where the waymarks head right into the trees (as indicated by a PNRC signboard). They cross the highway shortly after and then continue northeast, following and intermittently cutting across the bends in a broad *piste forestière*. Having quit this for the last time, the GR then swings decisively south, zigzagging up through some majestic old pines towards the tree line. Just before reaching the pass, **Bocca Palmenti** (1640m; 2hr 15min), look out for a dressed-stone spring to the left of the path. Denuded by severe overgrazing, the col can be hot work and you'll be glad of the chance to cool off before pressing on south to the **bergeries d'Alzeta** (1553m).

Beyond the shepherds' huts, the tree cover returns slightly, masking the views down the vertiginous Fiumorbo Valley to the east coast, visible for the first time on the GR20. The path remains shaded most of the way to the **bergeries de Cardu** (1515m; 3hr 15min), where there's another spring and a signboard pointing way down the mountain to the village of **Ghisoni** (see p.320) – a route waymarked in yellow, which drops 865m in around one hour thirty minutes.

The remaining one hour fifteen minutes to **E'Capannelle** (1586m; 4hr 30min) continues to contour through pine forest and skirts a third *bergerie* at **Scarpacceghje** (water available), before climbing to follow briefly a surfaced road. Having left it, the waymarks then descend across open maquis to the fringes of the ski station.

E'Capannelle

Presiding over a horribly scarred hillside strung with rusting ski lifts and pylons, the former ski station at **E'Capannelle** is not the most inspiring stop on the GR20. However, you can luxuriate in clean dormitory accommodation or over a hot meal at the (none-too-friendly) **Gîte d'Étape U Fugone** (☎04 95 57 01 81; €31 per head; May–Sept). Even if you're only passing through, it's hard not to be tempted on to their sunny deck for a reviving pit stop. In addition to the usual range of drinks, meals and hot snacks can be ordered here from a limited menu of mostly local specialities. They also sell a good selection of **trekking supplies** from the bar.

Most GR20 trekkers, however, head for the newer **refuge U Renosu** (supplies and hot meals available), further up the hillside (turn right when you first reach tarmac above E'Capannelle, instead of following the waymarks straight across the road). It's spick and span, and offers hot showers and meals.

Stage twelve: E'Capannelle to refuge de Prati

A choice of two very different onward routes presents itself at E'Capannelle. Contouring around the northern flank of the Fiumorbo Valley, the conventional itinerary proceeds in very much the same vein as the previous *étape*, at least as far as Col de Verde, where a pleasant café-cum-refuge makes a nice spot to refuel ahead of the ensuing one hour forty-five minute climb up to the refuge de Prati. If, however, you're hankering for a return to more typical GR20 scenery, consider the longer and more dramatic variant over the top of **Monte Renoso**, Corsica's fifth-highest mountain and the last summit over 2300m reachable from the path. As the latter option takes a couple of hours longer than the normal route, walkers who choose it tend to prefer to bed down for the night at Col de Verde rather than press on to Prati. Either way, it's worth bearing in mind the length and overall difficulty of stage thirteen, which is a tough one to combine with its predecessor. Plenty of trekkers do walk all the way from E'Capannelle to the refuge d'Usciolu in a day, but invariably regret it.

E'Capannelle to Col de Verde: the low-level route

The waymarks follow the line of the old ski lift uphill from E'Capannelle initially, peeling left after the second pylon to crest a spur. After a short descent down the other side, you arrive at the picturesque **bergeries de Traghjete**, whose stone huts huddle beneath the snow-flecked crags of Renoso, visible for the first time above. A short but fairly steep descent from here down the side of

> **Stage summary**
> Walking time: 5hr
> Distance: 19km
> Total ascent: 850m
> Total descent: 620m
> Highest point reached: Refuge de Prati (1820m)
> IGN Map reference: #4252 OT

a stream gully brings you to the **Pont de Casaccie** on the main D168. The GR20 uses it to cross the stream, and then drifts back into the forest off the right side of the road shortly afterwards.

Once clear of the tarmac, the path locks into a level gradient of around 1500m which it more or less maintains for the next couple of hours, rising and falling periodically to ford the succession of streams that slice through it. At the two hour forty five minute mark, the path emerges briefly from the forest to cross a cropped clearing, the **Plateau de Gialgone**, where a PNRC signboard indicates the turning for Monte Renoso (this is where you'd have rejoined the main GR20 if you'd followed the variant over the mountain).

A gradually steepening descent takes you back into the forest from the plateau and down to cross the Marmano stream via a **footbridge** (1390m), from the far side of which the route swings insistently east. Ten minutes or so further down the trail, look out for a sign nailed to a tree to the left of the path marked "**Le Sapin de Marmano**". Until a bolt of lightning lopped nearly 3m off its top, this mighty fir was allegedly the tallest in Europe at 56m, with a girth of 6.3m.

Having reached the top of a low rise, the **Col de la Flasca**, the red-and-white waymarks drift down the line of a wooded combe. However, at various points they get muddled with an older routing of the path, which meanders northeast along the ridgetop (where you might be lucky to come across glades of giant yellow gentians). Either way, keep heading downhill and you'll eventually end up on the D69 at **Col de Verde** (Bocca de Verdi in Corsican; 1289m; 4hr 15min).

A welcome opportunity to break for coffee and stock up on supplies for the next leg is provided by the *Refuge San Petru di Verdi* (☎04 95 24 4 82, ⓦwww .boccadiverdi.com; late May to mid-Oct), a seasonal café that also operates a little refuge. Rates are standard: €7 to pitch a tent, €13 for a bed, or €34 for half board, with a good evening meal. A modest selection of provisions (including quality local charcuterie and cheese) is on sale at the bar, where you can also order hot meals and snacks.

E'Capannelle to Col de Verde: high-level variant

The high-level variant from E'Capannelle, via the summit of Monte Renoso, is an altogether more challenging and memorable route than the lower one, although it does add at least half a day's walking to the *étape*. Most people who follow it end up spending the night at Col de Verde, making up time by leapfrogging Prati to reach Usciolu the next day.

Cleaving straight up Renoso's scarp ridge from the *station de ski*, the route skirts the Lac de Bastiani before swinging south over the summit, after which it keeps

> **Stage summary**
> Walking time: 6hr 30min
> Distance: 16km
> Total ascent: 815m
> Total descent: 1110m
> Highest point reached: Monte Renoso (2352m)
> IGN Map reference: #4252 OT

to the massif's watershed ridge before delving steeply downhill to a beautiful hanging valley on the far side. From there it bends east to rejoin the main GR20 at the Plateau de Gialgone, around five hours after leaving E'Capannelle. The route is well cairned throughout and easy to follow, but don't underestimate the dangers of the broad, shelving summit stretch in particular, which, like Monte d'Oro, is especially vulnerable to rapid changes in weather because of its proximity to the sea. Mist and cloud can sweep in to obscure the ridge in minutes, in which case you'll need IGN map #4252, a compass and adequate navigation skills and equipment to get you off the mountain in minimal visibility.

Weather permitting, the payoffs are some magnificent views of southern Corsica from one of the island's most highly rated ridge walks, and the chance to explore an exquisite hidden valley carpeted with *pozzi*. In addition, you'll have the satisfaction of knowing you've followed the route originally envisaged by the GR20's mastermind, Michel Fabrikant; the lower-level one was initially intended only as a bad-weather alternative.

Col de Verde to refuge de Prati

The remaining portion of stage twelve takes you 550m higher up the watershed to Bocca d'Oro. From the café at the col, head along the *piste* that rises from the far side of the road and keep an eye out for the point five minutes later where the waymarks veer left into the woods. Zigzagging up the side of the stream valley swathed in mixed beech and pine, the path emerges from the tree line after around thirty minutes and then begins to swing east into a sweeping traverse of the valley head. The final push to the pass is quite hard going, but the great views back over Monte Renoso provide regular excuses to stop.

Having reached **Bocca d'Oro** (1840m; 1hr 30min), you'll notice a dramatic change in landscape as the mountainside falls steeply away to the eastern plains and Ligurian Sea. On a clear day, the Tuscan coast is visible on the horizon as you drop gently across closely cropped grass, studded with outcrops of wind-eroded granite, to the hut.

Refuge de Prati (1820m; 1hr 45min; good range of supplies) is optimally placed to make the most of the wonderful views. It was completely rebuilt in

▲ Bergeries de Pozzi

2000 after a fire caused by a lightning strike and now ranks among the more attractive huts on the route, with 22 beds, a well-equipped kitchen and breezy deck. Facing due east, this is a perfect place to watch the sunrise over the sea, but if you're camping or bivouacking be warned that the site tends to be a very windy one and that there's very little in the way of shelter. Prati's unusually exposed, remote position, high in the mountains amid open grassland, explains why it was chosen as parachute drop zone during World War II, when Allied aircraft supplied the Corsican Resistance with arms, munitions and supplies – as recalled by a small plaque nearby.

Stage thirteen: Refuge de Prati to refuge d'Usciolu

Few sections of the GR20 convey quite as vividly as this one the sense of walking along an island watershed. For most of the day you'll be high up on the windy ridge dividing the Taravo Valley from the eastern plain, clambering over exposed outcrops, squeezing through narrow crevices and trying to stay upright on some skiddy inclines. Water is predictably scarce: you'll need at least enough to see you through the first two hours and thirty minutes, when the path reaches a spring near the Col de Laparo.

> **Stage summary**
> Walking time: 4hr 45min
> Distance: 10km
> Total ascent: 760m
> Total descent: 830m
> Highest point reached: Punta della Capella (2042m)
> IGN Map reference: #4253 ET

Having passed the memorial plaque to the Corsican Maquis at Prati, the waymarks make for the outcrop to the south and get stuck straight into the convoluted climb to the **Punta della Cappella** (45min), reached after an enjoyable traverse of a small, steep-sided cirque. At 2042m, the *punta* is the penultimate landmark above 2000m crossed by the GR (the last is Monte Incudine); scramble up to the summit itself, just to the right of the path, for the best of the day's views.

From here on, the route snakes insistently southwards, switching to alternate sides of the ridgeline via a series of rocky depressions. One or two passages require some simple handholds, and there are a couple of steep, gravelly zigzags as you drop from the Punta di Campitello (1937m) to the Col de Rapari, an open, grassy balcony offering a fine view over the Taravo Valley.

A much gentler descent from there takes you past some dramatically wind-bent beech trees to the largest gap in the ridge at **Bocca di Laparo** (1525m; 2hr 15min), where the orange waymarks of the **Mare a Mare Centre** cross the GR20. These lead down the side of the valley to **Cozzano** village (see p.323) in around two hours and thirty minutes, but leave you with a lengthy detour to rejoin the GR20; by dropping off the path, you also miss the most inspiring stretch of the *étape* between Col de Laparo and Usciolu.

From the col, the waymarks delve once again into the trees via a winding, moss-covered mule track that looks as ancient as the hills. The trail carries on at contour level for another twenty minutes or so before bending decisively into the line of the mountain for the long, hard ascent back up to the ridge. On windless days, this can be a killer climb, hampered by clouds of flies, but en route you pass a magical little hollow filled with asphodels – the obvious place to break before the final push to the top. Having reached the ridge, however, the waymarks continue to climb in earnest, only levelling off at the **Bocca Punta Bianca**, from where you gain an impressive view north.

After one further, more gentle, ascent – to **Bocca Furmicula** (1950m; 4hr) – the rest of the *étape* is plain sailing in fine weather, but beware if storm clouds are threatening as you drop downhill towards the refuge: this stretch is notorious for lightning strikes and at least two GR20 trekkers have been killed here in the past few years.

The **refuge d'Usciolu** (1750m; 4hr 45min) is a model hut in every way, with a magnificent view southwards across the Coscione Plateau to Monte Incudine and a *gardien* who brings a great sense of vocation to his work. His little shop (evenings only) stocks an excellent range of reasonably priced provisions (including fresh bread), packed up by mule from Cozzano every day. You can also order filling bowls of hot vegetable stew (order in advance on arrival; €9) and even send postcards and letters, complete with a special "Refuge d'Usciolu – GR20" postmark. The only catch is the congestion of the camping/bivouacking area, where flat ground and space are at a premium.

Stage fourteen: Refuge d'Usciolu to refuge d'Asina

Three distinctly contrasting landscapes characterize stage fourteen, as the GR20 makes its way across the last of the watershed's major massifs, **Monte Incudine**. The first is a knife-edge ridge known as the **Arête a Monda**, through whose pinnacles, tilting slabs, boulders and weirdly eroded buttresses the waymarks

Stage summary
Walking time: 6hr 30min
Distance: 17km
Total ascent: 1000m
Total descent: 1230m
Highest point reached: Monte Incudine (2134m)
IGN Map reference: #4253 ET

trace an ingenious course before dropping sharply back to the tree line. Between it and the pale grey mountain wall bounding the southern horizon stretches a broad area of moorland called the Plateau de Coscione, where for centuries shepherds from surrounding valleys have brought their flocks in summer. The GR20 cleaves diagonally across the middle of the depression in a little over an hour, and then bends east to attack the mountain, the last significant obstacle of the route.

The top of Incudine, however, feels frustratingly far off for the first couple of hours of the *étape*. Progress along the arête, reached after a short initial climb from the refuge d'Usciolu, is hampered by the vast outcrops jammed along it. But the waymarking is superb throughout, picking an inspired path that switches repeatedly from one side of the ridge to the other. In the thick mist that frequently shrouds this ridge you'll certainly be glad of them. Periodically obscured by the billowing cloud, glimpses of the Taravo Valley and Plateau de Coscione through gaps in the arête remind you that you're still at 1800m. Only after skirting the **Punta di a Scadatti** (1834m; 1hr 30min) to pass through the Brêche di a Petra di Leva does the route begin to yield ground.

At the **Bocca di l'Agnonu** (1570m; 2hr 10min) – shortly after passing a **spring** on your right – the GR20 finally hits a more or less level gradient. A PNRC signboard stands at the pass, pointing the way southwest to **Zicavo** (see p.323), the largest village in the Taravo Valley, which lies at the end of a two-hour downhill walk.

Most walkers, however, press on through the atmospheric beech woods and mossy boulders lying beyond the pass to a forested rise from which is revealed a fine view over the **Plateau de Coscione**. The next hour or so takes you across the rolling heath and numerous streams dissecting it to a **junction** (1450m; 3hr 15min), where the liaison path from Zicavo rejoins the GR20. Follow the *piste* downhill from there to the Furchinesu stream, crossed via the GR20's final cable bridge.

From here on, it's uphill all the way to the top of Monte Incudine, an easy ascent of around two hours and fifteen minutes in total. Once out of the woods lining the Furchinesu, the first landmark you pass is the ruined refuge of **I Pidinieddi** (1623m; 4hr), the remains of which lie scattered around a grassy hollow. Ten-minutes' walk further uphill, behind a coppice of trees, flows the **spring** that used to serve the hut; take on enough liquid here to get you over the mountain, as there are no more water sources beyond this point.

From the spring, the path strikes straight up the mountainside until it reaches the ridgetop at **Bocca di Luana** (1805m), where it veers south-southwest to follow the ridge all the way to the **summit** (2134m; 5hr 30min), marked by a crucifix. In clear weather the views, which encompass all of Corsica's southern tip, and even the coast of distant Sardinia, are magnificent, not least of all because of the Aiguilles de Bavella, which you see looming above the watershed for the first time here.

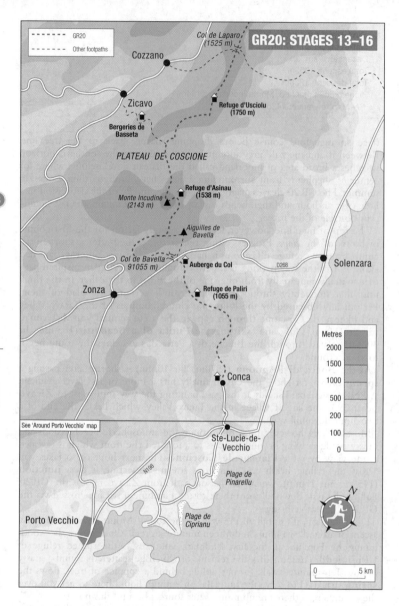

The descent from Monte Incudine follows a gentle incline at first until the waymarks reach a niche in the ridge, where they switch suddenly eastwards into a drop of what looks like an alarming gradient. This descent, down a messy mixture of sharp-edged boulders, slabs, grit and scrub, takes around one hour fifteen minutes in dry weather; in the rain you should negotiate it with extreme caution.

Visible an hour or so before you reach it, the **refuge d'Asinau** (1538m; 6hr 15min; some basic supplies) sits at the foot of Monte Incudine, surrounded by odorous alder scrub at the head of an overgrazed valley. It's a wild spot soaked in high-mountain atmosphere – the last such hut on the GR – but once again sheltered, flat camping and bivouac space is at a premium; if you aim to sleep outside, get here fairly early in the day. Some basic provisions (including cold Pietra beers) are sold by the *gardien*, but the welcome and prices are far more enticing at the **bergeries d'Asinau** (☎06 17 53 98 92), ten-minutes' walk further down the mountain, which offers proper mountain cooking, camping space and bunks indoors.

Stage fifteen: Refuge d'Asinau to refuge de Paliri

Moving on from Asinau, you can either trudge the long, flat, slow route along the side of the valley and around the spur to the Col de Bavella, or else bite the bullet and opt for the so-called **Variant Alpin**, a much steeper alternative that takes you through the heart of the Aiguilles before dropping down the other

> **Stage summary**
> Walking time: 6hr
> Distance: 18km
> Total ascent: 710m
> Total descent: 860m
> Highest point reached: Foce Dinosa (1206m)
> IGN Map reference: #4253 ET

side to the pass via a dramatic couloir. Don't let the name intimidate you – it's actually less nerve-wracking than several passages you'll already have covered. That said, the initial approach to the needles is steep, and one of the pitches involves clambering up another fixed chain.

Aside from the great views over Incudine, the chief incentive to choose the latter route is that it's simply far more fun than the conventional one, which is in essence a dull plod as far as the col, where the two paths merge. From here on, the GR waymarks follow an ancient transhumant corridor – much of it with original paving stones and buttressed corners intact – through the magnificent red cliffs and pine forest of Bavella, a landscape emblematic of the island's mountains since Edward Lear sketched it to such dramatic effect at the end of the nineteenth century.

Refuge d'Asinau to the Col de Bavella via the low-level route

After crossing a level stretch through the boulder field beside the refuge d'Asinau, the red-and-white waymarks descend at a gradually steepening gradient down the line of the hillside to a path junction, where a liaison route to the village of Quenza (see p.224) peels off the GR20. Shortly below it, you ford the Asinau to begin a short climb up the opposite side of the valley through silver-birch forest. At the 1382m mark (only 70m higher than the river), the path hits a level that it keeps to for most of the remaining route to the mouth of the valley.

The first and only real landmark of note along the way is the **junction with the Variant Alpin**, reached after one hour. Beyond it the path undulates across a succession of shallow clearings and side valleys, gradually descending as it rounds the spur of the mountain.

Having crossed the Caracuttu stream and dropped to 1005m, you then turn northeast and dig into the thirty-minute climb to the pass up the flank of the Ceca la Volpe ravine. As you do so, keep a close eye on the waymarks or you could end up drifting down sheep tracks at contour level to the stream, leaving you with a stiff scramble to regain the path. With the imposing Aiguilles looming over the main road, the statue of Notre Dame de la Neige at the **Col de Bavella** hoves into view after three hours and fifteen minutes from the Variant Alpin junction. A full account of Bavella village, just below the col, including accommodation reviews and transport details, appears on p.228.

Refuge d'Asinau to Col de Bavella via the Variant Alpin

Designated by yellow paint flashes, the Variant Alpin zigzags steeply uphill from its bifurcation with the main path, one hour into stage fifteen, through a long coppice of birch trees. Once you're clear of the woods the gradient eases a little as the route bends into a long southerly traverse across boulders and juniper scrub, with towers VII, VI and V of the Aiguilles rearing vertically above. Having skirted the base of tower IV (Punta di u Pargulu), the waymarks then regain the watershed at **Bocca di u Pargulu** (1662m), a spectacular pass from which you get a marvellous view back across the Asinau Valley to Monte Incudine.

From there, the variant drops steadily south past the east side of towers III and II. You'll need handholds at several points, most notably a large tilted slab crossed with the help of a ten-metre **fixed chain**. Beyond it, a succession of steep pine- and boulder-covered slopes leads to a second pass below tower I, **Bocca di u Truvunu**, from where a sustained scramble down a narrow couloir funnels you to the Col de Bavella. Allow at least three hours for this variant section.

Col de Bavella to the refuge de Paliri

The final leg of the *étape* takes around on hour forty five minutes of mostly unstrenuous walking to cross the Crête de Punta Tafonata, the jagged ridge

▲ The Col de Bavella

dividing the gorge north of the col from the wilderness area to its east. A spring stands at the trailhead, next to the *Auberge du Col*, from where you follow a winding *piste* for ten or fifteen minutes until it meets a path junction, marked by a PNRC signboard. Bear left here (a right turn would take you to the Trou de la Bombe, a walk described on p.228) and follow the red-and-white waymarks as they drop downhill to cross a stream and, shortly afterwards, join another *piste*.

Before beginning the last short climb of the *étape*, you might feel like a swim, in which case head upstream from the bridge where the *piste* crosses a small river; hidden among the trees are some waterfalls with a couple of deep pools.

The 200-metre ascent to the **Foce Finosa** (1206; 1hr) is rewarded with a panoramic view over the wild country crossed by the GR on its last stage to Conca. Numerous large boulders provide vantage points over the valley during the descent, which brings you to the **refuge de Paliri** (1055m; no supplies) after 45 minutes.

Eager to polish off the final *étape* before nightfall, many trekkers hurry through Paliri. But the GR20's last hut, which stands slap in the centre of a spectacular forest wilderness, makes an ideal base from which to explore one of Corsica's most dramatic and distinctive landscapes. On all sides vast red cliffs soar above the pines, some pierced by weird holes from which you might see climbers dangling on ropes a thousand or more feet off the ground.

Despite the proximity of the busy road, barely any day-trippers make it out here, so savour the isolation and grandiose scenery while you can; the coast and its crowds lie only half-a-day's walk away.

Stage sixteen: Refuge de Paliri to Conca

The final stage of the GR20 continues southeastwards along the old transhumant route formerly used by shepherds from the coast around Conca to herd their sheep to the high summer pastures of Incudine and Coscione. The consequent heavy grazing has over the centuries had a devastating impact on this rocky hinterland: greenery is scarce and signs of human settlement virtually nonexistent. The ghostly ambience is underlined by the ghoulish rock formations flanking much of the path, and by the ranks of charred trees lining the lower reaches of the valleys – the result of a huge bush fire that swept through here in 1985.

As the peaks of Bavella recede into the haze behind you, the forest gradually peters out to be replaced by Corsica's famous maquis, which reasserts itself here for the first time since the climb out of Calenzana, at the very start of the walk. The return of the **heat**, too, will take you back to the rigours of that initial ascent. With bodies well adjusted to the cooler climes of the interior, many trekkers succumb to sunstroke and severe dehydration during the latter stages of this *étape*; so carry plenty of liquid (at least double what you've been carrying in the mountains) as there's only one spring along the route and it's easy to miss.

Stage summary
Walking time: 5hr 15min
Distance: 12km
Total ascent: 520m
Total descent: 1360m
Highest point reached: Refuge de Paliri (1213m)
IGN Map reference: #4253 ET/#4254 ET

A leisurely descent through well-shaded forest gets the stage underway, as the waymarks drift down the floor of the valley below Paliri. From stream level, a short ascent brings you to a gap in a prominent rocky spur affording uninterrupted views over the **Punta d'Anima Damnata** (1091m), the conical hill immediately northwest that's become a climbing hot spot. Once through the niche, you then start to contour around the rim of the valley head, with Monte Bracciutu dominating the landscape to the north.

After an hour, the path bends decisively south around a spur, which it crosses at the **Foce di u Barcciu** (907m). This point marks the start of the GR20's last significant ascent, which starts gently enough but steepens considerably towards the top, with the mule path cutting in zigzags to the pass, **Bocca di u Sordu** (1040m; 1hr 45min). From the far side, a fine view unfolds of Conca's deserted hinterland, bounded by the blue Golfe de Porto Vecchio in the distance.

The next stretch takes you across a small, sun-bleached plateau scattered with extraordinary rock formations, from the edge of which the waymarks drop sharply downhill to the ruined *bergeries* at **Capeddu** (850m; 2hr 15min), where you'll find the only dependable spring of the *étape* (look for the path leading north off the GR20 and follow it for 100m; the spring is on its left) and a permitted camping/bivouacking area. The descent continues in earnest from there, dropping 250m or so in less than thirty minutes through fire-blackened forest to ford the Punta Pinzuta stream, which the path first climbs above and then recrosses shortly after.

Having crossed the stream a second time, you have to pull up a short, steep ascent to reach another pass, beyond which the route enters a long, sweeping traverse of a valley at contour level. This section through the maquis can be particularly hot work in the afternoon, when the sun will be directly ahead of you. But by now, a narrow, door-sized gap in the shadowy ridge ahead will be clearly visible. The final pass of the GR20, **Bocca d'Usciolu** (587m; 4hr 15min) provides an appropriately distinctive landmark at which to pause to contemplate your achievement: 170km distance covered, with some 19,000m of ascent and descent, over some of the roughest terrain in Europe.

Below you, spread out in the shadow of Punta d'Ortu, lies the village of Conca (252m; 5hr 15min), reached after an easy forty-minute descent through dense maquis. Close to the road, a dressed-stone spring marks the official end of the walk and the termination of the trusty red-and-white waymarks. To find the *gîte d'étape*, just keep plodding downhill along the lanes – the locals will wave you in the right direction. For an account of **Conca**, see p.261.

The Mare a Mare, Tra Mare e Monti, and Isula–Corti trails

For all its undeniable attractions, the GR20 affords a very unrepresentative picture of the island. To get a taste of the real *Corse profonde* – its sleepy granite villages, chestnut orchards, ancient mule paths and river valleys – you have to drop off the GR onto the network of lower-altitude trails. Waymarked in orange, the **Mare a Mare** ("Coast to Coast"), **Tra Mare e Monti** ("Between the Mountains and the Sea") and **Isula–Corti** (L'Île Rousse–Corte) paths may not present such a physical challenge as the GR20, but – as their names imply – they're no less compelling and many people find them a lot more enjoyable. Aside from the more subdued nature of the terrain (much of which is dominated by the sea), Corsica's cross-country routes are serviced by a network of well-set-up little *gîtes d'étape* where you can end a day's trekking with a carefully cooked meal and bottle of wine, sleep on a mattress and carb up the following morning with a full French breakfast.

Supplies are available in village shops most days, and you can expect a lot more contact with local people than you get up in the high mountains. One of the principal motivations for establishing these routes in the first place was to provide a source of income for the depopulated villages along them, and it's fair to say you receive a much warmer and more genuine welcome while walking in the Corsican interior than is par for the course on the coast or GR20.

The outlines featured below will give you a rough idea of what to expect on each of the routes, along with essential practical information to help you get to the trailheads, book accommodation and find supplies. Whichever itinerary you choose to follow, take along the relevant IGN **maps**, the FFRP's topo-guide, *Corse: entre mer et montagne*, or Trailblazer's *Corsica Trekking* (see p.425). The latter two publications include all the maps you'll need, along with stage timings and a wealth of background information on the areas crossed.

The Tra Mare e Monti Nord

The **Tra Mare e Monti Nord** is the oldest and most famous trail in Corsica after the GR20, zigzagging down the northwest coast from Calenzana to Cargèse via Galéria, Porto and Évisa. It's also one of the few waymarked routes on the island that rarely strays far from the sea, so the views are superb from start to finish. Chief among the highlights are the beautiful Scandola nature reserve, with its outlandish red cliffs; Girolata, a superbly isolated fishing village otherwise accessible only by boat; and the astounding views over the Grande Barrière and Golfe de Porto to be had from Capu di Curzu on stage five. Elsewhere, you get to walk through old-growth Laricio pine forests, cross time-worn Genoese footbridges, and swim in some of the loveliest natural river pools in Corsica.

One factor you should certainly bear in mind when contemplating this route is the **heat**, which renders it all but off limits between mid-June and October. Early spring, when the coastal flora is at its most colourful, is the best time to trek along the west coast.

Tra Mare e Monti Nord practicalities

The Tra Mare e Monti Nord is broken into ten stages (3hr 30min & 6hr 30min), which take between seven and ten days to walk. *Gîtes* punctuate every *étape*, although there are comparatively few places to re-provision; you'll probably find yourself making a detour to Porto to shop. ATMs are also thin on the ground; once clear of Cargèse, Porto and Galéria are the only places to stock up on cash.

For details on how to travel to and from the trailheads by **public transport**, see the relevant accounts on p.164 (for Cargèse) and p.129 (for Calenzana). Regularly updated timetable information is also available online at ⓦwww .corsicabus.org. SAIB (☎04 95 22 41 99 or 04 95 21 02 07, ⓦwww.auto carsiledebeaute.com) is the bus company covering the west coast, with services between Ajaccio and Ota via Cargèse running twice daily in July and August, with 1–2 services daily Monday to Saturday during the rest of the year. You can also get to Marignana and Évisa from Ajaccio with Autocars Ceccaldi (☎04 95 21 38 06 or 04 95 21 01 24), whose minibuses operate year round (daily Mon–Sat). Alternatively, several car rental companies (including Hertz) have facilities in Cargèse, allowing you to drop cars that you may have collected elsewhere.

Tra Mare e Monti Nord gîtes d'étape

With the exception of Cargèse, which has a clutch of small hotels (see p.165), every stage of the Tra Mare e Monti is covered by a *gîte d'étape*. However, demand for beds frequently outstrips supply, especially between May and mid-June and during September, when you shouldn't expect to find a free space unless you've pre-booked. Alternative accommodation is available only at Calenzana, Galéria, Évisa and Cargèse; elsewhere you might have to be prepared to bivouac or camp.

Calenzana *Gîte d'étape municipal* ☎04 95 62 77 13. Large, impersonal place with four-bed dorms. Usually crammed, because it also serves the GR20. Limited camping space. May–Sept. See also p.130.

Bonifatu *Auberge de la Forêt* ☎04 95 65 09 98. Well-run *gîte* with particularly good restaurant but unappealing campground to the rear. April–Oct.

Tuarelli *L'Alzelli* ☎04 95 62 01 75. Gorgeous location beside a deep stream where you can swim. Their terrace is also pleasant, and the food good. April–Oct.

Galéria *Chez M. Rossi* ☎04 95 62 00 46. Friendly place 1km southwest of the beach and village centre, with large garden for tents. April–Oct. See also p.140.

Girolata *Le Cabane du Berger* ☎04 95 20 16 98. The nicest of the pair in this village, with wooden cabins set under eucalyptus trees behind the beach. Their (optional) half board isn't up to much, though. The same applies to *Le Cormorant*

☎04 95 20 15 55, overlooking the jetty, where half board is obligatory.

Curzu ☎04 95 27 31 70. Modern three-storey building on the southwest side of the village, next to the main road. Provisions available. March–Oct.

Ota *Chez Félix* ☎04 95 26 12 92. Occupying a prime spot with fine views over the valley from its sociable terrace. All year.

Chez Marie (*Le bar des Chasseurs*) ☎04 95 26 11 37. Pleasant enough, and a good fallback if *Chez Félix* is full. April–Oct.

Marignana *Ustaria di a Rota* ☎04 95 26 21 21. Arguably the most convivial stop on the route. In addition to a quality Corsican restaurant, they've a well-stocked bar and even a small concert hall. April–Oct.

Revinda *E'Case* ☎04 95 26 48 19 or 06 82 49 95 65. A prime spot high above the west coast, with the character of a mountain hut more than a *gîte*. Meals available. April–Oct.

The Mare a Mare Nord

Scenic diversity is the hallmark of the **Mare a Mare Nord**, which begins at Moriani-plage on the east coast and winds west through the heart of the mountains to Cargèse. After a prolonged initial climb from sea level to enter the Bozio region, the path passes through a succession of hill villages to Corte, and then presses up the old Genoan mule track along Tavignano gorge to reach the Niolo Valley via the Col de l'Arinella. With the dramatic Monte Cinto and Paglia Orba massifs looming to the north, the trail then crosses the Col de Verghio into the Spelunca gorge, dropping through Évisa and Marignana (where it joins the Tra Mare e Monti) to follow deserted ridgetops and forested valleys back down to the sea.

No two days of the route are alike, and following it gives a vivid taste of the Corsican interior. But for an even more intense feeling of wilderness, the **Mare a Mare Nord Variant**, which peels off the main path after three stages and bypasses Corte in favour of the isolated forest area further south, is the one to go for. Crossing the watershed at Onda, where it intersects with the GR20, the variant presents more of a challenge as it passes through comparatively few villages. Accommodation and re-provisioning opportunities are few and far between, but the payoff is a feeling of remoteness you rarely experience on more frequented routes.

The **downside** of the Mare a Mare Nord as a whole is the couple of relatively dull stages towards the start of the walk. With a little more time, however, it is possible to avoid these by combining the principal route and its variant to create a giant **circular itinerary**, starting in Cargèse and progressing east to Corte, where you can jump on a train to Vivario and pick up the onward section back to Marignana. **Another variation** would be to follow the GR20 from A Sega in the Tavignano Valley and walk to Col de Verghio via the beautiful Lac de Nino instead of the Niolo.

Mare a Mare Nord practicalities

Both **trailheads** are readily accessible by public transport (see p.170 for Cargèse and p.287 for Moriani), and you can jump on or off the main path at regular intervals during the summer, when the Niolo Valley is served by bus (see p.324). The variant section, however, crosses a total backwater where you'll have to hitch if you decide to leave the path. Finding food can also be a problem on the variant: from June until September, supplies are sold (at inflated prices) at the *bergeries* below the refuge d'Onda, but beyond there the only place you can buy provisions before Marignana is the village shop at Pastricciola (open Tues, Thurs & Sat only).

Pressure on *gîte* beds isn't too bad on this route, at least until you reach Marignana, from where the hostels serve two different walks and are thus correspondingly popular.

Mare a Mare Nord principal gîtes d'étapes

I Penti *Luna Piena*, Santa-Reparata-di-Moriani ☎04 95 38 59 48. Privately run twenty-bed *gîte*, with great views of the eastern plain.

Val d'Alesani ☎04 95 35 94 74. Municipal *gîte* with twenty beds.

Pianello ☎04 95 39 61 35. Municipal *gîte*, in the first Bozio village of the route.

Sermano ☎04 95 48 68 08. Matchless views of the interior range, dominated by Monte Rotondo and Corte in the foreground, from this cosy *gîte* with only sixteen places.

Corte *U Tavignano* ☎04 95 46 16 85. Secluded in woods behind the citadelle. See also p.305.

Calacuccia *Couvent St François di Niolu*, ☎04 95 46 11 73. Double rooms as well as dorms, and fully equipped kitchen (but no meals), 1km west of Calacuccia in the hamlet of Sidossi. See also p.298.

Albertacce ☎04 95 48 05 60 or 04 95 48 08 05. Basic hostel on the roadside, with small dorms but good self-catering kitchen. See also p.300.

Évisa *Sarl u Poghju* ☎04 95 26 21 88. Very comfortable place, just below the village centre, offering better-than-average food. See also p.161.

Marignana See p.161.

Revinda See p.165.

Cargèse See p.165.

Mare a Mare Nord Variant gîtes d'étape

Poggio-de-Venaco ☎04 95 47 07 45 or 04 95 47 03 00. Close to Corte, with sixteen beds.

Santo-Pietro-di-Venaco ☎04 95 47 07 29. Not the most inspiring of locations, but large and well equipped.

Vivario See p.317.

Onda See p.354.

Pastricciola ☎04 95 28 90 83, or leave a message on ☎04 95 10 05 56. 1km from the

centre of village, and a bit institutional, but friendly, and there's a washing machine.

Guagno ☎04 95 28 33 47 or 06 81 61 21 21. Municipal *gîte* with two fourteen-bed dorms and lower-than-average rates, but no meals.

Letzia ☎04 95 26 63 24. Fully equipped self-catering chalets in woods next to a riding centre, run by the local *mairie*, at bargain rates. Reserve ahead.

The Mare a Mare Centre

The **Mare a Mare Centre** footpath cleaves diagonally across the middle of Corsica, between Ghisonaccia on the eastern plain and Porticcio at the southern tip of the Golfe d'Ajaccio. Accessible to all from late April to November, it sees relatively few hikers, though the route is as varied and scenic as any on the island, with some particularly memorable stretches along remote ridges overlooking the sea.

The trailhead is 2.5km south of Ghisonaccia on the N198, near a bridge called Pont de l'Abatescu, which you can reach on any of the buses running between Bastia and Porto Vecchio. From here the path cuts across fruit orchards and vineyards, nurtured by the River Fium'orbo, from which this region takes its name, to begin a gradual ascent of the coastal range.

Once over the Col de Laparo (1525m), where the route crosses the GR20, you enter the backwater region of Haut Taravo, named after the river that drains into the Golfe de Valinco near Propriano. From there the path heads west via remote Cozzano and Tasso villages to Guitera-les-Bains, where it climbs out of the Taravo Valley and over thickly forested spurs into Frasseto. Exposed ridges characterize the remaining few stages of the trail as it strikes north from Quasquara to scale the rocky Punta d'Urghiavari, before bending southwest to cross the main Ajaccio–Bonifacio road at the Col St-Georges. From here, another sharp ascent takes you onto a high ridge, and the path gives little ground until its junction with the Tra Mare e Monti trail near the isolated village of Bisinao, where it swings northwest towards Porticcio.

The most obvious **variation** for the Mare a Mare Centre would be to combine it with a few *étapes* of the GR20, with which it intersects at Col de Laparo. Following the route from west to east, instead of the conventional east-west direction, you can build on your altitude gain (and improved fitness) by swinging north along the GR20 to the refuge de Prati (see p.358) and press on from there towards Col de Verde. Weather permitting, the superb high-level variant over Monte Renoso (described on p.356) would provide the ideal culmination of this extremely varied route.

Mare a Mare Centre practicalities

The Mare a Mare Centre has grown in popularity over the past three or four years, but it's still one of the quietest waymarked paths on the island. That said, you'd do well to reserve your *gîte* beds in advance, as there is little by way of alternative accommodation in most villages. Although divided into seven stages (of between 3hr and 6hr 30min), the itinerary may be completed in six days by combining the first two *étapes*, making a longer-than-average first day from Ghisonaccia to Catastaghju (7hr).

There are **grocery stores** at Cozzano (stage two) and Sampolo (early in stage three), but none after that. This is one route on which you'll save yourself a lot of effort by eating in the *gîtes d'étape*, which all serve filling hot meals each evening (with advance warning). **Buses** connect Cozzano with Ajaccio (daily Mon–Sat with Autocars Santoni ☏04 95 22 64 44 or 04 95 24 51 56), and you can travel to and from the Col St-Georges on any of the services running between the capital and Propriano/Porto Vecchio in the south (see pp.263–264).

Ghisonaccia See p.270.

Serra-di-Fiumorbu ☏ 04 95 56 75 48 or 06 81 04 69 49. A stone building on the village outskirts with twnty five beds.

Chisà ☏ 04 95 56 36 61. Private *gîte* with eighteen bunk beds, close to one of Corsica's top *via ferrata* (see box, p.269).

Catastaghju ☏ 04 95 56 70 14 or 04 95 56 10 89. Dorm accommodation for twenty four in a converted hydroelectricity station.

Cozzano *Bella Vista* ☏ 04 95 24 41 59. Set in a gorgeous village, this is one of the friendliest and best-run *gîtes* in Corsica, with twenty six beds, camping space and a couple of doubles, as well as top-notch cooking. See also p.323.

Tasso ☏ 04 95 24 52 01. Four- to six-person dorms containing twenty two beds. Well set up for self-caterers, but they also offer half board.

Guitera-les-Bains ☏ 04 95 24 44 40 or 04 95 24 42 54. Small dorms, camping space and a very pleasant terrace.

Quasquara ☏ 04 95 53 61 21. Dorm space for thirty three and a well-equipped kitchen.

Col St-Georges ☏ 04 95 25 70 06. A small but very swish *gîte*. Somewhat marred by its location on the side of a main road, but with a fine, very Corsican *auberge*.

Porticcio See p.192.

The Tra Mare e Monti Sud

The **Tra Mare e Monti Sud** hiking trail runs from Porticcio to Propriano, divided into five relatively easy stages of between three hour forty five minutes and six hours. The scenery along the route, which winds southwest along the ridge dividing the Golfe d'Ajaccio from the Golfe de Valinco, is nowhere near as dramatic as on the Tra Mare e Monti Nord trail, but the gentle, maquis-covered hills and rocky coastline make it an enjoyable hike that will particularly appeal to less experienced walkers. It also takes you within striking distance of beaches at Capo di Muro, the prehistoric site at Filitosa, and the picturesque resort of Porto-Pollo. The only real drawback is that, unlike most of the long-distance footpaths in Corsica, this one does not have *gîtes d'étape* at each stage, which means you have to shell out on hotels or campsites for at least three of the four or five nights.

To create an excellent ten-day walk across the south of Corsica, you could combine this route with the Mare a Mare Sud (see below), which begins at its terminus, in the hamlet of Burgo near Propriano.

Tra Mare e Monti Sud practicalities

The trail's only two **gîtes d'étape** are at Bisinao (☏04 95 24 21 66) and Burgo (☏04 95 76 15 05). Both are heavily booked during the summer, when you should reserve at least a couple of weeks in advance to ensure a bed. For reviews of hotels and campsites in Porticcio, Côti-Chiavari, Porto-Pollo, Olmeto and Propriano, see the relevant accounts.

The Mare a Mare Sud

The **Mare a Mare Sud**, which meanders between the gulfs of Valinco and Porto Vecchio in southern Corsica in four to five days, is a relatively gentle route that takes you through the prettiest corners of southern Corsica. Encompassing the deep-blue inlets of the coast and the pale-grey peaks of the Alta Rocca region, its landscapes are unremittingly beautiful and unspoilt. This is a particularly good option for forest lovers: long stretches of the path wind through tracts of ancient oak and pine forest, regularly crossing streams and rivers where you can swim and sunbathe miles from any road. Several prehistoric sites – including the wonderful Cucurzzu remains at Levie – and a well-preserved Pisan chapel also lie within a stone's throw of the route.

Mare a Mare Sud practicalities

Divided into five stages of between four and six hours, the Mare a Mare Sud can be attempted at any time of year, even high summer, thanks to the amount of tree cover along the route. Its **trailheads** are both some way inland. As neither is served by public transport you'll have to brace yourself for a long walk or else catch a taxi. From Porto Vecchio, the start of the path at **Alzu di Gallina** takes between one hour thirty minutes to two hours to reach on foot. Striking uphill through maquis and then monotonous pine forest, the first *étape* is a bit dull and many people elect to skip it by hitching or catching a bus to Ospédale (see p.261) and continuing from there. If you begin the walk at Propriano, you'll have a 2hr 30min hike along the road to reach the start of the path at **Burgo**: follow the N196 for thirty minutes until you reach a Total petrol station, and turn right along the D257, following the road for 7km until you see the *gîte* on your left. The trailhead lies a little further up the road on the opposite side.

Buses connect many of the villages on the path with Propriano and Porto Vecchio, allowing you to join and leave the route at several points. Autocar Ricci's service (year round Mon–Sat; ☎04 95 76 25 59) stops at Sainte-Lucie and Levie; for Quenza, pick up Balési Évasion's minibus (July & Aug Mon–Sat; Sept–June Mon & Fri only).

Mare a Mare Sud gîtes d'étape

The Mare a Mare Sud's modest length, coupled with the proximity of its trailheads to some of Corsica's finest beaches, ensures it receives a steady stream of walkers from May onwards. Beds in the *gîtes* are thus at a premium, so book well ahead and expect to have to pay for half board, which is obligatory in most of them. The only hotel along the route is at Quenza (see p.225), but there is a pleasant *chambre d'hôte* in Sainte-Lucie (see p.220) and plenty of shops, restaurants and cafés elsewhere.

Burgo *U Fracintu* ☎04 95 76 15 05, ℱ04 95 76 14 31. Sixty beds in two-, four- and six-person dorms in a large *gîte* overlooking the valley. Half board obligatory (€29–39 depending on size of dorm).
Cartalavonu *Le Refuge* ☎04 95 70 00 39. Situated high in the massif d'Ospédale in a converted summer *bergerie*. Half board is optional; for details of the nearby *ferme auberge*, see p.261.
Levie *Bienvenue à l'Alta Rocca* ☎04 95 78 46 41. Not the most inspiring *gîte* on the route (it's run by the local municipality), but it's on the edge of the area's liveliest village. See also p.221.

Quenza *Corse Odyssée* ☎04 95 78 64 05, ℱ04 95 78 61 91. Tucked away a kilometre or so northeast of the village; follow the signs up the road beyond the *Auberge Sol e Monti*. See also p.225.
Sainte-Lucie-de-Tallano *U Fragnonu* ☎04 95 78 82 56, ℱ04 95 78 82 67. A converted water mill on the edge of the village. See also p.220.
Serra-di-Scapomena ☎04 95 78 64 90, ℱ04 95 78 72 43. Four-bed dorms and a superb east-facing balcony. April–Oct.

Le Sentier Isula–Corti

Cutting across the island from Pascal Paoli's port, L'Île Rousse, to his former capital, Corte, the **Sentier Isula–Corti** is the PNRC's newest waymarked route. As yet, few people seem to know of its existence, yet the itinerary – stringing together no fewer than five distinct micro-regions, tracts of extreme wilderness and some of Corsica's most remote villages – takes in more diverse landscapes than any other, as well as two contrasting historic towns.

Once clear of the coast, the route zigzags through the olive orchards of the Balagne (just skirting the area recently devastated by fire) to the cubic crow's-nest village of Speloncato, and thence over the famous Bocca di Croce d'Olu into the Giunssani – a Mediterranean Shangri-La of chestnut forests and mountain streams. A long dog-leg southeast to the mouth of the Asco Valley then leads due east into the deep trench at the island's heart, flanked by the Cinto massif, and over the Bocca di Serra Piana (1846m) to a magnificent hidden valley where you're unlikely to see another soul all day. From there, another stiff climb takes you into the Niolo, and eventually across the Bocca di l'Arinella to the Tavignano valley, where the route follows the ancient paved mule track down through the gorges and Laricio pine forest to Corte.

Running roughly parallel with the GR20 most of the time, this route has some challenging *étapes* – not least the twn hour stage from Asco to Corscia, in the Niolo, and the following day's eight hour fifteen-minute trek to the *Refuge A Sega*. Moreover, the almost total absence of dedicated hikers' hostels or *gîtes d'étapes* along the way means if you want to do it cheaply, without resorting to hotels and restaurants, you'll have to carry a heavy rucksack over some demanding terrain.

Isula–Corti practicalities

The Sentier Isula–Corti is divided into seven stages of between four hour fifteen minutes and ten hours – two of them excruciatingly long. Given the shortage of inexpensive accommodation along the route, it's tempting to ignore the PNRC's restrictions and take along a tent or bivvy bag and camp in remote areas for at least a few nights.

Getting to the trailheads at L'Île Rousse (see p.142) and Corte (see p.323) couldn't be easier: both are served by frequent buses and trains (except on Sundays and out of season, when services are scaled down). You'll need two **maps**: IGN topo-map 25 #4249 and #4250 OT. A leaflet outlining the route is also available from tourist and PNRC information offices.

Isula–Corti gîtes d'étape

Only three refuges-*gîtes d'étapes* serve the Sentier Isula–Corti. For the rest of the itinerary, you'll have to splash out on one of the pleasant country hotels listed below (although some walkers camp or bivouac illegally).

Asco See p.295.
Corsica ☏04 95 48 02 04. Small, municipal *gîte* in one of the island's highest villages.
Corte See p.306.
L'Île Rousse See p.125.
Moltifao See p.294.
Olmi-Capella See p.137.

Refuge A Sega ☏06 10 71 77 26. Modern refuge, deep in the Tavignano valley, 4hr walk from the nearest road. See also p.311.
Speloncato See p.135.

Contexts

Contexts

History

Corsica has always been an island of particular strategic and commercial appeal, with its sheltered harbours and protective mountains, set on the western Mediterranean trade routes within easy reach of several colonizing powers. Greeks, Carthaginians and Romans came in successive waves, landing on the eastern coast, driving native Corsicans into the high interior and battling against new predators in their turn. The Romans were ousted by Vandals, and for the following thirteen centuries the island was attacked, abandoned, settled and sold as nation-states and empires squabbled over Europe's territories, and generations of islanders fought against foreign rule and against each other. In the light of this turbulent past, it seems inevitable that Corsica's early history, unexplored until the twentieth century, should have its own pattern of invasion and occupation.

Beginnings

For thousands of years, the relics of Corsica's **Stone Age** were simply accepted as an inexplicable aspect of the island's landscape. In 1840 Prosper Mérimée, then Inspector of Historic Monuments, described the simple **menhirs** (from the Celtic *maen hir* – "long stone") of the southwest and tabulated various primitive stone monuments elsewhere in Corsica, but the origins and functions of these stone slabs and figures remained unknown until 1954, when French archeologist Roger Grosjean set about excavating and recording the megalithic sites. Only when his excavations started in earnest did a picture emerge of a complex prehistoric society that developed its religious and cultural framework over several millennia.

The first settlers

It's now believed that Corsica's **original inhabitants** arrived from northern Italy in the **seventh millennium BC**, long before the monument-building era. Making their shelters in caves and under cliffs, they survived by hunting, gathering and fishing. A thousand years later came new settlers with new skills, building villages, planting crops and herding cattle. The practice of **transhumant pastoralism** – driving sheep to graze on the uplands in summer, then down to coastal pastures in the winter – may have been started in this era, and is still followed by Corsican shepherds to this day. In the **fourth millennium BC**, the creators of the island's **megalithic** buildings migrated into the Mediterranean area from Asia Minor and the Aegean. There are numerous interpretations of the stone monuments and tombs that were erected during the next 2000 years, but the most widely held opinion is that they were connected with the veneration of ancestors and the spirits of the dead, and perhaps centred on an Earth Deity or Mother.

At first the dead were buried in underground tombs or **cists**, and were represented, commemorated or maybe guarded by single menhirs placed nearby. Clusters of these tombs and menhirs have been found in the southwestern Sartenais region and near Porto Vecchio. Cist burial later gave way to the custom of setting stone sarcophagi or **dolmens** (table stones) above ground and covering them with earth; around a hundred of these, measuring about 2m by 2.5m, have been discovered (now exposed after the erosion of the soil), one of the best examples being at **Fontanaccia**. At a later stage the menhirs acquired human forms and features: some were given swords or daggers, some were carved with rudimentary shoulder blades or ribs, and no two statues were the same. The function of these eerie warrior figures, most of which were found at **Filitosa** (see p.206), can only be imagined. Suggestions range from representations of dead spirits to trophies of war, each one marking a defeated invader.

The Torréens

The culture embodied by these carved menhirs reached its peak towards 1500 BC, when new aggressors – portrayed, perhaps, by the stone warriors – landed in the south and made their first base near Porto Vecchio. Naming this civilization the **Torréens**, after the dry-wall **torri** (towers) they raised in various parts of the island, Roger Grosjean posited that they were the same people as the sea-going Shardana who are known to have attacked Egypt in the late second millennium BC, and that the bronze weapons with which they subdued the islanders were the weapons depicted on the sword-bearing menhirs of Filitosa.

Their towers, each one built around a central cavity with smaller chambers to the sides, were found to contain remnants of fires, and may have been used to cremate the dead or even sacrifice the living. Fragments of the earlier, Neolithic structures, perhaps destroyed as the Torréens advanced along the island, were incorporated in their walls. Grosjean has traced the invaders' progression to the west, as they drove the megalithic natives further into the interior and finally to the north, where the natives were left to pursue their own beliefs and practices in peace. Stone menhirs were still being created in northern Corsica as the Iron Age got under way, centuries after the Torréen invasion, while in the south of the island – according to Grosjean – rivalry between Torréen settlements precipitated another migration, this time south to the island of Sardinia.

Greeks, Romans and Saracens

In 565 BC, Corsica's first major colony was founded at Alalia (Aléria) by Greek refugees from **Phocaea**. For a few decades these settlers made a successful living, planting vines and olive trees and enjoying a brisk trade in metals and cereals, but within thirty years they were fighting off an invading fleet of **Carthaginians** and **Etruscans**. By 535 BC, devastated by their losses in battle, the Greeks had abandoned Alalia to the Etruscans, who in turn were briefly succeeded by Carthaginian settlers in the third century BC.

By now Corsica had attracted the attention of the **Romans**, who sent in troops under the command of Lucius Cornelius Scipio in 259 BC. The indigenous islanders, enslaved or driven into the mountains by each successive invading power, joined forces with the Carthaginians and their leader Hanno to resist Roman occupation. Although the east coast was soon conquered and settled, it took another forty years before Corsica (together with Sardinia) could be brought within Roman administration, and another century of rebellion passed before the island's interior was overpowered.

For more than five hundred years Corsica remained a province of the Roman Empire. A string of ports was established along the south coast – subsequently flattened by invasion and malaria – and a settlement built at **Mariana**, to the south of present-day Bastia, though Aléria remained the largest settlement. From the third century AD onwards, **Christianity** was introduced to the island and bishoprics were established at Mariana, Aléria, the Nebbio, Sagone and Ajaccio.

This comparatively stable period in Corsican history came to an end as the Roman Empire disintegrated and the **Vandals** started to harass the coast. By 460 AD the Vandals were established on the island, only to be defeated by Belisarius and his Byzantine forces in 534, but absorption into the Byzantine empire did little to protect Corsica from the Ostrogoths and later from the **Lombards**, who managed to annex Corsica in 725 – by which time the coastal settlements were suffering frequent raids by the Saracens (or Moors). In 754 Pépin the Short, King of the Franks, agreed to hand Corsica over to the **papacy** once it was free of the Lombards; when the Lombards were driven out twenty years later, Pépin's son, Charlemagne, honoured the promise.

Within thirty years of its transfer to papal sovereignty, parts of Corsica were being overrun by the **Saracens**. These invaders retained their grip for another two centuries, despite the brief triumph of **Ugo della Colonna**, reputedly a Roman aristocrat sent to "liberate" the island by Pope Stephen IV, but more likely a semi-legendary figure based on Count Boniface of Lucca, who gained a foothold on the island in 825, building the fortress of Bonifacio on its southern tip.

Whatever the facts may be, Ugo della Colonna became a useful point of reference for the local Corsican families, who began to assert their authority as the Moors retreated under pressure from an allied force of Pisans and Genoese at the start of the eleventh century. During the Saracens' rule, the native islanders had been confined to the interior, where they had developed a system of administration based on mountain communities, with elected leaders who took every opportunity to make their status hereditary. This period saw the rise of such mighty clans as the **della Rocca** and **Istria** families, the dominant dynasties among the feudal lords known as the **Cinarchesi**, most of whom claimed descent from Ugo della Colonna. As their feuds and rivalries intensified, some swore allegiance to the pope, who in 1077 placed Corsica under Pisan protection; others turned for support to the Genoese, who claimed their own right to the island.

The Pisan period

In 1133, Pope Innocent II split Corsica's bishoprics between Pisa and Genoa, an action that did nothing to stem the enmity of the two republics. For two centuries, while Corsica remained **officially governed by Pisa**, the Genoese stayed on the offensive, capturing Bonifacio in 1187 and Calvi in 1268. Nevertheless, the Pisans were able to impose a framework of government built around the local parish or **piève**. A massive programme of church-building got under way, each church providing the focus for its *piève*, which in turn linked several village communities.

In the meantime, the Corsican nobles continued to flex their muscles. **Sinucello della Rocca**, a vassal of Pisa who held lands in the southwest, took advantage of the running dispute with Genoa and made his own bid for power, taking arms against other Corsican nobles and switching his loyalties between Pisa and Genoa as necessary. He eventually gained control of almost the whole island, drawing up a constitution and earning the name **Giudice** (Judge) for his sense of justice, but his success had made him few friends, and the rival *signori* soon turned against him. When Genoa defeated the Pisan fleet at

Meloria in 1284 and finally took control of the island, della Rocca retreated to his original base in the southwest and was eventually betrayed by his own illegitimate son. Captured by the Genoese, he died in prison in 1306.

The Genoese period

Despite **Genoa**'s decisive victory at Meloria, the republic's struggle to control Corsica was by no means over. In 1297, the island, along with Sardinia, was handed by Pope Boniface VIII to the **kingdom of Aragon**, setting off yet another territorial war – one that was to rumble on for two hundred years more. While Genoa held fast against Aragonese attempts to realize their claim to Corsica, the *signori* continued to fight it out among themselves. A people's revolt led by **Sambocuccio d'Alando** drove out the battling nobles of the northeast, and led to a political split between two areas of the island. In the northeast, the area known as *Diqua dai Monti* ("this side of the mountains"), the ancestral lands were taken over by village communities to form the **terra di commune**, officially protected by the Genoese, who founded and fortified Bastia in 1380. The southwest – *Dila dai Monti* – remained the **terra dei signori**, ruled in effect by the Cinarchesi, who looked to the more distant power of Aragon for support.

Generations of *signori* kept up a relentless effort to bring the whole island under their rule. Backed by Aragon, **Arrigo della Rocca** gained considerable successes against the Genoese in 1376, and then his nephew, **Vincentello d'Istria**, gained control of most of the island as viceroy of the king of Aragon from 1420 until 1434, when he was captured by Genoese forces and publicly beheaded. In 1453, in a bid to overcome such ambitious nobility, Genoa put Corsica into the hands of the **Bank of Saint George**, a powerful financial corporation with its own army. For ten years the bank imposed a tough military government, building a series of coastal watchtowers, restoring battered fortifications and containing the fractious warlords.

Sampiero Corso

Events in Europe brought this era to an end: **Henry II of France**, at war with Charles V, struck a blow against the Habsburg emperor's Genoese allies by sending a fleet to capture Corsica. Leading the invasion was mercenary **Sampiero Corso**, who took possession of the entire island except Calvi and Bastia. French rule lasted all of two years, before Corsica was passed back to Genoa under the Treaty of Cateau Cambresis in 1559. Corso, however, was rather less inclined to relinquish his supremacy, and led a successful uprising against the Genoese in 1564, again securing control of most of the island. He was finally defeated by a vicious Corsican custom – the **vendetta** – according to which any act of violence or dishonour had to be avenged by the victim's relations. Corso was murdered in 1567 by the brothers of his wife Vannina d'Orso, whom he had strangled in the belief that she had betrayed him to his Genoese enemies. His killers were heftily rewarded by the Genoese.

Genoese consolidation

In the late **sixteenth century** the Corsican population was reeling from years of war, pirate attacks, famine and malaria. The Genoese republic, now governing the island directly, was finally able to impose an administration of sorts. A governor was installed in Bastia to oversee the network of provinces and parishes, leaving local government to the Corsican communities and their assemblies (*consulta*). Attempts were even made to clamp down on the vendetta, but with no success – hundreds of murders were committed each year in the name of honour.

Nevertheless, in comparison with the previous pattern of civil war and invasion, the 170 years of direct Genoese rule were relatively peaceful. Corsicans enjoyed a certain degree of freedom to run their own affairs, and the rural economy developed and prospered – factors that were eventually to undermine the Genoese supremacy. Influential families, beneficiaries of the boom in agricultural trade, formed an articulate and ambitious new class. Excluded from the top ranks of government and resentful of Genoa's trade monopolies and high taxes, they provided the leadership for a Corsican society growing in political maturity and aspirations. Circumstances came to a head in the early eighteenth century, when discontent exploded into armed rebellion.

The Wars of Independence

The hated Genoese taxes were the trigger for **revolt in 1729** when, having suffered a series of failed harvests, one village near Corte refused to pay. Its defiance developed into a full-scale uprising and the reinforcements sent in to suppress it were soon overpowered. Rebellion spread quickly across the island and was formalized in **1731**, when a popular assembly declared **national independence**, adopting a constitution and forming a parliament with a representative from each village. The Genoese, besieged in their coastal fortresses, turned for help to Emperor Charles VI, who responded with six battalions, which helped recapture St Florent and Algajola from the insurgents. Under pressure from the emperor's troops, the Corsicans agreed to a settlement in 1732, winning several concessions from the Genoese, including access to public office.

The fighting resumed as soon as the emperor's soldiers had withdrawn, but the rebels made little progress, being short of resources and blockaded by a Genoese fleet. Salvation arrived in 1736 in the bizarre form of **Théodore von Neuhof**, a Westphalian adventurer brought up in the French royal court, who had spotted in Corsica's chaos an opportunity for glory. Having persuaded Tunisian financiers to back his venture, von Neuhof sailed into Aléria with ample supplies of money, arms and ammunition. The rebels had little choice but to accept his offer of support and they crowned him **king of Corsica**, though his authority was severely restricted by a new constitution, an executive council and an elected legislature. King Théodore's reign lasted eight months, by which time a lack of military success and depleted funds had provoked the hostility of many Corsicans; in November 1736 their monarch left the island, promising to find new allies.

Still the Corsicans and Genoese were in stalemate, each side unable to raise enough funds or forces to influence events decisively – until, in 1738, Genoa appealed to Louis XV of France and received several regiments commanded by the Comte de Boisseux. The following year, after the deployment of a further detachment of French troops, a thousand Corsicans were forced to flee the island. Among the refugees was **Giacinto Paoli**, one of the first leaders of the revolt, who went into exile in Naples with his teenage son Pascal.

The French pulled out of Corsica in 1741, but before long the major European powers were fighting over the island again, hoping for a strategic advantage in the War of the Austrian Succession. A British fleet carrying Austrian and Sardinian troops joined forces with the Corsican patriots, who elected **Gian'Pietru Gaffori** their commander. The 1748 Treaty of Aix-la-Chapelle marked an end to British involvement in the struggle, but the Corsicans continued their campaign, drawing up a new constitution in 1752. Gaffori led a determined drive against the Genoese, eventually capturing their stronghold at Corte, despite the fact that his son had been abducted and held hostage within the city walls. His heroic reputation among the Corsicans was matched by that of his wife, who prevented her household from surrendering to enemy troops by threatening to light a barrel-load of gunpowder and blow them and herself to smithereens.

Paoli's independent Corsica

The rebels lost their dynamic commander in 1753, when Gaffori was assassinated, and in 1754 **Pascal Paoli**, son of the exiled Corsican leader, was called back to Corsica to take over leadership of the rebellion.

Paoli returned with a keen sense of constitutional theory and a thorough political education. Having been elected leader of the nation in 1755, he introduced a constitution according to which every man over 25 had a vote and every parish could send representatives to the Public Assembly, which in turn elected an executive council of state. Paoli himself was in charge of military and foreign matters, but all other policies required the Assembly's agreement. Rapid steps were taken to boost the islanders' flagging morale and pitiful resources: schools were built and a university was founded in Corte; a mint and a printing press were established; mines and an arms factory were put into production. The death penalty was rigorously enforced for vendetta killings, which finally began to decline. Under Paoli's command the Corsican patriots and their enlightened system of government found admirers among the liberals and radicals of Europe. Jean-Jacques Rousseau toyed with the idea of moving to the island and writing its history; James Boswell came to meet Paoli and sang his praises in his journal of the visit, published in 1768 (see p.420).

In the meantime, events were overtaking the Corsicans. French forces occupied five coastal towns in 1764, and in **1768** the **Genoese ceded their rights** to the island, selling their claim to France under the Treaty of Versailles. An invading force landed within a month of the treaty being signed, taking possession of Cap Corse. Paoli's men – and women – kept up the pressure, hiding out in the maquis and launching guerrilla attacks on the French, but when a new detachment of troops was sent in there was little hope for the Corsicans, who suffered a terrible defeat at the **Battle of Ponte-Nuovo** in May 1769. Pascal Paoli had to flee to England.

French rule to the twentieth century

Though sporadic resistance continued even after Paoli's departure, Corsica was brought fairly painlessly within the monarchy as a Pays d'État, with its own biennial gathering of churchmen, nobles and commoners. As part of its programme of assimilation, the French offered Corsica's noble families scholarships to its prestigious military schools. Among the successful applicants was the son of Paoli's ex-secretary – **Napoléon Bonaparte**.

During the next twenty years of rule by the French monarchy, the drive for independence gradually subsided and, when the revolutionaries ousted Louis XVI in 1789, Corsica urged the Assembly to make the island a fully integrated part of the French State. The royal ban imposed on political exiles was lifted, and Paoli returned to be elected president of the Corsican Conseil-Général. His authority was at first accepted by the Paris Convention, but soon Paoli fell out of favour after a Paris-instigated campaign to conquer Sardinia ended in failure. When it became known that Paoli was to be arrested, the Corsican Assembly came to his defence, naming him **Father of the Nation**. Paoli's supporters turned on the French and pro-French on the island; the Bonaparte family, who had long since transferred their loyalty to France, left their Ajaccio home to the looters and were hastened to Toulon by Napoléon, by then serving in the French army.

The Anglo–Corsican interlude

Aware of the superior strength of French forces, Paoli called on his old English allies for help, and in 1794 **Sir Gilbert Elliot** arrived with reinforcements who quickly captured St Florent, Bastia and Calvi (where Nelson lost the use of one of his eyes). In return for this intervention, Britain demanded a stake in the island's government, and in June **1794** an **Anglo–Corsican kingdom** was proclaimed.

To the bitter disappointment of Paoli and his supporters, Sir Gilbert was made viceroy of the new kingdom, with the power to dissolve parliament, nominate councillors and appoint the highest officers of state. When the Corsican members of parliament responded by electing Paoli their president, Sir Gilbert threatened to pull out his troops, and they were forced to back down. A series of riots followed, and a nervous Sir Gilbert persuaded the king to exile Paoli once again – this time for good. But the damage was already done: Paoli loyalists joined the French in their attacks on British soldiers, and in September 1796 Sir Gilbert and his troops sailed away, leaving the island to be retaken by France.

The Napoleonic era and its aftermath

Apart from a brief stay in Ajaccio in 1799, **Napoléon** paid scant attention to his homeland during his period of power. A number of uprisings on the island during the 1790s were put down with brutal force, and opposition to Napoleonic rule led to widespread revolt by an alliance of Royalists, Paolists and British supporters in 1799. This, too, was stamped out and its leaders executed. In 1801 the constitution was suspended and Général Morand arrived to administer a harsh military rule. His reign of terror lasted until 1811, when the almost equally unpopular Général César Berthier took his place. In the same year the island was made a single *département* of France (it had been divided into two in 1796), with its capital in Ajaccio. Resistance to the French continued, and in 1814 the citizens of Bastia appealed to Britain to intervene on their behalf. A detachment of British troops was sent, but in April of that year Napoléon abdicated and the soldiers were recalled.

After 1815 and the **restoration of the French monarchy**, the governing state made some attempts to develop the island's economy, opening mines and foundries, setting up a railway, introducing an education act, and building roads and schools. But most of their schemes had little success, and Corsica remained a marginal and largely neglected part of the country. For Corsicans, the real opportunities lay in France, and young islanders began to turn away from the old villages, seeking their careers and education on the mainland. The romance and drama that visitors such as Edward Lear and Prosper Mérimée discovered in mid-nineteenth-century Corsica veiled a grim picture of poverty, malaria and violence – vendetta, though on the decline, was still claiming up to 160 victims a year (see p.216). In the last half of the century, **emigration** surged so dramatically that within sixty years the population had been halved.

The twentieth century

In 1909, as a result of a commission set up by Georges Clemenceau, French minister of the interior, the French government promised more investment and development for Corsica. This plan, however, was shelved with the outbreak of **World War I**, which itself reduced Corsica's population still further, taking over 20,000 lives (a higher per capita casualty rate than any other part of Europe).

During the 1920s and 1930s Mussolini set his sights on Corsica, and while the Nazis were busy invading France, 85,000 Italian troops descended on the island. They were later joined by a force of 10,000 Germans (who dug into the far south to defend the Straits of Bonifacio) – an occupying force of around one to every two islanders. With the Italian surrender in 1943, Kesselring's Ninth Panzer Division and the remaining German troops on the island were evacuated from the east coast, while the Corsican Resistance and Free French troops attacked them from the hills. By mid-September, Corsica had become the first *département* of Metropolitan France to be liberated. Allied troops and air forces moved in, and from 1946 kick-started the postwar economy of the island by clearing the east coast of malarial mosquitoes.

In the postwar years, Corsica was earmarked by the French government as a target for development, and in 1957 two state-sponsored organizations were set up to exploit its potential: **SOMIVAC** – the Société pour la Mise en Valeur Agricole de la Corse – introduced modern agricultural techniques; **SETCO** – the Société pour l'Équipement Touristique de la Corse – provided funds to build a tourist industry. Both organizations met with considerable distrust, seen as threats to an ancient way of life that had evolved and survived during centuries of hostile occupation. Nevertheless, the development gathered pace and, after 1962, when Algeria gained its independence, the situation was complicated by a massive influx of *pieds-noirs* refugees from the ex-French colony. Over 15,000 settlers poured into Corsica during the next twenty years, many of them buying up the newly developed land and hotels, adding to Corsican fears of losing control of their resources. Summer **tourists** began to arrive in steadily rising numbers, topping the half-million mark in the early 1970s (and now heading for two million annually).

Calls for autonomy

It was against this background of insecurity and mounting frustration with the ineffectiveness of Paris's half-hearted economic policies that demands for greater administrative power were increasingly voiced from the 1960s. Led by the **Simeoni brothers**, Max and Edmond, a party of nationalist students known as L'Action Régionaliste Corse (**ARC**) started to call for decentralized government, for restrictions on the east-coast tourist developments, for a Corsican university (Paoli's had been closed by the French), and for compulsory schooling in Corsican language and history.

A number of more radical **autonomist movements**, varying in tactics and demands, entered the political scene, and from the mid-1970s these won substantial support for their manifesto of a national assembly and demand for investment in controlled development and protection of the land. Meanwhile, following the **Aléria siege** of 1975, when two policemen died in a shoot-out with armed separatists (see p.272), a group of activists operating as the **FLNC** (Fronte di Liberazione Naziunale di a Corsica) embarked on a programme of bombing campaigns, targeting the tourist villages and foreign-owned properties that they believed were destroying Corsica's land and culture.

In the early 1980s the autonomists profited from a change of policy in France favouring increased decentralization. A Corsican university was re-established in 1981, providing a channel for the ambitions and political ideas of the younger generation. In the following year, Corsica became the first of the French regions to be granted a National Assembly, with limited powers over policy, administration and finance. Nonetheless, benefiting from close links with the IRA, a more ruthless and efficient FLNC intensified its paramilitary activities. Dozens of explosions heralded the election of 1984, as allegations of fraud and corruption were levelled against the politicians.

In 1987, **Charles Pasqua**, the (then) minister of the interior, mounted a clampdown on the FLNC. At the same time, nationalist political parties continued to poll around seventeen percent of the vote in elections, though a crisis was brewing that would inflict considerably more damage to the nationalist movement than any of Pasqua's heavy-handed tactics. Following a period of deepening political divisions, in 1990 the movement split into two opposing factions: **Cuncolta** and their armed wing, the FLNC Canal-Historique; and the **MPA**, whose paramilitary group dubbed itself the FLNC Canal-Habituel.

Soon an all-out blood feud erupted between the two, which claimed hundreds of lives and sent the murder rate spiralling to thirty per year. Visitor numbers dropped back to their lowest levels in a decade, while the French government seemed content to watch from the wings as the paramilitaries destroyed each other far more effectively than the security forces had been able to do.

Public opinion on the island had by now started to swing decisively against the FLNC and its various splinter groups, with the overwhelming majority of Corsicans opposed to independence from France. What little support for the armed struggle remained evaporated almost completely in February 1998 after the government's most senior representative in Corsica, **Préfet Claude-Érignac**, was gunned down while leaving the opera with his wife. Three days after the atrocity, the island's trade unions and most of its political parties staged a fifteen-minute silence calling for an end to the violence.

The dramatic swing of support away from the separatists in the wake of the Érignac murder, however, was to be short-lived. Érignac's successor, Préfet **Bernard Bonnet**, a hardliner dispatched by Prime Minister Lionel Jospin to impose law and order on the island, soon became embroiled in scandal after it was discovered he had ordered the destruction by undercover gendarmes of an illegal beach shack near Ajaccio. The Affaire de la Paillote, as the scandal was dubbed by the press, threatened for a while to implicate even the Elysée Palace when Bonnet accused Jospin of using him as a fall guy for his moribund Corsica policies.

Since the time of the ancient Greeks, Corsica has been regarded as strategically vital for control of the Mediterranean's seaways, and **World War II** was no exception. Claiming the island had to be secured to protect his North African colonies, Mussolini – who had long regarded Corsicans as Italians in all but name – dispatched a "Liberation Force" of 85,000 troops in the autumn of 1942. By that time, however, the Allies had already invaded North Africa and were mustering for an attack on southern Europe. Neither Mussolini nor Hitler knew where this was to begin, but Corsica, within easy reach of both the French and Italian coasts, was an obvious *point d'appui*. In fact, Churchill and Roosevelt had already settled upon Sicily as the landing site, and in order to throw the Axis off the scent had ordered that resistance activities in Corsica be stepped up as a diversionary tactic.

As the submarine, *Le Casabianca*, surfaced for the first time off the island's coast in December 1942, its crew and captain, **Jean L'Herminier**, can have had little inkling that their top-secret operation was in essence the start of wide-scale strategic deception. Backed by the American Secret Service, the **"Pearl Harbour"** mission (see p.158) was the first of a dozen or so similar landings in which agents, arms, munitions and money (provided mainly by the British and Americans) were ferried from Algiers to supply the nascent Corsican Resistance. Further consignments were flown in by the RAF as the partisan networks, marshalled by emissaries sent by rival Free French generals **de Gaulle** and **Giraud**, became better established. As well as putting in place a force that might later tie down occupying troops and armoured divisions, the hope of Allied Command was to fool the Germans into redeploying resources away from the real invasion site in Sicily.

Other, smaller-scale, feints were devised by Churchill's secret service. The most famous of them (the subject of the postwar best-seller, *The Man Who Never Was* by Ewen Montagu) was the beaching near Huelva in Spain of a corpse in naval uniform carrying faked dispatches which confirmed Eisenhower's army was set to attack southern Europe through the French Riviera. Among the many repercussions of this splendid *ruse de guerre* was that Hitler did exactly as Churchill had intended by ordering the reinforcement of Sardinia and Corsica in 1943.

When it became clear, in July of that year, that Eisenhower's invasion of Sicily was after all the Allies' main thrust, the Führer changed tack, removing his forces from Sardinia to fortify Corsica, from where they could more easily be removed to the Italian mainland ahead of the Allies' advance. This gave the British and Americans a golden opportunity to destroy Marshal Kesselring's Ninth Panzer Division as it lumbered unprotected by air support along the exposed, flat shoreline of Corsica's east coast. The Allied air force, however, had its hands full already, and the job of forestalling what soon become a full-scale retreat fell to the Corsican Resistance, beefed up by a French colonial force from North Africa.

By the summer of 1943, some 12,000 partisans had been placed under arms on the island, organized into regional cells by the left-wing **Front National**. Known as the **Maquis** after the dense scrub in which most hid out, the Resistance bided its time in the bush while waiting for the green light from Algiers. This eventually came with the capitulation of Mussolini's successor, Marshal Badoglio, in September 1943, just as the Germans were retreating up the east coast from Sardinia.

The surrender placed the Italians in an awkward position. Reviled by the islanders but no longer allied to the Germans, many Italian troops regarded

Corsican retribution as less of a risk than Nazi justice and mutinied or fled to the mountains to join the Maquis. In the event, their mistrust proved well placed. Following a fierce fire fight outside Bastia, Hitler personally ordered the execution of the captured Italian officers, but Kesselring's general, **Von Senger und Etterlin**, ignored the Führer's instructions, sending the prisoners directly to Leghorn (Livorno) instead where no such orders existed.

By mid-September, the German evacuation had reached its peak, with 3000 troops per day being airlifted or shipped off the east coast. Meanwhile, the Maquis and Free French army (dispatched by Général Giraud from Algiers and now numbering some 6600 men) had fought their way northeast through the interior from Ajaccio and were closing in from the hills behind Bastia. Strafed by the Allied air forces, and torpedoed by British submarines in the Tyrrhenian Sea, the retreating German army was effectively surrounded by October 2. By the time Von Senger und Etterlin stepped onto his launch to leave that night, approximately 27,000 German troops and up to 100 tanks had been removed to safety, for the relatively cheap price of a handful of ships (and one million litres of top Corsican wine, which rampaging German troops poured down the drains before they left).

Corsica was officially liberated on **September 16, 1943**, but was not yet out of trouble. Due to crossed wires in Allied Command, American bombers mounted a devastating broad-daylight raid on October 4 – as most of Bastia was partying in the streets. Hundreds were killed, and the Vieux Port, in particular, took a dreadful pounding. This fatal error soured celebrations on the island, and did little to calm the nerves of de Gaulle, who was already in a fury. Credit for the Liberation had gone to his arch rival, **Général Giraud**, who had dispatched the Free French troops without consulting the Committee of National Liberation, or CFLN (the de facto government in exile) in Algiers. Much to his right-wing adversary's chagrin, Giraud had also allowed the communist-dominated Front National to take control of communications and local government on the island, setting a potentially undesirable (from de Gaulle's point of view) precedent for the future recapture of French territories. ("He has stolen my Corsica!" de Gaulle is famously said to have cried.)

Backed by Roosevelt, Giraud was much more popular than de Gaulle – according to one eminent British historian, not least because "he grew a very large moustache and laughed at other people's jokes, whereas de Gaulle wasn't much of a success at either". Ultimately, however, charm proved powerless in the face of the future French president's wiliness, and within six months an outmanoeuvred Giraud was sacked from the CFLN and consigned to political obscurity.

De Gaulle's anger at the way Corsica had been liberated may go some way to explaining why this episode in the history of World War II rarely occupies the place it deserves in the history books. But the liberation provided an important platform for the ensuing invasion of southern France. Corsica became the Allies' key maritime and secret service base in 1944, and a vital staging post for craft bound for Italy. An additional, often forgotten, fact is that the liberation of the island could not have been achieved without the help of several thousand Arab and West African soldiers, hundreds of whom died in battle alongside Corsican partisans. A memorial on the **Col de Teghime** honours their bravery in the face of a considerably larger and better-equipped German army.

Matignon and beyond

It is impossible to say how much of the mud stuck to Jospin, but L'Affaire de la Paillote certainly did little to enhance the prime minister's hitherto squeaky-clean image in the eyes of French voters. More certain is that anti-French feeling intensified on the island in the wake of the Bonnet revelations, and that to seize back the initiative the Jospin administration had to come up with something visionary.

The deadlock seemed at last to be broken with the so-called **Matignon Accords**, a portfolio of radical proposals offering major new devolutionary concessions to the nationalists in exchange for peace. These included the transfer to an elected assembly on the island of responsibility for culture, education and regional development and greater legislative and regulatory powers.

Gaullist opposition to the package was predictably bullish: Jospin's plain-speaking, staunchly Republican interior minister, **Jean-Pierre Chevènement**, resigned over the bill, which he and his right-wing Jacobin cronies condemned as "a victory for blackmail by a violent minority of Corsicans ... a cowardly abdication of state responsibility (and) ... a bomb beneath the French Republic". His warnings that Jospin's line on Corsica would inevitably lead to calls for greater devolution by other French minorities seemed to come true in August 2001 when delegations of Bretons, Savoyards, Catalans and Basques convened with local nationalists in Corte.

In Corsica itself, however, the eighteen-month Matignon talks were hailed as a major step forward. Nationalist violence subsided, a ceasefire held and the separatists finally got together to discuss the fine print with government representatives. In May 2001, the French parliament gave the green light to the package, followed by a vote of approval by the Corsican regional assembly.

The success of the Matignon Accords, however, depended entirely upon the strength and resolve of Jospin's government, and both started to waver badly the following year. During the run-up to the 2002 elections, moderate nationalists began to withdraw their support, complaining that the text of the accords didn't go far enough. Then the upper house of parliament in Paris watered it down further, removing some of the proposed powers. Finally, France's Supreme Court declared the whole process unconstitutional.

With the victory of Jacques Chirac and the resounding defeat of Jospin in the presidential election of June 2002, Matignon looked doomed. Violence once again erupted ahead of the first visit to the island of Chirac's tough homeland security tsar, Nicolas Sarkozy. This was followed at the peak of the tourist season in August by a *nuit bleue* (nocturnal press conference) called by a coalition of paramilitary groups to announce the end of their ceasefire; more bombs and rocket attacks ensued.

The nail in the coffin for Matignon came soon after when the newly inaugurated prime minister **Jean-Pierre Raffarin** visited Corsica. He used the opportunity to declare that his government would not honour promises made by the previous administration and proposed instead a pan-French plan for limited devolution to all regions. Even the most moderate of moderate nationalists were furious. Leader of Corsica Nazione, Jean-Guy Talamoni, summed up the widespread resentment when he insisted that the island would not consent to being "lumped in with some uniform and general decentralization programme".

For a more detailed account of the recent armed conflict with the French state, see "The Corsican troubles" on p.392.

The 2003 referendum

A compromise was eventually reached in the form of a broad package of constitutional changes specifically tailored for Corsica, which the government proposed should be put before the island's electorate in a **referendum**. It included plans to merge Corsica's two *départements* and foster greater parity for women in parliament (Corsica at the time had only one female councillor and no MPs), as well as provision for a beefed-up regional assembly with control over education, culture, transport, industry and, most significantly, tax.

Despite Chirac's passionate opposition to Corsican autonomy in general, and his predecessors' Corsica policies in particular, the initiative was based loosely on Jospin's Matignon Accords, which interior minister Nicolas Sarkozy tweaked after visiting the Scottish parliament, seen by the Elysée Palace as a potential model. Both men campaigned hard for a "yes" vote in the run-up to the referendum, asserting that a Corsican parliament with more power was the best way to ensure the island's inhabitants remained French.

On the island itself, however, parties on both left and right remained split, and the vote – scheduled for July 6, 2003 – looked to be finely balanced. In the event, the government's proposals were narrowly defeated, by 51 percent to 49. A grim-faced Sarkozy said on television the next day that he now felt "nothing more could be done for the place", and indeed, government policy since has been moribund.

Many commentators at the time claimed one contributing factor for the "no" vote was the high-profile arrest, on the eve of the referendum, of Corsica's most wanted nationalist terrorist, **Yvan Colonna**. The goatherd from Cargèse had been a fugitive since the murder of Préfet Érignac in 1998, and his capture, just as the island was about to go to the polls, was widely interpreted as an attempt on the part of the French government to assert that a "yes" vote would not mean "giving in to terrorisim". If the arrest was politically timed, then the move backfired badly. Despite condemning Colonna's alleged crime, even moderate nationalists on the island reacted with indignation at what they dismissed as a blatant public relations manoeuvre. The gesture may well have provoked some Corsicans who might otherwise have voted for the plan to turn against it.

However transitory the factors that brought about the "no" vote, its impact has been long lasting. Rebuffed in its attempts to grant greater autonomy to Corsica, the French government has instead redoubled its crackdown on corruption and organized crime. Among the most high-level arrests were that of nationalist paramilitary supremo **Charles Pieri**, who, along with 21 associates (including the president of Bastia's premiership football club, SCB), was alleged to have managed a huge extortion and money-laundering racket designed to generate funds for the armed struggle. Pieri's arrest provoked a predictably angry response from the FLNC-U (currently the most potent paramilitary force on the island), and the number of bombings, machine-gun and rocket attacks on state symbols and institutions soared through 2004 and 2005, as Corsica seemed to return to the bad old days of the mid-1990s.

The 2005 ferry dispute

More recently, French government policy came into violent conflict with Corsican workers after it was announced that the loss-making ferry company, **SNCM**, would be privatized. To oppose the move, which critics claimed would cost more than four hundred jobs, a strike was called by the powerful CGT

Union, crippling Marseille and other French ports. Then, in September 2005, Corsican sailors commandeered a ferry, the **Pascal Paoli**, sailing it to Bastia from the mainland to publicize the dispute.

Following a brief standoff, in which riots and street demonstrations turned the centre and port of Bastia into something resembling a war zone, special forces and hundreds of CRS police were called in to reclaim the vessel and subdue the crowds that had gathered to protest. The twenty mutinous crew members were duly arrested, but TV pictures of them kneeling before heavily armed French soldiers on the decks of the Pascal Paoli succeeded in galvanizing public opinion on the island to an extent hitherto undreamed of by the unions. A general strike and mass demonstrations were swiftly planned, and amid the build-up to these, with nationalist ire mounting by the hour, Sarkozy made a tactical retreat and released the sailors – a move which caused widespread euphoria across the island.

Devolution and the environment

One of the principal debates surrounding the issue of devolution in Corsica is its potential impact on the environment. Corsica welcomes nearly two million visitors annually, yet the level of development, even on the coast, remains relatively restrained. The paramilitaries' predilection for blowing up foreign-owned villas and holiday complexes generally takes the credit for this, but the truth is that it is French environmental law which has kept the concrete at bay. As well as forbidding any permanent construction within 100m of the shoreline, the stringent *lois littoral et montagne* obliges developers to obtain state approval for any project inside an area designated as environmentally fragile or of outstanding natural beauty. All 360 of Corsica's *communes* fall into such categories.

However, in discussions leading up to the Matignon reforms, environmentalists repeatedly raised the spectre of what might happen if the island's newly elected representatives, endowed with powers to circumvent the *lois littoral et montagne*, were unable to resist pressure from developers. One of their prime responsibilities, after all, would be the regeneration of the island's economy. Corsican landowners are understandably licking their lips at the prospect of devolution: many have already been courted by investors, along with local politicians and developers, all of whom stand to make fortunes if the current building restrictions are ever relaxed.

Such concerns reflect not only the fragility of the island's natural environment, but also the chronically depressed state of its economy. Tourism and related industries currently account for between ten and twelve percent of GDP, while agriculture earns a paltry one to two percent. Unemployment may be nonexistent for three months over the summer, but in winter rises to nearly ten percent – which doesn't take into account the huge numbers of islanders who migrate to the Continent to work off-season. Another revealing statistic is that over thirty percent of all those employed in Corsica work for local councils. Industry generates only seven percent of GDP, with barely one percent of companies boasting a workforce of more than fifty people. In short, Corsica produces very little and would be economically unviable were it not for tourism and the vast subsidies from both the French State and EU.

If the island were ever to gain the legislative and regulatory powers its politicians and nationalist paramilitary groups demand, its elected representatives would be under great pressure to deliver tangible results. Couple this with the potentially huge sums of venture capital waiting in the wings, and you'll see why even some confirmed nationalists regard the future of Corsica with some trepidation.

Stalemate

At the time of writing – with Sarkozy installed in the Elysée Palace in the wake of the 2007 presidential elections, and Corsican rates of inflation and unemployment the highest in France – the devolutionary process seemed utterly deadlocked. To reclaim lost popularity after the 2003 referendum debacle and Pieri show trial, nationalist paramilitaries shifted focus to that perennial vote-winner, the issue of French-owned second homes on the island. A veritable tide of middle-class buyers from the continent have built holiday villas in Corsica over the past decade, pushing up property prices beyond the reach of the average islander. By the summer of 2007, ten houses per week were being blown up by the FLNC and its various splinter groups.

The campaign succeeded: public opinion has once again rallied behind the nationalist cause at a time when Paris seems clueless about what to do with Corsica in the long term. Other than sporadic reports of bombings – or bombers accidentally blowing themselves up – the only time the island has made national headlines over the past few years was when a TV telephone hoaxer pretending to be the Quebecois premier got presidential candidate Ségolène Royal to agree that "Corsica should be independent". Sarkozy responded by saying that "for me, Corsica isn't a joke … It's the Republic" – a statement of platitudinous resolve that encapsulates current government thinking on the thorny "*problème corse*".

The Corsican troubles: an overview

To the outsider, Corsica may seem peaceful enough. But you don't have to look too hard to find signs of the thirty-year conflict being waged between local nationalist extremists and the French State. On the outskirts of larger villages high walls and electric fences surround fortified gendarmeries; bullet marks mar the facades of many post offices, banks and government buildings; black graffiti deface most road signs; and the rubble of bombed-out holiday villas dots coastal landscapes from Cap Corse to the Bouches de Bonifacio.

Spawning more than five hundred bombings, arson and machine-gun attacks annually, the conflict, which in the past decade has descended into factional

The Moor's head

You can't travel far in Corsica without coming across the island's ubiquitous national symbol, the Moor's head. Depicting the profile of a young black male with a white scarf, or bandeau, tied behind his head, this enigmatic image crops up everywhere, from car stickers to key rings, postcards to football pennants. Yet its origins are obscure, shrouded in a mixture of myth and historical fact.

The first concrete associations of the Moor's head with Corsica date from the early seventeenth century, when it featured on German maps of the island. This inspired Théodore von Neuhof to use the image on the single silver coin he had minted to mark his short reign as king of Corsica. Not until November 24, 1762, however, was it declared the official symbol of Corsican Independence, at the instigation of Pascal Paoli.

The choice of the Moor's head seems somewhat strange, given the fact the symbol was known to have originally come from Spain and was at one time synonymous with the threat of colonial rule. It first came to the region on the battle standards of the Crown of Aragon, who ruled neighbouring Sardinia following the expulsion of the Saracens during the Crusades. Indeed, the white bandeau, which on Aragon standards was drawn covering the eyes rather than the forehead, is believed to symbolize the defeat of the Muslims and their forced conversion to Christianity, while the four heads featured on the dragonese arms refer to the legend of the four Muslim chiefdoms killed in the Reconquista of Spain.

The association of the Moor's head emblem with the defeat of the Saracens during the Middle Ages finds echoes in an old Corsican legend. In the story, a young woman named Diana from Aléria, on the east coast, was abducted by Moorish pirates and taken to Grenada. However, her fiancé, Paoli, managed to free her and, after crossing the Sierra Nevada, returned safely to Corsica. The king of Grenada, Mohammed Abdul Allah, was furious at being outwitted by a peasant and instructed his top general, Mansour ben Ismail, to recapture the fugitives dead or alive. After landing at Piana on the west coast, the Moors are then said to have raped and pillaged their way across the mountains to Aléria, where they were engaged, and eventually defeated, by a courageous Corsican army. In the course of the battle, Paoli avenged Diana's abduction by slaying Mansour and parading his disembodied head at the end of a stick around the entire island – whence the now famous image.

In more recent times, the Moor's head has been appropriated by the nationalist movement as the unofficial emblem of the Corsican Independence struggle. Wherever you find a French tricolore, you're almost certain to see a black-and-white Moor's head flag flying provocatively nearby.

infighting among the islanders themselves, has left few families unscathed. Since 1986, the murder rate in Corsica has run at an average of between thirty and forty per year – for a population of 260,000.

The chances of your getting caught up in any violence while on holiday are virtually nil, but the Corsican troubles remain a defining feature of island life, as integral to local society as the sectarian war of Northern Ireland or the Mafia's presence in Sicily, with which *le problème corse*, as the troubles are euphemistically dubbed on the mainland, shares many similarities.

The roots of nationalism

Although Corsica has always maintained its own culturally distinct way of life, the conviction that the islanders' unique language and customs should form the basis of an individual nation is a relatively new phenomenon. Not until the Wars of Independence and rise of **Pascal Paoli** (see p.284) in the mid-eighteenth century did nationalism gather any momentum, inspired by widespread outrage at the atrocities perpetrated by the French in the wake of the Genoese withdrawal in 1768. Before this time, any seeds of nationalist consciousness that may have taken root were stifled by instability or foreign oppression. Since the time of the Romans, Corsica has witnessed 19 changes of overlords, 37 popular revolts and 7 spells of outright anarchy.

The other force that has traditionally mitigated against the emergence of a unified Corsican nation has been **clannism**. In common with many Mediterranean societies, the island has always been riven by internal divisions: between families, hamlets, villages, valleys, and between coastal peoples and shepherds in the mountains. All too often, these differences were perpetuated by **vendettas** resulting from some kind of perceived slight to an individual or family's honour (see p.216). The prevalence of such feuds, which were commonplace until the end of the nineteenth century, ensured that mutual mistrust, suspicion and the readiness to resort to violence became firmly ingrained in the Corsican psyche.

Economic decline

The **revival** of Corsican nationalism in the twentieth century emerged essentially as a response to the island's steady economic decline under French rule. Whereas the Genoese had instigated a coherent and productive agricultural policy (whence the vast chestnut forests of Castagniccia and olive groves of the Balagne), the only distinguishing feature of their French successors' approach to the island's economic woes was **neglect**. With its agricultural produce no longer in demand, Corsica's crops literally withered on the vine.

Emigration, to the cities of the mainland and French colonies in Africa and the Americas, left whole regions perilously underpopulated by the start of the twentieth century. The world wars took their toll, too. Per capita, Corsica lost more of its menfolk on the battlefields of Europe than any other *département* in France. Experience of the wider world also encouraged those who survived to emigrate after demobilization. Between 1937 and 1956, census figures show the island's population dropped to a little under 76,000, while during the 1960s port records registered 10,000 more annual departures than arrivals.

The effect of such widespread emigration on the Corsican economy was devastating. Not only were there now fewer hands to work what little land remained under cultivation, but the drop in population also meant a much smaller labour pool, discouraging potential investors. By the mid-1960s, the island was officially the poorest *département* in France, importing six times what it exported, yet with a cost of living thirty percent higher than the average on the mainland.

The response of the French government to such poverty, however, continued to lack vision, while makeshift decisions issued by Paris throughout this era compounded Corsica's economic problems. Eager to put it on a par with the rest of the country, **de Gaulle** whittled away at the island's special fiscal exemptions, which had been in place since 1811, imposing duties on public transport and gambling, as well as tobacco and alcohol. As a result, the cost of transporting goods to Corsica increased, further worsening the balance of payments and contributing to inflation. To Corsicans, it seemed as if France was actively penalizing the island for being an island. To rub salt into the wound, neighbouring Sardinia, which also had become depopulated and poor, began to thrive from the 1950s on, thanks to massive investment and dispensations from the Italian government, which had put its economy on a level playing field with that of the mainland.

The rise of the FLNC

The adoption of violence by Corsican nationalists arose out of a widespread sense of frustration and powerlessness in the face of continued French indifference. Peaceful protests had consistently failed to galvanize Paris. Strikes called by an increasingly militant workforce in the early 1960s proved little more than a shot in the foot: when dockers downed tools in 1961, the resulting disruption provoked two major Italian shipping firms to remove their operations from the island altogether.

The mounting dissatisfaction may have rumbled on without erupting for another decade, had it not been for a string of controversies that struck in quick succession during the early 1960s. The first was the arrival, in 1962, of 15,000 *pieds-noirs*. The influx of newcomers provoked alarm among Corsican traditionalists that the island was being used as a "dumping ground" at the cost of indigenous culture and was losing control of its resources. Fears of exploitation were whipped up further the following year, when the government announced it wanted to export cheap **electricity** generated in Corsica to Sardinia. Considering Paris's long-term economic neglect, the plans were regarded as adding insult to injury.

The gravest insult to Corsican pride around this time, however, came direct from de Gaulle himself. When world opinion made it impolitic to stage **nuclear tests** in the French-occupied Sahara, de Gaulle and his team of military advisers chose **Argentella**, southwest of Calvi, as a potential atom-bomb testing site. News of the plans was greeted with public outrage in Corsica. An island-wide general strike and referendum showed unanimous opposition to the proposals, and 30,000 demonstrators took to the streets of Ajaccio and Bastia (the largest crowds to gather on the island since Liberation Day in 1943). De Gaulle, however, refused to back down.

At this point, local "vigilance committees", monitoring government surveyors on the northwest coast, lost patience with peaceful protest and took the law into their own hands. Armed patrols located a couple of engineers, and nearly killed them (even though, as it turned out, the men had nothing to do with the nuclear tests). The remaining government technicians were immediately recalled to Paris and the Argentella project was shelved.

Aside from being a rare example of how – at a time when anti-nuclear protesters were in prison in both the US and UK – a small population was able to reverse the nuclear policy of a national government, the Argentella episode marked a watershed in the island's history: it was effectively the first time since the Wars of Independence that Corsicans had taken up arms against the French State.

ARC and the Aléria siege

The impetus Corsica needed finally to launch a nationalist political party came with the return from the mainland of radicalized students after the university-led revolution in Paris of **May 1968**. In its infancy, the nationalist political scene was dominated by two groups: right-wing conservatives from established bourgeois families, and a smaller contingent of young Maoists and Trotskyists. The latter emerged as the dominant force in the **ARC** (L'Action Régionaliste Corse), founded in 1967. Regaled by the stirring, newly revived **polyphony** singing of groups such as Canta U Populu Corsu, its conferences resounded with the rallying cry "*I Francesi fora!*" ("French out!").

Direct conflict with the French government, however, didn't come until 1975, when the radical armed wing of the ARC, led by the **Simeoni brothers**, occupied a wine cellar near **Aléria** on the east coast to voice their anger at Paris's lack of action over a wine-adulteration scandal. A 1250-strong force of armed police was dispatched by Giscard d'Estaing to break the siege, and during the shoot-out that followed two policemen were killed.

In the wake of Aléria, on the anniversary of the Battle of Ponte-Nuovu (when Pascal Paoli's army was routed by the French) a clandestine nocturnal press conference – or *nuit bleue* – was held by balaclava-wearing nationalist gunmen to announce the formation of the Fronte di Liberazione Naziunale di a Corsica, or **FLNC**. The stated aim of the (then) poorly equipped, poorly trained paramilitary group was total freedom from French dominion.

The early years of armed struggle: 1976–82

The first two years of **armed struggle** were relatively restrained, with attacks directed against strategic government targets, such as Ajaccio airport, where an Air France Boeing 707 became an early casualty of the conflict. But after 1978 the tone became more militant. A right-wing anti-separatist group, **SAC** (Service d'Action Civique), believed to have been covertly funded by the government, was attempting to infiltrate and sabotage the FLNC, who responded by setting up a unit called **Secteur V**, charged with mounting bomb attacks on the mainland.

Proof that Paris and the SAC were in cahoots came in 1980 with the capture of three active French secret service agents in **Bastelica** (see p.195). The men were taken at gunpoint to the *Hôtel Fesch* in Ajaccio, and held until the building was stormed six days later. No one was killed, but the nationalists involved were seized and sent to swell the growing ranks of Corsican prisoners in mainland France.

The debacle infuriated the FLNC rank and file, and plunged the island into its worst spell of nationalist violence to date. This period also saw the spread of **racketeering** as the FLNC's principal means of raising funds. Protection money was increasingly demanded of hotels, restaurants and other tourist-oriented businesses across the island, while hold-ups and armed robberies proliferated.

By the beginning of the 1980s, however, it was clear that small-time villains had started to cash in on the troubles by running rackets behind a veneer of FLNC "respectability". In order to differentiate the *pur et dur* (pure and hard) from the *truands et petits voyous* (crooks and little yobs), the leadership imposed what it called **impôt revolutionnaire** (revolutionary tax). "Contributors" were notified when their payments were due in the magazine *Ribombu*, mouthpiece of the FLNC's newly formed political wing, **A Cuncolta di i Cumitati Naziunalisti**, or Cuncolta.

With the election of François Mitterrand and his socialist government in 1981, hopes were high that some kind of solution to *le problème corse* might at last be attainable. Corsica was granted its own **Assemblée Régionale** the following year (months ahead of any other region in France), and behind-the-scenes talks were held with the FLNC. Despite this, nationalist attacks continued to spiral, with eight hundred in 1982 alone.

The Pasqua crackdown

The situation seemed to have reached a stalemate by 1985, when Jacques Chirac's Gaullist home affairs minister, **Charles Pasqua**, instigated a crackdown on nationalist activities under the slogan "*Terroriser les terroristes!*" ("Terrorize the terrorists!"). Journalists who didn't tow the government line were purged, overtly nationalist music groups such as I Muvrini were banned and "Wanted" posters stuck everywhere. Suspected FLNC activists were rounded up and tension rose to a new high.

Meanwhile, in a bid for greater respectability, the FLNC declared a **war on drugs**. "*A droga fora!*" replaced anti-French invective as the graffiti writers' preferred slogan, and brutal summary justice awaited anyone identified as a dealer. But the campaign looked to be running out of control when two Tunisian immigrants accused of trafficking were gunned down in January 1986, provoking outrage both on the island and in mainland France.

From this point on, the **bombing of holiday villas** became the FLNC's prime propaganda ploy. Justified by the nationalists' claims that Corsica needed to be protected from foreign "influences" in general and modern architecture in particular, the nationalists' destruction of second homes on the island was, and continues to be, a vote winner. No islanders like to see ugly new buildings appearing along the coast, least of all ones occupied only for a couple of months each year, so when the FLNC reduces them to rubble they are regarded by many Corsicans, even those who may not otherwise support nationalist terrorism, as providing a much-needed service. Of course, house bombing also provides a potent lever with which to extract "revolutionary tax" from holiday-home owners.

Break-up of the FLNC

The late 1980s saw a marked softening of the French government's line on Corsica. With the backing of Mitterrand and his new socialist prime minister, Michel Rocard, home affairs minister **Pierre Joxe** visited the island nineteen times during his tenure. For the first time, recognition of *un peuple corse* (a Corsican people) and special status for the region, such as that enjoyed by former colonies L'Île de la Réunion and Martinique, were mooted.

The FLNC, however, procrastinated about how to respond to the new initiative, paralysed by mounting divisions between its hard- and soft-liners. Joxe began to lose patience as the disputes over his proposals intensified. Eventually, the strain exploded with the departure of one of the Front's key military leaders, **Pierrot Poggioli**, to form a rival nationalist party, L'Accolta Nazionale Corsa, or **ANC**. One of the most respected old guard of the early FLNC era, Poggioli condemned the "Mafia-ization" of the separatist movement and the corrosive effects of "revolutionary tax".

Intelligence reports, meanwhile, hinted at a massive **build-up of arms** in Corsica, but with the nationalists in apparent disarray, an all-out internecine feud rather than an intensification of violence against the state seemed the more likely outcome.

The Ribombu incident

The catalyst for the **break-up of the FLNC**, and the ensuing war between its respective factions, came at the end of 1990. Bastiais hardliners, marshalled by one of Cuncolta's leaders, **Charles Pieri**, tried forcibly to take over the movement's paper and main mouthpiece, **Ribombu**. When its editor realized what was happening, he telephoned the head of Secteur V in Ajaccio, charismatic Aléria veteran **Alain Orsoni**, who immediately travelled north to intervene. The two factions traded insults, but it was Pieri and his men who were left humiliated after Orsoni accused them of betraying FLNC activists while in police custody. The gauntlet had been thrown down.

Ripples from the "*Ribombu* incident" rocked the movement to its grass roots. Within a few months, the FLNC had split into three groups, each with its own political wing. Led by Alain Orsoni, the **MPA** (Mouvement Pour l'Autodétermination) lined up alongside **FLNC-Canal Habituel**, while **Cuncolta** aligned itself with the **FLNC-Canal Historique**. The rogue element in the equation was Pierrot Poggioli's ANC and its small *bras armé* (armed faction), **Resistenza**, which initially sided with the Canal-Historique but would later switch to Orsoni's camp.

The lines were now drawn for a bloody vendetta-like feud. Murders multiplied across the island as activists were picked off in tit-for-tat killings and reprisals, known as *règlements de compte* (settling of scores). Each faction's business interests were also targeted in a protracted bombing campaign.

One of the major flash points in the conflict occurred in May 1995, when the 35-year-old leader of Cuncolta, former primary schoolteacher **François Santoni**, and his friend, Gallo, ran into an ambush while motorcycling on the outskirts of Ajaccio. Gallo was killed in the encounter, but Santoni escaped. The next day, FLNC-Canal Historique vowed to track down all seven members of the hit squad involved, suspected to be from the MPA/FLNC-Canal Habituel. Consequently, the summer of 1995 was the bloodiest in living memory. Fifteen key figures, and dozens of minor activists in the nationalist movement, would be murdered, while those who survived were forced into hiding.

1996: Tralonca and the Bastia bombing

President Chirac and Prime Minister Juppé's public response to the relentless violence in Corsica was to initiate another law-and-order crackdown, declaring that it was "unacceptable for there to be one set of laws for Corsica and another for mainland France". Meanwhile, their junior ministers – as it later transpired – pursued secret negotiations with the terrorist groups, striking deals to secure an uneasy peace.

The most tangible result of these covert talks was the now famous *nuit bleue* at **Tralonca**, near Corte, when, on a freezing January night in 1996, six hundred FLNC-Canal Historique commandos gave a press conference to announce a temporary **ceasefire**. Armed to the teeth with Kalashnikovs, Israeli sub-machine guns, grenades, new flame throwers and AK47s stolen from the UN in Bosnia, the balaclava army presented a chilling photo opportunity for invited journalists. The promised truce, however, didn't last long.

Six months later it was broken in the most dramatic fashion, with the explosion of a **car bomb in Bastia**. The intended target was **Charles Pieri**, Cuncolta's national secretary. Timed to detonate in broad daylight as he was leaving the headquarters of his security firm in the Vieux Port, the device killed one Cuncolta member, Pierre-Louis Lorenzi, and injured fourteen innocent passers-by. Pieri himself sustained extensive injuries, but survived.

This was the first occasion in the history of Corsica's recent troubles that a large bomb had exploded during the day in a busy public place. The prime suspects were Orsoni's MPA/FLNC-Canal Habituel, but they moved swiftly to deny responsibility, raising suspicions that the attack had been an act of "outside provocation". One prominent MPA activist said it was "inconceivable" that such indiscriminate violence could have been perpetrated by Corsican paramilitaries. The finger of blame thus shifted towards the government, or some kind of anti-separatist group.

Contrary to expectations, the Bastia bombing did not spark off a spate of reprisal killings. The possibility that the attack may have been the work of *agents provocateurs* rather than merely another *règlement de compte* seemed to jolt the paramilitaries into realizing the extent to which their factional infighting was playing into the hands of their enemies. For a while, it seemed as if the attack on Pieri might shock the warring wings of the FLNC into another ceasefire.

Apart from costing the paramilitaries dozens of their best men, six years of intense internecine war had left the political process in disarray. No one seemed to know any longer who was negotiating with whom, or why, or what the ultimate aims of the armed struggle were. Part of the problem lay in the fact that many of the sources of conflict back in the early 1970s no longer existed. Since the inauguration of the FLNC, the government had shown itself willing to address the island's problems: two general amnesties had been called, Corsican had been recognized as an official language and the university at Corte resurrected.

Vast sums had also been poured into developing the island, to reduce unemployment and promote a sustainable economy. Corsica today boasts four international airports, eight maritime ports, high-specification trunk roads and ample, inexpensive air and sea links with the mainland, bankrolled by vast handouts from both the EU and national government. Around 500 million euros of direct subsidies and a further 1.32 billion euros of local government funding come to Corsica each year, making it the most heavily subsidized region of Europe. Corsicans are also exempt from social security contributions, and the island as a whole enjoys preferential tax status.

The majority of islanders benefit directly from this special treatment, and from state employment (one third of the total workforce is employed by the government or government-funded local councils), as well as welfare handouts of various kinds. It's hardly surprising, therefore, that public support for independence has gradually diminished over the past two decades. These days only the hardest of hardliners in the movement favour complete secession.

The new pragmatism is most vividly reflected in the agendas of Corsica's myriad nationalist parties, who have consistently polled between 15 and 25 percent of the vote in regional elections. The most moderate among them is the UPC – direct successor to the original autonomist party, the ARC. While the dust was still settling after the Bastia bomb, its annual convention in Aléria set out a list of **key demands** from the French government. These ranged from greater tax-raising and legislative powers for the *assemblée régionale*, to a lower rate of VAT on the island, mandatory teaching of the Corsican language in schools, a special Corsican *carte d'identité* and recognition of *le peuple corse* as a "national minority".

Juppé's revenge

In late 1996, during a period when France's new right-wing Gaullist government was constantly reaffirming its refusal to negotiate with terrorists, an

Manifeste pour la Vie

Among the few local voices courageous enough to speak out against nationalist violence has been that of "Manifeste pour la Vie" ("Demonstrate for Life"), a women's movement launched in Ajaccio in January 1996. One of its founder members was Laetitia Sozzi, whose husband, Robert, a former paramilitary, was shot after denouncing links between the FLNC and corruption in the building industry. At the core of the movement is its rejection of what it calls "the establishment of a system based on terror".

In the late-1990s, Manifeste's demonstrations consistently attracted crowds of thousands – an impressive statistic, given that any woman who marched behind the banner of *"Non à la loi des armes"* ("No to the rule of the gun") knew that by doing so she was opening herself to intimidation from the paramilitaries. Anonymous phone calls, letters and death threats were, and continue to be, directed against Manifeste activists, while Cuncolta's newspaper, *Ribombu*, has several times indulged in vitriolic attacks, subsequently condemned by La Ligue des Droits de l'Homme (League of Human Rights) as "shameful and archaically misogynistic". More recently, the local headquarters of a pro-Manifeste trade union was also sprayed with bullets; another found a bomb outside its Ajaccio office. Such intimidation, however, did not prevent women activists from gathering over 5000 signatures in a petition condemning paramilitary activity – an unprecedented achievement on an island where speaking out against violence is regarded as taboo.

unexpected twist came about when the prime minister himself, Alain Juppé, became embroiled in a scandal after the Cuncolta leader, François Santoni, claimed he had had secret talks with the government.

The most sensational of Santoni's accusations centred on the *nuit bleue* at **Tralonca**, which, he claimed, had been staged with the full connivance of the government. The prime minister had allegedly wanted a big turnout to ensure that the FLNC's rank and file would not later be able to disassociate themselves from the ensuing ceasefire. Juppé vociferously denied the charges, but the mud stuck.

Santoni's revelations had apparently been prompted by the prime minister's orders that participants of the Tralonca *nuit bleue* should be arrested – regarded by the FLNC as a flagrant betrayal of the covert agreement. Soon after, the city hall in Bordeaux, where Juppé is mayor, was bombed, and death threats issued to the French premier. But the FLNC clearly underestimated the prime minister's stomach for a fight. The personal attacks merely seemed to steel Juppé's resolve to defeat the terrorists.

Within a couple of months, he ordered a massive **crackdown** on lawlessness and corruption in Corsica, during which police raids netted all but one of Cuncolta's leaders, including Santoni, who was charged with extortion offences after the owner of the **Sperone golf course**, near Bonifacio, had gone to the police about protection threats he had received. To everyone's amazement, the response from the paramilitaries was muted. The rate of attacks on mainland France dropped, and no general strike was called on the island itself, where there seemed to be a tangible shift in public mood away from the nationalist cause.

The Érignac murder

The general election in June 1997 of a socialist government under **Lionel Jospin** coincided with the announcement by FLNC-Canal Historique of yet another **ceasefire**, this time allegedly to encourage concessions from the new administration. When these failed to materialize, however, the truce was called off and bombings resumed.

Thus it was initially the FLNC-Canal Historique who were to be held responsible for the brutal murder of the French government's most senior representative in Corsica, **Claude Érignac**, gunned down in front of his wife while leaving a classical music concert in Ajaccio on February 6, 1998. The FLNC-Canal Historique, however, surprised everyone by condemning the attack. That no one admitted responsibility for the highest-profile assassination in the island's history was widely regarded as symptomatic of the indiscipline and confusion that had overtaken the separatist struggle.

After a fifteen-month investigation, police arrested eight men but announced that their prime suspect for the murder was a goatherd from Cargèse called **Yvan Colonna**, an activist from one of Corsica's more militant breakaway terrorist groups. Colonna evaded capture for more than five years, hiding out in remote *bergeries*. His eventual capture, on the eve of a major referendum on devolution in 2003 (see p.403), is thought to have been a determining factor in the defeat of the government's proposals.

L'Affaire de la Paillote

The hunt for Érignac's murderer was a top priority for the man sent by Lionel Jospin to replace him. Heralded as an "iron fist" to clean up the island, 53-year-old **Préfet Bernard Bonnet** was a less sympathetic, less diplomatic character than his predecessor who, in his first year as governor, mounted a heavy-handed crackdown on violence, corruption and organized crime: dozens of prominent figures were detained; banks and local development funds investigated for fraud; and several buildings belonging to or built by known mobsters bulldozed.

Such tactics were expected to upset powerful players on the island, so little heed was paid on the Continent to rumours claiming Bonnet – and more specifically the much loathed GPS, an elite squad of paramilitary police which he'd insisted on deploying when he took up office – had stoked the flames of division within the nationalist movement by mounting undercover operations. Such rumours would soon come home to roost in dramatic fashion.

On the night of April 19, 1999, three men wearing black balaclavas landed an inflatable Zodiac on **Cala d'Orzu** beach, on the south side of the Golfe d'Ajaccio (see p.193). They carried with them incendiary devices and jerrycans of fuel, which they used to blow up a shack-restaurant (*paillote*) called *Chez Francis*, leaving behind them a note accusing its owner, Yves Feraud, of being a "cop grass". On an island inured to such attacks, the photos of the resulting destruction might normally have made it onto page three of *Corse-Matin* and then been forgotten. Within days, however, police investigating the crime scene made an extraordinary revelation: articles found amid the débris on the beach (a blood-soaked jacket, an army commando knife and government-issue two-way radios) suggested this was no Mafia or militant separatist attack, but some kind of bungled police operation.

Reaction on the island quickly turned from extreme amusement to indignation and outrage. Nationalists had long claimed the state had been waging a "dirty tricks" campaign and suspicion soon circled on Bonnet and his henchmen. Soon after the firebombing, three GPS agents were arrested. Next to be picked up, to the amazement of the national media, was their boss, **Col Henri Mazares** (Corsica's chief of police), who was promptly charged with arson.

More incriminating revelations followed as the bonfire of "**l'affaire de la paillote**" spread upwards. Mazares eventually admitted his complicity in the attack on *Chez Francis*, but he also insisted he was acting under orders and could prove it. When Bonnet himself was then called in for questioning and held, the nationalist press had a field day: "Bonnets by day – balaclavas by night!" ran one Cuncolta headline.

The préfet denied any involvement to begin with, mounting a brief hunger strike in his VIP Paris prison cell. But as more and more evidence came to light he changed his tune and instead accused the prime minister of masterminding his "judicial and media lynching" as a cover-up for the government's flawed Corsica policies.

Jospin responded by sacking Bonnet, whose arrest he described as "a heavy blow to the state, the Republic, the government and to Corsica". The scandal, however, continued to rear its head throughout the following year as the trials of the various agents and police officials implicated rumbled on. In the end, the disgraced préfet was given a three-year prison sentence. Jospin's credibility, and that of his interior minister, took a huge knock and may well have played a significant part in the socialist government's resounding defeat in the elections of 2002. On the island itself, thousands took to the streets calling for greater autonomy. Having dipped in the late-1990s with the upsurge in FLNC violence and murder of Préfet Érignac, public support for the nationalists' cause was once again on the rise.

The Matignon Accords

To regain some of the ground lost by Bonnet's bungle, Jospin tried a more softly-softly approach over the following eighteen months. Offered as a trade-off for peace, his package of far-reaching devolutionary measures – known as the **Matignon Accords** (discussed in more detail on p.388) – were well received by most nationalists and seemed the best hope for decades of breaking the political deadlock. Even hard-line separatists met with state officials to discuss the portfolio, while the French parliament gave its blessing in a ground-breaking vote.

While these political discussions were being held, the FLNC feud had entered a new and seemingly conclusive phase. At the centre of the power struggle was **François Santoni** – now released from prison after the Sperone golf course scandal – and former Cuncolta national secretary **Charles Pieri** (the activist injured in the Bastia Vieux Port car bombing). The political rivalry between the two men took on a sexual dimension after Pieri became involved with Santoni's former girlfriend, Marie-Hélène Mattei, a nationalist lawyer who'd also served time over the Sperone extortion.

The gloves came off after Pieri took over as head of Cuncolta from his arch adversary. Santoni's revenge was a whistle-blowing book about the FLNC and its corruption by **organized crime**. Co-authored with fellow dissident nation-alist Jean-Michel Rossi, *Pour solde de tout compte* took the form of an extended interview with journalist Guy Benhamou in which the two spilled the beans on the inner workings of the paramilitary groups – the personal feuds, corruption, covert negotiations with the French State and overall lack of ideological direction. By naming names and generally discrediting the FLNC, Rossi and Santoni were breaking the island's age-old, sacred *loi de silence* – the punishment for which they had themselves, by their own admission, meted out in the past.

It was therefore no surprise when, in August 2000, news broke that Rossi and his bodyguard had died in a hail of bullets over their morning coffee outside the *Bar Piscine* on the main square in L'Île Rousse. Pieri could not be connected with the murder, but soon after was imprisoned for "criminal association" and possession of illegal firearms.

Santoni, who by then had formed his own breakaway political group and armed wing (Armata Corsa), must have realized he was living on borrowed time. His revelations, both in *Pour solde de tout compte* and subsequent inter-views in the press, were calculated to create the maximum embarrassment among his enemies. An attempted assassination had nearly succeeded in 1995, and others were bound to follow. "Those who killed Jean-Michel Rossi would like to finish the job with me," he told reporters in the spring of 2001. "I will make headlines soon."

And so indeed he did, on August 17 of that year, when gunmen descended on a wedding he was attending in the south Corsican village of Monaccia-d'Aullène and shot him dead. In Paris, those opposed to Jospin's Matignon Accords seized the incident as a stick with which to beat the prime minister's Corsica policies. His former interior minister, Jean-Pierre Chevènement, who'd resigned over the proposals, claimed the murder emphasized "the illusions on which the Matignon process rests. By giving the priority to a violent minority, which continues its blackmail through terror, the Government has shut itself in a frightening head-to-head encounter with them. The process itself engenders violence."

Pegged to the waning popularity of Jospin and his socialist government, the Matignon talks gradually ground to a halt after key parts of the initiative were watered down. With his resounding defeat at the polls in June 2002, and the inauguration of a more staunchly Republican cabinet opposed to any special treatment for Corsica, any significant breakthrough seemed unlikely. After one of the longest collective ceasefires in the history of the island's armed conflict, car bombs and rocket attacks once again boomed through the streets of Ajaccio at the height of the tourist season.

The referendum and "The trial of nationalist banditry"

The renewed violence, however, seemed only to stiffen the resolve of Chirac and his interior minister, Nicolas Sarkozy, to break the impasse. Within six months of taking office, their government announced a package of **devolutionary proposals** (ironically, based on the Matignon Accords) which it was hoped would end Corsica's problems once and for all. Having set aside his instinctive dislike of devolution, the president was determined the Corsican electorate should realize that this was their golden opportunity for lasting peace.

On the day of the referendum (July 6, 2003), however, the proposals were narrowly defeated. One of the key factors that may have clinched the "no" vote was the arrest the day before of **Yvan Colonna** – the goatherd wanted for the 1998 murder of Claude Érignac. Colonna had been on the run for more than five years by this stage, the object of France's biggest ever manhunt. More than eight million phone calls had been examined, countless locations searched and hundreds of potential sympathizers detained for questioning – to no avail. The big breakthrough eventually came in the winter of 2001, when undercover police started to notice friends and relatives of the suspect switching off their mobiles before making odd trips into the maquis – presumably so as to remain untraceable. Finally, some two years later, after staking out more than two hundred remote *bergeries* on the island, police suspicions that their man was hiding out bandit-style in the maquis, rather than in the South American rainforest or on the mainland, as many had believed, were borne out when an infrared camera hidden in a stone hut outside Porto-Pollo picked up an image of a man fitting Colonna's description.

If his arrest was meant to reassure a hesitant electorate that, in spite of its support for a pro-devolutionary "yes" vote the government had no intention of getting soft on terrorism, it backfired badly. Instead, many Corsicans reacted with indignation, feeling the whole affair had been stage-managed to fool them into siding with the government, and reacted by voting "no" instead.

While Colonna and those accused of sheltering him awaited trial in Flery-Marogin prison outside Paris, Corsica slipped into a period of troubled uncertainty. With no fresh ideas to loosen the political deadlock, government efforts to resolve the island's problems were focused again on its law and order issues – specifically, corruption and extortion.

The change of tack by Paris soon bore fruit. Its first high-profile casualty was **François Nicolai**, president of Bastia's premiership football club, SCB. A representative of one of the club's main sponsors (the French high-street tour operator, Nouvelles Frontières) claimed he had been forced by Nicolai to sign a £300,000-per-year protection deal to halt "nationalist bombings" of the firm's offices in Corsica and on the mainland. The ensuing investigation showed that under Nicolai's direction, SCB had been used as a front for many other extortion rackets and frauds. Twenty-one suspects were rounded up altogether – among them no less than **Charles Pieri**, the FLNC-UC's group commander and principal fundraiser, and his daughter, Elodie – and charged with extortion, misappropriation of funds, financing terrorisim, and associating with criminals related to a terrorist organization. The FLNC-UC responded by declaring an end to their eighteen-month ceasefire: a major bombing campaign erupted, and on March 11, 2005, five people (including two babies) were injured by flying glass when a bomb exploded outside the Public Works Depot in Ajaccio.

"**The trial of nationalist banditry**", as Bastia's chief prosecutor billed it, unveiled for the first time in court the kind of nationalist-separatist corruption described by Rossi and Santoni in *Pour solde de tout compte*. Pieri was alleged to have set up a dodgy security firm who had paid its employees to carry out bomb attacks on clients. He had also run a nonexistent "cleaning company" (numbering SCB among its customers), through which millions of euros of illicit money bound for the paramilitary movement had been laundered. Much of the cash had also ended up in Pieri and Nicolai's own pockets, spent on flashy cars and boats. At the end of the five-month trial, Charles Pieri was found guilty and sentenced to ten years in prison. His associates were sent down for similarly long stretches. The FLNC-UC, meanwhile, intensified its attacks.

From January 2006, French-owned holiday homes became the new target of nationalist ire – a ploy always guaranteed to garner support for the island's nationalist paramilitaries. By the following year up to ten villas per week were being blown up by the FLNC's various factions. Although generally supported by Corsicans, the campaign has done little to depress house prices – its stated aim.

Prospects for peace

At the time of writing, in late 2008, the prospects of Corsica's paramilitaries renouncing the armed struggle seem as distant as they have at any point in the past 25 years. Few would deny that the French State, while lavishing funds and tax exemptions on the island, has failed to devise an effective and lasting economic strategy. But this does not explain why so many initiatives by a string of successive administrations have failed, nor why violence continues to be the island's predominant response to its political differences with the motherland.

To understand the real roots of *le problème corse* you have to look to Corsica's traditional culture. As Nicolas Giudici, one of the most respected commentators on the troubles, has pointed out, "Corsica is an ancient Mediterranean society, convinced of the legitimacy of its ways of doing things – which means factions, clans, infighting and vendettas."

Compounding the persistence of clannism in Corsica is the fact that nowadays the potential pickings of patronage and corruption are richer than ever before. Since 1994, billions of euros have poured in from the EU, to augment the 500 million euros of state subsidies the island receives each year and the 1.5 billion euros of funding for its bloated bureaucracy. "The vast proportion of (this money)", admitted a government report in 2002, has been "misappropriated" by corrupt mayors and paramilitary movements.

The trial of Pieri also underlined how far **organized crime** has taken over the nationalist movement, which these days seems less dominated by political ideology and visions of a better future than by the macho, violent culture of the island's past. Adherence to the old ways, however, is not going to be relinquished overnight on an island where clan rivalries and mistrust of government are firmly rooted, nor where anyone who openly opposes the paramilitaries effectively risks their life.

Corsican wildlife

The **Parc Naturel Régional de la Corse**, established in 1972, now embraces about a third of Corsica, largely down the mountain spine but reaching the sea in the northwest. Managing important sites such as Scandola, the Restonica Valley, the Finocchiarola isles in the north and the Îles Lavezzi in the south, the park authorities ensure the survival of the mouflon and other endangered species, and increase the accessibility of the wildlife of Corsica, through the publication of excellent books and booklets and through the maintenance of footpaths. The ruggedness of Corsica's heartland naturally restricts intensive exploitation, but even in areas where human intervention has occurred the island's terrain is extraordinarily rich. The lush chestnut woodland of the Castagniccia, for example, is the result of plantation, and the tangled, headily scented maquis which clothes more than half of Corsica might seem a natural cover, but is in fact what comes in after fire or on abandoned grazing land.

The habitat zones

Corsica's landscape has three well-defined **habitat zones**, the lowest of which is the Mediterranean zone, which runs from the sea to an altitude of 1000m. Corsica is noted for its clean seas and varied marine life. At places along the coast you'll find pristine sand dunes, lagoons and estuaries, all three of which are now hard to find elsewhere in the Mediterranean. Trees sometimes grow right at the edge of the beach: the highly resinous **Aleppo pine** prefers rocky ground at this level, while the **stone pine** (or umbrella pine) is often seen growing singly but sometimes in groves – some of the best specimens are at Palombaggia beach near Porto Vecchio. Stands of tall Australian **eucalyptus** can also be found in many places, planted in the late eighteenth century to rid localities such as Porto, in the northwest, of malaria.

However, the typical indicator of the Mediterranean climate is the **olive tree**. Solitary specimens can be found everywhere in Corsica's Mediterranean zone (the oldest giant is near the deserted convent below Oletta at the foot of Cap Corse), while the largest groves are in the Balagne and near Propriano. At these lower altitudes erect "funeral" cypresses are often planted alongside family tombs. Three species of oak also identify this zone – the **cork oak** (its trunk dusky red when newly stripped), the evergreen **holm oak** (which has spiny leaves on sucker shoots and is found in both shrub and tree forms) and the **kermes oak** (rarely tree-sized, and with holly-like leaves).

Introduced shrubs and trees that thrive in this Mediterranean climate include **orange** and **lemon** in groves and gardens, red or purple **bougainvillea** in gardens, **palms** in town squares, pink and white **oleanders** and the gigantic cactus-like **Mexican agave** on roadsides.

Another characteristic of the Mediterranean zone is that the **maquis** springs up after fire or when fields or open grazings are abandoned. Its most easily recognized plants are the shrubs of the **cistus** family, carrying pink or white flowers with crumpled petals, which are shed at the end of each day. Some cistus have highly scented gummy stems and leaves – the Montpellier cistus, which likes acid granite soils and has masses of small white flowers, is perhaps the most fragrant of all. Cistus bushes often indicate open, newish maquis, which in time will grow into an all-but-impenetrable scrub, with yellow-flowered **brooms** (some of which are wickedly thorny), the taller **strawberry tree** (the red strawberry-like fruits are edible but pappy), the pungent **mastic** and **myrtle**, **rosemary** and white-flowered **tree heather**, which grows 2m tall or more. In the "tall" maquis, cork, holm oaks and other trees come in, and as their crowns broaden they begin to shade out the shrubs below them, until eventually woodland or forest results.

Towards the top of the Mediterranean zone these trees might be joined by **maritime pine**, which unusually keeps large cones of different ages on its branches, and it retains those branches even when they are starkly dead – the Restonica Valley has many examples. **Sweet chestnut** also makes an appearance (it is most widespread between 500m and 800m), as does bracken. Groves of ancient chestnuts can be found near most of the hill villages, where the production of chestnut flour used to play an important part in the economy. Nowadays the chestnuts are given over to pigs (and pâtisseries), and many of the trees display dead, antler-like branches as a result of attacks of mildew and parasites.

At around 1000m, the **mountain zone** succeeds, as oaks and chestnuts give way to forests of the native, tall-trunked **Laricio** (or Corsican) **pine**, perhaps mixed with **beeches** and **firs**. The Aïtone, Valdo-Niello, Bonifato and Tartagine are among the most magnificent of these forests, featuring centuries-old Laricio pines reaching up to 40m that are the tallest conifers in Europe.

Above 2000m stretches the **alpine zone** – open and largely rocky, perhaps with scatters of ground-hugging bushy alders, and often with a wonderful variety of flowers.

Wild flowers

Many Corsican plants are distinctive of the island – of the 2000 species of **wild flowers** found here, eight percent are native to Corsica or shared only by Corsica and Sardinia. Which species you'll see will depend on the soil, the bedrock, the altitude and, of course, the time of year. Spring is glorious, with wild flowers everywhere, and many species celebrate a "second spring" after the summer drought: **cyclamens** and **autumn crocus** appear with the autumn rains, for example, and the handsome **bush spurges** of Cap Corse are in vivid green leaf in winter and spring, but reduced to bare twigs in summer.

Flowers of the Mediterranean zone

On the seashore in summer, the dramatic **yellow-horned poppy** is worth looking for, with its very long curved seed pods. Colourful **sea stocks** and **sea lavender** grow on shingle and on rocks, where carpets of **stonecrop** – with fleshy red leaves and heads of small blue flowers – also make a handsome showing. The **sea holly**, one of the most beautiful of all wild plants with its grey-green spiny leaves and blue flower heads, sometimes forms low mats a couple of metres across – you'll see it on the open sands at Cargèse, for example. Here and at the back of other sandy beaches you can also find the white **sea daffodil** flowering in August, and almost anywhere you might come across carpets of **Hottentot fig**, with its brilliant lilac or yellow-orange flowers.

In spring, various wild flowers brighten the clearings among the colourful **maquis** shrubs. If the maquis is invading old grazing land, or if the open patch is overgrazed and impoverished, there will probably be **asphodel** growing; its delicate white flowers are withered husks by summer, although the tall spikes remain. Many of Corsica's fifty or so species of **wild orchid** flower in the maquis: one of the most handsome is the pink **butterfly orchid**, and there are always a good number of the unmistakeable hooded **serapias** group, which are purple or dark red. French **lavender** is common, its small, almost black flowers carried below striking purple sails, and in some areas wild **gladiolus** can be seen along the roads or even as a weed in the ploughed fields – it has smaller flowers than the garden hybrids but is easily recognizable.

The verges and rocky cuttings of roads and lanes through the maquis and between the fields are home to **wild pinks** (some of the mountain pinks are endemic to the island), **ferns**, **honeysuckle** and **eglantine** (a wild white rose looking rather like cistus). Wild **asparagus** is often found growing around the olive groves, while in spring **tassel hyacinths** and white **Florentine iris**, the original fleur-de-lis, flower on open soil (the iris is also popular in gardens).

Flowers of the mountain and alpine zones

In the chestnut woods and amongst the pines of the mountain zone grow the handsome green tufts of the **Corsican hellebore**, a poisonous species endemic to Corsica and Sardinia. **Foxgloves** may be found here, and in spring scatters of **cyclamen** mix with **violets** along the stream-sides, together with hosts of delicate white or lilac **anemones** in some areas. **Autumn crocus** and **squill** also flower here and elsewhere towards the end of the year. Wherever you find beech trees at this height, you might look for wild red **peony**.

Although the mountain zone is harsh, there can be a surprising variety of flowers when the snow melts, many of them endemic – indeed, half of those you see might grow only in Corsica and Sardinia, such as a Corsican alpine groundwort and a blue mountain columbine. And many common enough in the Alps are not found here, suggesting that these two islands separated from mainland Europe at a far-distant time in the past.

Birds

As a result of the closed breeding of its resident island populations, Corsica's **birds** often display certain differences from those of mainland Europe. Songbirds such as the blackbird have a song that's distinct from that of related European species, and the birds' normal habitats are in many instances extended in some way. In Corsica the blackbird ranges from coastal maquis to the high mountains, while the explosive "chetti" call of the small brown **Cetti's warbler** is heard not only in the reed beds around the coastal lagoons but also in the maquis up to 500m. The most-renowned Corsican example is the elusive **Corsican nuthatch** of the Aïtone and other high pine forests. The **treecreeper** is another, while there are also forms of **great spotted woodpecker** and **wren** shared with Sardinia. Corsica is the place to add the **Dartford warbler** to your list – it is a localized and rare resident in the south of Britain; here it is common in the coastal maquis but as a darker, smaller subspecies.

Because of its position, Corsica is probably visited by the majority of trans-Mediterranean **migrants**, many of which make landfalls on the headlands or lagoons. The **spring** and **autumn** list includes common and curlew sandpiper (the latter is the commonest migrant wader here), reed bunting, marsh and Montague's harriers, pied flycatcher, grey heron, black kite and tree pipit. Of the birds that come to **winter** on the island, the sparrow-like dunnock is one of the commonest in the maquis, and amongst the other regulars are snipe, cormorant, common starling, gannet, pochard, tufted duck, teal, black-necked grebe, redwing and song thrush. Others such as the wood pigeon are resident, but numbers swell in winter, when incomers fly in to gorge on the plentiful crops of acorns.

Seabirds and wetland species

In general most **coastal birdlife** is centred on remote headlands and islands. Scandola, for example, has osprey, peregrine, rock dove and blue rock thrush (which also nest on bare slopes inland to 1800m). Shearwaters nest in some places, but you'll see fewer **gulls** than you might expect. Herring gulls nest at Scandola and Capo Rossu and other remote sites, and you may spot the Mediterranean gull (black-headed in summer) and the slim-winged Audouin's gull, which nest on several offshore islands. Shags, too, nest on rocky shores and are often seen flying low over the sea.

Despite widespread drainage for vineyards, fruit and other crops, the string of lagoons off the east coast remains one of the most extensive wetland units of the whole Mediterranean, attracting great crested and little **grebes**, pochard and mallard, and the water rail with its incredible pig-like cry. Reed, moustached, Cetti's and other **warblers** call from the reed beds, while marsh harrier and hobby hunt across them. In winter, Biguglia and the other lagoons are an important station for ducks, grey heron, wintering kingfisher and others.

Maquis species

The **maquis** in its various forms offers ideal nesting for **warblers** and birds such as red-backed shrike, pipits, buntings and even the highly colourful bee-eater. The **linnet** picks out more open areas, as does the **stonechat** and the red-legged **partridge** (the grey has been introduced for shooting in some places). These birds all follow the maquis as it spreads up the valleys and slopes inland, but where it grows tall and is invaded by holm oak and other trees (as seen in the Fango Valley, for example) the scrub warblers such as Dartford and Sardinian leave, while the blackcap and subalpine remains. Being evergreen, the maquis maintains its insect larder in winter, when many of its resident birds are joined by migrant cousins.

Kestrel and buzzards (widespread but nowhere very common) patrol above the maquis, as does red kite, which prefers the lower scrubby maquis to the taller growth. At night the clear, bell-like notes of the **Scops owl** and the call of the nightjar echo across the maquis, mingling with the constant croaking of frogs.

The chestnut groves are comparatively empty of birdlife, but look for the endemic **treecreeper** here, and also the **mistle thrush** and the **wryneck**, the last now rare almost everywhere.

Mountain species

In the **mountain** and alpine levels, grey wagtail and dipper forage in the spray of the torrents, where the crag martin is often seen as well. The pine forests have **goldcrest**, **coal tit** and the endemic **nuthatch** – this last, found from the Tartagine in the north to Ospédale in the south, is smaller than its mainland cousins and is more often heard than seen. Sparrowhawk and goshawk have a presence in these pine woods, as does the crossbill.

A feature of some parts of the **high mountains** is *pozzines* – small tablelands of peaty turf cut by meandering streams. Here **lark** and **wheatear** are often seen, with even blackbird and chaffinch if there are scrubby alders for cover. The blue rock thrush, though nesting on the coast at Scandola and elsewhere, can be met as high as 1500m. The central mountains are the domain of the yellow-beaked **alpine chough** and the rare **lammergeier** and **golden eagle**. Bonelli's eagle is reported from the Asco Valley, but it is not known if it nests.

Garden species

Gardens attract many birds, such as blackbird, warblers, hooded crow and turtle dove – the latter are widely shot when they fly in in spring, but there are always some to be heard in summer. (The collared dove is a recent colonist and still uncommon.) Gardens also attract the spotted flycatcher – the Corsican form scarcely lives up to its name, with few if any speckles, but it is quickly recognized by its lively fly-catching sorties, usually returning to the same post. In the Nebbio and a few other spots, the **hoopoe** (with its dramatic crest) is also seen in gardens at dawn. The towns attract **house martin** and **swifts** – both the familiar Eurasian swift and the similar pallid swift.

Mammals

Woodmouse, shrew, rabbit, brown hare, weasel and hedgehog are as familiar in Corsica as elsewhere in Europe, but there are no squirrels. Squirrel-like nests in shrubs or low trees may be those of the black rat, while a sighting of a small brownish animal with squirrel-like bushy tail would be the **fat dormouse**, though it is shy and nocturnal. The slimmer **garden** (or **oak**) **dormouse**, with white underside to body and tail, is also resident. Both these animals may search houses for a hibernation den in autumn, and you often hear them scratching around in the attic. Bats are common everywhere: in the gorge of the Bonifato forest behind Calvi, for example, they swarm out at sunset.

The fox is seen, and there are reports of a wild cat in remote parts of the island such as the Aïtone Forest – it may turn out to be a tribe of striped feral cat, domestic stock now living wild. There are similar indecisive reports of pine marten in these forested areas.

Around five hundred **mouflon** – a wild sheep, the males sporting massive curved horns – are found in two main areas: at Asco and at Bavella. They might be the relic of an original wild population that began to be domesticated in Neolithic times, or they may be the descendants of escapees from those first domestic flocks.

The **sanglier** (wild boar) is found throughout the maquis and in the lower mountains, and has something of a cult status in Corsica. Many villages organize weekly hunts over the winter, culling an estimated 10,000 each year from an average population of 30,000. Even though the males are smaller than their continental cousins, the Corsican boar can still reach 80kg, and is a formidable animal, being armed with tusks for rooting and grubbing – you'll come across the disturbed ground during walks in the maquis. It is a Corsican habit to let domestic **pigs** roam free in the chestnut and beech woods on the mountain flanks, so there is certainly interbreeding between boar and pig, yet about forty percent of the wild-boar stock remains untainted.

The native **red deer** – the smallest of all red deer – became extinct only a few decades ago, but some Sardinian stock can be seen in a paddock near Quenza in the south, from where they are released into the surrounding forest.

A checklist of wildlife sites

Forests

Aïtone Magnificent specimens of Laricio pine; in the remoter reaches (towards Monte Cinto), wild boar, eagle and mouflon. See p.162.

Bavella Impressive though fire-damaged hunting reserve; chance of sightings of mouflon and eagle. See p.229.

Bonifato Classic "chaos" of rocks and forest, pines and maquis. See p.139.

Castagniccia Chestnut woods. See p.276.

Ospédale Pines and other trees. See p.261.

Tartagine Bat caves and magnificent pines. See p.138.

Valdo-Niolo The largest of the island's forests, with fine examples of Laricio pine. See p.301.

Vizzavona Some of the finest pines and beech. See p.317.

Other wildlife zones

Vallee de l'Asco Possible sightings of mouflon, eagle, lammergeier; Corsican nuthatches can also be sighted amid the Laricio and maritime pine forest at the head of the valley. See p.293.

Biguglia and the east coast lagoons Birdlife. See p.70.

Bonifacio Limestone cliffs with rare flowers. See p.242.

Calanches de Piana Flowers and coastal birds. See p.154.

Cap Corse Remote maquis, good for birds (maybe eagles attracted by remoteness); nature reserve on Finocchiarola isles. See p.71.

Désert des Agriates A largish area of thin maquis growing on rocky, impoverished terrain; good for flowers and nesting birds. See p.98.

Fango Valley Good walking through mix of maquis and forest habitats. See p.140.

Îles Lavezzi Nature reserve off Bonifacio. See p.251.

Niolo Alpine choughs and other mountain birds. See p.297.

Restonica Corsican and maritime pine. See p.312.

Scandola Supreme nature reserve of international importance; classic lava-column geology; osprey and other birds; marine life. See p.153.

Offshore, the common and striped **dolphins** and the common **porpoise** patrol, if no longer as regularly or in the numbers that were once seen. The endangered monk seal of the Mediterranean was last seen in Corsican waters in 1982. The **fin whale**, however, is often seen with young off Cap Corse in springtime.

Reptiles and insects

Corsica's hot rocky landscape suits reptiles, and **lizards** are always seen scuttling across walls and rocks. The **Tyrrhenian wall lizard** is a sometimes abundant species found only in Corsica and Sardinia, and the mountain lizard is also endemic, but their variable colouring makes identification of lizard species difficult. Their cousins, the plump but flattened **geckos**, are most often noticed high on room walls and ceilings, which they patrol after sunset, dealing with mosquitoes and other irritations.

There are no poisonous snakes on the island. The **grass snake** is seen in damp places, while the **whip snake** – a slender snake often with a barred pattern – is found on sunny hillsides and other dry habitats. It will attempt to bite if annoyed – its French name is *coléreuse*, "quick-tempered one".

Hermann's tortoise used to be a common sight, but its numbers have dwindled dramatically over the past decade because of forest fires, habitat destruction and competition from aggressive, non-native Florida turtles. To reverse the trend, two centres for tortoise breeding and release have been created: one near Ajaccio (see p.173), and one at Moltifao in central Corsica (see p.294). The European pond **terrapin** might be seen in secluded pools and other still waters that have overgrown banks.

Endemic to the island is the **brook salamander**, olive-grey and brown and with a clear yellow stripe down its spine, found near running water up to 2000m. The rather larger **fire salamander**, with dramatic black and yellow skin, might also be seen.

Most piercingly vocal are the **edible frog** and the **common tree frog**, which has enormous vocal sacs for its small size. The **green toad**, with spotted green and white skin and shrill warbling call, is also reasonably common.

The frog chorus takes over from the summer daytime chorus of the **cicadas**, especially loud in the vicinity of their favourite umbrella pines. The cicadas are just one of a host of grasshoppers, bushcrickets, beetles, bees and **butterflies** that make Corsica so fascinating for anyone with any interest in natural history. Some butterflies will be familiar from northern Europe, such as the migrant painted lady and the red admiral. Of the Mediterranean species, one of the most handsome is the large and strong **two-tailed pasha**, which feeds on the strawberry tree of the maquis. **Hummingbird hawk moths** of various kinds are commonly seen in gardens, hovering in front of the flowers.

Damselflies and mayflies are a common sight dancing over the streams, and the dramatic and fierce **hawker dragonflies** – a birdwatcher's insect if ever there was one – may spend the day hunting across the maquis, far from water.

Geoffrey Young

Corsican music: "Les Polyphonies Corses"

Powerful and mysterious, the spiralling harmonies of **Corsican polyphony** are redolent of both the island's dramatic landscapes and the deep-rooted pride and passion that have always made its inhabitants a people apart. Popularity waned by the end of World War II, however today *polyphonies* are increasingly widespread, strengthening the identity on an island whose struggle for greater autonomy with the French State still erupts into periodic violence.

Polyphonic roots

"It was like hearing a voice from the depths of the earth; a song from the dawn of time; from a beginning that one never dares believe is accessible." So wrote Dorothy Carrington in 1948, after her first encounter with Corsican polyphony. Invited to attend Mass on Christmas Eve at a remote village in the mountains, she was enthralled when, instead of the organ music she expected, otherworldly a cappella singing swelled through the little Baroque chapel. In its counterpoint of familiar cadences with heavily ornamented, improvised harmonies, she discerned traces of Genoan madrigal, Gregorian plainchant, the call of an Arab *muzzein*, Roman liturgy and, just below the surface, something wild and strange resonating from the pit of Corsica's pre-Christian past.

Dorothy Carrington's first taste of polyphony came at a time when the form was on the verge of extinction, practised only by a scattering of old men in poor granite villages depopulated by two world wars and mass out-migration. In more prosperous times, when the island's olive groves and chestnut forests fed a thriving export market, polyphony accompanied most aspects of life. Shepherds sang to while away long evenings in lonely *bergeries*; farmers sang to the rhythms of the threshing circle; and everyone listened to polyphony in church, where Mass was traditionally sung by the men standing close together in the tight circle in front of the altar, with their eyes closed and hands cupped over their ears.

What really set the island's singing tradition apart was its unique sound, best exemplified by that most Corsican of forms, the **paghjella**. Death and separation were generally the inspiration for this profane song style, charged with strong emotions of love, loss and lament. *Paghjellas* are traditionally sung in three parts: the *seconda* leads the melody, joined soon after by the anchor notes of the *bassu*, delivered in a more plain style; over the top of these, the *terza* adds a complex counterpoint of fluctuating notes, much embellished and with a slight drag, or *ribuccata*, setting it apart. The staggered entries and overall absence of a strict meter mean these elements swirl around each other, occasionally drifting into dissonant overlaps that sound very foreign indeed to the Occidental ear.

Sacred Corsican song, such as would be heard in the island's churches and monasteries, tended to be more formal and in Latin, though elements of *paghjella* style (and Corsican lyrics) inevitably crept in (generally in proportion to how far into the mountains the Mass was performed). At major religious festivals – saints' days or the processions of hooded penitents which mark

Easter in many Corsican towns – the singing was performed (and still is) by lay brotherhoods, or **cunfraternitia**.

Cunfraternitia also provided the musical accompaniment for funerals. But at the wake afterwards, a single female relative would sometimes sing a **voceru**, its time marked by the stamping of feet or thump of gun buts on floorboards. If the deceased was a victim of a vendetta murder (an all too common occurrence in Corsica until well into the twentieth century), the improvised dirge would become a searing incantation whose verses not only registered the pain of bereavement but also the urgency of revenge, aimed at spurring the surviving men to retribution.

A third type of song, known as **chiami e rispondi** ("questions and answers"), took the form of a competition in which two male contestants had to improvise a dialogue (usually of ritualized insults) in strictly rhyming verse. They could sing about anything, but it was popular to aim abuse at the assembled company or else declaim about political issues. Agricultural fairs, such as **Santa di u Niolu** in the Niolu Valley, were – and remain – the main stages for this peculiarly Corsican genre.

The Riacquistu

Even long before the two world wars decimated Corsica's rural population, the days of the island's singing tradition were numbered. Realizing this, a pair of musicologists dedicated their careers to recording those polyphony singers and songs that survived in the island's remotest villages. The work of the first, folklorist **Austin de Croze**, went largely unnoticed when it was published around 1900. But thanks to phonographic and radio technology, field recordings made between 1948 and 1963 by one **Félix Quilici** enabled, for the first time, authentic polyphony to reach audiences whose only exposure to Corsican music had hitherto been garishly dressed folk troupes in the variety theatres of Paris.

However, public reaction to Quilici's compilations on 78rpm and later broadcasts for Radiodiffusion France was far from positive, veering from scepticism to xenophobia, and eventually – on the island itself – naked embarrassment. "Ah, nos pauvres oreilles!" ("Our poor ears!") declared one critic; "Que vont penser de nous les continaux?" ("What will the continentals think of us?") wondered another. All the same, Quilici's archive would prove a musical gospel for later generations.

One of the groups featured most prominently in it was a trio from Tagliu village led by *seconda* **Ghjuliu (Jules) Bernadini** (whose sons would go on to become Corsica's most commercially successful musical export, I Muvrini). But it was the famous broadcast of one of Bernadini's own compositions, *Lettr'a fritellu* (Letter to my brother) – written to mark the political imprisonment of a friend in 1974 – which is widely credited with first coupling polyphony with **nationalist politics**.

Throughout the 1970s, resentment at France's economic neglect of the island, and the way Corsica's language and culture had been suppressed, gradually coalesced into a fully fledged nationalist movement. Big rallies were held in Bastia and Ajaccio in which groups singing patriotic songs and old-style polyphony became an essential feature. None turned in more emotive performances than **U Cantu U Populu Corsu** ("The Corsican People Sing"), a bearded array of young radicals in flared jeans who were eventually banned by the French state for associating with the armed struggle then being waged by the paramilitary FLNC (Fronte di Liberazione Naziunale di a Corsica).

Others stepped in to take their place, however, and by the end of the decade, polyphony was not only synonymous with nationalist politics, but also cool again. Whereas the Bernadini boys used to practise secretly up in their village to avoid being teased at *lycée* in Bastia, by the early 1980s they were centre stage in a movement to reclaim the island's traditional culture, a movement dubbed the "**Riacquistu**".

Tradition versus evolution

An unwieldy ensemble of around thirty individuals, U Cantu U Populu Corsu fragmented after recording nine albums, its key members heading off to pursue their own musical agendas. At the root of the split were disagreements between the "traditionalists", who wanted to adhere closely to the old repertoire and singing styles, and the "evolutionists", who wanted to spread their musical wings. To some extent, this debate has dogged the island's music ever since. Mixing polyphony with other forms or styles, even the use of modern instruments, is seen by some hardliners as a kind of betrayal. It explains why, in their album cover notes and interviews, Corsican artists are always at pains to reaffirm the importance of their roots, even while departing radically from them – hence the all but mandatory inclusion of the Corsican "national anthem", **Dio vi salvi Regina**, and some visual reference to the **Corsican flag**, the Moor's head (see p.392).

One of the original Cantu members who has largely followed the traditional path is **Jean-Paul Poletti**. After completing formal music studies across the Tyrrhenian Sea in Florence, he returned to Sartène, famous for its blood feuds and granite tower-houses, to form the **Chœur d'Hommes de Sartène** and, later, a dedicated polyphony school. The choir's perfectly drilled harmonies provide a beautiful underscore for Poletti's powerful, operatic tenor voice, and their recordings are justifiably considered some of the most polished and pure to date.

At the opposite end of the island in the Balange region, another attempt to research and revive traditional Corsican music is a project called **E Voce di u Commune**, based in the pretty *village perchée* of Pigna. An association of instrument makers and musicians, the group not only refined regional polyphony but also the making and playing of local instruments, including the Corsican lute-like *cetera* (a type of cittern), the *pifana* (an aerophone made from a goat's horn) and *cialamella* (a kind of crude reed instrument), all of which had disappeared long before Quilici's field recordings were made. The results can be heard on the albums of the village ensemble, **A Cumpagnia**, and at the annual **Festivoce** music festival, held at the height of the *grandes vacances* in August.

While many singers and groups still do stick staunchly to traditional polyphony, most have at some point dabbled with other idioms. Among them is Poletti's erstwhile Cantu partner, **Petru Guelfucci**, a part-time beekeeper from the village of Sermano near Corte, whom many regard as "the other" *plus belle voix corse*. One of the founder members of the traditional ensemble **Voce di Corsica**, Guelfucci has paid his dues to old-school polyphony, but has tended since towards more mainstream French *chanson*, recording covers of Brel, Brassens and Ferré classics. Despite some success on the Continent (and, more improbably, in Quebec, where he briefly became a top-selling artist), his career has never reached the heights of that other great Corsican *chansonnier*, **Tino Rossi**, whose warblings made him a household name in France in the 1930s.

The other main Cantu spin-off was the group **Chjami Aghalesi**, a core of around fifteen singers who started out with the old repertoire, but soon began experimenting with original material and different musical styles (notably South American). They were also the first all-male group to record with women, collaborating with Patrizia Poli and the Nouvelles Polyphonies Corses (see p.418). Their greatest hour, however, was a cover version of Luis Llach's song "L'Estacos", re-dubbed "Catena" ("Chains"), which became a nationalist rallying cry in the elections of 1992.

Another outfit which began life as a conventional polyphony choir but has since evolved into something much more distinctive is **A Filetta** ("The Fern"). Under the direction of the masterful **Jean-Claude Acquaviva**, they first attracted attention performing at the Easter Passion performances in Calenzana through the 1980s, then went on to carve out an international career recording ambient movie scores (including the soundtrack of Eric Valli's hit docupic, *Himalaya*).

Girl power and beyond

Polyphony has always been regarded as a male domain in Corsica. It was acceptable for women in traditional society to sing at home, and perhaps at funerals, but certainly not in front of the altar. Only in 1992 were such attitudes challenged head on when the all-woman polyphony group **Donnisulana** released a traditional album, *Per Agata*, of spine-tingling brilliance, silencing in an instant the boys-only brigade with its emotional intensity and harmonic precision. Made as a memorial to a mutual friend, *Per Agata* brought together the finest female voices on the island, including the internationally famous mezzo-soprano, **Jacky Micaelli**.

Its triumph coincided with the arrival on the scene of another (predominantly) female group, **Les Nouvelles Polyphonies Corses** (NPC). From the outset, NPC were flamboyantly unconventional. With back-up from traditionalist Jean-Paul Poletti on the one hand, and experimental collaborators such as Hector Zazou, John Cale and Patti Smith on the other, they took polyphony into hitherto unimagined realms, laying it over electronically generated keyboard washes, Georgian choirs, Moroccan oud riffs and flamenco percussion – to great effect. As the **Trio Soledonna**, they've continued to evolve their sound with bolder compositions backed by a broad canvas of musical inspiration from across the globe.

In purely commercial terms, however, no Corsican group has hit the big time quite like cross-over maestros **I Muvrini**. The two "Little Mountain Sheep" from Tagliu, sons of the great Ghjuliu (Jules) Bernadini, were the first to effectively combine the traditional Corsican polyphony learned from the older generation with electric guitars, synths, bass and drums. French folk instruments (accordion, hurdy gurdy and bagpipes) also feature in the mix, overlayed by soaring harmonies and Corsican lyrics typically recalling forgotten places and ways of life. It's a sound that's unlikely ever to break into UK or US World Music markets, but the Muvrinis play sellout stadium gigs across France and Germany. Moreover, their success is a source of considerable pride on the island, encouraging a new wave of Corsican groups to experiment with their musical inheritance.

Discography

CD racks in music stores and supermarkets on the island tend to be dominated by compilations of forgettable Corsican schmaltz and I Muvrini albums, but you can usually track down some quality polyphony if you dig around. If all else fails, search ⓦ www.amazon.co.uk or www.amazon.fr, where you'll find most of our recommendations available through secondhand dealers.

Compilations

L'Âme Corse (Auvidis, France). An excellent all-rounder from Corsica's chief label, featuring the pick of the island's living vocal talent. You also get a couple of unusual instrumental tracks thrown in – all recorded to high standards.

Corsica/Sardinia (WDR/World Network, Germany). Members of Cantu and A Filetta teamed up in 1995 to record eight well-known hymns and a *paghjella* for this compilation, which also includes a couple of tracks from Donnisulana's benchmark album *Per Agata*. Not the most inspiring of selections, but the only one offering polyphony from both Corsica and Sardinia.

A Filetta

One of only two professional choirs on the island, A Filetta infuse traditional polyphony with a wonderfully dark edge. Collaborations with film score composer Bruno Coulais (*Himalaya*; *The Chorus*) have brought them international acclaim and enough clout (and budget) to experiment with both radical a cappella and lush orchestral arrangements.

Intantu (Olivi Music). A state-of-the-art album, both in terms of its vocal performances and choice of material. The songs cover the full gamut of forms, ranging from an old-style *paghjella* to gut-wrenching political *lamenti* penned during the *riacquistu*, plus a handful of the group's trademark modern compositions. Polyphony at its most versatile, lyrical and powerful.

Jacky Micaelli

Widely held to be the finest living female vocalist on the island, mezzo-soprano Jacky Micaelli has always included traditional Corsican a cappella in her repertoire, and her involvement with Donnisulana lent a gravitas to the group which helped female singers break through insular chauvinism.

Corsica Sacra (Auvidis). Pure polyphony, accompanied by intimate trios of male and female voices. The arrangements of both old and original compositions are beautifully stark, allowing the full expressiveness of Micaelli's voice to shine through.

I Muvrini

As I Muvrini, Bernadini brothers Jean-François and Alain have become a national institution. In the early 1990s, their trademark mix of polyphonic vocals with a modern band sound struck a chord both on the island itself and with expatriates living across the water in metropolitan France, eventually snowballing into a mass popularity that has broken all records and many musical boundaries along the way.

À Bercy (Columbia). This live recording, made at a celebratory concert in Paris in 1996, captures the Muvrinis on the crest of a musical wave, and is pretty much what they still sound like today. Opening with one of Jean-François' poetic laments, it's essentially a "greatest hits" selection which you'll either love or loathe depending on your tolerance of electronic keyboard chords and slow rock rhythms.

Pulifunie (ImcdPoly). Just to prove they can do the old stuff too: inspirational polyphony just as their dad and uncles taught them, only slightly marred by overbaked studio reverb.

Jean-Paul Poletti et le Chœur d'Hommes de Sartène

Along with A Filetta, Poletti's choir is Corsica's polyphonic flagship – a prominence it fully merits. Unlike Acquaviva's ensemble, though, this one has stuck resolutely to its roots, singing traditional repertoire in textbook style.

Cantu di a Terra (Accord). A definitive album in all respects: flawless renditions of sacred and profane songs, led by Poletti at the peak of his vocal prowess. Moreover, the recording quality is superb.

Trio Soledonna/Les Nouvelles Polyphonies Corses

Sisters Lydia and Patrizia Poli, with friend Patrizia Gattaceca, caused a sensation when they teamed up with Jean-Paul Poletti and singers from his Scola di Cantu, world music producer Hector Zazou and a bunch of talented musicians from across the globe to form Les Nouvelles Polyphonies Corses. The group was a runaway success, superimposing expansive *paghjella*-style vocals over an electro-acoustic backdrop. They've subsequently tended more towards pure a cappella, but as the Trio Soledonna, the original female core of the group now sings with instrumental musicians, to great effect.

Le Meilleure des Nouvelles Polyphonies Corses (Universal). Their "best of" album (though compiled before the 2001 release of *Isulanima*) charts NPC's evolution from Zazou to Trio Soledonna days. Throughout, the harmonies are razor sharp, the singing warm and seductive, and the arrangements highly original.

Isulanima (Philips France). The pick of the Trio's offerings. Traditional musicians from Spain, Greece and the Maghreb were recruited to infuse the Corsican harmonies with a pan-Mediterranean feel, and although a little glossy in places, the mix works well.

Voce di Corsica

Voce di Corsica assembled in 1990 around former Cantu vocalist Petru Guelfucci. Nearly all the members of the group, from the villages of Sermanu and Rusiu in the Bozio near Corte, were sons or nephews of singers who had featured prominently in Félix Quilici's 1960s field recordings – in fact, some of the older ones actually appeared themselves in the archives, singing as teenagers.

Polyphonies (Sony). With its distinctive black cover and strident graphics, this became a landmark polyphony album when it was released in 1990. Featured are traditional pieces, both secular (*paghjella*, Tuscan-troubador songs and madrigals) and sacred (hymns and death laments), alongside new compositions. One of the top half-dozen pure polyphony recordings ever to come out of the island.

Books

Very few books about Corsica have been written in English, and the great majority of them are out of print, so you'll have to resort to secondhand bookshops or the internet if you want to get stuck into most of the titles listed below. Those currently out of print are marked "o/p" in the reviews that follow. For the benefit of fluent French readers, we've also included a handful of French titles, which you can buy in any good bookshop in Corsica and mainland France or order via the internet at Ⓦ www.fnac.fr. In the UK, virtually any French book in print may be ordered from The European Bookshop, 5 Warwick St, London W1R 5RA ⓣ 020/7734 5259, Ⓦ www .eurobooks.co.uk. Best among the bibliographies of writing about the island is the World Bibliographical Series' *Corsica*, compiled by Grace L. Hudson, which you should be able to get hold of through any academic library. Titles marked 🏃 are particularly recommended.

Travel

James Boswell *An Account of Corsica: the Journal of a Tour to that Island and Memoirs of Pascal Paoli* (In Print Publishing, UK). Typically robust account of the author's eventful trip to the island in 1765 to seek out Pascal Paoli in his hideout at Sollacaro. The meat of the book lies in its expansive description of the encounter with the charismatic rebel leader, but the travelogue leading up to it proves more entertaining. After the journal's publication, Boswell became famous as an advocate of Corsican independence.

Thomasina M.A.E. Campbell *Notes on the Island of Corsica* (Hatchard, London, UK; o/p). This quirky 1868 travelogue, by an indomitable Scottish lady who was a friend of Edward Lear, begins with the caveat: "To the genuine British grumbler (who ought never to leave England unless accompanied by his own cook and a cow, and frequently not even then) Ajaccio says 'Remain At Home!' ". It proceeds in rambling fashion, with greater attention to the minutiae of travel and flowers than history and culture, but includes some entertaining episodes. This is unavailable, according to Amazon.

🏃 **Dorothy Carrington** *Granite Island* (Penguin). Published originally in French, *L'Île de Granite* is a portrait of Corsica woven around Lady Rose's first visit of 1947 (when she "rediscovered" the Filitosa menhirs), with experiences, meetings and historical asides drawn from later decades adding depth. Although something of a historical document itself these days, it remains by far the most erudite and rounded account of the island ever written, in any language.

Sir Gilbert Elliot *Life and letters of Sir Gilbert Elliot first Earl of Minto from 1751 to 1806* (Longmans, London, UK; o/p). Sir Gilbert became viceroy of the island during the Anglo-Corsican interlude and this book, compiled by his great-niece, collates his most memorable correspondence from the period, framed by a contextual essay and short biography. As interesting for its insights into the historical personalities of the era (including Paoli) as its vivid evocations of the mountains and forest.

Gustave Flaubert *Voyage dans les Pyrénées et en Corse* (Flammarion, France). Flaubert's parents promised him a trip to Corsica if he passed his baccalaureate, and this book is an account of the trip the young novelist-to-be subsequently made in the summer of 1840. Full of freshness, sensuality and descriptions of the island's landscape and people, it follows the 19-year-old's progress across the Pyrenees to the Mediterranean, with a poignant interlude describing his secret love affair with a beautiful Peruvian woman in Marseille.

Richard T.N.B.C. Grenville *The private diary of Richard, Duke of Buckingham and Chandos* (Hurst & Blackett, London, UK; o/p). Regarded as the first modern-style tourist to visit the island (in 1828–29), the Duke of Bucks arrived in Ajaccio by yacht and conducted a tour with his eye more on Corsica's landscape, village life and banditry than its lofty historical figures, which makes this a much more original read than most of its predecessors.

Edward Lear *Journal of a Landscape Painter* (Century, UK; o/p). After Boswell, the book that first brought images of Corsica to a mass readership in England. Lear visited the island in the 1860s, and produced a work remembered less for its lacklustre prose than beautifully atmospheric engravings, prominently featured by Dorothy Carrington in *Granite Island*. A collector's item these days, but available through many libraries and well worth tracking down.

Alan Ross *Time Was Away – A Journey Through Corsica* (Collins Harvill, UK; o/p). Dour, essentially impressionistic account of a visit to Corsica in 1947, while the island was still "sunk in a post-malarial torpor". In later years, the author admitted to being "over-influenced by the travel books of Graham Greene and detached camera-eye style of Christopher Isherwood", but his account makes an interesting snapshot, even if it doesn't stand much comparison with Dorothy Carrington's book, researched the same year. Illustrated with bold woodcuts by artist John Minton.

History and society

Dorothy Carrington *The Dream Hunters of Corsica* (Phoenix). Based primarily on first-hand interviews conducted between 1947 and 1995, this popular, accessible compendium of folklore expands with characteristic elegance on *Granite Island*'s coverage of matters occult, notably *mazzeri* – "dream-hunters" who can foresee death – and the evil eye.

Dorothy Carrington *Napoleon and his Parents on the Threshold of History* (Viking/Nal-Duhon; o/p). Lucid study of Napoléon's early years in his native country, from the Battle of Ponte-Nuovo until the death of his father in 1785, derived from the archives of Prince Napoléon and other previously unconsulted private collections. The most thorough work on this period, illustrated with facsimiles of little-known documents.

Philippe-Jean Catinchi *Polyphonies Corses* (Cité de la Musique/Acte Sud, France). Concise, richly illustrated history of Corsican song, from timeless shepherds' *paghjella* to Tino Rossi and I Muvrini. Most of the tracks on the accompanying CD are very much in the field recording mode, but still represent the broadest cross-section of traditional Corsican music so far compiled on a single disc, and the explanatory notes are more copious than usual.

Maurice Choury *Tous Bandits d'Honneur!* (La Marge Éditions, France). Popular history of Corsica's

"Almost colourless, its outlines uncertain, it swam in the early morning mist, a creation half-materialized, an ectoplasm of the sea in trance." Dorothy Carrington's first sight of Corsica in 1948, as recounted in *Granite Island*, has about it the air of a prophetic vision; and so indeed it must have seemed twenty years after the fact, when she settled down in a gloomy basement in Ajaccio to sieve through two decades of discoveries, encounters and wonderment. Distilled into three hundred pages of unfailingly elegant prose, the book she eventually published in 1971 – a heady mix of travelogue, historical tract and ethnography – provides a compelling portrait of an island poised on the brink of massive change, as its traditional ways were about to be subsumed by modernity. For the first time since Boswell's *Journal*, it brought Corsica to the attention of an international public, and reminded Corsicans themselves of the richness of their cultural heritage – a service for which the islanders, even those who may never have set eyes on the book, remain grateful. Decorated Chevalier de l'Order des Arts et des Lettres and granted an honorary doctorate by the University of Corte, Dorothy Carrington is still a household name in her adopted home, where she lived and wrote for nearly fifty years.

The future author of *Granite Island* was born **Frederica Dorothy Violet Carrington** at Perrott's Brook in Gloucestershire in 1910, into a landed family. Her father, a hero of the Boer War, was a friend and comrade of Cecil Rhodes, her mother a glamorous Edwardian hostess with a passion for liberal politics, music, painting and the ballets of Diaghilev. Both parents, however, died prematurely, and the young Dorothy found herself packed off to wealthy relatives in rural Gloucestershire. But she was never one for the sedentary hunting and shooting life and escaped as soon as she could to study English at Oxford. It was there she first met the dashing but impoverished Austrian Franz Von Walschutz, with whom she eloped first to Paris, and later to Rhodesia (Zimbabwe).

The thrill of life on an African farm having subsided, Dorothy left Von Walschutz and returned to London's prewar arts scene, mixing with an international bohemian intelligentsia. It was while organizing an exhibition in 1942 that she first met the surrealist painter Francis Rose. The son of a wildly beautiful Franco-Spanish arts impresario, Laetitia Rouy, Rose had grown up in Paris knowing Sarah Bernhardt, Jean Cocteau and Isadora Duncan, and had designed sets and costumes for Diaghilev while still in his twenties. It was said to have been in praise of a retrospective show of his work that his eventual patron, Gertrude Stein, made her famous remark, "A Rose is a Rose is a Rose".

Francis and Dorothy fell in love to a background of the London underworld. Though both from aristocratic families, neither had a penny to rub together during "that bitter, gritty spring", as she would later describe it, living on a diet of dandelion leaves picked amid the wreckage of the Blitz. Undeterred by their poverty, Rose proposed on the London underground in 1943, and they celebrated their engagement at a

struggle against the Axis forces, June 1942 to October 1943, focusing mainly on the socialist Front National's contribution to the Resistance. Choury was one of the leaders of the Maquis and offers a vivid insight into the compelling, often tragic events leading up to the island's liberation.

Vincent Cronin *Napoleon* (Fontana/ HarperCollins). Enthusiastic and accessible biography, recently repub-lished in paperback, which attempts to explain the life of France's great emperor in personal as well as military terms. Arguably the best route into this crowded field.

Desmond Gregory *The ungovern-able rock: a history of the Anglo-Corsican Kingdom and its role in Britain's Mediterranean strategy during the* down-at-heel café in the docks. The waiter that night was a Corsican, Jean Cesari, who on subsequent visits impressed and befriended the couple with his ability to conjure French baguettes from war-time rations, and with his stories of his romantic homeland – of its grandiose landscapes, chestnut gathering in the snowy mountains, mysterious "dream-hunters" and romantic *bandits d'honneur*. Cesari also talked of the enigmatic standing stones scattered under the olive trees on his cousin's farm, many of them carved with faces and weapons. Fresh from editing an anthology of travel writing (*The Traveller's Eye*, published in 1947) and eager for her own real adventures, Dorothy was hooked.

So it was, at the end of 1947, that Lord and Lady Rose set off – titled, but with virtually no money – in search of Cesari's menhirs. They carried with them little more than two suitcases crammed with sugar and coffee, then unavailable on the island. In the wake of World War II, Corsica was a land that had altered little in a century or more. At first the Roses revelled in its simple pleasures and Mediterranean exoticism, marvelling at the wonderful mountains, Genoese citadelles, turquoise water, and the singer-poets who wandered from house to house improvising verses in Corsican. With food straight from cottage gardens and orchards, they ate better than they had for years; in an interview forty years later, Dorothy fondly recalled how, if they needed salt, they'd "scrape some off the rocks with a teaspoon".

But Francis, hankering for the sophistication of London and Paris society, soon grew weary of life in Corsican peasant villages and left his wife to her new passion. In truth, he was gay and the marriage, which had never been an entirely happy one, was effectively over. Having retired to Britain, Lord Rose became a poverty-stricken, camp recluse in Surrey, where he is said – in homage to the *fin-de-siècle* Parisian surrealists he so admired – to have attended church dressed in a Mexican sombrero, leading a cat on a gold chain.

Dorothy, meanwhile, felt reborn. In Corsica she had at last found her life's work, a field equal to her appetite for hidden history and travel. The menhirs talked of by Jean Cesari did indeed turn out to be every bit as extraordinary as she had hoped, and it was she who first recognized their significance, persuading Roger Grosjean – the man generally credited with the "discovery" of Filitosa (see p.206) – to begin archeological digs (a fact still not mentioned by the site's guides). Later, she unearthed in forgotten archives a copy of Pascal Paoli's original Constitution of Independence, and showed the world how it had been a model not only for its French equivalent but also the Constitution of the United States of America.

Dorothy Carrington lived the rest of her long life in Ajaccio, producing a succession of erudite volumes on Corsica (notably on Napoléon and the island's disappearing occult traditions). She died seven months after her ninetieth birthday, surrounded by her books and a handful of Francis Rose's paintings, working on the same antiquated typewriter with which she had written *Granite Island*.

revolutionary war (Associated University Press, Toronto; o/p). The definitive account of Britain's short and ultimately fruitless rule of Corsica, which involved historical figures such as Nelson, Sir John Moore, Admiral Hood and Sir Gilbert Elliot.

Moray McLaren *Corsica Boswell: Paoli, Johnson and Freedom* (Secker & Warburg, London; o/p). Fellow Scot McLaren follows in the footsteps of Boswell, giving as he does so a readable account of the island's history and condition in the 1960s. He then pursues the story back to Britain, through Boswell's fund-raising campaign for the patriots to Dr Johnson's famous meeting with Paoli, and the rebel leader's eventual exile in London. An ambitious work that was the first in English to unravel the legacy of James Boswell's visit and subsequent espousal of the partisans' cause.

Aylmer Vallance *The Summer King* (Thames & Hudson; o/p). Popular, illustrated biography of Théodore von Neuhof, self-styled "King of Corsica", which attempts to separate the wheat of fact from the chaff of fiction put about by the man himself during his chequered lifetime. Also worth tracking down if the subject grabs you is Valerie Pirie's *His Majesty of Corsica* (Collins, UK; o/p), written a couple of decades earlier, in 1939.

Paul Silvani *Et la Corse fut Libérée* (La Marge Éditions, France). Written in 1993 and now available in a fully revised second edition (2005) this prize-winning history of the

liberation quickly established itself as the classic version, drawing on recently released records, contemporary documents and first-hand accounts to reconstitute the dramatic events of 1942–43.

Peter Adam Thrasher *Pascal Paoli: an enlightened hero 1725–1807* (Constable, London; o/p). The best English-language biography of the great man, covering events from his birth in Castagniccia in 1725 to his death at the age of 82 in London. Some of Thrasher's conclusions have been contested by later historians, but as an introduction to this revolutionary French thinker, whose achievements ultimately had a bearing on both the French and American constitutions, it's hard to beat.

Literature

Gabriel Xavier Culioli *La Terre des Seigneurs* (Lieu Commun, France). Phenomenally successful novel following the evolution of a family through a century of Corsican history. Full of fascinating background on island politics, village life and the impact of emigration and the world wars on traditional society. The present edition republishes the (lengthy) introductory essays from previous ones – vivid historical testaments themselves, as a member of Culioli's family was imprisoned in the 1990s for terrorist offences.

Alphonse Daudet *Letters from my Windmill* (Penguin). Inspired by a visit to the island in the winter of 1862, Daudet's most famous anthology of short stories includes his tale of a lonely Corsican lighthouse keeper on the Îles Sanguinaires, near Ajaccio, and a chilling account of the sinking of the *Sémillante*, in which 773 troops and sailors en route to the Crimean War

were drowned – the Mediterranean's worst ever maritime disaster.

Guy de Maupassant *Un Bandit Corse et Autres Contes* (Marzocchi, France). Maupassant, France's most illustrious short-story author, spent two months in Corsica in 1880, and the lively tales in this anthology were all inspired by his visit. The *Bandit Corse* has become a classic, and is said to have been avidly read by the *bandits* themselves after its publication.

Prosper Mérimée *Colomba* (Hachette, France). Short novel loosely based on a real-life blood feud that divided the village of Fozzano in the 1830s. A son returns to Corsica and is expected to avenge the death of his father. Though far from historically accurate, the story vividly evokes the violent spirit of the times and was a roaring success for Mérimée, inspiring a mini tourist invasion in Fozzano.

Walking and climbing

🏃 **David Abram** *Corsica Trekking: GR20* (Trailblazer, UK). Trailblazer's guide to the island's most illustrious long-distance trek. Even allowing for our inevitable bias (it's written by the same author as this Rough Guide), this is the most comprehensive book of its kind in English, with over 200 pages of lively route descriptions and background features, plus 32 hand-drawn trekking maps listing stage times and other points of interest. You also get a handy full-colour field guide to common Corsican flora.

Robin G. Collomb *Corsica Mountains* (West Col, UK). Covers all the routes up principal mountain peaks (and many obscurer ones), with information on different approaches and ascents, backed up with line diagrams, though the information on the island's footpaths is patchy and more than a decade out of date.

Féderation Française de la Randonnée Pédesetre/Parc Naturel Régional de Corse (FFRP, France) *Corse: entre mer et montagne* and *Corse: a travers la montagne corse*. This pair of colour topoguides, co-published by France's national trekking authority and the PNRC, splices together excerpts of the relevant IGN maps for the island's main trails with bare-bones route descriptions and other practical info. Accurate and lightweight, they've been the benchmark guides for years, although neither is currently available in English. You can order them at ⓦ www.ign.fr.

Flora and fauna field guides

Bertel Brun *Birds of Britain and Europe* (Hamlyn). The classic tome on the subject, showing most of the species you're likely to come across.

Burton, Arnold & Ovenden *Field Guide to the Reptiles and Amphibians of Britain & Europe* (HarperCollins). The indispensable companion for those wishing to differentiate Tyrrhenian from Bedriaga's wall lizards, and many more besides.

Davies & Gibbons *Wild Flowers of Southern Europe* (The Crowood Press, UK). Some 200 pages shorter than Grey-Wilson & Blamey's guide, but nicely designed, concise and photographic, with coverage of pretty much every flower you can expect to encounter.

🏃 **Grey-Wilson & Blamey** *Mediterranean Wild Flowers* (HarperCollins). The definitive guide, though at 560 pages it's a bit heavy to lug around on walks, and doesn't come cheap.

Higgins & Riley *Butterflies of Britain and Europe* (HarperCollins). Essential reading for keen butterfly spotters.

Jacquie Grozier *Birdwatching Guide to France South of the Loire* (Arlequin Press, UK). Includes a site guide to the island's ornithological hot spots.

Thibault & Bonaccorsi *Birds of Corsica* (BOU, UK). Written by Corsica's most eminent ornithologists, this essentially academic study lists all 323 species present on the island and places them in the wider context of the Mediterranean.

Language

Language

Language

T op of the nationalist agenda since the 1970s has been the revival of the Corsican language, which has survived despite repression by successive ruling powers. Travelling around the island's more rural areas, you'll regularly hear its distinctive rhythms and intonations – spoken by young as well as old. An estimated seventy percent of locals claim to be fluent speakers, but few use the language in their day-to-day lives and the trend is definitely a downward one. As a visitor, you can expect to get by well enough with French; English tends to be spoken only in the coastal resorts, and even then not all that well.

The Corsican language

Corsican, originally a Latin-based language with resemblances to Romanian, developed an Italianate vocabulary and syntax during Pisan and Genoese occupation. Arabic and French influences have added to the complexity of the tongue, which was predominantly an oral one until around two hundred years ago – hence the confusing variety of spellings for place names, which endure despite periodic attempts at standardization. The commonest variants come about through the transposition of ll and dd – as in *casteddu* and Buildings and monuments are often labelled in different languages (San Pietro/San Pietru), and on maps you'll find mountain passes, rivers and regions marked in a mixture of Italian, French and Corsican – the u ending (pronounced as in English "zoo") is a frequent indicator of Corsican usage. Deep in the country, many old people are still easier with Corsican than French, so a few phrases will be met with surprise and pleasure. Pronunciation is generally as for Italian, but look out for two tricky clusters of consonants – chj/chi and ghj/chi, pronounced "ty" or "dy".

Corsican words and phrases

Basics

yes	iè	here	custi
no	nò	there	custà
OK	và bé	this	quellu/quella
please	fate u piacè	that	quessu/quessa
thank you	a' ringraziavvi	now	ora
where	induve	later	dopu
when	quandu	open	apertu
what	chi	closed	chiusu
how much	quantu	with	cù

429

without	senza	week	simana
good	bonu	month	meze
bad	male	yesterday	ieri
big	grande/maio	day before	avant'ierisera
small	piccola/chjucu	night	a notte
cheap	bonu mercatu	car	a vittura
expensive	cara	girl	zitella
hot	caldu	boy	zitellu
cold	fredda	it's good	he bonu
more	piu	something	qualcosa
less	menu	I want	vogliu
nothing	nulla/nunda/nudda	next week	simana'dopu
today	oghje	next month	meze'dopu
tomorrow	dumane	morning	a mane
day	ghjurnu	evening	a sera

Greetings and responses

hello	bonghjornu	I (don't) understand	(nò) capiscu
goodbye	a'vedeci	Do you speak English?	parla inglese?
good evening	bona sera	My name is …	me chjamanu …
goodnight	bona notte	What's your name?	cumu a chjamanu?
sorry	me dispiace	I am English	sò Inglese
excuse me	scusame	Let's go	andemu
How are you?	comu sì?		

Questions and requests

Do you have?	avetene?	with shower/bath	cùllad uscia/ bag-narola
Give me (one like that)	datemi		
That's enough	basta	It's for one person/ two people	ci ne vole una/duie persona
What would you like to drink?	chi vulete beie?		
		How long are you staying?	quantu ci avete da stà?
I'd like a lemonade/ coffee	a me una limnata/ caffè		
		For one night/ one week	pé una notte/una semana
How much?	quantu costanu?		
Is there …?	c'he …?	It's fine	và bé
a room	una camera	It's too expensive	he troppu caru
with two beds	cù duie letti		

Directions

Where is …?	induv'é …?	How long will it take to get to Ponte Leccia?	quantu ci vole à ghjunghje à u Ponte à a Leccia?
It's near	he vicinu		
It's far	he lontana		
left	sinistra	What's the time ?	chi ora he?
right	dritta	It's three o'clock	sò trè ore
straight on	sempredrittu		

Months and seasons

January	ghjennaghju	September	sittembre
February	febbraghju	October	ottobre
March	marzu	November	novembre
April	aprile	December	dicembre
May	maghjiu	winter	imbernu/ingnernu
June	ghjiugnu	spring	veranu
July	ghjugliu	summer	estate
August	aostu	autumn	auturnu

Numbers and days

1	unu (una)	21	vintunu
2	dui (duie)	22	vintidui
3	trè	30	trenta
4	quattru	40	quaranta
5	cinque	50	cinquanta
6	sei	60	sessanta
7	sette	70	settanta
8	ottu	80	ottanta
9	nove	90	novanta
10	dece	100	centu
11	ondeci	101	cent'e unu
12	dodeci	102	cent'e dui
13	tredeci	Monday	luni
14	quattordeci	Tuesday	marti
15	quindeci	Wednesday	mercuri
16	sedeci	Thursday	ghjovi
17	dicessette	Friday	venneri
18	diciottu	Saturday	sabatu
19	dicennove	Sunday	dumenica
20	vinbti		

Words of the countryside

bird	acellu	plateau	pianu
mountain	montane	cliff	scuglialu
mountain pass	bocca/foce	bridge	ponte
mountain peak/summit	capu/cima/ monte/punta	river	fiume
		tree	arburu
forest/wood	furesta/valdu	beach	a marina
lake	lavu	village	u paese

French pronunciation

One easy rule to remember is that **consonants** at the ends of words are usually silent. *Pas plus tard* (not later) is thus pronounced "pa–plu–tarr". But when the following word begins with a vowel, you run the two together: *pas après* (not after) becomes "pazaprey". **Vowels** are the hardest sounds to get right. Roughly:

a as in hat	I as in machine
e as in get	o as in hot
é between get and gate	o, au as in over
è between get and gut	ou as in food
eu like the u in hurt	u as in a pursed-lip version of use

More awkward are the **combinations** in/im, en/em, an/am, on/om, un/um at the ends of words, or followed by consonants other than n or m. Again, roughly:

in/im like the an in anxious	on/om like the don in Doncaster said by
an/am, en/em like the don in Doncaster	someone with a heavy cold
when said with a nasal accent	un/um like the u in understand

Consonants are much as in English, except that: ch is always "sh", c is "s", h is silent, th is the same as "t", ll is like the y in "yes", w is "v", and r is growled (or rolled).

Learning materials

Rough Guide French Phrasebook (Rough Guides). Mini dictionary-style phrasebook with both English–French and French–English sections, along with cultural tips for tricky situations and a menu reader.

French Experience (BBC Books). Crammed with authentic, modern materials and learning practices, the BBC's latest French self-tutor, accompanied by audiocassettes, CDs and a TV series (on video), makes the competition look dowdy and dated.

A particularly upbeat volume 2 includes sections on French from around the Francophone world. Easily the best choice for beginners and intermediate learners.

Collins French Dictionary (Collins). The best two-in-one reference tool for learners, with over 80,000 entries, 120,000 translations and a user-friendly grammar section.

Mini French Dictionary (Harrap/Prentice Hall). French–English and English–French, plus a brief grammar and pronunciation guide.

Basic words and phrases

French nouns are divided into masculine and feminine. This causes difficulties with adjectives, whose endings have to change to suit the gender of the nouns they qualify. If you know some grammar, you will know what to do. If not, stick to the masculine form, which is the simplest – it's what we have done in this glossary.

For specific hiking vocabulary, see p.330.

today	aujourd'hui	in the morning	le matin
yesterday	hier	in the afternoon	l'après-midi
tomorrow	demain	in the evening	le soir

now	maintenant	big	grand
later	plus tard	small	petit
at one o'clock	à une heure	more	plus
at three o'clock	à trois heures	less	moins
at half past ten	à dix heures et demie	a little	un peu
at midday	à midi	a lot	beaucoup
man	un homme	cheap	bon marché
woman	une femme	expensive	cher
here	ici	good	bon
there	là	bad	mauvais
this one	ceci	hot	chaud
that one	celà	cold	froid
open	ouvert	with	avec
closed	fermé	without	sans

Numbers

1	un	21	vingt-et-un
2	deux	22	vingt-deux
3	trois	30	trente
4	quatre	40	quarante
5	cinq	50	cinquante
6	six	60	soixante
7	sept	70	soixante-dix
8	huit	75	soixante-quinze
9	neuf	80	quatre-vingts
10	dix	90	quatre-vingt-dix
11	onze	95	quatre-vingt-quinze
12	douze	100	cent
13	treize	101	cent-et-un
14	quatorze	200	deux cents
15	quinze	300	trois cents
16	seize	500	cinq cents
17	dix-sept	1000	mille
18	dix-huit	2000	deux milles
19	dix-neuf	5000	cinq milles
20	vingt	1,000,000	un million

Days and dates

January	janvier	September	septembre
February	février	October	octobre
March	mars	November	novembre
April	avril	December	décembre
May	mai	Sunday	dimanche
June	juin	Monday	lundi
July	juillet	Tuesday	mardi
August	août	Wednesday	mercredi

Thursday	jeudi	November 23	le vingt-trois novembre
Friday	vendredi	1997	dix-neuf-cent quatre-vingt-dix-sept
Saturday	samedi		
August 1	le premier août	2000	deux mille
March 2	le deux mars	2001	deux mille un
July 14	le quatorze juillet	2010	deux mille dix

Talking to people

When addressing people you should always use Monsieur for a man, Madame for a woman, Mademoiselle for a girl. Plain *bonjour* by itself is not enough. This isn't as formal as it seems, and it has its uses when you've forgotten someone's name or want to attract someone's attention.

excuse me	pardon	please	s'il vous plaît
do you speak English?	vous parlez anglais?	thank you	merci
how do you say it in French?	comment ça se dit en français?	hello	bonjour
		goodbye	au revoir
what's your name?	comment vous appelez-vous?	good morning/ afternoon	bonjour
my name is ...	Je m'appelle ...	good evening	bonsoir
I'm English	Je suis anglais(e)	good night	bonne nuit
Irish	irlandais(e)	how are you?	comment allez-vous?/ça va?
Scottish	écossais(e)		
Welsh	gallois(e)	fine, thanks	très bien, merci
American	américain(e)	I don't know	Je ne sais pas
Australian	australien(ne)	let's go	allons-y
Canadian	canadien(ne)	see you tomorrow	à demain
a New Zealander	néo-zélandais(e)	see you soon	à bientôt
yes	oui	sorry	pardon, Madame/ je m'excuse
no	non		
I understand	je comprends	leave me alone! (aggressive)	fichez-moi la paix!
I don't understand	je ne comprends pas		
can you speak slower please?	s'il vous plaît, parlez moins vite	please help me	aidez-moi, s'il vous plait
OK/agreed	d'accord	help!	au secours!

Finding the way

bus	autobus/bus/car	train station	gare (SNCF)
bus station	gare routière	platform	quai
bus stop	arrêt	what time does it leave?	il part à quelle heure?
car	voiture	hitchhiking	autostop
train	train	on foot	à pied
taxi	taxi	where are you going?	vous allez où?
ferry	ferry	I'm going to ...	je vais à ...
boat	bâteau	I want to get off at ...	je voudrais descendre à ...
plane	avion		

the road to ...	la route pour ...	how many kilometres?	combien de kilomètres?
near	près/pas loin	how many hours?	combien d'heures?
far	loin	straight on	tout droit
left	à gauche	on the other side of	à l'autre côté de
right	à droite	on the corner of	à l'angle de
what time does it arrive?	il arrive à quelle heure?	next to	à côté de
a ticket to ...	un billet pour ...	behind	derrière
single ticket	aller simple	in front of	devant
return ticket	aller retour	before	avant
validate your ticket	compostez votre billet	after	après
valid for	valable pour	under	sous
ticket office	vente de billets	to cross	traverser
		bridge	pont

Questions and requests

The simplest way of asking a question is to start with *s'il vous plaît* (please), then name the thing you want in an interrogative tone of voice. Similarly with requests. For example:

where is there a bakery?	s'il vous plaît, la boulangerie?	where?	où?
which way is it to the Genoan watchtower	s'il vous plaît, la route pour la tour génoise?	how?	comment?
		how many/how much?	combien?
we'd like a room for two	s'il vous plaît, une chambre pour deux?	when?	quand?
		why?	pourquoi?
can I have a kilo of oranges?	s'il vous plaît, un kilo d'oranges?	at what time?	à quelle heure?
		what is/which is?	quel est?

Accommodation

room for one/ two people	chambre pour une/ deux personne(s)	blankets	couvertures
double bed	lit double	quiet	calme
room with a shower	chambre avec douche	noisy	bruyant
room with a bath	chambre avec salle de bains	hot water	eau chaude
		cold water	eau froide
for one/two/x two people	pour une/deux/trois nuit(s)	is breakfast included?	est-ce que le petit déjeuner est compris?
can I see it?	je peux la voir?	I would like breakfast	je voudrais prendre le petit déjeuner
room on the courtyard	chambre sur la cour		
room over the street	chambre sur la rue	I don't want breakfast	je ne veux pas de petit déjeuner
first floor	premier étage		
second floor	deuxième étage	can we camp here?	on peut camper ici?
with a view	avec vue	campsite	camping/terrain de camping
key	clef		
to iron	repasser	tent	tente
do laundry	faire la lessive	tent space	emplacement
sheets	draps	youth hostel	auberge de jeunesse

Driving

service station	garage	to put air in the tyres	gonfler les pneus
service	service	battery	batterie
to park the car	garer la voiture	the battery is dead	la batterie est morte
car park	un parking	plugs	bougies
no parking	défense de stationner/ stationnement interdit	to break down	tomber en panne
		gas can	bidon
petrol station	poste d'essence	insurance	assurance
fuel	essence	green card	carte verte
(to) fill it up	faire le plein	traffic lights	feux
oil	huile	red light	feu rouge
air line	ligne à air	green light	feu vert

Cycling

to adjust	ajuster	inner tube	la chambre à l'air
axle	l'axe	loose	dévissé
ball bearing	le roulement à billes	to lower	baisser
battery	la pile	mudguard	le garde-boue
bent	tordu	pannier	le panier
bicycle	le vélo	pedal	la pédale
bottom bracket	le logement du pédalier	pump	la pompe
brake cable	le cable	rack	la porte-bagages
brakes	les freins	to raise	relever
broken	cassé	to repair	réparer
bulb	l'ampoule	saddle	la selle
chain	la chaîne	spanner	la clef
frame	le cadre	to straighten	redresser
gears	les vitesses	stuck	coincé
grease	la graisse	tight	serré
handlebars	le guidon		

Health matters

doctor	médecin	stomach ache	mal à l'estomac
I don't feel well	je ne me sens pas bien	period	règles
medicines	médicaments	pain	douleur
prescription	ordonnance	it hurts	ça fait mal
I feel sick	je suis malade	chemist	pharmacie
I have a headache	j'ai mal à la tête	hospital	hôpital

Other needs

bakery	boulangerie	to drink	boire
food shop	alimentation	camping gas	camping gaz
supermarket	supermarché	tobacconist	tabac
to eat	manger	stamps	timbres

bank	banque	telephone	téléphone
money	argent	cinema	cinéma
toilets	toilettes	theatre	théâtre
police	police	to reserve/book	réserver

A food glossary

Basic terms

Always call the waiter or waitress Monsieur or Madame (Mademoiselle if a young woman), never Garçon, no matter what you were taught in school.

pain	bread	cuillère	spoon
beurre	butter	table	table
oeufs	eggs	la carte	menu
lait	milk	l'addition	the bill
huile	oil	chauffé	heated
poivre	pepper	cuit	cooked
sel	salt	cru	raw
sucre	sugar	fumé	smoked
vinaigre	vinegar	salé	salted/spicy
bouteille	bottle	sucré	sweet
verre	glass	emballé	wrapped
fourchette	fork	à emporter	takeaway
couteau	knife		

Snacks

un sandwich/ une baguette	a sandwich	omelette	omelette
jambon	with ham	nature	plain
fromage	with cheese	aux fines herbes	with herbs
saucisson	with sausage	au fromage	with cheese
à l'ail	with garlic	salade de	salad of
au poivre	with pepper	tomates	tomatoes
pâté (de campagne)	with pâté (country-style)	betteraves	beets
		concombres	cucumber
		carottes râpées	grated carrots
croque-monsieur	grilled cheese and ham sandwich	épis de maïs	corn on the cob
		crêpe	pancake
croque-madame	grilled cheese and bacon, sausage, chicken or an egg	au sucre	with sugar
		au citron	with lemon
		au miel	with honey
oeufs	eggs	à la confiture	with jam
au plat	fried	aux œufs	with eggs
à la coque	boiled	à la crème de marrons	with chestnut purée
durs	hard-boiled		
brouillés	scrambled		

Soups (soupes) and starters (hors d'oeuvres)

bisque	shellfish soup	rouille	red pepper, garlic and saffron mayonnaise served with fish soup
bouillabaisse	Marseillais fish soup		
bouillon	broth or stock		
bourride	thick fish soup	velouté	thick soup, usually fish or poultry
consommé	clear soup		
pistou	parmesan, basil and garlic paste added to soup	assiette anglaise	plate of cold meats
		crudités	raw vegetables with dressings
potage	thick vegetable soup	hors d'œuvres variés	combination of the above, plus smoked or marinated fish

Fish (poisson), seafood (fruits de mer) and shellfish (crustaces or coquillages)

anchois	anchovies	langouste	spiny lobster
anguilles	eels	langoustines	saltwater crayfish (scampi)
araignée	sea spider		
barbue	brill	limande	lemon sole
bigourneau	periwinkle	lotte	monkfish
bonite	Mediterranean or "skipjack" tuna	loup de mer	sea bass
		louvine, loubine	similar to sea bass
brème	bream	maquereau	mackerel
cabillaud	cod	merlan	whiting
calamar	squid	mérou	grouper
carrelet	plaice	moules (marinière)	mussels (with shallots in white wine sauce)
claire	type of oyster		
colin	hake	murène	moray eel
congre	conger eel	oblade	silver bream
coques	cockles	oursin	sea urchin
coquilles St-Jacques	scallops	palourdes	clams
crabe	crab	poulpe	octopus
crevettes grises	shrimp	praires	small clams
crevettes roses	prawns	raie	skate
daurade	sea bream	rascasse	scorpion fish
denti	dentex	requin	shark
éperlan	smelt or whitebait	rouget	red mullet
escargots	snails	sar	silver bream
espadon	swordfish	saumon	salmon
flétan	halibut	seiche	cuttle fish
friture	assorted fried fish, usually whitebait	sole	sole
		St Pierre	John Dory
gambas	king prawns	thon	tuna
hareng	herring	truite	trout
homard	lobster	turbot	turbot
huîtres	oysters		

Fish cooking terms

aïoli	garlic mayonnaise served with salt cod and other fish	fumé	smoked
		fumet	fish stock
béarnaise	sauce of egg yolks, white wine, shallots and vinegar	gigot de mer	large fish baked whole
		grillé	grilled
		hollandaise	butter and vinegar sauce
beignets	fritters	à la meunière	in a butter, lemon and parsley sauce
darne	fillet or steak		
la douzaine	a dozen		
frit	fried	mousse, mousseline	mousse
friture	deep-fried small fish	quenelles	light dumplings

Meat (viande) and poultry (volaille)

agneau (de présalé)	lamb (grazed on salt marshes)	langue	tongue
		lapin, lapereau	rabbit, young rabbit
andouille, andouillette	tripe sausage	lard, lardons	bacon, diced bacon
bœuf	beef	lièvre	hare
bifteck	steak	merguez	spicy, red sausage
boudin blanc	sausage of white meats	mouton	mutton
boudin noir	black pudding	museau de veau	calf's muzzle
caille	quail	oie	goose
canard	duck	os	bone
caneton	duckling	porc	pork
contrefilet	sirloin roast	poulet	chicken
coquelet	cockerel	poussin	baby chicken
dinde, dindon	turkey	ris	sweetbreads
entrecôte	ribsteak	rognons	kidneys
faux filet	sirloin steak	rognons blancs	testicles
foie	liver	sanglier	wild boar
foie gras	fattened (duck/goose) liver	steak	steak
		tête de veau	calf's head (in jelly)
gigot (d'agneau)	leg (of lamb)	tournedos	thick slices of fillet
grillade	grilled meat	tripes	tripe
hâchis	chopped meat or mince hamburger	veau	veal
		venaison	venison

Meat and poultry dishes

bœuf bourguignon	beef stew with Burgundy, onions and mushrooms		with wine, onions and mushrooms
		merguez	spicy, north African-style lamb sausages
canard à l'orange	roast duck with an orange-and-wine sauce	steak au poivre (vert/rouge)	steak in a black (green/red) peppercorn sauce
cassoulet	casserole of beans and meat	steak tartare	raw chopped beef, topped with a raw egg yolk
coq au vin	chicken cooked until it falls off the bone		

Meat cooking terms

blanquette, daube, estouffade, hocheôt, navarin, ragoût	all are types of stew
aile	wing
carré	best end of neck, chop or cutlet
civit	game stew
confit	meat preserve
côte	chop, cutlet or rib
cou	neck
cuisse	thigh or leg
épaule	shoulder
médaillon	round piece
pavé	thick slice
en croûte	in pastry
farci	stuffed
au feu de bois	cooked over wood
au four	fire-baked
garni	with vegetables
gésier	gizzard
grillé	grilled
magret de canard	duck breast
marmite	casserole
mijoté	stewed
museau	muzzle
rôti	roast
sauté	lightly cooked in butter

For steaks:

bleu	almost raw
saignant	rare
à point	medium
bien cuit	well done
très bien cuit	very well cooked
brochette	kebab
beurre blanc	sauce of white wine and shallots, with butter
chasseur	white wine, mushrooms and shallots
diable	strong mustard seasoning
forestière	with bacon and mushroom
fricassée	rich, creamy sauce
mornay	cheese sauce
pays d'Auge	cream and cider
piquante	gherkins or capers, vinegar and shallots
provençale	tomatoes, garlic, olive oil and herbs

Fruit (fruit) and nuts (noix)

abricot	apricot
amandes	almonds
ananas	pineapple
banane	banana
brugnon, nectarine	nectarine
cacahouète	peanut
cassis	blackcurrants
cérises	cherries
citron	lemon
citron vert	lime
figues	figs
fraises (de bois)	strawberries (wild)
framboises	raspberries
fruit de la passion	passion fruit
groseilles	redcurrants and gooseberries
mangue	mango
marrons	chestnuts
melon	melon
myrtilles	bilberries
noisette	hazelnut
noix	nuts
orange	orange
pamplemousse	grapefruit
pêche (blanche)	(white) peach
pistache	pistachio
poire	pear
pomme	apple
prune	plum
pruneau	prune
raisins	grapes

Terms:

beignets	fritters
compôte de ...	stewed ...
coulis	sauce
flambé	set aflame in alcohol
frappé	iced

Vegetables (légumes), herbs (herbes) and spices (épices)

ail	garlic	persil	parsley
algue	seaweed	petits pois	peas
anis	aniseed	pignons	pine nuts
artichaut	artichoke	piment	pimento
asperges	asparagus	pois chiche	chick peas
avocat	avocado	pois mange-tout	snow peas
basilic	basil	poireau	leek
betterave	beetroot	poivron (vert, rouge)	sweet pepper (green, red)
carotte	carrot		
céleri	celery	pommes (de terre)	potatoes
champignons, cèpes, chanterelles	mushrooms of various kinds	primeurs	spring vegetables
		radis	radishes
chou (rouge)	(red) cabbage	riz	rice
choufleur	cauliflower	safran	saffron
ciboulettes	chives	salade verte	green salad
concombre	cucumber	sarrasin	buckwheat
cornichon	gherkin	tomate	tomato
échalotes	shallots	truffes	truffles
endive	chicory		

Terms:

beignet	fritter
farci	stuffed
gratiné	browned with cheese or butter
jardinière	with mixed diced vegetables
à la parisienne	sautéed in butter (potatoes); with white wine sauce and shallots
parmentier	with potatoes
sauté	lightly fried in butter
à la vapeur	steamed
Je suis végétarien (ne). Il y a quelques plats sans viande?	I'm a vegetarian. Are there any non-meat dishes?

(continued from vegetables table)

épinards	spinach
estragon	tarragon
fenouil	fennel
flageolet	white beans
gingembre	ginger
haricots	beans
verts	string (French)
rouges	kidney
beurres	butter
laurier	bay leaf
lentilles	lentils
maïs	corn
menthe	mint
moutarde	mustard
oignon	onion
pâte	pasta, pastry

Desserts (desserts or entremets) and pastries (pâtisserie)

bombe	moulded ice-cream dessert
brioche	sweet, high-yeast breakfast roll
canastrellis	Corsican speciality

biscuits, sometimes made with chestnut flour, flavoured with eau de vie, white wine, lemon or nuts

charlotte	custard and fruit in lining of almond fingers
crème Chantilly	vanilla-flavoured and sweetened whipped cream
crème fraîche	sour cream
crème pâtissière	thick, eggy pastry-filling
crêpes suzettes	thin pancakes with orange juice and liqueur
fromage blanc	cream cheese
glace	ice cream
ile flottante/œufs à la neige	soft meringues floating on custard
macarons	macaroons
madeleine	small sponge cake
marrons Mont Blanc	chestnut purée and cream on a rum-sponge cake
mousse au chocolat	chocolate mousse
palmiers	caramelized puff pastries

parfait	frozen mousse, sometimes ice cream
petit Suisse	smooth mixture of cream and curds
petits fours	bite-sized cakes/pastries
poires belle Hélène	pears and ice cream in chocolate sauce
yaourt, yogourt	yoghurt

Terms:

barquette	small boat-shaped flan
bavarois	refers to the mould; could be a mousse or custard
coupe	serving of ice cream
crêpes	pancakes
galettes	buckwheat pancakes
Gênoise	rich sponge cake
sablé	shortbread biscuit
savarin	filled, ring-shaped cake
tarte	tart
tartelette sarrasin	small tart

Corsican starters and charcuterie

cannelloni al brocciu	pasta stuffed with *brocciu* and mint with tomato sauce
omelette al brocciu	omelette filled with *brocciu*
suppa di pesce/ soupe de poisson	fish soup served with toast and garlic

suppa Corsa/ soupe Corse	vegetable soup with beans
coppa	smoked pork shoulder
figatellu	pork liver sausage
lonzu	smoked pork fillet
prisuttu	cured ham

Corsican main dishes

aziminu	rich, heavily spiced, garlicky fish stew
bianchetti	little fish fried in batter
cabrettu a l'istrettu	strongly spiced kid stew
formaghju di porcu	pork brawn seasoned with onion, garlic, pepper and maquis herbs
fritelle di gaju frescu	fritters made with chestnut flour and *brocciu*

lasagne di cignale	wild boar lasagne
pulenta	Corsican polenta, a mash made of chestnut- or maize-flour
pivarunata	peppery beef and potato stew with pimentos
stifatu	a roll of stuffed meats – goat, lamb and sometimes blackbird – served with grated cheese

tianu d'agnellu	lamb stew	tianu di pisi	onion, carrot, pea and tomato stew
tianu di cingale/ sanglier en daube	wild boar stew with potatoes	tripette	tripe in tomato sauce
tianu di fave	pork and bean stew		

Corsican cheese, puddings and digestifs

brocciu	soft white cheese made with curds	fromage Corse	uniquely flavoured indigenous hard cheese
canistrelli	soft shortbread-type biscuits made with white wine and honey	vin de myrte	a "firewater" eau-de-vie liqueur flavoured with wild myrtle berries often drunk as a digestif
fiadone	tart filled with brocciu		
fritelli/beignets	small doughnuts, sometimes made with chestnut flour		

Glossary

arrière pays hinterland

AOC Appellation d'origine contrôlée; hallmark guaranteeing authenticity of origin

à l'étage on the corridor

au feu de bois wood-baked

belle époque the "golden era" (of the late nineteenth century)

bergeries stone shepherds' huts or sheepfolds

bloc sanitaire toilet block on campsite

boucle circuit, or round walk

buvette mobile snack and drinks stall or caravan

camping à la ferme farm campsite

châtaigneraie chestnut grove

chef lieu administrative headquarters of a rural area

commune traditional Corsican parish, or administrative area

criques small bays

étapes stages of a walk

falaises cliffs

fontaine spring

gardien/gardienne warden (of a refuge)

maison d'Américain grand house built by returning emigrants on Cap Corse

navette shuttle bus or boat

paillote beach café-restaurant

passeghiata evening stroll in the town or village square traditionally enjoyed by Corsicans of advanced years

pied dans l'eau beside (literally "foot in") the water

piste unsurfaced track

pozzines or **pozzi** winding watercourses and mountain pools, separated by lush, spongy turf

produits du terroir local produce

séchoir drying house (for chestnuts)

serrer à droite veering to the right (of a road) when confronted by oncoming traffic on the wrong side of the central white lines

signori Corsican aristocracy

sous-préfecture modern administrative sub-division

tafonu naturally formed hole in rock

villages de vacances holiday village or camp

villages perchés old villages sited on outcrops or rock spurs

vracs plastic or glass containers for wine

Travel store

ROUGH GUIDES

Small print and

Index

A Rough Guide to Rough Guides

Published in 1982, the first Rough Guide – to Greece – was a student scheme that became a publishing phenomenon. Mark Ellingham, a recent graduate in English from Bristol University, had been travelling in Greece the previous summer and couldn't find the right guidebook. With a small group of friends he wrote his own guide, combining a highly contemporary, journalistic style with a thoroughly practical approach to travellers' needs.

The immediate success of the book spawned a series that rapidly covered dozens of destinations. And, in addition to impecunious backpackers, Rough Guides soon acquired a much broader and older readership that relished the guides' wit and inquisitiveness as much as their enthusiastic, critical approach and value-for-money ethos.

These days, Rough Guides include recommendations from shoestring to luxury and cover more than 200 destinations around the globe, including almost every country in the Americas and Europe, more than half of Africa and most of Asia and Australasia. Our ever-growing team of authors and photographers is spread all over the world, particularly in Europe, the USA and Australia.

In the early 1990s, Rough Guides branched out of travel, with the publication of Rough Guides to World Music, Classical Music and the Internet. All three have become benchmark titles in their fields, spearheading the publication of a wide range of books under the Rough Guide name.

Including the travel series, Rough Guides now number more than 350 titles, covering: phrasebooks, waterproof maps, music guides from Opera to Heavy Metal, reference works as diverse as Conspiracy Theories and Shakespeare, and popular culture books from iPods to Poker. Rough Guides also produce a series of more than 120 World Music CDs in partnership with World Music Network.

Visit www.roughguides.com to see our latest publications.

Rough Guide travel images are available for commercial licensing at www.roughguidespictures.com

Rough Guide credits

Text editor: Lucy White, Róisín Cameron
Layout: Jessica Subramanian
Cartography: Rajesh Mishra
Picture editor: Mark Thomas
Production: Rebecca Short
Proofreader: Margaret Doyle
Cover design: Chloë Roberts
Photographer: David Abram
Editorial: **London** Ruth Blackmore, Andy
Turner, Keith Drew, Edward Aves, Alice Park,
Jo Kirby, James Smart, Natasha Foges, Emma
Traynor, James Rice, Emma Gibbs, Kathryn
Lane, Christina Valhouli, Monica Woods, Mani
Ramaswamy, Harry Wilson, Alison Roberts,
Joe Staines, Peter Buckley, Matthew Milton,
Tracy Hopkins, Ruth Tidball; **New York** Andrew
Rosenberg, Steven Horak, AnneLise Sorensen,
Ella Steim, Anna Owens, Sean Mahoney, Paula
Neudorf; **Delhi** Madhavi Singh, Karen D'Souza,
Lubna Shaheen
Design & Pictures: **London** Scott Stickland,
Dan May, Diana Jarvis, Chloë Roberts, Nicole
Newman, Sarah Cummins, Emily Taylor; **Delhi**
Umesh Aggarwal, Ajay Verma, Ankur Guha,
Pradeep Thapliyal, Sachin Tanwar, Anita Singh,
Nikhil Agarwal

Production: Vicky Baldwin
Cartography: **London** Maxine Repath, Ed
Wright, Katie Lloyd-Jones; **Delhi** Rajesh
Chhibber, Ashutosh Bharti, Animesh Pathak,
Jasbir Sandhu, Karobi Gogoi, Alakananda
Bhattacharya, Swati Handoo, Deshpal Dabas
Online: **London** George Atwell, Faye Hellon,
Jeanette Angell, Fergus Day, Justine Bright,
Clare Bryson, Áine Fearon, Adrian Low, Ezgi
Celebi, Amber Bloomfield; **Delhi** Amit Verma,
Rahul Kumar, Narender Kumar, Ravi Yadav,
Debojit Borah, Rakesh Kumar, Ganesh Sharma,
Shisir Basumatari
Marketing & Publicity: **London** Liz Statham,
Niki Hanmer, Louise Maher, Jess Carter,
Vanessa Godden, Vivienne Watton, Anna
Paynton, Rachel Sprackett, Libby Jellie, Laura
Vipond; **New York** Geoff Colquitt, Nancy
Lambert, Katy Ball; **Delhi** Ragini Govind
Manager India: Punita Singh
Reference Director: Andrew Lockett
Operations Manager: Helen Phillips
PA to Publishing Director: Nicola Henderson
Publishing Director: Martin Dunford
Commercial Manager: Gino Magnotta
Managing Director: John Duhigg

Publishing information

This sixth edition published May 2009 by
Rough Guides Ltd,
80 Strand, London WC2R 0RL
345 Hudson St, 4th Floor,
New York, NY 10014, USA
14 Local Shopping Centre, Panchsheel Park,
New Delhi 110017, India
Distributed by the Penguin Group
Penguin Books Ltd,
80 Strand, London WC2R 0RL
Penguin Group (USA)
375 Hudson Street, NY 10014, USA
Penguin Group (Australia)
250 Camberwell Road, Camberwell,
Victoria 3124, Australia
Penguin Group (Canada)
195 Harry Walker Parkway N, Newmarket, ON,
L3Y 7B3 Canada
Penguin Group (NZ)
67 Apollo Drive, Mairangi Bay, Auckland 1310,
New Zealand

Cover concept by Peter Dyer.

Typeset in Bembo and Helvetica to an original
design by Henry Iles.

Printed and bound in Singapore

© David Abram/Rough Guides, 2009

No part of this book may be reproduced in any
form without permission from the publisher except
for the quotation of brief passages in reviews.

464pp includes index

A catalogue record for this book is available from
the British Library.

ISBN: 978-1-84836-051-8

The publishers and authors have done their best
to ensure the accuracy and currency of all the
information in **The Rough Guide to Corsica**,
however, they can accept no responsibility for
any loss, injury, or inconvenience sustained by
any traveller as a result of information or advice
contained in the guide.

3   5   7   9   8   6   4   2

Help us update

We've gone to a lot of effort to ensure that the
sixth edition of **The Rough Guide to Corsica** is
accurate and up to date. However, things change
– places get "discovered", opening hours raise
– notoriously fickle, restaurants and rooms raise
prices or lower standards. If you feel we've got it
wrong or left something out, we'd like to know,
and if you can remember the address, the price,
the hours, the phone number, so much the better.

Please send your comments with the
subject line "**Rough Guide Corsica Update**"
to @mail@roughguides.com. We'll credit all
contributions and send a copy of the next edition
(or any other Rough Guide if you prefer) for the
very best emails.

Have your questions answered and tell others
about your trip at
@community.roughguides.com

Acknowledgements

Thanks to Michel Sabatini, Nicholas Piobetta, Marcel Lafranche, Lina Soveria, Claire Carnell and the staff of Simpson Travel for some great steers; and VM and baby Morgan UAM for road-testing some of them with me. At Rough Guides, thank you to Lucy White and Roísín Cameron for getting the book back on track after a late start, and for their conscientious editing of its new streamlined incarnation. Thanks also to Mark Thomas, for freshening up the photos.

Readers' letters

Many thanks to the following readers for taking the trouble to write to us with feedback on the last edition:

Mr and Mrs AT Canton; Stuart Elliott; Per Goller; James Muller and Ulrika Wernmark; Peter Ryan; Michael and Victoria Steward; Kenneth Richardson; Mr and Mrs SL Strack; and Edwin Whitaker.

ROUGH
GUIDES

SMALL PRINT

Photo credits

All photos David Abram © Rough Guides except the following:

Title page
GR20 sign © Combre Stephane/Alamy

Full page
Bonifacio © Jon Arnold Images/Alamy

Introduction
Mouflon sheep © Dave Watts/Alamy
Outdoor café at L'Île Rousse © Yadid Levy/Alamy
St-Florent Harbour © Combre Stephane/Alamy
Genoese watch tower © De Agostini Picture
  Library

Things not to miss
02 Bastia Harbour © Robert Harding Picture
  Library/Alamy
04 Calvi © Robert Harding Picture Library/Alamy
13 Corsican wine © Lucy White
18 Diving © Waterframe/Alamy

Wild Corsica section
Trekking on Monte d'Oro, Corsica © Janos
  Csernoch/Alamy
Hiking on the GR20 © Jef Maion/Alamy

Mountain biking © Jaileybug/Alamy
Woman preparing to dive © Jupiter Images/Alamy
Diver inspecting wreck © WaterFrame/Alamy

Traditional Corsica section
Religious procession © Arco Images GmbH/
  Alamy
Traditional bread © Lucy White
Polyphony singing in church © Michael Jenner/
  Alamy
I Muvrini poster © Lucy White

Black and whites
p.144 Calanches Rocks © Jon Arnold Images/
  Alamy
p.172 Market selling cheeses © FAN Travelstock/
  Alamy
p.200 Filitosa Menhir © CuboImages srl/Alamy
p.266 The Via Ferrata © Ashley Cooper/Alamy
p.290 Lac de Nino © Jef Maion/Alamy
p.319 Cascade des Anglais © Jef Maion/Alamy
p.326 GR20 © Jef Maion/Alamy
p.336 GR20 © Jef Maion/Alamy
p.342 Bridge near Bonifatu © GP Bowater/Alamy

SMALL PRINT

Index

Map entries are in colour.

INDEX

C

Map symbols

maps are listed in the full index in coloured text

– – –	Chapter boundary	⛪	Convent/Monastery
═══	Major road	📡	Radio mast
══	Minor road	✈	Airport
▬▬	Pedestrianised road	✈	Airfield
▬▬▬	Steps	★	Bus stop
- - - -	Footpath	🅿	Parking
▬●▬	Railway	Å	Camping
▬▬	Wall	▒	Winery
- - - -	Ferry route	(i)	Tourist office
▬▬	River	⊠	Post office
♦	Place of interest	@	Internet access
▲	Peak	⊞	Hospital
≈	Pass	◉	Accommodation
⩘	Escarpment	■	Restaurants
⚓	Viewpoint	✡	Synagogue
⌒	Cave	▬	Building
⌂	Refuge hut	⊥	Church
⚱	Waterfall	⊡	Cemetery
▮	Tower	▦	Park
⚑	Lighthouse	▨	Marshland
⚲	Church (regional maps)	▦	Beach